SECOND EDITION

Human Behavior and the Social Environment

A Social Systems Model

WAYNE A. CHESS
JULIA M. NORLIN
University of Oklahoma

Allyn and Bacon
BOSTON LONDON TORONTO SYDNEY TOKYO SINGAPORE

Series Editor: Karen Hanson
Series Editorial Assistant: Laurie Frankenthaler
Production Administrator: Annette Joseph
Production Coordinator: Holly Crawford
Editorial-Production Service: Laura Cleveland, WordCrafters Editorial
   Services, Inc.
Cover Administrator: Linda K. Dickinson
Cover Designer: Suzanne Harbison
Manufacturing Buyer: Louise Richardson

This textbook is printed on
recycled, acid-free paper.

Library of Congress Cataloging-in-Publication Data
Chess, Wayne A.
   Human behavior and the social environment : a social systems model
/ Wayne A. Chess, Julia M. Norlin. — 2nd ed.
      p.   cm.
   Includes bibliographical references and index.
   ISBN 0-205-12824-6
   1. Social service.   2. Social systems.   3. Social systems—
Mathematical models.   4. Human behavior.   I. Norlin, Julia M.
II. Title.
   HV40.C53   1990
   361.3'2—dc20   90-41979
                                                                   CIP

Printed in the United States of America

10 9 8 7 6 5 4 3 2 1   95 94 93 92 91 90

Photo Credits: Part II, p. 113—© Susan Lapides 1980; Part III,
p. 203—© Susan Lapides 1982; Part IV, p. 279—© Susan Lapides
1980; Part V, p. 369—Peter Main/The Christian Science
Monitor.

Contents

Chapter 15
The Community as a Social System   395

Chapter 16
The Community Problem of Child Abuse and Neglect: A Practice Application   423

Index   439

Preface

Human Behavior and the Social Environment: A Social Systems Model is written primarily for those preparing for a career in social work or one of the other social professions. The task we faced as authors was how to organize and present knowledge about human behavior that would help in this quest to become an effective professional practitioner. Our initial task was to assess where the profession of social work is in terms of its own development, and particularly in its efforts at knowledge building. In Chapter 1 we share our thoughts with you. We hope this assessment makes sense to you and "fits" with where you are and where you want to go professionally.

We believe the profession is actively engaged in a process of self-examination. This self-examination process has resulted in identification of several areas in which substantial agreement exists, as follows:

1. Social work as a helping profession is characterized by great variations in the types of human problems and opportunities we address, the methods we use, and the settings in which we work. Although these variations are a source of important differences among us, they can and should be the source of our greatest strengths.
2. Given the variety of the forms of practice characterizing the profession, general agreement does not yet exist on our overall purpose, our special methods, and the specific knowledge base from which our knowledge and skills are derived.
3. The social work profession must assume the primary responsibility for identifying and developing its own knowledge base, one suited to its special features and including its many forms of practice.
4. The profession should concentrate knowledge-building efforts by identifying a common perspective on human behavior, one that incorporates the notions of wholeness and interdependence, and one that views human behavior in a social environment.

Given this assessment, there are a number of quite different ways to organize the bewildering amount of knowledge about human behavior that includes the role of the social environment. Some of the usual organizing schemes involve the life cycle, a problem-solving approach, analysis of the normal and abnormal, and an examination of human diversity, among others. For example, many human behavior courses bear significant responsibility for content on human diversity. An examination is made of ethnicity, gender, culture, and sexual preferences among people, and the behavioral and practical applications are explored. Hence, many human behavior textbooks are organized around diversity themes. Other human behavior courses and textbooks are organized around the life cycle. Still others combine two or more organization schemes. In this book, we settled on the use of the system to provide the basic organizing scheme. Believing the key characteristic of the profession stems from the word *social*, we further focused our attention on the social system. In short, recognizing the huge, but relatively unorganized, literature available on human behavior, we have used the social system as the tool for organizing this knowledge.

In a manner of speaking, the social systems model is essentially content- or information-free. By this we mean that the model is not to be confused with a comprehensive theory of human behavior; rather it can be likened to a special vehicle or carrier to which various substantial theories can be added and applied to a specific area of practice. For example, the Curriculum Policy Statement of the Council on Social Work Education (CSWE) specifies that students need knowledge of the individual as he or she develops over the life span. In this edition, we have included a new part focusing on the individual. In Chapter 10 of this new section, we include life-span-development content as set forth in psychosocial theory. In short, we take psychosocial theory and incorporate it into the social systems model. We include other developmental theories as well, for example, psychoanalysis, cognitive development, and moral development.

Content dealing with social work values, women's issues, human diversity, and the needs of special populations also are called for by CSWE. We approach these content requirements by outlining important lines of theory development that can be used to meaningfully address these needs within a systems perspective. Moral development theory, for example, as outlined by Lawrence Kohlberg, is used as the framework for dealing with issues concerning values and ethics as they pertain to moral issues confronted in social work. This content is also new to this edition.

To the Instructor

First, we want to thank those of you who took time to send us your comments and suggestions on the first edition of this book. These suggestions served as the primary basis of the changes incorporated in this edition. We are also mindful of your concern about the costs that students bear in needing to buy several books for their courses on human behavior. By expanding on content dealing with life-span development, values, women's issues, human diversity, special-population needs, and so on, we hope to have addressed this problem. Now, we hope the need for additional content can be more focused on the special interests of instructors and the needs of a given course.

Our selection of references has, to the extent possible, taken into consideration the issues of cost and accessibility. For example, we have made extensive use of the most recent edition of the *Encyclopedia of Social Work*. We believe these references will be easily available to both faculty and students.

We believe our approach to the organization of human behavior content is somewhat different than those generally taken. One of the differences is in the role the instructor can take in presenting this material. The social systems model is intended to be flexible, giving the instructor considerable latitude as to the additional content to be added.

In other words, the model provides a foundation upon which the instructor builds, thereby incorporating her or his own approach to knowledge building for practice. The book can serve as a primary text for a single course in human behavior that deals with the knowledge base for working with individuals, families, groups, organizations, or communities. It can also be used as a primary text for courses in each of these areas.

In the latter instance, such a course might focus on the knowledge base for work with individuals and families. In this case the instructor might select psychosocial theory as a substantive theoretical orientation; psychosocial theory would be viewed as a narrower range theory employed within the social systems model. Certainly not every theory or set of concepts pertaining to human behavior will fit within the assumptions and concepts that make up the model. But we believe the model provides the instructor with considerable latitude in how a course might be organized and taught, in order to capitalize on the instructor's special areas of expertise.

Some instructors may find the concepts new or at least not as familiar as, perhaps, those associated with the more traditional or usual lines of theory development in social work. If this is the case, you may want to spend some additional time at the beginning of the course becoming acquainted with the model. As an aid we have constructed an Instructor's Manual we believe you will find useful.

Our experiences over the last decade with this model suggest that students benefit from moving back and forth between conceptual content and practical applications of that content. The model is a conceptual tool—one that by its nature is abstract. Initially some students have difficulty with its abstract qualities and have trouble linking the model to their practice. It is here that the role of the instructor is vital, and the linking is accomplished in part through the use of many practice examples. The test makes extensive use of examples, but they need to be augmented by the instructor.

We would also like to note that, as accreditation site visitors, we have noticed that a large number of social work education programs identify social systems as the organizing theme of their curriculum. This book provides a conceptual foundation for several programs that have used it in an early testing process. Presenting the model and its theoretical supports in a basic human behavior and social environment course allows the model to be further utilized in other curricular areas. It has been our experience that, once mastered, the social systems model provides a way of thinking about the curriculum as a whole.

To the Student

We are delighted at your interest in the social work profession. It has been our experience that the people attracted to social work or one of the other social professions share a common calling to help others. The desire to be of help to others is one of the best and most important of all the reasons to choose one's life work. Also, most of us already in, or planning to enter one of the helping professions are intrigued by the reasons people behave as they do; not just why others behave as they do, but why we—you and I—do the things we do. Most of us also agree that this curiosity about people and their behavior is a good thing. In short, to be an effective professional helper you need to have an understanding of human behavior and, most important, you need an understanding of yourself. If it were otherwise, social work would not be a professional effort.

In writing this book, we have made some assessments of the social work profession—of where it is and where it is going. In part this assessment is based on our continuing research on current practices in social work; a much larger part is based on our conversations with colleagues and in reading what they write. We believe you are joining the profession at an exciting and important time. We have also made assumptions about you the reader, some of which we have just shared with you. We know that you bring to this class varying quantities of relevant life experiences, a value system, and knowledge of various theories of human development and behavior. We also know that you bring with you something of your own perspective about why people behave as they do. Our intent is to help you build on that knowledge.

The approach we have selected is premised on some of our own assumptions as to why people behave as they do. We label this a *social systems perspective*. We believe that most of the assumptions and ideas that form this perspective are widely shared in social work but perhaps not spelled out in quite this way. Based on this perspective, we have constructed a way of modeling human behavior in the social environment. Quite simply, it is a way of thinking about humans in interaction with each other. We believe the model has application for examining and better understanding social behavior in a variety of forms and levels. For example, it can be used to better understand your own behavior and that of your client in a helping relationship. It can also be used to better understand why people who make up an agency or a community behave as they do.

Considering the nature of the model and its varied applications, it is very general and abstract. Given its conceptual nature, we encourage you to become acquainted with the vocabulary and the meaning attached to the concepts. As an aid, we provide a glossary of terms at the end of most chapters. In most instances the concepts we use relate to some behavior that is characteristic of people in social interaction. Here we suggest that you search for a behavioral application of the concept within your own relationships with people, organizations, and communities with which you are familiar. For those not familiar with systems thinking, once the concepts start making sense, their interrelationships become clear. Many of our students have likened it to turning on a light. We hope you, too, find it useful.

Acknowledgments

When so many people are involved, it is hard to know where to start and then when to stop saying thanks. Our greatest debt is to the many writers from whom we have borrowed. Here we have to assume full responsibility for how their ideas have been expressed and, in some instances, built upon, but the basic ideas belong to others—to Freud, Tönnies, Cooley, von Bertalanffy, Lewin, Maslow, Allport, Parsons, Erikson, Watson, and Skinner—to mention but a few. We also owe a special debt to the hundreds of former students who took our human behavior courses over the last decade and who joined our struggle as participants and colleagues in helping develop the social systems model. In our combined forty years of teaching, many social work educators have unselfishly helped us as we shaped this social systems model. We would especially like to thank our staff and faculty colleagues at the University of Oklahoma School of Social Work for their review, comments, and suggestions over the years. For this edition we offer a special thanks to some of our new faculty, particularly Don Baker and Jay Memmott. Thanks also go to our department secretarial staff, Donna Vaughn and GariAnn Mullins, for their help.

Colleagues outside the school have also helped us with the ideas and have reacted and made suggestions on the many drafts of the manuscript. In this regard we wish to thank those members of the Kansas Council on Social Work Education who have assisted over several years. David Norlin has been a reviewer and has worked through content problems through years of use in the classroom. The Baccalaureate Program directors have given us the opportunity through round table discussions to work out conceptual problems. To that organization and to the members who have struggled with us, thank you. We are especially appreciative to our reviewers: Ronald Federico, Holly VanScoy, and Elizabeth D. Hutchison. Two colleagues and good friends have been especially helpful and have devoted hours of work to our manuscript: Siri Jayaratne and Ron Federico. The book is much better because of their critiques.

We also want to say thanks to Patsy Sellars-Bacon and Suzanne Koenig, two of our graduate assistants, who contributed in at least a dozen different and helpful ways. Finally, a thanks to Betty Bellis and Karen Hanson: Betty, who helped type both editions of the book, and Karen, who has served as our editor for Allyn and Bacon during both of the editions. Working is fun when you have the support and help of people like those who have been a part of this effort.

PART I

OVERVIEW

The Social Systems Model

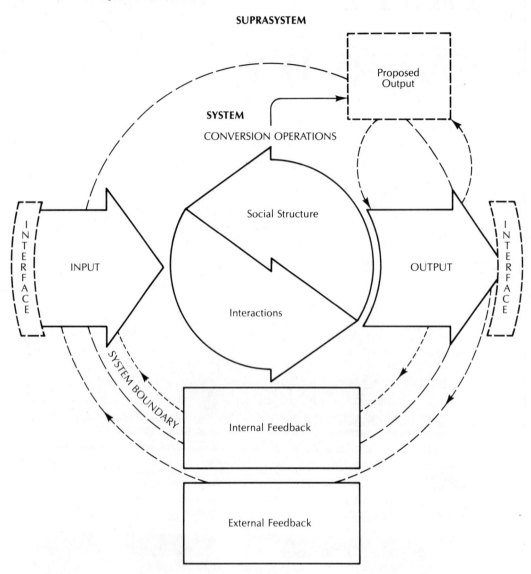

We would prefer to be sitting with you and exchanging ideas about ways of organizing knowledge that would be helpful in the practice of social work. This book resulted from such conversations between ourselves and from subsequent conversations with colleagues and particularly with students. Now we have the opportunity to share our ideas with you. The question is how to go about sharing these ideas in a helpful way through this book. Our decision is to write in the first person—something not typically done in texts. But given the inherent problems of communicating the abstract and conceptual nature of the content, we feel that to write as if we were actually talking to you personally is useful.

In Part I we provide an orientation to what the book is about and the ideas we hope to communicate. To accomplish this, we have organized the material into four chapters.

Chapter 1, as might be expected, is entitled Introduction. We decided to accomplish this introduction through a series of questions starting with What Is This Book About? The kind of questions posed are the kind we would want answered. The chapter also provides a brief introduction to the social systems model.

A social systems perspective is presented in Chapter 2. Here we are concerned with a general approach to the study of human behavior in the social environment, identifying the basic assumptions and lines of theory development that form the foundations of a social systems perspective. It is the extension of these assumptions and theories that has helped us shape a social systems model.

Chapter 3 is a comprehensive presentation of the model and the eight concepts that comprise it: (1) boundary, (2) suprasystem, (3) interface, (4) inputs, (5) outputs, (6) proposed outputs, (7) conversion operations (structure-interactions), and (8) feedback.

Chapter 4 concludes Part I. Here we identify the behaviors deemed common to all social systems. The approach we use builds from the work of sociologist Talcott Parsons. Four problems that every type of social organization must constantly and effectively address in order to survive and develop are: (1) goal attainment, (2) integration, (3) pattern maintenance, and (4) adaptation. We believe the similarities in behavior exhibited by systems dealing with these four problems have important implications to the helping professional.

Chapter 1

Introduction

OUTLINE

What Is This Book About?

This book is about the study of why people behave as they do and the application of this knowledge to the professional practice of social work. We are using the word *about* advisedly. By this we mean that the book introduces you to a way of organizing the large body of knowledge available about human behavior in a manner that should be helpful in your practice. We call the approach a *social systems model*.

The book is also about interdependence and wholeness. This idea of interdependence and wholeness as a way of looking at ourselves and our relationships to others is perhaps best expressed in the words of the great English poet John Donne (1571–1631):

> No man is an island, entire of itself;
> Every man is a piece of the continent, a part of the main;
> If a clod be washed away by the sea, Europe is the less,
> as well as if a promontory were,
> as well as if a manor of thy friends or of thine own were;
> Any man's death diminishes me, because I am involved in mankind;
> And therefore never send to know for whom the bell tolls;
> It tolls for thee.

Devotions XVII

The social systems model that we develop is a way of thinking about this idea of wholeness and human interdependence. Before talking about the model itself, some additional questions and answers should help in understanding the origins of this idea and its application to professional social work practice.

Who Is the Intended Audience?

The primary audience for the book is students in social work programs and in other schools and departments that prepare people for careers in the helping professions. A secondary audience is that group of professionals already in practice who are interested in the use of a social systems model as a way of grounding their own approach to practice. A more general audience is those who are intrigued with why people behave as they do and who are interested in exploring ways of better understanding themselves and those around them.

Why Did We Decide to Write This Book?

The book is our way of sharing an approach we have found helpful for organizing the large amount of knowledge of human behavior that is useful to the practice of social work. The approach provides a way of integrating existing information into a base for practitioners to employ in their own professional development.

Social workers and other helping professionals are called upon daily by their clients for assistance in dealing with every imaginable kind of problem or opportunity. To be of help, the worker must have a general grasp of an enormous amount of information about human behavior, along with skills in making effective use of that knowledge. First as students, then as practitioners, and finally as teachers, we each struggled with the problem of grounding our practice in a knowledge base that made sense to us and that we could communicate to others. After joining the same faculty and having similar teaching assignments, we discovered that we had come to similar conclusions. We called our approach a *social systems model* and have used this model in our classes for more than fifteen years. Over these years our students have served as a laboratory for the development and testing of the model. Much of this testing took place in practice and internships as students applied the model to their own cases, agencies, and communities. What started as a ten-page handout grew into this book.

Our reason for writing this book was not to provide another review of psychological and sociological theories and other knowledge developed outside of social work, but rather to provide an approach for organizing and building a knowledge base for the practice of social work. Our model starts where we believe the profession is undertaking its major knowledge-building efforts, that is, seeking understanding of human behavior by focusing on the relationships people have with other people, groups, and organizations that constitute their social environment.[1]

What Do Social Workers Do?

Social workers help people live more personally satisfying and socially useful lives. We do this by working in **direct practice** with clients and/or in **indirect practice** by working with or through groups, organizations, and communities. In short, social workers seek improvement in the quality of human life.[2]

Identifying where social workers work and the practice methods used can be helpful in describing more specifically what social workers do. The following two tables are drawn from our national studies of social work practice conducted with our colleague, Dr. Srinika Jayaratne.[3] The respondents were from a randomly drawn sample of members of the National Association of Social Workers (NASW), the majority of whom held Master of Social Work (MSW) degrees. Table 1.1 displays data for 1981, 1985, and 1989. As indicated by this table, mental health is the dominant setting, accounting for 28.4 percent of our 1981, 27.1 percent of our 1985, and 30.6 percent of our 1989 respondents. We should also note that there are a number of different types of mental health settings

TABLE 1.1 Practice Setting for NASW Members Employed Full Time, 1981, 1985, and 1989

	1981		1985		1989	
Category	*Number*	*Percent*	*Number*	*Percent*	*Number*	*Percent*
Mental health	195	28.4	156	27.1	194	30.6
Health care	97	14.1	88	15.3	108	17.0
Family service	61	8.9	52	9.1	56	8.8
Child welfare	54	7.8	54	9.4	48	7.6
School social work	52	7.6	36	6.3	41	6.5
Aging services	32	4.7	19	3.3	21	3.3
Private practice	21	3.1	40	7.0	22	3.5
Substance abuse	15	2.2	9	1.6	18	2.8
Corrections	14	2.0	5	0.9	9	1.4
Industrial/business social work	3	0.4	9	1.6	9	1.4
Developmental disability	–	–	15	2.6	21	3.3
Social work education	–	–	33	5.7	27	4.3
Other	144	20.9	58	10.1	60	9.5
Total	688	100.0	574	100.0	634	100.0

included in this category, for example, state mental hospitals, community mental health centers, guidance clinics and out-patient mental health clinics. Mental health, like the other categories, is a general heading for agencies serving clients with similar problems and requiring similar professional services.

We have included data from three of our studies to help show both the breadth of practice and recent trends. For example, our 1981 and 1985 data suggested that private practice appeared to be a rapidly developing area in social work. In 1981 just over three percent of our respondents reported they were in full-time private practice. This figure more than doubled, with seven percent of our 1985 respondents indicating that they were in private practice full time. Our 1989 data show respondents in full-time private practice at roughly the same level as in 1981. The early years of the Reagan presidency were associated with a strong movement toward the privatization of social services. The growth of private practice in social work was a part of that general move. The 1989 data do not indicate that this trend is continuing. The finding is an interesting one, but more research will be necessary to determine if this movement by social workers into private practice has run its course.

Health is an area that is evidencing steady upward growth. These data suggest that in 1989 nearly half (47.6 percent) of all social workers who were members of NASW worked in either health or mental health settings.

Table 1.2 summarizes the practice methods utilized by our respondents. We indicated earlier that social workers help people by working "directly" with them and/or by using "indirect" methods. This table is helpful in comparing the two different but complementary approaches. For example, casework is the principal method of direct service while administration is principally an indirect service. The typical test used to distinguish between a direct or an indirect form of practice is whether or not the helping method employed involves face-to-face contact with a client. A caseworker will have face-to-face contact with her or his client, for example, in helping a client deal with a drug abuse problem. In contrast, an administrator will typically not work directly with clients but rather will work through her or his own staff and through other agencies and groups on behalf of clients.

We have again provided data for three time periods to suggest the dynamic nature of social work practice. Of particular importance are changes that appear to be taking place in the use of direct versus indirect practice methods. A suggestion of this change is that in 1981, 41.0 percent of our respondents were engaged in casework (a direct practice method); by 1985 this percentage had dropped to 29.4 percent, and by 1989 it was back up to 36.9 percent. In contrast, 27.8 percent of our respondents in 1981 reported they used administration as their principal practice method (an indirect method); this percentage increased to 36.5 percent in our 1985 study but was down to 21.1 percent in 1989. When these two tables are compared, the surprising finding is not the stability evidenced in the settings in which social workers practiced over the periods surveyed, but the changes in primary methods used by social workers within those settings.

The practice method trend that bears watching is case management. In our 1981 study we did not include case management as a response category. In our review of the individual schedules we were surprised to find the number of people who included case management under the category "Other." In 1985 and 1989, we added the case management category (as well as policy analysis and teaching), and the number of respondents

TABLE 1.2 Practice Method of NASW Members Employed Full Time, 1981, 1985, and 1989

	1981		1985		1989	
Category	*Number*	*Percent*	*Number*	*Percent*	*Number*	*Percent*
Casework	280	41.0	168	29.4	234	36.9
Group work	13	1.9	5	0.9	21	3.3
Community organization	8	1.2	7	1.2	5	0.8
Administration	189	27.8	209	36.5	134	21.1
Supervision	70	10.3	49	8.6	63	9.9
Case management	–	–	29	5.1	57	9.0
Policy analysis	–	–	9	1.6	13	2.1
Teaching	–	–	28	4.9	35	5.5
Other	121	17.8	68	11.9	72	11.4
Total	681	100.0	572	100.0	634	100.0

reporting case management as their primary practice method rose from 5.1 percent in 1985 to 9.0 percent in 1989. These data suggest some changes may be occurring in the provision of direct services by social workers. Some interesting questions arise. For example, are the knowledge and skills needed to practice casework the same as those needed to practice case management?

We want to caution our readers with the reminder that our respondents are those holding membership in NASW and tend to have MSW degrees. We have no way of knowing whether this apparent shift is occurring among social workers who are not members or who hold the baccalaureate degree in social work. While we are confident that the findings from our studies can be generalized to the membership of NASW, only time and additional research will determine whether the shifts in practice methods suggested by these data are occurring and are significant in the preparation of students for practice. However, we would observe that those utilizing indirect practice methods do not employ the same knowledge base as those providing direct services.[4]

Before moving on to the next question, we want to emphasize two points that are useful to keep in mind when thinking about what social workers do. First, the great diversity in the needs for which social work services are sought results in social workers doing a great number of different things. Second, people's needs are constantly changing which in turn influences what social workers do. The implications are that social work is a dynamic profession and that what social workers do is constantly changing.

What Do Social Workers Need to Know to Practice?

We hope that our reply to the previous question "What Do Social Workers Do?" has suggested an approach to the answer. More important, though, is recognition that a final answer does not exist. Social work is a young, dynamic, and important profession. Its change and growth will constantly require new knowledge and render some existing knowledge irrelevant. Our general position is that growth of the knowledge base for practice goes hand in hand with practice itself, each contributing to the other and affecting the other. Ralph Tyler, in writing about the attributes of a profession, put it nicely:

> Without theory, practice becomes chaotic, merely a collection of isolated, individual cases. Theory gives meaning and clarity to what would otherwise be specific and isolated cases. On the other hand, without practice, theory becomes mere speculation. The realities of practice provide a check upon pure speculation, a test of the adequacy of theory and also, practice provides the problems which must be dealt with by any comprehensive theory.[5]

Our reply to this question so far, while perhaps making sense, does not really provide much guidance to a professor who must offer instruction in the knowledge base of practice. Nor is it of much help to students interested in the relevance of what they are being taught to today's demands of professional practice. In our 1989 study we decided to ask our respondents which theories of human behavior they use in their practice. Table 1.3 displays our findings.

Since respondents were asked to check each theory that applied, column totals are not meaningful. Each percent figure represents the proportion of respondents who use the theory. For example, 41 percent of all respondents indicated that they use psychosocial theory, thus 59 percent do not. We inserted the eclectic category merely to determine the proportion of social workers who consider themselves eclectics (those who would select from a number of theories the one considered most helpful for a given application). These data suggest that 40.5 percent of our respondents consider themselves eclectics while 59.5 percent do not. Our own position would be that anyone indicating use of two or more theories in his or her practice would, by definition, be an eclectic.

These data confirm what we had assumed: that a large proportion of social workers have an eclectic approach to practice. The data also suggest that psychosocial theory is used more frequently than any other. The next most frequently used theory is social systems (31.5 percent of our respondents).

We will, in the chapters ahead, be introducing you to most of the theories identi-

TABLE 1.3   Theories Used by Members of NASW Employed Full Time, 1989

Theory	Number	Percent
Psychosocial	260	41.0
Eclectic	257	40.5
Social systems	200	31.5
Psychoanalytic/Psychodynamic	126	19.9
Behavioral	120	18.9
Humanism	58	9.1
Ecological	50	7.9
Gestalt	29	4.6
Other	37	5.8

fied in this table as well as some others. What is important to note in Table 1.3 is the number of theories used and that no single theory is used by a majority of social workers. When combined with the two previous tables these data give some idea of the richness and diversity of the practice of social work. These data also suggest how difficult it is to provide social work students the specific kinds of theoretical knowledge needed to practice. The approach we will be developing in this book builds off this diversity. Simply put, we will be providing you a model into which you can fit any of a number of different theories.

Where Are the Knowledge-Building Efforts of the Profession Now Centered?

From our contacts with colleagues and our review of the literature, we believe a clear consensus is forming indicating a reaffirmation of the profession's historical position that knowledge building be focused on the interplay between people and their environments. By reaffirmation, we wish to convey that this position was part of the origins of the profession. Mary Richmond, the acknowledged founder of the profession, put it this way as she discussed the underlying philosophy of the casework method in social work:

> Individual differences must be reckoned with in every field of endeavor, but the theory of the wider self, though it has of course other implications, seems to be at the base of social case work. We have seen how slowly such work has abandoned its few general classifications and tried itself to consider the whole man. Even more slowly is it realizing that the mind of man (and in a very real sense the mind is the man) can be described as the sum of his social relationships.[6]

Over seventy years ago Mary Richmond also lamented the failure to link our knowledge of social behavior to practice.[7] Just as there is an emerging consensus on the focus of knowledge building, so is there growing agreement on the necessity of linking our knowledge-building efforts to the practice of social work. This movement is most clearly expressed in the notion of "empirically based practice."[8]

We believe that this consensus on focus is broadening and that it is part of a larger and intensified search for agreement on the profession's purpose, sanctions, values, and methods, as well as its knowledge base.[9] We consider this a healthy and significant phase in the profession's growth.

It is important to understand where social work has been so that we can grasp where it may now be going. The profession has multiple beginnings and has focused on "doing." We left the task of knowledge building to those in psychiatry, psychology, and sociology, among others. In recent decades there has been a vast increase in the growth of knowledge as well as in the forms taken in social work practice. Tensions have increased around the problem of what to borrow and from whom. The problem of a "goodness of fit" has also become an issue, as well as the question, "Does it work?"[10] It is these issues and problems that now seem to be moving social workers, particularly those in social work education, to assume greater responsibility for building a knowledge base more clearly related to what we do. In so doing, it is also squarely replying affirmatively to the long-standing and nagging question, "Is social work a profession?"[11]

What Are the Differences among Concept, Theory, Perspective, and Model?

These four terms may be familiar to you, but reviewing them will help us think about current knowledge-building efforts in social work. Although some writers use these terms synonymously, we make distinctions among them that help in building a knowledge base to practice.

Briefly stated, a concept is an idea that is used to describe something we wish to communicate. A theory is also an idea, but one that not only describes but offers a proposed explanation for the idea being advanced. A perspective represents a very broad and general view in which everything contained in that view is seen in its proper relationship. A model is a simplified representation of something real.

Concept

Concepts are the building blocks for theories.[12] A concept is a special kind of "idea," for example, social systems is a concept. The idea being expressed is that many groupings of people are characterized by systemlike features in their relationships with each other—they can be viewed as interdependent and interconnected parts of a whole. In other words, the actions of any one member of the group tend to affect the actions of other group members. Familiar groupings in which there are interdependent relationships among members include such diverse examples as a family, a worker and client, the congregation of a church, the staff of a mental health center, and the residents of a community.

Unlike a theory, a concept does not explain; it only gives a name to an idea. In the example of the social system, the idea being advanced is that many human groupings exhibit features of systemlike interdependence and wholeness. No explanation is contained in the concept as to why this presumed interdependence exists. As we will see in the next section, a theory addresses the "why" question. For now let us stay with the notion of concept and our example. You might say to us, "I am not sure that I understand what is being added here. You seem to be saying that you can call a family or any such group a social system. It seems to me that you are making things more complicated than they need to be. Why not just call a family a family?" We would agree with you if all we were doing was substituting one name for another. What is being added is a focus on a characteristic possessed by most families, and, indeed, most other forms of human groupings—the sense of interdependence and wholeness that members exhibit. By giving a name and thereby focusing on these characteristics, we are led to ask questions: What accounts for this appearance of interdependence and wholeness? Do all human groupings exhibit such characteristics? Does this apparent interdependence and wholeness have effects on the individuals who comprise the group? If so, what are the effects? These are the kinds of questions that lead to theory construction.

Theory

A **theory** is an idea that offers an explanation for the idea itself. A theory is comprised of a set of related assumptions and concepts. In our example, a theory would represent an explanation of the idea behind the concept of social system. For example, a theory would propose answers to the questions noted previously concerning the effects of the interdependence of group members on the group itself (group development) and on those individuals comprising the group (individual development). In recent years, a number of system theories have been advanced, particularly pertaining to the family.[13] Some have moved beyond attention to any one type of group, seeking instead to use system concepts to formulate a more general theory of human behavior.[14] These efforts have been helpful, but to date none of these theories has received general acceptance as constituting the base for the practice of social work.

Before discussing the more technical aspects of a theory, let us examine theory as an everyday way of thinking. For example, most of us have heard or been a part of the following exchange many times: "What do you think she (or he) sees in him (or her)? My theory is that. . . ." Offered is an explanation or a "personal theory" about some behavior of interest. Comprising this explanation is a series of observations about the couple involved. Probably also contributing to the explanation are some basic assumptions about human nature held by the person offering this explanation, for example: "After all, you know how men (women) are!"

What we call scientific theories hold much in common with the thinking just described. Typically, a theory results from a series of careful observations a person makes of behaviors or phenomena of interest. It is important to keep in mind that theory development does not take place in a vacuum, but builds on existing knowledge and beliefs; these we will refer to as **assumptions**.

In our opinion it is useful to view assumptions (beliefs) as comprising the foundations upon which theory development takes place, particularly in the social sciences. It is on this foundation that the person develops or specifies a series of concepts that help to describe the phenomenon being observed; next the person indicates the relationships presumed to exist among these various concepts in terms of the effect being explained by stating a hypothesis. These hypotheses or statements are then tested to be proven or disproven using the methods of science.

We have noted that in the social sciences, assumptions form the foundations upon which theory building takes place. Sigmund Freud's psychoanalytic theory can provide a familiar example of this point. He made the assumption that there were just two basic psychological motives, sexuality and aggression, which were in turn related to one's underlying animal nature. This assumption is a major part of the foundation of psychoanalytic theory.[15] Many of the concepts and relationships that comprise this theory, for example, infantile sexuality, id, and Oedipus complex, are to be understood within the context provided by this motivational assumption. Assumptions such as Freud's are broad in scope and, by their very nature, do not easily lend themselves to direct scientific verification. Such an assumption can be thought of more as a belief or a "given" than a scientific assertion.

Our stress on the importance of assumptions in understanding and evaluating theories pertains to the general process of knowledge building and some differences that may exist in this effort between the physical and social sciences. In thinking about possible differences, it is important to remember that the methods of science have their clearest origins and applications within the physical sciences. Social scientists have borrowed these methods and have sought to apply them to social phenomena—human behavior. Many argue that there are problems of fit, which are a function of the qualitative differences between the phenomena studied. Consequently, great care has to be used in the application of methods derived from the physical world to the social. For example, three quite different objects fall from an apple tree at the same time: a leaf, an apple, and a child. Assuming all of the physical conditions are known, the law of gravity can predict precisely the conditions of the fall and, under specified conditions, the time that each will strike the ground. While for certain purposes the identical behaviors of these three objects may be useful to know, in others the similarities are irrelevant. The child differs *qualitatively* from the other two objects; the fall has meaning to the child, but not to the other objects. In the case of the child, falling to the ground may have been a response to mother's call to dinner or an attempt to show off to his or her friends. Any attempt to understand the conditions of the child's falling from the tree that does not consider the child's social environment (mother or friends) would miss the critical features of the fall.

In the study of human behavior, we make assumptions that are different from those typically made in the physical sciences, and these assumptions might have important consequences to the methods used in theory construction and testing. In the preceding example, an underlying assumption might be that all human social behavior has meaning both to the person exhibiting it and to those affected by it. Such an assumption probably never occurred to Sir Isaac Newton in his studies of gravity and motion. But given this assumption, any theory of human social behavior must include attention to consciousness of self and others. More will be said of this assumption later when we distinguish between open and closed systems. It is enough to say at this point that most theory construction in the physical sciences has been based on the assumption of a closed system, for example, control against external influences on the subject matter. Our approach to knowledge building assumes the opposite position, an open system. In other words, human social behavior is to be understood by viewing the individual and the influence of her or his social environment.

For many the pursuit of a common knowledge base that would serve to ground social work's various practice methods was the search for one grand theory. To date and as suggested by the data displayed in Table 1.3, this search has proved unsuccessful but has served to suggest another strategy, a search for a common perspective.[16]

Perspective

A **perspective** is a way of looking at things as a whole. In contrast to theories, perspectives tend to be much broader in scope and do not attempt to explain or predict. Many people in social work are no longer concerned with finding a theory or set of theories to provide the scientific base for the general practice of social work. Part of the difficulty has been that previous grand theory searches have not recognized the great diversities that exist in practice and the profession's current state of development.[17]

Consensus now seems to be forming that the search for unity in the profession be concentrated on finding a common perspective. Ann Minahan, a well-regarded social work scholar, describes the need for a common perspective:

> Before applying theories to situations, we need to use a perspective for looking at situations of concern to social workers—situations that flow from our focus on interactions of persons and their environment and our purpose to promote mutually beneficial interactions. Our perspective needs to be broad enough to help us identify and view all pertinent interactions in specific situations. We need a perspective that helps us think about interdependence and connectedness.[18]

We share her position. For us a perspective, while focusing on wholeness, will also contain a set of broadly based assumptions and related concepts. A perspective differs from a theory in that it is a "viewpoint," a way of describing something of interest in general terms; it does not offer in researchable terms an explanation of the view. A perspective does provide a broad framework within which theory development can and should take place.

In Chapter 2 we sketch a social systems perspective. For us it is a way of thinking about human behavior and the social environment and is preliminary to developing a social systems theory.

Model

To **model** something is to create a likeness, usually a simplified version of something that is real. Models can take an infinite number of forms, ranging from the very simple to the extremely complex. For example, a doll is a model—in most instances a miniature and simplified representation of a person. The doll can have many important uses, ranging from being a child's toy to a medium of communication in play therapy between a therapist and a disturbed child. The simulators used in driver education classes are also models. They are more complex than the doll and incorporate both key features of a car and selected driving conditions, or the car's environment. By simplifying, through a representation of both the automobile and driving conditions, the simulators become helpful tools in teaching us how to drive.

The models mentioned so far have physical properties; for example, plastic used in fashioning a doll. Models can also be comprised of sets of interrelated ideas (concepts), or theories, or can be drawn from a particular perspective. The model in this book is just that sort of model—a way of modeling human behavior and the social environment. Like any other model, it is a simplified version of something real. As indicated earlier, there is an enormous amount of knowledge pertaining both to human behavior and to the social environment. The problem is that this knowledge exists in bits and pieces, and there is the added problem of how relevant much of this knowledge is to the practice of social work. We deal with these problems by selectively drawing from an enormous array of knowledge that is deemed useful in describing human behavior *and* the social environment.

There is an old saying in social work—"Start where your client is." This has been our intent. For us there is a consensus within the profession that future knowledge-

building efforts should focus on understanding human behavior as it is shaped by interactions with the social environment. Our approach is to model this interaction as a
social system. Like an overlay, this model can then be applied to any form of human
association with interdependent features.

We first identified a perspective about human behavior and the social environment
and labeled this a social systems perspective. Based on this perspective, we then fashioned a model that simulates the various groupings in which our clients exist and the
methods we use to help them. The model is like a basic framework to which various
concepts and theories can be added differentially in accordance with practice needs. The
number of concepts and theories added is determined by the person using the model.
The more concepts and theories added, the more complex the model.

What Is the Social Systems Model?

The **social systems model** is a way of looking at people, the many kinds of groupings
that people form, and the effects of these associations on human behavior. In short,
it is the approach we use for examining the interrelationships between human behavior
and the social environment. These groupings take many and varied forms ranging from
the family to gangs, counseling relationships, agencies, and society as a whole. Because of
their common ordering features, each can be modeled as a social system in a manner
that is useful to the practice of social work.

Before describing the model, we want to share an assumption we hold about such
groupings or more generally about human behavior and the social environment. The
assumption is that the individual is both the *cause* and the *effect* of all such groups. There
is a circular relationship between the individual and the groupings of which the individual is a part; each affects the others. The family can be used to illustrate this point. It is
the individual's need for a sense of belonging, a sexual partner, and a stable, caring
intimate relationship within which to raise children that helps explain the existence of
the family as a basic and universal type of human grouping. It is in this sense that persons and their needs can be viewed as the *cause* for the creation of the family. Similarly,
for most people, the relationships among family members represent a vital and ongoing
influence in shaping their own sense of selfhood. This is most clearly evident in the
impact the family has on children, that is, its socialization function. It is in this latter
sense that the individual as a distinct human personality can be viewed as an *effect* or an
outcome of the various groupings of which she or he is a part.

For us the assumption of the individual being considered both the cause and effect
of all forms of human groupings was the first step in operationalizing what is meant by
"human behavior and the social environment." This assumption established the logic for
viewing the individual and the social environment in which the individual has existence
as a whole or in John Donne's words as "a part of the main." We build on this logic by
also considering the various groupings that humans join together to form as separate
and distinct social entities, such as families, organizations, and communities. These
larger social entities too have social environments and therefore must be viewed as
wholes comprised of interdependent parts.

The social systems model is comprised of eight major concepts. Each of these concepts represents a set of ideas about the characteristics we believe are possessed by all human groupings exhibiting the qualities of wholeness and interdependence. The eight concepts are: (1) boundary, (2) suprasystem, (3) interface, (4) inputs, (5) outputs, (6) proposed outputs, (7) conversion operations, and (8) feedback. Figure 1.1 displays the model and indicates the relationships among these eight concepts. The model conveys our approach for conceptualizing the notion of human behavior and the social environment. The large central figure is a subject system, for example, a family. The small circles are components of the system's **suprasystem**, for example, a family's social environment (other individuals, families, organizations, and so on, to which the family is functionally linked). The basic notion is that the system is functionally linked to other social systems through what we term *output-input* exchanges. The area outside the suprasystem is desig-

FIGURE 1.1 The Social Systems Model   *Know for test*

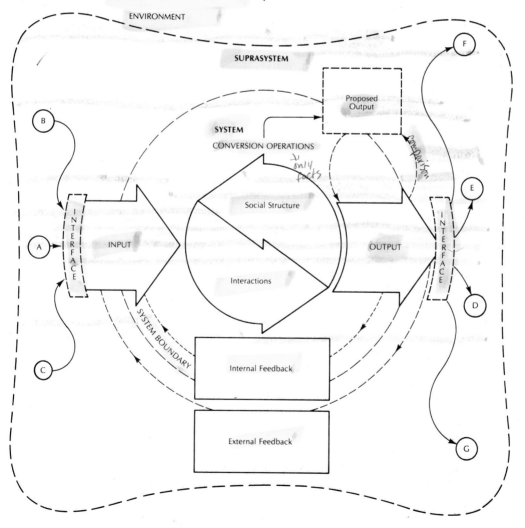

ENVIRONMENT

SUPRASYSTEM

Proposed Output

SYSTEM

CONVERSION OPERATIONS

Social Structure

INTERFACE

INPUT

OUTPUT

INTERFACE

Interactions

SYSTEM BOUNDARY

Internal Feedback

External Feedback

nated as environment. This larger environment affects the system and its suprasystem, but we treat these influences as secondary.

We were faced with a dilemma in thinking about how best to present to you an initial application of the model. Since most of you are social work students, we thought that an application to a case comprising a social worker and client might be most meaningful. The problem was in finding the kind of case that each of you could relate to meaningfully. Since some of you may not be seeing clients yet, we settled instead on using your school or department of social work as a primary example. Not only is this a "system" to which each of you can relate, it is one that is vitally affecting you as a person. This interchange between the person and the systems of which he or she is a part and their mutual effects is what the model seeks to illustrate.

In this initial application think about yourself as a student and thus a member of the system. Also think about the school as a system, a separate and distinct social entity that also possesses a social environment. Finally, when thinking about yourself, your fellow students, and your professors, think in terms of the specific roles that each of you play. Simply put, a social system is a system of interconnected and interdependent roles that individuals take on and enact.

We will use the eight concepts to describe the model. While for purposes of introduction we will be examining them one by one, they are interdependent parts of a whole. It is the eight concepts *and* the relationships among these concepts that comprise the social systems model.

Boundary

The **boundary** defines the subject system. In so doing, it also defines the appropriate roles that will be enacted by those comprising the system, for example, student, professor, secretary, or department chair. Like our skin, one purpose of a boundary is to protect the system so that its function is not adversely affected by external influences. The boundary accomplishes its purpose largely by controlling internal and external exchanges between the system and its relevant social environment (suprasystem). For example, if you are a student in this school you must have gone through an admission process, paid your fees, and met all the system requirements needed to become a student, a member of the system.

Now for a universal behavior associated with a boundary: All social systems possess boundaries and actively maintain them. In our example, if you refused to pay your student fees or failed to meet some other critical system standard, you would soon experience some of the school's boundary-maintaining behaviors; in other words, you would lose your status as a member of the system. It is important to remember that each of the concepts comprising the model seeks to describe a characteristic social behavior exhibited by *all* forms of human groupings.

Let us now return to our example. To assist in maintaining its boundary, your school/university probably issued you a student identification (I.D.) card. This card identifies you and your student role to other members of the system. A boundary-maintaining behavior would be your use of this card to check a book out of your library. You are a member of the system and thus have certain rights and responsibilities not held by nonmembers. In short, boundary-maintaining behaviors serve to distinguish insiders from outsiders. In our example, the I.D. card is an artifact indicating the presence of a boundary. The card is not the boundary itself—boundary is a relationship concept—it is not anything physical. It is your use of the card that illustrates the presence of a boundary.

To understand the universal nature of these concepts, think of your own family as the subject system. How are its boundaries evident and maintained? In considering the concept of boundary, remember that every social system is deemed to be dynamic, constantly changing and developing; this means that its boundaries will also be constantly changing. In our own birth families and in growing up, we each had to abide by family rules, some of which served a boundary-maintaining function. For example, many of our birth families felt it important that all family members have dinner together. It was a strict rule that we be home by 6:00 P.M.—that was dinner time! All family members respected the importance of sharing dinner together so we all arranged our schedules accordingly. The preservation of this time by all family members would evidence a boundary-maintaining behavior. Also, if we had friends in the house, at 6:00 P.M., it was time for them to leave (unless "invited" to join the family for dinner). Remember, boundaries serve to define and help preserve and develop the social system. Again think of your own family and especially how boundaries change. To understand the idea, look back at your early and later dating practices and the role of your family. What were some of the rules and how did they change? Specifically, what purpose did these boundary-maintaining rules perform with respect to your family as a whole? What were the effects of these rules on you as a person? How did they change as you grew older?

Suprasystem

The system's social environment, or the larger system of which the subject system is a part, is called the **suprasystem**. Like the system itself, the suprasystem is composed of member units. In this model, every system will have identifiable people, groups, and organizations to which it is functionally linked. In a manner of speaking, the concept of suprasystem gets at the notion of "social" in social work and "social" in social environment.

In our example, selected departments or colleges within your university would probably comprise parts of your school's suprasystem, as would those social agencies that provide internships or practica for students. In Figure 1.1, the suprasystem is conveyed by the broken line surrounding the subject system. In an actual application of the model, each of the small circles contained in Figure 1.1 would refer to specific organizations or groups that comprise part of your school's suprasystem. We will use our own school as an example. As a department of the College of Arts and Sciences, our college office has a vital effect on what can and cannot be done at the school because, for example, the monies that support the program are provided by the college. Simply put, to understand the behaviors of our school requires an understanding of the relationship between our school and the college office. Another example would be our relationship with a community mental health center where a number of our students have their practicum placements. This is a separate and distinct agency but one that is vitally linked to our educational program. Again, to understand our school would require an understanding of some of the relationships we have with key agencies and groups that while external to the school, have a vital effect on what we do.

The concept of suprasystem helps to identify another universal behavior: *All* social systems are open as opposed to being closed. They relate to other social units that are external to them through input-output exchanges; that is, one system's output is input to another system. When you graduate and leave the school (an output), you will enter a social agency as a new social work professional (an input).

In thinking about concepts like suprasystem, it is important to remember that you are using a model as a representation of something real. It is no more than a tool to help you categorize your observations. In so doing, the model becomes a way to better understand the social organization to which you are applying the model, be it a helping relationship, a family, or a community.

Again, think about your own birth family. In trying to understand what your family was like, what were the key external influences that helped shape it through the years? In short, what key individuals, groups, and organizations comprised its suprasystem?

Interface

Interface identifies a boundary shared with another system, one that comprises part of its suprasystem. Some of the terms we are using and their meanings may be new to you, and may appear more complicated than they really are. For example, the term *interface* is no more than a name for the idea that relationships people have with each other and with groups comprising their social environment are distinctive, not all the same. What this means is that in order to understand the behaviors of a system it is necessary also to understand the distinctive relationships it has with those other systems that comprise its suprasystem (social environment).

We define *suprasystem* as the larger system of which the **subject system** is a part. The subject system will have an interdependent relationship with each of the other organizations and groups that comprise its suprasystem. That part of the relationship that defines their mutual boundary and specifies the conditions and arrangements for their cooperative work is what we term *interface*.

The universal behavior to be noted here is that boundaries are always jointly maintained. In our example of a school, the contracts it has with social agencies that provide practicum settings would represent an interface. Here we would expect that both the school and the agency would abide by the agreements set forth in the contract; they thus jointly share the boundary-maintaining function. An interface may be evidenced by informal or formal agreements, or both. In Figure 1.1, interface is represented by the arrows that connect the smaller systems with the subject system. The connecting points can be viewed as their common boundary.

The concept of interface may be a difficult one to grasp. For us it is a helpful way to individualize relationships. While the concept has applications at the individual level, for example, between two individuals in their spousal roles of wife and husband, our interest is the relationship feature that connects the subject system to a *specific* system in its suprasystem. Once again think of your own family and those individuals and groups that you earlier identified as comprising its suprasystem. Can you think of an example of interface, a jointly shared boundary? A typical example would be the sharing of special occasions with one or more other families as would be the case if your family and your maternal grandparents spent Mother's Day together. These are special times, with each family setting the time aside to be together to reaffirm their special relationship. Each family maintains this boundary that connects their family with others. Your authors are both grandparents. A special kind of interface for us is the one that connects our respective families to our children and their families. Keep in mind that interface refers to a common boundary and that in maintaining that common boundary, common roles are specified along with acceptable and unacceptable behaviors. Simply put, the interface between our families and our children's families defines in part our role as grandparents. In one instance, this means under no circumstances can we give the grandchildren candy. In another, certain television programs are off limits.

If boundaries are not mutually maintained, problems develop that tend to create instability and disorganization. This disorganization can affect one or all of the groups that share a common boundary as well as the individuals who comprise such groups. As you move into practice, you are going to encounter a variety of human problems that result in part from the breakdown of boundaries that were to be mutually maintained, as, for example, in the sexual abuse of children.

Input

Inputs represent all the incoming resources, including individuals, who after some conversion process become the system's output. The concept of input helps us convey the interdependent relationships that we believe characterize all forms of human groupings because one system's input comes from another system. The notion of input also helps us to further develop the open system features of this model. Earlier in developing the concept of suprasystem, we identified the universal behavior as "All social systems relate to their suprasystems through input-output exchanges." Here we develop the input side of the exchange. For us the notion of exchange is central in both describing the model and in identifying a key dynamic undergirding human behavior and the social environment, that of exchanging something for something else.

Now let us explore the concept of input by further developing our example. While a bit awkward, think of yourself as an input to your school. As a matter of fact, you and your fellow students are your school's most important input. Your school can be usefully thought of as having been created as the means of preparing you and others to become social workers. Using the same idea but with a different example, a client entering into a helping relationship with a worker would represent the key input into that helping system. Similarly, the specific form of the helping system will be determined largely by the needs of that client and the helping capabilities of the worker. Here we have the start of an exchange.

Now let us take these two examples and return for a moment to the concepts of suprasystem and boundary. Prior to your acceptance into the school, you were part of the school's suprasystem. In a conceptual sense, you can also be thought of as the output of some other system, for example, a family, a junior college, another university, or an agency you left upon deciding to return to school to get your social work degree. In each of these instances you represent an important connection as you move between systems. You are the output of one and the input of another. Also, the school has a boundary to screen its inputs, one that determined whether you possessed the qualifications to enter the system. In this same fashion and prior to acceptance, a client is part of a helping system's suprasystem. The client can also be thought of as representing an output of a system, perhaps one associated with the problem for which the client is seeking help; for example, a family-related difficulty. To become an input, the client must pass through a boundary, a screening process aimed at determining whether the system is an appropriate one. The point here is that interdependent relationships exist between every system and its suprasystem; each is dependent upon the other in some manner and each is part of a whole.

Output

Output is the name given to inputs following completion of a processing cycle. In discussing the concept of input we made the point that it helped us operationalize the open systems features of this model. The same thing is true for output; here we are dealing with the other side of the exchange. Rather than taking something in from the suprasystem (an input), something is being exported; we term this an output. It is through the notion of input-output exchanges that an explanation is offered to a general ordering process evident in social life. This idea of exchange also offers meaning to the words of John Donne that introduced this chapter: "No man is an island, entire of itself; Every man is a piece of the continent, a part of the main."

Now let us develop the concept of output by using your school. Just as you were your school's most valuable input, upon receipt of your professional degree you become its most valuable output. You become an output in the sense that you have been "processed" and you leave the system. Given the purposes of professional education, we would expect that you and most of your classmates will take positions in social work agencies. We will also assume that you have, through your schooling, acquired the knowledge and skills to practice effectively in your new position. We are again back to the output-input relationship between systems. Now you are an output of the school as well as an input to the agency that has employed you. You are a vital connector of the two. On the output side, each is dependent on the other, and each is a part of the whole. In the same sense, upon completion of a counseling relationship, a client is an output of that helping system; the client will represent an input into one or more new or existing systems. Also as a result of the helping system, the client should be better able to function in these other systems.

The whole idea of thinking about people in input and output terms may be uncomfortable for some of us and may seem mechanical. The problem we faced as authors was finding terms and existing concepts that could be applied to any type or size of social system. For example, just as you with your newly acquired knowledge and skill can be thought of as an output of your school, so can a comprehensive plan to combat the problem of the homeless be thought of as an output of a community. On still a larger scale and in negative (dysfunctional) terms, racist or sexist policies and practices (such as apartheid) can be viewed as a societal output. Again, what we are using are sets of concepts that can be appropriately applied to a social system of any size and degree of complexity.

Proposed Output

Purpose and *goal* would serve as synonyms for our use of the term **proposed output**. There is a widely held assumption among social scientists that individuals behave purposively. We extend the same notion to all the forms of human association that individuals join together to form. It is this assumption of purposiveness in human associations that serves as the basic organizing scheme of the social systems model.

A word of caution is indicated here. We are not limiting the concept of proposed output to explicitly stated or even consciously held goals. The point being made is that purposiveness in social behavior is deemed to be universal and is operationalized in this model by the concept of proposed output.

Before moving on to the examples, we want to link the model to existing theory. The model offers a way of thinking about relationships, about the interdependence of people. Within the general framework provided by the model, there are many different approaches for seeking more in-depth understanding of the specific behaviors being exhibited by a person. It is through the use of existing theories applied *within* the model that one can extend and increase the usefulness of the model. For example, psychoanalytic and humanistic theory both assume that behavior is motivated and purposive. While sharing similar assumptions, the general perspectives held about human behavior, its motivational sources, and its goals are quite different. By selectively and appropriately adding such theories, the model takes on more varied and situationally specific applications. We will be reviewing various theories and their applications to this model throughout this book. We now want only to establish that the concept of proposed output is used to operationalize the universality of purposiveness in human social behaviors.

Now let us return to our example. Just as you as an individual have personal goals that led you to seek a professional education in a school of social work, so does your school have goals. These goals pertain to the kinds of knowledge, skills, and values that the school believes you should possess at the time you graduate. Where are these goals derived? They represent an informed judgment by your faculty as to what is needed to effectively practice social work. They have most likely been influenced by suggestions offered by previous groups of students, agencies that employ the school's graduates, the school's accrediting organization, and funding agencies, which are the agencies and groups that comprise the school's suprasystem.

The goals (proposed output) of a social system, as distinguished from those of an individual, will be shared by those comprising the system. It is the sharing of goals that helps provide the cohesiveness needed for the system to be sustained and to function. An example related to practice can help make the point. It is axiomatic in social work practice for the worker to actively involve the client in setting the goals for the helping relationship. To the extent that these goals are mutually held and supported by the client, the worker, *and* those comprising the helping system's suprasystem, the system is off to a good start. To the extent this is not true or does not develop, we predict difficulties resulting in diminished system success.

Conversion Operations

The processes by which a system transforms its inputs to outputs are called **conversion operations**. The process itself can be very short or very long. In our example of your school, processing lasts about two years. In a helping or counseling relationship, the process may be completed in one interview or continue for a year or more. In the case of a marriage (or family), the processing may last a lifetime. As we will see later, the purposes of the system will be a vital determinant of the length of the processing cycle. Also, most cycles are comprised of subcycles, which in turn produce outputs; for example, your semester grades, or, in a helping relationship, the completion of the assessment phase (cycle). The universal behavior associated with this concept is that every form of human grouping exists to achieve some (shared) purpose and will have identifiable and understandable means for pursuing its purpose(s). Conversion operations is the label that we give this process. Again caution is in order. While we indicate that this process is an identifiable and understandable one, it does not follow that in any given instance it is either fully identifiable or understood. For example, what is the effect of your family on you as a person? The family, as we will show later, can be modeled as a social system. Personhood or sense of self can be treated as one of its outputs. For example, your parents probably had some goals for you—some aspirations that in part guided family interactions. What were they in your case? What were the effects of family life on you and your development? What about your own goals? How have your goals and those of your family meshed? Any problems? Most of us have thought about and have searched for answers for these and similar questions. Many of the clients you will see will also be searching for answers to these kinds of questions.

The questions we have just posed are complicated ones. In the vernacular of the model, we can view ourselves as outputs from a number of systems, including family, school, and work, to mention but a few. The more difficult problem is understanding the processes that produce the output. These are the system's conversion operations. The model provides a basic organizing scheme that is useful descriptively; however, it does not answer the questions of "how" and "why." There are a number of important lines of theory development in the social sciences that, when used within the framework provided by the model, do address the "how" and "why" questions. We will be reviewing some of these theories in later chapters.

It is important to keep in mind that the model is generic. It seeks to identify a basic form of ordering that is characteristic of all types of human groupings. In other words, the pattern that is modeled will be identifiable at the individual, family, group, organizational, and community levels. This means that at each level of application all concepts that comprise the model will be used. While at each level there will be the counterpart of conversion operations, the lines of theory development to be applied to explicate these operations will be specific to the level of application.

We need now to introduce two subconcepts useful in describing key features of a conversion operation: structure and interactions. Structure refers to behavioral guides; interaction refers to the behavior itself. As we all know, what we expect people to do and what they actually do are two quite different things. Let us return to your school as an example. The conversion operation is the sum total of all the teaching and learning experiences that the school (the system) provides you in your quest for a professional education. It is the means through which you achieve an intended end state, a professional degree. Structure is evidenced in such things as the organization of curriculum and the sequencing of courses, as well as the sequencing of learning experiences within a course. Structure can be likened to a map. Within a course, the syllabus or course outline is another key indicator of structure. The syllabus should indicate both the educational goals (proposed output) and, like a map, the means the professor intends to use to achieve those goals.

Roles are the dominant structural features used in this model; in fact, a social system can be thought of as a system of roles. Simply put, a role is a set of behaviors expected of a person occupying a position in a social system. Roles link positions together functionally. In other words, a role is the way you expect your professor to act, and it is the way the professor expects you as a student to act. It does not follow that roles are going to be played out in the expected manner. Playing them out is what we mean by interactions, the actual behavior occurring between two or more people enacting system roles.

The central point we want to get across is that if we know the roles and other important structural features of a social system, we have a pretty good idea of how people will be expected to behave toward one another. Based on how we expect people to behave in a specific social system (structural expectations), we then secure information as to how they actually behave (interactions). In most instances we do not rely just on information obtained from the person enacting the role (our client), but from other relevant sources as well, those in related roles. We also will usually obtain information on the expected and actual role behaviors from those who comprise the suprasystem. In a way it is like putting a jigsaw puzzle together. By assessing both anticipated and actual behaviors of the system and its suprasystem, what had before looked like bits and pieces now looks like a whole; it is systemlike.

Feedback

The frequency in use of the term **feedback** in everyday conversation is probably a good measure of the extent to which systems thinking is penetrating our way of everyday life. In our modeling of social systems, feedback has a very specific meaning. It is information on the extent to which output conforms to proposed output. You might, as we develop the notion of feedback, wish to reexamine Figure 1.1. Proposed output (goals) is shown in that figure by a rectangularly shaped box (broken lines). It is connected by arrows to output. The comparison starts with what was intended. This in turn is examined in terms of what actually happened, which is the actual output. Feedback or the results of this comparison are then cycled back as one type of input. Figure 1.1 shows two lines of feedback, one occurring within the system, the second from outside, from the suprasystem. Internal feedback deals with comparisons from those who comprise the subject system. External feedback results from the comparisons made by those who comprise the system's suprasystem.

Feedback, as used in this model, links all of the other concepts together in a manner that highlights the qualities of interdependence and wholeness. Recall that it is these same qualities that we believe are evident in all forms of human groupings.

To explain the concept in terms of your school, if there is a good fit between the knowledge and skills you acquire and the knowledge and skills the employing agency expects you to possess, the feedback loop is working. If severe differences develop between what the agency expects its workers to possess and what the graduates of the school actually acquire, a feedback problem is evidenced and needs to be addressed in some manner. As indicated, feedback will always be generated from both internal and external sources. Internal sources are those people who are members of the system. An example is your feeling about whether the school is actually meeting its goals: Are you getting from the school what you expected and conveying this information to an appropriate source? An external source would be the evaluation of the school's performance provided by an accreditation site visit team from the Council on Social Work Education. In both instances, feedback would be the comparisons made between proposed output (goals and objectives) and actual output.

We have now completed our reply to the question, "What is the social systems model?" It is an approach that models human social behavior as a social system. It is also an open system, which means that the approach to building an understanding of human behavior and the social environment simultaneously addresses behaviors occurring within the system and between the system and its suprasystem. Now to our final question in this chapter.

Can the Individual Be Modeled as a Social System?

Earlier we made the point that from our position, upon which we have constructed our model, the individual is both the cause and the effect of all forms of human groupings, from the family to society itself. In this model then, the individual is always a part of the social system, never the whole system. Our interest is in understanding the effects of the various human groupings on the individual and the individual's effects on the human associations of which she or he is a part. We consider this interplay to be the focal point for knowledge building in social work and the foundation which informs practice. Therefore an individual cannot be modeled as a *social* system.

For some this assumption that the individual is both the cause and the effect of all forms of human association is a difficult and perhaps a troublesome notion. Grasping the implications of this point is critical in building a knowledge base for the special contribution that social work makes in the helping professions. While the individual client's well-being is always the central concern, the professional helping effort starts with the recognition that the person is a physical, psychological, spiritual, and social being: each is part of the whole. However, it is the understanding of the person as a social being that constitutes the main area for the contribution of the social work profession. The individual social worker can then be expected to possess expert knowledge about the social determinants of behavior and their implications in the helping process. This does not mean that the social worker ignores the physical, psychological, and spiritual dimensions of the individual. It does mean that the social worker possesses an area of expert knowledge in the same sense as the physician, psychologist, and minister. What it also means is that there will be instances in which the social worker will function as a team member and will contribute her or his special knowledge to a team effort. In other instances where the social dimensions of the case are primary, the social worker can be expected to assume the primary helping responsibility.

SUMMARY

In this chapter we posed a series of questions, the answers to which provide an introduction to the book. In replying to the first question, "What is this book about?", we identified the foundations upon which an approach to knowledge building useful to the practice of social work can be developed. The path taken is embodied in a social systems model that focuses on the dynamic interplay between the person and those who comprise that person's social environment.

In addressing the questions dealing with our audience, why we undertook to write this book, and the nature of social work practice, we identified the richness and the diversity of practice and the problems these features pose to those who are preparing for careers in social work. We believe that most if not all social workers have struggled at one time or another with their own professional identity. Because we do so many things for so many different kinds of clients we sometimes stop and ask ourselves, "Just what do we social workers do that is different from what other professional helpers do, like the psychiatrist, psychologist, or minister?" The approach developed in this book represents our answer to this nagging question.

The answers supplied to the questions dealing with what social workers do and where the profession is focusing its knowledge-building efforts are the origins of the ideas upon which the social systems model is based. Rapidly emerging, in our view, is a consensus on the mission of the profession that is a reaffirmation of its historical attention to help based on a perspective that views the person within a social environment; it is a view that incorporates the features of interdependence and wholeness. To us this means renewed attention to the "social" in social work.

We complete our overview by replying to the questions about the ideas that comprise an approach to knowledge building in social work and a description of the model itself. In short, the model is based on a social systems perspective, a way of looking at human behavior in the social environment. The model builds from a belief that the social worker's special area of expert knowledge and practice competence stems from an understanding of the person as a "social being." The mission of social work is thus understood as directed toward an improvement in the quality of human life by assisting people to become and maintain their social competence, their sense of themselves as social beings. We pursue this effort through both direct and indirect practice methods.

The answer to the chapter's final question, "Can the individual be modeled as a social system?" is "No." This question and its reply are intended to serve as a transition to the next chapter, which introduces the perspective upon which the model is based. *Social* means the involvement of others; it is the ordering of the person's involvement with others that we will be modeling in the chapters ahead.

Our reply to the question about the relationship of the individual and the notion of a social system is also intended to identify one of the most critical implications in the use of the model. Just as the individual's behavior is to be understood in terms of its social context, the same is true of the family, the agency, the community, or any of the many groupings that individuals join together to form; each is to be understood as having been affected and being affected by a social environment. Each is part of a larger whole; each is "a part of of the main."

GLOSSARY

Assumption A belief or supposition that something is true. An example of an assumption in psychoanalytic theory is that all behavior is motivated.

Boundary The external limits of a system, the region which separates the system from its suprasystem. A marriage license or contract sets a family apart as a system.

Concept A mental construct or idea derived from or associated with a theory, perspective or model.

Direct practice The form of social work practice that involves direct client contact, usually face to face, for example, casework.

Feedback The return of information to the system as input. This information pertains to the extent to which actual output conforms to proposed output. A social worker's agency supervisor provides feedback to her or him regarding her or his work with a family.

Indirect practice The form of social work practice that only involves indirect contact with clients. For example, social work administration is conducted on behalf of clients but does not usually involve direct contact with them.

Input All of the resources, including people, that are required by a social system to accomplish its purposes. Money appropriated to an agency is a vital input.

Interface A boundary segment which is shared and maintained by two systems, for example, a contract between a school of social work and a child welfare agency through which the agency would provide practicum placements for the school's students.

Model A representation of something real, for example, a social systems model is a representation of a social organization.

Output System inputs are processed by the system and they become outputs, for instance, the status of a client's problem at the time of case termination.

Perspective A way of viewing things broadly so that their relationships and relative importance are understood.

Proposed output A statement of what a system intends to accomplish, a system's goals and objectives, for example.

Social system A social entity characterized by individuals or other social units possessing functionally interdependent relationships with each other, for example, a family, agency or community.

Social systems model A particular representation of a social system.

Subject system A specified social system to which the model is to be applied, for example, the Arnold family.

Suprasystem That aspect of the social environment to which a subject system is functionally linked; for example, birth families are relevant parts of a family's suprasystem.

Theory A logically derived set of assumptions and concepts used to explain something, for instance, psychoanalytic theory.

NOTES

1. See, for example, the overview provided by Donald Brieland, "History and Evolution of Social Work Practice," *Encyclopedia of Social Work*, vol. 1, (Silver Spring, Md.: National Association of Social Workers, 1987), 739–754.

2. For the quality of life focus see, particularly, "Working Statement on the Purpose of Social Work," *Social Work*, 26, no. 1 (January 1981): 6.

3. For a discussion of this research and the source of these tables see Wayne A. Chess, Julia M. Norlin and Srinika Jayaratne, "Social Work Administration 1981–1985: Alive, Happy and Prospering," *Administration in Social Work*, in press.

4. See Rosemary C. Sarri, "Administration in Social Welfare," *Encyclopedia of Social Work*, vol. 1, (Silver Spring, Md.: National Association of Social Workers, 1987), 27–40.

5. Ralph Tyler, "Distinctive Attributes of Education for the Professions," *Social Work* 33 (April 1952): 61.

6. Mary E. Richmond, *Social Diagnosis* (New York: Russell Sage Foundation, 1917), 368.

7. Ibid., 365–370.

8. For an historical account of the general position taken here see: Donald Brieland, "History and Evolution of Social Work Practice," 739–754. In the same volume, see also the article by Carol H. Meyer, "Direct Practice in Social Work: An Overview," 409–422; and Scott Brear's "Direct Practice: Trends and Issues," 393–398.

9. Brieland, "History and Evolution of Social Work Practice," 739–754.

10. See, for example, Joel Fischer, "Is Casework Effective? A Review," *Social Work*, 18, no. 1 (January 1973): 5–20; and C. Brewer and J. Lait, *Can Social Work Survive?* (London: Temple Smith, 1980).

11. An early and important reference point on this issue can be found in the presentation made by Abraham Flexner in his 1915 National Conference of Charities and Correction presentation, "Is Social Work a Profession?" One of the issues addressed was that social work lacked educationally communicable techniques.

12. The position is a generally held one. See for example, William B. Sanders and Thomas K. Pinkey, *The Conduct of Social Research* (New York: Holt, Rinehart and Winston, 1983), 23–24; and Grace Ganter and Margaret Yeakel, *Human Behavior and the Social Environment: A Perspective for Social Work Practice* (New York: Columbia University Press, 1980), 3–7.

13. For an example, see Norman J. Ackerman, *A Theory of Family Systems* (New York: Gardner Press, 1984).

14. Ray Grinker, Sr., (ed.), *Toward a Unified Theory of Human Behavior* (New York: Basic Books, 1967).

15. For a discussion of this point see Barbara M. Newman and Philip R. Newman, *Development Through Life: A Psychological Approach* (Chicago: The Dorsey Press, 1987), 65–73.

16. Anne Minahan, "Theories and Perspectives for Social Work," *Social Work* 25, no. 6 (November, 1980): 435.

17. See Scott Briar, "In Summary," *Social Work*, 22, no. 5 (September 1977): 415–416.

18. Minahan, "Theories and Perspectives," 435.

Chapter 2

A Social Systems Perspective

OUTLINE

Background

In this chapter, we present a social systems perspective. The model that was introduced in the previous chapter has its origins in this perspective. Recall that a perspective provides a broad approach to an understanding of some matter of interest, in which everything is seen in a logical relationship to everything else.

Our social systems perspective builds from assumptions that we make about the world in which we live and why we humans behave as we do. These assumptions are drawn from several lines of theory development, most notably general systems and field theory. Drawn from these and other theories are a series of concepts. In short, we have borrowed a set of assumptions and concepts from several lines of theory development and from our own experiences and fashioned a social systems perspective from them. From this perspective we have constructed a social systems model, which is a teaching, learning, and organizing tool.

Before proceeding with a discussion of the assumptions and concepts that comprise the social systems perspective, we want to share with you some key definitions, the origins of these definitions, and how they are related to the professional practice of social work.

Definitions

Writers in the social sciences and in the applied professions tend to apply different meanings to the same term. For example one author has collected over fifty definitions of "system."[1] To confront this problem we are making a special effort to be as clear as possible in our definitions and then to use these definitions as consistently as possible.

The definitions included in this section represent a simple classification scheme for the various forms of human associations. We would prefer to present a generally recognized typology, but unfortunately none exists.[2] Given this situation, our task has been to create a typology suited to the purposes of this book. We have been guided in this process by the work of a number of writers, but most notably by the history of social work's definitional and classification issues.[3] Specifically, the struggle to conceptualize forms of practice intervention suggests to us an approach to classifying human groupings. These forms of intervention have been identified as social work practice methods. The principal ones are social casework, social group work, social administration, and community organization; simply put, the corresponding focus of intervention is the individual, the social group, the social agency (the formal organization), and the community. To us, this method orientation represents an implicit recognition of the existence of several levels of social organization relevant to the practice of social work.

Our typology or classification of social organizations is based on characteristics that we believe affect relationships among those who comprise these social groupings: (1) the extent to which **expressive** (personal) versus **logical** (rational) **actions** dominate; (2) the extent to which relationships among members develop naturally (self-organizing) or are formally constituted;[4] (3) the extent to which the organization's purposes are inclusive (broad) or exclusive (narrow); and, (4) the extent to which the organization's actions are affected by place (location). Given its special importance to social work practice, we have included the family as a subtype of the social group. The classification system and definitions that follow are based on this view:

1. *Social Organization.* Any social entity comprised of two or more persons/social units who share purpose, who show functionally interdependent and reciprocal relationships, and where the social organization itself has functional and reciprocal relationships with its social environment.
2. *Social Group.* A form of social organization comprised of two or more members who identify and interact with one another on a personal basis as individuals, possess a shared sense of the group as a social entity, are affected by the group-related actions of members, and in which expressive (natural) actions dominate.
3. *Family.* A social group characterized by an actual or perceived sense of kinship among its members.
4. *Formal Organization.* A form of social organization deliberately and formally created to achieve relatively specific and delimited goals.
5. *Community.* A form of social organization that is territorially based and through which most people satisfy their common needs and desires, deal with their common problems, and through which they relate to their society.

As indicated by this classification system, social organization is the general term used for describing the multiple forms taken in what has been earlier described as human groupings and/or associations. The definition of a social organization provides the foundation for our approach to a basic or generic social systems model. The typology derived from this definition of social organization also recognizes and builds on the social work practice methods of casework, group work, administration, and community organization.

In conclusion, we want to call to your attention the key attributes in our definition of social organization. These features have been incorporated into a perspective that espouses that all such organizations can be viewed as social systems. First, "social organization" is a term given to a social entity, something that has existence. It is a whole unto itself and is thus distinguishable from those persons or other social units that comprise it. Second, it is composed of at least two persons. This means that size is an organizational characteristic. The lower parameter of size is specified, the upper limit is not. For example, in this definition, a society would be considered a form of social organization, as would a community and a family; an individual would not.

Third, the member components of a social organization can be either individuals or groupings of individuals who have functionally interdependent relationships; these groupings are referred to as "other social units." Typically in small and relatively simple social organizations like a friendship group, there is little functional differentiation (role specialization). The member components can be most usefully thought of as individuals who essentially interact with one another as total personalities, thus expressive actions are dominant. On the other hand, in a large and relatively complex social organization like a mental health center, there is much greater functional differentiation; in these organizations, rational actions dominate among members. Also, the member components of the larger, complex organization can be more easily understood by treating them as groupings of individuals who perform similar functions. In this instance, there will be specific individuals who by reason of their position can be thought of as representing major units of the center; chief of outpatient services or director of social services, for example. In other words, in large social organizations there is a tendency for interactions among people to be guided more by the position they hold than by who they are as persons. This is made possible because the organization itself has been formally constituted, as have the relationships among its member parts, such as the various administrative units comprising the organization.

Fourth, the order that characterizes the relationships among the organization's member components is derived from the specific function performed by the organization. The notion of function that we are using has many similarities with the structural-functionalist tradition in sociology but also has some important differences.[5] It is sufficient to understand that here function should not be thought of as functional in a value sense but more in terms of purposive acts.

Our usage of function here is in the context of social groupings. Simply stated, it means that all such groupings involve some form of coordinated efforts by members in the pursuit of group purpose. It is this purpose or function performed that results in the evolvement of specialized functions to be performed by group members. Thus, the ordering, the social interaction that occurs both with the group itself and between the group and its social environment, is ultimately related to the function being performed by that group.

In summary, forms of human association not possessing the four features set forth in our definition would not be defined as social organizations. The point is that the social systems model can only be applied to those forms of human association meeting the definition of a social organization. For example, a typical movie audience would not be considered a form of social organization, and thus the social systems model would not be useful in examining the behavior of such an audience. The people attending are there for personal reasons; there is not a shared purpose that links people making them dependent upon one another. In the absence of a shared purpose, there will not be any internal or external ordering that will result in a sense of "wholeness."

Assumptions

In the previous pages, we defined social organization and several subtypes of social organizations. The following assumptions begin our effort to identify key features of our perspective of social organizations as social systems.

1. *There is an underlying intelligible general order in the world to which all matter relates.* This is the assumption on which the search for a general perspective of order is based. This assumption has two principal and interrelated parts. First, a general order exists. Second, this order is understandable to humans. Implied in the latter is a value judgment; that it is desirable to seek understanding of this general order. For us, the initial assumption is the most important with all others emanating from it. From both a philosophical and a practice position, the assumption of a general order conveys meaning or purpose. The pursuit of understanding of the general order becomes a pursuit of the meaning to existence. Later in this chapter we will provide an overview of general systems theory. It is basically a theory of order and extends this assumption in terms of its practice relevance.

2. *The whole is greater than the sum of its parts.* The general order is that of wholeness and is not to be explained through a process of reduction or disassembly. The order is comprised of parts and the ordered relationships among parts. The general order is to be understood as a whole. This does not mean that understanding and knowledge building cannot proceed by the process of disassembly. It can and has, but disassembly is incomplete. Through the processes and methods of science, we have acquired bits and pieces of knowledge. General systems theory seeks the common threads of order that are contained in these pieces and seeks to form and explain ever larger wholes.

The sense of this second assumption is that the world in which we live is a whole, something greater than just the sum of its parts. There is a subtlety involved in this assumption that is not clear to some people. The meaning of greater is not to be understood in linear terms, or as quantitatively more of the same. In other words, the assumption is not of the order that $1 + 1 = 3$ or 4 or any other number greater than 2. What is intended is that something higher is created, something that is qualitatively different than just the sum of its parts, $1 + 1 = A$.

For example, hydrogen and oxygen atoms can be combined to form water. While water results from the combining of hydrogen and oxygen atoms, something new is created. This new entity has properties that are qualitatively different from its predecessor parts; we cannot drink or wash our clothes with hydrogen and oxygen. So it is with social organizations; when people come together they form something different, a new whole. This new whole has properties that are different from those of the people who comprise it.

3. *All forms of human social organization exhibit key features of the general order as well as those distinctive to humans and to the several classes of human social organization.* Just as the human is greater than the sum of his or her parts, so are the various types of associations that humans join with each other to form. The most important of these associations is the family. This assumption holds that the family is not to be understood by understanding the individual humans who comprise it. It is something greater than the sum of its members. The ordering of relationships among its members will exhibit features of the general order, those distinctive to humans and those distinctive to the family as a form or class of social organization.

For us, the family is the prototype human organizational form. This means that the basic forms of ordering found in the family will be exhibited in all other, so-called higher and more complex forms of human association. In this sense, the common pattern of ordering to be found in the family can be thought of as isomorphic in social organization.

While the family is considered the prototype of all forms of human groupings, there have evolved more complex levels of human social organization. Assumption 3 holds that these so-called higher levels evidence the common ordering features found in the family, and also those characteristics that are specific to the specified level; for example, the formal organization. The development of a social systems theory is directed in part toward the specification of these distinctive features and the determination of a means of classification that expedites theory-building efforts.

4. *The individual is both the cause and the effect of all forms of human social organization.* We identified this assumption earlier and repeat it here because, in association with the other assumptions identified, it constitutes the foundation of our social systems perspective. Contained in this assumption is the belief that the individual is not born with a residual sense of selfhood or personality that evolves essentially unaltered over time into a mature and distinctive person. Selfhood for us is a process that develops over the life span and its distinctive features are socially acquired and developed. By this we mean that at any one time our sense of selfhood is the effect of that process. Specifically then, our sense of who we are is a socially acquired meaning, one that is constantly changing, constantly developing.

We are by no means denying the importance of the genetic and the various physical determinants of the human personality. For us they provide the basic parameters and likely channels along which development takes place. In accordance with this assumption, they do not account for the unique qualities that each of us possesses as a human being. The specific qualities of humanness we possess are socially acquired from other humans. The transmission process is social and takes place within and between the myriad of social organizations in which the individual is embedded.

Assumption 4 recognizes that each of us is born into and becomes part of an ongoing culture. As we grow and develop we become the carrier of that culture. Importantly, the social organizations of which we are a part (for example, the family) are also carriers of that culture. For us, this assumption forms the philosophical foundation for social work's focus on human behavior in the "social environment." To recast this idea, there is an ongoing and reciprocal relationship between the individual and the social environment of which the individual is a part. Each is a cause, each is an effect, of the other. Our understanding of human social behavior and our ability to use this understanding in professionally helpful ways start from this position.

5. *Social organization is characterized by varying degrees of functional interdependence both in the relationships among the member units of the organization and in the relationship between the organization and its environmental setting.* Here our concern is with the ordering in human relationships and the dominant characteristic, which is interdependence. Interdependence is twofold: there is an interdependent relationship among the members or the social units comprising the organization and between the organization and those social units comprising its social environment. Given the assumption of interdependence as the dominant feature of relationships, social systems becomes a universal way to characterize all forms of social organization.

Assumption 5 is important in terms of the implications it contains—that the individual is dependent on others, and that he or she is incomplete and completeness in its many forms is achieved through relationships with others. We have defined these relationships as resulting in social organizations. Here we are identifying an assumption that helps extend the notion that the individual is both the cause and the effect of all forms of social organization. Conceptually speaking, individuals come together because of their own incompleteness, and they form social organizations. In a cyclical manner, the individual acts on the organization and the organization acts on the individual. It is in this cyclical sense that the individual is viewed as both the cause and the effect of all forms of social organization. In systems language, we say that the individual is always both an input and an output to those social organizations of which he or she is a part.

This assumption also establishes the position that every form of social organization will display two related levels of ordering; one internal, the other external. The internal ordering identifies the functional relationships that exist among those who are members of the specific social organization. The external ordering links the subject organization functionally to its social environment. This distinction between internal and eternal ordering has important implications to knowledge building and to the practice of social work. As a practical matter, the internal ordering should be thought of as narrower in scope and more functionally interdependent when compared to the features of the external ordering.

6. *When fully developed, all forms of social organization display self-maintaining and development characteristics.* This assumption holds that once developed, a social organization takes on a life of its own. The system and its suprasystem relationships possess a propensity to grow, to develop. What "fully developed" means is an empirical question, as are the concepts of "self-maintaining" and "development." This assumption is getting at the notion that social organizations are dynamic, not static. They are proactive and there is a discernible development or growth pattern that can be understood.

Social organizations have been defined as social entities that cannot be understood by simply seeking an understanding of those individuals and groups of individuals who comprise them. But like the individual, no social organization is complete or autonomous; each is part of a larger whole and each has a cyclical and functionally interdependent relationship with this larger whole. In a conceptual sense, each is both the cause and the effect of the other.

Theory Development and the Social Systems Perspective

We have provided a review of the central assumptions that undergird and support a social systems perspective. Now we turn to the concepts that build from this foundation. Although we have taken these concepts from several lines of theory development, they form a system of thought or, more precisely, a perspective about social systems.

An overview of three lines of theory development follows. General systems theory has furnished most of the previously named assumptions and many of the concepts to be related. Here our debt is to one of the great thinkers of this century, Ludwig von Bertalanffy.[6] In addition to our coverage of general systems theory, we provide reviews of field theory and humanism.

You will have noted that we speak of a line of *theory development* as opposed to simply a *theory*. By this we mean that theory development is dynamic; it is ongoing. If it is in an area of interest and the line of thinking is deemed helpful, the chances are that a number of people will be making contributions. Also, researchers will be systematically testing its various propositions to determine whether these assertions are correct. The point here is that in most important areas of theory development, you will find a number of theorists who share similar but not identical views. In some instances these differences will be vigorously debated. These differences and the arguments being made can be troublesome and confusing to some readers.

Our approach to this problem is to focus on the person generally recognized as the major contributor or founder of a specific line of theory development. We will also seek to identify what we consider to be the major assumptions and concepts associated with that theory. Finally, we hope to convey that knowledge building is exciting. Its aim is to learn more about the world in which we live. For the helping professional, the focus is on why people behave as they do and on ways of assisting people to live more personally satisfying and socially useful lives.

General Systems Theory

General systems theory is a theory of organization; it has been likened to a science of wholeness. Frequently it is asserted by those who use systems concepts that "the whole is more than the sum of its parts." General systems theory proposes to explain why this is so. Its founder was a theoretical biologist named Ludwig von Bertalanffy (1901–1972). Born and educated in Austria, he became dissatisfied with the ability of linear-based, cause-and-effect theories to explain the growth and change he saw in living organisms. It occurred to von Bertalanffy that an explanation of this growth and change might lie in the relationships and interactions between those parts comprising the organism rather than in the parts. In other words, the search for understanding should focus on the order among the parts, not on the parts themselves. It was an idea that revolutionized science. Up to this point in time and based on a conception of linear causation, scientific exploration occurred largely through a process of reductionism, that is, seeking an understanding of the whole by understanding all of its parts. An example would be a person taking a clock apart to understand how each part related to every other part. In this example, the whole is represented by only the sum of its parts.

The intellectual foundation for general systems theory was set forth by von Bertalanffy in 1928; but it was not until the publication of *General Systems Theory* in 1968 that a complete statement of his theory became generally available.[8] Because of the revolutionary nature of thought in general systems theory, it has taken on the qualities of a social movement for many people.[9] Not only has it caused a rethinking of basic tenets throughout the scientific world, it has also provided a new vocabulary for people in all walks of life; for example, the popular use of terms such as inputs, outputs, and feedback. General systems theory has become more than a theory, it has become a way of thinking—a very broad perspective of the world in which we live.

The aim of general systems theory is the formulation of the principles of organization. Given the massiveness of the subject matter, these principles have to be stated in high levels of generality. For example, the principles must be as applicable for the study of organizational features of the atom as for the study of organizational qualities of the universe. Similarly, these same principles must hold for all those studying human behavior, from the psychologist studying the individual to the sociologist studying societal behavior.

Given the complexity and revolutionary nature of von Bertalanffy's thinking, it would be useful to identify some of the concerns he had and some of the assumptions that underlie his position. In our opinion, there are parallels in the concerns expressed by von Bertalanffy and others associated with the development of general systems theory and by those in the helping professions. Both groups have struggled with the mass and maze of theory development and its utility in explaining the behavior of living things.

Assumptions

Earlier in this chapter we identified a series of assumptions upon which our social systems perspective is based. We also indicated that these assumptions are related to general systems theory or even more broadly to a general systems perspective. The most fundamental of these assumptions is the existence of a general and understandable order to the world in which we live. Science and application of the scientific method is premised on this assumption. From this position, the task of science is to seek an understanding of this order. Scientists have gone about this task in modern times by "staking out a territory" and proceeding to investigate that territory through a process of reduction. The process was pursued by reducing the subject matter into ever smaller and more manageable parts; it was a process of simplification. For some like von Bertalanffy, this approach posed a problem and resulted in a growing fragmentation in knowledge-building efforts. Most of us can identify with the insight on this problem expressed by Peter Checkland, a general systems theorist: "Although I usually have difficulty remembering what I did last Tuesday, I have a clear memory of a school science lesson in the 1940s when the chemistry master put into my astonished mind the idea that Nature did not consist of physics, chemistry and biology: these were *arbitrary* divisions, man-made, merely a convenient way of carving up the task of investigating Nature's mysteries."[10]

Commenting on this process of knowledge building by arbitrarily "carving-up" a territory, Bennis and others observed, "Perhaps nowhere is the abyss between formal logic, and reality more evident than in man's attempt to order knowledge about his own behavior. There are today twenty-four (24) divisions within the American Psychological Association, and these are presumably logically separable from each other as well as from the subdivisions of sociology, anthropology, political science and psychiatry."[11] In short, general systems theory represents a reaction to the fragmentation that was occurring in scientific thought based on reductive and linear-based reasoning. Instead, a way of thinking that focused on "wholeness and causality" in interactive rather than in linear terms was offered. Here at last was also a way of viewing human behavior that focused on the person and his or her situation as a whole; it was a way of thinking that the profession of social work had advanced from its professional beginnings.[12]

Let us return now to the assumption of a general order. There is a subtlety involved; for many (including us), the order comprises a whole. Many people who think and write about such things do not necessarily share this added notion of wholeness. For us it is critical and it establishes the foundations for the next assumption—the whole is greater than the sum of its parts. If indeed this assumption is correct, a problem is introduced by efforts aimed at understanding this whole by a process of taking it apart piece by piece. Even if each part is understood in its entirety, the sum of this understanding does not explain the whole; it is more. In practice terms, if we are confronted with a serious family situation for which help is sought, we make this same mistake by seeking to only understand the individuals who comprise the family. The family is a whole and is not to be understood by understanding only those individuals who comprise it; it is more.

It was Aristotle who first framed the argument that the whole is greater than the sum of its parts. Thus, it is not a new argument but for many centuries it was dismissed. Our intent here is not to trace this fascinating argument through the history of science; it is, rather, simply to observe that von Bertalanffy and others have reintroduced the argument in general systems theory.[13] We also believe that this same argument is being advanced by those in social work who say that a holistic approach is needed to understand human behavior.

Now let us stop for a moment and draw an implication from the material just reviewed. In short, we do not believe that the day will come when human behavior will be understood in terms of the laws of physics, reduced to explanations based in the chemical and physical properties of the body. Our position can be easily misunderstood; enormous strides have been made in science through this relentless process of reduction and more will be made. The point is that this process is incomplete and poses particularly troublesome problems to the quest for learning more about living things. There is much more to be learned and perhaps new ways of thinking about life can be helpful.

We have touched on the first two assumptions associated with the social systems perspective. Rather than continue our effort of tying each of these assumptions to general systems theory, suffice to say that the remaining ones are derived from the first two. The central idea behind assumptions three through six is that social organizations exhibit features of general order and other features that are distinctive to humans as a species. Implicit in this notion is some hierarchy of wholes; each higher level has an ordering that is characteristic of lower levels as well as features that are distinctive to its level. The classification system of social organizations introduced earlier in this chapter stems from assumptions three through six. More of this later; now let us review some concepts that build off assumptions one and two, dealing with order and wholeness.

Concepts

The social systems perspective is comprised of a series of assumptions and related concepts. We have already introduced you to the eight concepts that comprise the social systems model. In the paragraphs ahead we will identify additional key concepts that together help comprise the social system perspective and which are tied most centrally to general systems theory. While the concepts will be identified and described, it is important to remember that all interrelate. Each is dependent upon others; together they are a whole, a system.

Emergence

The concept of emergence is helpful to thinking in general systems terms. A whole possesses **emergent properties** that are distinctive—properties not possessed by the parts comprising the whole.[14] These properties have emerged from the relationships that developed among the parts comprising the whole. In a manner of speaking, they are lost or cease to exist when the whole is separated into parts. Here a typical example is water. It has solvent properties and a taste not found in the oxygen and hydrogen that combine to form water. Another and dramatic example of this notion is life itself. According to the theory of mechanism, life ultimately is reducible to physiochemical events and laws. The contending position is the organismic (systems) one.[15] Life is an emergent state, one found in the organization of parts, not in the parts themselves. Love, as expressed in a human relationship (a family) is a familiar and important example of the notion of emergence. Love is not a property of the individual. While love affects the individual, it is a property of a relationship, not of the individual as such. This basic notion has a variety of practice implications. For example, if in a helping relationship the problems center on properties of a particular relationship, intervention aimed only at the individuals involved is likely to be problematic: The problem and the properties of the problem are elsewhere. In the social systems model, we further develop this notion of emergence by arguing that the system is not to be understood except in relationship to its suprasystem. In other words, there are properties of this larger whole that can only be found and understood by examining the subject system and the relationships with other social units that comprise its suprasystem.

Open Systems

Fundamental to general systems theory is the concept of **open systems.** This concept conveys that systems are dynamically connected to the environments of which they are a part. In other words, there is an ongoing exchange between the subject system and its environment. Figure 2.1 conveys the point by contrasting an open with a **closed system.**

The notion of an open system is a very simple idea, but a very powerful one. It encompasses an approach to the study of order that has both internal and external dimensions. To help operationalize *open* we use the concepts of inputs and outputs. We intend to use analogies drawn from the physical sciences sparingly, but this one seems quite appropriate here. When you were in grade school, one of your early science lessons probably introduced you to the process of photosynthesis. Here your teacher sought to link together systematically the organic and inorganic parts of the world. He or she described to you how the chlorophyll found in the cells of green plants converts sunlight, water, carbon dioxide, and other elements (inputs), into food for the plant and in the process releases oxygen (output) into the environment. Oxygen in the air then becomes an input that helps sustain animal life. This exemplifies a fundamental form of ordering based on an open system formulation of exchange.

General systems theory holds that all systems be viewed as open. We take this premise and include it as a component of the social systems perspective. Simply put, all social systems secure inputs from their environment (suprasystem). These inputs are the necessary resources required for the survival and development of the system itself. The system will then process these inputs, retain some, and then release the rest into its environment (suprasystem) as outputs.

The important point to be drawn from this concept of an open system is that it is a way of thinking and is distinguishable from a closed system perspective. Thus, in an open systems formulation, the explanation of the system's behavior must consider these openness properties and the exchange arrangement that the system has with its suprasystem. Not so in a closed system formulation.

Negative Entropy-Entropy

These two concepts present opposites and are related to the previously described notions of open versus closed systems. The theory in support of these two concepts is quite

FIGURE 2.1 Open and Closed Systems

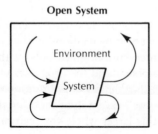

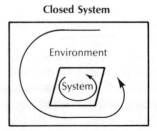

complicated. Our interest at this point is only in a way of thinking. In this case we are concerned with how growth and development occurs in social systems (negative entropy) and its opposite, how disorganization and the "death" of a system occurs (entropy).

In closed systems terms, **entropy** is a measure of disorder.[16] The origins of the concept are to be found in the second principle of thermodynamics. This principle holds that the general trend of events in physical nature is toward states of maximum disorder and the leveling down of differences. In practical or layperson's terms, things wear out, run down, decompose. This is true of all matter—our world, our universe, as well as the house in which we live, and the car that we drive. The process of entropy, then, refers to a process in which order is lost, in other words, the process of disorganization.

General systems theorists, von Bertalanffy in particular, argued that in living things a process of ordering, not disordering, was evident.[17] This reverse process or increase in ordering is called **negative entropy.** In defense of this position von Bertalanffy cited the evolutionary process, the development of ever higher forms of life from the amoeba to the human. We would add that all forms of social organization possess the potential for growth and development (assumption six—pertaining to the growth and development characteristics of social organizations). For example, think about a close personal or love relationship that you have with another person; this system or social organization had a beginning and over time it has grown and become more complex and more important. It is this capacity for growth and development that social organizations possess which we wish to understand and model. What are the conditions or principles that account for this capacity, or its reverse: How do we account for the disordering process we observe in human relationships at all levels from personal to societal?

The concepts we are discussing are both abstract and complex. Some try to express these ideas in mathematical formulas. Our interest is quite different and much more modest. For us the concepts are no more than a way of thinking about life and about professional practice. For example, the more closed a system, the more limited are its exchanges with its environment. The risk is one of "getting out of touch," "getting old before your time," "becoming obsolete," losing order. At a societal level we would cite Russia and China as examples; both societies are "shifting" and become more "open" in system terms. Likewise, marriages that fail and friendships that are lost can also be viewed in terms of being open or closed—exhibiting entropic or negative entropic characteristics. We might add that systems can get in equally severe difficulties by becoming too open. This observation leads us to a discussion of the concept of steady state.

Steady State

The final concept to be addressed in this section on general systems theory is **steady state**. In practical terms it can be thought of as a condition of the health of a system. At a more technical level, it pertains to the constancy of a favorable balance of input and output exchanges a system has with its suprasystem.[18] Favorable balance refers to a dynamic exchange process in which the balance is in favor of negative entropic forces, those promoting an increase in ordering rather than in disordering. In words that we are all familiar with, if you are paying out more than you are taking in you are headed for trouble. This point holds whether it is money, love or anything else that is involved in exchanges. The point also holds whether we are talking about an individual, a family, an agency, a community, or a nation.

The notion of a steady state incorporates the thinking behind such concepts as an open or closed system and entropy versus negative entropy. Later we will develop the theoretical support for our use of this concept in the social systems model. For now we want you to think of this term as a way of dealing with the dynamics in human relationships. As a person, a member of a family, a professional helper or agency administrator—the question is, how do we stay on course? In systems language the question is, how is steady state developed and maintained. The concept of steady state supplies us with a way of thinking about the ordering arrangements both within the system and between the system and its suprasystem and how they are maintained.

In this section on general systems theory we have sought to identify key concepts along with some related assumptions that have helped us form a perspective on the way social systems behave. While these concepts have been borrowed from general systems theory, they have applications when applied to individuals and all of the social organizations that people join to form. While some of these terms may be new, we encourage you to learn their meanings and the ideas behind them. They help form the building blocks for the social systems perspective. Next we review field theory and the contribution it has made to the social systems perspective.

Field Theory

In a memorial address at the 1947 convention of the American Psychological Association, Tolman summed up the contributions of Kurt Lewin (1890–1947) by noting, "Freud, the clinician and Lewin, the experimentalist—these are the two men whose names will stand out before all others in the history of our psychological era."[19]

Lewin is not classified as a general or social systems theorist; his quest might be best described as the "purification" of psychology. He believed that each science seeks to purify its own concepts and in so doing tends to segregate itself from the others. So, according to Lewin, any idea of a unification of all sciences through development of a general (systems) theory was wishful thinking. Lewin's contribution to our effort at forming a social systems perspective stems from the fact that he was one of the earliest psychologists to hold that human behavior could be usefully studied only by viewing the individual in an environmental context. More importantly, he supplied the concepts and the experimental approaches to undertake studies from this perspective. Lewin's mark on the behavioral sciences is still seen in the familiarity of some of his concepts and the related terms he coined, for example, *groups dynamics, sensitivity training, life space,* and *action research.*[20] His commitment to the importance of theory in knowledge building and the application of that knowledge to the problems of everyday life is perhaps best reflected in his often quoted remark, "There is nothing so practical as a good theory."[21]

Lewin was deeply influenced as a student and a young scholar by **gestalt psychology,** and the development of his holistic approach for the study of human behavior bears its mark. Our interest in Lewin's work stems not only from his attention to the study of human behavior in an environmental context, but also from the extensive research that he and his students accomplished in support of this contention. Lewin thus became one of the first theorists to provide empirical support for a social systems perspective to the study of social organizations.

While best known as a psychologist, Lewin held that it is possible to construct a general social psychological theory that would apply to the study of the group, family, formal organizations, and the community, as well as the individual.[22] His development of field theory was premised in part on this assumption. It also suggests to us that Lewin's work can be usefully viewed as a precursor to social systems theory (a theory yet to be fully developed).

Lewin's quest for a general theory for psychology was associated with his search for a branch of mathematics that would provide the precision needed to express and test his various constructs. The best known of his mathematical expressions is $B = F(P,E)$ or B (behavior) equals F (the function) of P (the person) and E (environment).[23] Lewin assumed that the person and the environment can be treated as an interdependent whole. This whole becomes the **life space** (LSp) of the person. Mathematically it is expressed as $B = F(P,E) = F(LSp)$. According to Lewin, "The task of explaining behavior then becomes identical with (1) finding a scientific representation of the life space (LSp) and (2) determining the function (F) which links the behavior to the life space. This function F is what one usually calls a law."[24]

We cite Lewin's mathematical expression because it embodies the central point developed in this book: Human behavior or the behavior of any social organization is to be understood in terms of the function and reciprocal relations it has with its social environment. For us, field theory supports the contention that social organizations can be viewed as open systems, and that the behavior of a subject system is to be understood in terms of the interplay between the system and its suprasystem.

Unlike Freud and many other theorists, Lewin did not search for behavioral determinants in the individual's past, his or her genetic legacy or his or her capacity to learn and reason. Behavior, according to Lewin, depends not on the past or the future but the here and now, or in his terms, "the present field." This is not to say that there cannot be unconscious determinants contained in the present field. What is central, though, is that the person's current situation (his or her life space) is the point where professional intervention becomes focused.

Assumptions

Lewin's work provided help to us in formulating several of the assumptions that introduced this chapter. While he is best remembered as a psychologist, he held that his concept of the field as a behavioral determinant also applied to the various groups that individuals join together to form (assumptions four and five). We are not, however, suggesting that Lewin's field theory shares all the same assumptions as undergird the social systems perspective. Rather, we are saying that Lewin's work helped us in formulating a social systems perspective. Field theory also helped us develop our assumption pertaining to the cause-and-effect relationship between the individual and the group. It was unfortunate that Lewin died so young (at age fifty-six) because in the years immediately preceding his death his interest was focusing on groups and larger systems and their effects on those who comprise them. Even so, his research in field theory offers avenues for investigating features contained in a social systems perspective.

Concepts

In the development of field theory, Lewin derived a series of concepts and definitions that are instructive as well as relevant in forming a social systems perspective. Included are such familiar concepts as field, needs, goals, tension, tension systems, and equilibrium.

Field

For our present purposes *field* and *life space* can be considered as essentially synonymous. The field is the environment in which the individual or other social unit is located and related behaviorally. **Field theory** holds that the individual (and other social units) cannot be conceived apart from some sort of environment.[25] Another useful way of thinking about field is as that environment which serves as the source for observational data pertaining to a subject system.

More so than any other line of theory development, field theory and the notion of field helped us in constructing our notion of suprasystem. Like field, suprasystem is the larger context that includes the subject system and which serves as the course for observational data.

Needs

Lewin distinguished two categories of human **needs**: genuine and quasi needs.[26] **Genuine needs** have their clearest origins in an inner state of the individual and can be likened to what Abraham Maslow called "physiological" or survival level needs, like hunger.[27] **Quasi needs,** on the other hand, are derived from sources external to the person and pertain to specific intentions of the individual. Quasi needs have their roots in genuine needs but are of a second order, for example, hunger is a basic need; deciding on what to have for dinner to satisfy that need, or in which restaurant to dine would serve as an example of a quasi need. In other words, the decision or the intention of an individual to do something causes a quasi need to be created. By their nature, quasi needs are much more frequently experienced and are less stable than genuine needs.

In our view, it is useful to think about genuine needs as having their origins in the nature of man. Quasi needs, on the other hand, are affected in their expression by the field and by the larger culture of which the person (and social system) is a part. Of interest is Lewin's theoretical position that the tension or energy patterns behind quasi needs and genuine needs are identical. Therefore, according to this position, a need of any order or description exists only when it upsets an equilibrium within the person. In other words, being hungry becomes motivational only when it disturbs a person's inner state and results in the creation of a tension system that, in turn, causes the individual to take actions to restore equilibrium. Also, Lewin's formulation simplifies the study of needs as sources of motivation by holding a universal explanation of how need satisfaction takes place.[28]

Lewin's concept of needs provides a way of thinking about human motivation and possible linkages between internal and external sources of motivation (the distinction drawn between genuine and quasi needs). Lewin's work and that done by Maslow (to be discussed next) have shaped our way of thinking about the role played by needs in a social systems perspective.

Goals

In Lewin's formulation, needs arise out of a sense of disequilibrium within the life space and serve to energize, organize, and focus behavior. While we do not share Lewin's conception of an equilibrium theory as a way of viewing the origins of human actions (preferring the more dynamic conception of steady state), his general thesis is important, particularly his attention to the role played by **goals**. In this formulation, goals can be viewed as the correspondents of needs—genuine or quasi needs. Similarly, the achievement of a goal is essentially equivalent to need satisfaction. While Lewin uses the term *goal* in a much broader sense than is used in our systems perspective, the underlying point is the same. In both instances, goals are end states that serve an organizing function for those seeking their accomplishment. From this perspective it matters little whether the goal is as narrowly conceived as being on time for an appointment or as broad as wanting to become a good social worker. The underlying dynamics are essentially equivalent. In both instances the goals represent end states that serve to organize, that is, they provide an order to those behaviors needed to achieve the end state. In a social systems perspective, goals should be thought of as constituting a proposed output of a cycle of system operations.

Tensions

With the foregoing features of field theory as background, we found Lewin's theory of psychological "tensions" helpful in developing the outcome orientation that characterizes our social systems perspective. These so-called **tensions** energize the person with respect to the pursuit of goals. In Lewin's formulation, these same processes can be assumed to operate in groups and in other forms of social organization as well as within the individual.

At this point, it would be useful to introduce the notion of psychological tensions through a story told of Lewin.[29] He was said to be constantly searching through everyday experiences for insights to better understand human behavior and to help in the construction of field theory. The story goes that Lewin and his students would frequently meet in a cafe and discuss their ideas over coffee and rolls. On one of these occasions and after several hours of discussion, one of the group members had to leave and so asked for the check. Although the waiter had not kept a written record, he made his calculation quickly and presented the group with an exact bill. Lewin observed this and after about a half-hour called the waiter over and asked him to produce the bill again. The annoyed waiter replied, "I don't know any longer what you people ordered, you paid your bill."[30] It was as though a state of tension had existed in the mind of this waiter that helped him keep track of his transactions with the group. Once he had completed his service, this tension state dissipated and was directed elsewhere, to another group of customers.

In the previous example, one can envision a whole series of related activities that comprised the waiter's relationship with this group; that is, consistent with his role as a waiter, he engaged in an ordered set of activities with these customers. These activities culminated in a final event, the rendering of a check and the payment for services provided. Here the goal was the receipt of payment. Lewin was intrigued with what he had observed, and this experience eventually led to the famous studies of tension systems conducted by Zeigarnik.[31] Done under Lewin's supervision, these studies constituted a test of the proposition that an individual's intention to accomplish a specific task corresponds to the creation of a psychological state within the person, a **tension system**, and that the need to discharge this tension results in goal-directed activity until the task has been completed. According to Lewin's thesis, the adoption of a goal causes a person to create a system or an ordered set of behaviors to be engaged in until the goal is achieved. To the extent that the goal remains unfulfilled, it will maintain an influence over the person's thoughts and behaviors. Once fulfilled, the tension is released and the energy becomes available for other actions—the need has been satisfied. We find this general notion helpful and believe the concept of what Lewin calls a tension system has appropriate applications to all forms of social organization.

Bluma Zeigarnik, one of Lewin's students, conducted her famous studies between 1924 and 1926. Her study was concerned with the effects on the person of unfinished tasks. Much like the question raised by the story of the waiter, at issue was whether a person under experimental conditions would be more likely to remember an unfinished or a finished task. Here the proposition was that the unfinished task would more likely be remembered because the tension system created by its adoption would not have been released, and the need would remain unsatisfied. This proposition was supported under a variety of different conditions and variations.[32] Other researchers have conducted similar or related studies which corroborated these findings.[33] The so-called *Zeigarnik effect*, the preferential recall of uncompleted tasks, has served as empirical support for Lewin's contention that a correlation exists between the release of the tension state and the satisfaction of a need. This finding has served as a cornerstone for research and theory building up to the present time. For example, the Freudian proposition that "slips of the tongue" and dreams are manifestations of unconscious tension states seeking discharge are viewed as pertaining to this same phenomenon.

These findings, while focused on the individual and that person's life space, take on greater significance with Lewin's contention that the group and other forms of social organization could be studied as social entities utilizing the principles and concepts underlying field theory.[34]

Field theory has served a useful transition function in moving from contributions made to a social systems perspective derived from general systems theory to those made by psychological and sociological theories. As indicated earlier, we do not believe a social systems theory applicable to the professional practice of social work exists; given this position our effort is to start with a social systems perspective. It is in this effort that we have found Lewin's work very helpful. First, field theory is an open systems formulation, one that views the individual in relationship to a social environment; indeed, Lewin extends this basic formulation to various forms of social organization like the family, an agency or a community. The behavior of each is to be understood as a function of a field of forces. It was this contention of field theory that was of major assistance to us as we developed the concept of suprasystem and cast it within a social systems perspective.

Second, Lewin establishes a linkage between the concepts of needs (human motivation), goals (human purpose), and tension systems (energized patterns of activities directed toward goal achievement) that we have found helpful and have generalized as part of a social systems perspective. Specifically, this linkage helped us develop the functional orientation of the perspective. Also, the linkage of the tension systems to goals helped us conceive of the social system operating in natural cycles, with each cycle being related to a goal state (or a subgoal state).

Third, Lewin undertook the task of subjecting his various concepts to empirical investigation. While our current interest is not in examining the research in support of the social systems perspective, the effort made by Lewin is noteworthy and awaits further attention. Maslow's need theory has been mentioned in connection with Lewin and is discussed next.

Humanism

The final line of theory development to be reviewed in this chapter is humanism. It is from this tradition within psychology that we borrow concepts that provide the social systems perspective with its humanistic features.

Humanism is sometimes referred to as the "third force" in modern psychology.[35] A brief review of the notion of the third force may be helpful in distinguishing this line of theory development. Briefly stated, psychoanalytic theory and behaviorism represent the two forces that historically have been most influential in psychology. These same two lines of theory development have dominated approaches used by professional helpers. The third force, humanism, is seen by its adherents as a kind of synthesis of the other two and represents an alternative way of understanding human behavior. The contributions of both psychoanalytic theory and behaviorism are recognized and built on in **humanistic theory** but in a manner that seeks to address their perceived deficiencies. In psychoanalytic theory, these perceived deficiencies pertain to a psychology fashioned from the study of the mentally disturbed, that is, the neurotic and psychotic. Psychoanalytic theory also postulates that human behavior stems from unconscious sexual and aggressive drives. In turn, these drives are to be understood in terms of humanity's legacy in the animal kingdom.[36] The behaviorist, according to the humanist position, also emphasizes the human continuity with the animal world. Much of the theory building on the part of behaviorists is seen as coming from the study of animals—dogs, chickens, rats, pigeons, and monkeys—rather than the study of humans. Also criticized are the quantitative methods employed by behaviorists. The humanists do not feel that psychology should be constructed through the use of statistical averages any more than from a study of the mentally ill.[37]

The third force focuses on the "humanness" of mankind and the wholeness of the individual as opposed to some particular feature of the individual such as cognitive development, for example.[38] In a sense, humanism is as much a way of thinking as it is a distinctive line of theory development. Perhaps because it is less rigorously defined and more general than psychoanalytic or behaviorist theories, many professional helpers have adopted it as a general guide to practice.

Many writers and theorists are identified with humanistic theory, including, among others, Carl Rogers, Gordon Allport, Charlotte Buhler, and Abraham Maslow.

Our principal attention will be to the contributions of Abraham Maslow. Born in Brooklyn, New York, Abraham Maslow (1908–1970) was well informed in both psychoanalytic and behaviorist theory. It was Maslow's concern about the deficiencies in these theories that led to his formulation of a humanistic theory.

Assumptions

Humanistic psychology focuses on wholeness and is congruent with the assumptions contained in the social systems perspective. The central contribution of humanism to these assumptions has to do with its attention to human potential, growth, and its proactive formulation of human behavior. Our assumption that all forms of human organization display self-maintaining and developing characteristics borrows heavily from humanistic psychology, particularly, the work done by Maslow. What we have done is simply to extend this idea to all the forms of human groupings that individuals join together to form.

In introducing humanism and its contribution to the social systems perspective, it should prove useful to elaborate a bit on its central assumptions and ties to field theory. The central assumption in humanism is the distinctiveness of humankind, not the similarities that we have with animals. The study of lower forms of animal life have no place in the construction of a humanistic psychology. Perhaps the central theme linking theorists of this tradition is the assumption that humans have an inner drive directing them toward self-fulfillment. In fact, some label this general tradition in psychology as *fulfillment theory*.[39] Maslow's theory of the hierarchy of needs is perhaps the clearest presentation of a human drive toward fulfillment, the need to become self-actualized.[40]

Humanism in the tradition of Maslow asserts that a psychology of human behavior should be developed by the study of the healthiest of humankind. It was through the study of those who were self-actualized that Maslow fashioned his need theory.[41] Consistent with this view of a drive toward self-actualization, Maslow assumed that one's inner nature is good or at least neutral as opposed to being bad, or comprised of animal-like aggressive and sexual impulses. Also stressed in humanism is the individualistic nature of the human; each person is unique. Specifically, Maslow held that the understanding of human behavior starts with acceptance of an essentially biologically based inner nature and that each person's inner nature is part unique and part species-wide.[42]

For us, humanistic psychology and field theory have a number of similarities. Both have been influenced by gestalt psychology (a holistic orientation) and give central attention to such key concepts as needs and goals. While labeled a "third force," we view humanistic and field theory as precursors to development of a social systems theory. Maslow's words make the point: "The general point of view that is being propounded here is holistic rather than atomistic, functional rather than taxonomic, dynamic rather than static, dynamic rather than causal, purposive rather than simple-mechanical."[43]

Concepts

A brief review of some of the central concepts used by Maslow in formulating his need theory should prove useful in demonstrating their tie to a social systems perspective.

Need

The concept of **need** pertains to an internal stimulus of genetic origin, a source of motivation directed toward the survival and development of the human. For Maslow, need represents a central organizing concept, one that he uses to identify the distinctive qualities of humankind. Given the genetic basis of human needs, for Maslow these needs provide the foundation for a "system of intrinsic values."[44] Postulated is a hierarchy of needs that forms the foundation for a hierarchy of values; it is these values that constitute the essence of human nature. Needs and the means through which needs are satisfied become the medium for individual development, but even more importantly, for the development of humankind itself.

Hierarchy of Needs

Maslow identifies five need levels: survival, safety and security, social belonging, self-esteem, and self-actualization. These needs are arranged in a hierarchy from those that are most basic and related to satisfaction of survival imperatives (such as food) to self-actualization (the realization of one's unique potential). In conceptualizing this need structure, it is useful to view these needs as instinct remnants with the lowest level needs (survival level needs) most like instincts. At each higher level, the needs are less like instincts; by this Maslow meant that they were more easily overcome by adverse environmental conditions.

The lower level needs in the hierarchy are labeled *basic* or *deficiency* needs and include survival, safety and security, social belonging, and self-esteem. Self-actualization is called a *meta* need. Meta or growth needs transcend the basic needs of the individual and deal with the capacity of the person to become all that he or she can be.

Prepotency Principle

A critical feature of Maslow's hierarchy of needs is what he calls the *prepotency relationship* among the need levels. A synonym for **prepotency** would be gaining dominance. Maslow contended that once a lower need level is essentially satisfied, the need loses its power to motivate the individual and the next higher need level gains dominance, or becomes prepotent.[45] Once all deficiency needs are essentially satisfied, the need for self-actualization gains dominance. The five need levels identified by Maslow and the notion of prepotency are illustrated in Figure 2.2.

Survival Needs

The needs comprising this level are based in the physiological requirements of the human body. These needs include food, water, air, sex, and rest, among others. Sex is included as a **survival level need** in the sense that the continuation of the species depends on the reproductive capability. In accordance with the prepotency principle, once the survival level needs are satisfied they lose their dominance in shaping behavior. Hunger is often used to illustrate a survival level need; that is, the degree of its intensity and how this intensity is lost once hunger is satisfied. Thus, a person who is truly hungry is dominated by the need; it is all the person can think about. However, once the hunger and related survival needs are satisfied, the need loses its dominance and is replaced by a higher level need.

FIGURE 2.2 Maslow's Prepotency Principle

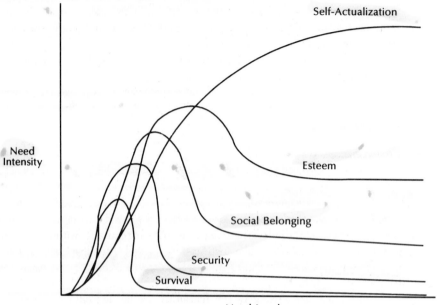

Maslow is helpful in formulating an approach to the study of both the behavior of the individual and societies. In short, Maslow argues that the opportunities for need satisfaction should be treated as a basic human right. In its essence, the argument is that to become truly human, these needs must be satisfied, and so it is a societal responsibility to create those arrangements that facilitate the satisfaction of these needs. While this point is peripheral to our main discussion, we do want to call to your attention this aspect of Maslow's argument. We also want to make the observation that the provision of social welfare services appears to incorporate a priority hierarchy similar to the one proposed by Maslow. For example, the provision of public assistance programs is basically aimed at meeting the survival level needs of eligible recipients for food, clothing, and shelter, and these needs are met before social belonging needs are met. We will have more to say about the usefulness of Maslow's ideas in a later section of this book when we deal with an application of the social systems model to the community.

Safety and Security Needs

Once survival level needs are essentially satisfied, the individual becomes conscious of the need for personal safety and the protection of his or her belongings; these needs become prepotent. When people are frightened, much of their behavior can be understood as efforts aimed at seeking a safe and secure environment. While not as dominating as survival needs, the pursuit of **safety and security needs** can account for important aspects of a person's behavior.

It is important to note that Maslow did not relate his need theory to age levels or to maturational stages. In other words, the young child or the old person may each be seeking to satisfy their respective survival or safety needs. Similarly, just as one may progress up the need hierarchy, so can one "progress down."

Maslow also extended the human need for orderliness and predictability as facets of the need for safety and security. Here again we find a theorist arguing the existence of a human need for order and a propensity to create order. We have found this idea advanced by Maslow a useful one, and it is incorporated in our perspective. Simply put, humans both seek and create order; we are system creators, it is a part of our "nature."

Belongingness and Love Needs

The need to belong, to be loved, becomes prepotent once safety and security needs are largely satisfied. It is important to distinguish between one's sexual needs and love. Sex is a physiological need; love is a relationship need. In its most healthy expression, sexual intimacy occurs within a loving relationship.

Maslow's contention that **belongingness and love needs** are genetically based and therefore universal among humans has been helpful. For us this position offers further theoretical support for the need to look at human behavior within a social context. To become human one must enter into relationships with others. It is only through other people that our need for a sense of belongingness and love can be satisfied. In Part II, The Social Group, we build on Maslow's contention by arguing that the social group offers the primary vehicle through which our sense of self, our sense of humanness, is both acquired and supported throughout life.

Esteem Needs

The notion of esteem as used by Maslow includes both self-respect and respect from others. This need becomes prepotent once love and belongingness needs have largely been satisfied. The concept of **esteem needs** is essentially synonymous with the idea of mastery and a sense of competency. In other words, it is not enough to be loved and to possess a sense of belonging; one needs to feel good about oneself in order to possess self-esteem.

Esteem needs along with those needs lower in the hierarchy are classified as basic or deficiency needs. In other words, from the humanist position, one is not truly human if one's esteem needs are not met.

Self-Actualization Needs

There is a qualitative break between self-esteem and **self-actualization needs**. Self-actualization needs are growth needs.[46] Because of major environmental barriers, few people ever truly become all they are capable of becoming. Much of Maslow's later works are concerned with self-actualization needs. He attempted to define the conditions of being in a state of self-actualization. His list of "being" values included, among others, wholeness, completion, beauty, truth, uniqueness, and self-sufficiency.

Self-actualization needs are highly individualized and personalized and cannot be satisfied by others in the same way that lower level needs are. At this level, the person must feel that satisfaction is accomplished largely from that person's own efforts. Maslow's need hierarchy can also be viewed as a dependence-independence continuum.

This notion of a continuum reduces the emphasis on the prepotency principle but retains some of the key ideas embodied in Maslow's work. The notion of a continuum is in keeping with some of the more recent research in operationalizing Maslow's work.[47]

Figure 2.3 illustrates Maslow's hierarchy of needs as well as the related notion of a dependence-independence continuum.

Humanistic psychology and Maslow's need theory in particular have contributed significantly to our social systems perspective. Humanistic theory stresses the distinctive features of the individual as opposed to qualities that may be found in other forms of life. While we support the supposition that common patterns of ordering exist in all life, this is not the subject matter of the social systems perspective. Here our concern is with those patterns that distinguish human forms of social organization. In the most fundamental sense, these features are found in the individuals who comprise such organizations. Employing the previously discussed concept of emergence, these qualities possessed by all humans account for the special ordering features possessed by the various classes of social organization such as, for example, the family.

We find Maslow's contention of a hierarchy of human needs a useful concept. For us, whether these needs are of genetic origin or deeply rooted in culture is not central. What is central is a dynamic conception of human behavior and one that has a positive developmental thrust—self-actualization. These qualities aside from their conceptual utility provide a firm ideological foundation for a professional practice aimed at improv-

FIGURE 2.3   Maslow's Need Hierarchy

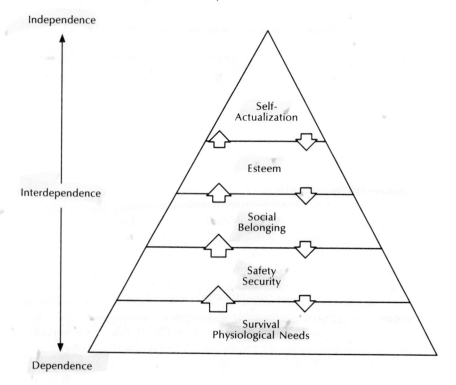

ing the quality of life. It is in this sense that we incorporate the general notion of a positive thrust toward growth and development as part of a social systems perspective.

SUMMARY

The purpose of this chapter was to present a social systems perspective, a general way of looking at human behavior in a social environment. Introducing this chapter were a series of definitions representing a classification system of social organizations. In short, the perspective developed in this chapter pertains to this classification; it is a way of thinking about these various forms of human groupings by treating them as social systems. Next we identified a series of general assumptions or beliefs that we hold about the nature of the world in which we live and about how we as humans behave. These assumptions were drawn largely from general systems theory and what might be described as a systems philosophy.

The bulk of the chapter was devoted to a review of several lines of theory development that have supplied key concepts contained in the social systems perspective. The theories reviewed included general systems theory, field theory, and humanism. In each instance we selected a major theorist to anchor our discussion of concepts. We might have selected other theories or other theorists to identify the same or similar concepts. The issue is not so much the theory or the theorist but the idea behind the concept; the search is for a way of helping us think about the interplay that takes place between humans and the social environments we inhabit, a social systems perspective.

This chapter serves as a background for the remaining parts of the book. In the next chapter we describe in detail the basic social systems model. While based on a social systems perspective, it represents a particular way of modeling the interaction that takes place between a social organization and its social environment. Here we will also be introducing other concepts that extend those previously identified or those that help develop the model's practice relevance.

GLOSSARY

Belongingness and love needs This third need level of Maslow becomes prepotent when safety and security needs are largely satisfied. This need is typified by affiliation, intimacy, caring, loving.

Closed system A theoretical state in which no external forces are deemed to influence the behavior of a system.

Community A form of social organization that is territorially based and through which most people satisfy their common needs and desires, deal with their common problems, and relate to their society.

Emergent properties Characteristics possessed by a social system that are not characteristics of the member components of that system. These so-called new features arise from the relationships that form the system, for example, the whole is greater than the sum of its parts.

Entropy The disordering process in systems; or, a measure of disorder in a system.

Esteem needs The fourth of Maslow's need levels is concerned with our need for self-respect and respect from others. This need level dominates after the social belonging and love needs are largely satisfied.

Expressive actions In human social relationships those actions that are guided by personal determinants as opposed to logical considerations.

Family A subclassification of the social group in which ties of actual or perceived sense of kinship are held.

Field theory A theory of human behavior that holds that behavior is a function of the person and his or her psychological environment. In this formulation the environment is conceptualized as a dynamic and energized field of forces.

Formal organization A form of social organization deliberately and formally created to achieve relatively specific and delimited goals.

General systems theory A theory of organization that deals with the formulation and derivation of the principles of all forms of order.

Genuine needs In field theory, a motivational state based on internal (natural) determinants and related to the maintenance of the person's well-being, for example, hunger.

Gestalt psychology A line of theory development that views the human as an organized whole.

Goals The end states sought by a social system, essentially synonymous with the concept of proposed output in the social systems model.

Humanistic theory A major branch of modern psychology called the "third force" (the other two forces being psychoanalysis and behaviorism). This psychological approach views humans as having a natural tendency toward "actualization," growth, fulfillment of basic potential. It views basic human nature as positive.

Life space A concept in field theory that comprises the person and his or her psychological field.

Logical actions Social actions within relationships based on reasoned choice. Logical actions represent the antithesis of expressive (natural) actions in social systems.

Needs An internal state of an individual pertaining to requirements for a state of well-being, for example, an internal motivational state.

Negative entropy The growth and development process in social systems resulting from their capacity to obtain energy inputs from their environment (suprasystem); it is the ordering process in social systems.

Open systems Systems that engage in exchanges with their environments and where these exchanges are needed to be mutually deterministic.

Prepotency A concept related to Maslow's Need Theory. This concept simply means that a lower level need dominates our attention and motivates us until it is satisfied, that is, it is prepotent.

Quasi needs In field theory, need states that develop as a consequence of genuine needs; they are the equivalent of the specific intentions of an individual.

Safety and security needs The second of Maslow's five need levels, these needs dominate or become prepotent after survival needs have been met. Individuals at this need level are concerned with personal safety, protection of belongings, orderliness, predictability.

Self-actualization needs The growth, meta, or being needs that are qualitatively different from Maslow's four lower or basic need levels. These being needs are highly individualized, personalized, and internalized. Few individuals become truly self-actualized.

Social group A form of social organization composed of two or more members who identify and interact with one another on a personal basis as individuals, possess a shared sense of the group as a social entity, are affected by the group-related actions of members, and in which expressive (natural) actions dominate.

Social organization Any social entity comprised of two or more persons or social units who share purpose and evidence functionally interdependent and reciprocal relationships, and where the social unit itself has functional and reciprocal relationships with its social environment.

Steady state A condition of well-being possessed by a social system and one marked by continuity of exchanges between the system and its suprasystem.

Survival level needs The most basic human needs according to Maslow, these needs constitute the first of five need levels. These needs include, among others, food, water, air, sex, and rest.

Tension system The psychic energy associated with a need state within a psychological field (field theory).

NOTES

1. See S. V. Yemelyanov and E. L. Nappelbaum, "Systems, Purposefulness and Cognition," in *Systems Research II: Methodological Problems*, ed. J. M. Gvishiani (New York: Pergamon Press, 1985), 95.
2. Later in this volume we will be discussing approaches to the classification of social organizations. The point being made here is that there is no generally recognized classification of social organizations currently available. For those interested in a review of approaches to a classification, see, for example, W. Richard Scott, *Organizations: Rational, Natural and Open Systems* (Englewood Cliffs, N.J.: Prentice Hall, 1981), 28–53.
3. For an overview of the profession and its development, see Donald Brieland, "History and Evolution of Social Work Practice," *Encyclopedia of Social Work*, vol. 1, (Silver Spring, Md.: National Association of Social Workers, 1987), 739–754.
4. For a discussion of the notion of self-organizing, see J. B. Probst, "Some Cybernetic Principles for the Design, Control and Development of Social Systems," *Cybernetics and Systems* 16, no. 2–3, 1985, 171–180.
5. See Nicholas Timasheff, *Sociological Theory: Its Nature and Growth*, 3rd ed. (New York: Random House, 1967), 216–263.
6. For a review of General Systems Theory and notation of the role played by von Bertalanffy, see Peter Checkland, *Systems Thinking, Systems Practice* (New York: John Wiley & Sons, 1981).
7. Ludwig von Bertalanffy, *General Systems Theory: Foundations, Development, Applications* (New York: George Braziller, 1968).
8. Ibid., 10–29.
9. Ervin Laszlo, *Introduction to Systems Philosophy* (New York: The Free Press, 1972).
10. Checkland, *Systems Thinking, Systems Practice*, 4.
11. Warren G. Bennis, et al., *Interpersonal Dynamics*, 3rd ed. (Homewood, Ill.: The Dorsey Press, 1973), v.
12. Mary Richmond, *Social Diagnosis* (New York: Russell Sage Foundation, 1917).

13. Bertalanffy, *General Systems Theory*, 55.

14. See, for example, the discussion of emergence in F. Kenneth Berrien, *General and Social Systems* (New Brunswick, N.J.: Rutgers University Press, 1968), 61–62.

15. Bertalanffy, *General Systems Theory*, 39–44.

16. See for example the discussion of entropy in Ervin Laslow, *The System's View of the World* (New York: George Braziller, 1972), 34–46.

17. Bertalanffy, *General Systems Theory*, 39–44.

18. For a useful discussion of steady state in the sense we are using it, see Walter Buckley, *Sociology and Modern Systems Theory* (Englewood Cliffs, N.J.: Prentice Hall, 1967), 52–58.

19. Alfred J. Marrow, *The Practical Theorist* (New York: Basic Books, 1969), ix.

20. See, for example, Kurt Lewin, "Experiments in Social Space," *Harvard Educational Review*, 9, 1939: 21–22.

21. Marrow, *The Practical Theorist*.

22. Ibid., 166.

23. Kurt Lewin, "Behavior and Development as a Function of the Total Situation," in *Manual of Child Psychology*, ed. Leonard Carmichael, 2nd ed. (New York: John Wiley & Sons, 1954), 918–919.

24. Ibid., 919.

25. Sylvia Hazelman MacCall, "A Comparative Study of the Systems of Lewin and Hoffka with Special Reference to Memory Phenomena," in *Contributions to Psychological Theory*, vol. II, no. 1, (Durham, N.C.: Duke University Press, 1939), 12–14.

26. Ibid., 946–948.

27. Abraham H. Maslow, *Motivation and Personality*, 2nd ed. (New York: Harper and Row, 1970), 35–38.

28. Kurt Lewin, *Field Theory in Social Science*, ed. Dorwin Cartwright (New York: Harper Brothers, 1951), 274–297.

29. Marrow, *The Practical Theorist*, 26–28.

30. Ibid., 27.

31. Ibid., 40–47.

32. Ibid.

33. Joseph de Rivera, ed., *Field Theory as Social Science: Contributions of Lewin's Berlin Group* (New York: Gardner Press, 1976), 49–150.

34. de Rivera, *Field Theory*, 144–146.

35. See, for example, Frank Goble, *The Third Force* (New York: Grossman, 1970); and Daniel N. Robinson, *Systems of Modern Psychology* (New York: Columbia University Press, 1979).

36. Gable, 4–6.

37. Ibid., 13–21.

38. Ibid., 13–21.

39. Sometimes this general line of theory development is referred to as fulfillment theory. See discussion in Barbara M. Newman and Philip R. Newman, *Development Through Life: A Psychosocial Approach*, 3rd ed., (Homewood, Ill.: The Dorsey Press, 1984), 26–29.

40. Maslow, *Motivation and Personality*, 97–104.

41. Ibid., 149–180.

42. Ibid., 35–38.

43. Ibid., 299.

44. Ibid., xiii.

45. Ibid., 36–38.

46. For particular attention to the notion of self-actualization, see Abraham H. Maslow, *The Farther Reaches of Human Nature* (New York: Penguin Books, 1976).

47. See particularly Clayton P. Alderfer, *Existence, Relatedness and Growth* (New York: The Free Press, 1972); and Wayne A. Chess and Julia Norlin, "Toward a Theory and Methodology for Need Assessment: Experiences under Title XX" (Norman, Okla.: School of Social Work, 1978).

Chapter 3

The Social Systems Model: Components

OUTLINE

Introduction

Chapters 1 and 2 have established a foundation for an in-depth presentation of the social systems model. In these chapters we provided a review of knowledge-building efforts in social work, described relevant characteristics and trends in current practice, and presented a perspective on human behavior and the social environment. Before proceeding, we want to recapitulate two points that bear on the approach we have taken in modeling social organizations as social systems.

First, social work is a "social" profession. Our expert knowledge is in the area of social behaviors and their effects. We deal with these behaviors at the individual, group, agency, and community levels. Second, we use the social relationship as our medium for helping; again, we use the relationship at all levels of our work. We are in the business of "fixing" social systems and we are also system creators. It is this latter point that we believe is sometimes overlooked. From the inception of the profession, the forming of a relationship has been recognized as the means used for understanding and for helping our clients. The point is that to form a relationship is to create a new social organization, that is, a helping system. In a manner of speaking, the relationship is to the social worker what the scalpel is to the surgeon, the law to the lawyer, and the Bible to the minister; it is what we use in helping our clients—the tools, the medium.

The social systems model is our way of operationalizing social in social work and social in social relationship(s). The term social pertains to the natural relationships that develop among humans in meeting common needs and in advancing their sense of well-being, both individually and collectively. In short, the profession of social work seeks to understand this natural helping and development process and through this understanding social workers seek to systematically and purposively use it to advance the well-being of people.

The social systems model for us serves as a way of modeling the natural relationships existing among people. It is through an understanding of the natural processes that socially link people together that we are able to understand the vast number and types of formed relationships. By formed relationships, we are contrasting those natural self-organizing relationships, such as friendships or love relationships, with those that are consciously and deliberately constituted to achieve some social end. These formed relationships would include such diverse examples as professional helping relationships, social service agencies, and international manufacturing companies. By understanding the pattern of behaviors common to all forms of human association, as well as those that are distinctive to the special types or classifications of such associations, we are provided a very powerful tool to use for human betterment.

As noted earlier, the systems model can be likened to a tool. As used in this book, it provides a framework and focus for organizing the vast amount of knowledge and theory currently available about human behavior and the social environment. By systematically ordering this knowledge in terms of its application to the practice of social work, we increase its relevance and provide direction for future knowledge-building efforts.

In Chapter 1, Figure 1.1 was used to introduce the social systems model. The purpose of that presentation was to introduce you to the eight concepts that comprise the model and their relationships. Through Figure 3.1, we want to build on our earlier introduction and to provide a comprehensive presentation of the model. As part of this building process, we want to incorporate content from our perspective on social systems as presented in Chapter 2. There we defined a social organization as "any social entity comprised of two or more persons/social units who share purpose, who show functionally interdependent and reciprocal relationships, and where the social organization itself has functional and reciprocal relationships with its social environment." In Figure 3.1, we focus on the functional and reciprocal relationships that social organizations have with their social environments. Through this diagram we start our effort at operationalizing the assumption that "the individual is both the cause and the effect of all forms of social organization."

Stated simply, the sources of need satisfaction, opportunity exploration, and assistance for dealing with social problems are always deemed to exist external to the individual (any social unit). In the parlance of the model, this means in the suprasystem. This notion is incorporated within Figure 3.1 by the large broken arrow moving toward the input side of the model and labeled Needs/Opportunities/Problems. These constitute the conditions or deficits in the suprasystem that give rise to or continue the existence of the social system. In other words, it is these external conditions that cause or motivate the individual to join with others for purposes of need satisfaction, opportunity exploration or problem solving.

The second large broken arrow moving away from the social system identifies the

FIGURE 3.1 System Suprasystem Relationships

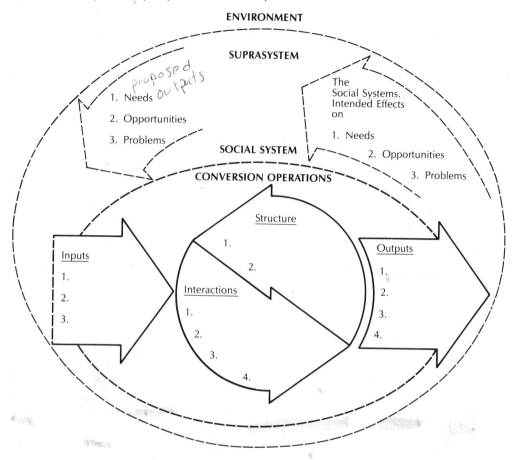

intended effects and/or purpose of the social system. These effects are always deemed to apply to conditions existing in the suprasystem, those that resulted in the creation and continuance of the social system. In the language of the model, this refers to proposed (task) outputs. Note that the arrows move in a cyclical fashion. The system comes into existence and is sustained by conditions existing in the suprasystem. The system affects its suprasystem which in turn affects the system. In this modeling, causation is a reciprocal and cyclical process. Using an earlier example, your school of social work came into existence because of the need for professionally skilled practitioners. This need exists external to the school. The school's graduates are expected to impact on this need. Assuming the actual impact is positive, there will be a continuing and most likely an expanding need for skilled social workers—again, each impacts and causes changes in the other.

At the individual level, the application is conceptually more complex. Suffice to say at this point that the individual as a human personality always exists external to a subject system. The individual enacts a role within a social system. The social system impacts the total person. Think of your relationship with your family, the subject system. You play many roles independent of your role as a family member. In these other roles, for example, as a student, you are part of your family's suprasystem. The family is going to affect you in these roles and vice versa. This point will be developed more extensively when we study the family.

Now we are ready to start our in-depth presentation of the model. One of the difficulties posed in undertaking a description of the model is knowing where to start. Each concept is linked to every other concept, so it becomes difficult to focus on any one part of the model without referring to all other components. To do so would prove confusing. We ask for your tolerance and that you bear in mind that our initial task is one of conveying the meaning of the particular concept under discussion. The second and more important task is to show how these concepts are interrelated and how they provide an approach to an understanding of a dynamic whole, the actual social organization to which the model is being applied. To help accomplish the second task, we will stop from time to time to summarize the concepts already covered and show by examples how they are interrelated.

We start our discussion with the concept of *boundary*. The reason for doing so is that boundary identifies the social organization that is to be modeled—it defines the subject system.

Boundary

Recall from our brief introduction of the model in Chapter 1 that the concept of boundary is used to identify a specialized aspect of the system's structure, that which distinguishes it from its suprasystem. Boundary serves three major functions. First, it defines and helps to provide a sense of the social organization's identity. Second, boundary controls the internal and external exchanges that every social organization has with its environment. Third, it provides the overall definition (boundary) of the roles to be played by those who comprise the system.

With respect to the first function, each social organization is considered a social entity, something beyond those individuals and other social units who comprise it. Boundary identifies those organizational features that bind the units together and that create the identity outsiders have of the organization. This aspect of the boundary function might be likened to those behaviors that result in the creation of an image, a sense of the wholeness or identity of such organizations as your family, your school or your community.

With respect to the second function and as shown in Figure 3.1, we define social organizations as being functionally linked to their environments. In using the model, organizations are regarded as open systems so as to depict this functional linkage with their environments. This linkage is always selective so that control of the exchanges between the organization and its social environment is of vital importance to its health and well-being. This filtering or control process is treated as a function of boundary. Through these control processes, the boundary shields the internal components and their relationships from harmful or disruptive external influences. Similarly, boundary-maintaining efforts permit exchanges with those external units that are deemed functional.

We have likened a social system to a system of interdependent roles as distinguished from interdependent individuals. This distinction helps get across the idea that each of us plays many different **roles**; for example, family member, student, employee, or friend as we move from one type of grouping (system) to another. In each of these roles we behave in accordance with a set of expectations specific to that system. As you leave one role, such as spouse, and assume another as student, you are passing out of the boundary of one system (the family) and through the boundaries and into another (the school). While you are the same person, you are quite different in one role as opposed to the other. In fact, many of the behaviors associated with one role would be completely out of place in the other. The third function of boundary then is to provide the definition of the roles appropriate to the system in which you are taking a part. In this same sense, boundary-maintaining behaviors not only serve to provide the overall definition of the appropriate roles but help assure that the performance of these roles is in accordance with that definition.

This is all very abstract and general. Given the generic nature of the model, the ideas expressed have to be applicable to all systems, from a casework relationship to the United Nations. Practically speaking, think of boundary as the "gatekeeping" function and one that is universal to every form of human grouping. Remember, boundary is simply the name given to an idea about a behavior assumed to be a universal characteristic of social systems. The behavior will always be enacted by a member or members of the subject system; it is never anything physical. To get the idea across, assume for a moment a spousal role (or any role involving an intimate relationship with another person).

> You are in a large room with lots of people. You notice from across the room that a woman/man is behaving very seductively toward your spouse. The feelings that you have and the action that you take get at our notion of boundary and boundary-maintaining behaviors. If you are like most of us, you will move toward your spouse and this new acquaintance and behave in subtle and not so subtle ways to suggest to your partner some "definitions" or redefinition of her or his role, vis-à-vis this system.

With the previous example as background, we will offer another in more detail. In this instance, it involves a mother attempting to discipline her child when her own mother seeks to intervene on the child's behalf: "Susan, you're much too hard on Amy. I remember when you. . . ." Angrily Susan interrupts her mother. "Mother, you stay out of this. Amy is my daughter!" Susan's words, "Mother you stay out of this. Amy is my daughter!" are a boundary-maintenance statement. These words plus Susan's **affect** (emotion) will probably be sufficient, at least in this instance, to have Susan's mother withdraw from a system that does not include her. For purposes of developing this example, let us assume that Susan and Amy constitute a subsystem of a larger system, the

Robbins family. In addition to Susan and Amy, there is another child, John. In this example, Susan, her mother Virginia, and the other members of Susan's birth family would constitute another system. Within the Robbins family and in this example, Susan is enacting the role "mother" vis-à-vis Amy who is in the role of "daughter." Susan plays a crucial role in the socialization of Amy, and part of this is accomplished through disciplining Amy when she has done something wrong. Any external influence which would negate or distort this relationship can be viewed as disruptive, and efforts will be made to reject or thwart the unwanted influences—this is what we mean by boundary and boundary-maintenance behaviors.

In the example of the Robbins family, the notion is stressed that boundary is a social, not a physical feature of structure. This is not intended to mean that physical structures cannot be used to help perform the boundary-maintenance function. To help make the point, let us assume that the Robbins family lives in a small home in a residential area of their community. There have been robberies and occasionally rapes in the vicinity of their home. Fearing both for their personal safety and their belongings, James, Susan's father, installed dead-bolt locks on the front and back doors. In this example, the door and the dead-bolt locks represent physical structures that can be employed in the boundary-maintenance function for the Robbins family. It is the social function served by the door and the locks that is included in the concept of boundary, not the door or locks as such. To state the point otherwise, the doors to the house could stand open day and night and the locks unused; thus, no boundary-maintaining function would be evidenced. In this model, it is the social meaning attached to behaviors that defines the concept of boundary. Also it is the collective set of behaviors that performs the function of boundary maintenance that serves as an organization's boundary.

We have illustrated the concept of boundary as applied to the family when viewed as a social system. The point to remember is that the concepts comprising the model are considered universal and that the behaviors identified in the model are present in some form in every social organization displaying features of interdependence and wholeness. Let us use two other types of social organizations to illustrate the concept of boundary: a university and a nation.

In accordance with our definitions, a university would be considered a formal organization. Given its relatively large size and complexity, the boundary-maintenance function of a university is likely to be evidenced in formally constituted means of determining who are the insiders and outsiders. For example, university students will typically be issued identification cards and these cards in turn must be shown to remove books from the library, to obtain tickets to athletic events, and to enroll in classes. Again, while the card has a physical existence, it is the social behavior attached to how the card is used and the meanings that are associated with these behaviors that evidence boundary and the presence of boundary-maintaining behaviors.

The uses of a passport can be understood in boundary terms when the model is applied to behaviors between nations. With a passport, an individual can pass from one country to another, that is, pass across the boundary separating one country from another. Again, it is the social behaviors that result from use of the passport that evidence the presence of a boundary. The example of a passport can also be instructive in identifying some of the more specified functions performed by a boundary. A boundary always serves a filtering or controlling function, that is, deciding who gets in and who is kept out. In conducting the boundary-maintenance function, representatives of the host system may specify certain temporary roles that an individual may enact while in the host system. For example, the person crossing a boundary from one country to another may engage in sightseeing but will be denied the right to vote in that country's elections or to work.

From a practice perspective, the concept of boundary can be helpful in identifying the existence of and the kinds of relationships that comprise an organization with which you may be working, for example, a family. If there is little or no evidence of the boundary-maintenance function among family members, this may suggest a weakness of relationships among its members or that this is a family (social organization) in name only. Also, the form and level the boundary-maintenance function takes can be instructive in better understanding some of the key relationships of those involved. In our example, the bluntness and affect associated with Susan's remark, "Mother, you stay out of this," may tell you something useful about Susan's relationship with her daughter as well as with her mother. Our only caution would be not to come to any conclusion based on any one comment or set of behaviors. Boundary and boundary-maintenance behaviors should be viewed as distinctive features of ongoing relationships, those that help identify and maintain the system by controlling transactions with outsiders. It is this general pattern of behaviors called boundary maintenance that provide useful insights to the helper.

Suprasystem

The determination of boundary serves to establish and define the existence of a social organization. As applied in the model, everything inside the boundary constitutes the subject system; those social units that are external and to which the system is functionally linked represent its suprasystem. In an application of the model, the notion of suprasystem defines the external system of which the subject system is the central part. The components of the suprasystem are always specific, as are the relationships that exist between these components and the subject system. It is useful to view the suprasystem as the designation, by the user of the model, of parameters of external sources of data needed to understand the behaviors of the subject system, for example, the needs that exist to which the subject system is functionally linked. The concept of suprasystem builds on the assumption that no form of social organization is self-sufficient. In the paragraphs ahead, we further develop the position that social organizations can be understood as a means or as a social tool that humans join together to form in order to meet some of their common needs and desires and to deal with an ever-changing environment. For now, we only assume existence of "functionally reciprocal" relationships between every social organization and its environment.

In developing this model, we have chosen to focus on the social environment as opposed to everything that comprises the environment, for instance, its other social and physical features. The decision was based on practical considerations and pertains to the model's focus on human behavior and the social environment. This decision does not mean that consideration will not be given to other features of the environment. It does mean that the focus of the suprasystem is on selected social components. The other features are treated as essentially contextual or setting factors; they are important, but secondary. In Figure 3.1, the environment is the larger context in which the suprasystem and system are embedded.

Before proceeding, it will prove helpful to place our use of the concept of suprasystem in a larger context. Here the sociological concepts of society and culture are helpful. While in this text we will not be modeling a society as a social system, we do consider society as a distinctive form of social organization. In fact, our position is that the society is the most dominant, inclusive and self-sufficient of all forms of social organization. It is in this sense that the society can be usefully viewed as a larger whole of which all systems and suprasystems contained within it are to a lesser or greater extent functionally related.

With this as background, let us now define **society** and **culture**:

Society Society is the most dominant, inclusive, and self-sufficient of all forms of social organization. It is composed of a specified group of people and other social units who share a common culture.

Culture Culture is a general set of shared meanings held by a specified group of people and other social units and serves as a foundation for their organized way of life.

With the definitions of society and culture as background, let us develop further the concept of suprasystem. To do this, we will return to our example involving Susan and her mother. Susan in her role as Amy's mother was interacting with a vital person in the suprasystem when she warned her own mother, "Mother, you stay out of this." Social interactions among members of the Robbins family enacting their family roles with outsiders constitute their suprasystem interactions. Susan's statement can thus be viewed as part of an interaction between a system and its suprasystem, and as indicated earlier, these interactions would be mutually determinant. By this we mean that the interaction would have an effect on Susan's mother, on Susan herself, and on the system(s) of which they are a part. In the latter case, let us make the assumption that this interaction helped to further define Susan's role toward her mother as well as to further define her own role as mother with respect to Amy. To complete the illustration, let us also make the assumption that this same interaction served to redefine Susan's mother's role both toward Susan and toward Amy, her granddaughter.

Now let us link this interaction between Susan and her mother to our previously defined concepts of society and culture. We are developing the conceptual connection between system, suprasystem, and the larger environment of which these systems are also a part. Here our attention is to the society and its culture. System and suprasystem do not exist in some fashion suspended in space. Conceptually, they too are part of a larger whole. Susan did not invent the mother role nor is her instruction of Amy about the roles of child, daughter, and female her own creation. These roles are cultural roles and are widely shared in a given society. Most likely Susan acquired her particular understanding of the role of mother (as female and daughter, for example) largely from her own mother.

Thinking in terms of cultural influences on system-suprasystem relationships is helpful in terms of practice applications of the model. Recall that while culture provides a set of shared meanings for the people who comprise that society, there is great diversity within a culture, including our own. It is useful to think of the American culture as comprised of a general set of shared meanings and within this general set, more specific subcultures. For example, Susan's gender, color, ethnic background, social class, and religious background will all affect her conception of herself and her relationships with others. These features will be most evident in what we describe as system-suprasystem relationships. Sensitivity to these diversities is fundamental to the use of this model.

Interface

We have completed discussion of two of the concepts comprising the systems model, boundary, and suprasystem. For us it was difficult to decide where to undertake our discussions of interface. In the model, interface represents the designation of a common boundary between a subject system and another system comprising part of its suprasystem. Given this property, locating the discussion immediately following suprasystem seemed logical. However, interface deals with the features of these common boundaries that permit input-output exchanges between the subject system and those with whom it is engaging in input-output exchanges. With this problem identified, keep the concept of interface in mind in the following sections in which the system's inputs and outputs will be discussed.

Earlier we used an exchange between Susan and her mother to illustrate both boundary maintenance and suprasystem. We will develop this exchange to illustrate our use of the concept of interface. Recall that Susan's statement, "Mother, you stay out of this. Amy is my daughter!" was used as an example of boundary maintenance. In effect Susan was telling her mother that she was interfering and that she had no right to do so. In this statement, Susan was reaffirming (maintaining) her family role vis-à-vis her daughter. In this example, we wanted to get at the general function of boundary, protecting the subject system from external influences that could be disruptive. This same exchange serves as an example of an interface. It does so because it represents a specific exchange between representatives of two systems (the Robbins family comprised of Susan, her daughter, Amy, and son, John, and Susan's birth family comprised of her two parents, Virginia and James).

In distinguishing between boundary and interface, think of interface as reflecting the interests of two distinct systems. To some extent, this notion of interface is captured in Roman mythology by Janus, the god of gates and doorways. Recall that Janus had two faces looking in opposite directions. Boundary is an aspect of a system's internal structure and the boundary-maintaining behaviors are always oriented to these internal needs; it is the face of Janus that looks into the system. Now think of "inter" in the literal sense of the word—between or among. As with the god Janus, it faces in two directions and represents a way of reconciling and dealing with contending interests. Interface is the concept that helps us construct the specific interactions that take place between a subject system and the specific individuals, groups, and organizations that comprise its suprasystem.

Now, let us continue the interactions between Susan and her mother and father, Virginia and James. In response to being told to "stay out of this," Virginia, after a moment of hesitation and being a bit hurt says, "Susan, I am sorry; I didn't mean to interfere. You know that James and I love you, we love you all (referring to Robbins family members). Look, why don't we all go shopping and have lunch; you know I promised James that I would buy Amy and John new fall school clothes." The response is a boundary-maintenance statement from Susan's mother's position, but one that reaffirms the special relationship between the two families (systems), their mutual love and need for each other. To conclude this exchange, let us assume that Susan smiles and says, "Mom, I am sorry for being so abrupt. I didn't mean to hurt you. I love you and I know you didn't really mean to interfere. Lunch sounds great; where shall we go?" The exchange between Susan and her mother provides an example of interface. The boundaries of the two systems are reaffirmed, but more importantly, features of the agreed-upon relationship between the two systems are specified, that is, what is permissible and what is not. Here we make the assumption that Susan and her mother enjoy having lunch together. Also assumed is that Susan and her children have come to terms with accepting as helpful (functional) the clothes and other purchases made by Susan's parents. Such purchases could, of course, be treated as interference and be rejected. In such an instance, the behavior would be treated as boundary-maintenance.

The concept of interface is applicable to all forms of social organization when treated as social systems. For example, the purchase by the Robbins family of a new car from their local Chrysler dealer would be evidenced by an interface between two systems. Here it would take the form of a purchase agreement. The interface would be formalized and represented as a contract. This purchase agreement (contract) would recognize the rights, interests, and all other pertinent matters agreed upon by the two parties. At an international level, the search for an agreement between Russia, the United States, and other countries seeking arms control, particularly nuclear arms, represents a search for an interface, an arms agreement.

It is important to remember that interface refers to agreements, formal and informal, made between two or more systems to jointly maintain and/or support some aspect of a relationship. The reasons or motivation for doing so may be quite different for the parties involved. For example, the United States and Russia would each decide that it was in their own best interest as well as in the best interest of the rest of the world to enter into and jointly support an arms agreement. At another level, each may find other advantages to such an agreement; perhaps Russia might find the agreement useful in dealing with the Chinese.

Interface, like boundary, however, is only evidenced in social behaviors between two or more social units. Agreements may be set forth in a formal contract as in the case of a car purchase or an arms agreement between two countries, but interface is only evidenced in the actual behaviors that link specified social organizations with each other. It does not follow that people or organizations always behave toward each other as expected. What can be said is that when there are unexpected behaviors that are deemed threatening, boundary-maintenance behaviors will become evident. As with all of the concepts comprising the model, interface is dynamic. These common features of boundaries are always changing, sometimes expanding, and sometimes being terminated, as would be the case in a change of employment by a family member, or a scrapped arms agreement, for example.

Input

We identify two requirements associated with the development and maintenance of all forms of social organization. First, a perceived need, problem, or opportunity causes a given social organization to come into existence. In this sense, the organization can be viewed as a response to this condition (see Figure 3.1). The organization can be as simple as two people forming a friendship, such as a social group resulting from the social belonging and/or love needs of two individuals; or, it can be as complicated as the United Nations, formed from a need to promote world peace among all nations. Second, once formed the social organization must have resources to sustain itself and to perform its functions. Here we return to an earlier assumption that no social organization is self-sufficient, and thus to survive it must continually be supplied with resources that are external to itself. As developed in the model, these resources are secured through input-output exchanges between the system and its suprasystem.

The two requirements just identified result in the designation of two forms of input: (1) signal, sometimes called task; and (2) *maintenance*. We will treat signal and task as synonymous terms. **Signal inputs** represent that category of inputs resulting from the perceived need, problem, or opportunity that the social system seeks to address. **Maintenance inputs** are those resources required to meet the perceived need, deal with the problem, or explore and capitalize on an opportunity. In other words, signal inputs, through a conversion process made possible because of the maintenance inputs, result in task outputs.

The term *signal inputs* is used because of the meaning attached to the word signal, a sign or a notification to act. As we will see later on, in large and complex forms of social organization, it is sometimes very difficult to distinguish between signal and maintenance forms of input. For example, in a hospital (a social organization) patients in a need state would represent signal inputs, and staff would compose part of the maintenance inputs. A sick or injured patient coming into the hospital through the emergency room will signal or activate the system to receive and treat the patient. Particularly in formal social organizations like a hospital, signal inputs occupy a temporary role. Also, the role is essentially assigned and largely defined by the boundary-maintenance function of the subject system.

In a practice application of this model, clients will always constitute the signal inputs. The helping staff and all of the other resources required to accomplish the helping effort are designated as maintenance inputs. In more precise terms, signal inputs are represented by the client and the condition or situation for which the client is seeking help. Recall that in the model, every system performs a boundary-maintenance function. In the example of the hospital, the emergency room staff will first provide an assessment of the patient's condition and, based on that assessment, decide what needs to be done. One possible action would be to admit the patient to the hospital. This assessment represents a boundary-maintenance function and the decision to admit would cause the patient to be treated as a signal input. Conceptually speaking, we can say that the intake function in all human service agencies is a boundary-maintenance function, the purpose of which is to screen signal inputs. Also, if a client is admitted into the system, the assessment process provides specification to the role the client is expected to play. It also helps the client understand the counter roles (for example, doctor, nurse, and social worker), that he or she will likely encounter.

The hospital example deals with the concept of input that comes into an existing form of social organization. The notion of input also applies to the creation of new forms of social organization. Rather than a hospital, let us use the example of a family counseling center. This is also an existing social organization, but through discussion of a case, let us think about how new social organizations are consciously formed. Our case will be the Arnold family, consisting of Bill, twenty-three, Sarah, nineteen, and their only child, Donnie, age 2. The couple has been married three years. The family was referred to the agency by the court because of Sarah's physical abuse of Donnie. Prior to the referral, the court placed Donnie temporarily in a foster home and referred his parents, Bill and Sarah, to the counseling center for assessment and assistance if indicated. The family assessment was conducted by Ms. Pat Gray, a social work practicum student. Following the assessment, an agency staff meeting was held. The assessment indicated sufficient family strengths, including an interest in securing help with the problem, for the case to be accepted for family counseling services. As a result of the agency staffing of this case, Pat Gray was assigned as the social worker and as a student she was to work closely with her practicum supervisor, Joan Seavers.

In the above case example, a social organization as we have previously defined it does not yet exist. But the decision by the agency to accept the case for family services indicates that the intent is for one to be created. By this we mean that the helping relationship that Ms. Gray seeks to establish with Bill and Sarah Arnold represents the intent to form a social organization. If Ms. Gray is successful in forming this social organization, it can be modeled as a social system. Conceptually speaking, the social organization to be formed is the medium through which our agency worker, Ms. Gray, will seek to help the Arnold family. In effect, a specialized helping organization is being formed as a tool to intervene in ("fix") another organization, the Arnold family. What we will be doing in order to explain the model is to treat this newly formed social organization as a social system.

At this point, it should prove useful to summarize the concepts discussed so far in this chapter by applying them to this case. The system boundary will develop around the three people who will comprise this emerging system: Pat Gray the social worker, and Donnie's parents, Bill and Sarah Arnold. Constituting its suprasystem will be the important individuals, families, agencies, and others who are functionally linked to this newly formed system. A synonymous term borrowed from Lewin would be the "field" for this system. In our example, the key features of the suprasystem will likely include the family counseling agency itself, particularly Pat's practicum supervisor; the court; Donnie; and the foster parents, among others. Interface would be represented by the common boundaries shared by this system with each component that comprises its suprasystem, including Pat's supervisor, for example. Recall that the model is simply a specific way to organize thinking about something that is real. In this instance it is the professional helping relationship being established by Ms. Pat Gray to assist the Arnold family. The formulation of the suprasystem is made by Ms. Gray as part of her assessment of this case.

Building on our example, Bill and Sarah Arnold in their roles as clients will constitute the signal input into this emerging social organization. Maintenance inputs include Pat Gray in her role as student social worker, and all of the resources (for instance, an office, secretarial support, and time), necessary to support Ms. Gray and her helping efforts. Everything that Ms. Gray will require in this helping relationship will be labeled as maintenance inputs.

We have attempted to illustrate in this example the functional connection on the input side that every form of organization is deemed to have with its environment, that is, those resources obtained from the suprasystem that help constitute and sustain the subject system. There should also be a word of caution here. We are taking certain liberties with the model to assist in explaining it. In the above case, we have talked about forming a system and the so-called inputs required. Technically, the model is a way of viewing existing organizations that display characteristics of interdependence and wholeness. So, while it is useful to think in systems terms as to why organizations form, the model is only applicable to mature organizations. The model does not yet have a developmental application.

Output

We described the concept of input in terms of the resources required by a system to operate. Conceptually, it illustrates the dependent relationship that every social organization has with its environment. Now we move to the other end, the output side of the social system. The concept of output represents the functional tie that every form of social organization has with its social environment. The notion of output also helps to identify the dependent relationship that the suprasystem has with the subject system.

In the previous section, we identified two classes of inputs: signal and maintenance. Three classifications of output were specified: task, maintenance and waste. A **task output** is a signal input after system processing. Earlier, signal input was illustrated by a person being admitted to a hospital. For purposes of developing this example, we will call our patient Art. At the time of his release from the hospital, Art in his patient role would be considered as task output. More specifically, the task output in this instance would be Art's physical status in relationship to his physical status at the time of admission. At the time of his admission, Art's physician, along with the assistance of other members of the hospital's staff, made an assessment of his physical status that established baseline information on the condition that resulted in his need for hospital care—a heart attack. The physician formulated treatment goals (proposed output) and a course of treatment suited to achieving the goals. Conceptually, these goals represented the doctor's view of the likely course of Art's problem as a consequence of his treatment plan, and what Art's condition should be at the time of his discharge from the hospital. His actual condition at the time of discharge would be labeled *task output*.

The hospital with all of its component parts constitutes the system, and boundary maintenance will be evidenced in a determination of Art's eligibility for admission. Functionally relevant people, families, agencies, and others external to the hospital represent its suprasystem. In this model, Art comes to the hospital from its suprasystem. Having suffered a heart attack, Art is no longer able to fulfill his usual family roles. Therefore, Art represents an output of the family as well as an input to the hospital. Given this position, the two systems are functionally linked.

Art's admission to the hospital is not without conditions. Art's expectations and those of his family about their respective roles and responsibilities and those of the hospital constitute a portion of what we earlier termed interface. Similarly, the hospital has its rules and expectations as to the roles to be played by Art and his family along with what its own role will be if Art becomes a patient. Among other matters, his family will be expected to honor visiting hours, and Art will be expected to behave as a patient, that is, act in accordance with the role of patient. Art and/or his family are also expected to pay for his hospital stay. With Art's admission, he becomes a signal input to this system, and his payment for care becomes a portion of the system's maintenance inputs.

At the time of discharge, Art becomes a task output of this system. Similarly, Art represents an input to his own family, a vital part of the hospital's suprasystem. Our patient has made good progress and has recovered from his heart attack to the point that he can be cared for by his family. Also we assume that by reentering his family, he is able to assume some of the duties associated with the various family roles he plays. In this example, we have tried to illustrate some of the system concepts, but do so in a way that illustrates the input-output connections that characterize the general social ordering described in our social systems perspective and their specific application in this model.

Before leaving our hospital example, we should note that it is possible to develop the example into one emphasizing the hospital as a large formally constituted social organization. In such an application, signal inputs would be represented by all the patients admitted during an interval of time, perhaps a year, and task outputs would be the status of all those patients at the time of their discharge. Part IV of this book deals specifically with such applications.

Our emphasis so far has been on task outputs. Now let us turn to the notion of **maintenance outputs**. The model's open system qualities recognize not only the functional effects of the system on its suprasystem but the reverse effects as well. Recall that each system is envisioned as possessing functional ties with its suprasystem, and these ties are mutually deterministic. In other words, just as task outputs will affect the system's suprasystem, so task outputs affect the system itself. Maintenance outputs is the concept that embodies these reciprocal effects.

For purposes of developing the concept of outputs, let us return to the example involving the Arnold family. Here we illustrate, through use of a social work example, the distinction between task and maintenance outputs. The social system being modeled is a social organization comprised of Pat Gray, a student in the role of family social worker, and Bill and Sarah Arnold in their roles as clients. The purpose of the helping relationship is the development of this family so that it provides a safe and loving environment for Donnie, their son. Conceptually, the term task output refers to the status of signal inputs at conclusion of a processing cycle. As a practical matter, the cycle can be as short as the conclusion of a session in an ongoing helping relationship—"How do you feel about what we talked about today?"—or the conclusion of the relationship with the closing of the case. For purposes of simplification, let us apply the notion of output to the termination of the Arnold case.

Under such a scenario, output would be the status of the Arnold family in terms of the capacity of Bill and Sarah in their parental roles to provide a safe and loving family environment for their son, Donnie. Depending on how the original goals were stated, the goals may have included the return of Donnie to his parents and the reassignment by the court of parental rights to Bill and Sarah Arnold. Task outputs would be the actual status of the Arnold family at the conclusion of their work with Pat Gray. The output would be stated or recorded in terms of the goals of their services contract, which would be proposed output (more will be said of this later when we discuss proposed output and feedback).

The clearest example in this case of a maintenance outcome would be the increased knowledge and professional helping skills acquired by Ms. Gray in working with Bill and Sarah Arnold. In this application, Ms. Gray and all the resources required to sustain the system are viewed as maintenance inputs. Here maintenance outputs is the term used to identify the effects of these resources on the system itself. While the principal justification for the use of maintenance inputs is their contribution to what we label as task output, they have other important justifications as well. Specifically, they serve as investments in strengthening and developing the system itself.

Note that in the previous example we are not saying that task outputs would be represented by Ms. Gray's effect on Bill and Sarah nor that maintenance outputs would be Bill and Sarah's effects on Ms. Gray; that would be a linear, not a systems formulation of effects. In other words, these effects involve the totality of system-suprasystem influences and they are reciprocal and mutually deterministic.

Up to this point we have focused on positive characteristics of output. In human services work, task output will always be represented by the condition of the client or some designated social unit like the family following a processing cycle. The client may be better, the same, or worse. The important point is that task output, when applied to a human service agency, is an appraisal of the client following a processing cycle. The appraisal is in terms of those conditions that brought him or her to the agency or into a helping relationship, and it is concerned with those positive or negative changes associated with the helping process. Similarly, a maintenance output is an assessment of the helping system itself following a processing cycle. This assessment may indicate that the system itself may be better, the same, or worse. Using our student worker, it may be that the case turned out badly and in part she blamed herself for "mishandling" the situation. Here we would have an example of a negative maintenance outcome.

All forms of outputs are conceptual designations. The model user has the final say in the specification of the concepts and the organization of data that will fill out and operationalize these ideas in a particular application. In some instances, task outputs can be objectively represented, for example, a client did or did not obtain a job, remain drug-free, or return to a drug habit. In the Arnold case, Donnie's return home or his continuance in foster home care could be accepted as an objective indication of output. Frequently though, in human service applications of the model, output will be represented by a *perception* of what occurred as a result of the intervention process. In the Arnold case, Ms. Gray's evaluation as stated in her discharge summary represents largely her own perceptions of what happened. Similarly, Bill and Sarah Arnold have their own perceptions of outcome. These perceptions may be very similar or they could be quite different. The selection of what constitutes an appropriate specification of output falls upon the person using the model.

Now we turn to our final classification of output, **waste**. The concept of waste is simply an attempt to capture all forms of a system's output. We use the notion of waste as a designation of inefficient, ineffective, or inappropriate use of resources in terms of the production of task and maintenance outputs. A simple example would be the time and related resources utilized on behalf of a client who after one or two interviews fails to return and who obtains no benefits as a consequence of agency contact. As we will later see, waste plays a critical role in feedback, the return of output information that is fed back into the system as input. The designation of waste represents a judgment by the person employing the model of the noneffects and the negative effects that the system itself has on its task and maintenance outputs. Staff burnout would be an example of waste in an agency application of the model. Burnout is a negative maintenance outcome, one that diminishes the helping capacity of the system. It also represents a negative effect on the person experiencing burnout.

Proposed Output

The social systems model is premised on existence of an underlying order evident in all forms of social organization. This order derives from purposes shared by those individuals and other social units who comprise a social organization, be it a friendship group, a client-worker treatment relationship, a family, an agency, or a community. The concept of proposed output is that feature of the model that incorporates this assumption of purposiveness. In the broadest sense, proposed output is a structural feature of the model and a part of the system's conversion operations. However, because of its importance, it will be discussed separately and before we undertake our discussion of conversion operations.

Output was reviewed in a previous section and was defined as the actual effect that a system has both on its suprasystem (task outputs) and on itself (maintenance outputs). In contrast, proposed output represents the future effects that the system proposes to have on its suprasystem and on itself. We are not suggesting a tight fit between these intentions and actual effects, far from it. We are saying that the model is based on a perspective that holds that some level of shared purposes is necessary for the development and the continuance of all forms of social organization. And, while shared purposes may not be fully realized, these purposes provide a guide to the understanding of behaviors.

The term *proposed output* is a generic one used in input-output oriented systems models. **Goal** is a more familiar term and our use of goal is similar to the way Lewin used the concept in field theory.[1] Briefly stated, goals represent statements of a future effect or future state of the system. Most importantly, goals organize and give focus to the relationships among those comprising a social organization. The following are some frequently heard goal statements: "Some day we are going to be rich"; "Go for it"; "Let's win the next game"; "This agency is dedicated to improving the quality of life of its clients";

"We're going to do something about the drug problem in this town." Goals always deal with a future state but the future can be an hour or ten years away; the exact time parameter is not a central issue. For example, the statement "Let's have pizza for dinner" can be a goal. If the statement represents one mutually held by family members, the chances are quite good that the family will enjoy a pizza dinner together.

While a goal must be shared in order to represent proposed output, it does not follow that to share means to verbalize the goal, to systematically go about securing a commitment to that goal, or for that matter that agreement exists on how to accomplish a shared purpose. In most informal organizations like a friendship group, the goals are not usually verbalized as such. Rather, they are mutually understood and are evidenced by the interactions among group members. The following statement is an example of a mutually held goal: "Lunches together are always so much fun; let's get together again next Tuesday, same time, same place." The statement suggests that those having lunch together had fun. While not stated as such, their shared goal is one of having fun, enjoying each other's company and feeling good about themselves by feeling good about each other. The assumption is made that all those who participated shared a sense of mutuality, a feeling of being accepted as a person. We would further assume that if one or more members of this friendship group did not share in this sense of belonging, then the likelihood is that they would eventually leave the group; it would not be meeting their needs (goals).

Where do goals come from and how do they become shared? A simple answer to the first part of this question would be that, conceptually, goals have their origins in: (1) the problematic or opportunistic conditions perceived to exist in the environment; and (2) the needs or wants representing internal conditions of the individuals or the social units comprising the subject organization, for example, a need to be loved. The second part of how goals become shared is the more difficult of this troubling question. A practical response would be that goals become shared when those comprising the social organization define a problem or opportunity similarly or conclude that mutual action toward the same goal would be in their best interest. In a structural sense, the model only assumes existence of some level of shared purposes. In the chapters ahead, we will explore some of the lines of theory development that seek to explain how shared goals evolve.

Before moving on to examples of goals or proposed output, it would be useful to tie in the concepts of culture and values to our use of the term proposed output. Culture, as you recall, represents a set of shared meanings held by the people comprising a society. These shared meanings provide the clearest source of the ordering that links systems to their suprasystems and to the larger environment. **Values** are a special feature of culture; they represent those shared meanings about what is desirable and undesirable in social life. Values affect both the selection of the means and ends of social behaviors. In the sense of an end state, values are synonymous with goals that are stated at high levels of abstraction. The notion of values as a key aspect of structure is a very helpful way of examining the goal framework that binds people together in common pursuits.

At this point, a practice application showing how cultural values help to shape proposed output should be helpful. A value that undergirds the foundation of all forms of social work intervention is that social work practice is focused on improving the quality of the client's life.[2] Given this position, we can now say that "improvement in the quality of life" represents the highest or most comprehensive goal statement undergirding all professional helping efforts. The point is an important one in the sense that it provides a common focal point to professionally sanctioned helping efforts irrespective of method, field of practice, or client group. Also, when applied in a practice case, this common goal statement provides the basic focus for the ordering of the social systems model. Thus, the task of the professional worker becomes one of assisting clients to operationalize how the quality of their life can be improved in their particular instance. We will term this process of operationalizing goals as one of constructing a hierarchy of outcomes.

Just as cultural values represent end states (for example, adding quality to human life), some values also pertain to means. In developing the systems model we hold that the determination of end states affects the selection of the means to be used to accomplish those ends. To develop the practice relevance of this point, let us again return to a cultural value to which the profession of social work firmly subscribes, "each individual has a right to self-determination." This value can be treated as either a means or an end. For purposes of illustration, we will treat the value of self-determination as a means. By putting the two values together we can characterize practice intervention in social work as always focusing on improving the quality of the client's life and always employing methods (means) that recognize, to the extent possible, every person's right to be self-determined. In the most fundamental sense then, these two values will shape the formulation of proposed output in every practice application of the model. Similarly, these two cultural values as incorporated into a helping profession provide an approach to understanding the ordering process that should be evident in specific practice applications of this model.

We will use the Arnold family again to illustrate the concept of proposed output. In developing the concept we will employ the notion of a hierarchy of outcomes as a strategy for operationalizin   mission of improving the quality of life. For the purpose of the application we wil. ... d to add some additional content to the case.

Recall that the case involves child abuse and that the principals include Donnie, the injured child; Pat Gray, the student social worker; and Donnie's parents, Sarah and Bill Arnold. The agency involved is the Westwood Child and Family Center. In more detail the relevant events leading up to the judge's referral of the case are as follows:

Bill, age twenty-three, is a truck driver and is away from home a great deal. Sarah is nineteen; she married Bill while she was a junior in high school. The couple had known each other for some time and had dated "seriously" several months prior to marriage. While they each loved the other, Sarah was not much interested in school, had never gotten along with her mother, and so was anxious "just to get away from home." For her, Bill was someone who loved her, but he also provided a way to escape from a very unpleasant home situation and from school, which she considered a "waste."

Donnie was not a planned child. On the one hand, Sarah was delighted with the pregnancy; on the other she was sick a good part of the time and didn't like what the pregnancy "did to my body." As a consequence of these experiences, Sarah "swore" she would never get pregnant again. Sarah also felt confined with Donnie, largely because Bill was on the road so much. As a long-distance truck driver, Bill might be away from home a week at a time.

The event that led to court action was an outburst of anger in which Sarah struck Donnie with her fist and burned him with her cigarette. The couple had been arguing over money. Rather than continue the argument, Bill, as he did frequently, just walked out of the house. Sarah was furious. Donnie was crying and attempted to crawl up on his mother's lap; she kept pushing him down. "Get away from me," she yelled. After several more attempts to crawl up on her, Sarah struck out, hitting him with her fist and yelling, "I told you to stay down." Donnie, frightened and hurt, only screamed louder. In response, Sarah thrust her cigarette at Donnie burning him on his arm and chest.

Immediately following her attack on Donnie, she stopped in shock and horror at what she had done. Sarah ran screaming from the house to a neighbor. Together, Sarah and her neighbor took Donnie to the emergency room of their local hospital. Sarah tearfully told the emergency-room physician what had happened. The doctor explained that he was required by state law to report the incident through the "Child Abuse Hot Line" to the county child welfare office.

Donnie was treated and detained at the hospital. Following emergency investigative procedures by the local child welfare agency, Donnie was removed from his parents' custody and under a court order was temporarily placed in a foster home. In the adjudication hearing that resulted in the temporary placement of Donnie in foster care, the judge mandated that the couple seek help with their personal difficulties as a condition for subsequent consideration of the return of Donnie to their care. It was in this manner that the bewildered Sarah and Bill Arnold arrived at the Westwood Center.

At intake, the family was seen by Ms. Pat Gray, a social work practicum student. The assessment revealed that as a child Sarah had been abused by her own mother. She vividly recalled these experiences and how she swore she would never hurt a child of hers. The act of abusing her own child, with the loss of control it evidenced, was frightening. On the other hand, she wondered about her own mother and the stress she may have been under. She explained to Pat Gray, "I really never thought about the problems my mother had and what she must have thought about herself when she lost control."

The assessment of Sarah and Bill both as individuals and a family showed considerable strength. The evaluation of Donnie by the child welfare agency revealed that Donnie was physically, socially, and psychologically developing normally. There was no evidence that Donnie had suffered any previous abuse.

Following a staffing conference, the center accepted the Arnolds for family services. Ms. Pat Gray was assigned as the worker and since she was a student she was to work closely with her practicum supervisor, Joan Seavers.

In this example, a social organization as we have defined it does not yet exist. But, the decision by the center to accept the case for family services indicates that the intent is for one to be created; that is, the helping relationship comprised of Pat Gray, the student social worker, along with Bill and Sarah Arnold. Given Donnie's age and his placement out of the home, he will not be included in the helping system about to be created.

The first interview following the decision to accept the case was used by Pat to help answer questions raised by Sarah and Bill about what would be involved in their family counseling sessions and more particularly to agree on the goals of what Pat referred to as their "services contract." In so doing, Pat defined her role as the family services worker and their roles as clients. Pat also helped Sarah and Bill to understand her role with respect to the court and the child welfare agency.

Earlier in this chapter, Figure 3.1 was used to illustrate the purposiveness and cyclical characteristics of the social systems model. Figure 3.2 applies these characteristics to the helping relationship that has been formed to assist Bill and Sarah Arnold deal with their problem. In short, we are modeling the Arnold case. Our focus will be on how goals can be formulated (proposed output). We will illustrate this for you by a technique we call constructing a **hierarchy of outcomes**.[3]

In Section I of Figure 3.2 under "Problem Conditions," we summarize the problems being faced by the Arnold family. Conceptually, the Arnold family exists in the suprasystem of the Westwood Child and Family Center. This agency came into existence to help families deal with problems such as those confronting the Arnolds. In this case, the problem conditions include: (1) physical abuse of Donnie; (2) financial stress; and (3) loss of self-esteem (Bill and Sarah). For purposes of this illustration, we are assuming that these problems have been jointly defined and agreed upon by the Arnolds and Ms. Gray during the problem identification and assessment phase of their work together.

The subject system then, is comprised of Ms. Pat Gray and Bill and Sarah Arnold. This system has been formed under the auspices of the Westwood Child and Family Center; its purpose is to assist Bill and Sarah Arnold to deal with the identified problems.

The signal inputs to this new system will be Sarah and Bill in their problem/client roles. The chief maintenance input is the social worker, Pat Gray. Additional maintenance inputs include such agency resources as Ms. Gray's office, clerical support, and supplies.

Key features of this new system's suprasystem will include, among others, the Westwood Child and Family Center (particularly Pat Gray's supervisor), Donnie and his foster parents, the judge who referred the Arnolds to the center and the protective services worker who is supervising Donnie's foster home placement (not shown).

The system's task output in its final form will be the status of the problem conditions as set forth in the services contract. More specifically, task output will be represented by the status of these conditions identified within the goal structure of the services contract. Maintenance output in its final form will be the condition of the maintenance inputs, for example, Ms. Pat Gray at the time this case is terminated. Typically, maintenance outputs are not specified in a services contract. The effects of this case on Pat Gray will likely be addressed within the supervisory relationship that Ms. Gray has with her practicum supervisor, Joan Seavers. There will also be waste. We will not, at this point, concern ourselves with the conversion operations of the model, except to note that the goals, or what we call proposed output, are an aspect of the structure of these operations.

In Section II of Figure 3.2 the concept of proposed output is diagrammed utilizing the

Know for test

FIGURE 3.2 Conceptualizing Proposed Output as a Hierarchy of Outcomes

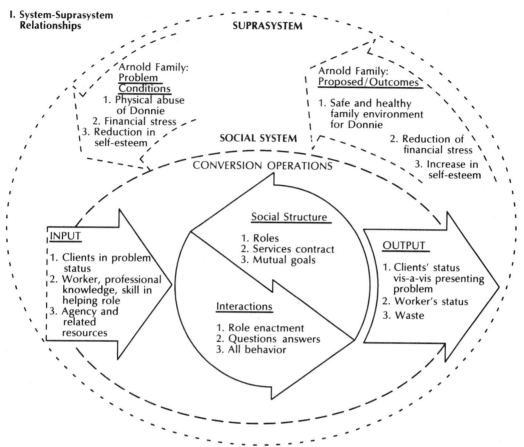

I. System-Suprasystem Relationships

SUPRASYSTEM

Arnold Family:
Problem
Conditions
1. Physical abuse of Donnie
2. Financial stress
3. Reduction in self-esteem

Arnold Family:
Proposed/Outcomes
1. Safe and healthy family environment for Donnie
2. Reduction of financial stress
3. Increase in self-esteem

SOCIAL SYSTEM

CONVERSION OPERATIONS

INPUT
1. Clients in problem status
2. Worker, professional knowledge, skill in helping role
3. Agency and related resources

Social Structure
1. Roles
2. Services contract
3. Mutual goals

Interactions
1. Role enactment
2. Questions answers
3. All behavior

OUTPUT
1. Clients' status vis-a-vis presenting problem
2. Worker's status
3. Waste

II. Proposed Output as a Hierarchy of Outcomes

*Mission

Goal 1   *Goal 2   Goal 3

*Objective 1   Objective 2   Objective 3

*Activities   Activities   Activities

Definitions:

1. Mission: A broad philosophical and inspirational statement of intended output which guides all practice activities.

2. Goals: Long-range qualitative statements of intent pertaining to a component or aspect of the mission statement.

3. Objectives: Statements of intended accomplishments that are specific, attainable, appropriate, and measurable.

4. Activities: A program or plan of (professional) services directed toward accomplishment of each objective.

(Continued)

FIGURE 3.2 (*Continued*)

III. Proposed Task Outputs

MISSION: To improve the quality of life of the members of the Arnold family through the provision of family counseling services

GOAL 1. To achieve a safe and healthful family environment for Donnie (return of Donnie to his family).

GOAL 2. To stabilize the family's financial situation.

GOAL 3. To increase the levels of self-esteem of Bill and Sarah Arnold within their parenting roles.

OBJECTIVE 1 (Goal 2). To increase the Arnold family's amount of annual household income by 20 percent ($7,000) by June 30, 19__ (specified date).

OBJECTIVE 2 (Goal 2). To decrease the Arnold family's annual household indebtedness by 30 percent ($3,000) by December 30, 19__ (specific date).

OBJECTIVE 3 (Goal 2). To increase the savings of the Arnold family from none to $2,000 annually by December 30, 19__ (specific date).

ACTIVITIES (Objective 2):

1. Ms. Gray will explain the basic notion of a family budget and provide the Arnolds with sample budgets.
2. Sarah and Bill Arnold will devise and mutually agree upon their own family budget. The budget will be in place by September 30, 19__ (specific date).
3. Each week the couple will examine and mutually agree upon any changes to be made in budget expenditures and share their decision with Ms. Gray.
4. Sarah and Bill Arnold will consolidate their loans into an extended payment plan consistent with their income. This loan consolidation will be accomplished by October 11, 19__ (specific date).

IV. Proposed Maintenance Outputs

MISSION: To improve the quality of life of the Arnold family through the provision of family counseling services.

GOAL 1. To increase Ms. Gray's knowledge and skill in the provision of family counseling services.

GOAL 2. To increase Ms. Gray's knowledge of community services pertaining to the needs of the community's abused and neglected children.

GOAL 3. To increase Ms. Gray's sense of competence as a professional social worker.

OBJECTIVE 1 (Goal 2). By May 1, 19__ (end of practicum), Ms. Gray will be able to diagram the community child protective service system.

OBJECTIVE 2 (Goal 2). By May 1, 19__ (end of practicum), Ms. Gray will have updated the agency's resource manual dealing with child protective services.

OBJECTIVE 3 (Goal 2). By May 1, 19__ (end of practicum), Ms. Gray will have completed a needs assessment of the community's abused and neglected children.

ACTIVITIES (Objective 2):

1. Assign Ms. Gray the Arnold family.
2. Have Ms. Gray personally visit each community agency providing child protective services.
3. Have Ms. Gray meet with the center's research director to design an approach for updating the agency's resource manual pertaining to abused and neglected children.
4. Others.

technique known as a hierarchy of outcomes. Adjacent to the diagram are definitions of the terms applied to each level of the hierarchy. Up to this time we have used the terms proposed output, goals, purposes, mission and objectives synonymously. These terms now take on more specialized meaning when used in the manner indicated in this diagram.

You should also be alert to the qualitative break that occurs in the hierarchy between statements of objectives and activities. In keeping with the position developed in the social systems perspective, **activities** always represent the means selected to accomplish the ends designated at the objective level in the hierarchy of outcomes. Activities refer to the set of tasks that are performed in order to reach an objective, such as weekly family counseling services. Sections III and IV of Figure 3.2 provide examples of proposed output utilizing the notion of a hierarchy of outcomes. Section III specifies examples of proposed task outputs while Section IV contains examples of proposed maintenance outcomes.

Earlier we made the point that there is consensus within the profession that the overall **mission** (purpose) of social work is to help improve the quality of life of those we serve. Building off of this position, we particularize it by naming the client(s) in the mission statement, at the first or highest level in the hierarchy: "to improve the quality of life of the Arnold family through the provision of family counseling services." Note the relationship of means to ends established in the statement. The end state is the improvement in the quality of life of the Arnold family; the means for doing so is through the provision of family counseling services. The end state becomes the basis for constructing proposed task output statements; the means statement serves as the basis for constructing the proposed maintenance output statements. The inclusion of the means statement also establishes the social work domain for helping people improve the quality of their lives—the provision of social services. There are many professions that exist to help people improve the quality of their lives; social work is the lead profession for helping people do so through provision of social services.

In our example, and for the reasons cited above, there is a common mission statement out of which both task and maintenance outcomes are derived. The second level in the hierarchy we label the goal level. These are always broad qualitative statements and in task outputs these identify the domain of life to be addressed. The general domains for attention are identified in the assessment phase of the helping process. In this example, we make the assumption that Ms. Gray and the Arnolds mutually agreed on the areas of their family life with which they are asking for assistance. The three areas are identified in the goal statements. A useful way of organizing an approach to assessment and for constructing the goal level of the hierarchy is to rephrase the mission statement in terms of a question. In this instance it would be, "How can the quality of life of the members of the Arnold family be improved through the provision of family counseling services?" The answer in this instance identifies three domains: (1) family relationship; (2) finance; and (3) feelings about self.

The same process identified in operationalizing the mission statement into goals is used in constructing statements of **objectives**. Here the selected goal statement is converted into a question. In the example of goal 2 it becomes, "Given my knowledge of the Arnolds and their situation, how can I help them stabilize their family financial situation?" The answers become the objectives or level three in the hierarchy of outcomes.

The three objectives falling under goal 2 represent Ms. Gray's and the Arnolds's answer to the previous question.

The number of goals and objectives comprising the hierarchy represents a judgment of the worker. Typically, the number is reflective of the degree of complexity of the case and the expected length of the helping process. Our interest here is merely to share what we believe to be a helpful approach for operationalizing proposed output in the systems model. We also want to emphasize that the specificity characterizing the objective level of the hierarchy is absolutely essential in making practical use of the model. Objectives within this model are always specific, attainable, appropriate, and measurable.

With activities, we move from statements of future desired states to how to get there—the means to be employed to achieve the proposed output. As we will see in the next section, activities, or the sets of tasks to be performed, provide a key structural feature of the conversion operations of the model.

In constructing a hierarchy of outcomes, every objective will have a (planned) set of activities or tasks to be performed as the selected means for the achievement of an objective. In a helping relationship, the total of all activity sets would comprise the worker's intervention plan, the means to be used in accomplishing the objectives (proposed output) of the helping process. In Section III, under Proposed Task Outputs, we have selected objective 2 to use as the example (the indebtedness problem). The activities here are organized around helping the Arnold family learn to budget their money. Again, it is important to remember that for illustrative purposes, we are developing only parts of the hierarchy of outcomes as applied to the Arnold case.

Section IV applies the notion of a hierarchy of outcomes to proposed maintenance outcomes. Here the focus is on Ms. Gray, the social work practicum student, and her supervisor, Ms. Seavers. The maintenance output statements (if they were in written form) would be found in the practicum supervisory contract between Ms. Gray and Ms. Seavers. The process of constructing the maintenance outcome statements is the same as illustrated with the task statements. Consistent with one's assessment of the needs involved and one's professional orientation, the highest level statement is converted into a question. The answer(s) to the question becomes the construction of the next lower level.

Recall that our mission statement read "to improve the quality of life of the Arnold family through the provision of family counseling services." The task output statement focused on the Arnold family (the signal or task input into the system). In constructing the maintenance output statements, the focus shifts to the maintenance inputs—the resources that result in the "provision of family counseling services." Ms. Pat Gray is the most important of these resources. In constructing the goal level, Ms. Gray would say to herself, "In order to increase the quality of life for the Arnold family, how can I increase my capacity to provide family counseling services?" We make the assumption here that Pat Gray has discussed this matter with her practicum supervisor, Ms. Seavers, and the mutually agreed-upon goals, objectives, and activities have resulted from that process.

Stressed in this section is the mutuality of this process of goal setting. The helping process in social work is dynamic, not passive; the client is an active participant in this social process. It is not like going to your doctor and getting a prescription to take care of a sore throat, a situation in which the patient role is essentially passive. You and the doctor do not usually jointly decide which drugs he will prescribe and you will take. The social work helping process is different; it is a mutual process. Again returning to our perspective on human behavior, if the helping process is conceived as a mutual process, it follows that those participating must share a mutually held set of intentions. In systems terms, this is what we mean by proposed output.

Conversion Operations

Conversion operations is the name given to the concept that embodies the arrangements systems have for transforming their inputs to outputs. Sometimes in systems literature, these arrangements are treated as a *black box*. This notion has some useful practice implications so we will spend a moment developing the idea behind it. In short, the black box refers to "hidden and mysterious" processes and structures that produce an output which cannot be entirely explained.

The idea of the black box is based on a very simple kind of relationship, that between input and output. In this sense, the notion operationalizes a great deal of everyday common sense thinking or what might be called *practice wisdom*. In terms of social intervention, whether at the individual, agency, or community level, some things just seem to work while others do not. It is rather doubtful that a practitioner in a given case can explain all the necessary details as to why the intervention plan was or was not successful. However, the astute and experienced practitioner does learn over time that certain things work with certain clients in certain situations. The practitioner may not fully understand why and on a very practical level it may not be necessary to know why, "it just works." In effect these practitioners are utilizing the notion of the black box.

The home gardener might provide a familiar example of the black box concept. The gardener wants fresh tomatoes as output. Knowing the relationship between input and output, the gardener plants a seed (black box) into the soil (part of the suprasystem). Certain other inputs are provided in the form of light, moisture, fertilizers, and, perhaps, insecticides. Assuming reasonably favorable conditions in the suprasystem, the black box will process inputs in ways of unknown and perhaps little concern to the gardener. In about sixty days the black box delivers its output—ripe tomatoes.

The black box concept is prevalent in a person's daily life, for example, in driving a car, baking bread, taking aspirin, or utilizing a personal computer. Again, the person is interested in results, not the means by which results are obtained. In systems thinking, the notion of the black box can be thoughtfully employed and may provide a shortcut in problem solving. A related value and one of importance is that understanding input-output relationships becomes a way of starting to think in systems terms. As this way of thinking becomes progressively more useful, the practitioner is likely to become more curious and may seek to examine some of the contents of the black box. With this in mind, we will develop the concept of conversion operations as our approach in describing how systems convert their inputs to outputs.

Our discussion of a system's conversion operations is divided into two interrelated sections under the headings of Structure and Interactions. Our general approach to the conceptualization of structure and interactions builds on assertions made by Lewin in field theory. We found Lewin's use of the concepts of goals and needs helpful as organizers of behaviors. This position is generally supportive of the one taken in the construction of this model which views organizational behaviors as purposive. The outcome orientation of the model embodies this assumption. As just described in the section on proposed output, the function (purpose) performed by a system, vis-à-vis its suprasystem, is the primary source of the ordering exhibited by that system. As used within the concept of conversion operations, structure refers to that aspect of order that is evident in the conversion of the system's inputs to outputs. This ordering can be usefully thought of as based on the interrelated sets of activities required to achieve the system's proposed outputs. These activities are evident in the relationships that guide interactions among those who actually comprise the system.

The conversion operations of a system should not be envisioned in linear terms, that is, a step-by-step progression from input to output status. Also, structure is constantly being altered as a consequence of the actual behaviors of people carrying out roles. Just as structure as an underlying order shapes behaviors, so do actual behaviors shape this underlying order in reciprocal and ongoing ways.

We start discussion of the conversion operations with the concept of structure. In doing so, it is a little bit like attempting to answer the question, "Which came first, the chicken or the egg?" Structure and interactions are like two sides of the same coin, but unlike a coin they are constantly changing with each affecting the other in a cyclical fashion. In the paragraphs ahead we will attempt to explain why this is so.

Structure

In earlier sections we discussed boundary, interface, and proposed output. In this model each of these concepts pertains to a specialized aspect of the system's structure. In this section we will build on these earlier discussions involving structure but our focus is on those features that pertain to the conversion of inputs to outputs.

Specifically, the concept of structure refers to the arrangements of patterns, formal or informal, that affect and give direction to social interactions within the system and between the system and its suprasystem. Included in structure are such things as social roles, service plans, formal administrative arrangements, relevant aspects of culture, values, time, budget, plans, space, and ties with other systems in the social environment. In effect, social structure is a way of describing the underlying order of the social system. Again recall that social systems are viewed as dynamic, constantly changing. From this point of view, this underlying order is also constantly changing. It is this conceptualization of the underlying order that serves as a determinant or a guide to system behaviors and what we refer to as the *structural dimension* of the system's conversion operations.

Roles represent the system's most important structural feature and thus a logical place to start our discussion. To introduce the concept of role, let us turn for a moment to the insights on human behavior offered by Shakespeare. The following quote is from *As You Like It* (Act 2, Scene 7):

All the world's a stage,
And all the men and women merely players;
They have their exits and their entrances;
And one man in his time plays many parts,

In the first line, if we were to substitute "suprasystem" for "stage" we would be getting close to our contention of the interplay between a system and its suprasystem. The stage and its props help shape the behaviors of those on stage and the perceptions held by the audience of what is happening. The reference in the second line to players suggests a script. The notion of a script is very close to what we mean by structure—the guides that help shape human social behaviors. Finally, "part" as used by Shakespeare is essentially what we mean by "role." Each script will contain many roles, and in life people play many different roles in many different scripts.

We want to hastily add that our notions of structure and particularly that of role are far more dynamic and much less tightly drawn than indicated in the preceding passage. What does not come through in this passage is how much each of us is shaped by the events that surround us, and how we play and innovate and thus shape the roles we are given to play.

The insight offered by viewing a society's social life as ongoing is, from our perspective, constructive. Each of us is born into an ongoing stream of social life. The socialization process that occurs in childhood is a preparation for assuming a place in this life. We will then depart, but this social life will continue. It is the notion of shaping and being shaped that pertains to our use of structure in this model. Now, with the insights offered by Shakespeare serving as a context, let us continue our examination of structure.

In the model, roles and sets of roles rather than individuals are the main structural features. Further, the focus is never on the role as such, but rather on the relationships that link roles together in ever larger wholes. Roles, as used in this model, always have two dimensions: The first pertains to the expected behaviors associated with the subject role, the second to the expected behaviors of the counter or reciprocal role. Role is a social or relational concept. These built-in expectations that functionally link roles are called *structure*. From this position, one can consider a social system as a system of roles.

Individuals (people in interaction) represent the components of social organizations, so when the model is applied to a specified social organization, it is the person or the set of people in roles that becomes a focus of attention. Before proceeding further, let us define some key terms that will be involved in subsequent discussions: **norm, role**, and **status position.** We have found the approach taken by Alvin Bertrand helpful in the formulation of the concept of role. For Bertrand, roles are comprised of a set of norms and can be thought of as a required or acceptable behavior for a given interactional situation.[4] Roles then are sets of norms assigned to a position in a social system. Conceptually speaking, roles are derived from functions to be performed and the role itself represents the expected behaviors associated with performance of some system-related function.

The role of mother is a useful one to use to distinguish between the concepts of norm and role. As employed here, the role of mother is comprised of a series of functionally interrelated norms. The function being performed is "mothering," that is, caring for a dependent child to see that the child not only survives but develops in accord with his or her potential. The norms are the expected behaviors in the specified interactional situations of a mother carrying out this role in relationship to her child. Like the role itself, the norms comprising that role are culturally defined. These norms represent the generally accepted way of caring for the child through adulthood and beyond. The norms comprising the role of mother will vary with the child's age, developmental status, how other family roles are being played and particularly the subculture to which the system is related. For example, norms associated with the role of mother to her infant daughter would be to feed her at regular intervals, change her diapers promptly when they are wet or soiled, hold and caress her, and in other ways show that she is wanted and loved. It is the sum total of all of these norms that comprise the role "mother." We have described a traditional conception of the role of mother as the primary care giver. Attesting to the dynamic nature of the concept of role is the extent to which the role of mother is changing. Typically, this traditional role of mother as primary care giver has been assumed by the female. In growing numbers of American families, males are assuming this role. In others, the norms associated with the role of mother are being reassigned so that the mothering/caring functions are being redistributed; both parents are sharing this role.

There is little need for the concept of status position when applying the model to simple and relatively undifferentiated social organizations. In such applications, the system is most easily viewed as a system of roles. It is with larger and more functionally differentiated organizations that the concept of status position becomes helpful. A status position is comprised of a set of functionally interrelated roles. In such applications it becomes useful to view the system as comprised of a system of status positions or simply of positions.

We will again use the Westwood Child and Family Center to illustrate the concept of status position. The center is comprised of a total of twenty professional and staff positions. Structurally, the center can be viewed as comprised of twenty different status positions with each position in turn comprised of several roles. Recall that Ms. Joan Seavers is Ms. Gray's practicum supervisor. Ms. Seavers is employed by the center as a case supervisor. She supervises four other staff family therapists in addition to her practicum responsibility. Ms. Seavers also carries a small caseload. Conceptually, Ms. Seavers occupies a (status) position within this social system. This position is comprised of a series of roles including, among others, practicum supervisor to Pat Gray, supervisor of four other staff therapists, and family services worker (her own caseload). Ms. Seavers might well have other roles in this system; for example, member of the center's Executive Committee, or Chairperson of the center's Community Relations Committee. It is the sum total of these agency roles that comprises her (status) position. Importantly, each of these roles is related to some function performed by this agency. As we will see later, the notion of status position is very close to what is usually thought of as a position identified in an agency's organization chart.

The concept of status position becomes helpful in describing complex social systems in which various functions are performed. Each role within a given status position becomes linked with other roles and dedicated to the performance of some specialized function.

While the concept of role is central in a structural presentation of the model, the focus is always on the relationships among roles. Here the concept of **role reciprocality** is helpful in getting at the functional and reciprocal nature of the relationships that comprise the system. Bertrand identified the following characteristics as comprising role reciprocality: "(1) certain rights and duties are involved between two roles, (2) these roles are located in separate status positions; and (3) the two roles represent specialized aspects of the same functional process."[5]

Now, let us summarize some of the points that bear on the concept of structure as employed in the model: (1) the member components of social systems are roles which are functionally and reciprocally linked to each other; (2) the norms or expected behaviors comprising each role are, like the role itself, derived from the larger culture to which the system is functionally related; and (3) while the individual enacts a role, the behaviors associated with that role are derived primarily from the functional requisites of the system itself. With this as background, how inputs are converted to outputs is to be understood in part by understanding how roles are functionally and reciprocally linked to each other.

Up to this point, the discussion of structure has centered on role and related concepts. We have pointed out in this discussion that roles have their origins in the wider culture. Nevertheless, it is within the specific social organization to which the model is being applied that the more detailed attributes of roles and their relationships to each other have their specific meanings.

Now, to develop the points just mentioned, let us again refer to Ms. Gray's supervisor, Joan Seavers. The origins of Ms. Seavers's role as a social worker were acquired during her graduate education. Further, the school that Ms. Seavers attended utilized a social systems model to conceptualize practice and as a framework for organizing practice knowledge and skills. By adopting this model, Ms. Seavers shaped her own role as a practitioner and similarly her conception of the client role. Through her practicum experiences in school, she developed her sense of the role of supervisee and the counter role of supervisor. By the time she joined the center's staff as an employee, she had a firm sense of many of the professional roles that were to comprise her status position within this agency. In fact, her decision to accept the position at the agency represented a judgment on her part of a good fit between her own conception of her professional self and what the agency was looking for in a professional staff member. As a staff member within the agency, Ms. Seavers's roles are being shaped even further by agency policies, including fee schedules, service contracts and other agreements the agency holds with other community agencies, and personnel policies.

Given Ms. Seavers's use of a social systems model, she is aware that many physical aspects of the agency and her own office will also shape the roles she plays. The way she has decorated her office and located furniture has all been done with the thought of how these features will affect her role as a family services worker and the roles her clients will enact.

More specific to input-output features of structure, Ms. Seavers's assessment methods, her use of a hierarchy of outcomes to form intervention goals with her clients, as well as her use of a service contract all represent structural features of her role as a family services worker. Given her leadership responsibility in the helping process, she also assumes some preliminary responsibility for helping her clients develop their respective roles in the helping process. Similarly, in her role as a practicum supervisor for the School of Social Work, Ms. Seavers is helping to shape the professional role of her student, Ms. Pat Gray.

Interaction

Interaction is the second of the two concepts that comprise the system's arrangements for transforming its inputs to outputs. Whereas structure is used to designate all of the features that represent the underlying order guiding social behaviors, interactions are the behaviors themselves. Given this position, structure is always anticipatory, whereas interactions are always the meanings attached to the actual behaviors. Strictly speaking, both structure and interactions are sets of meanings; structure represents the normative expectations of those about to be involved in an interactional situation, or in retrospect what was expected to occur; interactions are the meanings attached to the behaviors, that is, the words and emotions (affect) actually exchanged by those participating in the exchange or affected by it. Here, the idea of emotion, or what we refer to as affect, is important. Just as there are behavioral expectations associated with role performance, so are there expectations about the affect. The display of appropriate affect in carrying out a role has special significance for those in the helping professions. If a client does not display affect appropriate to the role in a specific interactional situation, it is a possible indication of an emotional problem. The point we wish to make is that the concept of structure helps you think about what might be expected in behaviors and affect in a given interactional situation. Your set of expectations then becomes the basis for drawing comparisons between what might have been expected and what actually occurred.

To develop the distinctions between structure and interactions, we will again turn to the Arnold case. Sarah's abusive acts toward Donnie served as the catalyst for the referral of Sarah and Bill Arnold to the Child and Family Center. In a manner of speaking, Sarah's abuse of her son violated community norms pertaining to parent-child relationships—the role of mother. In this society, acts of physical and sexual abuse against children are considered so serious as to represent a violation of law, and the perpetrator is subject to criminal prosecution. That is what has happened in this case. Given the nature of the present problem, Pat Gray, our student social worker, would explore how Sarah and Bill viewed their parenting roles during her assessment of the Arnolds. In the course of her assessment, Ms. Gray would compare her own professional conception of these roles with that described by the Arnolds. In this instance, the normative standards held by Ms. Gray would represent structure. The questions she poses to the Arnolds about their own parenting roles will have this structure as their "source" but the discussion between Ms. Gray and the Arnolds would represent "interactions."

Now let us turn to another example of the relationship between structure and interactions. Here let us assume that as part of their services contract the Arnolds and Ms. Gray agreed to meet at the center for one hour each Wednesday at 4:00 P.M. for their family counseling sessions. All parties agreed that if something should come up that would affect this meeting time, the other party would be notified. These agreed-upon arrangements contain two important components of structure. First, in this model time and space are always important features of structure. Time and space will always shape social behavior. Time tells people when they will meet and how much time they will have together. Space similarly affects behaviors. For example, we expect that Ms. Gray's decision to have the family sessions at the center rather than at the Arnold home represents a professional judgment aimed at the "structuring" of the helping system. By this we mean that the setting and atmosphere at the center are different from those at the Arnold home and will hold different meanings for those participating. Second, the services contract agreed upon by Ms. Gray and the Arnolds is also an important structural component of this helping relationship. In addition to setting conditions around time, it establishes the goals and objectives as well as the means (activities) to be employed in their work with each other. Agreed-upon means and ends are integral to a professional helping relationship and the discussions which occur between Ms. Gray and the Arnolds are guided by this feature of structure.

Even in the theater, actors seldom play their roles precisely as they are set forth in the script and guided by stage props. In real life, there is far greater divergence between what is expected in role behavior and what occurs. People are always surprising each other by not behaving in an expected manner. Some of these surprises are pleasant while others are not. Again, it should be acknowledged that roles and other structural features are modified through interactions. In an application of the model, departures from normative expectations are frequently significant and become content for the worker to explore.

For example, after several weeks of being prompt for their appointment, on a Wednesday the Arnolds do not show up, nor do they call. This behavior is an example of what may be an important departure between the structural expectations and the actual behaviors. At issue is the meaning that Ms. Gray will attach to this behavior (or the absence of an expected behavior). Ms. Gray is confronted with a number of possible meanings. The explanation could be as simple as car trouble at a location where there is no telephone. Or the behavior may suggest that the Arnolds (one or both) are angry with Ms. Gray and are using this method of expressing their feelings. In any event, she will make a professional assessment as to the meaning of this behavior (interaction) and this meaning (an aspect of structure) will in turn affect or guide her subsequent interactions with the Arnolds. In this example, there is another departure from expected behaviors; the Arnolds also have a contract with the local court that mandates their participation in family services as a condition for the possible return home of their son, Donnie. Ms. Gray is also involved in the contract with the court; her responsibility is to notify the court in the event the Arnolds violate their services contract. In this latter instance, the contract with the court is part of the interface, a mutual boundary between the court and the Westwood Child and Family Center. This feature of structure will affect Ms. Gray's interactions with an important feature of their suprasystem.

Feedback

Each concept comprising the model is a representation of some characteristic about how all social organizations are believed to behave within their social environments. We make the assumption that all such organizations have ongoing functional relationships with other individuals, groups, and agencies that comprise their social environments. These relationships are deemed to be cyclical and mutually determinant, as opposed to being linear in nature. In other words, the relationship is like a loop with the return segment of the loop back to the subject organization labeled as feedback. Simply put, feedback provides the necessary information to answer the questions "How are we doing?" and "What is going on?" Not only do we make the assumption that all forms of social organization have information exchanges of the type described, but that it is through this information exchange that the organization makes adjustments and is able to maintain its functional fit with its social environment; this condition is labeled steady state. If this information exchange is impeded, distorted, or ignored, it becomes problematic to the organization and unless corrected can lead to the termination of the organization.

Our use of the concept of feedback contains three key features. First, the concept is applied only to a system's output; second, the information generated is always in reference to the system's proposed output; and third, feedback is always considered a maintenance input.

Feedback is always evaluative in nature and pertains to the differences between what was proposed and what actually happened. Frequently, the analogy of a furnace's thermostat is used to illustrate feedback. The thermostat is a heat-sensing device typically located in an area representative of a desired temperature. A person sets the thermostat at the desired temperature level. When the surrounding temperature drops below the desired level, an electrical contact is made which in turn causes the furnace to turn on. The furnace continues to warm the space to the desired level. Once the air surrounding the thermostat reaches the desired level, the electrical contact is broken, which automatically turns the furnace off. The output of the furnace is heat, the proposed output is a predetermined room air temperature. The thermostat measures output against what is intended. Once the intended heat level is reached, it signals the system that for the moment its job is done and so its output of heat ceases. The thermostat is a sensor used to determine desired conditions. Once these conditions have been reached, it sends information (input) back to the system. Based on this input, the furnace ceases, at least temporarily, its work. The use of the thermostat is helpful both in explaining the concept of feedback and in drawing the contrast between a physical and a social process. Certainly the physical process of maintaining a desired functional relationship between the furnace and its environment is a more precise one than can usually be accomplished between social organizations and their environments.

The use of the thermostat is also helpful in illustrating how feedback influences system inputs. In the case of the thermostat, it determines whether electricity, an input, will be supplied to the system. In the case of a social process, the influence on inputs is much more subtle and complicated.

The social systems model distinguishes two types of outputs, maintenance and task; therefore, there will be two levels of feedback. Maintenance feedback is internal and deals with the status of the system itself and results from the comparison of proposed maintenance outputs with actual maintenance outputs. Task feedback is external and deals with the status of relationships between the system and its suprasystem. Here, proposed task outputs are compared with actual task outputs.

Feedback can also be categorized as being negative or positive. At this point we need to caution you to set aside your definitions of negative as bad and positive as good. We are using positive and negative in a mathematical sense. Positive merely means an increase in the direction of something being measured. Negative means a decrease in whatever it is that is being measured.

Of the two types of feedback, **negative feedback** is the more familiar one. It simply refers to the self-correcting information that is fed back into the system dealing with the deviation between what was proposed as output and what actually occurred. For example, if you are working with a client who is subject to outbursts of anger, you may have agreed upon an objective dealing with the reduction of the number of and severity of these outbursts. Let us say that your objective was that by the third week of working together these outbursts would have diminished from ten per week to five. At the end of the third week the outbursts had been reduced from ten to seven. Your objective had been five but the actual reduction was seven, or two short. This information reported back to you by the client is an example of negative feedback. The content of the information deals with the deviation between what was proposed and what actually happened. The deviation from the baseline of ten was in the right direction even though it was two short of your objective. This is negative feedback in the sense that there were fewer outbursts than at the baseline (ten). You were also short of your objective by two.

As evidenced by the above example, negative feedback is that information that pertains to the reduction of deviation from a set baseline and a system's objective. The amount of reduction is *not* the central idea in the use of this term—it is direction. So in the above example you could have exceeded your objective with the client not evidencing any outbursts—the reduction being from ten to one. Here, you exceeded your objective of a reduction from ten to five. It is still negative feedback; the data suggest you were more successful than you had estimated. Negative feedback is designed to show you the progress being made in the accomplishment of the system's objective. If this progress is being evidenced, it indicates that your original assessment was probably correct and that the activities (services plan) that you and the client are engaging in to deal with the problem are having the intended effects.

Positive feedback is the reverse, it is information that shows that the deviation from the baseline to the sought-after level is increasing (+), not decreasing (−). If, in our example, the number of outbursts had shown an increase from ten to fifteen, that information would be treated as positive feedback. What it tells you is that something else is probably going on that you have not fully taken into account. In this situation, you need to be very attentive. These data may suggest that your initial assessment was incorrect or that you need to take another look at the activities comprising your services plan.

The notion of positive feedback is how we emphasize the open systems and dynamic nature of the model. Negative feedback is tied to a specific conception of what a system intends to accomplish. The purpose of negative feedback is to supply information helpful to correct deviations from that *proposed*. While this kind of self-correcting information is critically important, it introduces a conservative bias to the model. In systems language, negative feedback tends to maintain and confirm the system in a particular condition. These processes are referred to as **morphostatic.**

We are surrounded by evidence of social change; sometimes this change is volatile and tends to be destabilizing both to individuals and to the groups that people join together to form. Positive feedback is the name given to the information pertaining to the system output that is not confirming and does not contribute to the maintenance of a particular condition. Processes contributing to system change are called **morphogenetic.** They inform the system that it is sometimes necessary to change if steady state is to be maintained.

Earlier we cautioned you not to equate negative and positive feedback with bad or good news. Simply treat the data as information upon which to render a professional judgment.[6]

To further develop and contrast negative and positive feedback, we will return to the Arnold case. Recall (Figure 3.2, Section III) that task goal 2 dealt with stabilizing the family's financial situation—an area of stress. Objective 2 involved an effort to reduce the amount of family indebtedness by 30 percent or $3,000 by December 30, 19___. For the purpose of illustrating negative feedback, let us assume that on December 30, 19___, the debt had been reduced by 25 percent or $2,500. While the amount of indebtedness was not reduced as much as was proposed (25 percent versus 30 percent), substantial progress was achieved. This progress suggests that the original assessment was on target and that the selected activities used to achieve the objective worked. Let us also assume that in the judgment of Ms. Gray and the Arnolds, there was a corresponding reduction of family stress related to financial matters. We might also assume that Ms. Gray was feeling good about herself in her role as a family counselor. Here, all is going according to plan; feedback (negative) is confirming to the system and its activities.

Now, let us illustrate positive feedback with the same goal and objective structure but with a different scenario. Recall that Sarah Arnold quit school in the eleventh grade after she and Bill married. Sarah had considered her school work a "waste"; it seemed to have little relevance to her. The family assessment conducted by Ms. Gray was essentially premised on the reunification of the family with the return of Donnie. This was to be accomplished by reducing the causes of family stress, specifically, financial stress, by helping the Arnolds improve their parenting skills and more generally to increase understanding and support of each other's needs and concerns. In this scenario, Sarah would continue in her role as primary care giver to Donnie and as housewife. However, in the revised scenario, Sarah really enjoyed her work with Pat Gray dealing with budgeting and the general management of household expenses. She shared with Ms. Gray that she had always been good with numbers but saw little relationship between this natural talent and her math courses in high school. She also shared that while she dearly loved Donnie and Bill, there had to be more to life than "washing clothes, cleaning house, and baby sitting." She confided, "It seems as though all I do is give, give, give. I need my own space and some time to take care of me."

As a consequence of discussing the whole matter of managing family finances, Sarah decided she wanted to go back to school. Bill thought this a good idea so they, on their own, took out a loan for $3,500 to help cover her school expenses. So rather than a reduction in debt (negative feedback) there was a significant increase in family debt (an increase in the deviation from the objective—positive feedback). In addition, a family friend offered Sarah an assistant bookkeeping job in her place of business. As a consequence, the Arnold family's annual income was increased by 40 percent ($14,000), so carrying the added debt was not a problem. Given the progress made by the family, Donnie was returned home. Child-care arrangements made it possible for Sarah to continue her work and to pursue her efforts at obtaining a GED. She also attended some vocational education classes to increase her bookkeeping skills. Most importantly, as a consequence of their work with Ms. Gray, both Sarah and Bill were feeling much better about themselves and Donnie seemed delighted with being in child care. In a matter of speaking, steady state had been achieved but by quite a different route.

Feedback in the second scenario would suggest that not only were there quantitative but qualitative differences in output from that proposed. While there was an increase in debt, her new job made the debt manageable. This is an example of positive feedback in the sense that the output was the opposite of that expected (the debt level increased instead of decreasing). The output included actions that were not anticipated but were highly relevant to the original problem situation. Importantly, the positive feedback suggested that the original problem definition and assessment did not fully take into account this family's potential, especially Sarah's. Ms. Gray read the positive as well as the negative feedback and, in conjunction with the Arnolds, reworked their services contract and its goals and objectives.

Under the second scenario, Ms. Gray not only revised the services contract with the Arnolds, but began a reassessment of her own career plans. She had entered the school of social work because of an interest in becoming a family therapist. As a consequence of her experience with the Arnold family and related experiences, she became more interested in women's issues. She explained her interest to her supervisor saying, "I wonder how many Sarah Arnolds there are out there, trapped by lack of experience, education, and opportunities? The more I think about this, the more I am intrigued with community organizing work and research. I might even want to go and get a doctorate."

The point being developed is that positive feedback is concerned with information that gets cycled back that is not confirming of the original assessment and intervention plan (activities directed toward achievement of objectives). It suggests that something else is going on that needs to be taken into account. In our second scenario, the changes that were occurring, while quite different from that specified at the objective level of the hierarchy of outcomes, were fully consistent with the goal of achieving "a safe and healthful family environment for Donnie" and an improvement in the "quality of life for the Arnold family." Most importantly, the positive feedback led to a reconstruction of the family roles enacted by Sarah and Bill. The decision by Sarah to take a full-time job as a bookkeeper led to a restructuring of all family roles. In a manner of speaking, this was a destabilizing period for all. Here, destabilizing should not be thought of as good or bad. Conditions were changing which resulted in a reconstituted system, one that survived.

Similarly, this process had a destabilizing effect on our practicum student, Ms. Gray. Again, the disordering process in her own life should not be thought of as good or bad; the notion of positive feedback is simply a way of viewing forms of information that don't fit. This kind of feedback contributes to a deviation from a premise—whatever that premise might be. In the case of Ms. Arnold, it dealt with her role as a traditional housewife and mother; with Ms. Gray, it dealt with her conception of herself and of her goal to become a family therapist.

It is important to point out that while our examples have had happy endings, they could have had unhappy endings as well. Feedback is information that is fed back into the system and is used to maintain steady state. Negative feedback will always pertain to the extent that output conforms to what has been proposed. Positive feedback also can contribute to steady state but suggests that something else is going on that needs to be addressed. Also, left unattended both negative and positive feedback will lead to a disordering of the system and eventually its destruction.

Finally, a word about waste. Earlier, we defined waste as the designation of inefficient, ineffectual, or inappropriate use of resources in terms of the production of task and maintenance outputs. The concept of waste is simply a convenient way for the model user to account for all of the resources employed in producing a specified output. It is feedback that provides the information upon which the designation of waste depends. Both negative and positive feedback can produce waste and it is calculated when output is compared with proposed output. If at the end of the case, Ms. Gray, in comparing what was proposed and what actually occurred, concluded that she could have better handled the case, there was waste. If not, there was no waste. If she felt she could have better handled the case, she would want to determine as precisely as possible which things went wrong or could have been better handled. This information or waste gets fed back into the system as maintenance input and should help her do a better job next time.

SUMMARY

The preceding pages have provided an in-depth presentation of the eight concepts that comprise the basic social systems model. The concepts are boundary, suprasystem, interface, input, output, proposed output, conversion operations, and feedback. Of these eight concepts, seven deal directly with relationships between a subject organization and its social environment. In systems language, boundary distinguishes the system from its suprasystem. Suprasystem is the designation of the system's functionally relevant social environment. Interface is the common boundary shared by the system and one or more other social units comprising its suprasystem. Input represents the resources utilized by a system, all of which are derived from its suprasystem. Output is the effect of the system on its suprasystem. Proposed output is a statement of the system's intentions. And finally, feedback is information on the effects of the system on its suprasystem and on itself. Only the concept of conversion operations deals with the internal activities of the system—how input is transformed to output.

We have relied primarily on social examples of these concepts rather than those drawn from the physical sciences. In so doing, we have also sought to recognize the common applications of these concepts to physical as well as social phenomenon. We have, however, concentrated on the features that are distinctive in their application to social organizations.

Our use of the Arnold case as a practice example has served two purposes. First, it became a way for us to maintain a practice orientation to this material. Second, it provided us the opportunity of stressing that professional social work involves the creation and uses of various forms of social organization as the medium of intervention, whether at the individual (clinical), organizational (social administration), or community level (community practice). In the Arnold case, Ms. Gray's task was to form a helping relationship with Sarah and Bill Arnold. In the language of the model, she created a social system of which she was a member. The purpose of this system was to help "fix" another system, the Arnold family.

In Figure 3.3, we have used the helping system created by Ms. Gray to illustrate graphically some of the relationships between the concepts that relate this system to its suprasystem. While not highlighted in our discussions, on a conceptual level the Arnold family itself represents an important suprasystem relationship. In this connection we distinguish between the roles played by Sarah and Bill in the helping relationship with those that they play in their family. More will be said about this feature when social groups are discussed in Part II.

FIGURE 3.3 The Helping Relationship as a Social System

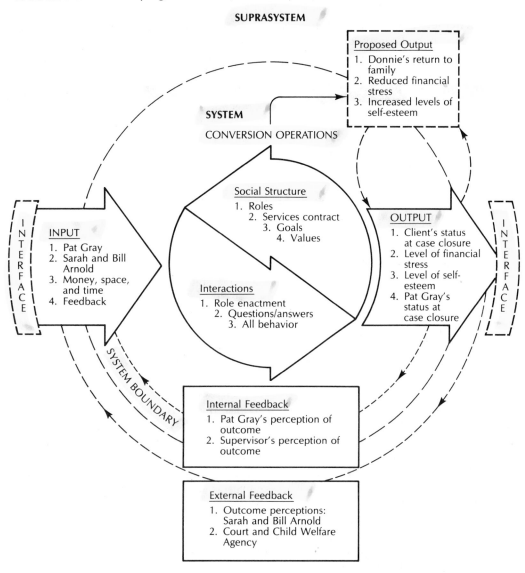

GLOSSARY

Activities   An organized set of intended or actual actions that take place in social systems and constitute the means to obtain the proposed output.

Affect   The feelings or emotion expressed by a person and observed and interpreted by others.

Culture   A set of shared meanings held by a specified group of people that serves as the social foundations for their organized way of life.

Goal   A proposed future state to be achieved through pursuit of functionally related activities. Within a hierarchy of outcomes, goals represent long-range qualitative statements of intent pertaining to a component or aspect of the mission statement.

Hierarchy of outcomes   An approach to formulating proposed output in the social systems model.

Maintenance inputs   That classification of inputs that sustain and enhance the system and that, following a cycle of system activities, may be designated as maintenance outputs.

Maintenance outputs   The designation of maintenance inputs following a cycle of a system's conversion actions.

Mission   A broad philosophical and inspirational statement of proposed output which guides all practice (system) activities.

Morphogenesis   Those influences, processes, and variables that contribute to the structural change of the system. These influences are evident in positive forms of feedback.

Morphostasis   Those influences, processes, and variables that contribute to the maintenance of the existing state of the system. A synonym would be "homeostatic" influences, such as the effects of negative feedback.

Negative feedback   A return of information to the system evidencing a reduction in the deviation between actual and proposed output.

Norms   The usual behavior associated with role enactment in a prescribed interactional situation.

Objectives   In a hierarchy of outcomes, those statements of intended accomplishment derived from a specific goal. These statements are specific, attainable, and measurable.

Positive feedback   A return of information to the system evidencing an increase in the deviation between actual and proposed output.

Role   A structural component of a social system. Roles are comprised of functionally integrated sets of norms and represent expected behaviors of the person enacting the prescribed "role."

Role reciprocality   A mutuality of exchange in pursuit of shared purpose. The exchange will evidence three characteristics: (1) certain rights and duties involving two or more roles are recognized and accepted; (2) these roles are located in different status positions; and (3) these roles represent specialized aspects of the same functional process and are directed toward the same or comparable goals.

Signal inputs   That classification of inputs that the system processes and that become task inputs.

Society A group of people who share the same culture. Functionally, a society is the most dominant, inclusive, and self-sufficient of all forms of social organization.

Status position A location in a social system comprised of two or more roles.

Task outputs The designation of signal inputs following a cycle of a system's conversion actions.

Values Shared meanings as to what is desirable and undesirable in social life.

Waste The designation of inefficient, ineffective, or inappropriate use of inputs.

NOTES

1. See discussion of field theory in Chapter 2. For a discussion of the notion of goal within field theory, see Kurt Lewin, *Field Theory in Social Science,* ed. Dorwin Cartwright (New York: Harper & Brothers, 1951), 39–42.

2. A discussion of this point is found in Chapter 1. See particularly, "Working Statement on the Purpose of Social Work," *Social Work* vol. 26, no. 1, (January 1981): 6.

3. Beulah R. Compton and Burt Galaway, *Social Work Processes,* 4th ed., (Belmont, California: Wadsworth Publishing Co., 1989), 486–495.

4. Alvin L. Bertrand, *Social Organization: A General Systems and Role Theory Perspective* (Philadelphia: F. A. David Company, 1972), 34–37.

5. Ibid., 38.

6. See, for example, Lynn Hoffman, "Deviation-Amplifying Processes in Natural Groups," in Jay Haley, *Changing Families* (New York: Grune & Stratton, 1971), 285–311.

Chapter 4

The Social Systems Model: Systems Dynamics

OUTLINE

Introduction
Goal Attainment
Integration
Adaptation

Pattern Maintenance
Summary
Glossary
Notes

Introduction

Chapter 3 introduced in detail the eight concepts comprising the social systems model. Each identifies what we consider to be a feature common to all forms of human groupings. Taken together, these concepts provide a way of describing and modeling the qualities of wholeness and interdependence found in the various forms of human social organizations. The model also identifies some of the behaviors deemed universal among these human groupings. For example, all social systems possess a boundary and will expend resources in the performance of the boundary-maintaining function. Another example is that all social systems relate to their suprasystem (environment) through input and output exchanges. If we are correct in our approach, then any form of social organization possessing the features of wholeness and interdependence will display these behaviors. Combined with more narrow ranging theories, such as humanistic or field theory, the model can become a very powerful tool for both knowledge building and for the practice of social work.

In this chapter, we want to move beyond the descriptive features of the model and its capacity for incorporating other theories. Here, our interest will be in the further development of the model itself. Specifically, we want to identify an approach for understanding why human groupings behave as they do. Again, our search will be for universal behaviors, those that will be evidenced by all forms of human social organization displaying the critical features of wholeness and interdependence. For example, these behaviors should be exhibited by such diverse human groupings as found in a casework relationship, a family, a welfare department, a community, or a society. We have labeled these behaviors *social systems dynamics.*

In beginning our discussion, let us first link the approach to some material developed earlier. In our presentation of a social systems perspective, we defined steady state as a condition of well-being. This condition is achieved and maintained by continuity of input and output exchanges that occur between the system and its suprasystem. Simply put, our approach to the formulation of systems dynamics is based on how such systems become and stay healthy.

Like the model itself, the concept of steady state has its origins in general systems theory.[1] A way of thinking about steady state is to contrast it with a more familiar term, homeostasis. Recall that **homeostasis** is a state of equilibrium produced by a balance of functions and related properties of a system. Perhaps the most widely used example is body temperature. Think of the human body as a system. This system operates at its best when all of its subsystems are in a homeostatic or optimum state, such as when the body temperature is 98.6 degrees Fahrenheit. Whenever there is a deviation from this homeostatic state, infection for instance, a series of body processes will be activated that will attempt to restore this balance. The relationship of homeostasis to health or well-being is evident whenever we see a doctor for an examination. Typically she or he will check our temperature, blood pressure, heart rate, and other vital signs. All of these provide measures of the extent to which our body is in a homeostatic state. Deviations from this optimum state suggest that something may be wrong—we may be sick.

There are several characteristics of homeostasis that are important to keep in mind as we develop the concept of steady state. First, the term homeostasis is premised on the notion of a fixed optimum state or balance. Second, deviations from this state are viewed as unbalancing or evidence of a disordering process. Disordering in the sense we are using it here represents a deviation from the ordering that produces and maintains the homeostatic state, for example when body temperature deviates from 98.6 degrees.

Third, the homeostatic state results from and is maintained by a series of counterbalancing system processes. In this sense, it is a dynamic process, but one that is directed toward the maintenance of a relatively fixed state.

Fourth, the term *homeostatic* is borrowed from the physical sciences, specifically biology and physiology. Its application is in what we would describe as essentially closed systems and its operation in humans is essentially automatic in the sense that the processes resulting in homeostasis are not under direct or conscious control of the individual.

Fifth and finally, the homeostatic process operates through a feedback system. While much remains to be learned about the processes involved, deviations from the optimum state are fed back through control systems that in turn activate those processes that will counter the causes of deviation. The effects are directed toward the return of the system to a fixed state.

The notion of homeostasis as an equilibrium-seeking model has been applied to the study of human behavior. For example, in classical psychoanalytic theory, the natural state of the organism is at rest. The primary determinants of behavior are innate sexual and aggressive drives. These drives, when activated, upset an **equilibrium** or homeostatic state. The effort of the organism (ego) is to contain these drives and to restore the organism to a state of equilibrium. In short, homeostasis provides a reactive approach for modeling human social behavior. Steady state, in contrast, offers a proactive approach. Again, we will return to an earlier point to develop this idea.

In Chapter 2, A Social Systems Perspective, the following assumption was identified: When fully developed, all forms of social organization will display self-maintaining and development characteristics. There is a related assumption that we now wish to identify, and it applies to our perspective on individual behavior as well as to the behaviors of all social organizations. The assumption is that the natural state of both the individual and of all forms of social organization is proactive rather than reactive. As just noted, some theorists argue that human behavior is either internally or externally stimulated; a response is made to a stimulation and the individual returns to a passive mode or a state of equilibrium.[2] We do not find this perspective a useful one on which to develop the model or explore theories based on this contention. Our position is consistent with general systems theory as advanced by von Bertalanffy. He viewed all living organisms as intrinsically active, as opposed to passive. "The stimulus (i.e., a change in external conditions) does not cause a process in an otherwise inert system; it only modifies processes in an autonomously active system."[3] We hold that in humans the same premise holds for internal conditions (that is, those stimuli having their direct origins in genetic or physiological conditions within the individual). Here we find the work of Maslow helpful, particularly his conception of a hierarchy of human needs. Included in this hierarchy are basic and growth needs—a drive toward self-actualization.[4] Our task then has been to find a way of incorporating and operationalizing these ideas in the social systems model. In the context of this chapter, it has been a search for a way of describing the dynamic nature of social systems.

In our contemplation of systems dynamics, we again find the thinking of von Bertalanffy helpful. He, like Maslow, was quite critical of psychology and the social sciences generally. His criticisms were pointed and at times harsh. The following is an example:

> Let us face the fact, a large part of modern psychology is a sterile and pompous scholasticism which, with the blinders of preconceived notions or superstitions on its nose, doesn't see the obvious; which covers the triviality of its results and ideas with a preposterous language bearing no resemblance either to normal English or normal scientific theory; and which provides modern society with the techniques for the progressive stoltification of mankind.[5]

Central to von Bertalanffy's concern was a view of the human as some sort of super robot, one that was programmed to respond to stimuli; with rest being the natural state of the person.[6] Essentially the model was that of homeostasis. As you might imagine by now, von Bertalanffy's position was directly opposite that of the conventional wisdom. For him the natural state of a system was one of disequilibrium. He referred to this condition as a "steady state."[7]

Now, from the position of homeostasis as a reactive approach and steady state as a proactive approach for modeling systems dynamics, we will contrast the two and the five points developed earlier. First, and in contrast to homeostasis, steady state is not a fixed state. The point of orientation is not an internal state of equilibrium. The orientation is external. The steady state is an adaptive or functional adjustment between the subject system and its suprasystem.

Second, since the notion of steady state is not premised on a fixed and optimum state, there is not an assumed fixed order that maintains such a state. It is important to keep in mind that for many, general systems theory represents a different way of thinking. As an example, steady state is premised on a disequilibrium model. Rather than a fixed order, this order is constantly changing. Change then is an inherent feature of the model—everything is in the process of change, of becoming. From this position, deviation from an existing state does not in itself indicate a disordering process. Deviation from a previous state is, in fact, assumed.

Third, like homeostasis, steady state is developed and maintained by ongoing counterbalancing system processes. This is a dynamic process, but one that produces a constantly changing rather than a fixed state.

Fourth, steady state is an open system, not a closed system concept. By open system, we mean that the subject system is in constant interaction with its suprasystem through a process of input-output exchanges. Unlike the processes associated with homeostasis, steady state in a social system is not an automatic, programmed set of processes. The actions relate instead to cognitive processes entered into and acted out by those who comprise the social system.

Fifth, and like homeostasis, steady state is developed and maintained by a feedback system. Unlike a closed system, where the feedback loop deals with the effects of internal processes, steady state in an open system deals with the effects of both internal and external processes. Recall from our earlier discussion in the social systems model that feedback loops deal with both maintenance (internal) and task (external) outputs. There are also two types of feedback, positive and negative.

With the contrasting of homeostasis and steady state as background, the next step for us has been to operationalize steady state. We have likened steady state to a system's condition of well-being. The task for us has been to find a way of formulating how systems maintain a state of well-being. Similarly, the loss of steady state is the loss of system status. Figuratively speaking, the loss of system status means the death of the system.

It is in the writings of the well-known sociologist Talcott Parsons (1902–1979) that we found the idea that has proved particularly helpful in operationalizing steady state. Parsons spent much of his adult life in what might be described as helping to formulate a general theory of action.[8] In his theory-building work, he used the social system as a basic organizing scheme. In fact, one of his most important works is titled *The Social System*.[9] As an approach to the understanding of the actions of social systems, Parsons suggested use of a **four-problem paradigm**.[10]

The four problems are labeled goal attainment, integration, adaptation, and pattern maintenance. In brief, the system must make satisfactory progress in accomplishing its task goals; that is, it must meet minimum suprasystem expectations (which is the **goal attainment** problem). The system must also make satisfactory progress in accomplishing its maintenance goals; that is, it must meet the minimum expectations of its member units (the **integration** problem). The system must, in an ever changing environment, maintain those basic patterns that provide for its unique identity (the **pattern-**

maintenance problem). Finally, the system must recognize and deal with a volatile and unpredictable external environment and seek to adapt this in ways that promote its goal attainment activity (the **adaptation** problem). These four problems according to Parsons are confronted by all social systems; in this sense they are universals. Problem-solving efforts by the social system to deal with these problems result in the development of specialized structures. In this sense, Parsons' four-problem paradigm suggests an approach for the study of the development of social systems. Also of interest to us was that these four problems are never really solved; they must be contended with throughout the life of the system. While these four problems can be separated for analytical purposes, they are all related to maintaining the system's qualities of interdependence and wholeness. As a consequence, the dynamics of system behaviors are to be understood as efforts aimed at developing and maintaining a steady-state relationship in optimizing these four problem-solving efforts.

While at first appearing complicated, the ideas advanced by Parsons are very helpful and have a common sense quality to them. The apparently complicated features are more illusory than real. In addition, the assumptions and concepts advanced by Parsons in his general theory of action are compatible with our social systems perspective and the model itself. In fact, the general theory of action that he pursued can be likened to a general theory of human social behavior. While not based in general systems theory as advanced by von Bertalanffy, it has many similarities. Specifically, Parsons's works embrace the notion of an open systems approach to the study of social organization. He also viewed system-environment interactions in functional terms.

In developing the four-problem paradigm, Parsons held that social systems can be thought of as organizing around two major axes.[11] The vertical axis serves to provide the system with its external and internal references. In conceptualizing the vertical axis, it is useful to think of it as extending through the system and connecting the system to its suprasystem in a hierarchical manner. The horizontal axis is designated as *instrumental-consummatory* and comprises the means-ends dimensions of organizational relationships. It is also useful to view this axis as extending through the system and connecting it with other systems horizontally. In this formulation, **consummatory** designates the end state being sought (goal) and **instrumental,** the means being used to achieve the goal. In the language of the social systems model, consummatory refers to the proposed output and instrumental to the set of activities being employed to accomplish proposed output.

When dichotomized, these two axes produce a matrix that defines four functional problems that every social organization must successfully address to maintain steady state. Figure 4.1 presents the matrix and the labeling of these four functional problems: adaptation, goal attainment, pattern maintenance, and integration.

In the paragraphs ahead we will be dealing with these four problems and their relationships. Our approach will be to formulate each as a problem-solving question.

Goal Attainment

THE PROBLEM: How to Optimize Task Outputs in a Manner That Satisfies Suprasystem Expectations

The problem posed in goal attainment provides a useful starting position. It also identifies the controlling variable in the model, task output. Social organizations are social tools deliberately created as means to respond to some opportunity or problem perceived to exist in their social environments. Given this purpose, goal attainment represents both an external and a consummatory function. It is external in the sense that the opportunity or need that caused the system to be created exists in the suprasystem (see Figure 3.1). It is consummatory in that goal attainment represents an attempt to satisfy that opportunity or need. It is important to note that satisfaction, as we are using the term here, is not experienced by the system but by the social units that are a part of the suprasystem, or those who make use of the system's task outputs. This is the notion of output-input exchanges that we discussed earlier. It is also a way of looking at the ordering that is evident in the relationships between systems and their suprasystems.

To put this point in a practice context, resolution of the goal attainment problem is to be found in the perceptions held by the client or his or her representatives, not the worker. The distinction between signal and maintenance inputs is helpful. In human service agencies, clients are always the signal inputs. Following conversion operations, clients leave the system as task outputs and enter and/or become part of the system's suprasystem. It is in this sense of consummation that the problem of goal attainment is to be understood—have suprasystem expectations been consummated? In the client's view have the goals of the helping system been attained?

Earlier, Lewin's field theory was reviewed. His use of "goals" and tension systems can be helpful in understanding what we mean by the goal attainment problem.[12] Recall the story told of the waiter's annoyance at being asked by Lewin to recompute the bill that he and his students had incurred at the cafe. We pointed out that the waiter's issuance of the bill and its subsequent payment represented goal attainment in this system. The waiter's behaviors and those of his customers could be understood in this context. Once the bill was presented and payment made, the tension system that was organized around this goal was released and the energy was now available for other work. Here goal attainment would be evidenced by the level of satisfaction Lewin and his students had as customers. Conceptually speaking, once the bill had been paid, they were no longer part of this system but represented its task output. It is in this sense that goal attainment is always external and consummatory.

The problem of goal attainment deals with suprasystem expectations. It is these expectations that the system must satisfy, at least to some extent, if the system is to

FIGURE 4.1 Parsons's Four-Problem Paradigm

	Instrumental	Consummatory
External	Adaptive Function	Goal-Attainment Function
Internal	Pattern Maintenance Function	Integration Function

survive. We will be discussing the means used for goal attainment later when adaptation is addressed. It is the sister problem to goal attainment.

To illustrate the problem of goal attainment, let us return to the use of an earlier example, the Arnold case. It is important to recognize that the Arnold case represents a formed social organization as opposed to one that developed naturally, the Arnold family itself. We will discuss these distinctions and their implications later. With the Arnolds, goal attainment expectations would be tied to the goals agreed upon by the social worker, Pat Gray, and Sarah and Bill Arnold. Goals pertaining to financial stability, reuniting the family, and increased levels of self-esteem in their parenting roles were included. The fulfillment of these goals at a level deemed satisfactory for this system is an example of the goal attainment problem. The level of goal attainment represents one of the sources contributing toward steady state. If the goals were not satisfactorily attained or if an excessive amount of resources had been expended in goal attainment activities, the assumption is that steady state would be threatened.

We applied the concept of goal attainment to the time of the Arnold family's case closure, the completion of the final goal attainment cycle. Conceptually it would have been just as appropriate to examine goal attainment status at the completion of an earlier cycle, for example, when a progress report was made to the court responsible for removing Donnie from his home. In the sense that we are using the concept of the goal attainment cycle, it means that the effects of that cycle on the suprasystem have been fed back into the system. The use of this information in terms of subsequent actions by the system affects its steady state.

The Arnold case represents a very small social organization, being comprised of three individuals, with each enacting his or her particular social role. We make this point because the activities associated with resolving each of these four problems can be viewed as causing the creation of four subsystems dedicated to these functions; that is, structural differentiation based on these problem-solving functions. In large formal organization, such specialized subsystems can be identified; for example, the assembly line through which a General Motors plant produces automobiles would be a specialized subsystem dedicated to the goal attainment function. Here goal attainment would be in the production of automobiles and the purchase of them by consumers. The problem is consummatory in the sense that these consumers must purchase their cars and be satisfied with their purchases. It is external because these consumers exist in the company's suprasystem.

Integration

THE PROBLEM: How to Optimize Satisfaction of the System's Maintenance Needs
The notion of integration is premised in part on the observation that the people who comprise social organizations share needs that are independent of the needs of the social organization itself. Further, these needs must be satisfied to some degree or the organization itself is adversely affected. Simply stated, people who work together in some kind of joint enterprise should enjoy their work together; if their various work roles are vitally

related and they cannot tolerate each other, there is likely to be a problem reflected in their capacity for coordinated and cooperative work.

At a conceptual level it is useful to view the components of a social system as having an affinity toward each other, in other words, being attracted to each other.[13] In this sense, the problem of integration is internal and consummatory. It is an internal problem in that the needs are those of the system itself; its components include but are not limited to the personally based needs of those individuals enacting social roles. The problem is consummatory in that it pertains to an end state, need satisfaction.

In order to develop this point, let us again return to the Arnold case. We have discussed the problem of goal attainment. We make the assumption that Pat Gray and Sarah and Bill Arnold each have personal needs and that their mutual work together must address these maintenance needs as well as the task needs of reuniting the family, that is, returning Donnie to the family. The need to create and sustain a helping system capable of dealing with the Arnolds's problem is a key feature of the integration problem confronted by Ms. Gray. Recall that the helping relationship is being formed as the means of helping the Arnold family.

Forming a helping relationship capable of sustaining this problem-solving work is more difficult than it may seem. For example, Pat Gray must be sensitive to her own belonging needs and her needs to feel good about herself. Her work with the Arnolds should contribute to the satisfaction of these personal needs, but certainly these needs are not the reason for this relationship. Pat also recognizes that Sarah and Bill each have personal needs that are independent of their roles as husband and wife and mother and father. These needs can be expected to intrude in some fashion on this helping relationship. By recognizing and responding appropriately to these needs, Pat will help build a trusting and helping relationship that will help solve their problems.

Pat also understands how easy it is for means to become ends. An example would be that Pat's own personal need to be liked, to have people depend on her, could distort the relationship so that it was used primarily to serve her needs rather than those of her clients. This is what is meant by a means becoming an end. Pat's practicum supervisor, Joan Seavers, also recognizes how easy it is for a new practitioner to become overinvolved in a case and to substitute means for ends. In her supervisory meetings with Pat we could expect that Joan would inquire about how Pat personally feels about Sarah and Bill and how these feelings are contributing to or perhaps distracting from the helping relationship.

Similar to the point made in our discussion of goal attainment, those activities associated with dealing with the integration problem cause the creation of a subsystem devoted to this effort. In the case of the Arnold family, the subsystem will be evidenced in the roles of those comprising the system. If the application were to a large formal organization, the subsystem might be represented by a department or some other administrative designation. Personnel departments in large organizations address integration problems; that is, they are typically devoted to addressing system needs as opposed to being primarily concerned with the production of task outputs. For example, personnel departments hire workers, deal with problems of morale, and try to promote job satisfaction.

Adaptation

THE PROBLEM: How to Optimize Goal Attainment by Modifying the Suprasystem or, if Necessary, the System Itself

The problem of adaptation is especially useful because it helps us focus on the dynamic qualities possessed by all forms of social organization. For example, there are times when most of us feel literally overwhelmed by all the things changing around us. We wonder if we will ever get caught up. Alvin Toffler, in his popular book *Future Shock*, captured for many people how rapidly our world is changing around us; he also helped us see how these changes are affecting us as individuals, as family members, as workers, and as members of our society.[14]

By focusing on the functional tie that every social organization has with its social environment, we are provided a way of grasping an insight on the process of change. If the world is changing around us, we are going to be caught up in these changes and be changed by them. In systems terms, this is what we mean by change being mutually deterministic. In other words, change is two way, not one way; the system changes (adapts) but so does its suprasystem. For many this is a troublesome and difficult idea. We believe the difficulty lies in the linear way of thinking that most of us have been taught. Simply put, something happens and we adapt to it, for example, loss of a job. In this formulation it would appear that adaptation is an internal problem—it happens within the system. For us this is not a useful or accurate way of viewing human behavior and misrepresents the functional linkage between humans and their social environment. A more useful approach is one that views humans in a proactive rather than reactive posture. Humans and by extension all forms of social organization are actively intervening with others who constitute their social environments; it is a dynamic process.

In this model, then, the problem of adaptation is an external one; the system is actively involved in seeking changes in the suprasystem that will facilitate goal attainment. We do not mean to suggest that the system does not adapt to changes that are occurring externally; it does. What we are saying is that these changes have reciprocal effects—they are not one way. We are also saying that the change process always assumes a proactive stance on the part of the subject system. The system is seeking the attainment of its goals. The means for accomplishing these goals always involves adaptation efforts. We might add here that some people, perhaps many, are reactive; perhaps this is why they have problems in attaining their goals. This same point holds for families, agencies, communities, and all forms of social organization. The point we want to stress is that the model assumes a proactive stance. If the model is applied to an organization, for instance, a family, that does not display this proactive feature, our guess is that the family will show problems in steady state.

We have used the Arnold case to illustrate at a direct practice level various systems concepts; we will return again to this case to discuss the adaptation problem. Before doing so, however, we will introduce some system concepts used by Pincus and Minahan in their text, *Social Work Practice: Model and Method*.[15] This book was perhaps the first practice text in social work to be clearly organized around a systems conception of practice. These authors identified four basic systems: the change agent system, the client system, the target system, and the action system.

If we were to apply these system terms to the Arnold case, Ms. Gray and the Westwood Child and Family Center would comprise the change agent system.[16] The client system is the expected beneficiary of the helping effort.[17] In this case, the ultimate beneficiary would be Donnie. It was Donnie who was injured and the intent of the helping process is to see that Donnie is not hurt again. The target system, according to Pincus and Minahan, are "the people the change agent needs to change or influence in order to accomplish his goals."[18] In this case, the target system is comprised of Sarah and Bill Arnold in their parental/family roles. Finally, the change agent works with the action system to accomplish the goals of the helping effort and to influence the target system.

While our social systems model does not use the same terms as advanced by Pincus and Minahan, the two approaches are quite similar. What they term action system describes what we are referring to as the adaptation problem. Recall that this problem is external to the subject system (a variation of what Pincus and Minahan label the target system). The problem is also an instrumental one; it involves the means to be employed in goal attainment. Pincus and Minahan put it this way: "The change agent does not work in isolation in his change efforts; he works with other people. We use the term "action system" to describe those with whom the social worker deals in his efforts to accomplish the task and achieve the goals of the change effort."[19]

The problem of adaptation recognizes the rapid changes that are taking place in the world about us. The problem also recognizes the critical role that agencies and other people play in helping or hindering our efforts at goal attainment. In the Arnold case, there are several key agencies that are external, that will influence the extent to which goal attainment (such as the return of Donnie to his parents) will take place. Included among others would be the court and judge who removed Donnie from his parents, and the child welfare agency that is supervising Donnie's foster placement. In the terms used by Pincus and Minahan, the relationships that Ms. Gray would form with the court and the child welfare agency would be labeled the action system.

In this application of the model, these two agencies represent part of the system's suprasystem; these same two agencies will be central to the resolution of the adaptation problem confronting Pat Gray. Neither Ms. Gray nor her agency have the authority to return Donnie to his parents. Ms. Gray's job is to help Sarah and Bill Arnold deal with the family problems that resulted in Donnie being removed from them. Once Ms. Gray is confident that Sarah and Bill Arnold are able to handle their parental roles, she must then convince (adapt to her view) the court and the child welfare agency that it is both safe and in the best interest of Donnie and all others that he be returned to his natural home. Thus goal attainment will depend upon Ms. Gray's ability to modify the suprasystem in the form of actions required of the court and the child welfare agency to return Donnie home.

Now let us move to General Motors, a large formal organization, to provide another example of the adaptation problem. To keep the example simple, let us say its goal is to make a profit for its shareholders through the sale of automobiles. With the goal attainment problem identified, adaptation pertains to efforts that General Motors must make to create an environment that will facilitate the sale of its automobiles *and* at a price that will result in goal attainment. All of the marketing, promotional, and lobbying activities engaged in by General Motors represent efforts by that organization to modify its environment in order to optimize goal attainment, sale of its cars. Simply stated, the problem is to convince consumers that they need to buy a General Motors car. Similarly, there are conditions in this external environment that will affect General Motors and the kind of cars it builds, including customer preferences, behavior of competitors, price of oil, and government regulations. General Motors is not simply going to manufacture cars and let them sit on the dealers's lots. It is going to actively seek to adapt the world around it in order to sell those cars, trying to convince the public that "This is a deal you can't refuse."

The Civil Rights Movement of the 1960s and 1970s also offers a way of examining the problem of adaptation at a societal level. Earlier the suprasystem was described as representing a larger order to which a subject system (as a subsystem) is functionally related. This larger order (society) can impact both positively or negatively on its subsystems and the humans who comprise it (minority groups). Racism and sexism are two negative features of this larger structure that can and do erode and diminish the quality of life of many citizens. If the Civil Rights Movement were viewed in social systems terms, goal attainment for that system would be an improvement at the societal level of the quality of life of Blacks and other minorities—more and better jobs, social justice, feelings of self-esteem, and more. In this case the suprasystem is deemed to possess racist structural features that are oppressive and demeaning in their impact. These structures are the object of change as the necessary means to bring about goal attainment in the form of an improved quality of life. The example of the Civil Rights Movement also helps to get across what we mean by a proactive stance. The means employed to accomplish goal attainment was at times confrontive and involved use of conflict strategies. Here conflict was viewed as instrumental—a means toward goal attainment.

Pattern Maintenance

THE PROBLEM: How To Maintain in a Constantly Changing and at Times Volatile Environment the System's Most Important Structural Features, Those That Provide Its Unique Identity

Just as every individual is different from every other individual, so is every social organization different from every other. Pattern maintenance is the continuing effort that must be made to preserve this distinctiveness. Like the other problems, maintaining this distinctiveness in a rapidly changing social environment is a difficult task. Have you ever had the feeling that you are being pulled in a dozen different directions or are having problems "getting it all together"? These expressions are getting at a problem faced by all social systems, that of maintaining their basic patterns of behavior. At an individual level it is maintaining who we are; at the organization level it is essentially the same thing, who we are as a family, an agency, or a community.

Pattern maintenance is an internal and instrumental problem. It is internal in the sense that it pertains to the maintenance of core structural features of the relationships among members of the system. Pattern maintenance is an instrumental problem in that it must be dealt with in order for the system to achieve its consummatory aims of goal attainment and integration. Just as values constitute the core internal features of the individual personality, so do values comprise the core internal structural features of a social system. Similarly, just as one's system of values is helpful in maintaining stability in a rapidly changing world, so does the system of values that comprises the internal structure of a social system provide stability. We are not suggesting that values do not change, they do, but less rapidly than other structural features.

Any attempt to understand the behavior of a social system includes and perhaps starts with an identification of the undergirding value system.[20] It is this value system that provides a point of orientation for understanding a rich array of patterns of integration. In so doing, it helps provide the system with a sense of identity both for its own members and for those who are nonmembers. It is the maintenance of this pattern that comprises the pattern-maintenance problem. An example using the value dimension of pattern maintenance can be illustrated in a family that has a strong moral code in which the use of drugs is considered both morally and legally wrong. A teenage member of that family finds himself under constant and severe pressure to try drugs: "It is cool," "It is in," "Be one of us." He or she is faced with a competing value system, one that is in opposition to the family's and the way he or she has been socialized. If he or she should "do drugs," not only will his or her own "steady state" be affected but that of the family as well.

There is another dimension to the problem of pattern maintenance that is referred to as *tension management*. In discussing the problem of integration, note was made of the usefulness of thinking of system components as having an affinity for each other. Like a magnet, this force (affinity) tends to draw member units toward each other. The notion of tension management or pattern maintenance is just the reverse. Conceptually speaking, it is useful to think of every system as also being characterized by a force that pushes member units away from each other as well. An example of these twin but opposite forces can be found in a marriage. Integration is the drawing together of the married partners in an ever closer and more intimate union. We can understand this force as an expression of their mutual love and their belongingness needs. Operating in the reverse is a force that pushes them apart. This force is an expression of their autonomy as individuals, their need for independence, and their respective needs to become self-actualized. The pattern maintenance problem is clearly stated in the two words themselves—pattern maintenance.

Social organizations are comprised of individuals or parts of individuals in the conceptual sense that a social organization is a system of roles rather than a system of autonomous individuals. The person playing a system's role is also an individual and has needs that are understood as part of his or her personality. The healthy individual has a conception of self or personhood that is independent of any of the organizational roles that he or she may play. Within an organization, the individual gives up a part of his or her autonomy to become a part of something larger; this is the force of integration. Similarly, the counterforce of drawing away arises from the person's sense of personhood, of independence, of wanting to maintain and enhance his or her autonomy. While we have used the individual as an example of the need for greater autonomy, we hold that this tension state characterizes any system component, be it an individual, an administrative unit of a formal organization, or a neighborhood within a community.

The problem of pattern maintenance evidences recognition of the inevitable pull of system components to become more autonomous. Unless this problem is controlled, the system pulls itself apart and steady state is lost. In conceptualizing steady state, it is useful to envision a hierarchy of structures comprising the structural pattern that must be maintained. In other words, some of these structural relationships are more important than others. In this connection, the centrality of these structures to the identity of the system determines their importance. We assume that if certain vital relationship features are lost, the system becomes something else or ceases to exist as a system.

Now let us return for a final time to the Arnold case to illustrate the problem of pattern maintenance. We can approach the problem with the following question: In this helping relationship, what is the fundamental structural pattern that Pat Gray, the student social worker, must maintain with Sarah and Bill Arnold if the goals are to be attained? The clue to answering this question would be found in the value system that Pat Gray brings into a professional helping relationship. The relationship (social system) she forms with Sarah and Bill Arnold should evidence a value system and code of ethics that will guide their work with one another. In fact, it is this pattern of ethical behaviors that forms the foundation of their relationship. It helps distinguish this as a professional relationship.[21] It is also this pattern that must be maintained that constitutes the essence of the pattern maintenance problem with which Ms. Gray must contend.

Another related example would be in the use of agreed-upon professional methods. The right to be self-determined constitutes a part of the mutuality in problem determination, goal setting, and intervention methods that caused the helping system to be formed in the first place. For whatever reason, if Ms. Gray sought to impose her own personal beliefs, values, and decisions on the Arnolds, it would represent a violation of this basic pattern and would be destabilizing to the system. Unless checked, the violation of the agreed-upon right to be self-determined would result in the loss of steady state. Under these conditions, if the system should continue it would no longer represent a professional social work relationship.

SUMMARY

This chapter has presented a summary of behaviors deemed common to all human forms of association meeting our definition of social organization. These behaviors have been described as constituting the dynamics of the social systems model. Just as survival is the imperative that the individual must address throughout life, so it is with all human forms of association. We take the position that all forms of social organization become social entities unto themselves, and they too must contend with maintaining their existence. Some of the survival problems are similar to those faced by humans but others are distinctive. For example, social organizations have no counterpart to the physical development pattern characteristic of humans.

Similarly, one can argue that the entropic process is more evident in individuals than their social organizations. With human beings, death is a certainty; we grow old and we die—if not by accident or some other event, then by a degenerative process. Not so with social organizations. First, they have no physical structures that will degenerate. Also, they, more than individuals, are characterized by negative entropy. As a consequence, some organizations have survived for thousands of years. For example, the

Catholic Church is approximately 2000 years old. Social organizations do die, but from loss of steady state.

Building on the insights of Parsons, we described a four-problem paradigm to characterize behaviors deemed common to all forms of social organization. The problems are goal attainment, integration, adaptation and pattern maintenance. The resolution efforts of these four problems result in behavior patterns common to all forms of human groupings displaying the features of interdependence and wholeness. Within these common patterns, each human grouping will exhibit distinctive patterns of its own. It is through an understanding of the general patterns and the distinctive features exhibited by a specified group that the knowledge building and practice applications derive. Utilizing the social system model, one can say that a subject system will always display behaviors that: (1) seek *goal attainment* or satisfaction of suprasystem expectations (its goals and objectives); (2) seek to *adapt* the suprasystem (and itself) in ways that facilitate goal attainment; (3) seek a level of *integration* that functionally aligns member units in ways that strengthen the system itself; and, (4) seek to *maintain those structural patterns* that provide the system its specific identity. It is the latter problem that is more fundamental and serves as the point of coordination for efforts directed toward the other three problems. The identification of common patterns of system behaviors is contributed to by the evolution of specialized structures within the social system. These structures are dedicated toward resolution efforts aimed at one or more of these problems. The evolution of these structures provides an approach for the study of organizational development and maintenance.

The four problems are all systematically interrelated. They are never finally solved, but they must be constantly addressed and the relationships among the various solutions optimized. Failure in any of the problem areas will result in loss of steady state or loss of order and thus the death of the system. The continuing resolution of these problems also creates the necessary conditions for growth and development.

The concept of feedback is vital in thinking about how steady state is maintained. The feedback loop associated with each of these problems is continually called upon to provide information on progress being made in dealing with each of the four problems. The feedback will be both positive and negative. It is the ability to understand this feedback and to make the necessary adjustments in order to optimize efforts at dealing with all four problems that results in steady state.

It is important to remember that these four problems are interrelated and that progress in dealing with one of these problems may create additional problems with one or more of the others. For example, Ms. Gray may be making important progress in dealing with the goal attainment problem by helping the Arnolds stabilize their financial situation, and increase their parenting skills and their sense of self-esteem. But by focusing on this element, she may have neglected her contacts with the judge who removed Donnie from the Arnold home and the child welfare agency that is supervising Donnie's foster home arrangements (the adaptation problem). In so doing, Ms. Gray may have complicated the attainment of the goal of returning Donnie to his family.

Finally, while there are four problems, the coordination of the efforts to deal with them rests in pattern maintenance. Part of the pattern-maintenance problem lies in developing and utilizing the feedback structures that permit the coordination of efforts at dealing with all four problems. It is in this sense that pattern maintenance is the most sensitive and important of the four elements of steady state.

GLOSSARY

Adaptation　Manipulation of the suprasystem as a means of facilitating accomplishment of a system's task goals.

Consummatory　A classification of actions directly related to attainment of a task goal.

Equilibrium　A state of balance or adjustment, typically achieved through opposing actions.

Four-problem paradigm　A conceptual designation of four problems that each social system must constantly address in order to maintain steady state.

Goal attainment　Satisfaction of the suprasystem's expectations of a subject system.

Homeostasis　A state of equilibrium typically formulated to describe the genetically based adaptive capabilities of organisms.

Instrumental　Actions necessary to help or facilitate accomplishment of a goal or end state; for example, a classification of means employed to accomplish a specified end.

Integration　The satisfaction of the system's maintenance goals.

Pattern maintenance　Protection of a system's core structural patterns, those that provide its unique identity.

NOTES

1. Ludwig von Bertalanffy, *General Systems Theory: Foundations, Development, Applications* (New York: George Braziller, 1968), 124-131.

2. Our view of the proactive conceptualization of humans and of all forms of social organizations is similar to that suggested by Walter Buckley, *Sociology and Modern Systems Theory* (Englewood Cliffs, New Jersey: Prentice Hall, 1967). See particularly the distinction that Buckley draws between the older notions of homeostasis and steady state on pages 52–53.

3. Ludwig von Bertlanffy, *Das Gefüge des Lebens* (Leipzig: Teubner, 1937), 133. The point can also be found in Bertalanffy, *General Systems Theory*, 209.

4. Abraham H. Maslow, *Motivation and Personality*, 2nd ed. (New York: Harper and Row, 1970), 35–38.

5. Ludwig von Bertalanffy, *Robots, Men and Minds: Psychology in the Modern World* (New York: George Braziller, 1967), 6.

6. Ibid., 3–52.

7. Bertalanffy, *General Systems Theory*, 208–213.

8. See particularly, R. Baum Laubser, and A. Effrat, *Explorations in General Theory in Social Science: Essays in Honor of Talcott Parsons*, ed. V. Lidz (New York: Free Press, 1976).

9. Talcott Parsons, *The Social System* (Glencoe, Ill.: The Free Press, 1951).

10. Talcott Parsons, "An Outline of a Social System" in T. Parsons et al., eds., *Theories of Society* (New York: The Free Press, 1961), 36–41.

11. Ibid.

12. Kurt Lewin, "Behavior and Development as a Function of the Total Situation," in *Manual of Child Psychology* (2nd ed.), Leonard Carmichael (ed.), (New York: John Wiley & Sons, 1954).

13. Parsons, *The Social System*.

14. Alvin Toffler, *Future Shock* (New York: Random House, 1970).

15. Allen Pincus and Anne Minahan, *Social Work Practice: Model and Method* (Itasca, Ill., 1973), 61.

16. The change agent, according to Pincus and Minahan, is the professional helper. In this case that person is Ms. Pat Gray. The agency that employs her and thereby is giving her the sanction to practice is the Westwood Child and Family Center. The professional helper and the agency providing the sanction and authority to practice become, in this instance, the change agent system.

17. The basic notions out of which these four system concepts arose are from the work of Lippit, Watson, and Westley in their book, *The Dynamics of Planned Change* (New York: Harcourt, Brace, & World, 1958). The term client system as used by Pincus and Minahan has further restrictions than implied here.

18. Pincus and Minahan, *Social Work Practice*, 58.

19. Ibid., 61.

20. Parsons, *Theories of Society*, 39.

21. See, for example, NASW Code of Ethics.

PART II
THE SOCIAL GROUP

The Social Systems Model

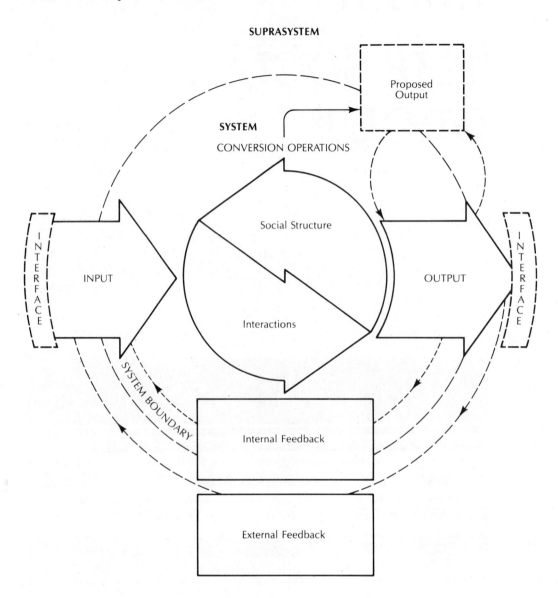

In Part II we develop the position that the social group represents a distinguishable form of social organization, one that can be usefully modeled as a social system. Building on the generic features of the model presented in Part I, this section is devoted to discussion of the special characteristics possessed by social groups and the implications of these qualities to the use of the social systems model. The family, one form that the social group takes, is given special attention.

Chapter 5 provides the introduction to the social group. The chapter builds from the definition of the social group and the lines of conceptual thought that serve as the foundations for this definition. Discussed in some detail are the concepts of Gemeinschaft, Gesellschaft, and primary and secondary groups. These seminal concepts are used to help distinguish the social group from other forms of human association.

In Chapter 6 we expand our discussion of the social systems perspective by concentrating on assumptions that help to distinguish the social group when viewed as a system. Building from these assumptions, two additional lines of theory development are identified, namely, exchange and symbolic interaction. We have found these two theories of particular help in explicating the features of social groups that distinguish them from other forms of human association.

The social systems model is applied to the social group in Chapter 7. A family, the Joneses, is used for illustrative purposes. Each of the eight concepts comprising the model is discussed through use of this family.

Chapter 8, an examination of the dynamics of the social group, concludes Part II. Here, as in Part I, the concept of steady state is used to illustrate the notion of system dynamics. Maintaining the continuity started in Chapter 7, the Jones family serves as the primary example for illustrating how social groups attempt to maintain steady state.

Chapter 5

The Social Group: An Introduction

OUTLINE

Review

Several assumptions about human social behavior were noted in Chapter 2, "A Social Systems Perspective." Of particular relevance here is: "All forms of human organization exhibit key features of the general order as well as those distinctive to humans and to the several classes of human social organization." We build from this assumption by taking the position that the distinctive features in human relationships are rooted in the basic interdependence of individuals on one another. Humans have survived as a species because of their ability to join with each other as a means of satisfying their own needs and of dealing with the problems and opportunities posed by their physical and social environments. It is the extension of this assumption, the interdependence and interactions that humans have with their environment, that forms the premise for the open systems conception of the model and of its cyclical nature.

Embedded in the notion of the interdependence of humans and their social environment is the assumed social or gregarious nature of people. This observation is certainly not a new one. For example, several centuries before the birth of Christ, Aristotle wrote, ". . . man is by Nature a social animal. Anyone who either cannot lead the common life or is so self-sufficient as not to need to, and therefore does not partake of society is either a beast or a god."[1]

What is meant by social nature and how is this nature expressed? There are no conclusive answers to these questions and the search encompasses much of the subject matter of psychology and sociology. What can be described are the lines of debate and inquiry in the pursuit of answers to these questions. Particularly important is information on theory development that affects the use of a systems model for the study of social organization. We have already reviewed some of these theories; our intent is to develop them further and add others in this chapter as they apply to the behavior of the social group. As noted previously, the work of Maslow clearly addresses the issue of social nature and his need theory places the source of belongingness needs in the genetic structure of the species.[2]

According to Maslow, the belongingness and love needs represent basic needs and become dominant when the individual's physiological and safety needs have been satisfied.[3] Human interdependence and cooperation become the chief means through which survival and safety needs are addressed. Once these needs are satisfied, the pursuit of belongingness needs and love needs takes on a different character. Human association is no longer a means, it becomes an end in itself. In other words, a sense of belonging or love can only be obtained from other humans. Thus, human association through social groups becomes both a means and an end in the satisfaction of social needs.

Just as some theorists, like Maslow, hold that human social behavior is tied to a genetic legacy, others take a counter position. They hold that human behavior can be understood by examining the individual's environment. Many holding this latter position argue that social behavior is learned behavior.[4] From this point of view, the history of humankind is not to be understood in terms of genetically based mechanisms but simply by the fact that social behavior "works." The position these theorists take is that cooperation with others has been necessary to solve the survival imperative at both the individual and the species level, but it is a learned behavior. So rather than a genetically based propensity to seek out and engage in social behaviors, humans possess a genetically based capacity to think, to reason, and to learn. This capacity distinguishes humans from all other forms of life and it is through this capacity to learn and to reason that the social behavior of humans is to be understood. Individual and cultural variations in behaviors are to be viewed from both a learning perspective and from the functions these behaviors are designed to serve. Similarities in patterns of human behavior within and between societies can also be explained in terms of the common problems faced, for example, survival. We will in Part III be reviewing some of the key psychological theories dealing with how humans learn.

For us, the argument as to whether social behavior is genetically based or learned is not central to our current purpose. What is important is recognition that it does exist and that it helps to account for our ability as a species to exist and, if numbers are an indication, to prosper. Sometimes it seems that we get caught up in negatives—our inhumanities. There are plenty of examples, as a reading of any newspaper will attest. What we lose sight of sometimes is our basic humanity. We have a social nature, the ability to conceive of others as well as ourselves as individuals, to have feelings toward other people, and to enter into relationships with them for the pursuit of shared purposes.

It is the social group that for us provides the clearest source of insights on our social behavior, our distinctive human qualities. Also, our position is that the social group is the first level of social organization. In a manner of speaking, the social group is the building block upon which all larger, more complex forms of social organization depend. We will start the inquiry by reviewing our definition of the social group.

Definitions

Earlier we offered a simple classification of social organization. Included was the definition of the social group:

> **Social Group** A form of social organization comprised of two or more members who identify and interact with one another on a personal basis as individuals, possess a shared sense of the group as a social entity, are affected by the group-related actions of members, and in which expressive (natural) actions dominate.

Based on this definition, our interest is in identifying the distinguishing features of the social group. These features help to differentiate the social group from other forms of social organization. It is these characteristics that we will be exploring because of the implications they have when the social systems model is applied to a social group.

We consider five characteristics possessed by the social group to be particularly important. They are:

1. *Size.* The minimum group size is specified but the maximum is not. As a form of social organization, the social group is small. The upper limit in size is constrained by the person-to-person nature of interactions that all group members have with one another. If this person-to-person feature is lost, the organization ceases to be a social group in terms of the definition.

2. *Goal Structure.* The social group is characterized by minimum levels of role differentiation. Interaction among members is essentially person-to-person, and as total personalities rather than in narrowly defined roles. As a consequence, the goal structure of the group tends to be implicit rather than explicit; that is, the goals are derived essentially from the needs, such as social belonging and love, of those persons comprising the group.

3. *Identity.* All members share a common group identity and perceive the group as a whole. This unity is most clearly expressed by the notion of "we" when reference is made to group-related activities. In addition, the social group has an effect on the selfhood possessed by its individual members.

4. *Effect on individual behavior.* The social group performs significant socialization and social control functions for its members. In short, every social group possesses a distinctive subculture, which includes a normative system that influences the group-related behavior of its members. These group norms are adopted, in part, by members (internalized) and become a part of the individual's own value system.

5. *Self-organizing.* The relationships among group members and the resulting interactions have their origins in the internal or natural state of the members. In this sense, social groups are self-organizing. The group-related actions are driven primarily by emotional as opposed to reasoned factors. Thus, relationships in social groups serve as an end, in and of themselves as opposed to being instrumental or a means to some other end. It is this self-organizing feature of social groups that helps distinguish what we label as a **natural group** from a **formed group**. Formed groups are consciously constructed to perform some group-related task.

The family is the prototype social group, but our definition includes a large number of familiar groups including the play group of the child, the teenage club (or gang), the friendship group of the adult, and the activity group. All of these groups are included in the definitions to the extent that the relationships among group members conform to the definition. For example, if the primary purpose of an activity group such as a bowling club were to teach people to bowl or to earn money for the club through tournament winnings, the group would not fit the definition. In this instance, instruction or earning money would have taken primacy over human association. Therefore, groups formed specifically to achieve what we have earlier defined as task goals would not be included in the definition of social groups. Among these formed groups would be committees, athletic teams, therapeutic groups, work project teams, and quality circles. It is possible that some formed groups would meet our definition of a social group. An example would be a high school athletic team that, while constituted to win games or events, gave primary attention to the personal association among members and winning was secondary. We consider the distinction made between social or natural groups as opposed to formed groups to be important, primarily because of the differential impact these groups have on their members.

In Part I we used examples of natural and formed groups. Relative to knowledge building, we consider the natural group the locus for theory construction. It is through our understanding of the natural group that we learn how to apply this knowledge, and utilize these implications in the forming of a casework relationship.

The conceptual foundation for the definition of the social group as used in this chapter has its roots in the writings of Ferdinand Tönnies and Charles Horton Cooley, among others. Because of the importance of the ideas introduced by Tönnies and Cooley, selected features of their ideas will be reviewed in the following sections. We are also indebted to them because their ideas on the characteristics of social relationships served as the cornerstone for the classification of social organizations used in this book. Tönnies and Cooley are also helpful in our effort to distinguish between natural and formed groups and how the former instructs us in the latter.

Gemeinschaft and Gesellschaft

Writing in the latter part of the 1880s, a German sociologist and philosopher, Ferdinand Tönnies (1855–1936), developed the concepts of Gemeinschaft and Gesellschaft to contrast two basic types of social relationships.[5] Tönnies used these concepts to describe what he viewed as qualitatively different relationships among people in traditional and predominantly rural societies versus those in more modern and industrialized societies.

Gemeinschaft   Gemeinschaft characterizes personal relationships that are entered into and enjoyed for their own sake. Such relationships evolve naturally, and actions are spontaneous (as opposed to being deliberated upon) and **cathected** (invested with emotional energy). These relationships are characterized as intimate, traditional, and informal.

The prototype Gemeinschaft relationship would be that existing between family members. Gemeinschaft relationships dominate in what we have defined as the social group.

> **Gesellschaft** Gesellschaft relationships are entered into as a means toward some other end. Such relationships are characterized by rational considerations and are calculated as the best means for achieving a determined end. These relationships are characterized as contractual, impersonal, voluntary, and limited.

The prototype Gesellschaft relationship is that between a buyer and seller. For example, an individual enters into a contractual relationship (means) with a real estate agent for the purpose of selling a home (end). Given the definition of Gesellschaft, we assume that the person wishing to sell the house would seek an agent possessing the skill, knowledge, experience, and other qualities associated with being a good real-estate salesperson. Any personal or Gemeinschaft features that might develop in that relationship would be secondary to its primary purpose—selling the house. This distinction between means and ends is fundamental in understanding the differences between these two types of relationships.

It is important to bear in mind that Tönnies was attempting to develop two analytically pure models for examining social relationships. He was living during a period of rapid change resulting from the effects of industrialization and urbanization and was interested in the human effects of these changes. In short, Tönnies observed that as social life became more complex and society more differentiated, there appeared to be a corresponding shift from Gemeinschaft to Gesellschaft types of relationships. As a practical matter, though, it should be understood that all human relationships will have Gemeinschaft and Gesellschaft qualities. In most instances one or the other will tend to dominate and thus distinguish a particular social organization. Gemeinschaft qualities are considered to dominate Gesellschaft features in social groups. This is not to say that in a given instance a social group might not evolve into a form of social organization in which Gesellschaft relationships dominate; however, if that occurs, it ceases to be what is here defined as a social group and becomes something else, for example, a formal organization or a formed group.

Natural and Rational Will

From time to time in the chapters ahead we will refer to the Gemeinschaft and Gesellschaft features of relationships. Because of the importance of these two types of relationships, it is helpful to tie these concepts to Tönnies's search for a deeper explanation of human behavior. He introduced his inquiry as follows: "What, why, and how do thinking humans will and want? The simple and most general answer is: they want to attain an end and seek the most appropriate means of attaining it."[6]

How do humans will and want? In addressing the question, Tönnies identified two contrasting types of will, one he labeled *natural*, the other *rational*.

Natural Will   Natural will is linked to the essence or underlying character of the person. In its most elementary or in its simplest form, it is expressed in the direct, naive, honest and emotional acts of the child.

For a child, the explanation for an action might be, "I did it because I wanted to." For an adult, an explanation of an act based in natural will would be, "It felt like the right thing to do."

Rational Will   Rational will is a contemplated choice, one in which the alternatives are weighed and a decision made as to the best means of achieving a specified end.

As in the case of the related concepts of Gemeinschaft and Gesellschaft, Tönnies formulated two ideal or pure forms of will. Like their relationship counterparts, these two conceptions of will can be viewed as contrasting points on a continuum that is used to examine how human choices that underlie social behavior are made and exercised. Tönnies stated his case:

> The general human volition, which we may conceive as natural and original, is fulfilled through knowledge and ability and is also fundamentally conditioned through reciprocal interaction with them. The whole intellect, even in the plainest man, expresses itself in his knowledge and correspondingly in his volition. Not only what he has learned but also the inherited mode of thought and perception of the forefathers influences his sentiment, his mind and heart, his conscience. Consequently, I name the will thought of in this latter sense natural will *(Wesenwille)*, contrasting it with the type of rational will *(Kürwille)*, in which the thinking has gained predominance and come to be the directing agent. The rational will is to be differentiated from intellectual will. Intellectual will gets along well with subconscious motives which lie deep in man's nature and at the base of his natural will, whereas rational will eliminates such disturbing elements and is as clearly conscious as possible.[7]

This passage by Tönnies is instructive in that it sets forth key dimensions of his conceptions of will. Natural will is the older of the two, having its origins in the very nature of men and women and subsequently developed in the cultural patterns that have evolved within societies over the centuries of human association. In a manner of speaking, natural will represents a collective wisdom passed on from generation to generation and is incorporated in the individual through the general socialization process. This form of will embodies a sense of tradition. Rational will is of more recent origin and is associated, in part, with the growing complexity of social life. It can be argued that rational and natural will have a common origin in an internal state of the human. Natural will, as evident in overt behavior such as an act of affection, is a relatively direct expression of this so-called natural state. In contrast, rational will is affected more by a reasoned assessment of the social, political, and physical environment, and a judgment of the possible effects of actions on the person's own goals, for example, when a woman makes a decision to pursue a professional career. Here the decision often results from a conscious consideration of the money to be earned, the status of the profession among one's peers, and the market demand for such professionals. In contrast would be the woman who simply assumes that as an adult she will marry, bear children, and take care of a home, her children, and her husband. In the latter instance, the reasoning would be that this is the way it has always been, and always will be; therefore, it is right. Recall that Tönnies was writing in the latter part of the nineteenth century and was contemplating the effects of rapid urbanization and industrialization on human association and the structure of society. During this time, people were becoming more mobile, the family was changing from an extended to a nuclear form, and people were increasingly depending on jobs for their livelihood. People were less likely to know one another, yet they were growing more interdependent. The conditions were thus established for new forms of association among people; it was these new forms of relationships that Tönnies labeled Gesellschaft. Because of their contractual and temporal features, these new forms of relationships seemed more functionally suited to the needs of people in a rapidly changing, mobile, and industrially based society.

The distinctions drawn between intellectual and rational will by Tönnies are particularly instructive. "Intellectual" is not used by Tönnies as a synonym for the ability to reason; rather it is being used as a more general statement of human capacity and the relationship of that capacity to behavior. Another way of looking at intellectual is as a state of relative richness of capacity, as distinguished from an analytical or reasoning capability. An example of intellectual will would be the works of a great artist or poet. The artist's creations are highly personal. The sources of the creative genius are not to be found in the artist's contemplative, technical, and analytical skills. The art object or poem is not manufactured, it is one of a kind; it is personal, inspired and an extension of the artist himself or herself. Here the art object is an intellect-driven expression of natural will. On the other hand, the decision by an engineer to design and manufacture a new computer to be used as a problem-solving tool would require, like the artist's creation, great intellectual capacity, but for the engineer it would be an expression of rational will; it is a reasoned act.

We again return to the essence of Tönnies's question—How do humans will and want? Let us attempt a reply by using the popular expression "Where there's a will, there's a way." The expression is helpful on two counts: It introduces the notion of the relative intensity of will or the degree of human determination (motivation); and the expression again deals with the relationship between means and ends. "Will" becomes that which is needed or desired, the end state, or in systems language, the proposed outcome. "Way" becomes the means for achieving the end state, or in systems terms the structure or approach to be used.

When the notion of intensity of human determination (will) is combined with the relationships between means and ends, two different courses of actions become possible. First, given a relatively fixed association between means and ends, any given action will require a particular level of intensity of will for the specified action to take place. An analogy would be flipping a switch—it's either on or off, the action either took place or it did not. In the second instance, no fixed relationship is perceived to exist between the means and the end. Here one might assume a more complex set of possible actions in which various levels of human determination become associated with different means to achieve the desired end state, for example, "How badly do you want it?" or "If you want it badly enough, you will figure out a way to get it."

In part, the means-ends relationships undergird the distinction made by Tönnies between natural and rational will. For example, in very stable and tradition-bound societies, there are relatively fixed ways of doing things, clearly established means for achieving a specified end—"This is the way we have always done it." In less traditional or in modern (open) societies, there are more options available to secure a desire or an end state. Simply put, natural will is associated with the relatively fixed connections between means and ends and rational will with those situations where alternative means are available to secure a given want.

It would be useful to pause at this point and identify some of the contributions made by Tönnies that have aided our definition and conceptualization of the social group. Here Tönnies's use of the social relationship to contrast the origins of human actions (will) and the expression and purpose of will in human association is useful. According to Tönnies, the patterned social relationships that comprise the social group result from natural will and are an expression of the mutual dependence humans have on one another and on their environment. This natural dependence is manifested and fulfilled by mutual performance—nothing more, nothing less. Here, in its strictest sense, is the purest example of the origin of relationships that result in the forming of social groups.

Using Tönnies's concepts and our definition, the social group arises out of those human needs associated with the expression of natural will, and the resulting relationships are Gemeinschaft in nature. The intimacy, the sentiments, the person-to-person nature of the relationship among group members have as their central function the affirmation of each person's existence as a human being. It is in this sense that these Gemeinschaft relationships serve as both a means and an end. Later in this section we will be building on Tönnies's concepts of natural will and Gemeinschaft to establish the position that the social group is the medium through which each person develops an identity as a person.

In other words, it is the Gemeinschaft relationship form rooted in natural will that is the primary medium of socialization in the young. It is through Gemeinschaft forms of relationships that an individual's sense of selfhood is initially developed. It is later in development that Gesellschaft types of relationships have their impact.

One final point needs to be made before moving on, and that pertains to Tönnies' use of the term **mutuality**.[8] Mutuality means to hold the same feelings each toward the other. This feature of mutuality, the sharing of sentiments, characterizes or is a condition of a Gemeinschaft relationship. We point this out because of the importance of the concept of mutuality as a necessary condition for a professional helping relationship. Tönnies's work represents one of the origins of this concept as applied to a therapeutic or helping relationship. In short, it is a relationship state in which the client and worker share a common or mutual sense of and respect for each other as human beings. It is through this capacity that the worker and client are able to achieve a common definition of the problem, a course of action to be followed, and a goal to be achieved. Recall also that the concept of mutuality includes the provision that the relationship can achieve its mutual intention only through mutual performance. Forming the professional relationship, which is essentially Gesellschaft by its contractual nature, incorporates Gemeinschaft features as necessary conditions for the achievement of its goals. This notion of mutuality as used by Tönnies serves as an example of how knowledge gained in the study of natural groups has applications to formed groups, such as the professional helping relationship.

Primary and Secondary Groups

The term **primary group** was coined by Charles Horton Cooley (1864–1929), an American social psychologist, and appeared in his first major work, *Human Nature and the Social Order.*[9] As with Tönnies, Cooley developed an evolutionary conception of social organization. Like other social scientists of their time, both were influenced by the rapid social changes associated with the industrial revolution, urbanization, bureaucratization, and centralization. Unlike Tönnies, Cooley focused his attention at the individual level, being interested in how the individual's personality was formed and in the general interplay between society and the individual. Cooley's evolutionary point of view followed two channels, the hereditary or physical origins and the social origins of human nature. He was strongly influenced by Charles Darwin in his evolutionary views of the "physical channel in human development,"[10] but it was his reasoning and the conceptual development of the social origins of human nature for which we are more indebted. Also to be noted was Cooley's focus on the wholeness of the human, physical, spiritual, and social spheres; each comprises a part of the whole. In introducing you to the notion of wholeness and order, we used the words of the poet John Donne, "No man is an island, entire of itself." Cooley introduces his idea of wholeness when applied to the human mind and social organization in a somewhat similar and thoughtful way:

> Mind is an organic whole made up of cooperating individualities, in somewhat the same way that the music of an orchestra is made up of divergent but related sounds. No one would think it necessary or reasonable to divide the music into two kinds, that made by the whole and that of particular instruments, and no more are there two kinds of mind, the social mind and the individual mind. When we study the social mind we merely fix our attention on larger aspects and relations rather than on the narrower ones of ordinary psychology.[11]

Cooley's sense of wholeness and the relationship of the individual to society is fully consistent with the systems notions being developed in this chapter, and in this sense we view Cooley's work as making a significant contribution to modern systems thinking.

Cooley's conceptualization has provided a useful point of departure for the development of our approach in defining and modeling the social group. Of central importance is Cooley's contention that the primary group provides the medium through which the human personality is formed and subsequently supported. It is Cooley's work that helps operationalize an assumption that comprises in part our social systems perspective. The assumption is that the individual is both the cause and the effect of all forms of human groupings. While Maslow's work in formulating need theory helped in dealing with the cause portion of the assumption, it was Cooley who dealt with the effect portion. In short, his position is that the primary group comprises the individual's earliest form of human association, typically the family or its surrogate. It is through this primary group association that the infant learns those specific behaviors, values, and other attributes that constitute humanness. In a larger sense, the child is able to learn and exchange meanings through the acquisition of language. Through language the child is able to form a sense of those around him or her and to evolve a sense of self. While the process of the child's development of language was not described in any definitive sense by Cooley, he viewed the process as an internalization of members of the group through some form of psychological or image representation. Out of these representations, the child is able to differentiate external objects, people, and things, as well as a sense of selfhood. The family is just one of the primary groups that constitute the social mediums through which the child and later the adult acquire humanness and a sense of self. While Cooley stressed the importance of the family as providing the critical primary group experience, it is just one of the many group experiences through which the human is socialized and through which personal development takes place throughout life. Cooley summarized his position as follows:

> It is the nature which is developed and expressed in those simple, face to face groups that are somewhat alike in all societies; groups of the family, the playground, and the neighborhood. In the essential similarity of these is to be found the basis, in experience, for similar ideas and sentiments in the human mind. In these, everywhere human nature comes into existence. Man does not have it at birth; he cannot acquire it except through fellowship, and it decays in isolation.[12]

Cooley's general thesis of the primary group and its relationship to personality formation has served as a useful point of departure for many writers. We generally agree with the thesis, and it has assisted us in developing our definition of the social group. Cooley's writings also serve as an important foundation for other assumptions we make about the social group and its function. These assumptions are as follows:

1. The social group is a universal form of social organization and is thus found in all societies and throughout recorded history.
2. The social group derives its basic character and form from the individuals who comprise it; but as a social entity, it is not explainable in terms of the sum of its members. It is more. It possesses emergent properties that become evident only through the relationships people have with each other.
3. Individuals derive their essential and common attributes of humanness through participation in social groups.
4. Humanness is both socially acquired and supported. It is a dynamic state of being and must be sustained by social interactions throughout the life cycle.
5. Ego, self, and personhood each represent the notion of a socially acquired identity. In short, it is a specific embodiment and expression of what is generally meant by

humanness. The uniqueness of the human personality results from a dynamic interplay of its physical, spiritual, and social dimensions, which are manifested and affected by the situational context.

These assumptions form ongoing themes that will be developed in later sections of this book. They also serve as important components of the foundation upon which the systems model is based, particularly as the model is applied to the social group.

SUMMARY

In this chapter, a definition of the social group has been offered, along with assumptions underlying this definition. We have concentrated on the works and key concepts of Ferdinand Tönnies and Charles Horton Cooley. These two theorists have been identified not only because of their historical significance but also because their key concepts remain today as important foundations to the study of all forms of human association including the social group. It is important for the reader to understand that there were many other earlier writers who might have been cited—Durkheim, Simmel, Dewey, and others. Our choice of theorists stems from a belief that future practitioners find it useful to deal with those whose seminal contributions are deemed central to the systems model.

We have also introduced in this chapter several additional concepts that are useful in thinking about characteristics seen in human relationships. These characteristics have helped form the foundations for the simple classification of social organizations used in this book. Gemeinschaft refers to those features of relationships having their origins in the basic social nature of humans. Gesellschaft can be usefully viewed as the polar opposite of Gemeinschaft relationship characteristics. We are in no way suggesting that you think in terms of good and bad; rather as natural and formed. By Gesellschaft, we refer to relationships that are contractual and voluntarily entered into to accomplish some mutually agreed-upon goal. These so-called formed groups have become necessary in a world that is growing ever more complex and impersonal, and changing ever more rapidly. It is these formed groups that do much of the work that is required to maintain our society. Gemeinschaft and Gesellschaft provide a way of examining and contrasting relationship features possessed in all forms of social organization.

Primary and secondary groups represent one of the earliest and most important efforts at classifying social organizations. For us, the classification scheme deals with how the basic qualities of humanness are transmitted and supported, and on how we as humans deal with our dependence upon each other.

While largely abandoned in the modern social science literature, we also introduced the notion of will as used by Ferdinand Tönnies. Understanding his use of the term is necessary in order to follow his thinking about human relationships. Also of importance in our view is a meaning associated with will; a proactive capacity contained within each person, that is, a "will" to live. We do not wish to argue pro or con on a doctrine of vitalism. Our argument is only directed toward support of a conception of humans that provides a proactive rather than a reactive stance in a search for understanding human behavior within a social environment.

GLOSSARY

Cathected A relationship or an object invested with emotional energy (feeling).

Formed group A group that is consciously created to perform tasks as the means used to accomplish a goal.

Gemeinschaft A type of relationship that is informal, personal, and entered into for its own sake (as opposed to a Gesellschaft relationship).

Gesellschaft A type of relationship that is formal, impersonal, contractual, and entered into as a means to another end (as opposed to a Gemeinschaft relationship).

Mutuality A sense of being mutual; two or more people holding comparable feelings toward each other. Within a helping relationship, it is the capacity of the worker and client to possess a sense of being mutual.

Natural group A group that is self-organizing as opposed to being consciously created. Natural groups and social groups are synonymous.

Natural will As used here, a view held by Tönnies of human volition based in one's basic (inherited) nature.

Primary groups Groups that form naturally and are based on the affiliation needs possessed by humans. They are primary groups in the sense that they are most important and the first form taken in human associations.

Rational will As used by Tönnies, human actions in which thinking and logic have gained dominance.

Secondary groups A loose categorization of all forms of human groups not considered primary. See Primary group.

NOTES

1. Aristotle, *Politics*, c. 328 B.C.

2. Abraham H. Maslow, *Motivation and Personality*, 2nd ed. (New York: Harper and Row, 1970), 77–95.

3. Ibid.

4. The position that social behavior is learned behavior is held in one form or another by a number of different theorists, particularly those classified as learning theorists. For a useful review of this position, see William C. Crain, *Theories of Development: Concepts and Applications* (Englewood Cliffs, N.J.: Prentice Hall, 1980).

5. Ferdinand Tönnies, *Community and Society*, ed. and trans. Charles P. Loomis (Lansing, Michigan: Michigan State University Press, 1957), 247–259.

6. Ibid., 247.

7. Ibid.

8. Ibid., 247–259.

9. Charles Horton Cooley, *Human Nature and the Social Order*, rev. ed. (New York: Charles Scribner's Sons, 1922), 32.

10. Ibid., 23–25.

11. Charles Horton Cooley, *Social Organization* (New York: Charles Scribner's Sons, 1909), 3.

12. Ibid., 30.

Chapter 6

The Social Group: Theoretical Support

OUTLINE

Practice in Search of Theory

In this chapter we identify those lines of theory development that help in the application of the social systems model to what we have defined as the social group. In the previous chapter we noted that the social group is the building block for the more complex forms of social organization, that is, the so-called formal organization, such as a social agency. Just as the individual is the component from which the social group is formed, so is the social group the component out of which higher, more complex types of social organization are either formed, or at least in part, comprised.

From a social systems perspective, this notion of higher forms of order developing from the adding of new member components and their resulting relationships is sometimes referred to as the emergent characteristic possessed by social systems.[1] In effect, the notion of emergence is related to the assumption that the whole is greater than the sum of its parts. In our approach to the study of the group, our position is that the group is a whole, an entity unto itself. In other words, when individuals form a group, something new emerges, something apart from the sum of the individuals who comprise it.

From the beginnings of social work, the group has been an area of professional concern, but practice has been hindered by the lack of a united theoretical approach.[2] In summarizing approaches to the development of group theory and research, Garvin identifies field theory, social exchange theory, and social systems theory as the main contributors.[3] We would add symbolic interaction theory to the list. Our approach to the study and understanding of the group builds on these theories, among others. In the pages ahead, we will be summarizing key features of exchange and symbolic interaction theory in terms of their use in the social systems model.

Exchange Theory

Central to a social systems perspective is the notion that all forms of social organization are comprised of interacting and interdependent parts. In developing a model of a social system intended to have practice relevance, it is insufficient simply to assume that the components are interactive and interdependent. The question is, why are they so? Perhaps an even more fundamental question is, how does social interaction get started? While there are no final answers to such questions, **exchange theory** offers an avenue of explanation that we have found useful. It is also one of the oldest theories of social behavior and perhaps the most straightforward. This latter characteristic makes it particularly appealing to students who are searching for the relevance of theory to practice.

Tönnies can again be helpful in setting forth the conceptual foundations of exchange theory. In drawing the distinction between natural and rational will and the resulting Gemeinschaft and Gesellschaft forms of relationships he observed:

> However, when I become conscious of my most urgent needs and find that I can neither satisfy them of my own volition nor out of natural relation, this means that I must do something to satisfy my need; that is, engage in free activity which is bound only by the requirement or possibly conditioned by the need but not by consideration for other people. Soon I perceived that I must work on other people in order to influence them to deliver or give something to me which I need . . . However, as a rule when one is not receiving something in a Gemeinschaft-like relationship, such as from within the family, one must earn or buy it by labor, service or money. . . . I now enter or have already entered into a social relationship, but it is of a different kind. Its prototype is barter or exchange. . . .[4]

As suggested by Tönnies, exchange theory appears to have its clearest application in the explanation of social organizations in which Gesellschaft relationships dominate. Our position is, however, that every social organization possesses both Gemeinschaft and Gesellschaft features and that exchange theory has applications to all forms of social organization possessing system features.

Exchange theory has its conceptual foundations in the needs that humans have for one another with exchange being the medium through which need satisfaction occurs. Because of the recurring nature of many human needs (for example, survival, safety, and social needs), individuals have an incentive to stabilize and perpetuate those exchange arrangements that are deemed mutually satisfying, useful, or otherwise necessary. Simply put, this process of stabilizing and providing continuity to these relationships results in social organization. From this perspective, the basic notions of the universality of human needs and the process of social exchange offer an important avenue for the explanation and explication of human interdependence.

The social systems model has a functional orientation, meaning that a social system can be understood by examining its effects on other social systems and vice versa. Recall that the systems model is premised on output and input exchanges between systems—the task output of every system represents a task input to other systems in its suprasystem. We believe that exchange theory offers a useful way of explicating these output-input relationships, by treating them as a form of exchange. Similarly, by examining these exchange arrangements and their effect on each other we can better understand why social organizations behave as they do and can construct a model that incorporates these behaviors.

In exchange theory, things possessing value are exchanged between the participating parties. These things can range from goods and services to sentiments and emotional supports. Items are exchanged that are perceived to have comparable value. The processes of exchange should not be thought of as a precise, conscious, calculation of the value of this versus that. In some instances this may be the case (for example, in the purchase of an object from a store), but what is being described is a much more general, unprecise, social process in which human emotional as well as logical considerations are involved in the assignment of worth.

The following example should help develop some of the basic notions behind exchange theory. On the first day of class, June Edwards and Margaret Rabovsky along with about thirty other students are in the process of introducing themselves. The professor has suggested that in their introductions, each take a moment to share with others why they are seeking a career in social work, what their current employment status is, if any, and what kind of professional position they will seek upon graduation. In introducing herself, Margaret indicates that she is from out of state and while not currently employed will need to find a part-time job to help meet school expenses. She explained that in her hometown of Columbus, Ohio, she had served as a volunteer at a school for the mentally retarded and hoped eventually to work professionally with physically and mentally handicapped children.

After class, June sought Margaret out and explained that she is currently working part time as a recreation aide at a children's convalescence center and that she understands there is an opening for another part-time aide. "It only pays minimum wage, but the staff is real nice and the kids are great. If you're interested, I can tell you who to call." "Am I!" was Margaret's response. She went on to say that she was recently divorced and while not getting assistance from her former husband she was being helped by her parents. "I am temporarily living with them and they are helping with tuition and books until I can get back on my feet." Margaret thanked June for the job lead and was anxious to know more about the work. It was getting close to noon and June said, "What are you doing for lunch? If you're not busy, we can talk about the job."

In the above example, we have a group of strangers meeting in their first social work class. Given their mutual interest in social work and the time they are going to spend in classes together, it seems inevitable that friendships among many of them will evolve. At issue is how social interaction gets started in the first instance—what is the "starting mechanism." Obviously there are a myriad of ways, but according to exchange theory there is a foundation principle—something is given of "value" by the person initiating the interaction to another. There is then the general expectation that the person who was the recipient will respond with something of comparable value. It is like returning something of comparable value to stay out of debt. Exchange theorists are not suggesting that the people engaging in social interaction are necessarily conscious about contemplating the exchange in these terms. They are saying that an examination of human interaction suggests that social exchange is a basic dynamic. In our example, June offers Margaret information about a possible job, a very helpful and courteous act. Margaret gratefully acknowledges the important information by thanking June. Margaret's acknowledgement made June feel good about herself and glad that she had taken the time to share the job information.

From the position taken in exchange theory, June, in supplying the information to Margaret, would hold an expectation that it would be gratefully or at least courteously received. In short, there was the expectation that a response would be made by Margaret and that the response would have value to June. In this instance, the grateful response by Margaret fulfilled June's expectation and confirmed her own sense of being a helpful and caring person. Margaret increased the value of her response to June by sharing information about her recent divorce and the role her parents are playing in helping her restructure her life. Margaret did not have to add anything about her personal life in her response to a stranger. By doing so, she further confirmed the value of June's information and in effect invited another response. June found Margaret's response confirming to her own sense of selfhood but also started to form a "first impression" of Margaret; it was a positive impression of someone that she might want to get to know better. She may have thought to herself, "Margaret seems to be an awfully nice person, it would be helpful if she could get a job out at the center. I bet the kids would love her."

The two did have lunch together. In the course of their conversation June shared more about the job with Margaret. In the exchange, each began sharing a bit more about themselves. The next day they sat next to each other in class and Margaret said that she had called the center for a job interview. What we have in the interactions between June and Margaret is the possible start of a personal friendship, a two-person group. If one does form, we would refer to it as a natural group. Its origins are found in the social needs that all people have for one another. Such a group would conform to our definition: "A form of social organization comprised of two or more members who identify and interact with one another on a personal basis as individuals, possess a shared sense of the group as a social entity, are affected by the group-related actions of members, and in which expressive (natural) actions dominate."

The conversations and other interactions between June and Margaret are common-place and occur throughout our lifetimes. Sometimes they are represented by a single exchange, some are continued on a casual basis, and a few result in the formation of a group. Our interest in exchange theory is that it offers an explanation of how social organizations form, an explanation having very wide application. Perhaps equally important, it also offers an explanation of why they don't form. For example, in the above exchange, consider what might have happened if Margaret's response had not met June's expectation, if Margaret had not "gratefully" received the information, but had responded: "A recreation aide, I'm not that hard up yet, but thanks!" Such a response would not only depreciate the value of June's information, but June herself, because she works as a recreation aide. We can surmise, based on this latter exchange, that the two would not have had lunch together. We might also guess that June would not be particularly interested in sitting next to Margaret in class.

The position being developed here is that social exchange can be viewed as representing a universal principle undergirding social life. It thus offers a framework for examining human social behavior at all levels. Here we need to be careful; we are not suggesting that the notion of exchange can explain all social behavior. We are saying that the notion of social exchange can be a useful and beginning building block for the study of social behavior. How does interaction lead to the kind of social relationships that comprise social groups? Exchange theory offers a way to help answer that question.

Before moving on, one additional point needs to be made. While our interest is in identifying the patterns that are common to the various forms of social organization, we are all individuals and as such we must not forget that in special ways we are all different from one another. It is the science of psychology which helps us understand these individual differences. June and Margaret are distinct human personalities. June sought Margaret out to talk with her. She did not have to do this; it was a voluntary act on her part. Margaret responded in a positive and enthusiastic manner. Again, this was a voluntary response on Margaret's part. Here we are not concerned with a psychological understanding of June or Margaret. Our focus instead is on understanding the interaction or the social exchange between June and Margaret. We might summarize this point by identifying another underlying assumption in exchange theory. People make choices in what they do and what they don't do, with whom they associate and with whom they do not associate. They choose among alternatives based on expected benefits related to their own needs, past experiences, and the range of options they believe are open to them. In short, people choose among alternative courses of action as they perceive them. The notion of "as they perceive them" is critical because it represents an appraisal of what is of value to them.

With our example of June and Margaret serving as a background, let us examine some of the ideas of those who have set forth the basic tenets of exchange theory.

Perhaps more than any other social scientist, George C. Homans is associated with the development of, and current interest in, exchange theory.[5] His approach to formulating exchange theory borrows heavily on behaviorist principles. Unlike many of his colleagues in sociology, Homans's interest was in the small group as opposed to the large and more complex types of social organization. Homans felt that understanding the more elementary forms of social organization would help in understanding the more complex forms—large formal organizations and societies. In other words, he believed that investigations of the small group could be used as the building blocks for helping to understand the behaviors of people and other social units in larger forms of social organization. Even more basic is Homans's belief that psychological generalizations are an important component of sociological explanations. Operating from this perspective, he frequently reminded his colleagues that no human form of social organization exists that is not comprised of individuals, and therefore sociological analysis should always consider individuals and their fundamental patterns of behavior.[6] This position by Homans is similar to the one we hold and accounts for the basic organization of this book.

One of the criticisms of exchange theory is its vocabulary; for example, the use of terms such as costs, benefits, and rewards. For many it sounds as though an economically based model is being used as a major explanation for social behavior. Given such an interpretation, many find the approach troublesome. Homans commented on this general reluctance by his colleagues to acknowledge the importance of exchange in the development of sociological theory:

In our unguarded moments we sociologists find words like "reward" and "costs" slipping into what we say. Human nature will break in upon even our most elaborate theories. But we seldom let it have its way with us and follow up systematically what these words imply. Of all our many "approaches" to social behavior the one that sees it as an economy is the most neglected, and yet it is the one we use every moment of our lives—except when we write sociology.[7]

A summary of the central propositions of exchange theory as set forth by Homans follows:

1. Social behavior is essentially based on an exchange of things possessing value. These things can be material or symbolic; for example, goods, services, or sentiments.
2. The provision of something of value from one person to another, when accepted (the initiation of a relationship) by the other, creates an obligation to reciprocate. The provision of something of value in return completes the first cycle of the exchange transaction.
3. The exchange process, once initiated, tends toward a balance—the exchange of things possessing similar value as perceived by those involved in the exchange. In short, the balance in terms of relative value becomes the central force in maintaining the equilibrium of the social interaction. It is through such a process that social organization is formed and maintained.
4. An exchange always involves both a cost and a reward to each person. Derived from this is the assumption that the relationship will be continued as long as the perceived costs of the exchange over time do not exceed its rewards, or that a more advantageous alternative is not available.
5. Dynamically, each person in the exchange seeks to maximize his or her return (reward less costs will equal the return).[8]

According to Homans, these general propositions of exchange are the basis for the development of social structure in small groups. Similarly, it becomes possible to derive more specific propositions from these as to how people behave in a small group. For example, in the third proposition, Homans argues that a person will try to see that no other person in a group secures greater profit (satisfaction). In other words, the group will tend toward a dynamic state of "balance" characterized by a sense of equity or fairness in exchange.

Before proceeding, we want to comment on the criticism that exchange theory appears to build off of an economic conception of social behavior. Costs, rewards, and benefits are certainly key concepts in economic theory and perhaps more useful words can be found to describe the dynamics of social exchange. For us, it appears more likely that economic theory has its origins in the fundamental patterns undergirding exchange relationships among humans, such as bartering. In short, it seems more likely that economic theory has its origins in basic human patterns of exchange, and represents an attempt at the rationalization of exchange relationships and their dynamics that extends beyond individuals to ever larger systems.

There are also reductionist and linear thinking traps to be avoided. Our interest in this section is the social group and the search is for a line of theory development that will help us better understand how social groups form and grow. Our contention is that social exchange theory can be useful in this regard. We will also be using the notion of exchange as we examine the behaviors of larger and more complex forms of social organization, for example, the formal organization. Such forms of exchange are not merely the extension of the forms of exchange found in social groups. These larger forms of social organization possess emergent features that will affect the dynamics of exchange.

It is useful to conceive of exchange theory as encompassing a wide range and multiple forms of exchange, from simple to complex. Also it is important not to limit the notion of exchange to just one set of activities, but rather to view it as a core event or set of events that frequently is associated with a range of supporting or related activities. Another more complex example can help develop this point. Susan and Bob are in marital therapy because of increasing interpersonal and sexual difficulties. Susan complains that she gets little pleasure out of their sexual relationship, and since she has gone to work, there have been increased interpersonal difficulties between her and Bob. These difficulties seem to center on how routine household duties are handled. Bob indicates that their sexual relationship had been quite good until recently, or at least as far as he was concerned. Now, he complains that Susan is always finding excuses, "She is too tired, has a headache — it's just one excuse after another." Bob also argues that many of their arguments start over simple things "like who does what around the house — and then it's downhill from there — we end up screaming at each other."

Bob and Susan married when she was a sophomore and he was a senior in college. Upon graduating, Bob found an excellent position as an accountant. Susan quit school to become a housewife. The first two years of marriage were fine, with Susan staying home taking care of the house and generally supporting her husband's career. She then became restless and generally bored, finally deciding to go back to school to complete her social work education. Following graduation she took a professional position in a child protective agency. Just as she was feeling better as a person, troubles started to increase with Bob. While on the surface Bob was supportive of her return to school and the pursuit of a career, he became annoyed at the demands her job placed on their home and personal life. For example, Susan occasionally had to respond during evenings and weekends to emergencies that arose in her work. Also, Bob complained about the TV dinners and that the house was always a mess. Susan, in turn, complained that Bob had promised to help more around the house after she returned to work, but in effect he still expected her to prepare meals and do most of the housework. As their personal tensions developed, she found their sexual relationship less and less satisfying. She also felt that Bob was becoming more demanding sexually, and "this has turned me off." From an exchange theory perspective, Susan and Bob's earlier relationship was typified by an exchange in which Susan's needs for economic and emotional security were provided by Bob. In exchange, she met his sexual and esteem needs through her supportive role as a wife and sexual partner. For a couple of years there was balance to this exchange. But as Susan became more self-confident and economically self-sufficient through her educational and professional achievements, the balance shifted, and the economic and emotional security provided by Bob became less important (possessed less value). Also, Susan found less pleasure in attempting to satisfy Bob sexually, developing the feeling that he was far less attentive to her sexual needs than she was of his. Their personal and situational needs changed, but there was not a corresponding shift in the way they responded to each other's needs. Unless Susan and Bob are able to adjust to each other's needs and establish a new working balance in this exchange, their marriage is likely to end in divorce.

The example makes several points. First, exchange relationships can become quite complex, forming a core around which many related activities revolve. Second, exchange relationships are dynamic in the same sense as the social organizations of which they are a part; these relationships are constantly changing, constantly developing. Once focused there is a strain toward balance in the exchanges but there are counter strains toward imbalance which we will soon discuss. Finally, and as suggested by Homans, social exchange has both its costs and its rewards. In our example, Susan is beginning to sense that the costs of her relationship are exceeding its rewards. The same thing is happening to Bob. Their marriage is in danger, and thus their mutual recognition of the need for help in the form of marital therapy. In the language of the model, steady state is being threatened.

Peter Blau has also made important contributions to the development of exchange theory. Unlike Homans, who concentrated his attention on the small group and simple levels of social organization, Blau focused on larger and more formally constituted social organizations.[9] While Gesellschaft types of relationships tend to dominate in such structures, we have found his writings helpful and applicable to the social group as well. Of particular help is Blau's attention to four processes comprising exchange: (1) transaction; (2) differentiation; (3) stabilization; and (4) organization.[10] We will review these processes and will conceptualize the first three of these processes as stages in group development. The last process identified by Blau is of somewhat different character from the other three and pertains to the view of exchange as a more general process leading to the creation of larger forms of social organization, for example, formal organizations. We will focus on the first three processes, which have more relevance to the social group.

Transaction

Transaction, the initiating phase of a social relationship, can be viewed as having its origins in the needs of the individual, and it is through interactions with others that need fulfillment occurs. In the most fundamental sense, exchange is rooted in self-interest—a person initiates interaction by giving something to another with the expectation of getting something needed in return. In an absolute sense, it is not necessary to assume any cultural or normative supports for the transaction process.[11] In other words, human interdependence is so fundamental to human survival that exchange becomes a medium to deal with survival issues. Culture can be viewed as developing in part out of this basic human interdependence and through the mechanism of exchange. There is a general cultural norm of reciprocity that is supportive of exchange. We will be treating reciprocity as does Gouldner, as a universal norm evident in one form or another in all cultures and throughout recorded history.[12] The universality of this norm can be understood in terms of its importance in the origins and support of a variety of forms of social structure. The norm of reciprocity is reflected in such Biblical assertions as "Do unto others as you would have them do unto you." While we will be focusing on the positive features of exchange as an approach to explaining social organization, there is a negative side that must be acknowledged, as in the familiar saying, "An eye for an eye and a tooth for a tooth."

The premise supporting the transaction phase is that the initiating person hopes that the offer of something of value to another will be accepted and thereby create a sense of obligation on the other to return something of comparable value. Each person is satisfying the other through an exchange, and through this process a social structure is created that will serve as a guide for subsequent exchanges. It should be noted that if the receiving person does not respond or offers something of less than the expected value, the relationship is likely either not to get started in the first instance or at least will be off to a shaky start. If the receiving person does respond and offers something of comparable value in return, then the counterpart of the original premise is established. Given the success of the first transaction, the conditions are established upon which subsequent exchanges can occur. Here, we have the possible start of a social group, whether it be two, three, ten or more people. Something new is being created. Its unity is in the relationship that binds those participants together in an interdependent way. Those participating in the exchanges are in effect producing something of use to each other. There is a subtlety involved, and it is seen most clearly in social groups, those in which Gemeinschaft features dominate. The exchange transactions among members create a level of interdependence that takes on a separate character. Not only do the members involved in exchange transactions derive something of value through their relationship with one another, but they also obtain something of value from a new entity being formed, a group; and thus a **synergic** effect in need satisfaction occurs. It should be noted that during this initial transaction phase, the relationships among those participating in the exchange are very fragile. Our earlier example of June and Margaret was intended to illustrate the transaction phase of social exchange.

Olsen, in reviewing Blau's work, identifies three principles associated with the transaction phase:

1. The greater the probability that a potential exchange transaction will prove more rewarding (benefits equal or greater than costs) to an actor, the more likely one is to initiate it.
2. The greater an actor's obligations to reciprocate for benefits previously received from another, the more likely that actor is to complete an exchange transaction.
3. An exchange relationship will be perpetuated as long as it proves rewarding to the participants, they have no other more attractive alternatives, and their needs and goals remain unsatisfied.[13]

The reader can safely make the assumption that in real life few exchanges get beyond the transaction phase on their way to a social group.

Differentiation

The notion of power plays a central role in the way Blau conceptualizes social exchange.[14] Given the premise that humans depend on one another for satisfaction of a variety of different needs, exchange theory becomes a way of conceptualizing the dynamics of this interdependence. Blau makes the point that the relative dependence that people have on one another can be viewed in terms of the influence or power that people have over one another. In other words, "Your need of what I have (your dependence on me) represents my power over you." Similarly, "what you have that I need (my dependence on you) represents your power over me." Assuming that the individuals entering into an exchange do so voluntarily, the transaction phase of the exchange process is marked by a balance. Here balance refers to the perceptions held by those involved in the exchange that the exchange is fair, that is, what the person is receiving through the exchange (relationship) is at least equal to what he or she is giving. If this were not the case, the exchange would not have been entered into in the first instance, or if an initial exchange proved disappointing from a balance perspective, it would not be continued.

Olsen is helpful in developing the notion of balance from a power perspective. From this position social exchange can be treated as balanced reciprocal influence characterized by: (1) voluntariness—each individual chooses to participate or not in the exchange; (2) stability—a stable pattern of exchange develops and persists over time; (3) *equity*—each participant perceives a sense of equality in relation to the other person(s) involved in the exchange; and (4) distributive justice—at any given time, the balance between what is given and received may not be equal, but over time it will even out.[15]

Given the changing needs of people and the differential access individuals have to resources, there is always a possibility that the exchange transaction will evolve from balanced reciprocal influence to unbalanced. In keeping with the name, **differentiation**, given this process, the exchange transactions will tend to become "differentiated" relative to the power possessed by each member over others involved in the exchange. Blau makes the point as follows:

> By supplying services in demand to others, a person establishes power over them. If he regularly renders needed services they cannot readily obtain elsewhere, others become dependent on and obligated to him for these services, and unless they can furnish other benefits to him that produce interdependence by making him equally dependent on them, their unilateral dependence obligates them to comply with his request lest he ceases to continue to meet their needs.[16]

When an exchange becomes unbalanced, or loses one or more of the previously defined characteristics of balance, one of several things may occur. Given other alternative sources of need satisfaction, the most likely outcome is for the exchange to be terminated. Perhaps of greater theoretical interest are those relationships that continue in some unbalanced form. The notion of balance (or what we choose to call steady state) suggests stability. Becoming unbalanced indicates instability. Thus, inquiry based on a social power perspective into unbalanced forms of exchange becomes a way of investigating destabilizing forces in social groups. For example, when one member of a group becomes more powerful than the other(s), for whatever reason, and the one(s) with lesser power remain(s) dependent on the more powerful one, the conditions exist for a coercive or exploitive relationship to develop. If this should occur, conflict is likely to result. One example would be a woman who is physically abused by her husband. From an exchange perspective, the relationship may initially have been in balance, with both enjoying the friendship, love, sexual behavior, and other qualities. But say that the husband, through his work, has had opportunities for other friendships and liaisons with other women. Because of this, these resources from his wife lose some of their value to him. She, in turn, by being confined to the house and not working, becomes more dependent on him but possesses diminished resources for exchange. Simply put, the exchanges become unbalanced. Tensions increase between the two, finally resulting in the husband physically assaulting his wife. The wife, who is without a job and without other family, is essentially without options. To call the police or to seek help is, from an exchange perspective, to place herself in even greater jeopardy, by risking the loss of economic security and whatever is left of the personal relationship with her husband. As we know from our own practices and from newspaper accounts, the woman's situation becomes desperate and sometimes desperate actions are taken.

Once an exchange transaction becomes unbalanced, Olsen suggests there will be a tendency on the part of the more powerful individual to maintain and otherwise to take advantage of the weaker one(s). The point here is that by capitalizing on the advantage, the more powerful individual secures his or her advantage and avoids the added costs of a balanced exchange. In this connection Olsen states the principle involved as follows: "To the extent that a relationship becomes unbalanced as a result of power differentiation and cannot be rebalanced in some manner, it will be transformed from reciprocal influence exchange to coercive control exertion."[17]

Before leaving the differentiation process as set forth by Blau and Olsen, we want to remind the reader of our preference for treating power as only one dimension of differentiation. Also, differentiation can be usefully treated as a phase in group development, one that will characterize development of all social groups as they move toward stabilization. Our position is that as the patterns of exchange become ongoing, role differentiation is an inevitable feature of the exchange process. Each person brings something to the group that is exchanged with that brought by others. A series of expectations is developed among those comprising the exchange. These sets of mutual expectations become the normative features of the roles comprising the exchange relationship. In a balanced reciprocal exchange, the values of these role features are essentially equivalent. Each person in the group is different in the sense that he or she brings something valued by other group members. In exchange terms, they give something of themselves to another and in return receive something of comparable value or perhaps of greater value.

Stabilization

The third process in exchange theory is aptly named and refers to those developments that seek to firm up the exchange transaction and to limit the destabilizing forces, such as power inequities, for example, that come into play. Given previously stated properties and principles underlying exchange, the assumption is that all exchange relationships surviving the first two stages of development will move toward **stabilization**. Olsen summarized the three principal ways by which stabilization occurs as the development of: (1) mutual trust, (2) shared norms, and (3) leadership.[18]

Given the dominance of self-interest in the first or transaction phase and the potential for power differentiation in the second phase, it stands to reason that the stabilization phase of an exchange relationship would be associated with the development of mutual trust. At this point it is useful to draw a distinction between mutual trust as it might be developed in Gesellschaft as opposed to Gemeinschaft groups. In Gesellschaft relationships the exchange represents a means to the achievement of some end. In other words, the exchange is dominated by logic, in the sense that there is a calculation of the means and ends and a decision is made. An almost infinite number of such relationships is possible. They can involve a single transaction and thus be very short term (for example, buying an item at a garage sale), or they can involve multiple exchanges and last a lifetime (as could be the case in services received from the family physician).

Here an observation is in order about the transaction phase: The greater the value of that being exchanged, the greater the likelihood of some formal specification of the details of the exchange. For example, in a garage sale, money is likely to be exchanged for the item. There is no guarantee and no objective standard exists upon which to measure the value of the object, for example, an old set of glasses. Here individuals only enter into the exchange if they each agree on the value of that being exchanged. On the other hand, if an apartment is being leased (exchanged for money), there is a likelihood of a much more elaborate and formalized set of conditions surrounding the exchange; in most instances, there will be papers signed by the two parties that set forth in detail the rights and duties of each. In short, in Gesellschaft relationships in which items of significant value are involved, the matter of mutual trust tends to be dealt with by an explication of the conditions and terms of exchange agreement. This agreement is then evidenced by a signed contract. If a disagreement should later arise, the signed contract becomes the basis for resolution or subsequent legal action. The growing use of prenuptial agreements is another example in which Gesellschaft as well as Gemeinschaft features would exist in the exchange relationship.

In Gemeinschaft relationships, the exchange serves as an end in itself as opposed to being a means to an end. This distinction is important in understanding the dynamics involved, particularly as they pertain to the stabilization phase. Given this distinction, the notion of a formal contract specifying the conditions and terms of the exchange is antithetical to a Gemeinschaft relationship. In other words, exchanges involving relationships possessing significant Gemeinschaft features are likely to be much more open, vague, and perhaps risky. In essence, what is being exchanged is some part of the self, as, for example, in a developing friendship group. As a consequence, the early transaction phase is likely to be characterized by low-risk forms of exchange. From this same low-risk perspective, if in the differentiation phase the exchange is becoming unbalanced and is taking on coercive features, one can get out of the relationship before suffering significant losses.

It would seem to follow that in an exchange in which Gemeinschaft relationships dominate, there would be a tendency for such exchanges to start on a low-risk level. It would also seem to follow that such exchanges would tend to be recurring in nature, especially those necessary to the satisfaction of social belonging needs. Therefore, mutual trust would tend to develop over time through the process of mutuality in need fulfillment. This process would tend to be associated over time with ever greater risk being taken by the parties involved in the exchange. A practice example would be a counseling relationship with a client unable to pay a fee, or at least a full fee. Based on an exchange perspective, the client could be expected to be very cautious in the transactional phase.

There would be mutual testing behavior, with the client being especially wary because of having so little to offer in the exchange. Given the inability to pay a fee, the client also runs the risk of becoming involved in a coercive type of relationship, especially if the client is a nonvoluntary one, for example, a client sent to the agency by the court because of child abuse. Given this situation, one should expect a good bit of testing behavior, with mutual trust developing slowly.

At a more general level, Blau comments on the development of mutual trust as a feature of the stabilization process:

> By discharging their obligations for services rendered, if only to provide inducements for the supply of more assistance, individuals demonstrate their trustworthiness, and the gradual expansion of mutual service is accompanied by a parallel growth of mutual trust. Hence processes of social exchange, which may originate in pure self interest, generate trust in social relations through their current and gradual expanding character.[19]

Olsen identifies three norms central in the stabilization process: (1) reciprocity; (2) fairness; and (3) distributive justice.[20] The notion of reciprocity has been identified by a number of sociologists as central to all forms of social organization; for example, Simmel has noted "the reciprocity of service and return service" and that "all contacts among men rest on the schema of giving and returning equivalence."[21] Some authors would consider fairness and distributive justice features of a general norm of reciprocity,[22] but for our current purposes it is useful to consider fairness and distributive justice as norms in their own right. Reciprocity means a mutual exchange. The key notion is mutual, and by this the exchange is bound and judged by the idea that what was given and what was received have comparable value. It is a norm in the sense that the meaning or reciprocity has been internalized, and thus one is morally obliged to return to the giver something having equivalent value.

The notion of fairness in exchange, while similar to reciprocity, is not so much grounded in the idea of mutuality as it is to some objective measure of equity. In this sense, the exchange would be in keeping with some established measure of equivalence and would be seen so by an impartial third party.

Once an exchange is enacted and deemed beneficial, there are conflicting forces at play. Through the differentiation process the possibility exists for one or more of the participants to seek an advantage and gain control in the relationship. While holding certain advantages for the more powerful person, the disadvantage has to do with the instability that the imbalance introduces. Stabilizing forces come into play through mutually satisfying exchanges and the development of mutual trust. Furthermore, as we just pointed out, the sharing of such norms as reciprocity and fairness facilitates the stabilization process in exchange. The norm of distributive justice mentioned earlier refers to a shared belief held by those participating in the exchange that, while the exchanges that take place day by day may not be equivalent, they will balance out in the long term. An example here would be the husband who works and supports his wife while she pursues her graduate education in social work. The bargain they have is that once she gets her degree and obtains a professional position, she will support him as he goes back for his master's degree in elementary education. Here the exchange is unbalanced and one-sided for a period of time and then unbalanced on the other for another period. But in the longer term the couple mutually benefits—there has been distributive justice.

Exchange theorists assume that the stabilization phase in the development of social relationships is accompanied by the evolvement of leadership roles. In the discussion of the differentiation phase, the tendency for an exchange relationship to become unbalanced was noted. This unbalancing was viewed as a result of the greater power that one person has over the other(s) in the exchange relationship. Countering this unbalancing threat is the tendency by members involved in the exchange to assume leadership and follower roles. By this we mean that an influence structure will emerge in which certain people will be recognized for the usefulness of their ideas or behaviors in facilitating the exchange process and its outcomes. In the social group, this is an informal process. As we will see later when we talk about the formal organization, the influence structure will have both formal and informal features. At this point, it is important to recognize that leadership, whether formally or informally established, is a social process, and as such, its effects are only evident in the behavior of the people involved. To put it another way, leadership only works if the lead is followed, if others are influenced and behave in the expected manner. Here the notion of legitimacy is important and simply means that the leadership actions being exercised are followed. In other words, by following the leader's suggestions, the role of the leader is legitimated and confirmed. In relationship to the exchange process, the leadership function focuses on securing the kind of conditions that stabilize exchange transactions, such as guarding against development of power inequities. Olsen states the principle as follows: "Exchange relationships become stabilized through time to the extent that they develop mutual trust, shared norms and legitimate leadership."[23]

In this section we have summarized key assumptions, concepts, and principles of exchange theory. In so doing we have sought to identify a line of theory development having application to social groups and other forms of social organization as well. For us, the exchange paradigm is useful in thinking about how relationships form and social organizations develop. The paradigm also has utility in viewing suprasystem and social system relationships. The social systems model builds off a functional conception of social organization; it is through forms of input-output exchange that systems relate to others who comprise their suprasystems. Exchange theory offers an avenue for exploring and developing this notion of exchange both internally and between the system and its suprasystem.

Symbolic Interaction Theory

Just as with the other theories reviewed, there is no such thing as a theory of symbolic interaction; it is more useful to think of a general line of theory development referred to as symbolic interaction. It follows that there are a number of theorists who have made contributions to this line of reasoning. The two best known and most important are Charles Horton Cooley and George Herbert Mead. We also want to note at this point that there were several major social work theorists who made important contributions to the development of the theory of symbolic interaction. Best known among these contributors was Jane Addams.[24]

Earlier we cited the distinctions that Charles Horton Cooley drew between primary and secondary groups. Recall that Cooley contended that it is through the medium of primary groups, particularly the family, that the individual acquires her or his distinctive human characteristics.[25] Also it is through such groups that these human qualities are supported and developed throughout the life cycle. It was Cooley's efforts at explaining this position that laid the intellectual foundations for the theory of symbolic interaction. While Cooley's contributions are of great importance, the acknowledged founder of the theory of symbolic interaction was George Herbert Mead.[26] It should be noted that Mead did not term his view symbolic interaction, but rather social behaviorism. His choice of words is instructive. Mead found behaviorist theory of great help as he sought to understand and account for the social behavior of humans. His concern, though, was with its narrowness, its strict attention to directly observable behavior. Mead held that the individual possesses an inner life and an emotional or affective dimension to existence that was not adequately addressed by behaviorism. In many ways, a strict behavioral orientation is like paying attention only to that part of an iceberg showing above the water, the part that is directly observable. **Symbolic interaction theory**, while incorporating much of the social learning features of behaviorism, also gives attention to the inner life of the individual, what we might term the antecedents of behavior. Using the analogy of the iceberg, attention is given to what lies both above and below the surface.

The most comprehensive presentation of Mead's work is to be found in *Mind, Self, and Society*.[27] The book was published in 1934, three years after his death. It is based on class notes assembled by his students at the University of Chicago.

It should prove helpful for us to identify what we consider to be the assumptions that form the foundations of the theory of symbolic interaction.[28] These assumptions extend those that comprise our social systems perspective:

1. The distinctiveness of humans derives primarily from their capacity to think, to communicate their thoughts with others and to act in accordance with their thinking. This assumption holds that only humans possess this capacity.
2. Selfhood, the ability of the person to conceive of her- or himself as an object (possessing a separate and distinct personality) is socially acquired, supported and developed throughout life. While the capacity to develop a sense of selfhood is genetically based, the self has no antecedent existence within the organism.
3. The capacity to think and to communicate is based on the ability to learn, retain, and to purposively use an enormous amount of information. This information is in the form of conventional meanings attached to symbols. A symbol is nothing more than a name, a dictionary meaning given to something real or imagined. The systematic structuring of these symbols by people sharing the same general culture is what we refer to as language, for example, the English language.
4. The relationship of thinking, feeling and acting is dynamic and cyclical. Human social behavior is a social process in which the individual (self) initiates an action and by both the consciousness (awareness) of self and of others, controls and modifies that act through completion. That is to say, the social act is modified or ad-

justed as it is being carried out by the person. This is accomplished by the person (self) constantly interpreting the reactions and the behaviors of those actually comprising or otherwise exerting an effect on the social interaction.

5. It is through the capacity to think symbolically, to imagine future states, and to take action in pursuit of such imagined states that provides the proactive foundation (motivational source) for human social behavior. It is therefore assumed that the human has the capacity to form in her or his mind future states of existence, to share these states with others for purposes of mobilizing mutual or social action required to pursue such states. In ordinary terms we refer to this as *thinking*.

6. Just as the individual possesses the capacity to contemplate future states so do the various social organizations that humans join together to form. It is this capacity that accounts for the proactive nature of all forms of social organizations—the family, the formal organization, the community, and society. In short, when a family member enacts a family role, that person is acting for the family as a whole.

Symbolic interaction theory makes use of a series of concepts, many with familiar names, but very specialized meanings. Resting on the assumptions just noted, these concepts and their interrelationships form the building blocks of the theory. In the paragraphs ahead we will summarize the more important of these concepts.

Symbol

A **symbol** is something, typically a word, that represents something. For example, the word "tree" serves as a name of something that has existence in our environment. There is common agreement in our society and among others who use the English language on the meaning of tree. As a consequence we can communicate with one another about "trees." The word "tall" is also a symbol but is of a somewhat different order. It does not describe a specific entity but rather a characteristic of some entity. For example, one would not say "there is a tall." Rather the symbol "tall" helps to describe something: a tall tree, a tall woman, or a tall building, for instance. We have evolved, and continue to evolve, an extensive set of symbols to communicate with each other. Importantly, symbols are not just meanings assigned to sounds (words), but to marks, gestures, facial expressions, and body movements (body language) as well.

The fact of the matter is that we humans have assigned symbols to every aspect of our physical, social, psychological and spiritual environment. By so doing, we can communicate with one another about everything imaginable. According to symbolic interactionists, humans construct a representation of reality through their language. From this position, humans relate to one another primarily in terms of these commonly shared meanings. In the most fundamental sense, social interaction becomes symbolic interaction.

More so than most other theorists dealing with human behavior, the symbolic interactionist ties language and more generally symbolic exchanges to behavior. Given this tie and the importance of language, one starts to get a different perspective on those who are handicapped in their capacity to learn and to communicate. We are not referring only to those who may be mentally and physically impaired, but to all those who have limited learning (educational) opportunities or experiences.

Socialization

The concept of **socialization** means to become social and, by extension, to become like other people sharing the same culture. Simply put, to become socialized is to become human. More technically, socialization refers to the social process through which individuals learn and internalize the values, beliefs, attitudes, knowledge, skills and behaviors of their society. It is in and through the socialization process that one learns to use symbols personally and socially.

Most people think of socialization in terms of the very young. Perhaps the trials and tribulations of parents attempting to toilet train their spirited two year old gets across the general idea. People in our society use a toilet to dispose of their body wastes. It is a learned behavior and most parents take the task of teaching toilet training to their young quite seriously. The example of toilet training is instructive in understanding the state of tension that inevitably exists between an individual's natural strivings and the relentless and powerful forces of socialization. Examples are the protests and tantrums of a child not wanting to go to bed, or the later pressures being felt by many young women and men from their families to settle down and get married (as opposed to an unmarried life spent pursuing a professional career).

In symbolic interaction theory, the process of socialization is life long. The key notion is that it is the symbols of one's culture that are learned, internalized, and become the basis of who we are and what we do as social beings. For example, whether born into an American, African, or Asian family, the infant arrives with essentially the same genetic capacities. While we may all be very much alike and in this sense equal at birth, we are subjected to quite different social experiences throughout the remainder of our lives. These experiences shape us in very real ways and, from the symbolic interactionist point of view, we become a product (an output) of these experiences. To put the matter in other words, the same infant raised in three different families, in three different cultures (social environments) would have become three quite different persons. Similarly, gender and its meanings will be different in each culture and to some extent within each family. A female raised in three different families and in three different cultures would have become three quite different women. In a manner of speaking, just as one learns to become a physician or a social worker, so does one learn how to be white versus black, woman versus man, or American versus Japanese. We do not wish to minimize the biological and physiological differences among people. We only wish to say that through the process of socialization we attribute different meanings to these differences. These meanings are also constantly changing; the meaning of being a woman today is far different for most people than it was twenty or fifty years ago. For example, the sense of selfhood of the women reading this book today is likely to be quite different than that held by their own mothers or grandmothers. Similarly, their daughters and granddaughters will view themselves in their gender roles quite differently.

The point we wish to make is that one's genetic heritage is not a central issue in symbolic interaction theory. Rather there is an acknowledgement that one's genetic heritage sets some broad and important parameters to development. What is central is the social environment in which we are raised. It is this social environment that is given meaning as a symbolic environment and which in turn defines who we are and shapes our perceptions of reality throughout life. Just as this social environment is constantly changing, so will our socialization be continuous and change our conception of who we are throughout life. For example, your conception of yourself as a woman or man at age twenty-five is likely to be quite different than it will be at thirty-five, at fifty, and at seventy-five. In part, this is because in our culture we view people differently at different stages in life. These cultural differences affect the views we hold of ourselves at different stages in our development.

Socialization is a form of social learning. It is social in the sense that it is part of an interactional process. The process is also cyclical and its effects are mutual. With the infant the process starts at birth, the relationship that is initiated is frequently referred to as bonding. In the traditional family the parents have acquired, in their own socialization process, notions of their respective parental roles, for instance, that of mother. They enact these roles with respect to the newly born infant. They hold, caress, feed, talk, soothe, and otherwise respond to the multiple needs of their infant. They also respond to the child's cries, smiles, noises, and movements as a parent. In so doing, they are learning and developing the parenting role with respect to their infant daughter or son. To put this another way, both the parents and their child are being socialized into their respective roles. This is what we mean by being mutual and cyclical. The mother responds, the child responds, and the child's response shapes the mother's next response. Each acts on the other, each is affected by the other.

Symbolic interactionists hold that socialization is essentially a cognitive process.[29] This being the case, early socialization is dependent upon the acquisition of language. To become socialized in the sense we are defining the concept, the infant must develop a capacity for self-reference. By this we mean, to distinguish between her- or himself and all other matter. This process is active during the early years of life. Mead suggested that this takes place through a two-stage process. First is the play stage. Here the child plays at being another, for instance, mother or father; the play is initially focused on significant (and interesting) people in the child's social environment. Second is the game stage, the beginning of group activity and group ordering.

In the play stage, socialization is occurring in the sense of learning roles that are critical in the life situation of the very young child. These roles are learned by taking and playing the role, for example, taking the role of mother. In so doing, the child will typically then enact two roles, her mother's and her own. In this play stage the young child is in the process of differentiating between herself and others; she is developing a sense of selfhood by playing at roles. To put this another way, she is evolving a sense of self by practicing her own role in reference to the counter roles of mother, father, and/or sister, among others. The key process is one of imitation, taking the role of another.

The second stage in this socialization process is much more complicated. In the first stage, the child plays both parts; saying something in one character and responding in the other. It is essentially a private form of play. The second is social in that it involves others. Mead puts it this way: "If we contrast play with the situation in an organized game, we note the essential difference that the child who plays in a game must be ready to take the attitude of everyone else involved in that game, and that these different roles must have a definite relationship to each other."[30] It is in ordering that the child must have a sense of herself and all the other players. Cognitively, the ordering in game play is much more complex than in individual play. The child must evolve a more differentiated sense of self to participate in a game than is needed at the play stage. Clearly it is with the family (or its substitute) and in small play groups that the child learns of herself and others. It is here that the sense of social ordering and the sense of one's relationships in that order have their origins. It is also in this capacity for sensing order that one evolves an ever more complex and differentiated sense of selfhood.

Self

As evidenced in our discussion, socialization and **self** are closely related concepts.[31] In the theory of symbolic interaction, it is the self that is created and developed throughout life via the socialization process. Socialization, in turn, takes place through social interaction. Let us pause a moment here and summarize the relationship between self, socialization, and social interaction. We have defined socialization as the social process through which individuals learn about and internalize the values, beliefs, attitudes, knowledge, and behaviors of their society. A social relationship is a cognitive and affective connection between two or more people in which each takes the other(s) into account in his or her thoughts and in relevant aspects of behavior. The extent and level of this connection is associated with the specific roles being enacted in the relationships, for example, mother and daughter or social worker and client.

In our definition of socialization we used the term to *internalize* values, beliefs, or attitudes. To internalize means to adopt, to take on, or in symbolic interaction theory, to incorporate into one's *self*. The first step in the socialization process becomes developing a self; it is this self that is socialized throughout life. Recall in symbolic interaction theory an assumption is made that at birth we do not have a residual self that is a part of our genetic heritage that then grows and develops like other parts of the body. What we do have is a brain and related capabilities that permit us to learn, to think, to feel, and to take others into consideration in a state of self-consciousness, and then to act in accordance with this state of self-consciousness. It is this capacity of being able to evolve a state of consciousness of one's self and others that the symbolic interactionists label self.

We have described the self as a process originating very early within the larger socialization process. Symbolic interactionists also use the concept of self as an outcome. The distinction is important in terms of the use we make of it in the social systems model, particularly as applied to the social group. At one level we can think of examining the socialization process at any point in time. The self can be usefully considered as the sense of selfhood that exists at that point. An analogy would be a movie that we interrupt for purposes of examining a frame. In this sense, the self is an outcome, effect, or product of the process up to that time. We use the notion of self as an output in a similar way. Social groups, particularly the family, are vital in the socialization process, particularly in a child's early development. Just as we might stop a movie and examine an individual frame, so can we examine a family at any point in time in terms of its effects on the development of self in any or all of its members. To help develop this point we will return to Cooley. In discussing the role of the primary (social) group in developing a sense of selfhood he noted:

> By primary groups, I mean those characterized by intimate face-to-face associations and cooperation. They are primary in several senses, but chiefly in that they are fundamental in forming the social nature and ideals of the individual. The result of

intimate association, psychologically, is a certain fusion of individualities in a common whole, so that one's very self, for many purposes at least, is the common life and purpose of the group.[32]

In a manner of speaking, we are modeling this process described by Cooley when we apply the systems model to a social group. At any point, a task output of the group will be the sense of selfhood possessed by its individual members that can be attributed to the interactions within the group. This idea is further developed throughout Part II of this book.

Now let's return to our description of the concept of self. To start, we will build on the insights provided by Cooley. An approach for thinking about the social origins of self are found in his well-known "looking glass self." "Each to each a looking glass reflects the other that doth pass."[33]

Cooley develops his point as follows:

As we see our face, figure and dress in the glass, and are interested in them because they are ours, and pleased or otherwise with them according as they do or do not answer to what we should like them to be; so in imagination we perceive in another's mind some thought of our appearance, manners, aims, deeds, character, friends, and so on, and are variously affected by it.

A self-idea of this sort seems to have three principle elements: the imagination of our appearance to the other person; the imagination of his judgment of that appearance, and some sort of self-feeling, such as pride or mortification. The comparison with a looking glass hardly suggests the second element, the imagined judgment, which is quite essential.

The thing that moves us to pride or shame is not the mere mechanical reflection of ourselves, but an imputed sentiment, the imagined effect of this reflection upon another's mind. This is evident from the fact that the character and weight of that other, in whose mind we see ourselves, makes all the difference with our feeling.[34]

We are all familiar with the extent to which we are influenced by the feelings of others, especially those who are very close to us. Cooley, however, is suggesting something much more basic, a way of thinking about how our sense of selfhood arises in the first place. For the moment though, let us explore a bit more the basic notion of a looking glass self. The sense of self is derived as follows: "I am what I think you think I am." From this perspective, the self is acquired externally as opposed to arising internally. It is acquired from others who have formed a conception of you as a person. Obviously this is not a direct transfer but a perception of a perception, or in the words used above: "I am what I think you think I am." Several features of this position are critical in the socialization process: (1) the sense of self is socially acquired, it is a learning outcome; (2) selfhood is acquired from multiple sources, not one, and these multiple sources have different valences (power) in the formulation process; (3) just as there is no single source from which the notion of selfhood evolves, the same sources can convey different and conflicting meanings to the person at different times (for example, "Do as I say, not as I do"); and (4) the notion of selfhood is based on a social process and that process is active throughout one's life. In other words, the conception of self is dynamic, always in a state of becoming. Given this dynamic character, the process must be supported throughout life or a loss of a sense of selfhood occurs.

The notion of the looking glass self should be thought of only as a starting place for exploring how our sense of selfhood is developed and sustained. Most of us feel that we have a much more integrated and stable sense of ourselves than is suggested by Cooley's analogy. On the other hand, think of the times we have said to ourselves or heard others say "I feel myself pulled in a hundred directions," "I've got to get myself together," or "I've got to find myself."

A number of scholars have built on Cooley's work, but none has made more of a contribution than George Herbert Mead. In thinking of self, his ideas of the "I and the me" are very useful.[35] In undertaking the review it is important to keep in mind that Mead is not suggesting the "I" and the "me" are structures within the brain, nor that the self is a physical entity located somewhere within the body. The self is a state of consciousness in which the individual is able to conceive of her- or himself as a separate and distinct person. The symbolic interactionists refer to this state of consciousness as the capacity to view one's self as a social object.

Mead's use of the "I" and "me" is simply an analytic device by which one is able to think about the self as both a process and an effect of the process. Simply stated, the I and the me comprise the self. An example of the basic notion involved would be "I wonder what he thinks of me?" In this sentence the "I" and "me" comprise the two components of self. Here, the "I" designates the subject phase of the process, the "me," the object phase. The "I" is that sense of self as perceived by the individual; it is always in memory and represents our historical sense of self. This perception of the "I" held by the other, from the view of the "I," constitutes the "me" in our question, "I wonder what he thinks of me?" In this sense, the "me" results from taking the role of the other and evaluating the action of the "I" within the framework of their relationship. The process in which the self evolves is not linear, it is cyclical and mutually deterministic. This sounds more complicated than it is. The point is that selfhood needs to be viewed as a process. At any stage in this process, the person has a sense of self. This sense of self is designated as the "I." The person in any social relationship has both a sense of self (the "I" component) as well as a particular sense of how another person may view her or him. This sense of another's view is accomplished by taking the role of this other person. The actual interactions that take place between the two people involved in the relationships will be affected by these prior perceptions.

At the completion of what we will designate as a **social act**, the completion of a cycle of activities within a **social relationship**, there will be an evaluation of what occurred. This is the feedback loop. Included in this evaluation will be a personal evaluation of the role you played as viewed by the person in the other role; this is the "me" part of the self. This impression then is merged into the self as a "me" within a specific role. This impression similarly affects the "I" part of the self if the relationship is a significant one. Finally, this merged sense of the "I" and "me" will form a foundation for the next encounter in this social relationship (an updated sense of self). In some relationships this process is a very conscious one, while in other relationships it is not. To say this another way, you leave an impression with the other person and that person leaves one with you. Your perception of the other person's impressions of you is termed the "me" in that role.

That impression of yourself will in turn affect your own more general impression of your "self."

Each of us is involved in many, many, relationships; some very important, some less so, many others of little consequence. We have isolated an example of an interaction in which the question posed was, "I wonder what he thinks of me?" This was done to illustrate the self as a process. Our sense of selfhood is effected in an ongoing way by a great number of social relationships with each having a somewhat different effect.

While the "I" and "me" are useful in examining the process of self-development, we all intuitively know that we are more than the sum of our social relationships. We do not bend and change with each new relationship. The self has, in most people, great stability. Mead's use of the notion of the generalized other is helpful in thinking about this stability: "The organized community or social group which gives to the individual his unity of self may be called 'the generalized other.' "[36]

Early in life this so-called generalized other is a composite sense of who we are as derived from the key people in our social environment, parents, other family members, and others with whom we have significant relationships. It is through these people that we learn about life and learn about ourselves. In the popular parlance, these people have served as role models.

Freud's use of the term *superego* is somewhat akin to Mead's use of the generalized other, that part of our self that serves as a conscience and sets ethical standards for behavior. We learn from others early in life general patterns of what is right and what is wrong from society's view. There is a value system and moral code that cuts across various roles that we play within our particular culture. This value system and morality is internalized and becomes part of our sense of self. Just as we may be affected in our behavior by specific others in our social environment, so will we be constrained by a generalized other. For the moment think of the "I" part of our self being constrained and influenced by both generalized and specific others, with the generalized others being something like our conscience. Again caution is indicated; while stable for most people, conceptions of what is right and wrong also change. The caution is that each of us will, so to speak, be guided by a generalized other. There is no single generalized other and for each of us this "other" also changes and develops throughout life.

Now let us pause in our development of the concepts and through use of an example integrate the concepts of symbol, socialization, and self. We have indicated that the development of a sense of self or selfhood is a part of the socialization process that we all have experienced. This process, at least in the early years, is most typically carried out through a social group, the family. Just as a child learns the names of all kinds of things, so does she learn her own name. For our example, let us call her Ann. All members of the family will use the same designation when communicating with her. She learns this designation (symbol) through repetition and reinforcement in the same manner that she learns the names of other objects in her environment. But there is far more to the process than merely learning her name. In referring to her, family members and others will convey a variety of related meanings attached to Ann and her behaviors, for example: "Ann's daddy's girl," "Mama loves Ann," "Ann, no!," "Ann wet her pants," "Ann's been naughty," and so on. Again, the messages are many and frequently evaluative in terms of what Ann should and should not do. Ann develops a sense of selfhood essentially derived from the meanings held of Ann by people who care for her and upon whom she depends, those with whom she has a relationship.

Early in Ann's life (and in the socialization process) the sense of self is relatively undifferentiated. As she grows into adulthood she will acquire many different roles, and her sense of self will become more complex. She will view herself as Ann the woman, Ann the friend, and Ann the student, for example. In conceptualizing the socialization process of self, the distinctions made between ascribed and achieved roles are important to grasp. An **ascribed role** is assigned to the person by others as a consequence of the person possessing a particular attribute. These assigned roles are normative and drawn from society itself. Typically these ascribed roles pertain to such things as a person's gender, age, race, or condition (such as handicapped), and life stage (for instance, a child). An **achieved role**, as suggested by the term itself, is attained, presumably by the individual involved. Examples of an achieved role would be a social worker, a college graduate, and/or a "mover and shaker," among many others. While conceptually both ascribed and achieved roles represent locations or structural positions in a social system, the concepts are helpful in understanding the process of socialization itself.

For example, Ann's conception of self will be strongly influenced by being female, a child, white, and from a middle-class family. She will be responded to in certain ways because prior cultural definitions exist for each of these ascribed roles, and the significant people in her life are, for the most part, going to apply these meanings to her. For example, "Good little girls don't sit that way," "Good little girls don't 'sass' their mothers," "Pretty is as pretty does." Especially in the early years of life, Ann, through her behavior, will be evaluated in terms of cultural norms or standards, that is, what good little girls should be like. She will learn something of what is expected in being a child, or in being a girl, in terms of how her own behavior corresponds to the standards of these ascribed roles held by her parents and others significant to her. In short, she acquires a sense of selfhood, but one that is substantially affected by prevailing norms, particularly those applying to the roles ascribed to Ann. She will develop a sense of self and become an individual different from anybody else, but, and this is frequently not understood, she will be much more alike than different from other white women of her age because she has been socialized into these key roles. The associated values, beliefs, and ways of behaving have become internalized and are like a second nature to her.

Let's return to Ann's early socialization process. Ann, like any very young child, is essentially and entirely dependent upon her parents to meet all of her needs—food, shelter, safety, and love. She has been born or has otherwise come into a particular family or set of caregivers. The point is that, so far, Ann has not had much say in her life and what happens to her. Her parents are very powerful, and she quickly learns lessons about what happens when she obeys and disobeys her parents. In general terms, obedient behavior is rewarded while disobedient behavior is not. In fact, depending on the level of disobedience, her misbehavior can result in various forms of punishment. Most children, but certainly not all, learn that life is a lot easier if they behave. In learning to behave, it becomes necessary for the child to have a conception of self, to be able to treat oneself as an object, and to symbolically imagine one's behavior in terms of all the applicable do's and don'ts. Assuming some reasonable level of parental consistency in these do's and don'ts and the resultant actions, Ann can imagine how her parents or others are going to behave toward her in an ever larger number of circumstances. By this symbolic representation of herself and all those relevant to her, she can symbolically try out a great range of behaviors in her mind. By so doing, she gains an ever larger sense of control over herself and others. In other words, Ann will learn how to think about herself in a large number of circumstances. By playing the role of others she can anticipate the likely consequences of her proposed actions and decide whether or not to do it. "I better not do it, mother will be furious and she will ground me for a month."

It also should be acknowledged at this point that there is no single, comprehensive, unified culture. Rather, there exists a general set of widely held meanings that provide a sufficient unity and integration so that people sharing the same culture can identify and communicate meaningfully with each other. The concept of culture should be viewed as dynamic, constantly changing, and constantly developing. The implications of the socialization process stem from these features; there is no single track that each person follows in terms of becoming socialized. There is, instead, great diversity in the transmission process, especially in a relatively open society such as ours. Given the pluralistic nature of the American culture, it is useful to think of each family, each social group, as having its own subculture. While drawn from and having much in common with the wider culture, it has its own unique features.

Using Ann as an example again, let us assume that she was born into a very religious family, each family member's role being highly prescribed within the definitions set by a certain denomination (Baptist, Catholic, Methodist, or Presbyterian, for instance). Also for illustrative purposes, let us assume that the family is middle class, urban, and midwestern. Each of these features of the family, particularly its religious and class background, contributes to development of specific aspects of a subculture that distinguishes this family as a social group from all other families. Here subculture represents a set of meanings derived from the larger culture but possessing its own distinguishing qualities. In our example, Ann's initial learning about and experiences with the wider culture will be through the special filter (subculture) of her own family. What she will learn as she grows older, meets other people, participates in other groups, and attends school, is that not everybody thinks alike; or, from a symbolic interactionist position, not everyone attaches the same meaning to symbols. In short, Ann will receive mixed messages about all that surrounds her—everything from what is right and what is wrong to who she is. Developing and maintaining a sense of self is no easy task. It is no wonder that children as well as adults experience problems in this process. Some of these problems become severe and, as members of the helping professions understand, require professional assistance.

Situation

From a symbolic interactionist point of view, all behavior occurs within some larger context; this context is called the **situation**. Every situation has many features; including time, location, physical objects, and, as we will see in a moment, roles. All of these features are interrelated and hold a meaning to the person who is involved in forming a definition of a specified situation. In other words, all social behavior derives from an individual's definition of the situation in which he or she will be interacting with others.[37] Through the process of socialization, each person acquires a vast repertoire of situations they have experienced, heard about, read about, seen acted out on television, or just imagined. This storehouse of memories provides the source of definitions that the person uses in any given social circumstance. Critical to this notion of situation is the attendant concept of self. In terms of defining a situation, the major consideration to be made is how the individuals doing the defining determine the role they are to play and how that role should be enacted within a given situation. In short, the defined situation is a major determinant of behavior.

Given this general approach to the understanding of human behavior, the coordination of social behavior depends in large part on the sharing of comparable definitions of the situation by those who will be interacting with each other. Conceptually, these common definitions result from the common experiences, the common learning, and the use of common symbols during the process of socialization. If a group of people who do not know each other are assembled, with each holding a different definition of the situation in which they are involved, a degree of socially awkward behavior might well result. What if the assembled people held such diverse definitions of the situation as a cocktail party, a funeral, a committee meeting, and a wedding reception. If you were in such a situation and had understood the situation to be a cocktail party for a politician, you would probably be wondering where the bar and hors d'oeuvres were located. Your preliminary definition would probably be shaken if the person standing next to you appeared somewhat puzzled and inquired where he might find the body of the deceased.

Central to the notion of the situation are the roles that are required in the defined situation. A person's definition of the situation establishes, at least in general terms, the role he or she is to play and the roles to be played by other people involved in the same situation. This formulation suggests an approach for understanding the social coordination that is evident in social life. In developing this position, it is important not to assign a narrow conception to the notion of situation; for example, a wedding or a specific meeting. Rather, situation should be thought of as a focal point or a point of orientation for a variety and usually an ongoing set of social interactions. Using the notion of a point of orientation, every situation will have a goal to which the various social interactions pertain. For example, a family's evening meal would be a situation. For most families it occurs at a typical time and place, and the roles of all family members as they pertain to this situation are mutually understood. Situations become linked for the individual, but the person's precise role for any given situation is derived from his or her definition of that situation.

For most adults, the situations they face are familiar ones. This is not to say that all situations are accurately defined or are routine. Life is full of surprises—some good, some bad. A surprise occurs when a defined situation turns out to have some novel features, that is, people not behaving in the expected way. An example of how situations are typically linked might be helpful. Barbara and Sam Jones have been married for five years. They live in a three-room apartment and both hold professional positions. Barbara is a clinical social worker at the Midtown Mental Health Center, and Sam is an accountant for the Biosk Corporation, a large steel-making firm. The example starts with the alarm going off at 7:00 A.M. Either Barbara or Sam is positioned to turn off the alarm (part of his or her role). The first situation to be faced is getting ready for work, which includes showering, using the bathroom, deciding what to wear, and dressing. Given that Barbara and Sam have been married several years, the chances are that their early morning routines are well established. They share a common definition of the situation and each knows what to expect from the other; that is, each knows the other's role and each expects that role to be carried out in the expected manner. Given the common definition of the situation, they take turns using the bathroom, showering, and accessing the clothes closet, and there is small talk about the day past and the events likely to occur in the day ahead. Soon they move from their bedroom to the kitchen, and the situation changes and becomes organized around having breakfast. Again, this situation has a definition, and their respective roles are mutually understood and carried out. Someone sets the table, someone prepares the food, someone brings in the paper, feeds and lets the pets out, and so on. If either Barbara or Sam should not carry out their role in the expected manner (satisfactorily), a point of tension between the two may arise: "Sam, have you fed the dog?" "Barbara, cool it! I'll feed the damn dog when I finish the paper!"

Once breakfast is concluded, the two start preparing for their respective work situations. Again the transition is likely to be relatively smooth, with both taking on different or modified roles, each suited to their definition of the situation about to unfold. They move out of their roles in the social group known as Barbara and Sam, the Joneses, to their roles in larger and formally constituted social organizations; for example, Midtown Mental Health Center and Biosk Corporation. Conceptually, when Barbara and Sam move out of their respective spousal roles, the roles in the social group known as the Joneses remain dormant until the two reactivate them through their mutual entry into another situation, when they return to their apartment that evening or if they meet for lunch.

For Barbara, the transition from the role of wife to the role of clinical social worker occurs almost automatically as she bids goodbye to her husband and enters the mental health center. Again it is a familiar situation; she knows generally what to expect in terms of how people will play their roles and how she will play hers. As she moves toward her own office, she picks up additional clues that help her define the upcoming situation; for example, remarks from the secretary and colleagues, seeing a familiar patient anxiously waiting to see her, or noticing yesterday's unanswered telephone calls. Typically there are continuities to situations that greatly facilitate the process of definition. As in the case of Barbara, it is almost as if she had stepped out of her clinician role at the end of the previous work day and stepped back into it at the start of the next work day with little or no loss of continuity. It is useful to think of the individual playing only one role at a time, but with the individual possessing great skill in moving in and out of roles as the situation dictates.

The point illustrated in the example of Barbara and Sam is that most situations confronting people are familiar, and over time people gain a pretty good idea of how they fit in. In other words, they have an overall grasp of each situation, of how all roles are generally enacted. Situations flow from one to another, and people adjust to the appropriate roles naturally and almost automatically. Importantly, social behavior is to be understood as influenced by the person's definition of the situation, and the definition not only means understanding one's own role, but having a general understanding of all the roles that are active and pertinent to the defined situation. In this sense, and in his or her own mind, the individual acts out his or her own role as well as the roles of others in the process of defining the situation. While roles are the most critical feature in defining the situation, there are other important components that shape behaviors (for example, time, space, and physical features).

Certainly not all situations confronted by people in social life are familiar and routine. Also, even seemingly routine situations have surprises. What the symbolic interactionists are suggesting is a general approach for understanding social behavior. Inherent in their position is a formulation of how the human memory functions. They suggest that the individual does not memorize bits and pieces of information that are somehow recalled and reassembled as needed; more likely memory involves the retention of larger and at least loosely ordered information. In addition, the ordering of the retained material probably contains some reference to the individual as a self (a social object) so that the memory has what might be termed a behavioral orientation. The issue of the structure of memory is not central here; what is central from this theoretical perspective is that the definition of the situation employed by the individual provides the orientation that results in that person's behavior. In the course of interactions occurring within that situation, the individuals constantly receive feedback as to how successfully or appropriately they are playing their roles in relation to the goal of that situation. Again, this process in most instances is subtle, and adjustments are made automatically. At other times the process may be anything but automatic and subtle. Rather than socially coordinated behavior associated with a stable relationship, conflict may arise, which leads to redefined and restructured roles or perhaps the termination of a relationship; for example, termination of a social group—a divorce in the case of the Joneses.

Social Act

The social act is the final concept to be reviewed in this section. We have left it for last because it serves a useful integrating function in helping to summarize the theory of symbolic interaction. The social act also is helpful in operationalizing the notion of conversion operations as used in the social systems model, particularly when applied to the social group.

Symbolic interactionists, along with many other students of human behavior, have sought approaches at the micro level for examining social behavior. Needed was a means for examining behavior that would preserve its wholeness, but at the same time permit identification of a unit of interaction that could serve as the building block for the larger study of the process of social interaction and social organization. Among social interactionists, this unit of behavior is labeled the social act.[38]

Earlier we used Sam and Barbara to illustrate the notion of situation as the context which helps define roles and provide direction for social interaction. Described in that example was a continuous stream of behaviors starting with waking in the morning, having breakfast, and going to work, among others. On the surface it appears as though the couple is involved in a continuing stream of activities, sometimes with each other, sometimes with others, and sometimes alone. On closer inspection, the stream of activities appears much more like a series of episodes of behavior joined together like links in a chain. There is evidence of purposiveness of behavior both within an individual link (having breakfast) as well as with the total chain of events for the day.

The social act can be usefully viewed as an episode or link in an ongoing chain of social behaviors.[39] Recognizing that much of social behavior is routine, the notion of the social act can be helpful in seeking understanding of the larger process of social interaction and social organization. The social act, at a minimum, will involve two people enacting separate but reciprocal roles. The act will have both a discernible beginning and an end. The social act, as it is conducted in a social group, will possess a cyclical quality. By this we mean the act is not linear, but circular in form. The end state of the act is not a final state but an intermediate one; it serves to conclude one set of interactions but in so doing sets the conditions or starting point for the next cycle.

For example, two friends (a social group) meet for lunch. Upon seeing the other, he or she says, "Hi, how has it been going?" The other responds similarly and they may shake hands or embrace momentarily; here we have the start of a social act. They have lunch together, conduct their business, or just enjoy each other's company. The episode concludes with the two saying, "Great lunch, see you later." Each then goes his or her own way with the likelihood that each will be involved in a series of such episodes each day. The use of an initial greeting and a goodbye in the example serves to get across the idea that the social act assumes a beginning and ending phase. The ending phase "Great lunch, see you later" was intended to get across the idea that the ending phase contains within it the condition for the next cycle. The next cycle could occur in an hour, day, week, month, or year or more. The connection that is deemed to exist in social relationships that links the social acts together in the form of an ongoing relationship is essentially independent of time. By this we mean that the relationship doesn't have a physical structure to it, rather a mental one. This relationship and their respective roles within the relationship exists in the minds of the two people involved. If they are close friends, they will think of each other while they are apart. In thinking of each other each will play themselves as well as the role of the other, and might communicate this: "I was thinking about you last night."

A social act will always occur in a specified situation. In other words, there will be a specific context in which the interactions will occur. This context will provide additional clues to the participants, not only to the role they are to play, but also provide details of how the roles are to be carried out. In our example, the social act took place at noon and in a restaurant. Time, spatial arrangements, the presence of other people, and the purpose of the meeting will all help shape the interactions that will take place. In the social systems model, the roles, the situations, and all of the conditions that will affect interactions are features of the structural components of the conversion operation. The actual behavior that transpires between the two friends having lunch is labeled interactions.

To extend the example, let us assume that the two friends are of the opposite sex; not only are they good friends but also have a sexual relationship with each other, are both lawyers, and employed by competing law firms. In the lunch setting their roles are shaped by that situation; if they happened to be facing each other in the court room or adversaries in a lawsuit, their roles would be shaped by that situation. Similarly, if they were spending the night together, that setting would shape their respective roles. In the example, we are dealing with the same two people, but they play quite different roles with each other depending on the situation and its definition. If their relationship is stable, the chances are that they move in and out of roles, and switch roles, quite naturally; for example, the roles of friends, sexual partners, and lawyers.

In describing the above relationship, we used the word stable. In the language of the model, the relationship (group) would be in steady state. Each of the two individuals has a good sense of self, and possesses the capacity in the relationship to take his or her own role and the role of the other as well. In this sense, they would be sensitive to the interests and needs of the other and to take the other in consideration in their own role enactments. This capacity of being able to act by taking into consideration the role of the other is sometimes referred to as mutuality. It is, as we indicated earlier, an important capacity to possess in working with clients in formed groups.

To conclude this discussion of the social act, we will elaborate a bit more on the dynamics of the interactions that are involved. First, there will be a communication (symbol/meaning) sent by the one initiating the interaction, for example, "Hi, how has it been going?" This communication is based on a definition of the situation, the role to be played toward the "other" and the other person's role toward the sender. To put the matter in other terms, the greeting contains within it an expectation of the type of response to be returned. Here the assumption is made by the initiating person that the other person has defined the situation and the role they are to play in a similar or compatible fashion. If the communication is received by the other in the expected way and the expected response sent, then the social act is well underway. The interaction will continue but with the same dynamics playing. If a communication is sent but not received in the intended way, we have the start of a communication problem. The response made in return is not confirming, which in turn will affect the next communication to be sent, and so on.

Again the notions of the "I" and "me" are useful in seeking an understanding of the basic dynamics involved in the social act. The message being sent is coming from the "I." As the message is being sent, it will be interpreted and modified based on how it sounds to the "me" who is taking the role of the other. Most of the time what we say coincides with what we thought we were going to say. Other times it does not. In such instances we may say to ourselves, "I can't imagine I said that." Also, we are all familiar with "slips of the tongue" that we have made. The point is that we are never quite sure of what we are saying until we actually say it. There is an evaluative process that involves the self and that part of the self that takes the role of the other.

The social act is concluded as the individuals move on to their next set of activities. Consciously or unconsciously, there is an evaluative activity that is associated with the closure. The evaluation includes the taking the role of the other and examining one's performance from that perspective. That evaluation is taken in and in some small way affects the self and the conditions for the next cycle.

SUMMARY

This chapter has introduced lines of theory development that, when placed in a social systems perspective, have helped us specify the distinctive features of social groups. While note has been made of the absence of general agreement on a theory of social groups, we believe the existing theories can be helpful to the practitioner. We have concentrated our review in this chapter on just two theories, social exchange and symbolic interaction.

Exchange theory offers insights into a variety of forms of human association. The theory also summarizes a great deal of "common sense" and offers an explanation for much that occurs in one's everyday life experiences. Its relatively straightforward qualities suggest that it would be a good place to start an explanation of the relationships between human behavior and the social environment. Simply put, the link between humans and their social environments can be understood as a form of exchange. "You have something I need and I have something you need, so let's get together." Certainly much of human behavior is far more complex than is suggested by this statement, but it does offer a useful starting place.

Exchange theory is more helpful in understanding the development of relationships within social organizations than between them. Nevertheless, the metaphor of exchange has utility in the understanding of relationships both within and between social organizations. In the latter case, exchange offers a way of explicating what we mean when we speak of the functional qualities of the model. In short, social organizations produce things that possess value to others in their social environments (suprasystems). These things are termed outputs and are exchanged for those things needed by the system to continue the exchange process.

Symbolic interaction theory helps to convey what we mean by the interplay between structure and interactions. Central in this construction are the concepts of self, situation, and social act. In symbolic interaction, self is the ability to see oneself as a whole, as an object in a social situation. We know and generally understand our own roles in life as well as those played by others. We can, by taking our own roles as well as those played by others, contemplate or imagine our behavior with others in advance of the actual interaction. As humans we have the capacity to think and to imagine as well as to act. In fact the latter is to be understood or conditioned by the former. From this perspective, social interaction is symbolic interaction.

For us, the single most helpful contribution of symbolic interaction theory is the explanation offered of how the self is formed and how it develops throughout life. In short, the sense of selfhood is a social outcome and most clearly one associated with the social group. This insight gives the social group its distinctive feature. Conceptually speaking, the person is both a signal and maintenance input to the social group. The task output of every social group is a sense of selfhood. It is through the social group, particularly the family, that the sense of self is both developed and supported throughout life. More will be said of this contention in the next chapter when the model is applied to a family.

We concluded our review of symbolic interaction by summarizing what is meant by the social act. It is the social act that provides the analytic tool for examining social interaction. At the micro level, it is the social act that operationalizes the concept of conversion operations as we use it in the social systems model. In a manner of speaking, the social act is the counterpart of a cycle of social interactions that we are seeking to model in the social group.

GLOSSARY

Achieved role A role that has been earned or is recognized as a consequence of meeting certain requirements. The role of professional social worker is an achieved role, that is, it is achieved as a consequence of meeting certain requirements.

Ascribed role A role that has been assigned and is not related to something consciously sought by the individual. Typically an ascribed role pertains to a characteristic possessed by the individual, for example, color, gender, or age. The role of woman is an ascribed role.

Differentiation A social process of increased specification usually related to or derived from the pursuit of some shared goal (purpose). Also, the second stage of exchange as used in exchange theory.

Exchange theory A social psychological theory that accounts for social organization by an exchange process.

Situation The larger context in which human behavior takes place and in which reciprocal influences exist between the individual and a relevant environment. The concept is associated with the theory of symbolic interaction.

Socialization The process by which the individual learns to think and act in accordance with prevailing norms, for example, cultural expectations.

Social act The smallest unit of interaction occurring with an ongoing social relationship in symbolic interaction theory.

Social relationship The cognitive and affective connection existing between two or more people in which each takes the other(s) into account in their thoughts and in relevant aspects of behavior (role enactment).

Stabilization A developmental stage or level in exchange theory marked by steady state in exchanges between a subject system and its suprasystem (the third stage).

Symbol A sign for which a shared meaning exists within a society. Typical symbols include, among others, words, gestures, marks, and body posturing.

Symbolic interaction theory A social psychological theory that accounts for social interaction and the development of social organization through an exchange of meanings as symbols. In the most fundamental sense, the notion of self is an acquired meaning. Reality, the perception of the real world, in effect is a system of meanings that is socially acquired and supported.

Synergic The effects generated by the interactions of two or more parts of a system. The effect cannot be produced by any of the individual parts acting alone.

Transaction The initial developmental stage or level in exchange theory. Premised in self-interest, exchange is sought by providing something of value to another with the expectation that something needed by the person initiating the exchange will be offered in return.

NOTES

1. The concept of emergence has several different meanings. In terms of its use here, see, particularly, James G. Miller, *Living Systems* (New York: McGraw-Hill, 1978), 28–39. Also see Walter Buckley, *Sociology and Modern Systems Theory* (Englewood Cliffs, N.J.: Prentice Hall, 1967). For a variation of this phenomenon see a discussion of emergent norm theory in Allan G. Johnson, *Human Arrangements* (New York: Harcourt Brace Jovanovich, 1986), 643–644.

2. See Charles D. Garvin, "Group Theory and Research," in *Encyclopedia of Social Work*, vol. 1, (Silver Spring: National Association of Social Workers, 1987), 682–696.

3. Ibid., 685.

4. Ferdinand Tönnies, *Community and Society*, trans. and ed. Charles P. Loomis (Lansing, Mich.: Michigan State University Press, 1957), 252.

5. Robert L. Hamblin and John H. Kunkel, eds., *Behavioral Theory in Sociology: Essays in Honor of George C. Homans* (New Brunswick, N.J.: Transaction Books, 1977).

6. Weldon T. Johnson, "Exchange Theory in Perspective: The Promise of George C. Homans," in Hamblin and Kunkel, eds., *Behavioral Theory in Sociology: Essays in Honor of George C. Homans* (New Brunswick, N.J.: Transaction Books, 1977), 78.

7. George C. Homans, "Social Behaviors as Exchange," *The American Journal of Sociology* 63 (May 1958): 606.

8. Ibid.

9. Peter M. Blau, *Exchange and Power in Social Life* (New York: John Wiley & Sons, 1964).

10. Ibid.

11. For a review of these processes see Marvin Olsen, *The Process of Social Organization*, 2nd ed. (New York: Holt, Rinehart and Winston, 1978), 96.

12. Alvin W. Gouldner, "The Norm of Reciprocity," *American Sociological Review* 25 (April 1960): 161–178.

13. Olsen, *Process*, 93.

14. Blau, *Exchange and Power*, 116.

15. Olsen, *Process*, 94.

16. Blau, *Exchange and Power*, 118.

17. Olsen, *Process*, 95.

18. Ibid., 96.

19. Blau, *Exchange and Power*, 94.

20. Olsen, *Process*, 96–97.

21. Georg Simmel, *The Sociology of Georg Simmel*, trans. and ed. Kurt H. Wolff (Glencoe, Ill.: Free Press, 1950), 387.

22. Gouldner, "Norm of Reciprocity."

23. Olsen, *Process*, 97.

24. Mary Jo Dugan and Michael Hills, eds., *Women and Symbolic Interaction* (Boston: Allen & Unwin, 1987), 3–15.

25. Charles Horton Cooley, *Social Organization* (Glencoe, Ill.: The Free Press, 1909), 23–31.

26. See, for example, Anselm Strauss, ed., *The Social Psychology of George Herbert Mead* (Chicago, Ill.: The University of Chicago Press, 1956), iv–xvi.

27. George Herbert Mead, *Mind, Self and Society* (Chicago: University of Chicago Press, 1934).

28. The assumptions are made by the authors and have no single source. Symbolic interaction has its foundations in the philosophy of pragmatism and is associated with the thinking of Charles Peirce, John Dewey and George Herbert Mead. For an interesting review of the origins of symbolic interaction see Hans Joas, *G.H. Mead: A Contemporary Re-examination of His Thought* (Cambridge, Mass.: The MIT Press, 1985), 33–63.

29. Mead, *Mind, Self and Society*, 135–226.

30. Ibid., 151.

31. John P. Hewitt, *Self and Society: A Symbolic Interactionist Social Psychology*, 3rd ed. (Boston: Allyn & Bacon, 1984), 91–143.

32. Charles Horton Cooley, *Social Organization* (New York: Scribner, 1902), 184.

33. Charles Horton Cooley, *Human Nature and the Social Order* (Glencoe, Ill.: The Free Press, 1956), 23.

34. Ibid.

35. Mead, *Mind, Self and Society*, 173–281.

36. Ibid., 154.

37. For a development of this idea see Johnathan H. Turner, *A Theory of Social Interaction* (Stanford, Calif.: Stanford University Press, 1988).

38. Hewitt, *Self and Society*, 65–70.

39. Ibid.

Chapter 7

The Social Group as a Social System

OUTLINE

Introduction

In this chapter we will model the social group as a social system. We begin by reviewing the definition of the social group:

> **Social group** A form of social organization composed of two or more members who identify and interact with one another on a personal basis as individuals, possess a shared sense of the group as a social entity, are affected by the group-related actions of members, and in which expressive (natural) actions dominate.

In Chapter 3 we introduced the eight concepts comprising the model and described the general features of each of the concepts. To illustrate the model we used practice examples; the Arnold family was one of the cases used. We now further develop the distinction between a **formed** group and a **natural** group, which we are defining as a social group. The Arnold family represents a social group, and would in Cooley's words also be a primary group.[1] In short, Gemein chaft relationships dominate in social groups. In contrast, the therapeutic group of which Sarah and Bill Arnold became a part represents a formed group. In such groups, Gesellschaft relationships dominate. The social organization is formed by the therapist as the medium through which specific therapeutic goals are to be pursued. We have not sought to devise a separate classification for such therapeutic groups but do distinguish such forms of social organization from the social group. Suffice it to say for the moment that we consider therapy groups as hybrids. By this we mean that the insights gained from understanding the dynamics of social groups served to help construct a hybrid or therapy group, one designed to bring about change through use of the personal relationship.

Our intent in the pages ahead is to examine the distinguishing features of the social group. In other words, the social group displays ordering features common to all forms of social organization; in addition they display those specific to the social group. The distinguishing feature of the social group is the dominance of Gemeinschaft relationships, and it is this feature that gives the so-called naturalness to these relationships. We will primarily use the family as the example of the social group. In doing so, we continue our use of the family introduced in the previous chapter, the Joneses.

Boundary

Boundary distinguishes the system from its suprasystem. Those people inside the boundary comprise the system; those individuals, groups, agencies, and others that are external but which affect the system's output and input exchanges represent its suprasystem. A description of boundary is more difficult. Unlike the shell of a chicken's egg or the skin of a human, the boundaries of social organizations, including the social group, cannot be seen, touched, heard, felt, or otherwise discerned by the human senses. This should remind us that, unlike the shell of an egg, groups and their boundaries do not have a physical existence. Boundary is a concept and pertains to particular social behaviors, those that bind the members of the system together; boundaries also have the particular function of controlling input-output exchanges between the system and its suprasystem. The distinguishing feature of the social group's boundary is the informal, Gemeinschaft quality of boundary-maintaining behaviors. In a social group, boundary is only evidenced in the boundary-maintaining behavior of its members.

In our definition of a social group, we indicated that group members "possessed a shared sense of the group as a social entity." This shared sense of the group is essentially what we mean by boundary. It represents a state of consciousness of the other members of the group—their common needs and interests, and the importance of the group to all members. Group members therefore interact differently with insiders than they do with outsiders. Those interactions with others that reaffirm the special relationships that insiders have with each other and deny such interactions with outsiders are labeled boundary maintenance.

Is boundary something real? Is it important? One way of addressing both questions is through an example. Think of a playground situation at the start of school—a young, mentally retarded child is being mainstreamed, meaning that the child is attending regular classes as opposed to being in a special class with other children who have similar handicaps. Our mentally retarded child approaches a group of children in his class, wanting to join their play. Noticing the approach, one youngster yells to his friends, "Hey, here comes the dummy!" Given this beginning definition of a situation, the chances are that the handicapped child will be taunted and otherwise excluded from this group because "he is not one of us." The behavior of the play group toward an outsider is a familiar but negative example of boundary maintenance. Is it important? We believe so; certainly if the social group is deemed to be fundamental in the development of selfhood, its dynamics need to be understood and its practice relevance considered.

Given this proposition, consider the impact over time on the development of a sense of self in this child who is being called "dummy," or worse, in situation after situation. In this connection, the proposition associated with symbolic interaction theory takes on special meaning: "I am what I think you think I am." Many similar examples could be cited, like those involving racism, sexism, and other forms of discrimination evidenced by the use of terms such as "nigger" and "babe." The main point is that boundary is evidenced only in social behavior, and these behaviors distinguish insiders from outsiders. One difficulty in the above example should be emphasized: it dealt with a negative set of behaviors. Boundary maintenance is crucial to the survival of any form of social organization; if there is no boundary, there is no organization. Therefore, every social system possesses a boundary and engages in boundary-maintenance behaviors.

With the above as background, let us proceed with a discussion of boundary and its characteristics. Boundary should always be considered a form of social behavior basically aimed at preserving the integrity of the group. A social group's integrity or essential identity is maintained largely by controlling input and output exchanges. Every group has a normative structure that affects the behaviors of its members. That aspect of the normative structure that pertains to the control of input and output exchanges represents boundary. Earlier it was stated that every social organization develops its own subculture. One aspect of this subculture is how its boundaries are defined and maintained, that is, how the key relationships among its member units (individuals in the social group) are handled. This aspect of the normative structure in a social group is played out in the roles people enact both with respect to group members and nongroup members, as in the example of children at play.

At a practical and applied level, almost every social organization has a name, such as The Joneses, The Rat Pack, or The Cubs, for example. The specification of boundary in any application of the model usually starts with the group's name. Simply put, all people holding membership, formally or informally, in the group, are insiders; all others are outsiders. Basically, the group-related behaviors that insiders have with or pertaining to outsiders are generally boundary-maintenance behaviors.

It should also be noted that boundary maintenance can involve use of a variety of physical barriers, symbols, and physical actions, as well as verbal and written forms of communication. The key is the social meaning attached to these. For example, in the traditional marriage ceremony the couple exchanges rings. The ring, an ongoing, unending circle, conveys the notion of oneness, that a new family (social group) has been created. The ring is usually made of gold or some other precious metal. Symbolically, the preciousness of the ring stands for the preciousness of the new relationship that has been formed. Wedding rings, by reason of the cultural meanings attached, can be viewed in this model as serving a boundary-maintenance function. By being worn on the third finger of the left hand it indicates to others that the person wearing the ring is married. Using our earlier example of Sam and Barbara, other women in the case of Sam, and other men in the case of Barbara, may be less likely to view them as "available" if they are wearing their wedding rings. Here the ring and its social meaning identifies and helps to maintain the special relationship that Sam and Barbara have with each other. Barbara and Sam also have their own apartment, a mailbox with both names on it, and perhaps dead-bolt locks on their door. Physical barriers like the door can be conceived as serving a boundary-maintenance function for the Joneses. The critical determinant is the meaning that Barbara and Sam attach to these barriers and related symbols and how they use them.

Suprasystem

In the previous section we made the point that the system's boundary serves to bound the system and thus to separate it from its surroundings. Conceptually, the notion of suprasystem is used to operationalize the position that every social organization with system properties has vital and ongoing relationships with selected organizations, agencies, and individuals in its environment. The concept of suprasystem is used to operationalize the relevant open system properties in this model. It is roughly comparable with the notion of social environment, as in the phrase, "human behavior and the social environment." Theoretical support for our use of this term is drawn largely from the concept of "field" as used in field theory. We also functionally define the relationship between the system and its suprasystem in terms of input and output exchanges, using exchange theory to help operationalize the concept of exchange.

In this section our special interest is in the social group. The question becomes, "What are the distinguishing features of the group that have implications in formulating its suprasystem ties?" Three features of the social group are particularly helpful: the social units comprising the group are always individuals; the relationships among group members are informal, usually face-to-face; and these relationships serve both as means and ends for the members.

Given that the member units of social groups are individuals (as opposed to groups of individuals), the suprasystem of the social group always includes other social groups to which the members belong. To illustrate this point, let us use the Jones family again. Barbara is a member of a number of other social groups, including her family of origin—her mother, father, and two sisters. To understand the Joneses as a social group requires some understanding of how the Joneses relate to other social groups that include Barbara and Sam as members.

Since social groups tend to be informally organized (the legal state of marriage represents a formal contract, but even here the relationships among family members tend not to be formally specified), their suprasystem relationships also tend to be informal. For example, Barbara and Sam alternate spending Christmas with their respective families; Barbara's parents one year, and Sam's parents the next. While such suprasystem relationships are not formally specified by a legal contract, they are no less firm and binding for the groups involved. For example, if Sam has a conflict between a planned overseas business trip and spending Christmas with Barbara and her family, the chances are that he is going to be confronted with a real dilemma.

In Figure 7.1 we present an **ecomap** depicting the suprasystem of the Joneses.[2] This figure builds off Figure 1.1 by specifying the system-suprasystem relationships of the Joneses. Here, rather than using letters to identify a suprasystem member, the actual system is identified. In the center is our subject system and surrounding it are the key

FIGURE 7.1 Ecomap: The Joneses

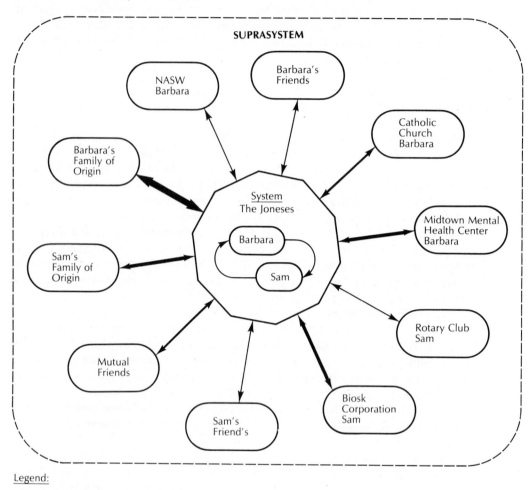

Legend:

← → = Thickness indicates current relative importance to subject system.

people, groups, and organizations having an impact on the behavior of the Joneses. The thickness of the connecting line designates the relative importance of that relationship to the lives of the Joneses at a given point in time. Arrows also move in both directions suggesting the mutual effects that these systems have on each other.

The figure is a composite portrayal of the components of the Jones's suprasystem. As will be noted in our next section, the actual influence of these other systems will vary depending on the cycle of activity that is being examined. For example, in one cycle perhaps only one suprasystem influence will be operative. The remaining members of the suprasystem, in a manner of speaking, will be dormant.

In our example involving the dilemma posed to the Joneses by the conflict between a Christmas trip to Barbara's parents and Sam's business trip, only two aspects of their suprasystem are involved. Here, leading in importance, is Barbara's family of origin, and the Biosk Corporation, Sam's employer. The remaining systems are essentially dormant in terms of their influence on the Joneses in this episode of their life.

Interface

Technically, interface refers to a boundary segment that a subject system shares with another system comprising a portion of its suprasystem. Operationally, think of interface as representing a set of mutual understandings held by two or more systems that guide their interactions with one another.

These understandings can be formal, such as a contract, or informal. In social groups, they are almost always informal. As part of a boundary, an interface serves to control input-output exchanges and seeks to exclude those influences that may be disruptive to the relationships among those sharing a common boundary. Of central importance in the use of this concept is the uniqueness attributed to each interface.

The social group is characterized by the dominance of Gemeinschaft over Gesellschaft relationships. Similarly, these Gemeinschaft qualities of relationships are evidenced in interface. We will develop these features with our family the Joneses. Barbara's parents are June and Phil West, and Sam's are Verna and Todd Jones. While the relationship among the three families has been cordial, Barbara has felt that she has never been fully accepted by Sam's parents, particularly by his mother, Verna. Sam and his mother have always been very close, and Barbara has surmised that Verna has felt that no woman was quite good enough for "her" Sam. The two sets of parents represent key parts of Barbara and Sam's suprasystem. Conceptually, the common understandings shared by Barbara and Sam as to their relationship with each of their parents is characterized by the term *interface*. These interfaces are distinctive, representative of the nature of the functional ties between the Joneses and their two sets of families. Using concepts drawn from symbolic interaction theory, the interface is evidenced in the particular spousal roles that Barbara and Sam play when dealing with their two sets of parents.

Every other year, Barbara and Sam spend Christmas with Sam's parents; the alternate year it is with Barbara's parents. Since Sam's parents live some distance away, they usually spend two days together. For reasons stated earlier, Barbara feels that "Two days are all I can take." Barbara and Sam have reached mutual agreement on alternating Christmas between the two sets of parents, a feature of the interface. They have also agreed on major aspects of their respective roles, especially as to how they are carried out when they visit Sam's parents. While Barbara would much prefer that she and Sam stay overnight at a local motel, she has agreed that they stay in his parents' spare room. Sam feels to do otherwise would hurt his parents' feelings. Barbara finds it particularly annoying during these visits that Sam's mother literally waits on him hand and foot. She is convinced that Sam's lack of help to her in the kitchen is a direct result of the way his mother brought him up. To deal with some of these concerns, Sam has agreed that he will be particularly attentive to Barbara's feelings and needs during these visits. In this connection, Barbara once observed to a friend, "The first time we visited I felt like an idiot. Sam spent most of his time with his mother; he acted like I wasn't even there. I told him later he had better treat me like his wife or I would never darken their door again."

In this example we have identified critical features of interface. The common boundary described was the one linking Barbara and Sam to his family. The interface is represented by selected features of the relationship between the two groups. Included would be the frequency of visits, living arrangements while they are there, and how the two families relate to each other. Both Sam and Barbara are close to their respective families. The ties they each maintain with their families are intended to be supportive of these relationships on the one hand, but not so intense as to be disruptive of the relationship that Barbara and Sam have with each other. The interface represents a kind of compromise, one that maintains and enhances their respective relationships with their families of origin, but also enhances their relationship as husband and wife.

On one visit and in Barbara's presence, Sam posed the following question to his mother, "Look, Mom, next year why don't you and Dad spend Christmas with us? We will invite Barbara's folks and we can all have Christmas together. Our house has plenty of room and you and Dad have always enjoyed Barbara's parents. I think it would be a great idea." In this instance and for quite different reasons, neither Barbara nor Verna thought it a great idea. While not mentioning it at the time, Barbara was furious that Sam raised the issue without consulting her in advance. Sam's idea presented a major change in the interface joining the Joneses with their respective families. Barbara was quite sure her parents would not like the arrangement. The day was saved when Verna replied, "Sammy, that is a good idea, but you know it really wouldn't be the same. When you're here, it's just like old times. You know, we have spent an awful lot of Christmases together in this old house!"

The above exchange highlights an important characteristic of an interface—the preservation of relationships both within and between the subject systems. In our example, it is clear that Sam's parents consider the Christmas visit by their son and his wife a special time and they look forward to it. Somehow a change in which they would share this visit with Barbara's parents in their son's home simply would not be the same; it would not be functional.

The example also helps to get across the notion that a system's suprasystem is always changing. Its composition and dynamics are best understood in terms of a specific cycle of system interactions. In the above example, it was a Christmas visit by Barbara and Sam to Verna and Todd Jones, Sam's parents. Our interest is in understanding Barbara and Sam from a systems perspective. Here we were provided some insights into their relationship by observing their interactions with Sam's parents. In this cycle of activities, the key suprasystem influence was Verna and Todd Jones, and to a lesser extent, Barbara's parents, June and Phil West. Other groups comprising the Joneses suprasystem were essentially dormant and irrelevant in understanding the interactions that took place in this cycle. Each cycle of interactions is likely to involve a somewhat different set of suprasystem influences, each having its own interface.

Figure 7.2 charts the system-suprasystem relationships in this cycle. The large circle connected by an interface with the Joneses is the senior Jones family comprised of Sam's parents, Verna and Todd. In this episode, Barbara's parents, while not physically present, affected in part the outcome of this cycle, which was the decision to continue the alternating visits to the two sets of parents at Christmas.

In this section we have attempted to highlight the Gemeinschaft nature of group behaviors and their meanings as evidenced in interface. Such behaviors are not to be understood in terms of their logic, but by the emotional and personal meanings they

FIGURE 7.2   Ecomap—Interface: The Joneses

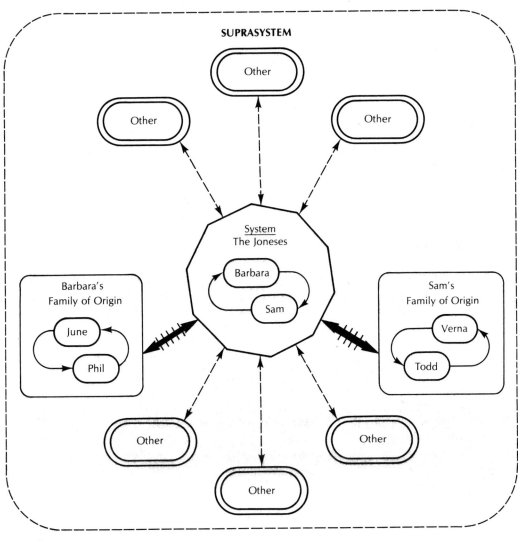

SUPRASYSTEM

Legend:

─┼┼┼┼─   = Interface

⬭   = Dormant Suprasystem Influences

◀──▶   = Thickness indicates relative importance

represent. The derivation of these behaviors is to be found in an underlying order and is to be understood in terms of the related goals of the subject systems.

Input

Inputs are always derived from the suprasystem and are classified in this model as being either maintenance or signal. Maintenance inputs are those that energize and operate the system, while signal inputs are processed by the system, resulting in its task output. The concept of input helps to illustrate the interdependence that every social organization has with its environment. It is through the use of this construct that we convey the position that all social organizations are both ultimately derived from and supported by organizations, groups, and individuals in their environment.

The distinctive feature of input when applied to the social group is that group members always represent both maintenance and signal inputs. This is the only form of social organization in which this is the case. The reason is found in the Gemeinschaft nature of relationships among group members; that is, the relationship serves as both a means and an end in itself. To restate the point, people become members of social groups because they enjoy one another's company, not just as a means to accomplish some other end. The group becomes the means by which members meet their social needs; the satisfaction of these needs then becomes the desired end state for group members.

In Chapter 2, A Social Systems Perspective, the following assumption was noted: "The individual is both the cause and the effect of all forms of human social organization." It is through an application of the model to the social group that we operationalize this assumption. The following example is offered to help develop the point.

Barbara and Sam met while in college, fell in love, and married. Barbara and Sam both represent input in the creation and continuance of the social group known as the Joneses. Conceptually, they represent maintenance inputs in their spousal roles because their spousal role relationship constitutes the group. It is their love, support, and attention to each other that builds (maintains) the group. Similarly, in the absence of their mutual love, support, and attention, the group will weaken and perhaps dissolve, for example, in separation or divorce. The group represents the means by which Barbara and Sam satisfy each other's needs, but the satisfaction of their respective needs also represents a primary function of the group. It is in the latter sense that Barbara and Sam as "selves" represent the group's signal input (and thus its task output). Recall that in symbolic interaction theory selfhood is viewed as a process. It is in this sense that Barbara and Sam each brought his or her own sense of selfhood into the marriage. Because of the importance of this relationship to each of them, the sense of selfhood of each is constantly being affected by their interactions with one another.

In using the model it is important not to think of inputs as occurring only at a single point in time, such as the time of group formation, for example. When systems are in an active mode, the concept of inputs represents the continuous process of infusion of information and resources from the suprasystem. Social organizations operate in cycles or through series of interconnected social acts; also at times social organizations are dormant, as, for example, when Barbara and Sam are in their work roles.

While developing the concept of interface, we described an episode in the lives of

Barbara and Sam during which they were spending Christmas with Sam's parents. This episode was treated as a cycle in the life of this family. Utilizing symbolic interaction theory, both Barbara and Sam entered that cycle with a conception of themselves in their spousal roles (maintenance input). Recall Barbara's later remark to a friend, "The first time we visited I felt like an idiot. Sam spent most of his time with his mother; he acted like I wasn't even there. I told him later that he had better treat me like his wife or I would never darken their door again." Her description describes essentially a negative effect on her sense of selfhood attributed to that visit—"I felt like an idiot." This statement represents a task output of this cycle, an effect on her self-esteem. The latter part of her statement pertains to the maintenance component of their spousal relationship—"he had better treat me like his wife or I will never darken their door again."

To develop this cyclical notion, consider the effect of paydays on family behavior. The money Barbara and Sam earn and apply jointly to meet family expenses would be treated as a maintenance input (the money they retain for themselves would not). The so-called family money is used to purchase food, pay the rent, and for a host of other family purposes. Whether Barbara and Sam are paid weekly, bimonthly, or monthly, there is a cycle of activities associated with the receipt and dispersal of this money. The example of a paycheck is helpful because for most people it illustrates the meaning of treating input as a resource that helps to energize and sustain a system during a cycle of activity. As with all forms of maintenance input, the amount of money devoted to the system is a critical determinant of system behaviors.

Suppose that Barbara and Sam want to purchase their own home. As a consequence of adopting this goal, they will most likely budget their money so they can save a portion of their income in order to make the necessary down payment. There will always be a critical relationship between a system's input and its outputs. In the case of money, the Joneses will learn that they cannot pay out more than they take in without experiencing some difficulties. The systems model incorporates this point—there will always be a relative balance between a system's inputs and its outputs. If this balance is upset, a threat is posed to what we describe as steady state. The loss of steady state results in the loss of system status.

Earlier we made the point that in modeling the social group, the individual group members represent both maintenance and signal forms of input. If either Barbara or Sam fails in providing maintenance inputs, their marriage will start experiencing difficulties. The familiar saying, "You can't get something for nothing" is relevant when applied to any form of input. Exchange, field, and need theories can help in further developing this point. For purposes of the example, let us say that both Barbara and Sam depend on one another primarily for satisfaction of their social belonging and love needs. Their marriage and their sense of relationship with each other are the means for achieving this satisfaction.

Barbara now finds herself being considered for a supervisory position at her agency. She is delighted at the prospect of this promotion, as is Sam. In the pursuit of the promotion, she spends increasing amounts of time on the job, brings work home, and takes on more work-related committee assignments. From a field theory perspective,[3] her work-related activities have taken on greater importance vis-à-vis other activities as she pursues the goal of a promotion. Similarly, there is a reduction in the amount of time, energy, and related maintenance inputs that Barbara provides to her marriage (reduction in the relative importance of activities devoted to family goals). Unless there is a redefinition of what Barbara and Sam expect from one another in the marriage, problems will arise between the two. From an exchange theory perspective, both are providing something the other needs, and in so doing are satisfying their own needs. If the exchange becomes unbalanced, difficulties will arise. Here the norm of distributive justice as we employed the concept in our discussion of exchange theory is useful.[4] If in their exchange relationship Sam believes that the unbalanced nature of the exchange is temporary and that in the longer term both he and Barbara will benefit (that is, Barbara's promotion will hasten the time when they can buy their home), their relationship will not be adversely affected.

The central point developed in the above example is the assumed relationship made in the model between inputs and outputs. The example has also been developed to highlight the position that inputs are always derived from the suprasystem. The most complicated point has to do with the individuals comprising social groups representing both signal and maintenance forms of input. In this latter instance and in our example, if Sam continues not having his needs met by Barbara, it can be predicted that his contributions to the marriage will be diminished (reduced inputs). There is a spiral-like phenomenon created between inputs and outputs that will pose a threat to the system. It should be noted that if Barbara and Sam have their needs fully satisfied (task outputs), they can be expected to put more of themselves into the marriage (increase in maintenance inputs).

Output

Exchange theory is helpful in conceptualizing output. Simply put, output is what the system produces and exchanges for its inputs. These exchanges take place with organizations, groups, and individuals within its suprasystem. Also, just as there are various forms of inputs, so are there classes of output. In this model we identify three forms: task, maintenance, and waste. Task outputs are signal inputs that have been processed through the system; maintenance outputs are maintenance inputs following a processing cycle; and waste represents a designation of inefficient and/or ineffective use of resources in providing both maintenance and task outputs. On a conceptual plane and over time, task and maintenance outputs should possess greater value than the original signal and maintenance inputs. It is in this sense that the system adds value and is functional. The system would thus be evidencing negative entropy; if the reverse is true and the value of a system's task and maintenance outputs is of the same or less value than the original signal and maintenance inputs, the system would be evidencing entropy, that is, a loss of order. In the latter instance, there is a threat to steady state.

When applied to the social group, the concept of task output will always refer to the state of individual group members following a processing cycle. This so-called state will always refer to what the group members expected from the group experience. Exchange theory is useful in identifying and specifying what *state* means. For a specific individual, it is what that person expected to derive from the group experience. The person has given; at issue is, What has she or he received in return and with what effect?

Intimacy and informality are hallmarks of the social group. Given these characteristics, the identification and specification of what an individual expects to obtain from the social group becomes problematic. It is highly unlikely that members of a social group will set forth a formal statement of what they individually and collectively expect to achieve from their group experience. Such a level of formality is antithetical to the character of the social group as we have defined it. However, we hold that each group member possesses a set of expectations of group outcomes. Further, we also assume that a general agreement exists among group members as to what they expect to receive from their association with each other. This does not mean that this outcome has been logically and rationally thought through by each group member; it would not be a social group if this were the case. For the individual, the task output of a group is essentially an emotional state, how the person feels about himself or herself and others. In this same sense, we hold that the individual assigns a value to his or her participation in the group.

In conceptualizing outcome for a social group, it is useful to do so both globally and for a specific cycle of activities. For example, on their tenth wedding anniversary, Barbara and Sam might reflect personally or with each other on what they expected from the marriage and what they have received. We would characterize this as a global assessment. On the other hand, an assessment of a cycle might be all of the activities that Barbara and Sam engage in relative to celebrating their tenth wedding anniversary. Suppose Sam was called away to an important business meeting and Barbara spent their anniversary evening alone. Both Barbara and Sam would probably assess the evening as a disappointment. The emotional states attributable to this situation are important. Let us say that Barbara was both angry and depressed over the situation. Barbara's emotional state would be considered a task outcome of this cycle of the group, as would Sam's. Given these two outcome assessments, it may well be that both Barbara and Sam's global assessment of their marriage would be very positive even though both would classify their tenth anniversary as a negative experience.

To return to the concept of output as applied to the social group, the sense of selfhood will always be a feature of output for group members. The impact on selfhood will vary among individuals depending on the group involved, along with a variety of other considerations. However, for most people and for most of the time, the family exercises the dominant influence in developing and sustaining a sense of self.

The notion of selfhood as a primary outcome of the social group is a complicated notion. Barbara and Sam not only are married and thus constitute a social group in accord with our definition, but they are also the most important people in each other's lives. While obviously not constructed as a formal output statement, both Barbara and Sam derive important parts (definitions) of themselves from their relationship with each other. Not only do they rely on each other for meeting their belonging and love needs, but for their self-esteem needs as well. Given the position taken in this model, that individual members of a social group constitute both maintenance and signal inputs, the so-called state of Barbara and Sam's marriage at any point in time would be considered a maintenance output. Similarly, the portion of Barbara and Sam's sense of selfhood derived from their marriage at any point would represent task output of their marital relationship. Our position in treating the acquisition and support of selfhood as a system's output has its foundations in the theory of symbolic interaction. Recall the statement, "I am what I think you think I am." In this example, Barbara and Sam have significance in each other's lives. The model provides a way of operationalizing this position.

In concluding this section, attention needs to be given to the notion of waste. Conceptually, some waste is always associated with the conversion of inputs to outputs. We will be drawing particular attention to this point when we discuss feedback. We now illustrate the concept of waste by Barbara's effort to secure a promotion. Let us say that Barbara did not receive the promotion. The time and effort she spent in the pursuit of the promotion that came at the expense of her family represents waste. Here we assume that no useful family outputs were achieved by this effort. Conceptually, waste is important because it becomes a means of accounting for a part of the discrepancy between a system's inputs and outputs. We can assume that both Barbara and Sam, and their relationship suffered somewhat from the experience, that there was essentially negative outcome to this experience. We would consider the resources used in this effort as waste.

Proposed Output

The preceding sections have contained references to proposed output. As discussed in Chapter 3, the concept of proposed output refers to the system's goal structure. It represents an approach to the operationalization of an organization's purposes. Our interest in this chapter is to examine the distinctive features of proposed output when applied to the social group.

We have already identified two of the most distinctive features of social groups: first, the Gemeinschaft nature of relationships among group members; and second, and linked to the first, that the individuals holding membership in the group comprise both its maintenance and its task outputs. More specifically, it is the individual's anticipated role performance within the group that constitutes the maintenance input. The signal input is the individual as a total personality, the self as a separate and distinct human being. Proposed task output is the person's sense of self that is expected to result from the group experience. Proposed maintenance outputs are represented by an expected future state of the system itself.

We will develop an example using Barbara and Sam to help explain the notion of proposed output. When the couple was contemplating their future relationship, Sam said, "Barbara, marrying you would make me the happiest man on earth." Conceptually speaking, Sam is contemplating a future sense of selfhood, one that will result in part from his relationship with Barbara. Here the social system will be the family we call the Joneses. In terms of the model, the Joneses as a family is more than Barbara and Sam in their respective family roles. This family, as viewed by this model, is a separate and distinct social entity. Barbara and Sam are also separate and distinct human personalities. Only a part of their lives are spent in their respective family roles; each plays many other roles in many other systems, for example, Barbara in her role as a social worker. In everyday language and in everyday occurrences we recognize and distinguish between ourselves and the various roles we play. In terms of means and ends, Sam's remark treated his relationship with Barbara as the means *and* the end state, his own happiness. Implicit in his remark would be the same end state for Barbara, the "happiest woman on earth." In both instances, the means is represented by their relationship as husband and wife, the Joneses.

Proposed maintenance outputs pertain to the future status of their relationship as members of the Jones family. The marriage vows that Barbara and Sam took contain statements of proposed maintenance outcomes, for example, that they will remain married "until death do us part." Proposed is a lifetime relationship as husband and wife. While this is a proposed goal, it does not follow that proposed and actual output are always the same. Nevertheless, this mutually held goal should shape the kind of relationship that develops.

In the earlier sections dealing with input and output, reference was made to money as another form of maintenance input. The money earned by Barbara and Sam that was jointly held and used for family purposes would indeed be considered as a maintenance input. If Barbara and Sam should establish a goal dealing with the disposition of family income, this would represent a proposed maintenance output; their previously mentioned goal of saving money for a down payment on a house would serve as a proposed maintenance output. Here we make the assumption that the purchase of the home will serve to strengthen family relationships. The key to the classification is in the purposes served by the money and/or related goods. If the intention of a given family is to accumulate wealth as an end in itself, the actual wealth accumulated at any point would be considered a task output; the intended amount to be accumulated would represent a proposed task output.

Before closing our discussion of proposed output and moving on to conversion operations, it is important to reiterate that proposed output always pertains to a cycle of activity. The cycle can be very short—a day or less; the cycle can also be very long—a lifetime. Proposed output is always related to the end state of a cycle. Finally, and because of the dominance of Gemeinschaft features of the relationships in social groups, proposed outputs are not usually formalized as a hierarchy of outcomes. This does not mean that the people comprising a group may not mutually hold very specific objectives. Also, the social relationships features that pertain to the mutual pursuit of these objectives can be Gesellschaft in nature. Here an example would be a decision by Barbara and Sam to save enough money to buy their own home by their third wedding anniversary. This was a logically and reasoned decision by the couple. In a manner of speaking, it was a businesslike decision based on income and tax considerations. Each payday they systematically deposited money in a savings account to be used for their down payment. Both the objective and the actions in pursuit of the objectives serve as an example of Gesellschaft features of a social relationship which in total is primarily Gemeinschaft in nature.

Conversion Operations

In an early chapter, conversion operations were likened to a black box. This box in the systems model represents the housing for the mysterious processes through which inputs are converted to outputs. In a social group application of the model, this wonderful box would contain the structures and processes that would carry out Cooley's assertion that through the primary group "human nature" comes into existence. As stated previously, there is no generally accepted explanation of the behaviors of social organizations in general or the social group in particular. Our use of the concept of conversion operations is simply a recognition that something happens to the individual as a result of participation in social groups. Similarly, through the personal interactions of its members, something happens to the group itself.

The approach we used for examining the conversion process involves use of two other concepts: structure and interactions. The notion of structure merely implies existence of an understandable order, the regularities characterizing the behaviors of all forms of social organization. As used in this model, structure is always anticipatory, it is never actual behavior. In contrast, interactions are the actual social behaviors of individuals acting as members of social organizations, for example, a family. Beyond the basic configurations and assumptions that comprise the model, it is the model user who selects appropriate theories and related knowledge sources for specific applications. Here we have found field, exchange, and symbolic interaction theories helpful.

Structure

Roles are always the dominant structural feature in any application of the systems model. Given that social groups are characterized by Gemeinschaft relationships, the portrayal of these role relationships diagrammatically is difficult. There have, however, been important effects in measuring and depicting these social relationships applicable to the social group. The general approach is known as **sociometry** and the actual graphical representation of these relationships is called a **sociogram.**[5]

Another useful approach for depicting structure in families is the genogram.[6] Here the focus is on kinship relationships both within the system and between the system, and those kinship relations that comprise parts of what we designate as suprasystem. We can show these relationships by using the Joneses. To help develop this aspect of structure, we are going to pick the Joneses up a little later in their marriage. Now they have a daughter, Ann, who is three months old. Figure 7.3 displays a genogram of the Jones family. Our subject system is comprised of Sam, Barbara, and their daughter, Ann. Both sets of parents and grandparents are shown along with other family members.

As indicated by the legend, a square denotes a male; for example, Sam; and the circle, a female, for example, Barbara. The horizontal line connecting a square and a circle indicates a marital relationship and the date of marriage, such as 6-15-84. The vertical line that descends from the couple indicates children of that marriage, for example, their daughter, Ann. A circle or a square that is crossed out indicates that the person named is deceased. An example is Todd's mother, Rose. The age shown, 73, was her age at death.

The genogram is not only a useful way of depicting the structural and kinship relationships within families, it has many helpful applications to social work practice with families. It presents a summary of important information on kinship relationships, including ages and marital status, to be used as a reference as well as a discussion guide for the worker and family members.

As evidenced by this genogram, we have much more information on the Joneses. Most important at this point is that with the birth of Ann, our social system has become more structurally complicated. The system now has three subsystems: (1) Barbara and

FIGURE 7.3 Genogram: The Joneses

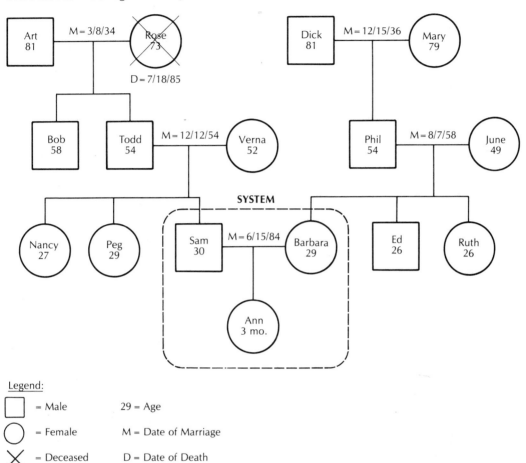

Legend:

☐	= Male	29 = Age	
○	= Female	M = Date of Marriage	
✕	= Deceased	D = Date of Death	

Sam in their spousal roles; (2) Barbara and Ann in the maternal parent and child roles; and (3) Sam and Ann in the paternal parent and child roles. To help keep the structure from becoming unnecessarily complicated, we will consider Barbara's location in this social system as her status position. This position is made up of two major roles, wife and mother. Similarly, Sam's status position is also comprised of two major roles, husband and father. For our immediate purposes, Ann's status position and role are one and the same, daughter. Figure 7.4 structurally portrays the Joneses as a social system with its three associated subsystems.

We have stressed in our discussion that group-related experiences are fundamental in the development of selfhood. Similarly, one's sense of selfhood is constantly changing and constantly developing; selfhood is a process, and for most people vitally related to the family roles they play. Figure 7.4 is helpful in developing this point because it illustrates the evolving nature of the group. Until the birth of Ann, Barbara and Sam related to one another only in the spousal roles. Now with Ann, new family roles are assumed.

FIGURE 7.4 The Jones Family: Subsystems

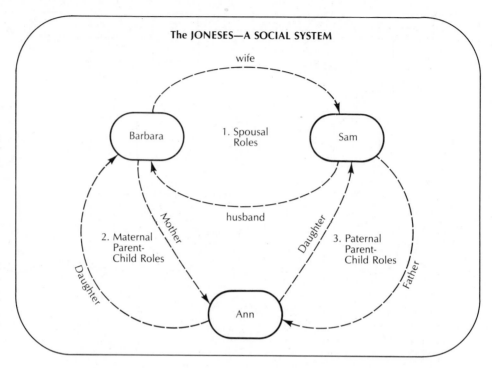

Life will not be the same for Barbara and Sam with the addition of their parenting roles. As a consequence, their own sense of selfhood will be different. Being a parent is now a vital part of their own sense of who they are.

In some ways, assuming a new role is like putting on a new suit of clothes; sometimes it takes a while to get used to your "self" in this new outfit. For many, the transition is an easy and a natural one. For others, it is less so, and some never are able to make the transition; they reject the role. Roles exist independent of the individual. An example is the parental role, a societal role for which there are normative performance standards. When Barbara and Sam became parents, they simply assumed their parental roles in relationship to Ann. They each had their own ideas not only of their own parental roles, but of the parental role of their spouse. They had learned their roles from their own parents and others while growing up. In enacting these roles, they will judge their own performances and their spouse's by these standards. For example, Barbara may state, "Sam is an awfully good father, he dearly loves Ann. We take turns getting up and feeding Ann and changing her diapers. It's a real partnership." Sam's sense of himself is going to be impacted not only by his own role performance but by those who are close to him and make their own judgments as to what kind of father he is, especially Barbara.

Symbolic interaction theory, particularly its attention to the idea of situation, is helpful in understanding the structural features of conversion operations. Recall that situation is the social and environmental context in which role enactments take place. In our use of the term, the situation is essentially synonymous with what we mean by structure. Here context includes not only the other individuals in their respective roles, but time, space, and all of the other environmental features that shape the perceptions of those who are enacting roles in a given interaction. For example, Barbara and Sam as human personalities will bring these parts (structural features) of themselves into any cycle of activity, for instance, having dinner together. Also shaping this situation is the amount of time they have for dinner—whether it will be rushed or leisurely; whether it takes place in their own home or a restaurant; whether their dinner spaces are cramped or comfortable, clean or dirty, drab or attractive; and other such situational features that affect role enactment.

Included in our conception of structure is proposed output. While for purposes of presenting the model we treat proposed output as a separate concept, it is a part of the system's conversion operations. Technically, proposed output or, more simply, goals, are always the desired future state that provide for the ordering and sequencing of interactions in any given cycle of a social group. More simply stated, the assumption is that all social behavior is purposive or goal directed. Therefore, every cycle of group activity will evidence this purposiveness. In turn, the purposiveness will shape the definition of the situation in which the interaction will take place. In our use of the Joneses, the goal of a cycle can be as simple as having breakfast together or as complicated and long term as living together "until death do us part."

Interactions

Earlier we had observed that social structures cannot be seen, touched, heard, tasted, or smelled. These structures exist in the minds of people and represent their perceptions of how they are to act in any specific interactional situation. Interactions are the actual behaviors that people engage in with one another. Interactions can be seen, heard, felt, tasted, and smelled. We see one another, we interpret gestures and body language; we hear what others say to us; and we embrace, kiss and touch one another. It is through our senses that we derive meaning that shapes our development of self and our view of others.

The model user knows that the actual behavior of a social group via the behaviors of those who comprise it will never conform exactly to its structure. Why? In the first place, structure is introspective; it exists in the minds of people and pertains to their perception of who they are, their sense of selfhood. This sense of self includes all the roles they are called upon to play and how their roles are to be enacted. Second, the individual also holds expectations of how counter roles are to be played. In real life, most of this behavior is spontaneous and flows naturally like the waters of a stream following the contours of the creek bed. It is important to note that the creek bed (like structure) is constantly changing as the water flows through it (like interactions). The metaphor of the creek bed is also helpful in conveying the interaction between the channels that guide the flow of water and the water itself—each acts on the other, each is influenced by the other.

Conceptually and theoretically it is helpful to equate interactions with symbolic interactions.[7] To develop the point we will use our social group, the Joneses. A simple example would be the goal the Joneses have of buying a home (a proposed output of this system). Each payday, Barbara deposits $400 of her check into a joint savings account.

This money will ultimately be used for a down payment on their house. This action on Barbara's part stems from the previously stated goal. Further, her role as wife now incorporates the expectation that she will make this monthly deposit. The role change stems from the newly adopted goal and serves as a guide to her behavior as well as Sam's. For example, the statement, "Barbara, how much do we have in the bank now?" incorporates the notion of symbolic interaction in the sense that Barbara and Sam have comparable meanings attached to such questions about the savings account. Another way to stating this shared meaning would be, "How much money do we have toward the down payment on our home?"

A more complex set of interactions would be those directed toward their mutual goal of self-actualization. This goal, unlike the house, is likely to remain a goal as long as this social group (marriage) is intact. Earlier the point was made that Barbara and Sam are the most important people in each other's lives. As a consequence, each makes a contribution to the need for self-actualization of the other. Given their importance to each other, their actual interactions are likely to contribute to and distract from the goal. Interactions associated with their mutual goal of self-actualization might be that Barbara and Sam set aside Friday night as time just for each other (structure). One Friday, Sam arrives home with a dozen roses. Barbara is taken back and asks, "What is the occasion?" His reply: "You are; it is just a reminder of what a wonderful wife and mother you are. I am probably the luckiest man in the world." The interaction includes the purchase and presentation of the roses to Barbara as well as her statement. For both Barbara and Sam, red roses are symbolic of their mutual love. (Sam has been surprising Barbara with red roses throughout their marriage.) The feelings engendered by this interaction make Barbara feel very good about herself, Sam, Ann, and their marriage.

This example can be useful when viewed as a social act, a cycle of activity occurring between Barbara and Sam. In a manner of speaking, the goal of this cycle is the reaffirmation of their love for each other and their own sense of selfhood. The cycle is diagramed in Figure 7.5.

Recall that in symbolic interaction theory, the social act is treated as the smallest interactional unit identifiable in an ongoing relationship. It will always involve at least two or more people, and although not necessarily made explicit, it will have a purpose, a beginning, and an ending point. The selection and the analysis of the social act is simply an approach to the study of the stream of human interaction that typifies the behavior of any given individual or social group. If the focus is on an individual, that person will be impacted upon by a variety of different groups of which she or he is a member. If the focus is on the group, the group itself will change and develop over time as the relationships among its members change and develop.

The Social Group

Our focus in this section is on the social group and our example is the Joneses. This episode is about five hours in length and primarily involves Barbara and Sam. Ann is only incidentally involved, but her involvement is shaped by the goal of the episode; which is the reaffirmation of the love that Barbara and Sam have for each other, the effects of this love, and the esteem and support it provides on the development of their respective senses of selfhood. The episode starts with Sam entering their apartment.

FIGURE 7.5 The Social Act: The Joneses

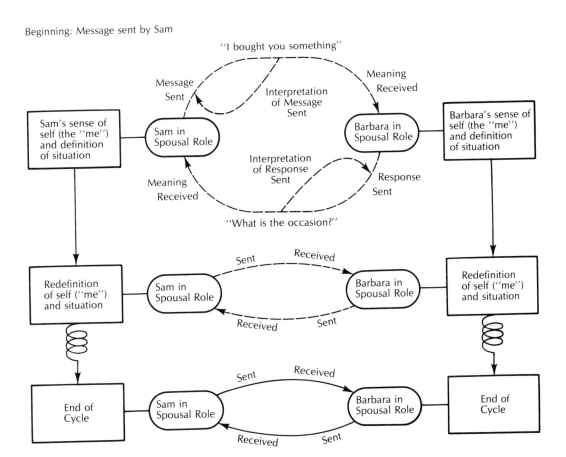

Purpose: To reaffirm marital relationship

Beginning: Message sent by Sam

Ending Point: Sleep following sexual relations

It is a pretty autumn day, things have been going well for Sam in his job, and it is Friday. Sam is feeling quite good about himself and his family. As he is contemplating his situation, he decides to stop on the way home and pick up a dozen red roses for Barbara and a cuddly teddy bear for Ann. Here Sam is moving out of his work role and is in the process of taking on his husband and father roles. His actions in the purchase of the flowers and the teddy bear stem from the contemplation of these roles and how they should be enacted when he arrives home. With Sam, this contemplation is a cognitive process. His actions in buying the flowers and the teddy bear result from playing his role, and that of both Barbara and Ann, in his own mind. He anticipates both Barbara's response and that of Ann when he presents them with their respective gifts. It is their anticipated responses that cause him to stop and make the purchases. Even though she is present only in his mind, he starts feeling warmly toward Barbara and says to himself as he is driving home, "She is a fine woman," and he smiles.

In the foregoing description, the cognitive process which involves Sam's thinking about himself and his family represents the evolvement of structure. The structure is the imagined roles that he plays out in his mind. These imagined interactions provide the guides to his behavior—structure always precedes and serves as the initial guide to the social behaviors. It is the playing out of the role that we label as interactions.

To return to our example, upon opening the door to the apartment Sam greets Barbara with a loving smile and says, "I brought you something." In Figure 7.5 this represents the start of the interaction. We have, in the development of the example, alluded to Sam's own sense of selfhood (he is feeling very good about his family). This sense of selfhood is summarized in the square on the left side of the figure. Sam's words of greeting stem from this sense of himself and his definition of the situation that is now unfolding. His words, "I brought you something," represent the message sent. The intended meaning is further communicated by his smile, by his movement toward Barbara, and by the roses he is about to present. The moment that Sam starts to speak, he is now hearing what he says and rendering a personal judgment as to whether this conforms to what he was intending to communicate. Here again, we have evidence of structure. Sam is judging what he actually hears himself saying (the meaning being transmitted to Barbara) against the meaning he was intending to convey. He mentally does this by playing his own spousal role and by simultaneously playing Barbara's spousal role.

These imagined roles represent the structural determinants in this interaction. The looping back of the message as shown in the figure represents this comparison that is constantly going on in social interactions. As indicated previously, Sam is taking the role of Barbara in this process even before she responds. In part, he does this by watching her face, her movements, and anything else that may provide clues to how she is receiving this message. This is a dynamic process, and as a consequence the actual words that Sam is using in conveying his meaning to Barbara may be altered before he completes his part of the interaction, and prior to the time that Barbara actually responds.

Barbara will derive her own meanings from the message being sent in essentially the same way as described for Sam. She will process a sense of self, a definition of the immediate situation. She will do so in part by playing her own role as well as that of Sam. This occurs almost instantly (this is not a new situation for either Barbara or Sam) so their interactions will tend to unfold in the way they have before. For purposes of this example, let us assume that she responds in the way that Sam has predicted. Her response, which is given with a smile is: "What is the occasion?", and is consistent with Sam's expectation. Just as with Sam, Barbara will not know exactly what her response is until she actually hears herself. Again, there is a looping back and an interpretation of Barbara's own words as soon as they are spoken and before there is a verbal response from Sam.

The interaction is now underway and both are defining the situation in essentially the same way. Sam's reply to Barbara's response is: "You are; it is just a reminder of what a wonderful wife and mother you are. I am probably the luckiest man in the world." This is the kind of response that Barbara was expecting and is affirming to her own sense of selfhood and their marriage. She smiles and interaction continues: Sam gives the new teddy bear to Ann and she squeals with delight. Again, the response is consistent with what Sam had anticipated. For a few minutes Sam and Ann play peek-a-boo. The couple then decides to have dinner at their favorite restaurant. They call their baby-sitter for Ann. They have a fun evening with much small talk and return home quite late. Sam takes the baby-sitter home. When he returns, Barbara and Sam sexually consummate the evening and go to sleep. The episode/cycle is now complete and is for both Barbara and Sam a great evening with both feeling good about each other and about themselves. In Figure 7.5, the final interaction closes the cycle but in a manner that is ready to start again as they pick up their spousal roles in the morning.

This episode, in a manner of speaking, went in accord with the script. The couple is feeling good about themselves, about each other, and the world in general. The system is in steady state. With a different scenario the outcome could have been quite different. It could have ended with an argument and sleeping in different rooms, or worse. What if after Sam's initial greeting—"the meaning sent"—Barbara had responded suspiciously, "What have you done now?" (that you are trying to relieve your guilt by giving me these roses). Sam is now caught off guard not having expected this response. His response would probably be a defensive one, expressing perhaps annoyance and emotional pain. Our interest here is not one of the content but the basic dynamics—the continuing interplay between structure and interactions in the system's conversion operations.

In our discussion of conversion operations, we have relied heavily on concepts drawn from symbolic interaction theory. In doing so we have sought to offer an approach to the understanding of the behaviors of the social group, particularly the family. We find symbolic interaction theory useful because it deals effectively with behavior at the small group level. The theory, or at least the concepts from it that we use, are fully consistent with the model and its basic assumptions. Symbolic theory, with its focus on interpersonal communications, is also especially helpful in terms of its application to social work practice.

While our focus is on the natural group, the application of the insights provided to the formed group is easily made. For example, the casework and/or therapeutic relationship is a social system. All the concepts comprising the model can be identified in a casework relationship if that relationship exhibits the characteristics of interdependence and wholeness. The conversion operations will be comprised of a services plan and its associated tasks and activities. This is the structural aspect. The actual behavior of the caseworker and client are the interactions. Here the concepts of situation and social act as drawn from symbolic interaction can be very helpful. The social act (cycle) can be a single session or the entire process ending in the closure of the case.

Feedback

Technically, feedback is that feature of structure that possesses the function of gathering and reporting back into the system the progress (or lack thereof) toward goal achievement. All forms of social organization are characterized by efforts aimed at determining the extent to which their functions are being performed satisfactorily. Here the notion of "satisfactory functional performance" pertains to relations within the organization (maintenance outcomes) as well as between the organization and other individuals, groups, and agencies in its suprasystem (task outcomes). As with other system features, the social group is distinguished by its informal feedback arrangements.

To develop the notion of external feedback, let us return to the Joneses. Recall that in our example Barbara and Sam have one child, Ann, and want to have a second, who they hope will be a son. Ann has two sets of grandparents who are both very proud of their granddaughter. Both sets of grandparents also hope that Barbara and Sam will have more children. In their case, gender is not an issue. They simply want more "grand-babies." Let us also say, for purposes of developing the example, that at the time of their marriage neither Barbara or Sam wanted children; they both had strong career aspirations and felt that having children would interfere with their career goals. After their marriage, and sometimes not too subtly, both Barbara's and Sam's parents inquired as to whether they had changed their minds about having children. In this instance, Barbara and Sam were receiving feedback regarding a goal that excluded having children; that is, their goal was not meeting suprasystem expectations.

Earlier we distinguished two forms of feedback, negative and positive. We cautioned at that time against equating negative with "bad" and positive with "good." Negative feedback simply refers to the kind of information that tracks the deviation from the current state to a desired state. The purpose of negative feedback is to provide information that can serve to reduce the variability from the actual state to the proposed future state. Negative feedback, in the manner that it is applied in this model, is always in relationship to proposed output, the goals of a particular cycle of system activity. Negative feedback provides the information necessary to keep the system moving toward its goal, to reduce the deviation (thus the negative or "−") between the desired state and the actual state. Ultimately, you want to reduce the negative deviation to the point that it is identical with the proposed state—no deviation.

Positive feedback also has as its reference point a specified future point, a goal state of the system. Positive feedback pertains to information that identifies an increase (thus, the positive or "+") in the variability between the current status of a system and its proposed future state. A reduction in the deviation or variability among a past state, the current state, and the proposed state indicates that progress is being made toward the specified goals. Positive feedback is disconfirming and suggests that progress toward that goal is not evident; the movement of the system is away from that goal.

An example of negative and positive feedback in a casework situation might involve a worker and a depressed client. One goal of this helping relationship might involve a decrease (−) in the number of times the client "breaks into tears" between sessions (the objective is to reduce the number of times this occurs to zero by a specified time). Starting with a baseline of fifteen times per week, the actual number of times the crying takes place compared to the objective would represent feedback. If at a particular session, the number of tearful times had dropped to eight, this would be an example of negative feedback. Unless there were information to the contrary, this would suggest that the activities comprising the services plan were working, that the number of episodes of crying were being reduced. If this progress continues, then the goal (objective) should be reached. The progress being made as evidenced by the negative feedback is confirming of the appropriateness and attainability of the goal.

Using the same example, positive feedback would be represented by an increase (+) in the number of crying episodes occurring between sessions, for instance, from fifteen to twenty. If these episodes continue to increase, the worker should start questioning the efficacy of the services plan or perhaps the assessment of the client that led to the services plan and its goal of reducing the crying episodes. Perhaps the client's depression is more severe than first indicated, and the worker should seek a psychiatric and/or a medical evaluation of the client's condition. Again, the point being made is that both forms of feedback are important but they mean different things. In a professional relationship, both are critical and necessary to monitor in order for the relationship to maintain steady state.

Now let us return to the Joneses and develop in this example the notions of negative and positive feedback. We had indicated that Barbara and Sam had decided at the time of their marriage they would not have children—a goal statement. Instead, they would both pursue their respective careers with their marriage supporting this goal. The interactions between the two of them and their friends confirming their goal of not having children and of pursuing their professional careers would be evidence of negative feedback. This type of feedback serves to reduce the variability between their goal and their present situation. The couple's use of birth control measures and their confirming messages to each other about their decision not to have children would evidence negative feedback confirming that goal.

There is, however, not full agreement on this system's goal by some key members of the suprasystem. Both Barbara's and Sam's parents were looking forward to being grandparents and were more than disappointed in the couple's decision not to have children. This disappointment, in the various ways that it was evidenced, would itself be feedback. It is positive feedback in the sense that it tends to increase the deviation from the goal of not having children. In this case it was successful in the sense that Barbara and Sam began to have doubts about their goal of not having children and the dedication to their own careers. As in this case, positive feedback tends to be disconfirming information about a system goal and suggests the need to reconsider system goals.

When Barbara's and Sam's parents learned that Barbara was pregnant, they were delighted and conveyed their pleasure in a variety of ways—Barbara's father promptly put a bumper sticker on his car that read, "Ask me about my Grandbaby," and Sam's mother crocheted baby blankets. Now we have confirming suprasystem feedback to the system. Here we have an example of the adoption of a new goal that is, more consistent with suprasystem expectations, that is, more functional. The feedback is now confirming. The feedback is technically negative in the sense that it shows a reduction (−) in the deviation between the system's goal and the current state of the system.

Important from a conceptual position is that feedback is always information fed back into the system. At the point of reentry into the system, feedback becomes designated as maintenance input. To illustrate the notion of feedback as a maintenance input we will provide a final example involving the Joneses. Recall that one goal of the Joneses was to purchase their own home. In pursuit of this goal, both Barbara and Sam decided on a savings plan in which there would be monthly deposits into a savings account. Their savings would then be used for a down payment on a house. Barbara checking their savings account would not in itself constitute feedback to this system because the information obtained was not shared with Sam and thus did not serve as a maintenance input. Recall that maintenance inputs serve to activate and drive the system. Feedback is always a vital maintenance input; its specific function is to help correct any imbalance that may be occurring in the system's pursuit of its goals. For example, if Barbara had found upon checking the savings balance that Sam had made a withdrawal, and had checked with Sam, this would be positive feedback because it represented an increase in variability between what was expected and what occurred.

In this situation, Barbara did check with Sam for an explanation. Since this information was fed back into the system, it served as a maintenance input for the next cycle of activity. Let us say that Sam offered a plausible explanation indicating that he had used the money to pay a bill because his bonus check hadn't come through yet, saying, "I thought I had mentioned this to you; I'll put the money back as soon as I get my check." A month later Barbara makes her usual deposit and finds that another substantial withdrawal has been made. With Sam's previous explanation and this new information, Barbara is likely to be very upset. As a consequence, she probably would confront her husband and demand to know why he had made the withdrawal. Barbara's confrontation with Sam would indeed be considered feedback, representing a major deviation from their goal (proposed output). Again, the feedback would represent a maintenance input, theoretically designed to get the system back on course. To extend the example, let us say that unknown to Barbara, Sam was on drugs and had started to use the money in their savings account to support his growing drug habit. Now let us suppose that after a series of heated exchanges over the bank withdrawal, Sam confesses to his wife that he is using cocaine and used their down payment money to buy "coke." Barbara is shocked, angry, bewildered, and at a loss as to what to do, what to say.

Given the nature of the problem, it appears as though the goal of purchasing their own home is no longer a realistic one, at least for the near future. Barbara and Sam will need to rethink the purpose of their relationship and establish some new goals; Sam may agree to seek treatment for his addiction and Barbara may agree to be supportive and to work toward meeting the cost of his treatment. Here we have a new goal structure and a whole new set of relationship changes between Barbara and Sam associated with the newly adopted family goal.

The adjustment that took place resulted from the positive feedback on the goal status of their down payment money. The feedback led to a major reworking of Barbara and Sam's relationship based on the establishment of new goals. Conceptually speaking, feedback, if not heeded, will lead to problems in the system's capacity to function and, if serious enough, to the dissolution of the system itself. In short, if the system ceases to be functional, sooner or later it ceases to generate the inputs required for its continuance, resulting in a loss of steady state.

SUMMARY

This chapter has provided an application of the social systems model. Focusing on the distinctive features of the social group, the eight concepts comprising the model have been described, and, through use of examples, have been systematically related to each other. The concepts comprising the model are boundary, suprasystem, interface, inputs, outputs, proposed outputs, conversion operations, and feedback.

We have distinguished the formed from the natural group. In our use of these terms, the so-called natural group is essentially synonymous with our use of the term social group. These groups form naturally in the sense that their origins and their purposes are to be found in the distinctive qualities possessed by all human beings. Perhaps Maslow more than any other theorist identified the need for belongingness and love,[8] and labeled it as one of the basic needs in his theory of a hierarchy of human needs. In our conceptualization of the social group we have also relied heavily on the contention made by Charles Horton Cooley that the distinctive qualities of humanness are socially acquired and supported through life by primary groups. What Cooley referred to as a *primary group* is very close to what we call the *social group*. It is this contention by Cooley that we have sought to operationalize in the model by considering the individuals who comprise social groups as representing both the group's signal and maintenance inputs, and the group's task outputs.

Our position is that formed groups, such as a therapeutic group or a helping relationship comprising the worker and the client, are distinguished from the social group by the types and purposes of the relationships utilized. Here we borrowed from the seminal works of Tönnies and his use of the concepts of Gemeinschaft and Gesellschaft. The professional relationship is essentially Gesellschaft in character, while the social group is dominated by Gemeinschaft relationships. We are also using the notion of "formed" advisedly when we apply it to the reasoned creation of groups to be used professionally. In such an instance, the worker forms a group as the medium through which the helping process is to be conducted, and borrows on her or his knowledge of the dynamics of the natural/social group in fashioning this medium of intervention. This professional, formed group represents a calculated mixture of Gemeinschaft and Gesellschaft features and is based on the needs of the client and the goals of the helping effort.

A number of different kinds of social groups have been used to help identify the distinguishing features of systems concepts. To help demonstrate the interrelationship or wholeness of these concepts, we made particular use of the Jones family. We could have used any other social group to serve this purpose. Our choice of a family as the principal example was intended to convey our belief that the family is the dominant form of social group and the one to which most of our readers can most easily relate.

We have also used concepts from exchange, field, need, and symbolic theories to extend the usefulness of the model when applied to the social group. In doing so we have sought to show how existing theory can be used to further develop specific applications of the model.

To conclude this chapter we present Figure 7.6 to model the Joneses as a social system.

GLOSSARY

Ecomap   As used here, a diagrammatic presentation of a system's suprasystem.

Formed group   As used in this chapter, a small group that has been created specifically

FIGURE 7.6   The Jones Family as a Social System

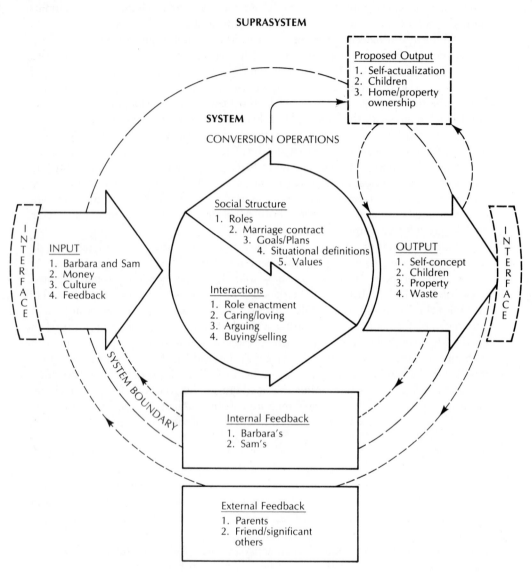

to accomplish some task. The helping relationship between a social worker and a client is an example of such a group.

Natural group   As used in this chapter, synonymous with social group. The designation has been made in order to draw a contrast between a natural and a formed group. Natural groups are characterized as self-organizing, while formed groups are intentionally organized.

Sociogram   A diametrical representation of social relationships in social groups. Special attention is given to the direction and intensity of these relationships.

Sociometry   The study of structure and function of small groups.

NOTES

1. Cooley's notion of the primary group was reviewed in Chapter 6; see Charles Horton Cooley, *Human Nature and the Social Order*, rev. ed. (New York: Charles Scribner's Sons, 1922).

2. An ecomap or ecogram, as they are sometimes called, is a way of graphically depicting what we refer to as a system's suprasystem. For a discussion of the ecomap as it is sometimes used in social work, see Beulah R. Compton and Burt Galaway, *Social Work Processes*, 4th ed. (Belmont, CA: Wadsworth Publishing Company, 1989.) For another representative family-centered presentation of this general approach to diagramming, see Evan Imber-Black, *Families and Larger Systems: A Family Therapist's Guide Through the Labyrinth* (New York: The Guilford Press, 1988), 9–13.

3. For a discussion, see Kurt Lewin, "Behavior and Development as a Function of the Total Situation," in *Manual of Child Psychology*, ed. Leonard Carmichael, 2nd ed. (New York: John Wiley & Sons, 1954), 918–948.

4. The norm "distributive justice" was discussed in Chapter 6. For a review of the concept, see Marvin Olsen, *The Process of Social Organization*, 2nd ed. (New York: Holt, Rinehart and Winston, 1975), 94–95.

5. See, for example, J. L. Moreno, *Who Shall Survive? Foundations of Sociometry, Group Psychotherapy and Sociodrama* (Beacon, N.Y.: Beacon House, 1953).

6. For a useful summary of the genogram applicable to social work practice, see Norman L. Paul and Betty B. Paul, "Death and Changes in Sexual Behavior" in *Normal Family Processes*, ed. Froma Walsh (New York, The Guilford Press, 1982), 229–250.

7. For useful overview of symbolic interaction theory and the use of situation see John P. Hewitt, *Self and Society: A Symbolic Interactionist Social Psychology*, 3rd ed. (Boston: Allyn and Bacon, 1984).

8. Maslow's need hierarchy was reviewed in Chapter 2. The basic reference for his work is Abraham Maslow, *Motivation and Personality*, 2nd ed. (New York: Harper and Row, 1970).

Chapter 8

The Social Group: Systems Dynamics

OUTLINE

Introduction: Steady State
Goal Attainment
Integration
Adaptation

Pattern Maintenance
Summary
Glossary
Notes

Introduction: Steady State

Chapter 4 served as an introduction to the dynamics of social systems as viewed by this model. We will briefly review that here as we consider the distinctive features of these dynamics as they are evidenced in the behavior of social groups.

Because of its small size, relative simplicity, and familiarity, the social group serves as a useful starting place to examine further the notion of system dynamics. In preparation for this discussion we have reviewed lines of theory development applicable to the social group, namely, exchange and symbolic interaction theories. These two lines of intellectual inquiry, along with others, have been useful in developing the social systems model. Up to this point our focus has been on the descriptive value of the model. The eight concepts comprising the model represent characteristics that we believe are possessed by all social groups exhibiting the qualities of interdependence and wholeness. The model therefore can inform practice by helping the worker categorize her or his observations, particularly in the assessment phase of the helping process.

Now our attention turns to the common action patterns exhibited by social groups. We have indicated earlier our assumption that all human social behavior is functional in its orientation, that is, it is goal directed. While the notion of being goal directed provides a useful starting place, the need is for a more comprehensive framework from which to view group behaviors. We also want to anchor our approach to the study of natural processes evidenced by healthy groups as opposed to one focusing on deviance and pathology.[1] In everyday practice the social worker is confronted with individuals, groups, families, and organizations, in various problem states. Our interest is in a way of formulating the natural state, one exhibiting the healthy patterns associated with growth and development, not the sick ones. Perhaps from this perspective we can learn more about the problem or deviant states. Perhaps even more important would be how we as professionals can capitalize on the healthy parts of relationship patterns as we construct our intervention strategies to deal with the less healthy parts.

We began our effort in formulating this sought-after condition of a group's well-being by giving it a name—steady state. Our particular formulation of steady state built on the ideas advanced by Ludwig von Bertalanffy in general systems theory. Borrowing from the work of Abraham Maslow, we made the further assumption that the natural state of all social groups would be proactive.[2] To constrast the conditions of being proactive and reactive we employed the term homeostasis. Recall that homeostasis is essentially a closed systems term, one in which the optimum state is fixed, an example being body temperature. System deviation is from a fixed state, and system responses are those that seek to return the system to a fixed state of equilibrium. Steady state is, in contrast, a state that is constantly in flux. The healthy state is one of change. The notion of "steady" refers to the continuity of input-output exchanges between the system and its suprasystem.

It was the work of Talcott Parsons in action theory that provided the basic outlines of an approach to modeling system dynamics.[3] Recall that Parsons identified what he considered to be four universal problems that confront all social systems in their quest to survive and grow. He labeled these as (1) goal attainment; (2) integration; (3) adaptation; and (4) pattern maintenance. These problems each have two major characteristics. First, the problem will deal with either internal relationships or external ones. Second, the problem will deal with the means being used or the ends being sought (see Figure 4.4, Chapter 4). Goal attainment is an external problem in that it deals with suprasystem expectations. It is also a problem dealing with the end states, the system's task goals.

The problem of integration is internal, dealing with the needs of the system itself. The satisfaction of these needs is the end state being sought, and is synonymous with the system's maintenance goals.

Adaptation is external in the sense that the problems primarily involve the system's external relationships. These are instrumental problems in the sense that they involve adaptation processes needed for the system to achieve its task goals.

The final problem, pattern maintenance, is internal and instrumental. It is internal in the sense that it deals with the problem of maintaining the core sets of relationships that bind system members to each other. It is their relationships that provide the system with its distinguishing characteristics. These problems are also instrumental in the sense that it is these key relationship features that serve as the means for the system to achieve its maintenance goals.

For many, the level of abstraction required to think in systems terms is difficult. This poses a problem to us as we seek to identify general patterns of social interaction that are applicable to all social groups. If the model is to inform practice, the patterns have to be applicable to any one of an infinite number of specific groups. As most of you have already determined, the four-problem paradigm that we are using introduces an even higher level of abstraction than the model itself. Our own experience is that the level of generality is only part of the problem; the larger problem is to break out of a mode of thinking that is linear and reductionistic. In short, it is not helpful to think in cause and effect terms and to separate out these four problems and address them as though they are independent of one another. These four problems are all interrelated so that efforts at dealing with one can affect the other three in either a helpful or adverse way. Once the reader becomes comfortable with the systems vocabulary and in thinking systemically, we believe the abstractness will cease to be a problem. Our hope is that the four-problem paradigm will help you to think in systems terms.

With the acknowledgement of the level of abstractness involved as background, let us now continue to develop the paradigm. In doing so, we will summarize the relevant features of each problem. To do this complicates our own argument to think in terms of wholeness rather than in reductionist terms. In doing so, we can only again caution at the onset that each of these problems is related to the other three. What we would seek would be system interactions that optimize the management of these four problems simultaneously.

Goal Attainment

THE PROBLEM: How to Achieve the Group's Task Goals, Specifically Member Needs for Self-Development

Social groups come into existence as a principal means of meeting the individual needs of their constituent members. Their continuance depends on at least minimal levels of need satisfaction occurring. The earlier definitions of role, norm, and role reciprocality should prove useful to you in conceptualizing the processes associated with the maintenance of steady state. Given the four-problem paradigm, the problem-solving efforts by the system differentiate roles among group members.[4]

Those role features specific to expected behavior in a given interactional situation are called norms. The notion of role reciprocality deals with the mutual expectations in role performance by those engaged in the same functional process; goal attainment, for example. Because of the small size of social groups, all members are likely to be involved in dealing with each of the problems associated with the maintenance of steady state. In other words, by examining the structure of the roles comprising a specific social group, one should be able to discern the normative features of those roles associated with dealing with each of the problems. This does not mean that each group member will be equally involved in dealing with each of the four problems. Much more likely, a given member of the group will have a lead responsibility with the other group members (or member) playing a secondary or supporting role. To summarize this point with respect to goal attainment, every social system will have roles or features of roles associated with addressing the problem of goal attainment. The distinctiveness of this feature in the social group is the informal nature of this aspect of structure.

Again, we will build on our earlier example of Barbara and Sam to illustrate the goal attainment aspect of steady state. Barbara has always taken pride in her long, peach-colored hair. She still recalls fondly those childhood memories of her mother brushing her hair and telling her how beautiful it was and telling her that she was "such a pretty girl." She has similar happy memories of sitting on her father's lap and having him stroke her long hair and call her "Peaches," a nickname that stayed with her through college. Sam also found Barbara's hair to be something special and was quick to compliment Barbara's effort at making herself more attractive by changing hairstyles. In goal-attainment terms, that part of Barbara's perception of selfhood related to her hair is dependent in part on the time she spends on her hair and Sam's reactions to this aspect of herself. These behaviors between Barbara and Sam stem from those structural aspects of their respective roles devoted to the goal-attainment function. (In this context, one goal of the system is the support and development of the sense of selfhood for both Barbara and Sam.)

Perhaps a negative example using the same problem would be instructive. Let us say that Barbara has just returned from the beauty shop and has had her hair cut and newly styled. She anxiously awaits Sam's return from work to see what he has to say, hoping that he will be pleased. Sam enters the apartment, says "Hi," moves on to the refrigerator, gets a can of beer, and then sits down in front of the television to watch a football game. A couple of minutes later, he yells to his wife, who is still in the kitchen, "Honey, how soon will dinner be ready? I'm starved."

Using symbolic interaction theory, Barbara had mentally defined a situation in which both she and Sam had specific roles to play. The goal of this situation, from Barbara's definition, was a positive and confirming comment about her new haircut and hair style. Conceptually speaking, because of Sam's importance to her and because of the importance of her hair to her concept of self, Sam's behavior in this situation is likely to be taken very personally. Sam came onto the scene, defined the situation differently, and proceeded to carry out his role in accordance with his definition (that is, Barbara's role as the cook who prepares dinner). Based on the earlier situation, Barbara is likely to be more than a little disappointed and perhaps annoyed with her husband. While perhaps not consciously, the absence of a positive response from Sam may even stir some self-doubts, for example, about her attractiveness to Sam.

Given the goal of this set of events (Barbara's definition), Sam, because of his insensitivity, is likely to receive feedback from his wife. In a more comprehensive application of the example, let us say that Barbara and Sam are increasingly less attentive to each other's needs and expectations; perhaps some of the "magic" has gone out of their relationship. This would be another way of describing a growing problem in goal-attainment efforts and thus a threat to the steady state of this system. The key in this formulation is conceiving the group as both a means and an end. In this scenario, the relationship as a means was not working; it was producing hurtful rather than helpful ends.

In summary, then, the concept of goal attainment is essentially synonymous with what we have earlier described as task output. The problem is that unless a system is able to achieve a satisfactory level of goal attainment, a threat is posed to its steady state. While seemingly a simple and common-sense concept, goal attainment is treated in this formulation as an external and consummatory function of the system. The subtleties of these distinctions will be developed as the other concepts comprising steady state are discussed. It is sufficient to note at this time that in our example the Joneses constitute the social system. Barbara and Sam are individuals who, when they are not playing their respective family roles, exist as human personalities independent of the social group called the Joneses. The effect of the marital relationship on Barbara and Sam as total personalities encompasses what is meant by *goal attainment*.

Conceptually, Barbara and Sam as total personalities exist as part of the system's suprasystem. In this sense, goal attainment is an external function, and since it is an effect, it is also a consummatory function of the system, an example being the effect of Barbara and Sam's marital relationship on Barbara and Sam as individuals. Another way of illustrating this notion would be a comment by Sam's mother to a friend: "Barbara has been good for Sam: he really settled down after he met her." In terms of the model, the comment suggests that the relationship between Barbara and Sam has had a beneficial effect on Sam as an individual, at least in the eyes of his mother. Conceptually speaking, the effect is not one-way—Barbara affecting Sam. Rather, the effect is an interactive one attributed to the system (the social group). In terms of the comment by Sam's mother, it represents a task outcome statement of the social group called the Joneses. In other words, Sam as an individual is a somewhat different person today than he was prior to his relationship with Barbara. It should also be noted that social groups can have negative as well as positive effects on those who comprise them. Here an evaluative statement by Sam's mother might have been, "He was a good boy until he met Barbara."

In our example of goal attainment we have relied heavily on the theory of symbolic interaction, particularly on the concepts of situation, self, and social act.[5] Whether consciously or not, both Barbara and Sam know they are good for each other. In their marriage they have each been supportive of the other and have given each other a sufficient amount of space to grow as a person. This notion of being supportive of the other and giving the other space to grow as a person is what we define as activities related to dealing with the goal attainment problem.

As a reader you might ask, what is the problem? *Shouldn't* Barbara and Sam be supportive of one another, with each giving the other space to grow as a person? Our reply is yes, but it is not always easy to do. For example, Barbara and Sam can be so caught up in their own needs that neither has as much time for the other as the other requires. Also, as we will see next when we examine the problem of integration, giving each other support and room to grow can come at the expense of the system's maintenance needs.

Integration

THE PROBLEM: How to Achieve an Optimum Alignment of Member Roles Relative to the Satisfaction of the Group's Maintenance Goals

The goal attainment problem, by reason of its external orientation, deals with each member's total sense of selfhood, and to a lesser extent with other roles he or she plays in other organizations; for example, the work role. With the integration problem, the focus shifts to the roles members play within the system itself, such as husband and/or friend. Here the problem becomes one of need satisfaction within the specified role in the group. Since all system roles are interrelated at the level of the social group, the problem is one of all group members feeling good about the group and good about themselves as group members.

Remember that we have assumed that, once formed, a social organization possesses a propensity for continuance and development. Our use of the concept of integration in the systems model builds on and helps to operationalize this assumption. If an organization is to attain its goals, its members must get along well enough with each other to work cooperatively. The means and ends formulation is useful in developing the notion of integration, particularly the consummatory function served. In addressing the problem of integration, the group itself becomes both the means and the end.

Integration is an internal function, that is, it takes place within the group and pertains most fundamentally to the state or quality of relationships among its constituent members. These structural relationships (roles) among members are the means; the strength, health, and quality, of these relationships also serve as ends. In the latter sense, how group members feel about the group itself can be treated as an end state, that is, the consummatory dimension of integration. From the perspective of the social group, we assume there is an optimum balance between how group members feel about the group and each other (consummatory dimension of integration), and the effect of the group on them as individuals (consummatory dimension of goal attainment). The following comment by a friend of the Jones family can be used to illustrate the sought-after optimum state: "Barbara and Sam are just super people; they are deeply in love and both are absolutely devoted to their daughter, Ann. Yet, I have never known two people more self-actualized." The comment is intended to get at the consummatory dimensions of both goal attainment and integration. Assuming that one goal of the social group known as the Joneses is the self-actualization of Barbara and Sam, the comment suggests progress toward goal attainment. Similarly, the comment indicates an ideal marriage. In terms of this conceptualization of steady state, the couple is solving the integration and goal attainment problems, and by inference, the adaptation and pattern maintenance problems as well. Recall that adaptation and pattern maintenance are treated as instrumental with respect to the problems associated with goal attainment and integration.

We believe it is useful to assume that there is a propensity for the roles enacted by those comprising the system to be constantly modified in search of an optimum fit. That is the search for the solution to the problem of integration. In discussing the goal attainment problem, we noted that Barbara and Sam have understood each other's need to grow as a person and the important role that each plays in helping the other. Barbara, for example, enjoys her career as a psychiatric social worker. She feels that she is quite skilled as a counselor and is able to be a positive influence in the lives of her clients. She also has aspirations to become a supervisor and secretly to become the director of a comprehensive mental health center. These aspirations for personal and professional development have time constraints and related requirements. Sam has been supportive of Barbara's work and has encouraged her to pursue these personal goals. Sam also has personal and professional goals that have significant requirements. There is never enough time to do everything. Sometimes Barbara is driven to seek personal development goals, which is the goal attainment problem, while at other times she feels that Sam and Ann need her in her spousal and parental roles. The tension between these demands is labeled **role conflict**. Our use here with the Joneses is to illustrate the **tension relationship** between the goal attainment and integration problem.

Given the example, you have probably already concluded that a solution to the integration problem can complicate finding a solution to the problem of goal attainment. By extending the example, we can see that the demands of the role of wife and mother can conflict with Barbara's pursuit of becoming self-actualized. Here we would have to assume that Barbara's pursuit of self-actualization involves roles outside the marriage as well as those inside; for example, being a social worker at the Midtown Mental Health Center. Similarly, Barbara and Sam's pursuit of self-actualization can adversely affect their marriage. The preceding conveys the interrelationship and tensions between the four problems comprising steady state.

Adaptation

THE PROBLEM: How to Modify the Group's Social Environment in Ways That Optimize Goal Attainment, Particularly in an Advantageous Exchange of Outputs for Inputs.

In the popular use of the term, adapt means to fit. This is also the technical meaning we ascribe to this concept in its use with the system's efforts in maintaining steady state. Given the dynamic formulation of the suprasystem, the model builds on the assumption that the fit between the system and its relevant suprasystem is always problematic; that is, what fit yesterday may not fit today. Given this position, the problem of adaptation is never solved in any absolute sense of the word. Like the other three problems comprising the paradigm of steady state, adaptation requires continuous attention by the system.

Conceptually, adaptation is treated as the performance by the system of external and instrumental functions. The function is external in the sense that the focus is on the relationships the system maintains with key components of its suprasystem; the function is instrumental since the actions pertain to the means employed in facilitating goal attainment. Implicit in the notion of goal attainment as used in the model is some form of exchange between the system and the suprasystem. In this context we have found exchange theory helpful, particularly the contention in that theory of the self-interest foundations of exchange.[6] Stemming from a self-interest orientation, adaptation is represented by all of those system actions that facilitate goal attainment. Included are those that generate the necessary inputs (maintenance and signal) required to sustain and develop the system.

For many people the word *adapt* is narrowly defined, being essentially viewed as one way. In other words, *to adapt* essentially means *to get along*. Used in a personal sense, it conveys the notion that the individual needs to change in order to get along with others. An example would be a mother's advice to her son: "Johnny, you are going to have to learn to get along." The point here is that for many people the notion of adaptation suggests that the external situation (suprasystem) is not subject to change; it is taken as a given. From this definition, it is the individual, group, or family that must change in order to accomplish the fit. This is not the meaning of the concept of adaptation as we are using it in this model. Building from the assumptions in exchange theory, we hold that the system's adaptation actions are proactive; the initial actions focus on modification of features (other systems) of its suprasystem. If these efforts prove unsuccessful, only then will the system modify its behavior in order to facilitate goal attainment or, if necessary, change or modify its goals. At an applied level, the assumption is made that the adaptive behaviors of most social organizations include changes within and between the organization and other organizations and individuals in its environment.

Adaptation actions in social groups are typically informal rather than formal. To illustrate the concept we will again model the relationship between Barbara and Sam. To develop the concept, we will pick up the relationship while they were in college, but prior to their marriage. After dating several months, both Barbara and Sam found themselves becoming emotionally involved. In both instances, this was the first time they had found themselves so intimately and deeply involved with another person. Both were a bit shaken by the intensity of their relationship and uncertain about what it meant. What they did know was that they wanted to spend as much time with each other as possible. Complicating their personal relationship were their different religious backgrounds. Barbara came from a devout Roman Catholic family while Sam's family was Methodist. Sam's family was active in their church but would not be considered deeply religious. Sam had relatively little interest in the church and had not attended church regularly since leaving home to go to college.

In contemplating their relationship and its future, Sam suggested to Barbara that she move in with him. Although she and Sam had been having sexual relations, the idea of moving in with Sam came as something of a shock. For Barbara, their sexual relationship was one thing, but living together was quite another. Foremost in her mind was the visibility this would give to their relationship and what her parents would say. After talking about the proposed living arrangement and working through their own feelings, Barbara consented and moved in with Sam. Conceptually, we can say the (task) goal of the system was the satisfaction of the couple's respective social belonging and love needs.

The problem of adaptation can be treated as the manipulation of the suprasystem in a manner that facilitates goal attainment. Simply put, the problem was getting their respective families (and friends) to accept and be supportive of their relationship and living arrangement. All of the activities that Barbara and Sam engaged in vis-à-vis their respective parents to obtain acceptance of their new relationship would be treated as adaptation.

We have stressed the input-output exchanges that each system has with its suprasystem. The situation being confronted by Barbara and Sam can illustrate this relationship. To develop the connection between adaptation and input, let us assume that both Sam's and Barbara's parents have been helping them meet the costs of their education. The lack of acceptance of this relationship by either or both sets of parents could affect the money available to meet the couple's living and college expenses (maintenance inputs). Given the above definition, Barbara and Sam's efforts to gain parental acceptance of their relationship now involves both money and emotional support. If their efforts to solve the problem of adaptation prove unsuccessful, and their parents withdraw financial support, either Barbara or Sam may have to quit school and go to work. The other option would be to heed the position of their parents and again live apart, or depending on the extent of the pressure, terminate their relationship. In both instances, coping with the adaptation problem will play a key role in dealing with their goal attainment problem. Securing parental acceptance of their relationship is the means for sustaining and developing their personal relationship which is the end or the goal they are mutually pursuing.

The example was selected because it helps illustrate the proactive stance that we attribute to this feature of how a system maintains steady state. The example is not intended to indicate that in each and every group there will be active efforts made to manipulate its environment in terms of facilitating goal attainment; nor does it follow that every group successfully solves the problem of adaptation. The concept of adaptation identifies an ever-present problem condition that must be addressed continuously and successfully if the system is to maintain steady state, and to survive.

Pattern Maintenance

THE PROBLEM: How to Maintain, in a Constantly Changing and at Times Volatile Environment, the Social Group's Most Important Structural Features

For readers familiar with action theory, the terms *pattern maintenance, tension management,* and **latency** deal with or are used to describe the fourth problem confronted by social systems.[7] We find the term *pattern maintenance* most useful in conveying the central notions involved. Nevertheless, for our purposes, the three terms can be treated by the reader as essentially synonymous.

The concept of pattern maintenance as used in this model is premised on the assumption that each social system will possess a hierarchy of relationship patterns. These patterns will vary in terms of their relative importance to the preservation and development of the system itself.

Just as individuals possess a value system that influences their behavior, so do the groupings that individuals join together to form. Selected values will be shared by the members of the group. In effect, these values become group values, and they in turn will effect interactions between group members and between group and non-members. In the latter instances some of these behaviors between group members and non-members would be performing the boundary maintenance function. Boundary-maintaining behaviors can, in selected instances, be useful in identifying efforts at dealing with the problem of pattern maintenance. For example, Barbara and Sam vowed to each other that they would be their only sexual partners as long as they were together. The value involved was the "rightness" involved in being each other's only sexual partners. This agreement becomes a shared value and one that they both considered as fundamental to their personal relationship and later on to their marriage. In this instance, the pattern-maintenance problem would include all of those efforts made by Barbara and Sam to guard against any violation of this aspect of their relationship. Here the assumption is made that this agreement is so important to Barbara and Sam that any violation of it would likely result in the termination of their relationship. This example would also pertain to the boundary-maintenance function. It is important to note here that boundary-maintaining functions, in many instances, also represent efforts at dealing with the problem of pattern maintenance; however, the problem of pattern maintenance deals with other system functions as well.

Exchange theory can be useful in helping to conceptualize the notion of pattern maintenance as a problem to be contended with in maintaining the steady state of a social group. In our presentation of the core concepts and assumptions in exchange theory, we identified four processes and likened the first three to stages in group development: transaction, differentiation, and stabilization. Recall that the stabilization phase is evidenced by the presence of mutual trust, shared norms, and development of legitimate leadership. We hold that a social group, as we have defined it, comes into existence only during the stabilization phase. The earlier stages might be referred to as presocial group status. Finally, we hold that in the formation of the social group, not all of the shared norms or the features of mutual trust are of equal importance or of the same order; there is a hierarchy of relative importance to these relationship features. The norms, trust levels, and leadership forms vary by group and particularly by the goals that guide group behavior. It is those norms and their undergirding values deemed central in the pursuit of the group's goals that constitute the pattern that must be maintained.

The following examples may prove helpful in identifying the notion of core values. For a neighborhood gang, a core value may be that, regardless of the price paid, no gang member ever "rats" to the police on another member (turns informer). To turn in another group member would constitute the most fundamental violation of trust and would destroy the gang. A group of high school girls may vow that no member will ever accept a date with another's boyfriend. Again, to do so would represent a fundamental violation of trust that might well lead to the dissolution of the group itself. The latter example can also be helpful in developing the related concept of tension management. Every social organization is comprised of individuals, and so the assumption is made that some level of tension between group and personal goals is inevitable. Just as there is an assumed affinity that draws group members together (integration, based in part on social belonging needs) so is there an assumed movement in the opposite direction in which members seek greater autonomy and control over their own lives (self-actualization needs). This movement by group members to increased levels of autonomy creates states of tension that must be managed if the system is to survive. An example would be a member of the girls' group who really wants to date her best friend's boyfriend. If she dates him, she runs the risk of destroying her friendship and being ostracized from the group.

We will use the Joneses to provide the final examples of pattern maintenance. Recall, from an earlier presentation, that Barbara had found that Sam had withdrawn money from their joint savings account and had lied to her about its use. This breach of trust is an example of a problem related to pattern maintenance. Unless Barbara and Sam can reestablish a sense of mutual trust, their relationship is threatened, or in systems language, there is a threatened loss of steady state.

The example illustrates a problem that arose after Sam had violated a core feature of their relationship, mutual trust. It is also important to relate Sam's act to a mutual goal of Barbara and Sam's, saving for the down payment for their first home. Assumed is that this goal was highly cathected, and Sam's action felt to Barbara like an attack on her as well as on their relationship. To put the matter otherwise, if Sam had lied to her, saying that he had to work on Saturday when in reality he was meeting some of his friends to go to the ball game, the problem with Barbara would probably have been much less severe. In this latter instance, Barbara may well have been quite angry, but would not have taken the action quite as personally as lying about the withdrawal of money from their joint savings account. Sam lied in both instances, but the lie about attending the ball game did not deal specifically with a highly cathected systems goal.

The examples of pattern maintenance used so far have dealt with specific problems that were seen to pose a threat to steady state. In constructing the systems model, we take the position that healthy organizations constantly expend energy in strengthening, through reaffirming actions, those values that are fundamental to their existence. As a consequence, this proactive or preventive feature is seen to characterize all social systems. Familiar examples of reaffirming actions at a societal level are the "Pledge of Allegiance" that children recite at the start of each school day or the "Lord's Prayer" that the congregation recites during their worship time together. An example at the level of the social group, using the Joneses, would be their regular church attendance and the actions by both Barbara and Sam to serve as leaders in their young adult Sunday school class. These actions reaffirm the Christian values undergirding their marriage and its linkage to church doctrine. Another example would be the Jones's mutual decision to rotate spending Christmas with their respective families. This family decision represents a reaffirmation of the importance of the family and of spending special times together.

The theory of symbolic interaction is useful in understanding the intent of the above examples. Group members' common understanding and level of cathexis of the words and actions is critical in pattern maintenance. Acts of reaffirmation then serve to clarify and strengthen those shared meanings and help to reduce the possibility of actions that will pose a threat to the maintenance of these patterns, for example, Sam's withdrawal of money from their joint savings account. Inattention to these mutually held values and reaffirming behaviors tends to weaken the patterns and pose a threat to steady state.

SUMMARY

The concept of steady state was employed in this chapter to describe system dynamics. The approach used to develop the notion of steady state builds from the four-problem paradigm originally formulated by Parsons in action theory. Our interest in this chapter was the development of the distinctive features of the dynamics of social groups. To help develop the basic ideas involved in steady state, extensive use was again made of examples, particularly the Joneses, believing the continuity of the example would help in understanding the interrelatedness of these concepts. For us the concept of steady state and the four-problem paradigm is helpful in describing what we mean by the assumption that all social organizations are in a proactive mode. The natural state of the social organization is one devoted to the search for the means of optimizing the resolution of the four problems identified as goal attainment, integration, adaptation, and pattern maintenance. In terms of dynamics, this conceptualization offers avenues of explanation as to how social organizations survive, change, and develop. Given the reciprocal and mutually deterministic features of the systems model, the concept of steady state offers an approach to the broader study of social change.

GLOSSARY

Latency   A concept in action theory referring to one of the four functional imperatives bearing on the survival of a social system. As used here, the term latency is synonymous with pattern maintenance.

Role conflict   The competing demands on the individual in enacting two different roles in which meeting the demands of one role is at the expense of the other. An example would be the conflict experienced by a woman in the role of mother and employee. The demands of her employer may be in conflict with her role as mother, for example, in being able to stay home with an ill child.

Tension management The term as used here is synonymous with latency and pattern maintenance.

NOTES

1. For a useful application of this notion of focusing on natural processes in healthy groups, see Froma Walsh, ed., *Normal Family Processes* (New York: The Guilford Press, 1982).

2. See particularly Chapter 2, "A Social Systems Perspective." Here we anchor this assumption in general systems theory and need theory as developed by Abraham Maslow.

3. References to the four-problem paradigm are derived from the work of Talcott Parsons and are related to the concepts associated with his pattern variables. A review of this material is contained in Chapter 4 of this book. To explore Parson's ideas, see particularly Talcott Parsons, *The Social System* (Glencoe, Ill.: The Free Press, 1951). See also Chapter 5 of Talcott Parsons, Robert F. Bales, and Edward A. Shils, *Working Papers in the Theory of Action* (Glencoe, Ill.: The Free Press, 1953).

4. This point was also dealt with in Chapter 4. In brief, the four problems confronted by every social organization can be viewed as causing specialized functions to be created within each organization to address each problem. In small organizations like the social group, this differentiation takes the form of features (norm structures) within the role structure of the group. For a discussion of this notion of functional differentiation within the small group, see particularly A. Paul Hare, "A Functional Interpretation of Interaction," in Herbert H. Blumberg, et al., *Small Groups and Social Interaction*, vol. 2 (New York: John Wiley & Sons, 1938), 429–447.

5. For a review of these concepts as used in symbolic interaction see John P. Hewitt, *Self and Society: A Symbolic Interactionist Social Psychology*, 4th ed. (Boston: Allyn and Bacon, 1988).

6. Exchange theory was reviewed at some length in Chapter 6. For an interesting but rather technical discussion of the self-interest characteristics in exchange, see Kenneth E. Boulding, *Ecodynamics: A New Theory of Societal Evolution* (Beverly Hills, Calif.: Sage Publications, 1978), 163–188.

7. For a useful discussion of pattern maintenance, as well as the other three problems, see Morris Zelditch, Jr., "A Note on Analysis of Equilibrium Systems," in Talcott Parsons and Robert F. Bales, *Family Socialization and Interaction Process* (Glencoe, Ill.: The Free Press, 1955), 401–408.

PART III
THE INDIVIDUAL

The Social Systems Model

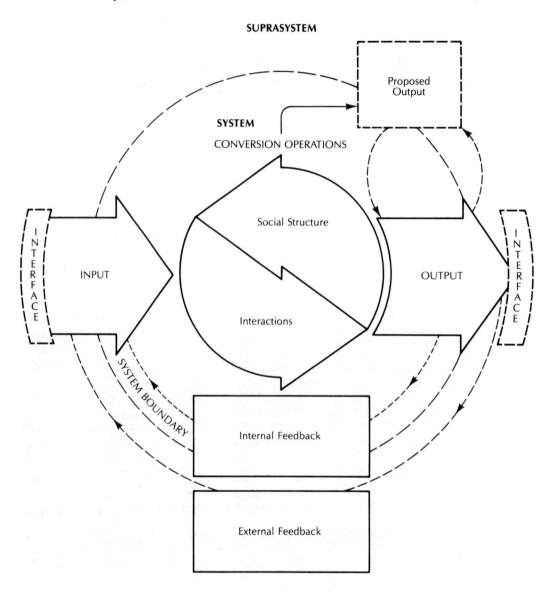

The basic position developed in this book is that the individual is both the cause and the effect of all forms of social organization. Given this position, our dilemma was whether to discuss the individual before or after discussing the social group. Obviously, our decision was the latter.

In Chapter 9, we introduce four lines of theory development utilized by social workers in their practice. The theories are: (1) psychoanalytic/psychodynamic theory; (2) behaviorism/learning theory; (3) cognitive development theory; and, (4) moral development theory. We have included these theories for two related reasons. First, they are core theories and are used by many social workers in their practice. Therefore, any student contemplating the professional practice of social work should have a general understanding of each of them. Secondly, each theory makes a special contribution to our total understanding of individual behavior. By understanding the theory, it is possible to selectively incorporate these theories into the social systems model for specific applications to practice.

In Chapter 10, we present psychosocial theory, but within the social systems perspective. In so doing, we build particularly off the contributions of Erik Erikson and his eight life stages. For us, the resolution of the psychosocial crisis associated with each stage can be usefully viewed as an output of that stage. Our research indicates that psychosocial theory and social systems theory are the two paradigms most frequently used by practicing workers. By framing a way of combining the two, we hope to make a contribution to advancing their use in the professional practice of social work.

Chapter 9

The Individual: Theories of Psychology Used by Social Workers

OUTLINE

Introduction

In this chapter, the focus shifts so that we can provide you with a review of psychological theories having relevance to the practice of social work. We have stressed the assumption that the individual should be viewed as both the cause and the effect of all forms of human association. While this book examines in detail these reciprocal effects, an understanding of the individual as a separate and distinct human personality is crucial in all forms of social work practice. It is the field of psychology that provides the avenues for this exploration. While, from our perspective, the individual cannot usefully be viewed as a social system, the individual in a role is always a member of such systems. Each of us has a physical, psychological, spiritual, and social existence. So, while this book focuses on the social, we are each a whole and it is the interplay of these four systems that comprises the whole of human experience.

Here we identify and develop the interface between the social and psychological. This does not mean that the counterpart interfaces between the physical and spiritual are less important; they are not. All practicing social workers need to be informed on the physical and spiritual dimensions of human life, but that is not the subject matter of this book.

A useful place to start our review of psychological theory and its interface with sociology is to draw a distinction between the two disciplines. Recall that both of these social sciences, like all other sciences, grew out of the study of philosophy. We humans have always been curious and have sought to understand the world about us as well as the purpose of human existence. As our knowledge increased, there was movement toward development of specialty areas of inquiry; sociology and psychology are two of the many domains of science that have evolved over the centuries. With psychology and sociology, the focus is on living versus nonliving matter. It is here that we get the distinction drawn between the so-called physical and social sciences.

Sociology is a science of social organization and social processes. The focus has tended to be macro, with primary attention being given to human societies. The word sociology was coined by Auguste Comte (1798–1857) as he sought to define a new social science. The tie between this new science and the older physical sciences is evidenced by his reference to sociology as "social physics."[1]

Psychology, in contrast, is a science of human and animal behavior. While the focus of psychology is on human behavior, the study of lower forms of animal life has been critically important in the development of this field.[2] For many psychologists, the study of lower and simpler forms of animal life has important implications in understanding human behavior.

In organizing our approach, a decision had to be made about which psychological theories to include and how to classify them. There are a myriad of theories and no widely accepted classification system. Our approach was guided by a judgment as to the practice utility of these theories and their usefulness in terms of the development of the social systems model. Here we relied on our research, as reported in Chapter 1 (see Table 1.3).

We have categorized the theories to be reviewed in this chapter as follows: (1) psychoanalytic and psychodynamic; (2) behaviorism and learning; (3) cognitive development; and (4) moral development. In tracking a line of theory development, it is important to distinguish between a line of theory development and a particular theorist. Suffice it to say that within any of the above classifications there will, in most instances, be a number of different theorists, each with his or her own particular area of emphasis or interest. In presenting each of these lines of theory development we will provide an introduction including some brief historical data about the leading theorist(s); a statement of focus; an identification of key assumptions and concepts; and, through a summary, identify its implications in the use of the social systems model and its contribution to the practice of social work.

Psychoanalytic and Psychodynamic Theory

We start our discussion with psychoanalytic theory for two reasons: the historical importance of psychoanalytic theory and the critical impact this line of theory development has had on the profession of social work. According to our research (see Table 1.3), in 1989 approximately twenty percent of our respondents indicated use of psychoanalytic theory in their practices.

Sigmund Freud was one of this century's greatest thinkers; and psychoanalytic theory, for many years, was the dominating influence in psychology. Not only did psychoanalytic theory greatly influence the development of the behavioral and social sciences generally, but western culture as well.

Social work was in a very formative stage of development when psychoanalytic theory impacted psychology and psychiatry in this country. The influence was particularly strong in social casework, the dominant practice method in social work for much of its history.[3] Psychoanalytic theory provided social work with a theoretical base to practice and the psychoanalyst/psychiatrist with a role model to emulate.

We have labeled this section Psychoanalytic and Psychodynamic Theory, and for the most part, will be organizing content around the theory as it was developed by Freud. As with other theories, there are a number of variations; most of the important ones were developed by students and colleagues of Freud. This general cluster of theories is frequently referred to as psychodynamic theory. **Psychodynamic** simply refers to cognitive, emotional, and motivational processes that consciously and unconsciously affect one's behavior. Before proceeding, we should also note that **psychoanalysis** is the method of treatment used which is based on psychoanalytic theory.

Sigmund Freud (1856–1939) is the acknowledged founder of psychoanalytic theory. He was born in Freiberg, now part of Czechoslovakia. At the age of four, he and his family moved to Vienna where he spent all but the last year of his life. Educated as a physician, his interest was research, particularly in the area of neurology. It was his fascination with the problem of hysteria that eventually led to his great contributions and to the development of psychoanalytic theory.[4]

Several things are important in tracking the development of psychoanalytic theory. First, its founder Freud was a physician, not a social scientist. His training was in the physical sciences, as was his orientation as a researcher. Second, he lived and practiced in Vienna during the latter part of the nineteenth and beginning of the twentieth centuries. His theory development was affected by the historical and cultural influences of his time. Third, Freud's theory building was grounded in his direct practice with patients who were largely women drawn from the middle and upper classes. In short, his theory was developed largely from clinical sources rather than from experimentation. His subjects were human, not animals; they were troubled people, not the mentally healthy.

Focus

Psychoanalysis, unlike some of the other theories to be reviewed, can be categorized as a general theory of individual behavior by its relative scope. It is a comprehensive theory dealing with intrapsychic determinants of behavior (motivation), psychopathology, and the treatment of psychopathology. There is little in the way of psychological behavior that cannot be explained by this theory.

Assumptions

The following five assumptions are those that we consider to be fundamental to this line of theory development:

1. Humans are animals and an understanding of human behavior builds from this heritage—the primary determinants of behavior arise from sexual and aggressive drives.
2. There are unconscious determinants of behavior.
3. Development is in accordance with the epigenetic principle and associated with sexual maturation.
4. All behavior, except that related to fatigue, is motivated.
5. Behavior is in accordance with the pleasure principle, the maximization of pleasure and minimization of pain.

In thinking about the assumptions undergirding psychoanalytic theory, we would like to again emphasize that Freud was a physician and his education was in the physical sciences. It is also important to keep in mind the state of science in the latter part of the 1800s. Freud was also influenced, like many of the other scientists of his time, by evolutional theory. He was particularly interested in the work of Charles Darwin and his findings dealing with the process of natural selection.[5]

Evolutionary theory is based on the assumption that there are natural laws which have application to all forms of life. Unlike the humanist, evolutionists are concerned with what humans have in common with all life forms; humans are animals and will exhibit patterns of behavior and development based on natural laws. For example, psychoanalytic theory incorporates the **epigenetic** development principle. The basic notion is borrowed from embryology and holds that organisms develop from an undifferentiated mass (fertilized egg) through a series of fixed stages to a mature state. These stages are separate and distinct, and no stage is ever skipped. Difficulties in one stage will tend to have adverse developmental consequences in subsequent stages. The latter point becomes especially important if the problem in development at a particular stage occurs early in that stage. For example, the organism's heart will be the first organ to form and function, followed shortly by the brain and spinal cord. Difficulties affecting development of the heart and central nervous system, especially early in the development of either stage, will have severe consequences to the developing fetus.

Freud extended the epigenetic principle to the psychosexual development of the human and postulated five stages of development.[6] Other theorists operating from the same assumption have advanced additional stages. For example, Erikson's developmental theory has eight stages[7] and Newman and Newman have ten.[8] It should be noted that as theorists have added stages they have also tended to add attention to the interplay between the individual as a physical and psychological being and the individual's social environment.

Freudian, or what might be termed classical psychoanalytical theory, assumes the existence of unconscious determinants of behavior. The unconscious can be likened to a "life force" composed of sexual and aggressive impulses. In fact, all behavior is assumed to have its origins in these animal-like instinctive impulses.[9]

Concepts

We find it useful to first identify the key assumptions that a theorist makes and upon which the theory builds. These assumptions form for us the foundation for a perspective on the phenomenon to be explained. The identification of concepts and their linkages builds off of this perspective and starts a process of operationalizing the basic relationships the theorist is seeking to explain. Freud was interested in the psychic determinants of behavior and so our review of the key concepts of psychoanalytic theory will be organized under five structural categories of these psychic determinants. The five areas are as follows: (1) the structures of the mind, (2) levels of consciousness, (3) stages of development, (4) dynamics, and (5) well-being.

Structures of the Mind

Freud identified three distinct components of one's "mental apparatus" and labeled them id, ego and superego.[10]

Id   The **id** corresponds to a life force and contains one's inherited instinctual urges. It is the primitive part of the human personality. It is unconscious and is driven by the pleasure principle. The concept of id builds off the assumption that a human being is first of all an animal, and is to be understood in terms of his or her biological and evolutionary origins. The id is comprised of aggressive and sexual impulses. In a manner of speaking, these impulses are part of one's animal origins and are to be understood in terms of their survival purpose, which is the perpetuation of the species through reproduction.

Ego   The **ego** represents that part of the id that has been socialized. While drawing its energy from the id, the ego is guided by the reality principle, the recognition of behavioral demands of the real world. The notion of the ego in psychoanalytic theory contains the recognition that a human being has the capacity to think, to learn, to reason, and to adjust one's behavior to the social environment, the "real world." While this cognitive capacity is not central in this line of theory, it represents an important building block used by later theorists. In a sense then, the ego mediates between the id and one's environment.

Superego   **Superego** is the third of the three concepts comprising the mind's structure. It can be likened to an incorporation within the person of parental attitudes and more generally of existing cultural standards. Like the ego, the superego is a part of the id; also like the ego, parts of it are unconscious. Sometimes the superego is likened to one's conscience. It is the superego that "lays the guilt trip" on the ego for doing things deemed wrong. In another sense, the superego can be likened to an *ego ideal,* a standard or conception of what the person can become if he or she tries. Again, this notion is not a central one in this line of thinking, but it does give evidence of attention to environmental effects on the individual and the evolvement of a morality system that impacts on behavior.

   The ego is the mediator between the id and the superego, being pushed from both sides but being guided by its own logic and sense of reality. Conceptually speaking, the ego may be strong or weak, and it is here that the practice implications most clearly emerge. There are also a series of concepts dealing with the means used by the ego to defend against the impulses of the id and the unrealistic expectations of the superego. Important in this sense is the concept of **defense mechanisms**. From this line of thinking, much of human behavior can be viewed as defensive in nature, a constant struggle among one's more basal, primitive impulses; unrealistically high expectations for one's self; and an ever-changing environment.

Alexander and Ross summarize Freud's structure of the mind and the interplay of the id, ego, and superego as follows:

> The id is the original powerhouse of the mental apparatus; it contains the inherited instinctive forces which at birth are not yet organized into a coordinated system. The ego is conceived as a product of development which consists in the adaptation of the inherited instinctive drives to one another and to the environment. The superego . . . represents the incorporation of parental attitudes which are determined by the existing cultural standards. After maturation, the ego becomes the dynamic center of behavior. . . . The ego's function . . . is to carry out . . . coordinated rational behavior and is aimed at maintaining a constant condition . . . within the organism. . . . In satisfying biological needs and in defending the organism against excessive external stimulation, the ego performs its homeostatic tasks with the help of four basic faculties: (1) internal perception of instinctive needs, (2) external perception of existing conditions upon which the gratification of subjective needs depends, (3) the integrative faculty by which the ego coordinates instinctive urges with one another and with the requirements of the superego and adapts them to environmental conditions, and (4) the executive faculty by which it controls voluntary behavior.[11]

Levels of Consciousness

Freud identified three levels of the consciousness of thought, the unconscious, the preconscious and the conscious.

Unconscious   Everyone, according to psychoanalytic theory, is born with an **unconscious**. The notion of the unconscious is essentially synonymous with the idea of a life force. In its essence, this life force is comprised of sexual and aggressive impulses that are animal-like in their origin. The unconscious is also comprised of desires, wishes, and experiences that are frightening and otherwise unacceptable to the individual. Through a process Freud termed **repression**, these thoughts are forgotten, and they become part of a person's unconscious.

The notion of an unconscious is important in that the individual lacks awareness of its content, but this content does affect behavior. For example, in this line of reasoning slips of the tongue are assumed to be caused by unconscious content or impulses striving for expression. As indicated previously, the id is that part of the mind that is entirely comprised of unconscious content and impulses striving for expression. There is also psychic energy expended to retain this content in the unconscious. The energy so expended is not available to do other work and so diminishes the basic supply of available energy.

Preconscious   The **preconscious** consists of thoughts and content that are not now in awareness. In a manner of speaking, they are in memory and can be recalled by the individual when needed. It is in this capacity for recall by the individual that this content differs from that which is in the unconscious.

Conscious Consciousness pertains to an individual's awareness, to the capacity to experience cognitively and emotionally what is going on. In a manner of speaking, consciousness means to be in control of one's experiences; to be **conscious** means to be aware of one's surroundings, to be able to process this information and to act accordingly. In Freud's formulation, the ego represents that part of the mind that contains the conscious and the preconscious as well as the unconscious components. It is the ego that processes information, interprets reality, and tends to act in relation to its perception of reality.

Stages of Development

Identified as a key assumption in psychoanalytic theory is that development, specifically human sexual development, is consistent with the epigenetic principle.

The basis of development stages in psychoanalytic theory is the contention that human sexuality develops in fixed stages and that these stages provide a foundation for the psychological development of the human. Consequently, the focus in psychoanalytic theory is psychosexual development, not physical, psychological, or psychosocial development. Freud labeled the generalized sexual energy comprising the id as libido. The attachment of libido to a specific part of the body resulted in creation of an erogenous zone or an area that, when stimulated, elicited highly pleasurable feelings. In short, classical psychoanalytic theory holds that there is a specific sequence in the development of erogenous zones corresponding to one's general sexual development. This general development pattern is merely part of the comprehensive maturational process guided by innate, biological factors.

Freud identified five stages in this development sequence: (1) oral, (2) anal, (3) phallic, (4) latency, and (5) genital.[12]

Oral Stage The **oral stage** is the first of the five psychosexual stages in development, covering the period from birth to about eighteen months. Initiated by the sucking reflex, the infant not only feeds but derives sexual pleasure from the sucking process itself. The newborn has no conception of self or others but the development of this vital social process gets started through the taking of nourishment. The oral period is of fundamental importance in the infant's development and a relationship prototype gets started that will have significance throughout life: the nourishing, caring, and protection offered by a mother or mother surrogate. In accordance with the epigenetic principle, problems in this stage of development have severe implications for subsequent stages and the general development of the human personality.

Anal Stage Next in sequence is the **anal stage**. It starts around the eighteenth month and lasts until the child is about three. Now it is the anal region that becomes energized with libido and the infant turns his or her attention to the pleasures associated with bowel movements and the fecal products produced. Guided by id impulses, the child will express pleasure through handling and smearing of her or his feces. Mother, of course, is less than enamored with this expression of pleasure and the socialization struggle starts in earnest.

The anal period coincides with the infant's growing capacity to differentiate himself or herself from the rest of the world. The infant's mother and other caregivers become objects in their own right and sources of pleasure and sometimes pain. Up to this point the infant has little control over life, but through the eroticism associated with the anal area, things begin to change. The young child now has something that he or she can control, his or her bowel movements. An important struggle develops, one that is deemed to have far-reaching implications in terms of the child's development. On the one hand, there are the id-related impulses associated with the pleasure of bowel movements and the play with feces; and on the other, there are the child's parents who are likely to have some distaste for anal matters. They will soon seek to impose their views and their behavior on the child. Thus, toilet training will start.

The parents are far too powerful, and the child will lose the resulting struggle. Sometimes the problems associated with this period are essentially resolved. Sometimes they are not, which leaves scars on the developing personality. The progressive development through these life stages is marred by problems, and the ego capacities or defenses are weakened. New and more sophisticated and effective defense mechanisms are acquired by the ego for successfully dealing with the special problems posed in each stage of psychosexual development. To the extent this is not the case, the ego will have growing difficulties contending with the ongoing battle between the id and superego.

Phallic Stage   The **phallic**, or what is sometimes termed the **Oedipal stage**, starts at around age three and lasts until six or so. It is at this time that the genital area becomes the important erogenous zone. Freud and many of his followers gave greater theoretical attention to the problems confronting the boy during this period than the girl. According to Freud, the young boy takes ever greater interest in his penis and the pleasure it gives him. The boy also takes an interest in the sexual equipment of others, both boys and girls. Now, more than earlier, psychological development takes a somewhat different track for males and females.[13]

Freud's use of the Oedipal complex that confronts boys at this time is instructive. Typically the boy's mother is his first love object; she has been his primary caregiver and he feels pleasure in her presence. His pleasure should not be thought of as an adult form of sexuality, but is nevertheless sexual in character. The young boy may want to continue to sleep with his mother but will be told "you're getting too big—you need to sleep in your own bed." What is not entirely clear to the child in this logic is why it is that his father can sleep with his mother but he cannot. His father is the rival for his mother's love. The boy wishes to possess his mother but cannot. Both his father's size and cultural prohibitions will make the boy's battle a lost cause. Important from a developmental perspective is the crisis created by the boy's sexual strivings for his mother and the reality that confronts him that he cannot have her. Many aggressive and sexual fantasies plague the young boy. He must learn to deal with this crisis and typically does so by repressing these feelings; that is, by burying them in his unconscious. Also, helping the child is a constantly growing superego, the internalization of parental and cultural prohibitions.

The young girl goes through similar experiences, but her attachment is to her father or his surrogate. Like her male counterpart, competitive feelings grow toward the parent of the same sex. In the case of the young girl, this period is often referred to as comprising the **Electra complex**.

Latency Stage   The next stage is one of comparative quiet and is labeled the **latency stage**. By now, the normally developing child has acquired a good ego-based defense structure and the power of the id-related aggressive and sexual impulses have become latent. This stage typically coincides with the start of school and lasts until puberty. Temporarily freed from the impulses of the id, the child is able to direct his or her energies outward toward the world. Typically, this is a time of learning and mastery.

Genital Stage   The latency period comes to an abrupt halt with the onset of puberty. For girls, this is roughly at age eleven and for boys puberty begins at about thirteen. The individual has entered the **genital stage**. Sexual feelings swell inside, but now both the girl and the boy are prepared in terms of their physical equipment to find a release for their sexual impulses. But the problem is more complicated; not only are the cultural and social barriers to be confronted, but the past and repressed feelings as well. The ego's defense mechanisms are severely tested. From a psychoanalytical and developmental theory perspective, this is a difficult, perhaps the most difficult, period in a person's life.

According to Freudian thought, the genital phase is the final stage in psychosexual development. The reawakened Odeipal and Electra impulses must be dealt with again. It is a difficult time for both the adolescent and his or her family. Typically the resolution is accompanied by the selection of a sexual partner, marriage, and movement away from parents.

In classical psychoanalytic theory, it is the early years that are the formative ones, particularly those preceding latency. The basic personality is formed early on. Freud had little to say about adulthood experiences; these experiences are deemed to have little effect on the person's basic personality structure. However, life's stresses and strains will tend to stir up earlier, unresolved conflicts which may tax the individual's defense mechanisms. Regression from a later to an earlier developmental state may occur.

The strength and capacities of these defense mechanisms are to be understood in terms of the previously mentioned life stages. As evidenced by Freud's clinical practice, some of these problems can be disabling, resulting in the development of neuroses or psychoses.

Dynamics

Central to psychoanalytic theory is the notion of a life force, an energy of genetic origin, that takes the form of instinctual sexual and aggressive impulses; these forces are constantly striving for expression. This force in humans results in the structuring of the mind into the id, ego, and superego. This life force is also affected by the basic maturational sequence that guides all animal development. In other words, the dynamics of human behavior have their origins in these sexual and aggressive drives, but their expression in behavior is modified by the interplay of the id, ego, and superego, and by the psychosexual stage of one's development.

Well-being

Psychoanalytic theory has its origins in the study of mentally troubled people; there is not a central concept that deals with a state of health or well-being. There are, however, two related concepts that pertain to the direction, conservation, and management of psychic energy: the pleasure principle and the reality principle.

Pleasure Principle   In formulating psychoanalytic theory, Freud advanced the **pleasure principle**, which he considered to be of genetic origin. Simply stated, the principle holds that organisms seek pleasure and avoid pain by the immediate discharge of their instinctive drives and tension states.

Reality Principle   Opposing the pleasure principle is the **reality principle**. Just as the pleasure principle guides the behavior of the id, the reality principle guides the behavior of the ego. The ego comprehends the demands and expectations of the environment. The reality principle is based on the recognition of the demands of the real world and that one's behavior needs to be adjusted to this reality. In effect, the ego learns and finds ways of postponing the immediate forms of gratification related to the pleasure principle in order to cope with the constraints imposed by those with which one has to get along.

The typical example used to illustrate these contending principles is the behavior of the young child. The youngster seeks immediate gratification of her or his impulses. The child soon learns that this pursuit of instant gratification can lead to serious problems with parents. Parents, in turn, are very powerful and can discipline in ways that are quite unpleasant. Here the adventuresome child learns about reality. As ego is strengthened, the reality principle gains dominance, but not control, over the pleasure principle.

Well-being, in a manner of speaking, is a state of equilibrium. The internal drives based on the pleasure principle are countered by the ego's adaptive arrangements, which in turn, are based on the reality principle. These two principles and their opposing actions are reflective of the homeostatic conception of well-being embodied in psychoanalytic theory.

Summary and Implications

We have in the past few pages sought to present an outline of the major features of psychoanalytic theory. It is a rich and historically important line of theory development. Our review has only touched on what we consider to be its core features. For many, modern psychoanalytic theory is still the theory of choice, particularly for those engaged in long-term individual psychotherapy. There are many versions of what can be labeled as modern psychoanalytic or psychodynamic theory. We will not attempt to summarize the current state of this theory except to note that there is a tendency to give more emphasis to the ego as an open personality system. This movement is in contrast to a semiclosed system devoted to the conservation of energy, as in the natural state of the organism when at rest. Also, there is a tendency by current theorists to emphasize growth and change capacities of the individual. This is in contrast to the homeostatic conception of well-being that typified earlier psychoanalytic thinking.[14]

The tie between psychoanalytic theory and the social systems perspective is indirect and historical. It is indirect in the sense that the life stage development model to be presented later has its origins in psychoanalytic theory. It is historical in that most of the other theories presented in this book, particularly humanistic and field theory, have been influenced, at least to some extent, by Freud's works. Earlier we mentioned the importance of psychoanalytic theory in the development of the casework method in social work. While this influence has been diminishing over the decades, psychosocial theory, a derivative of psychoanalytic theory, remains very influential.

Behaviorism and Learning Theory

Behaviorism and learning theory is the second general line of theory development to be tracked in terms of its contribution to the social systems model and to social work practice. For our current purpose, we are considering behaviorism and learning theory as essentially synonymous. We find it useful to view the development of this line of thinking as a response, in part, to psychoanalytical theory. For example, psychoanalysis was concerned with the internal determinants of behavior, the aggressive and sexual impulses comprising the id. Behaviorism is concerned with manifest behavior. A behavior is a fact and thus a point of departure for attempting to explain it. For the behaviorist, the determinants are to be found in the external situation of the person, not the person's inner life.

As with each line of theory development, there is a problem in labeling the line of inquiry and then deciding what to include and what to omit. This is particularly true for what we are choosing to label behaviorism and learning theory. Daniel Robinson aptly described the issue when he wrote:

> There is no doubt that the behaviorist perspective has been the dominant one in modern psychology, at least in the English speaking world, for the past thirty years. Despite the monolithic expression it has been given by its several influential spokesmen, it is a highly varied and shifting perspective. Behaviorism is not a single ism standing in defense of a short list of propositions. It is more a "culture" within psychology than a "school," more a habit of thought than a system. It is, therefore, with caution that one goes about saying what behaviorism is.[15]

What was true about the importance and diversity of behaviorism in 1979, when Robinson wrote these words, is at least equally true today. In the past several decades behaviorism has also become a dominant influence in social work, a part of a general move within the profession toward a more scientific approach to practice. In 1989, our research indicated that nineteen percent of all respondents utilized behaviorism and learning theory in their practices (Table 1.3).

In the beginning, behaviorism was devoted to building a scientific psychology by using the traditional methods and procedures employed in the physical sciences. John Watson (1878–1958), who can be termed the "father" of modern behaviorism, sought to rid psychology of its preoccupation with subjective theorizing.

Watson was born in a rural area of South Carolina near the town of Greenville. He attended Freeman University and went on to do graduate work at the University of Chicago, finishing his doctorate in 1903. Watson then took a teaching position at Johns Hopkins University, where he did his most important work. Watson led what is sometimes referred to as the behavioral revolt in psychology. His position was very clear: there was no place in psychology for the study of consciousness through introspection and other such methods.[16] He agreed that psychology should drop from its vocabulary such concepts as consciousness, the unconscious, mind, need, goal, emotion, and most, if not all, the concepts noted in the previous section on psychoanalytic theory. Psychology should, according to Watson, focus its effort on the understanding, prediction, and control of behavior.[17]

Modern behaviorism has its clearest origins in the work of the Russian physiologist Ivan Pavlov (1849–1936). Pavlov was fifty years of age when he began his now famous work on conditioned reflexes. Dogs salivate when food touches their tongues, a process that facilitates the ingestion of food. Pavlov observed that his dogs would also salivate prior to the presentation of food, apparently stimulated by the footsteps of those coming to feed them. In short, a physiologically or internally based reflex to food was being triggered or "conditioned" by a stimulus having no intrinsic relationship to the food, the footsteps.

A typical experiment employed to test his proposition would find Pavlov placing a dog in a harness within a darkened room. A light would be flashed on and seconds later food was placed in the dog's mouth. The dog would salivate as the food touched the tongue. This experiment would be repeated several times, and Pavlov found that the light alone would produce salivation. This serves as an example of the classical conditioned response experiment. Food placed on the dog's tongue represents an **unconditioned stimulus** (US). The light which preceded the feeding was a **conditioned stimulus** (CS). In other words, it was an added but unnecessary condition to produce the sought after effect of salivation. The salivation to the food was the **unconditioned response** (UR). The salivation linked to the presence of the light, but in the absence of food, constituted the **conditioned response** (CR). What Pavlov identified was an elemental form of learning.[18]

Watson built on the work of Pavlov and founded what we are referring to as the behaviorist tradition in modern day psychology. As with each of the other major theories, Watson is just one of many writers who has made contributions. Others include Edward Thorndike, John Dollard, Clark Hull, B.F. Skinner, and Albert Bandura, to mention but a few.[19]

Watson was an environmentalist and his position is clearly evident in the following famous quote:

> Give me a dozen healthy infants, well formed and my own specified world to bring them up in and I'll guarantee to take any one at random and train him to become any type of specialist I might select—doctor, lawyer, artist, merchant, chief, and yes, even beggar-man and thief, regardless of his talents, penchants, tendencies, abilities, vocations, and race of his ancestors.[20]

Watson understood that he was overstating his position, but nevertheless the quote conveys well his firm and, some would say, radical environmental position.

Focus

The focus of this line of theory development is on how behavior is influenced or regulated by environmental conditions. **Radical** or stimulus-response **(S-R) behaviorism** views environmental control as acting directly on the individual's behavior. **Methodological** or stimulus-organism-response (S-O-R) **behaviorism** views environmental-behavioral relationships as being mediated by the individual's symbolic or cognitive processes. **Behavior modification** is the application of this line of theory to the resolution of human problems.

Assumptions

Different behaviorists will start with their own assumptions. Our interest here is in identifying areas of general agreement, particularly as the assumptions would distinguish behaviorism from other major lines of theory development.

1. There is continuity between the species. Functional relationships between animal behavior and the environment also hold for human beings.
2. The conditions of the environment are the primary determinants of animal and human behavior.
3. The procedures of natural science (for example, systematic observation and experiment) provide the best way to understand behavior-environment relationships.
4. Both normal and abnormal behaviors are the product of behavior-environment relationships and can be modified by the manipulation of these relationships.
5. The individual's personality is the sum of her or his acquired behaviors and learned behavior-environment relations.

Behaviorism shared with psychoanalytic theory the premise that the study of humans starts with recognition that humans are animals. Consequently, experiments performed on animals have applications to humans, for example, Pavlov's work with dogs.

In many ways, the remaining assumptions, for example, that the individual's personality is the sum of his or her acquired behaviors, are the antithesis of positions held in psychoanalytic theory. In psychoanalytic theory, the personality is formed largely by internal, psychic determinants and the interplay between the id, ego, and superego, and environmental determinants of behavior are given little attention. Behaviorists, however, hold that the search for causation of behavior is not to be found in internal states of the individual (the unconscious), but in the person's external environment. In fact, behaviorists, in the tradition of Watson and Skinner, feel that attention to such internal states retards, rather than advances science.

Behaviorists do not assume that human behavior is shaped by life stages that follow the epigenetic principle. Rather, they hold that behavior is shaped by the environment in a continuous manner. From this position, behaviorists offer a process rather than a stage model for formulating their theory.

It is important in behaviorist theory that the human is being viewed as a reactive creature, reacting to stimuli located in the environment. This helps explain the assumption that the human personality is the sum of learned behaviors. This assumption is in contrast to one that would hold a proactive view of the human and the development of the self.

Concepts

The assumptions undergirding behaviorism are reflected in a large number of concepts. We will summarize those we consider to be most important. Before doing so, we want to draw a distinction between two important lines of thinking within the behaviorist framework. Earlier we noted the work of Pavlov and Watson. Their work was described as being in the classical conditioning tradition within behaviorism. Here use was made of the stimulus-response experiments and the associated concepts, such as the unconditioned stimulus (US) and the conditioned stimulus (CS). A second line of investigation, best demonstrated by the work of B.F. Skinner, is known as **operant conditioning**. In classical conditioning, responses are automatically elicited by known stimuli. In operant conditioning, it is not necessary to know the stimulus that elicits the response. The focus in operant conditioning is on the response and its consequences, not the eliciting stimulus. Skinner holds that behavior is shaped and controlled by its consequences.[21] In this formulation, what stimulated behavior in the first instance is not the central issue. It is what follows the behavior that influences its continuance or discontinuance. In short, behavior is determined by its consequences.

Reinforcement

Reinforcers are stimuli that increase the probability that a specified antecedent behavior will recur. **Reinforcement** can either be positive or negative. A **positive reinforcer** increases the possibility that the antecedent behavior will occur again. In negative reinforcement, the removal of an aversive or negative stimulus also increases the probability that the antecedent behavior will recur.

Reinforcement Schedules

A **reinforcement schedule** expresses the arrangement between behavior and its consequences over time. Examples of schedules include, among others, continuous reinforcement (every desired response is reinforced); a fixed ratio schedule (the reinforcement occurs after the subject makes a predetermined number of responses); and a variable-ratio schedule (the reinforcement varies for each trial).

Two classes of reinforcers are identified: primary and conditioned. A **primary reinforcer** is one that has natural reinforcing qualities. Here an example would be food (positive) or removal of pain (negative). Giving a dog a cookie when it sits is an example of use of a positive primary reinforcer. The behavior being reinforced is sitting.

A **conditioned reinforcer** is anything that signals that a reinforcer is available. For example, a smile or other such personal expression of approval or support when a mother feeds her infant would be a conditioned reinforcer (the food is the primary reinforcer).

Three things are important in both reinforcement and punishment: frequency, amount, and delay. Frequency and amount of reinforcement or punishment have a positive relationship to response strength; delay (time) has an inverse relationship.

For example, if a young child brings the evening paper to his father and is promptly rewarded by a hug and a smile, the chances are that the behavior will be repeated. On the other hand, if the father waits, and later hugs and thanks the child for bringing him the paper while the child is watching television, it is the act of watching television that will likely be reinforced, not the bringing of the paper.

Extinction

Extinction is the term applied to behaviors that fade away, that are reduced to their baseline or natural level of occurrence. In short, behaviors that are not reinforced become extinct. In practical terms, if a child throws a temper tantrum to secure parental attention and the parents consistently withdraw their attention from the child when this occurs, the tantrum behavior will fade or become extinct. The behavior is not being rewarded, therefore it becomes extinct. **Spontaneous recovery** is a related concept which holds that an extinguished behavior can spontaneously reappear under circumstances similar to those in which the behavior was originally reinforced.

Generalization and Discrimination

Generalization is the term applied to the process whereby a response generalizes across a class of stimuli. An example would be a young child who says "da da" when her father appears. Here the word "da da" has been reinforced and she has thus made the association between the words and her father. The child may then say "da da" when any adult male appears; the stimulus has been generalized to a class of stimuli—adult males.

Discrimination is the opposite process to generalization. It is the ability to respond only to an individual case from a class of stimuli; thus, the child says "da da" only when her father appears. In operant conditioning, generalization can refer to either generalizations across stimulus conditions or across responses.

Shaping

Shaping, as used in operant conditioning, is a method for establishing new behaviors. The notion of shaping or *successive approximation* helps convey the position that conditioning typically occurs through a gradual process rather than all at once. A desired behavior can be achieved through a series of steps, with each step representing progress toward achievement of the sought-after behavior. For example, teaching a son or daughter to catch a ball typically involves shaping. All of those behaviors that will lead to the ability to catch a ball are reinforced. Verbal cues and reinforcers might include: "Keep your eye on the ball when daddy tosses it . . . that a girl . . . Remember to keep your eye on the ball . . . Now put your glove hand out in front . . . that was good . . . you almost caught it that time . . . Don't close your eyes . . . there you're doing real good . . . You're going to become daddy's ball player," and other encouraging comments.

Punishment

For many, negative reinforcement and punishment are equated. As indicated earlier, negative reinforcement involves the removal of an aversive stimulus, not the addition of punishment for an unwanted behavior. An aversive stimulus is one that hinders or diminishes the value of a reinforcement being used to strengthen a given behavior. **Punishment,** on the other hand, is not designed to strengthen a given behavior, but to get rid of it. For example, a mother who insists on walking her daughter to school and finds her daughter balking and resisting going to school may herself be the problem. A friend suggests that she let her daughter go to school with some of her neighborhood friends rather than in her company. Implied in the example is that the daughter is embarrassed by her mother's presence. The decision not to walk her daughter to school would be an example of negative reinforcement, the removal of an aversive stimulus – herself. What is being reinforced in the example is the behavior of going to school. Punishment, on the other hand, would be spanking the daughter for resisting going to school in an attempt to get rid of an unwanted behavior.

Skinner believed that extinction was more effective than punishment in getting rid of an unwanted behavior. Simply put, punishment leads to escape from and/or aggression toward the punishing object; extinction does not.

Punishment and reinforcement can be best referred to as operations. Reinforcement increases the probability of a response while punishment is an operation that decreases the probability of a response. Within this context, it is useful to contrast a positive with a negative operation. A positive operation is one in which something is added to a situation. A negative operation is one in which something is removed. These concepts can be diagramed as follows:

		Effects on Behavior	
		Reinforcement (Increase)	Punishment (Decrease)
Modification to Environment	Positive (Add)	Positive Reinforcement	Positive Punishment
	Negative (Remove)	Negative Reinforcement	Negative Punishment

Summary

We have in this section briefly discussed key assumptions and concepts identified with a line of theory development labeled behaviorism and learning theory. While many have made contributions, our attention has been principally on the work of John B. Watson and B.F. Skinner. This line of theory is rapidly developing. The work of Albert Bandura in social learning is particularly noteworthy for a number of reasons, not the least of which is its open system, proactive view of human behavior.[22]

While not nearly as influential or as well known, behaviorism has a history in social work approximately as old as psychoanalysis. For example, in 1930, Virginia Robinson identified behavioral psychology (Pavlov and Watson) as one of two influential approaches for social work theory development (the other being psychoanalytic theory).[23] It was Edwin S. Thomas with E. Goodman who reintroduced behaviorism into social work through a series of workshops given in 1964.[24] It is also Thomas who is largely responsible for the resurgence of interest in behaviorism in social work practice.

Theories and theorists build off one another. Behaviorism and its emphasis on the environmental determinants of behavior was, in part, a reaction to the bias in psychoanalytic theory favoring internal and genetic explanations of behavior. In a dialectic model of change, psychoanalytic theory can be viewed as a thesis with behaviorism becoming the antithesis. Some have agreed that humanistic theory reviewed in an early chapter represents a process of synthesis.[25] We find the work of Ludwig von Bertalanffy and his formulation of general systems theory a useful example of a synthesis.[26] It was in this way that these theories helped inform our approach to the development of the social systems model and its open system with cyclical and steady state features.

In the next section, we will be reviewing cognitive development theory. We have separated the discussion of behaviorism and learning theory from cognitive development theory principally because the latter breaks away from the linear and reductionist thinking that characterized the early development of behaviorism.

Cognitive Development Theory

To cognize means to know. Thus **cognitive** theory development pertains to the steps involved in deriving meaning from experience: How do we come to know?

While there are a number of theorists who have made contributions to this line of thinking, none is better known and more highly respected than Jean Piaget (1896–1980). Born in Switzerland, Piaget, like Darwin, showed talent as a naturalist while still a child. Indicative of his talent and potential, Piaget published an article at the age of ten on an albino sparrow he had observed in a park. It was Piaget's skill in observation as a naturalist that was to serve him well later on in his work with children and how they learn.

As a young man, Piaget went to the Sorbonne in Paris where he worked in the laboratory of Alfred Binet. Studies were being conducted there on the nature of intelligence. In his work, Piaget sought to understand how children arrive at their answers to problems, how they reason. Just as the behaviorists hold that human behavior is shaped by environmental influences, the cognitive theorists hold that knowing is shaped by the interaction between the individual and the environment.

Focus

This is a theory of human development focused on cognitive processes. In this sense, it is a narrower range theory than those addressing a wider range of development processes.

Assumptions

As with other lines of theory development, not all theorists in a given category are going to operate from the same set of assumptions. Our interest is the identification of those who appear central to a given line of theory development.

For us, the following four assumptions form the foundation of this line of theory development:

1. Cognitive development occurs in an invariant sequence.
2. There is continuity in cognitive development, with each stage building on the former and representing ever more comprehensive and more complex ways of thinking.

3. Cognitive development is not governed by either internal maturation or external teaching, but rather by the individual, through his or her own activities.
4. Cognitive structures are created, developed, and modified by the interaction of the person and his or her environment.

We find the assumptions supporting cognitive development theory, as just noted, to be consistent with those comprising the social systems perspective. Particularly helpful is the position taken with respect to the interplay between the individual and her or his environment in the development of cognitive structures. While it is important to note that cognition is assumed to develop through a series of fixed and invariant stages, Piaget did not hold that these stages were genetically determined.[27] While cognitive development is considered a stage theory, Piaget was by no means a strict maturationist.

Cognitive theorists assume that people of different ages think differently. The position is tied to stages of development, but the central idea is that children think differently than do adults. At this point, it should prove useful to the reader for us to contrast assumptions made by cognitive theorists from those undergirding other lines of theory development. Central in psychoanalytical theory is the assumption that development is governed principally by a genetically based maturation cycle. At each stage, the individual is confronted with stimuli that have internal origins, but these influences on the personality are shaped more or less by environmental experience. A diametrically opposing position is held by the behaviorist. The maturationally based explanation is rejected and personality development is essentially grounded in a set of learned behaviors. Cognitive theorists in the tradition of Piaget hold that cognitive development is essentially a spontaneous process in which children build their own cognitive structures through their own experiences. It is this proposition that holds special interest for us. A proactive, as opposed to a reactive, position is taken in seeking to understand human behavior. The interaction between a human being and her or his environment is an active one. The natural state is one in which the child is actively exploring his or her environment. In so doing, the child is constantly building new cognitive structures and elaborating on older ones as a means of comprehending and coping with the environment.

Concepts

Building off the above assumptions are a number of important concepts. The most important are those that identify the four developmental periods. Before describing these, we will define Piaget's notion of stage and summarize some of the other key concepts associated with cognitive development.

Stage

A **stage** is a developmental level typically conceptualized in terms of epigenetic theory (the structural elaboration of the unstructured egg as opposed to the growth of a preformed individual). More generally, the notion of stage is linked to a basic organizational scheme that is distinctive in its own right, more complex than the previous stage but less complex than the next higher stage. A **stage theory** is one that employs stages as a fundamental organizing scheme in explaining growth and development. For example, cognitive development is a stage theory, behaviorism is not.

In cognitive development theory as advanced by Piaget, the distinctiveness of a stage is evidenced by:

1. The mode of thinking is qualitatively different at each stage.
2. There is internal organization to each stage; it is a whole unto itself.
3. The individual progresses through stages in a progressive and invariant way. No stage is skipped.
4. Each higher stage builds on and integrates with the next lower stage in a hierarchical manner; the stages are vertically as well as horizontally integrated.
5. The stages are specific to all humankind. They are not culturally based, and thus the same stages would be evidenced in all cultures.

Schema

The concept of **schema** is used in cognitive development theory to denote existence of a structure of thought or a perceived representation of reality in memory. In the social systems model, the concept of schema would be labeled as a structural feature, a guide to action that would be called forth in a specific interactional situation. In cognitive theory, the first schemata are tied to inborn reflexes like sucking. In this sense, schemata have their origins in a reactive stance of the child, such as the sucking reflex that occurs when the infant's lips are touched. Building on the reflex are a host of associated experiences upon which the child builds his or her own action schemata. The proactive posture in social development thus becomes evident.

Three related concepts are used in describing the development of cognitive structures: assimilation, accommodation, and organization.

Assimilation

Assimilation refers to the integration of new experiences and objects into an existing schema. For example, if the reader had been introduced earlier to general system thinking, the social systems perspective and model would be assimilated into an existing schema. In a manner of speaking, the new information would simply help elaborate on an existing frame of reference.

Accommodation

To accommodate means to adjust in order to accomplish a fit. Some new experiences or information simply do not fit into an existing schema or previous sets of related experiences. These new and novel experiences require the construction of new, or, more likely, the modification of existing schemata. This process is referred to as **accommodation**. To extend the example noted above, if you have not had previous experience in systems thinking, the content in this book will involve some accommodation process on your part. The content is not only new, it involves a different kind of thinking; thus it cannot simply be assimilated into existing cognitive structures. The task becomes more difficult and involves an expenditure of more energy with new and different structures being developed.

Organization

Organization as used here refers to a tendency to seek and build order. In other words, in cognitive development there will be an ever-present tendency on the part of the individual to seek coherence in schemata; in other words, to systematize observations and data in the development of cognitive structures. Piaget only made very sparing use of biological concepts in his work. He viewed the tendencies of assimilation, accommodation, and organization as biological tendencies apparent in all organisms. Thus the propensity to create order and for behavior to evidence this underlying ordering process is genetically determined.

Relative to our example of systems thinking, if the content is new and accommodation takes place, it will be followed by a reordering of relevant structures by the process of organization. This is the "aha" (it is finally making sense to me) phenomenon. For many students unfamiliar with systems thinking, the first part of the semester is a struggle as they attempt to fit the systems perspective into their usual way of thinking. Then something appears to happen quite spontaneously, "a light comes on."

The notions of assimilation, accommodation, and organization identify a general approach to ordering employed by Piaget. In the earlier chapter dealing with the social systems perspective, we identified an assumption dealing with the existence of a general ordering phenomenon. Piaget has specified in detail the ordering processes that he proposed as an explanation for cognitive development. Stated differently, human beings seek order; disorder is uncomfortable and, depending on its level, frightening. Recall that Maslow identified safety and security needs as the second level of needs following only physiological needs in relative importance. These safety needs include the need for structure and order.[28] People are self-organizing in terms of their own thinking as well as in the various groupings that they join together to form. Piaget gives us some clues about this basic ordering process as it is developed in the cognitive structures of humans.

Circular Reaction

The concept **circular reaction** is used by Piaget to describe learning activities in which the infant attempts to repeat an action (the circular action) that first occurred by chance. An example would be the infant's hand coming in contact with the mouth. The hand drops and the child tries (initially unsuccessfully) to repeat it. This is an attempt at coordinating two separate motor schemata—an arm movement and sucking. Piaget describes primary, secondary, and tertiary circular reactions, each involving a greater differentiation in sensory motor actions.

In a secondary circular reaction, the child chances onto events that are external. An example would be a movement in which the child studies a rattle in the crib. Interested in the noise, the child strikes to repeat the action. Tertiary circular reactions represent a further development of schemata. In tertiary circular reactions, the child experiments with different actions, each with a different outcome. For example, a child is sitting in her highchair playing with several objects. She pushes one off, watching it fall to the floor. She pushes another, again watching it fall. She then takes another object, leans over the chair, and drops the article to the floor. She repeats the action, but from a different angle, again watching the relationships between different moves and different outcomes. The schema is becoming ever more differentiated through her circular actions.

Stages

Piaget did not tie his stages to specific ages, believing that considerable variation occurs at the age when children enter a given developmental stage.[29] The suggested ages are offered only as a general point of orientation. The four cognitive stages identified by Piaget follow.

Sensorimotor Intelligence (Birth to Eighteen Months) As suggested by the phrase **sensorimotor intelligence**, development at this stage centers on sensory and motor schemata. Clearly evidenced in this developmental stage is the importance of sucking and its relationship to the taking in of nourishment and the related social experiences with caregivers. Sucking is just one of the senses being developed. In addition, there is the rapid development of motor skills and their impact on cognitive schemata. Important in thinking about this stage is recognition of the physical action basis for the development of these cognitive structures.

Piaget identified six substages occurring within Stage I: (1) reflexes, such as sucking; (2) primary circular reaction, which are successful cycles of action (beginnings of memory); (3) secondary circular reactions; (4) coordination of secondary schemata; (5) tertiary circular reactions; and (6) beginnings of thought.[30]

The sensorimotor stage builds on the genetically based reflex actions with which the infant is equipped at birth. Chance happenings resulting from these sensorimotor actions start a pattern of increasing elaboration (schemata). Very early on, the child demonstrates a learning/memory capacity through the repetition and elaboration of various sensorimotor-based actions. This stage ends (roughly at eighteen months) when a new capacity emerges, one that will separate the child from all other life forms: language.

Preoperational Thought (Eighteen Months to the Early School Years, Six to Eight) The notion of operations, as used by Piaget, refers to a transformation that is carried out in thought rather than in a physical action. In adult terms, one can become angry and strike the person who has angered her or him; or, it is to be hoped one can become angry, think about striking the person and decide on another course of action, or just walk off. Thinking about such events involves a representation of a situation and taking or not taking action based on the contemplation of a variety of possibilities and their respective consequences. Thinking, as just described, is a very complex set of operations. A child, according to Piaget, moves through a series of stages prior to achieving the kind of complex thought process described above.

With the term **preoperational thought**, Piaget identifies a transition between sensorimotor and operational thought. In the sensorimotor period, the child's mental development is concerned with the immediate environment. Initially, it is with explorations involving her or his own body. Later in this period, it broadens to include the child's immediate environment. Critically important in Stage I is the child's growing capacity to distinguish her- or himself from the environment. The child, through the elaboration of schemata, gains a growing sense of time, space, causality, and object permanence.

Early in life, things exist for the infant only to the extent that they occur within the perceptive field. In other words, the infant does not have a schema of a permanent object. Such schemata develop as a consequence of experience (learning) and maturational development. Piaget describes this phenomena of object permanence in experimenting with his own seven-month-old child:

> At the time of his feeding I show him the bottle, he extends his hand to take it, but at that moment, I hide it behind my arm. If he sees one end sticking out he kicks and screams and gives every indication of wanting to have it. If, however, the bottle is completely hidden and nothing sticks out, he stops crying and acts for all we know as if the bottle no longer existed, as if it had been dissolved and absorbed into my arm.[31]

The notion of object permanence is particularly helpful in differentiating between Stage I and Stage II, when the child becomes able to comprehend the existence of objects (including people) even though they may not be immediately present. For example, mother exists for the infant even though she is at work. Even more important, the child has learned that she or he is also an object.

In Stage II, a new form of thinking arises, one based on symbolic representations. Schemata based in sensorimotor representation must now accommodate new experiences. A reordering of thinking takes place (organization) in which symbolic structures gain dominance. During this time (the reordering of schemata), the child's thinking is illogical. It does not make much sense from an adult's perspective.

Our earlier review of symbolic interaction theory should prove helpful at this point. The child in Stage I is rapidly learning that all of the objects in her or his environment have names. Importantly, the child learns that she or he, too, has a name. In this way, the child's development of selfhood rapidly develops.

In the preoperational thought stage, the child is accumulating knowledge about many words and their meanings. At this point in development, the child is moving from single words to combinations of two or three words and then on to sentences. The child's verbalizations are reflective of the increasingly more complex thought structures that are forming.

Children at this stage are starting to use these symbols and their meanings as an early form of thinking. During this time, the child is imitating those around her or him and engaging in a variety of imaginary activities. The child's knowledge and skill building schemata are very much tied to perceptions of her or his own direct experiences with things in the world.

Concrete Operational Thought (Seven to Early Adolescence, Eleven to Thirteen) This period of **concrete operational thought** coincides with the early school years and is marked by a rapid development of cognitive activities. It is at six or seven that the child's cognitive schemes start to evidence the organization associated with thinking on a symbolic level. Prior to this time, the child's thinking has been essentially unsystematic, and lacking a common thread of logic. It is important to remember that developmentally, the child's first symbols are based in motor actions, not in linguistics. In the stage of concrete operations, physical actions begin to be internalized as mental actions (operations). It is at this stage that children are able to formulate classes or categories of objects. For example, a child at this stage would be able to sort a series of blocks of varying size and color easily when asked to do so. The child at the preoperational level would need to physically compare the blocks one with another in order to determine relative size and to sort generally in that manner. Now the child is able to keep the sorting schemes in her or his head and mentally make the comparisons. Behaviorally, the child at this concrete operational level will be able to coordinate thinking and acting much more rapidly and successfully than his or her counterpart at the preoperational level of thought.

Coinciding with cognitive development is a movement from egocentrism to a concern for others. At the first substage of the sensorimotor stage, movement is toward the infant's capacity for self-identification. Here the infant begins separation of self from the experienced environment. This has occurred in normal development by the time the level of preoperational thought has been reached. At the preoperational stage, the child is the center of her or his universe. Here we have solitary and imaginary play taking place. While a child may play in the presence of others, it is not until she or he achieves the level of concrete operations that she or he has the cognitive capacities to fully take the actions of others into her or his thoughts and actions. Now the child has the mental capacities to engage with others in game play. At this stage, cognitive and social development are rapidly occurring with each acting on the other. From a symbolic interaction position, the child is now developing the capacity of taking the role of another. The child is learning to look at things from another person's point of view.

Cognitive theory recognizes substages within each of the major stages. Our interest at this time is only to acquaint you with a line of theory development, not its substance. For this reason, we will be selecting as examples only content that will help you grasp the overall ideas being advanced by the representative theorist. For example, Piaget identified eight groupings of relationships that the child will grasp during the period of concrete operations, one being substitution (understanding that the expressions, $4 + 3 = 7$, $5 + 2 = 7$, and $6 + 1 = 7$ are all equivalent). He then defined five laws that would pertain to these eight groups. An example is the law of inversion (if $A + A_1 = B$, then $A = B - A_1$, or $A_1 = B - A$).[32]

Piaget, through his research and theory building, sought to map the development of mental capabilities. His work is of great consequence to educators, particularly those working with children. In thinking about his work and its implications, keep in mind the assumption upon which his theory builds, that cognitive development occurs through the child's own activities. In short, children are born inquisitive. They are, in this sense, proactive. The teaching and learning environment is fundamental. The period of concrete operations is critically important in developing a child's thirst for knowledge.

Formal Operational Thought (Adolescence through Adulthood) The final stage of cognitive development Piaget labeled **formal operational thought**. This stage starts around age eleven, coinciding essentially with adolescence and continuing throughout adulthood. It is important to recognize that cognitive development does not stop at adolescence, but develops throughout one's life. The person in this stage has the cognitive equipment to lead a full and productive life. While Piaget posited four stages of development, it does not follow that all people progress to the fourth, that of formal operations. Many people for many different reasons never reach the stage of formal operations.

In contrast to concrete operations, the person at the formal operations stage can deal abstractly with the logic of things. At this level of reasoning, the person develops the capacity to reason along multiple lines so that in any given situation the person is able to deal with all contingencies. The point has now been reached that thinking becomes detached from the here and now. There is the capacity for reflective thinking and contemplation of future states under various sets of circumstances.

Piaget believed that it is through social interactions with others that one achieves the formal operations level of cognitive capacity. People learn through their interactions with others of differing points of view and other ways of thinking. It is an open systems formulation.[33]

Piaget's work has implications for many other lines of theory development as well as for the various forms of professional practice like social work. For example, symbolic interaction theory is premised, in part, on a level of cognitive capacity that permits one to mentally play one's own role and the role of others as well. We commonly and casually refer to this as thinking about an upcoming situation. This capacity is essentially at the level of formal operations. Symbolic interaction also assumes a well-developed reflective and introspective capability in developing a sense of selfhood.

Summary

The social systems model operationalizes a perspective on the ordering of human relationships. This ordering can be applied to a relationship comprised of two people or to a society as a whole. In all instances, the order being described is social and ultimately exists in the minds of those who are enacting social roles. Structure, as order, is never anything physical. It is always social. Cognitive development theory supplies an approach to the study of the mental structures and processes. In so doing, it informs the social systems model.

We have taken the position that the individual derives her or his sense of humanness and selfhood through interactions with others. Piaget and others in this intellectual tradition help link cognitive and social development together; it is ultimately a social process, as is selfhood.

Cognitive development theory, in the past couple of decades, has had growing importance in social work; this has been particularly true in work involving children and adolescents. There is now a growing number of social workers who employ cognitive therapy in their work with a wide variety of different types of clients.[34] As with behaviorism, the growing interest in cognitive development theory seems tied to a general move toward a scientific base for practice.

Moral Development Theory

We will conclude our review of psychological theories by summarizing moral development theory. Morality, the role of values, and the relationship of cognitive states involving moral issues and behavior have been differentially approached within various lines of theory development. As we introduce this section, distinguishing between the concepts of values, morals, and ethics should be useful. Briefly, we consider a value to be a shared meaning as to what is desirable and undesirable in social life. For example, in this society, the importance of work is stressed. The societal value can be stated "to work is good, not to work is bad." Morals constitute a reasoned code of what is right and wrong which grows out of larger societal values and which pertains to interpersonal relationships, for example, being fair, honest, and just. Ethics deal with the conduct or specific moral choices made by a person within a situation involving relationships with others. For example, the National Association of Social Worker's Code of Ethics provides the practitioner a guide to help in professional work with clients.

In moral development theory, we are interested in the stages humans go through in developing their sense of what is right and wrong.[35] Because values and ethics are at the best of what we as social workers do, we will be examining the development of this reasoning capacity at all levels of interpersonal relationships, from the interpersonal to the societal level.

Earlier in this chapter, we provided a brief summary of psychoanalytic theory. While moral development is not a primary issue in this line of theory, the matter is contained in Freud's use of the concept of superego. Recall that the superego is roughly comparable to one's conscience. Simply put, according to Freud, an individual's behavior is viewed in terms of the ego's capacity of dealing with the demands of the id and the superego. Psychoanalytic theory, given its attention to the superego, offers an avenue of exploration for the study of moral reasoning and ethical behavior.

Likewise, the issue of morality and learned behavior has not been a central focus of behaviorism, at least by early writers. Skinner puts it thusly:

> In an operant analysis of the stimulus control of verbal behavior, we can identify the referent of abstract terms, but terms like "morality" and "justice" raise an additional problem. It can be solved by recognizing that the behavior we call moral or just is a product of special kinds of social contingencies arranged by governments, religions, economic systems and ethical groups. We need to analyze those contingencies if we are to build a world in which people behave morally and justly, and a first step in that direction is to dismiss morality and justice as personal possessions.[36]

Abraham Maslow considered moral behavior and its relationship to human needs within his basic formulation of a hierarchy of human needs. As with psychoanalytic and behaviorist theory, Maslow and humanistic theory do not give primary attention to moral development. The contribution that Maslow makes is the linkage he establishes between need satisfaction and one's value system. He summarized his argument as follows:

"The Instinctoid Nature of Basic Needs," constitute for me the foundation of a system of intrinsic human values, human goods that validate themselves, that are intrinsically good and desirable and that need no further justification. This is a hierarchy of values which are to be found in the very essence of human nature itself. These are not only wanted and desired by all human beings, but also needed in the sense that they are necessary to avoid illness and psychopathology.[37]

Clearly there is not a well-established line of theory development in psychology dealing with moral development. While not neglected, this content tends to be incorporated in theories of a broader range. For us, the clearest line of theory pertaining to moral development is to be found in the work of Lawrence Kohlberg.[38] We need at the onset to acknowledge that Kohlberg's work builds on and extends the work done by Piaget.

Lawrence Kohlberg was born in Bronxville, New York, in 1927. He attended Andover Academy in Massachusetts. Kohlberg, after a period of work on behalf of the Israeli cause, enrolled at the University of Chicago completing his baccalaureate degree in just one year. It was during his graduate education in psychology at the University of Chicago that he became familiar with Piaget's work. Kohlberg's interest was in the moral reasoning of children. This became the subject of his doctoral dissertation. His methodology was patterned after the work of Piaget and involved the interviewing of children and adolescents on moral issues. Kohlberg received his doctorate in 1958. He stayed on and taught at the University of Chicago before becoming a professor of education at Harvard.

Focus

As indicated by its title, moral development is a stage theory; it is linked to one's general cognitive development, but focuses on those processes associated with the development of moral reasoning and the ethical basis of behavior. It is a stage theory of narrow range.

Assumptions

Given the closeness of moral development and cognitive development, the same general assumptions are shared by these two lines of theory development. We have identified the following particular assumptions upon which we consider moral development theory to rest:

1. The progressive stages of human maturation are associated with capacities for progressively higher stages of moral reasoning.
2. Once the major moral premise of a person is understood, the solution to moral problems confronted by that person can be derived through laws of thought.
3. There is a link between moral reasoning and ethical behavior.
4. There is a greater tie between moral reasoning and ethical actions at higher than at lower stages of moral development.

Like Piaget, Kohlberg is not a strict maturationist. By this, we mean that Kohlberg does not believe that the stages of moral development he postulated are the direct result of maturation. While associated with human maturational processes, they depend upon a child's thinking about and experiencing, within a social context, moral problems. In short, moral development is a social process linked to the general physical, psychological, social, and spiritual development of the individual.

Given the narrow range of moral development theory, the assumptions tend to be specific and are approaching researchable propositions. There has been a significant amount of research done by Kohlberg and others in recent years. The focus of our presentation and space limitations do not permit a review of this research; however, it has been well documented by others.[39] Our interest is in the presentation of the basic outlines of this theory and linking it with the social systems perspective and to the practice applications in social work.

Concepts

Moral development theory shares many of the same concepts summarized earlier in our review of cognitive development theory. Our interest in this section will be with the six stages of moral development identified by Kohlberg. Like Piaget, Kohlberg developed his theory by interviewing children, initially ages ten to sixteen. Later, he expanded his research to include adults. Kohlberg was interested in how children think; more specifically, with how they mentally deal with moral issues and moral dilemmas. He sought to understand the pattern of thoughts that led to their conclusions. Given this approach, it is difficult to separate his theory from the methodology employed.

His assumption was that children at different stages of moral development would use qualitatively different forms of reasoning in dealing with the dilemmas. A typical approach would be to provide the child with a dilemma and then an interview guide would permit the probing of the reasoning involved. Based on the reasoning evidenced, a scoring guide would place the child at a particular stage of moral reasoning. The ethical dilemma that follows is one of the more famous ones posed by Kohlberg. It is entitled "Heinz Steals the Drug."

Heinz Steals the Drug
In Europe, a woman was near death from a special kind of cancer. There was one drug that the doctors thought might save her. It was a form of radium that a druggist in the same town had recently discovered. The drug was expensive to make, but the druggist was charging ten times what the drug cost him to make. He paid $200 for the radium and charged $2,000 for a small dose of the drug. The sick woman's husband, Heinz, went to everyone he knew to borrow the money, but he could only get together about $1,000 which is half of what it cost. He told the druggist that his wife was dying and asked him to sell it cheaper or let him pay later. But the druggist said: "No, I discovered the drug and I'm going to make money from it." So Heinz got desperate and broke into the man's store to steal the drug for his wife. Should the husband have done that?[40]

Kohlberg's model of moral development was comprised of three levels with each level consisting of two stages for a total of six. Earlier, Piaget had advanced a two-stage theory closely linked to his cognitive stages of concrete operations and formal operations.

Level I   Preconventional Morality

Stage 1   Here the logic is based on whether the behavior should be rewarded or punished. The orientation reflects a perception of what is right or wrong. There is little middle ground, reflecting the child's concrete operations mode of thinking. In short, good behavior is rewarded, and bad behavior is punished. Stealing is bad; therefore, since Heinz stole and thus did something bad, he should be punished. The issue is clear cut for the child operating at Stage 1: There are no mitigating circumstances.

For children at this stage, rules exist externally to them. These rules are fixed and one obeys them to avoid punishment. In Kohlberg's use of **preconventional morality**, he noted that the thinking which resulted from the logic used had not been internalized. The child does not yet possess a personal sense of the notion of conventional (customary or normative) standards.

Stage 2   In this egocentric stage, the central concern is: What is there to be gained? Here a self-interest orientation is evidenced. The child has gained an understanding that people hold different views and do things for different reasons. Again the child has not formed her or his own conception of right and wrong but does recognize that there is no single view. Reflecting the self-interest orientation of this stage, the child's thinking will tend to reflect egocentrism. "What was in it for Heinz"? Perhaps the end justified the means employed.

Level II   Conventional Morality

While level one rests on an egocentric sense of fairness linked to individual need, Level II evidences a logic based on fairness that incorporates shared conventions. Similar to Level I, the moral reasoning at this level still has external rules and **conventional morality** as its reference.

Stage 3   The concern of Stage 3 is approval, particularly of those in authority, such as parents, teachers, and God. Children who tend to give Stage 3 responses are entering adolescence. While their orientation is widening, they are very much concerned with the approval of others. In the case of Heinz's dilemma, they identify with his intention of saving his wife's life and his lack of options. They also tend to view the druggist as selfish and bad. Of the two, it is the druggist who is wrong and should be punished.

Stage 4   In this stage there is a growing concern about and respect for authority and the best interest of society. The young person is now evidencing a societal perspective. While still external, the young person's logic senses that the good of the individual is tied to the good of all, and thus the importance of maintaining order. With respect to Heinz, there remains sympathy for his wish to save his wife, but this is tempered by the view that what he did was wrong. The moral reasoning of this stage examines the need to rule by law. There would be anarchy if we all were guided by what we personally considered right and wrong as opposed to a common set of rules applicable to all regardless of the merit of individual motives.

Level III   Post-Conventional Morality

In Kohlberg's hierarchy of moral reasoning, **post-conventional morality** represents the highest or most advanced level of thought. Movement is away from a morality based in convention to one tied to the individual's own system of values and moral standards.

Stage 5   In Stage 5 there is a recognition that an orderly society is not necessarily a just society. In this stage, the reasoning becomes sensitive to an individual's rights but within a larger framework that seeks to advance the well-being of all. In a matter of speaking, there is a new perspective on what is meant by "improving the quality of life" and the concern is with how this might be accomplished for the benefit of all.

In the Heinz dilemma, respondents incorporating Stage 5 thinking seek to weigh the moral and legal issues involved. On the one hand, moral judgment holds that life is more important than property. On the other, there is the contention that social control binds us to live and behave within the law. If a law is not just, there are ways to change it using democratic processes. In fact, there is a responsibility to seek these changes in order to improve the quality of life of all. In the case of Heinz, judgment should consider his act within a broad social perspective. Both Heinz and the druggist have reasons for their actions. While there is a recognized need to hold Heinz responsible for his illegal act, the level of punishment should fully consider the reasons for his act.

Stage 6   Kohlberg's final stage is one that recognizes a system of ethical principals that apply to all people in all cultures. The principles of justice are viewed as universal; they apply to all humankind irrespective of gender, color, national origin, sexual orientation, or physical or mental condition.

The civil rights movement, the women's movement, the gay-lesbian movement, and the world-wide human rights movement all have relevance to the moral reasoning evidenced in Stage 6. The work and dedication to the civil rights cause by Martin Luther King and the life and work of Mahatma Gandhi are frequently used as examples to illustrate the moral right and responsibility for acts of civil disobedience. There is a principle of social justice that justifies the challenge of laws that are deemed immoral and hurtful, for example, laws that support apartheid.[41]

Gender-Related Differences

The work of Carol Gilligan is particularly important.[42] In *In a Different Voice* she examines possible gender differences and the development of psychological theory. Lawrence Kohlberg was a teacher, friend, and colleague of Gilligan. Her work particularly reflects issues related to Kohlberg's theory of moral development.

Earlier, we reviewed the concepts of Gemeinschaft and Gesellschaft and identified them as qualitatively defining different kinds of social relationships. These relationships and their use arise out of different ways of thinking about self and others. Recall that Gemeinschaft relationships are those natural relationships that are informal, personal, and that are entered into for their own sake; the relationships that serve as both a means and an end, such as a love relationship. Gesellschaft relationships are contractual in character; they are formal and impersonal and are entered into as a means to achieve some desired end, for example, an employment contract. With the notions of Gemeinschaft and Gesellschaft providing background, let us review some of Gilligan's findings.

To help develop her position, Gilligan used responses to Heinz's predicament. For our review, we will illustrate gender differences by examining the responses of two very bright and articulate children, Jake and Amy, both eleven. While arriving at similar conclusions, the logic they used is quite different. Consistent with the dilemma as constructed by Kohlberg, Jake focuses on a conflict between the value of life versus property. Jake argued as follows:

> For one thing, a human life is worth more than money, and if the druggist only makes $1,000, he is still going to live, but if Heinz doesn't steal the drug, his wife is going to die. (Why is life worth more than money?) Because the druggist can get a thousand dollars later from rich people with cancer, but Heinz can't get his wife again. (Why not?) Because people are all different and so you couldn't get Heinz's wife again.[43]

Jake develops his logic in math which he indicates is "the only thing that is totally logical."[44] He also takes the law and the possible actions of the judge into account, all from the above position. He reasons that laws are human creations and thus contain errors based on unforeseen circumstances. In this case, while Heinz did break the law, the judge should be as lenient as possible, recognizing Heinz's motive, the value of life over property. In Kohlberg's rating system, Jake's responses would be Level II (Conventional Morality), a mixture of Stages 3 and 4. Amy's response as to whether Heinz should steal the drug involves a different (Gemeinschaft-based) logic and is more tentative:

> Well, I don't think so. I think there might be other ways besides stealing it, like if he could borrow the money or make a loan or something, but he really shouldn't steal the drug—but his wife shouldn't die either.

Amy was then asked why she felt that Heinz should not steal the drug. Her reply does not consider either property or law but rather the effect that the theft could have on the relationship between Heinz and his wife. She reasons:

> If he stole the drug, he might save his wife then, but if he did, he might have to go to jail, and then his wife might get sicker again, and he couldn't get more of the drug, and it might not be good. So, they should really just talk it out and find some other way to make the money.[45]

Amy's moral reasoning builds on the human relationships that are involved. She views society as bound together through systems of human relationships, not an institutionalized system of rules and laws. She relates to a Gemeinschaft world, not a Gesellschaft one. The solution to this problem is to be found in a natural set of human relationships based upon mutual understanding and mutual respect. Amy reasons, "if

Heinz and the druggist had talked it out long enough, they could reach something besides stealing."[46]

Given Kohlberg's rating scale and definition of stages, Amy appears to be a full stage lower in development than Jake. Is the Gesellschaft-related logic of Jake superior or just different than the Gemeinshaft world of Amy? They do look at the world, at least through this dilemma, differently. For Jake, the dilemma is one of life versus property rights and an imperfectly written law. Amy sees it as a breakdown in human relationships. The means for resolution is the relationship; it is both the means and the end.

For us Gilligan's thoughtful work provides another way of examining structural patterns of interaction having relevance to the social systems model. Her work suggests that there may be quite different patterns of thinking that are gender-related. These differences may be helpful in exploring women's issues as they pertain to forms of discrimination and oppression. These differences in thinking may operate very subtly, and to the detriment of women in societies dominated by men. Gilligan develops her reasoning by comparing a hierarchical stage model evidenced in cognitive and moral development with that of a web. She frames women's issues as follows:

> The reason women's experience has been so difficult to decipher or even discern is that a shift in the imagery of relationships gives rise to a problem of interpretation. The images of hierarchy and web, drawn from the texts of men's and women's fantasies and thoughts, convey different ways of structuring relationships and are associated with different views of morality and self. But these images create a problem in understanding because each distorts the other's representation. As the top of the hierarchy becomes the edge of the web and as the center of network of connection becomes the middle of a hierarchical progression, each image marks as dangerous the place which the other defines as safe. Thus the images of hierachy and web inform different modes of assertion and response: the wish to be alone at the top and the consequent fear that others will get too close; the wish to be at the center of connection and the consequent fear of being too far out on the edge. These desperate fears of being stranded and being caught give rise to different portrayals of achievement and affiliation, leading to different modes of action and different ways of assessing the consequences of choice.[47]

SUMMARY

The work of Piaget suggests that cognitive development occurs in a fixed sequence. The progression is hierarchical and results in an ever more complex and differentiated set of structures. At the level of formal operations, the individual is able to think conceptually and symbolically, and is thus freed of thinking based on direct experience. The individual now possesses the mental capacities for both retrospective and future thinking, not only about self and others but all forms of human groupings, and thus can plan and work toward building a better future world.

Also recognized in the work of Piaget is the notion that cognitive development is a social process, one that is dependent upon interactions with others. We find cognitive development theory useful, not only because it supports the view that selfhood is an ongoing social process, but it also suggests that this occurs in fixed stages. Within the social systems model, this offers a structural dimension that incorporates the notion of life stages.

Kohlberg builds on the foundation of cognitive theory by charting moral development. Our interest in moral development is threefold. First, the profession of social work is grounded in a set of values and moral reasoning that focuses on an individual's right to be self-determined and to be allowed to achieve his or her full potential. This is the foundation upon which the professional helping relationship and the profession's use of the service contract builds. Kohlberg's work helps extend the reasoning upon which the value of self-determination, potentiality, human worth and dignity, and other social work values rest. At a more general level, the profession of social work is devoted to a set of moral principles that apply to all and have as their purpose an improvement in the quality of life for all people. This is the profession's highest statement of purpose. Again, Kohlberg's moral development theory helps operationalize the notion of social process by linking it to the highest level of moral reasoning and the involvement of a set of moral principles.

Second, while both cognitive and moral development theory are classified as psychological theories, individual development is recognized as a social process. This view, presented in cognitive and moral development theory, is for us one-sided and linear in its orientation. The impact that the individual as a psychological being has on the groups in which she or he is a member is not examined. The cyclical impact of the individual and the social environment is not addressed. The use of these two theories within the social systems model becomes a way of incorporating these reciprocal and dynamic influences.

For example, we hold that the various groups that humans join together to form evolve into a group culture which includes a value system. This system, especially in the family, becomes a reference point that affects the moral development of its members. This interplay between group (family) members and the individual members, particularly children, is especially important.

The social systems model also employs a four-problem paradigm (Chapters 4 and 8) to explain system dynamics. Pattern maintenance is one of the four problems comprising this paradigm. Kohlberg's work on moral development theory is helpful in thinking about the problem of pattern maintenance. Recall that the problem pertains to the maintenance of the core or most vital patterns of behavior that distinguish the subject group from others. In reviewing this problem, we mentioned that all systems possess a hierarchy of interactional patterns with those at the core being the ones that are most important to maintain; and if violated, the system risks losing steady state and thus ceases to exist. In most groups, this core pattern will be interlaced with moral values that are mutually shared, for example, trust, confidentiality, fidelity, honesty, justice, and respect, to mention but a few. It is the thinking and research performed by Kohlberg and others in this tradition that help us understand why these patterns are of such fundamental importance in the maintenance and development of the group itself.

Third and finally, it is in the area of moral development that we are able to examine some of the reasoning that may explain differences in thought by different people. Of special interest to us are the possible differences in the development of moral thought that may be gender related.

To conclude, in this chapter we have reviewed four lines of theory development in the field of psychology.[48] Like a prism, each offers a different view of human behavior. Each has importance in the field of social work, and each informs the social systems model in a somewhat different way. Cognitive development and moral development theories may be somewhat less known among social workers than psychoanalytic and behavioral theories. In addition to their use with the social systems model, these two development theories suggest that people do not all think alike. Aspiring social workers as well as those in practice are alert to the implications of this reasoning. Social work practice in all its forms is premised on the use of a relationship. The forming of a relationship is contingent upon the individuals involved being able to understand each other. Communication problems can stem from many sources because people do not all think the same way. One of the sources may well be gender differences in modes of thought that are present in all that we do.

GLOSSARY

Accommodation In cognitive development theory, the construction of new schemata or modification of existing schemata to adjust to new experiences or information.

Assimilation In cognitive development theory, the fitting of new experiences and objects into an existing schema.

Anal stage The second of the five psychosexual stages associated with psychoanalytic theory.

Behavior modification/therapy The treatment of problem behaviors usually by employing operant conditioning procedures.

Circular reaction In cognitive development theory, the term used to describe each learning activity in which infants attempt to repeat an action that first occurred by chance.

Cognitive theory Theory pertaining to the steps involved in deriving meaning from experience.

Concrete operational thought The third of Piaget's four cognitive stages. This stage starts at about age six and ends in early adolescence.

Conditioned reinforcer The concept is applied to anything that signals to the subject that a reinforcer is available.

Conditioned response (CR) In classical conditioning, the response evoked by a stimulus as a consequence of repeated association.

Conditioned stimulus (CS) In classical conditioning, the stimulus that produces the response as a consequence of repeated and systematic association.

Conscious The individual's capacity to experience cognitively and emotionally what is going on in the environment and to process and act in accord with this information.

Conventional morality   The second level of Kohlberg's moral developmental theory. Logic is based on fairness that incorporates shared conventions.

Defense mechanism   In psychoanalytic theory, the means used by the ego to defend against impulses of the id and the unrealistic expectations of the superego.

Discrimination   In behaviorism, the ability to respond only to an individual case from a set of stimuli.

Ego   In psychoanalytic theory, the part of the mental structure that has been socialized and experiences and interprets reality.

Electra complex   In psychoanalytic theory, this concept is the counterpart of the Oedipal complex. The daughter possesses an unconscious incestuous desire for her father along with animosity toward her mother.

Epigenetic   The notion that organisms develop from an undifferentiated mass through a series of fixed stages to a mature state.

Extinction   The assumption that behaviors that are not reinforced will reduce to their baseline or natural level of occurrence.

Formal operational thought   The fourth of Piaget's cognitive stages. Adult capacities of reasoning, abstraction and symbolization emerge. This stage begins at adolescence and continues through adulthood.

Generalization   In operant conditioning, the process in which a response generalizes across a class of stimuli.

Genital stage   The fifth and final stage in psychoanalytic theory.

Id   In psychoanalytic theory, the primitive part of the mental apparatus that contains inherited instinctual urges.

Latency stage   The fourth of the five psychosexual stages in psychoanalytic theory.

Methodological (S-O-R) behaviorism   The theory that environmental-behavioral relationships are mediated by an individual's symbolic or cognitive processes.

Oedipal stage   Alternative language for the phallic stage of development in psychoanalytic theory.

Operant conditioning   The position that behavior is determined by its consequences.

Oral stage   The first of the five psychosexual stages in development identified in psychoanalytic theory.

Organization   In cognitive development theory, the tendency to seek and build order.

Phallic stage   The third of the five psychosexual stages of development in psychoanalytic theory.

Pleasure principle   Freud's principle of psychoanalytic theory that holds that organisms seek pleasure and avoid pain by the immediate discharge of their instinctive drives and tension states.

Positive reinforcer   A stimulus that increases the possibility that an antecedent behavior will occur again.

Post-conventional morality   The third level of Kohlberg's hierarchy of moral development.

Preconscious   Thoughts and content that are not in the person's awareness but, unlike the unconscious, can be recalled by the individual when needed.

Preconventional morality   The first level of development in Kohlberg's theory of moral development.

Preoperational thought   The second of Piaget's four cognitive stages. This stage occurs from approximately eighteen months and ends during the early school years.

Primary reinforcer   A reinforcer that has "natural" reinforcing qualities.

Psychoanalysis   The method of treatment used which is based on psychoanalytic theory.

Psychodynamic   Cognitive, emotional and motivational processes that consciously and unconsciously affect one's behavior.

Punishment   The method of ending a given behavior by the addition of an unpleasant stimulus.

Radical (S-R) behaviorism   The theory that environmental control acts directly on behavior.

Reality principle   In psychoanalytic theory, the recognition of behavioral demands of the real world. The ego learns and finds ways of postponing the immediate forms of gratification related to the pleasure principle.

Reinforcement   A stimulus that increases the probability that a specified antecedent behavior will occur again.

Reinforcement schedules   The timing structures employed to increase the probability of a desired behavior. Schedules include continuous reinforcement, fixed-ratio schedule and variable-ratio schedule among others.

Repression   The manner, according to Freud, in which animal-like aggressive and sexual impulses are "forgotten" by an individual. These impulses then become part of the person's unconscious.

Schema   In cognitive development theory, a perceived representation of reality in memory.

Self-efficacy   A person's sense of confidence in his/her ability to perform behavior required in a specified situation.

Sensorimotor intelligence   The first of Piaget's four cognitive stages. This stage is from birth to eighteen months and development centers on sensory and motor schemes.

Shaping   The concept of reinforcing all behaviors that lead to desired end behavior.

Spontaneous recovery   The concept that extinguished behaviors can reappear under circumstances similar to those that originally reinforced the behaviors.

Stage   A developmental level tied to epigenetic theory.

Stage theory   A theory that employs stages as the organizing scheme in explaining growth and development.

Superego   The part of the mental structure in psychoanalytic theory that is likened to one's conscience. The superego contains a person's parental attitudes and cultural standards.

Unconscious   In psychoanalytic theory, this concept is synonymous with life force and includes sexual and aggressive impulses that are animal-like in origin, including desires, wishes and experiences that are frightening or unacceptable to the individual.

Unconditioned response (UR)   In classical conditioning, a physiologically or internally based response to an unconditioned stimulus.

Unconditioned stimulus (US)   In classical conditioning, the stimulus that evokes the unconditioned response, for example, a stimulus that produces a response prior to a learning opportunity.

NOTES

1. See *The Encyclopedic Dictionary of Sociology*, 3rd ed., (Guilford, Conn.: The Dushkin Publishing Group, 1986), 279.

2. *The Encyclopedic Dictionary of Psychology*, 3rd ed. (Guilford, Conn.: The Dushkin Publishing Group, 1986), 224–227.

3. For a general review, see Donald Brieland, "History and Evolution of Social Work Practice," *Encyclopedia of Social Work*, vol. 1. (Silver Spring, Md.: National Association of Social Workers, 1987), 739–754.

4. Freud's early work in hysteria was done in collaboration with Josef Breuer and resulted in the publication in 1895 of *Studies on Hysteria*. Later Breuer disassociated himself from Freud, from psychoanalytic theory and from what came to be known as the practice of psychoanalysis.

5. Charles Darwin, *The Origin of Species* (New York: Modern Library, 1859).

6. See, for example, Sigmund Freud (1920), *A General Introduction to Psychoanalysis*, trans. J. Riviere (New York: Washington Square Press, 1965).

7. Erik H. Erikson, *Childhood and Society*, 2nd ed. (New York: W.W. Norton & Co., 1963).

8. Barbara M. Newman and Philip R. Newman, *Development Through Life: A Psychosocial Approach*, 4th ed. (Chicago, Ill.: The Dorsey Press, 1987).

9. See, for example, Sigmund Freud, *Instincts and their Vicissitudes*, trans. J. Riviere, in *Collected Papers*, vol. IV. (New York: Basic Books, 1959).

10. For a useful and interesting summary, see F. Alexander and H. Ross, eds., *Dynamic Psychiatry* (Chicago, Ill.: University of Chicago Press, 1952).

11. Ibid., 9–10.

12. Sigmund Freud, "New Introductory Lectures on Psychoanalysis," in *The Standard Edition of the Complete Psychological Works of Sigmund Freud*, ed. J. Strachey, vol. 22, (London: Hogarth Press, 1964).

13. See for example, Sigmund Freud, "Female Sexuality," in trans. J. Strachey, *Collected Papers*, vol. V (New York: Basic Books, 1959).

14. For a positive critical review of psychoanalysis, see Marshall Edelson, *Psychoanalysis: A Theory in Crisis* (Chicago: University of Chicago Press, 1988).

15. Daniel N. Robinson, *Systems of Modern Psychology* (New York: Columbia University Press, 1979), 93.

16. See particularly, John B. Watson, "Psychology as the Behaviorist Views it," *Psychological Review*, 20, 1913.

17. Ibid.

18. For a review see Ivan P. Pavlov, *Conditional Reflexes*, trans. G.V. Ansev (London: Oxford University Press, 1964).

19. For discussions of their works, see Edwin G. Boring, *A History of Experimental Psychology* (New York: Appleton-Century-Crofts, 1957).

20. John B. Watson, *Behaviorism* (New York: W.W. Norton & Co., 1970), 104.

21. B.F. Skinner, *The Behavior of Organisms* (Englewood Cliffs, N.J.: Prentice-Hall, 1938) pp. 20–21.

22. Albert Bandura, *Social Learning Theory* (Englewood Cliffs, N.J.: Prentice-Hall, 1977).

23. Virginia Robinson, *A Changing Psychology in Social Work* (Chapel Hill, N.C.: University of North Carolina Press, 1930).

24. Eileen D. Gambrill, "Behavioral Approach," *Encyclopedia of Social Work*, vol. 1 (Silver Spring, Md.: National Association of Social Workers, 1987), 184–194.

25. See Frank C. Goble, *The Third Force: The Psychology of Abraham Maslow* (New York: Grossman Publishers, 1970).

26. Ludwig von Bertalanffy, *General System Theory: Foundation, Development, Applications* (New York: George Braziller, 1968).

27. For a discussion of this relationship, see Jean Piaget, "Piaget's Theory," in *Handbook of Child Psychology*, ed. Paul H. Mussen, 4th ed. (New York: John Wiley & Sons, 1983), 103–128.

28. Abraham H. Maslow, *Motivation and Personality*, 2nd ed. (New York: Harper and Row, 1970), 35–38.

29. Piaget, 109–112.

30. For a convenient and easily understood summary of Piaget's stage model, see Ruth M. Beard, *An Outline of Piaget's Developmental Psychology for Students and Teachers* (New York: Basic Books, 1969).

31. Sarah F. Campbell, ed., *Piaget Sampler: An Introduction to Jean Piaget Through His Own Words* (New York: Jason Aronson, 1977), 4.

32. Beard, *Piaget's Developmental Psychology*, 82.

33. Jean Piaget, *The Psychology of Intelligence* (London: Routledge & Kegan, 1950).

34. For a review of cognitive theory and its development in social work, see Edmund Sherman, "Cognitive Therapy," *Encyclopedia of Social Work*, vol. 1 (Silver Spring, Md.: National Association of Social Workers, 1987), 288–291.

35. For a social work application, see Diane de Anda, "Adolescents," *Encyclopedia of Social Work*, vol. 1 (Silver Spring, Md.: National Association of Social Workers, 1987), 51–67.

36. B.F. Skinner, *About Behaviorism* (New York: Alfred A. Knopf, 1974), 244.

37. Maslow, *Motivation and Personality*, XIII.

38. For example, see Lawrence Kohlberg, "Development of Moral Character and Moral Ideology," *Review of Child Development Research*, ed. M.L. Hoffman and L.W. Hoffman, vol. 1 (New York: Russell Sage Foundation, 1964).

39. See, for example, John C. Gibbs and Keith F. Widaman, *Social Intelligence: Measuring the Development of Sociomoral Reflections* (Englewood Cliffs, N.J.: Prentice-Hall, 1982).

40. Lawrence Kohlberg, "The Development of Children's Orientations Toward a Moral Order: 1 Sequence in the Development of Moral Thought," *Human Development* 6, 1963, 19.

41. Lawrence Kohlberg, *Essays on Moral Development*, vol. 1 (New York: Harper & Row, 1981).

42. Carol Gilligan, *In A Different Voice* (Cambridge, Mass.: Harvard University Press, 1982).

43. Ibid., 26.

44. Ibid.

45. Ibid., 28.

46. Ibid., 29.

47. Ibid., 62.

48. For a comprehensive review of lines of theory development in psychology, see Kenneth P. Hellner, *History and Systems of Modern Psychology* (New York: Gardner Press, 1984).

Chapter 10

Psychosocial Theory: A Social Systems Perspective

OUTLINE

Background

The previous chapter has provided an overview of several important lines of theory development in psychology now being used by practicing social workers. In this chapter we add another psychosocial theory. According to our research, psychosocial and social systems are the two theoretical paradigms currently dominating the practice of social work (see Table 1.3).[1]

In earlier chapters we indicated how various theories can be incorporated into the social systems model for purposes of conducting research, organizing knowledge, and to inform practice. Our effort in this chapter will be the incorporation of psychosocial theory. Before doing so, our first task is to provide additional background, including a definition of psychosocial theory.

Simply put, psychosocial theory has its origins in psychoanalytic theory and builds off the psychosexual stage features of that theory. The *Social Work Dictionary* does not offer an entry on psychosocial theory but does define "psychosocial development theory."

We consider the two as synonymous, with the notion of development simply incorporating the concept of life stage. The *Social Work Dictionary* provides the following definition:

> The concepts delineated by Erik Erikson and others to describe the various stages, life tasks, and challenges that every person experiences throughout the life cycle. The phases and life tasks, defined elsewhere in this dictionary, are; trust versus mistrust, autonomy versus shame and doubt, initiative versus guilt, industry versus inferiority, identity versus role confusion, intimacy versus isolation, generativity versus stagnation, and integrity versus despair. Some other psychosocial theorists describe different ages and life tasks.[2]

As suggested in this definition, the chief architect of this line of theory development was Erik Erikson. In a manner of speaking, he was to psychosocial theory what Freud was to psychoanalytic theory. So while there are a number of contributors to this line of theory development, our review will build mainly from the work of Erikson.[3]

Erik Erikson was born in Frankfurt, Germany, in 1902. Being of Jewish descent, he fled Germany with the rise of Nazism and settled in Boston. While in Germany, he studied under and was psychoanalyzed by Anna Freud, Sigmund Freud's daughter. Erikson's interest was with children and he became Boston's first child psychoanalyst.

His contributions in the development of psychosocial theory can be distinguished from the more classical psychoanalytical theory in two important ways. First, psychosocial theory focuses on the ego, not the id. While the id and the presence of unconscious determinants to behavior are acknowledged, it is consciousness and the role of ego that is stressed; in short, psychosocial theory is an ego, not an id, psychology. Second, the stages encompass the life span and focus on the interplay between the distinctive features of the stage and the psychological, social, and cultural experiences associated with each life stage. Erikson acknowledges the importance of sexual maturation, but his stage formulation is a psychosocial, not a psychosexual one.[4]

Recognition of life stages did not originate with Freud, but it was he who linked the idea with the maturational process and fashioned a psychology that embraced the stage concept. We will not attempt to track the origins of this idea but would like to share with you some lines from Shakespeare's "As You Like It." Earlier we used a portion of the following to develop the concept of role (see Chapter 3). It is through Jaques' commentary on life that Shakespeare offers his insights on "life stage" development:

> All the world's a stage,
> And all the men and women merely players:
> They have their exits and their entrances;
> And one man in his time plays many parts,
> His acts being seven ages. At first the infant,
> Mewling and puking in the nurse's arms;
> Then the whining school-boy, with his satchel
> And shining morning face, creeping like snail
> Unwillingly to school. And then the lover,

Sighing like furnace, with a woeful ballad
Made to his mistress' eyebrow. Then a soldier,
Full of strange oaths, and bearded like the pard,
Jealous in honour, sudden and quick in quarrel,
Seeking the bubble reputation.
Even in the cannon's mouth. And then the justice,
In fair round belly with good capon lin'd,
With eyes severe and beard of formal cut,
Full of wise saws and modern instances;
And so he plays his part. The sixth age shifts
Into the lean and slipper'd pantaloon,
With spectacles on nose and pouch on side;
His youthful hose, well sav'd, a world too wide
For his shrunk shank; and his big manly voice,
Turning again toward childish treble, pipes
And whistles in his sound. Last scene of all,
That ends this strange eventful history,
Is second childishness and mere oblivion;
Sans teeth, sans eyes, sans taste, sans everything.
("As You Like It," Act II, Scene VII)

Shakespeare spoke of the seven "ages" of man; Freud identified five, and Erikson, eight.[5] Shakespeare's ages spanned a lifetime; Freud's ended with adolescence. Shakepeare spoke of the various psychological and social experiences associated with each stage of life, while Freud's stages deal with the person's sexual development and related effects on psychological development. Erikson, building on Freud's insights, extended the stages to cover the life span, broadened the social determinants of behavior, and downplayed the importance of sex in the developmental process.

Before leaving Shakespeare's words it is useful to establish a further link with psychosocial theory and the systems model. Early in Jaques' soliloquy he notes:

And one man in his time plays many parts,
His acts being seven ages.

Several points can be drawn from the passage that are instructive. First, the universality of the seven ages. "All the world's a stage, and all the men and women merely players." Second, roles are learned and are enacted for each of the seven ages. These words remind us of the frequently heard parental admonition "act your age". This is suggestive of the wisdom of Shakespeare's insight, that there are roles appropriate for each of life's ages. Similarly, there are roles that are inappropriate. How many times have you heard (or said to someone), "You are too young (or too old) to do that"; or, "When are you going to grow up?" Third, the developmental process is cyclical, with a common beginning and a common ending. Both are characterized by helplessness and thus the need for others to meet even the most basic needs. In a manner of speaking, it is an open systems view of life and development, with the learned role being specific to each stage.

Many, if not most, psychological theories help us understand our individuality. Psychosocial theory, for the reasons suggested by Shakespeare, helps us examine the common patterns of behavior that provide the foundations upon which our individuality emerges and develops, stage by stage.

Focus

In relative terms, psychosocial theory is of narrow range, at least in comparison to psychoanalytic theory. The dominant organizing schemes are life stage and internal (psycho) and external (social) determinants of behavior (the psychosocial crisis). As originally formed, the focus of this theory is the individual. We will expand on this focus by emphasizing an open systems formulation and one that views the individual in proactive rather than reactive terms. In so doing, we maintain more of a dual focus, on the individual and the social environment. Through use of the social systems model we will show how each acts on the other and how each is affected by the other.

Assumptions

Given the origins of psychosocial theory, many of the assumptions deemed central to psychoanalytic theory should also apply. This is not necessarily the case. Erikson does not dwell on such notions as the unconscious, id drives, or the continuity of humans with the animal kingdom. His focus is on consciousness, the ego, and the interplay of internal and external determinants of an individual's behavior. The following assumptions are central for this presentation of psychosocial theory:

1. There are distinguishable stages of development over the life span of the individual—from conception to the end of life; these stages are universal.
2. These stages are linked to the more general maturational process and occur in an invariant sequence.
3. Each developmental stage is affected by the previous stage in a cyclical fashion.
4. The whole person must be understood, and the whole is comprised of the physical, psychological, social, and spiritual.
5. An understanding of a person's behavior must specifically consider the social context in which it occurs, as well as the life stage.
6. The ego, or self, develops and changes over the life span, and a sense of selfhood can be considered an outcome related to each life stage.

The assumptions build on and expand the more general assumptions previously identified with the social systems perspective (see Chapter 2). It is through psychosocial theory that we will examine an approach that helps us understand the sources of personality organization.

Concepts

Within the framework provided by the social systems model, three organizing concepts will be used to present psychosocial theory: (1) life stage, (2) psychosocial crisis, and (3) developmental activities.

Stage, as you will recall from the definition given previously, refers to a developmental level. **Life stage** as used in psychosocial theory means the same thing as stage. Theorists vary in the number of stages identified and the labels they attach to each stage. This can be confusing to the reader just being introduced to stage theories. With this in mind, we have prepared Table 10.1. Here we compare the stages used by Freud in psychoanalytic theory with the approach used by Erikson and generally referred to as psychosocial theory. We have also included the stage designations we used and a rough approximation of the age range of each stage.

Of the three organizing schemes, life stage is the most important and serves as the basis for presenting much of the content of psychosocial theory in this chapter. Utilizing a social systems perspective, the individual emerges from each life stage a different or at least a changed person. In essence, the difference results primarily from the resolution of the psychosocial crisis associated with the life stage.[6]

Psychosocial Crisis

The notion of **psychosocial crisis** has its origins in Erikson's work and is the concept used to designate the tension state that develops between the person and his or her social environment in each life stage. We suggest that you think of this concept as a particular way of operationalizing the basic notion of human behavior and the social environment. In short, this theory holds that in each stage of development the person experiences sets of internally based needs. These needs are associated with the maturational process. The

TABLE 10.1   Life Stages: Psychosocial Theory

Stage Designation	Approximate Ages	Psychoanalytic	Psychosocial
1. Infancy	birth–18 months	Oral	Basic Trust vs. Basic Mistrust
2. Post Infancy	18 months to 3	Anal	Autonomy vs. Shame and Doubt
3. Pre School	3–6	Phallic (Oedipal)	Initiative vs. Guilt
4. School	6–12	Latency	Industry vs. Inferiority
5. Adolescence	12–20	Genital	Identity vs. Role Confusion
6. Early Adulthood	20–35	–	Intimacy vs. Isolation
7. Middle Adulthood	35–65	–	Generativity vs. Stagnation
8. Late Adulthood	65–death	–	Ego Integrity vs. Despair

person also possesses certain developmental capacities and experiences with which to cope and satisfy these needs.

There will, in addition, be corresponding sets of expectations, interpersonal and social, that confront the person externally. While serving to drive the developmental process, these expectations are beyond or at least different from the capabilities and experiences currently possessed by the individual. It is the interplay of these conflicting expectations, desires, and demands that creates the psychosocial crisis. The idea of a crisis is a very helpful and powerful one in offering an explanation of a wide range of human behavior. Erikson, however, cautions against viewing the notion of a crisis as being something negative; it is merely the designation of the natural state of tension associated with the different sets of expectations and coping capacities associated with each life stage.

Erikson, building on the insights provided by Freud, identified a psychosocial crisis associated with each psychosexual stage.[7] His designation was in the form of a **polarity** evidencing what he viewed as the central developmental issue and the outcome parameters for dealing with the issue. By polarity, we mean that the resolution of the psychosocial crisis of each stage will result in an individual's possessing personality (self) features falling somewhere between the two opposing poles. For example, in Stage 2 (Post Infancy) the psychosocial crisis is autonomy versus shame and doubt. Recall that Freud designated this as the anal period. The youngster at this age is gaining an early sense of self, and finds pleasure with her or his own body products. The child also is now at the maturational level that permits a growing amount of control over bowel and bladder movements. This is one of the few areas in which the youngster is able to exercise control. The child's parents or their surrogates also have ideas of how, where, and under what circumstances bowel and bladder functions are to be performed. Here we have the classical conflict between the internally based needs of the child and the external societal demands for compliance with normative standards. More simply stated, the child will be trained in the use of the toilet to deposit body waste. The societal agents charged with this responsibility are the child's parents. While a difficult time for both child and parents, the crisis will be resolved and with mutual effects. With respect to the child, the stage will impact in terms of some combination of an internalized sense of autonomy, or shame and doubt.

Erikson, as well as others in his tradition, expanded on Freud's observations, with psychosexual development becoming psychosocial development. The central idea recognized by Erikson in Stage 2 was the child's rapidly growing but very fragile sense of self (autonomy). The oral and sexual features were only dimensions of a larger and more general process of becoming more autonomous. The very nature of the maturational process and the expectations of parents and others make the crisis of this stage inevitable. According to Erikson, it is a universal crisis faced by all youngsters of this age and their caregivers. The child emerges from this stage different than when she or he entered. The differences are concentrated within the polarity of autonomy or a lack of autonomy, and a personal sense of shame and doubt.

Applying the systems perspective to psychosocial theory requires some elaboration on the key concepts comprising the theory, increasing the emphasis on the social determinants of behavior and the open systems features of the model. Relative to psychosocial crises, our position is that the effects of the crises are always reciprocal and mutually deterministic. For example, the resolution of the youngster's crisis of autonomy versus shame and doubt will impact the child, other family members, and the family itself. These system changes in turn will affect the child and her or his capacity to deal with each of the subsequent life stage crises.

The formulation of the psychosocial crises by most early proponents reflects linear and cause-and-effect thinking. There is a clash of internal and external forces and an effect is produced. We believe a cyclical and proactive view is more useful. Similarly, this so-called effect of the resolution of a psychosocial crisis is not inalterable. In psychosocial theory, the effect is registered in the ego, or what we prefer to call one's sense of **self-hood**. As we have indicated earlier, consider the development of selfhood as a process. Psychosocial theory provides a way of examining this process from the perspective of a life stage. Within this context, think of the resolution of a psychosocial crisis as resulting in the acquisition of new or modified features of one's self. For example, in post infancy, a child may gain a sense of personal autonomy, but with some minor feelings of shame and doubt. This sense of autonomy then provides a structural feature of selfhood upon which future experiences will build or will undermine. In other words, subsequent life experiences can both contribute to the further development of this aspect of selfhood derived from the resolution of the psychosocial crisis, or distract from it resulting in, for example, a reduced sense of personal autonomy and an increase in self-doubt.

While not central in his work, Erikson clearly recognized the cyclical and mutually deterministic effects of social intervention. For example, he spoke of the importance of parents' confidence in themselves in their parenting roles.[8] This sense of **self-efficacy** in the parenting role, according to Erikson, is transmitted to the child and has meaning. The child's response will, in our judgment, tend to be confirming to the parents. We believe the reverse is also true, particularly in very young children. If the parents are anxious and unsure in their parenting roles, the child will mirror this anxiousness and uncertainty. In this scenario, the child's behavior tends to confirm the parents' perceptions of themselves and they continue to feel uncertain and anxious. Here some of the concepts previously reviewed in symbolic interaction theory can be helpful, such as "the looking glass self" (see Chapter 6).

Some digression is indicated at this point to support our contention of the importance of the notion of reciprocal and mutually deterministic effects in the formulation of psychosocial theory. It is useful to keep in mind that the theory describes a social process, but from the viewpoint of individual development. So just as the child struggling with the crisis of autonomy versus shame and doubt will be affected by the behavior of his or her caregivers, so will the caregivers be affected by the behavior of the child. These effects are then transmitted back to the child; it is a mutually shaping and ongoing process both within and between each life stage.

Perhaps an example drawn from our own research can help develop the point. As a general proposition, we believe that the social worker's own sense of personal confidence in his or her professional role is a key determinant in understanding the outcome of his or her work with clients. It is the same logic that was referred to above in noting the importance that Erikson attributed to parents' feeling confident in their roles. If a worker is anxious and unsure of her- or himself in the helping role, we believe this gets communicated to the client with adverse effects on both the helper and client roles. Again, each affects the other in an ongoing way. Our own research on this phenomenon to date has concentrated on these effects on the worker (the maintenance output). Our findings suggest that perceptions of competence have a buffering effect against burnout and are positively correlated with feelings of job satisfaction.[9] Our contention is that a cyclical and mutually deterministic conception of life stage development is more useful than one based on linear reasoning.

There is one further observation that we wish to make prior to concluding this summary of the concept of psychosocial crisis. A major criticism of Freud's work, for some, was that it was biased in terms of gender, race, class, culture, and other factors. Erikson understood this criticism and it explains in part his avid interest in anthropology and the other social sciences. He wished to formulate his ideas in a manner that would reduce such biases.[10] Keep in mind that much has changed since Erikson produced his important work over forty years ago.

We find Erikson's designations of the psychosocial crises at each life stage of great help, and representative of the magnitude of his many insights into human behavior. The specific designations of these stages are affected by cultural expectations and as such can be viewed as most representative of western and industrialized societies in the 1950s. Also, these societies have been dominated by males and so the labeling of the psychosocial crises will be influenced by this dominance. This does not diminish the importance or the existence of the so-called crises, it merely acknowledges that there is great diversity in our world and this diversity is constantly changing, as are the social expectations.

Developmental Activities

In psychosocial theory the label *developmental task* is frequently used to describe what we refer to as activities in the social systems model. Thus, for our purposes, developmental tasks and **developmental activities** refer to the same thing. Our use of the concept of activity has been described earlier in connection with the discussion of a hierarchy of outcomes (see the discussion of proposed output in Chapter 3).

In short, in psychosocial theory there are universal sets of activities (developmental tasks) that take place within social systems. These are the means the system employs to deal with the psychosocial crises at each life stage. It is a positive resolution of the psychosocial crises that is the implicit goal (proposed output) for each life stage. Recall that in the hierarchy of outcomes, activities are derived from goals and objectives. They are the selected means to be employed by the system to achieve its goal.

The power and the usefulness of psychosocial theory is in identification of a universal set of developmental activities that are employed at each life stage for dealing with the psychosocial crisis. These developmental activities are institutionalized into sets of roles associated with each life stage, for example, the typical family roles of mother, father, and child. These role sets then provide the basic structure through which the developmental activities are played out. It is useful to view these activities as part of a natural ordering that occurs between the person and his or her social environment at each life stage. This natural ordering is derived from a combination of the genetic equipment possessed by each human, the maturational development of the human (and which is part of this genetic equipment), and the cultural expectations associated with each society.[11] Again, while there will be variations of these activities within different cultures, these variations are within the so-called natural order; the order itself should be treated as a given. For example, all human infants require care arrangements or they will not survive. Every society will institutionalize arrangements for the care of its very young; these arrangements, for example, the nurturing role, constitute the natural ordering associated with dealing with the crisis of basic trust versus basic mistrust.

As with all the major concepts being defined, the notion of activities has its origins in the insights provided by Freud. Toilet training offers a familiar example of what we mean by a set of developmental activities. These activities are typically engaged in during the post infancy stage and, in part, serve as a means for dealing with the crisis of autonomy versus shame and doubt. There are other sets of activities as well; another example would be language training and development. A central point to remember is that these activities are social and take place between the individual and others playing a central, or at least a significant role in the development process. It is this social process that we model as a social system, for instance, a family.

The concept of activities serves to identify core patterns of behavior that are distinctive to each life stage and serve as a medium through which the psychosocial crisis is mediated. Importantly, the performance of these activities involves learning, and the involvement of even more complex cognitive states. Part of this learning involves the development of the ego, or what we call the self. These cognitive patterns and the related sense of selfhood are elaborated upon stage by stage.

The work of Hamachek is of interest here.[12] He has formulated by stage, behavioral expressions related to the polarity identified in each stage, for example, autonomy versus shame and doubt. People deemed to have a sense of autonomy "like to make their own decisions, particularly about matters important to them." In contrast, those who possess a sense of shame and doubt about themselves "prefer being told what to do rather than make their own decisions."[13]

In the sections ahead we will be discussing each of the life stages identified by Erikson using the organizing schemes noted above.

Infancy

In introducing infancy as a life stage, two points are particularly noteworthy. First, while this stage starts at birth, development begins at the point of conception. There is also more to this prenatal development process than the genetic contribution of the two partners. Research findings focusing on prenatal development suggest that the mother's psychological, physical, and social well-being are critically important to the developing fetus, and thus the use of drugs or smoking by the mother affects the fetus.[14]

Second, at birth the infant is far more advanced in development than is generally understood and thus early social experiences are more important than many parents realize. Freud and Erikson both recognized the importance of the early developmental stages, with perhaps infancy being the most influential of all. This position is in accordance with the epigenetic principle, and it also makes common sense from the position of psychosocial theory. If the general proposition is accepted that humanness is socially acquired, then it follows that the infant's early experiences with other humans are critical. Here the parental roles, particularly that of the mother or the primary caregiver, are critical. It is here that a context is formed to deal with the psychosocial crisis.

Psychosocial Crisis: Basic Trust versus Basic Mistrust

The family is the prototype social organization and is found in one form or another in all societies. While the family performs many functions, none is more important than serving as providers for the care and the protection of children. Be it a traditional nuclear family, a single parent family, an extended family, a foster family, or any of the other varied forms, it is the family that provides the social environment in which the **basic trust versus mistrust** crisis is played out. As developed in this book, the family in whatever form becomes the primary (not the only) social system for dealing with this crisis. In systems language, the infant and her or his parents in their parental roles become the primary inputs to the system. Much of the content developed in Part III, particularly Chapter 7, applies to our discussion here.

The term "basic," as in "basic need" used by Erikson, is instructive. The infant at this stage is entirely helpless; she or he would perish if not for the care and protection provided by other humans. The infant, while being of the animal kingdom, is also quite a different and special kind of social animal. This distinctiveness is to be found, in large part, in her or his social nature and the cognitive capacities that provide the basis for developing this social (human) nature. The medium for developing this capacity is the relationship; it is the primary way that all humans functionally link themselves with others. The most fundamental relationship is with the primary care giver, the person(s) who assumes the initial "mothering" or nurturing role. Since this relationship is the first, it becomes the prototype for future relationships. Trust as used here has several related meanings, such as confidence, reliability, predictability, and dependability. Basic means fundamental, the core or essence of trust. Recall that at birth the child is only equipped with a few genetically based capacities, for example, sucking. It is here that cognitive development theory is instructive, for it is through the maturation of the sensory and motor functions that learning proceeds. The infant can taste, feel, see, hear, and smell, but most importantly she or he can learn and attribute meaning to these early sensory and motor experiences. Basic trust or mistrust is a meaning that is learned and one that is attributed to a relationship. In the vocabulary of the systems model, a sense of trust or mistrust is an output of this stage; it is an attribute of the self and this attribute becomes an input for the next stage.

Developmental Activities

In psychoanalytic theory this is the oral stage, and most writers, including Erikson in the psychosocial tradition, acknowledge the importance of the infant's mouth during this formative period. The sucking response is part of the genetic equipment with which the infant begins life. Not only is the mouth used for taking in nourishment, it is through her or his mouth that the infant starts exploring the world.

Erikson, building on Freud's work, notes that while the mouth and oral activity are important, the infant's other sensory equipment is similarly important. Not only is the infant taking food in through her or his mouth, much more is being taken in via the eyes, ears, nose, and other organs.[15] Again, cognitive development theory is helpful in grasping the structures of thought that are occurring at this time via the sensory and motor systems.

During the initial phase of this eighteen month period, much of the family's (care giver's) activities are centered around feeding, holding, changing diapers, bathing, and otherwise attending to the physiological needs of the infant. It is when these activities are carried out that the infant deals with the crisis of basic trust versus mistrust. In the language of the systems model, these activities comprise the interaction portion of the system's conversion operations.

Recall that the infant is born with essentially a "clean slate"; there is no sense of self, of mother, of father, or anything or anyone else in the world. Most of these meanings are learned through activities (interactions) with others, and become part of the infant's growing sense of personhood. In this sense they are social experiences. The infant is hungry and is fed. It is how the infant is fed that creates the social experiences. The food fulfills a need and is thus pleasurable. Being held close to the parent's warm body and being rocked is also pleasurable. These experiences become linked as the cognitive structures evolve and out of these social activities a sense of trust or mistrust forms.

The infant comes to recognize mother and other family members and, through their caring responses to her or his needs, experiences pleasure, comfort and a general sense of well-being in their presence. A relationship, and a vital one, is underway. To the extent that the infant's needs are satisfied physiologically and socially, a sense of trust of others develops. To the extent that needs are not satisfied, or that there is an inconsistent pattern, a sense of mistrust evolves.

It is important to keep in mind that while psychosocial theory focuses on the interplay of internal and social experiences, the infant is learning about the world from her or his own experiences as well. So while the early experiences of the infant with family members is critical, the total environment that the child experiences is similarly important. It needs to be safe and stimulating. The child learns by and through the richness and diversity of this environment.

While the focus of psychosocial theory is on the individual, most of the experiences dealt with are social, so the effects are, from a social systems perspective, reciprocal and mutually deterministic. To illustrate these ideas, we will turn to the Jones family. Recall that Barbara and Sam were married while in college and both worked a while before deciding to have children. They were twenty-seven when they learned that Barbara was pregnant. Not only were Barbara and Sam delighted with the news, but both sets of parents and other family members were as well. Quickly Barbara became the center of attention of family members and friends. There was much talk, particularly among the women, about the pregnancy, visits to the obstetrician, and their own experiences while being pregnant. Sam wanted, to the extent possible, to share the birthing experience with Barbara. He attended the Lamaze classes with Barbara and both prepared for their future parenting roles. Thus there was an intensive socialization process underway long before Ann's birth. Not only were Barbara and Sam being prepared for their parental roles, but both of their parents were working through their own feelings about being grandparents; Ann was the first grandchild on both sides of the family. In short, both the social system and the key aspects of its suprasystem were in line with and supportive of the "new addition" to the system.

What has been depicted is a very supportive, if not ideal, environment for the birth of Ann. Extensive preparations had been made so that Barbara would be with

Ann during the critical first few months of her life. While Sam's company did not have paternity leave, he did use three weeks of vacation to stay home with Barbara and Ann.

Ann had her own room and Barbara took a three months leave from her job. She decided not to breast-feed Ann. In part this was based upon the decision that both she and Sam would share feeding and otherwise caring for Ann.

Barbara and Sam enjoyed holding, rocking, and constantly talking to Ann. Ann, in return, would smile and coo in response to the attention she was receiving. There were difficult as well as good times, but the care she was given was consistent and loving. Barbara and Sam had been well prepared and were confident in their parenting roles.

Barbara's return to work was especially difficult. She felt guilty about Ann being in a nursery daycare program. However, the decision to return to work was her own and fully supported by Sam. The Joneses' routine and lifestyle were significantly altered by Ann. For example, the couple had to get up two hours earlier so that Ann could be dropped off at daycare, the partying with friends on weekends came to an end, as well as the intimate dinners and special vacations they enjoyed together. The roles of the Joneses were both different and more complicated as a consequence of Ann's birth. Barbara and Sam were becoming different people as they assumed their parenting roles. In a manner of speaking, the social system known as the Joneses was different because it had added a new member and had adopted new goals pertaining to the raising of Ann.

Ann was confronted with the crisis of basic trust versus basic mistrust. Her parents were also dealing with a psychosocial crisis associated with the life stage of early adulthood—intimacy versus isolation. These crises were played out within the social system that was the Jones family—Barbara and Sam in their parental roles and Ann as their infant daughter.

Erikson made the point that the resolution of the crisis always falls somewhere between the two poles. In Ann's case, she experienced both feelings of trust and distrust, with the sense of trust dominating. Importantly, one can not know trust without some sense of distrust. Ann, as she grows older, will need to know when she can trust and when she cannot trust. Erikson put it as follows: "the human infant must experience a goodly measure of mistrust in order to trust discerningly."[16]

Before leaving the infancy stage and Ann, it is important for us to again remind you that we are seeking to describe a line of theory development from the perspective of health and well-being. Given that Ann is a healthy baby, cared for by loving, competent, healthy, and economically secure parents, the chances are that she is going to develop into a healthy, stable adult. Many (if not most) children are born into far less advantageous circumstances; some will be unwanted, others will be born to very young, poor, inexperienced parents. Others will not have parents at all. Some will not survive, but all who do, in accordance with this line of theory, will be faced with solving the psychosocial crisis of basic trust versus basic distrust.

Perhaps surprisingly, and in spite of all the environmental problems, most of these infants will, like Ann, solve the crisis on the positive side. The key for successful resolution is in both the richness of the environmental circumstances and the quality of the relationship with key caretakers. Perhaps a useful way of viewing this is from the assumption that there is a natural ordering (Gemeinschaft forms of relationships) and that it is when there is substantial deviation from this ordering that problems arise. Finally, it is

the natural ordering of developmental activities associated with dealing with the psychosocial crises that constitutes the conversion operations of the social system. In an application of the model, the cycle can correspond to the life stage or, at a micro level, to a
social act within the framework of a specific life stage, such as an episode dealing with the
"potty training" of Ann.

Post Infancy

Freud labeled this the anal stage because, through the maturational process, the child
now has gained control of her or his sphincter muscles. This level of control is important
to both the child and to her or his care givers. For the child, it is the beginning of a sense
of personhood, a state of existence independent of others in the environment. During
the first eighteen months of life, the infant existed largely by taking things in, not only
through the mouth, but through all of the senses. Mental capacities were rapidly developing through the maturation of sensory and motor systems. This first stage was labeled
sensory motor intelligence by Piaget and establishes the cognitive foundations for the
next stage of development—preoperational thought.

Erikson's contribution to psychosocial theory was recognition that a range of developmental changes were occurring and affecting the child during this period of post
infancy. Freud recognized and focused on the sexual maturation and its effects. Certainly
the child was interested in and at times preoccupied with bladder and bowel functions.
However, much more was happening. It is during this post infancy period that the child
is becoming mobile and is learning to speak. It is through language and the associated
imagery that the child begins the process of grasping her or himself as possessing a separate and distinct existence; the process is lifelong.

Psychosocial Crisis: Autonomy versus Shame and Doubt

It was the recognition of the struggle of developing a sense of **autonomy**, of separateness,
that led Erikson to define the psychosocial crisis of this stage as **autonomy versus
shame and doubt**. Recall that this is the stage of "the terrible twos." The normally
developing child is willful and quick to say "no"—even when no means yes! Not only is
the child grasping some of the implications of the control she or he has over her or his
body, but the impact that words have on others—especially "NO!" Being repeatedly told
"NO!" in a demanding voice by a two-year-old is, for many parents, a provocation—an
invitation to "show the little critter who is boss". Unappreciated in such circumstances is
the fact that the child and parent simply don't think the same way. For the child, the
immediate situation is "all there is"; there is no comprehension of the implications of
"NO" in the same sense that it is understood by the adult. The child has been repeatedly
told "NO!"—don't do this, don't do that—no!—no! At this point in development, the
child has learned the word no and at least some of its implications. It is, in the mind of
the child, a very powerful word, far more powerful than the word yes. It is a beginning
way that the child has of experiencing her or his own individuality—of becoming autonomous.

Parents (care givers) are society's agents for the socialization of the young. For some, we would hope, only a few, the provocativeness of the child at this age is evidence of something bad inside, perhaps evil; their task is to rid the child of this "badness." This can be likened to "breaking the will" of the child. While there may be many ways of doing this, one is to shame, to humiliate, to humble the child for their "wrong doings." Erikson describes shame and guilt in useful ways. For example:

> Shame supposes that one is completely exposed and conscious of being looked at: in one word, self-conscious. One is visible and not ready to be visible; which is why we dream of shame as a situation in which we are stared at in a condition of incomplete dress, in night attire, 'with one's pants down.'—
>
> Too much shaming does not lead to genuine propriety but to a secret determination to try to get away with things, unseen—if, indeed, it does not result in defiant shamelessness.
>
> Doubt is the brother of shame—
>
> This stage, therefore, becomes decisive for the ratio of love and hate, cooperation and willfulness, freedom and self-experience and its suppression. From a sense of self-control without loss of self-esteem comes a lasting sense of good will and pride; from a sense of loss of self-control and of foreign overcontrol comes a lasting propensity for doubt and shame.[17]

Developmental Activities

The activities of each lower stage serve as the foundation for activities of the next higher one. Critical in infancy was the development of trusting relationships, sensory/motor skills and the beginning differentiation of selfhood. It is the extension of these activities supported by the rapid maturational development of the child that the activities of post infancy build.

While each child has her or his own developmental pattern, most children around the age of one are standing alone and starting to take their first few steps.[18] In the stage of post infancy, the child starts by taking her or his first few awkward, hesitant steps; by the end of this stage they are running and jumping—in constant motion. The dominant theme underlying the activity patterns of this stage is the growing capacity of the child for self-care. In recognition of this growing capacity, there are the sets of societal expectations reflected in the parenting role. Youngsters of this age are expected to become more mobile and so this becomes evident in the behavior of parents. Much of family life at this stage is linked to helping the child become more mobile, to feed himself or herself, to develop toilet habits, to communicate her or his needs and wishes, to generally adapt to the behaviors society expects of post infancy. Importantly, many of the activities of this age are social—the child is learning how to become a person. Much of this is being accomplished through language development.

At the point of entry into this stage (eighteen months) most children will have a vocabulary of just a few words (roughly three to thirty). By the time they are ready for the next stage, their vocabularies will approximate a thousand words. Not only is the child rapidly learning new words, but a sense of selfhood as well. The world is being taken in by the child through the imitation of others, particularly parents and others having significance to the child. The post infancy period is also the time when the child starts engaging in solitary play. The child lives in part in an imaginary world. It is through this imaginary world that the child plays out what is happening around her or him. Here she or he plays house; in so doing the child is playing out what her or his understanding is of the role of mother, role of father, as well as her or his own role. Typically, the child will play all of the parts, including her or his own. In effect the child is learning the roles of those around her or him by playing them. It is here that the work of Piaget is helpful in understanding what is going on in the mind of the child. This is the stage of preoperational thought, learning by doing, by experiencing.

Let us turn to the Joneses and to Ann who is now three. She is the "apple of her daddy's eye" and a source of great pride for Barbara and for both sets of grandparents. Ann attends day care at the Children's Center, a program provided for the employees of the Midtown Mental Health Center, her mother's place of employment. Barbara was anxious for Ann to be with children from a variety of different cultural and socio-economic backgrounds. Center patients, staff and neighborhood residents all use the Children's Center. Given that the mental health center serves a low-income clientele, the children in day care were literally from every imaginable background.

In this scenario, the day-care center becomes an important part of the suprasystem for the Joneses. Ann spends over forty hours a week in day care or almost as many of her waking hours as she spends with her parents. Both Barbara and Sam initially held ambivalent feelings about the amount of time Ann spent in day care; Barbara had particular difficulty with day care, feeling somehow that she was compromising her relationship with Ann by not staying home "like a real mommy." Contributing to her feelings was her knowledge that Verna, Sam's mother, felt that her place was in the home taking care of Ann and her husband. Barbara understood her sensitivity around this point; nevertheless, each time they visited Sam's parents she had the sense that Verna was searching for evidence that Ann was somehow being adversely affected by her day-care experiences (a new feature in the interface between the Joneses and Sam's parents).

All the evidence was to the contrary. Ann looked forward to day care and, while the pace was hectic, all things seemed to be going well with the Joneses. According to Barbara, Ann was easy to toilet train. She had established bowel control by the time she was eighteen months and by twenty-four months seldom wet herself. Sam likened Ann's stubborn streak to Barbara, saying they appeared to be "out of the same mold." This stubbornness, evidenced by Ann's saying, and sometimes screaming, "No!" and stamping her little foot, reached a high point when she was about thirty months old and has since diminished. Barbara and Sam, for the most part, didn't react to these outbursts by Ann. They were firm in their dealings with her and when things became tense, would simply put Ann on a chair telling her that when she "settled down" she could then join the family again—"in the meantime—stay put!" In their private times together and thinking about how difficult Ann could be, they would console themselves with the expression, "this too will pass."

While acknowledging their "ups and downs," Barbara and Sam were feeling quite good about themselves and particularly about how well Ann was progressing. They reminded each other of their earlier decision not to have children. In Barbara's words, "While I love my work and I love being Sam's wife, Ann has given me something special. In a crazy way, by being a mother I think I now know what being a woman really is about."

The point we wish to emphasize in the example is the cyclical and interactive effects that family members have on one another in terms of life stage development. Not only is Ann dealing with a psychosocial crisis, but so are her parents (intimacy versus isolation) and grandparents (generativity versus stagnation). Each is having an effect on the other, but Ann, as the first child and grandchild, is, for the moment, a focal point.

Pre School

The third life stage corresponds to what Freud designated as the phallic or Oedipal stage. Recall that in psychoanalytic theory, as a result of the process of sexual maturation the sexual energy that was focused in the anal area shifts at this stage to the genitals. Youngsters, as they grow older, are curious about all parts of the body; now this curiosity centers on their genitals and the genitals of others. This interest is heightened by the pleasure that is associated with the manipulation of these special body parts. As is frequently the case, the child's parents are not as enthusiastic about this genital play as is the child, often saying, "Quit that"; "That's not nice!"; "Good little girls (boys) don't play with themselves!"; and other admonitions. Some of the parental admonitions to the young at this age are both frightening and bizarre, for example, references to castration; small wonder that the psychosocial crisis of this age deals with initiative and guilt.

Erikson, as he does at each stage, looks for a broader scheme than just the sexual one for characterizing the stage. The youngster at three is now quite mobile and, having shed diapers, is much more in control of his or her movements. The child seems anxious to test the limits of these new capacities. In a manner of speaking, and for the child, perhaps there are no limits: "I am Superman (woman)." Sometimes, and to the consternation of parents, the child is like a perpetual motion machine.

Psychosocial Crisis: Initiative versus Guilt

Erikson was a bit uncomfortable with the notion of initiative as he sought to frame this crisis. He observed:

> I know that the very word 'initiative' to many, has an American, and industrial connotation. Yet, initiative is a necessary part of every act, and man needs a sense of initiative for whatever he learns and does, from fruit-gathering to a system of enterprise.
>
> The ambulatory stage and that of infantile genitality add to the inventory of basic social modalities that of 'making,' first in the sense of 'being on the make.' There is no simpler, stronger word for it; it suggests pleasure in attack and conquest. In the boy, the emphasis remains on phallic-intrusive modes; in the girl it turns to modes of 'catching' in more aggressive forms of snatching or in the milder form of making oneself attractive and endearing.
>
> The danger of this stage is a sense of guilt over the goals contemplated and the acts initiated in one's exuberant enjoyment of new locomotor and mental power.[19]

The polarity is initiative and guilt. It is useful to think of guilt as associated with or as an adverse consequence of the initiative. The relationship between the crisis of each stage is important to keep in mind. The previous crisis dealt with autonomy versus shame and doubt. Here we make the assumption that eventually a positive resolution of this crisis was reached. The child, with this developing sense of autonomy, is now testing out her or his capacities and for her or him "the sky is the limit." The problem is that there *are* limits and the child will discover that she or he is not Superwoman or Superman, that she or he cannot fly and that dad or mom has already been spoken for. The key in resolving the crisis is to maintain the spirit of initiative and for the child not to have an overwhelming sense of guilt over the excesses that characterize the initiatives undertaken.

Given the systems perspective being applied, the resolution is a system outcome, the key system again being the child's family. To state the matter otherwise, the task outcome of this stage will be a sense of selfhood possessed by the child (Ann) as it pertains to the ratio of feeling **initiative versus guilt**.

Developmental Activities

At this time, much is going on with the child physically, cognitively, and socially. In a manner of speaking, initiatives are occurring in each of these areas. Similarly, there will be sets of developmental activities associated with each of the areas. Cognitively, this is the period that Piaget labeled preoperational thought. Learning is still very much linked to the here and now. This is important because one of the things the youngster is learning is gender. Ann, in our Jones family, has had many reminders of her gender from all the important people around her, such as, "Ann is Daddy's girl"; "Ann, good little girls don't do that"; "Ann, pretty is as pretty does"; and "Ann is such a beautiful little girl." Ann, who is now five, has her mother as a role model for what female as well as mother means. She has also observed with more than a casual interest the experiences of tenderness and love between her father and mother. With this in mind she announced that she too was going to marry Daddy when she got big. Simply stated, to understand sex as gender is to learn what male and female both mean. Complicating this understanding is that sex roles are constantly changing. Ann's sex role is not a given, it is something that she will learn; it is a meaning that she will acquire and the meaning will shift and change throughout her life. It will be influenced by her age, her race, the social class of her family, and generally by the normative standards evidenced in the Jones family and by other groups (systems) of which she will be a member.

The point here is that there are a host of activities that take place between the youngster and her or his caretaker that result in the acquisition of a perception of gender. This perception is a vital part of the acquisition and development of a sense of self. These activities, for the most part, occur within the family and the acquisition of the gender dimension of self can be usefully viewed as a system outcome.

Fortunately for Ann, both of her parents are confident in their respective sex roles and so she has had good role models for both sex roles. Ann, while not comprehending the genital basis of gender, does understand that, like her mother, she has a vagina, and later, when she gets "big," will have breasts like her mother. Her dad, like all males, has a penis. Barbara and Sam enjoyed and at times were amused at Ann's questions dealing with sexual matters, such as why females have a vagina and males, a penis. Her questions were answered in a matter-of-fact and simple way and this seemed to satisfy Ann, or at least until she could think of the next question. Barbara and Sam understood that Ann had no real comprehension of the genital basis of sex at this stage of her development. They also knew, or at least hoped, that in a few years Ann would be again asking them some of these same questions.

In concluding this discussion on activities, we want to call your attention to the moral development that is occurring at this time. Here the earlier discussions of the superego in psychoanalytic theory and moral development theory are pertinent (see Chapter 9). The child at the pre school stage has a sense of what is right and wrong, at least within the framework provided by their care givers. Recall that children at the pre school stage would be at what Kohlberg labeled as Level I, the Preconventional Level of moral development (see Chapter 9). This stage is marked by the child seeing rules as fixed and absolute. These rules are, in a manner of speaking, handed down by adults and other "absolute" authorities. It is within this context that it is useful to conceive of the sense of guilt that a child can develop at this stage when told that they are bad and should be punished. Again, it is important to be reminded that the young child and the adult do not think the same way. Parents need to be alert to and sensitive to these differences.

School

The stage we designate as school corresponds generally to the time the child is in elementary or grade school (between the ages of six and twelve). Freud labels this the latency period, essentially a quiet and dormant period in terms of psychosexual development. Although it may be quiet in terms of sexual maturation, it is anything but quiet with respect to the cognitive development that takes place. This stage ends with the onset of puberty at approximately age twelve, a bit earlier for most females and a bit later for most males.

Psychosocial Crisis: Industry versus Inferiority

This is a busy time for children, a time when they more formally start preparation for life as an adult. Erikson observed that the child in all cultures receives some systematic instruction during this period.[20] While many children have been in day care and thus away from their families during the day, school is different. It tends to be more formal and more evaluative in nature. There are tests, grades, "passes," and "failures"; it is for most children a more competitive environment than they have previously experienced. In most instances, children find themselves in classes organized by age and its associated expectations. Children are compared one with another and children compare themselves with others as well. It is for most children a difficult as well as an exciting and challenging time. Industry is expected and rewarded, lack of industry is not, but is nevertheless labeled; this child may be called "slow," "lazy," or "problem," for example. The outcome of this stage will be an aspect of selfhood containing some ratio of feelings of **industry versus inferiority**.

The child, by entering school, has also entered a major new social system, one that is more Gesellschaft in nature than the family. In the Jones family, Ann was Ann, the daughter of Barbara and Sam Jones. Now she takes on a more differentiated role, Ann the student. She is one of fifteen students in her class and one of 225 in Monroe Grade School. She is faced with a different arena in which to compete for attention and recognition.

The outcome of the psychosocial crisis of industry versus inferiority is now somewhat more problematic, in part because there are more social systems that affect or produce the outcome. The two principle ones for all are the family and the school, but there are others as well; the church, neighborhood, and school friendship groups would serve as examples. While for most children the family remains the dominant influence, the school is rapidly gaining in importance. There are also other factors that will impact on the outcome of this crisis, factors over which Barbara and Sam as well as Ann have little control. An example would be the quality of school program that is available both generally and specifically. In a specific sense would be the competence and sensitivity of the teacher, the equipment, supplies, and the teaching and learning environment that is available to the child. On a more general level would be the richness and diversity of the school system itself. Examples would include, among others, specialty programs available in athletics, music, and the arts. Other cultural features include the diversity of students and faculty in terms of gender, race, religion, social class, disabilities to which the child is exposed, and how the social system deals with these differences.

Developmental Activities

With each higher life stage, the number of social systems involved in dealing with the psychosocial crisis increases. Similarly, there tends to be greater structural differentiation occurring within the social systems themselves. As these systems become more structurally differentiated, there is an ever greater number of roles and their associated sets of activities that the child is called upon to master. The child will do better at some than at others. For example, one of your authors recalls a son coming home from second grade excited about what he had accomplished in school that day; he was first in his class! On inquiry, it turns out that he was the fastest runner in his class. While not indicating their disappointment, the hope held by his parents was that he might have been "number one" in arithmetic, or at least in spelling. Not so for the youngster and, as seen through the eyes of his friends, being the fastest runner in his class was by far a greater achievement.

It is during the school stage that the child evolves from what Piaget labeled as preoperational to concrete operational thought (see Chapter 9). It is through cognitive development that the child gains the mental capacities to deal with an ever more stimulating and complex environment. In part, it will be through the new cognitive capacities that the child will either be helped or hindered in dealing with the crisis of industry versus inferiority in this society.

The child's cognitive development will affect both the child's intellectual and social capacities. In earlier stages the child has acquired a sense of personal autonomy and initiative upon which this stage builds. As a part of this development, the child has acquired a personal sense of selfhood, including gender and some knowledge of the key roles played by others in her or his life; for example; mother, father, grandparent, other family members, and day-care teacher, to mention but a few. This knowledge has largely been accomplished through the process of imitation and identification. Also, the knowledge of these roles has been experienced as they relate to the child. The child's level of cognitive development is now permitting the child to mentally take the role of others in much more complex and interactive forms of problem-solving or goal-related activities.

To illustrate the basic notions involved, we pick up Ann, who is now eleven and a sixth grader at Monroe Elementary School. Our focal system will be a new social group, a girls' basketball team. The developmental activities that will be illustrated are those associated with learning a team sport. We will be interested in how, through game play, Ann will develop additional capacities to think representationally and, more generally, how the team experience will help her deal with the psychosocial crisis of this age.

Ann and her two best friends, Susie and Wendy, decided to join the school's newly formed girls' basketball team. Like both of her parents, she is physically well coordinated and assertive. By joining the team, Ann gets a first-hand lesson in interdependence. In this regard, she soon finds that her personal goals must be subordinated to those of the team. With the assistance of her coach, Ms. Bacon, she begins to understand her role on the team (Ann plays a guard position) in relationship to the roles (positions) played by her teammates. Ann is assertive like her mother, and loves to try to steal the ball from the opposing team. While supportive of her assertiveness, Ann's coach cautions Ann against taking frequent risks to steal the ball from opponents because, in so doing, her position on defense is left unguarded. Through coaching and game play, Ann learns the game and her role vis-à-vis the roles of other team members. Ann's cognitive stage (beginning of formal operational thought) now allows her to mentally take the role of others in ever more complex ways. She is able to explore representationally (mentally) the possible outcomes of her actions in relationship to total team play. Ann discovers that there are more opportune times than others to make steal attempts without jeopardizing her team's defense. In short, Ann is learning to mentally and simultaneously take the role of all her team members, and those of the opponents, into consideration as well as her own before she makes an attempt to "steal" the ball; she mentally becomes able to anticipate actions of others before they occur and by so doing, adjust her own actions.

Ann's teammates, who themselves are gaining skill in mentally taking the role of others, begin to adjust to Ann's assertive style of play as she adjusts to theirs. By the end of the season, the team is greatly improved. One by one, Ann's coach instituted specific defense and offense strategies (system structures). The coach was aware of the girls' expanding ability to think representationally and utilized this as new and more complex plays were introduced.

The experiences Ann had in playing her first year of competitive sports assisted her in the resolution of the psychosocial crisis of industry versus inferiority. She learned through basketball and a variety of other social experiences to work cooperatively with others toward a team goal, even with those girls that she did not especially like (a maintenance output). Here she recalls Ms. Bacon's frequent reminder, "remember girls, it's teamwork that wins games."

Ann also gained, as she developed her athletic skills through basketball, a greater mastery over her own body. She also learned how to lose as well as to win as a "good sport." Self-evaluation in a situation occupies a great deal of the school age child's thinking and Ann's coach was mindful of this as she worked with the girls. Similar to the leader of a therapeutic group, the coach guides the development of a group culture. A sense of cohesion is developed that will assist each member in gaining a sense of personal competence necessary to the development of self-efficacy (a task outcome of the group). This confidence in oneself, in turn, is vital to the resolution of the crisis of industry versus inferiority.

Both Barbara and Sam attended Ann's games. They marveled at how fast she was growing up. Their presence helped Ann and she would cast a glance to the stands after making either a bad or a good play. She also looked to her coach for reactions to both her good and bad plays. Ann was finding another important female role model in her life, Ms. Bacon. Ann's friendships also grew with her two special friends, Susie and Wendy. These friendships with Susie and Wendy were about to take on even more importance as Ann entered adolescence.

Adolescence

In classical psychoanalytic theory, this period is labeled genital, and ends the process of psychosexual maturation; the individual at this stage is physiologically capable of sexual reproduction. In accord with the psychoanalytic position, the latency period ends with an infusion of sexual energy marking the onset of the genital stage. More dramatically than the previous stages, the individual enters the stage as one person and completes it as another; the girl becomes a woman, and the boy, a man.

Erikson, as with the other stages, recognized the importance of sexuality. But there is much more going on. While the young person may be physiologically capable of sexual reproduction, there is more to adulthood than sexual capacity. The adolescent is continuing to seek a definition of self. At least for a little while, this process is going to be complicated by the rapid physical changes that are occurring along with the growing intensity of sexual impulses. Young women and young men need to get adjusted to their new bodies. Changes are also occurring cognitively; this is the stage of formal operations. For those who reach this stage, a whole new and important set of cognitive capacities are available to deal with the psychosocial crisis.

Psychosocial Crisis: Identity versus Role Confusion

Many, if not most, writers who deal with the period of adolescence treat it as a period of great change and turmoil. The child enters this period, and after eight or so years, emerges with an identity as an adult, ready to take her or his place in society. The stage can be usefully viewed as a period of transformation between childhood and adulthood. The medium of the transformation is, for most people, the social group. While the family remains important, it is the peer group that now plays a key role. Erikson sets the stage for dealing with the crisis of this age as follows:

> But in puberty and adolescence all samenesses and continuities relied on earlier are more or less questioned again, because of a rapidity of body growth which equals that of early childhood and because of the new addition of genital maturity. The

growing and developing youths, faced with this physiological revolution within them, and with tangible adult tasks ahead of them are now primarily concerned with what they appear to be in the eyes of others as compared with what they feel they are, and with the question of how to connect the roles and skills cultivated earlier with the occupational prototypes of the day. In their search for a new sense of continuity and sameness, adolescents have to refight many of the battles of earlier years, even though to do so they must artificially appoint perfectly well-meaning people to play the roles of adversaries; and they are ever ready to install lasting idols and ideals as guardians of a final identity.[21]

In Part II, The Social Group, we develop the position that selfhood is a process and can be usefully thought of as an outcome of the social group(s). To help develop this notion, we introduced you to the theory of symbolic interaction and notably the work of Charles Horton Cooley.[22] Recall that it was he who coined the words "the looking glass self."[23]

Cooley's observations are especially helpful in contemplating the psychosocial crisis of adolescence. An identity is being sought; the sense of identity that had evolved largely through the socialization efforts occurring within the family no longer fits the rapidly developing and changing teenager. A new identity is needed. This is the stage in life when the adolescent spends a good bit of time in front of the mirror checking on the physical changes taking place in her or his body; in many ways, the adolescent is also searching for an identity in the mirror: "Who am I?"

As suggested by Cooley, the adolescent searches particularly for identity within the peer group. Erikson speaks to the propensity for young people of this age to join together.

> Young people can also be remarkably clannish, and cruel in their exclusion of all those who are "different," in skin color or cultural background, in tastes and gifts, and often in such petty aspects of dress and gesture as have been temporarily selected as *the* signs of an in-grouper or out-grouper. It is important to understand (which does not mean condone or participate in) such intolerance as a defense against a sense of identity confusion. For adolescents not only help one another temporarily through much discomfort by forming cliques and by stereotyping themselves, their ideals, and their enemies; they also perversely test each other's capacity to pledge fidelity.[24]

Some psychosocial theorists, notably, Barbara M. Newman and Philip R. Newman, have given additional attention to the role of the group in the search for personal identity. Building on the work of Erikson, they propose that adolescence be divided into two periods, early and later adolescence.[25] The "nerd" or the "geek" are labels given to those who are unable to develop group identity. The psychosocial crisis of early adolescence in their scheme is labeled "group identity versus alienation."[26] The point they develop is that the search for personal identity by the adolescent involves two steps. First is the development of a group identity (the peer group). The so-called group identity then provides the framework for the second step, the acquisition of a personal sense of identity (self).

Developmental Activities

The developmental activities through which the psychosocial crisis is played out include a number of social systems, including the family, the peer group, the school, and the job, to mention but a few. In each, the adolescent plays a role. Each of these systems has its own set of goals which, as we have pointed out before, is the source of the role and the activities associated with playing that role. The problem is that the goals of some of these systems are in conflict with the other. The clearest example for most young people are the goals of the family versus the goals of their peer group. When there are conflicts in the goals of two or more systems and an individual is playing a role in each of the systems, there is inevitably some level of role conflict. For the adolescent as well as others, this situation gives special meaning to the expression, "being between a rock and a hard place." For most young people of this age, the solution involves an emancipation from the family as a necessary condition for solving the crisis of identity versus role confusion.

We now pick up Ann and the Jones family again. Ann is seventeen, living at home and is a senior at Midtown High School. She serves as vice president of her senior class, is a member of the Thespians Club and the school's basketball team, and works weekends as a cashier at Wal-Mart. Ann has dated since fifteen, having a couple of what she describes as "steady relationships," but is not involved in one at the moment. In sixth grade she developed a strong friendship with two other members of the basketball team, Susie and Wendy. Their friendship has persisted and intensified; they still refer to themselves as the "Fearsome Three-some." The name developed as a consequence of their "fearsome" behavior on the basketball court.

Barbara and Sam are now forty-five. In addition to Ann, they have a son, Paul, thirteen. Both sets of their parents are alive and enjoying good health. Barbara and Sam own their home and financially, as Barbara puts it, "We are able to make ends meet." Except for Sam's experience with drugs early in the marriage and a period of unemployment, the marriage has worked for both of them.

While at times "bumpy," there has been nothing of great consequence in Ann's experiences as a teenager. Ann received a car for her sixteenth birthday. She was disappointed that it wasn't new (it was a 1980 Chevy), especially since both Susie and Wendy had received new cars from their folks on their sixteenth birthdays. There were also family difficulties over a boy that Ann had dated. This problem was most serious to Sam, who did not like the fact that the fellow drove a motorcycle and wore an earring. Simply put and in Sam's words, "I just don't like and don't trust the kid. I can't imagine what Ann sees in him!" Barbara was far less concerned about the relationship than her husband and, for the most part, mediated the problem between the two.

Barbara's role shifted as Ann grew into a young woman. While still "Mom," to Ann she was also a friend and at least to some extent, a confidant.

Barbara and Sam had the usual aspirations and worries about Ann; a special concern was drugs. It was generally acknowledged that drugs were a major problem in high school. Drugs, premarital sexual relations, and moral and ethical matters generally were topics of conversation between Ann and her mother. Ann did try "pot," although she has as yet not admitted it to her mother. In discussing the matter with Susie and Wendy, she observed, "You know neither Mom nor Dad have ever asked me if I have tried drugs. I know where they are and I really appreciate the way they have handled this." Ann's own explanation is that she can get on her own high. In Ann's words, "Basketball is a high for me."

Ann is well on her way to successful resolution of the crisis of **identity versus role confusion**. She has been popular in high school and received honorable mention for all-state guard as a member of the school's basketball team. She is confident in her role as a woman and, while not as yet having a sexual relationship with a man, feels that she doesn't have any "hangups" about sex.

Ann feels as though she has been something of a disappointment to her family as a student. While considered a solid B student, she knows that her mother was "straight A." Compounding the problem is Ann's ambivalence about what kind of career she wants and even if she wants to go on to college. While her parents have been supportive of her dilemma, she knows it is troubling to them. In this regard, she is not likely to easily forget her dad's terse remark, "You know you can't make a living playing basketball." She does know that she needs to get away from home, to be on her own. Most of her friends are making plans for college, but she is not sure that she is ready for college. She likes work, but hasn't found anything that "turns me on." Ann does like to travel, but to travel, one needs money and she has none.

Early Adulthood

It is the addition of separate stages for adulthood that marks one of Erikson's most significant contributions to psychosocial theory. He was the first Freudian to do so. It was this attention to adulthood as well as to ego functions that helped to establish the beginnings of psychosocial theory and to distinguish it from psychoanalytic theory.

Through a satisfactory resolution of the identity versus role confusion crisis, the young adult is now prepared to assume her or his place in society. This typically includes the selection of a mate and a job. It is this selection process that contains the challenges for dealing with the crisis of this stage.

Psychosocial Crisis: Intimacy versus Isolation

The adolescent, particularly during the early years of the stage, is self-absorbed in the search for identity. The position held by Erikson is that a sense of personal identity is a prerequisite for intimacy. By intimacy, Erikson is conveying the capacity of giving oneself to a relationship in a full sense of mutuality. It takes a strong personal identity to do so; the danger is a risk of the loss of self in this process. It is the risk of identity in an intimate relationship with another that becomes a core issue in this crisis.

Erikson relays the story of an incident in which Freud was asked what the normal adult should be able to do well. Freud's answer was a simple one: "Lieben und arbeiten" (to love and to work).[27] This, for Erikson, gets at the heart of the crisis that must be dealt with at this age. He observed:

It pays to ponder on this simple formula; it gets deeper as you think about it. For when Freud said "love" he meant "genital" love, and genital "love"; when he said love *and* work, he meant a general work-productiveness which would not preoccupy the individual to the extent that he loses his right or capacity to be a genital and a loving being. Thus we may ponder, but we cannot improve on "the professor's" formula.[28]

We have, in earlier parts of this book, indicated that, from a social systems perspective, the individual is always a maintenance and a task output. At the end of each system cycle, there will be an effect on the system itself. In other words, the cycle of activities will affect the system roles being played by those who comprise it (maintenance output). An example would be the roles of those comprising the Jones family; those of spouse, parent, daughter, and son. Similarly, the system cycle will produce an effect on each of the family members in terms of their own sense of selfhood. In short, each cycle produces two effects, one in terms of the system role being played, for example, Ann the daughter of Sam and Barbara (maintenance output). The second effect is on the total sense of selfhood possessed by each system member, Ann herself (task output).

Now we return to the insights into human behavior offered by Freud and Erikson. To become truly human, one must be capable of loving. This means giving oneself to another, who gives himself or herself to you, and doing so with neither losing his or her own identity. There is still another part; to be able to give oneself to work and to do so without losing one's sense of personal identity, and still possessing the ability to maintain the loving relationship. The risks are considerable, but that is the nature of the psychosocial crisis of this age. How many times have you heard or perhaps said to yourself, "I am not ready to make this commitment."

We have, in developing the systems model, integrated some of the concepts borrowed from Abraham Maslow. Here Maslow's notion of a hierarchy of needs is instructive.[29] He contends that once survival and safety needs are satisfied, belongingness and love needs become dominant. While these needs will be addressed in a number of different ways, each will involve relationships with others. The most important and powerful of these will be through an intimate and continuous relationship with another person.[30]

Both Maslow and Erikson distinguish between the sexual expression of love in an intimate and loving relationship as contrasted to the sexual act in terms of a reproductive or recreational function. It is the former that is involved in resolving the crisis of **intimacy versus isolation**, while the latter is considered a negative way of dealing with it. Erikson posits the problem in this stage as the inability or unwillingness to enter and remain committed to an intimate relationship. The consequence is a growing sense of isolation and thus the diminishment of the potential of selfhood. While Erikson may be correct, an alternative position would hold that his conception is time and/or culture bound; there may be alternative ways of addressing intimacy needs.

Developmental Activities

While there are many sets of developmental activities to be mastered by the young adult, according to Erikson the two most important are in the domains of selecting a partner and a career. In some instances, one's career and one's partnership with another will be the same; for increasing numbers of young adults, both men and women, they are different. The two domains, in turn, involve new major social systems; the family is one, the second is work and usually the role of an employee. We will return to the Joneses in order to develop the concept of activities as they are applied at this age. Our focus this time will be on Barbara at the age of thirty-five. Recall that Barbara and Sam are the same age. Ann is now seven and Paul a vigorous three-year-old. In psychosocial development terms, we have a family of four with three different life stage crises providing for the dynamics of family life. The principal social system in which these crises will be played out is the same for each, the family. The particular suprasystems having importance will be determined by the specific family cycle or social act being modeled.

We pick Barbara up on the date of their fourteenth wedding anniversary. It is a Saturday night. The kids are in bed and she is alone. Sam lost his job at the Biosk Corporation when it was taken over by a large company. After a period of unemployment, Sam recently found a job as a salesman with another steel company. The job requires a great deal of travel, something neither he nor Barbara like. She is thinking back to their tenth anniversary and remembering that Sam had missed that date also, again because of his job. She is feeling a bit sorry for herself when the phone rings. It is Sam calling from Peoria. That afternoon, a dozen red roses had arrived from Sam, and at least for that moment, it had made her day. Sam had also been thinking about missing their tenth anniversary and said, "Look, I have to be in Chicago on Monday. Why don't you meet me there and we will take a couple of days and celebrate our anniversary." Sam was always surprising Barbara and she loved him for it. He continued, "I have already talked to Mom and she will take care of the kids. I know you have time coming at work. We haven't been to Chicago together since school—let's do it." After some protest that they couldn't afford it, Barbara agreed and added, "Sam, I really do miss you. Where will I meet you—the same place?"

After hanging up the telephone she smiled, and thought back over the past fourteen years. Barbara is now a supervisor at the mental health center. She enjoys her administrative duties but, at least for the moment, has given up her aspirations to become director of a mental health center. She reflects on the birth of Ann and Paul and how complicated life became, and on her eventual decision to be a wife and mother first, and to place her career second. She thought to herself "something had to be first, at least for now; but Sam owes me one. We have had a good marriage. He has been good for me and I know I have been good for him. I do miss him; I can hardly wait to get to Chicago."

Barbara then calls Sam's folks to confirm the babysitting arrangements. After completing the call, she decides to go on to bed; it has been a busy and complicated day. She stops and checks on Ann and Paul, who are asleep. "What a couple of little angels," and she smiles; "It has been a good life."

The point we are seeking to develop here is the successful resolution that Barbara has made to the psychosocial crisis of intimacy versus isolation. There have been good and bad times in the marriage and in her life. She has continued to develop personally and still enjoys an intimate and loving relationship with Sam. We highlight the latter point because for Erikson and many others in this tradition, a mature and satisfying sexual relationship is a primary measure of one's successfully solving this crisis.[31]

Middle Adulthood

For Erikson, the middle years of adulthood are of central importance, at least as important as any of the other life stages. It is here that the generations are linked in an evolutionary manner. The middle adult years become centered in preparing the next generation for their place in society. Here also is that period in which individuals who are successfully dealing with the crisis of this stage, are seeking ways of making our world a better place to live.

Psychosocial Crisis: Generativity versus Stagnation

The age span comprising this stage is thirty years, from age thirty-five to age sixty-five, the longest of all the stages. It covers for most people the most productive years of their lives. The notion of generativity identifies personal growth that evidences a sense of mutuality toward humankind while stagnation refers to a lack of such growth and a developing sense of personal impoverishment. The sense of generativity is typically experienced through work, civic activities, help of others, and through the raising and guidance of children. It is the latter area, the raising and guidance of children, that Erikson gives special attention. He does not, however, restrict the notion of generativity to the raising of one's own children, but to the general effort made by one generation to the betterment of life for the next.[32] The tie made by Erikson between the crisis of the previous stage, intimacy versus isolation, and this stage is important. Through the capacity of achieving a sense of intimacy, one is able to maintain a sense of personal identity yet become a part of a larger whole. The larger whole is the sense of mutuality with another person. The capacity contains the ability to recognize and be responsible to the needs of another and by the ability to give and receive. It is a state of maturity in which one is able to continue growing by giving.[33] By so doing, the foundation is set for the next stage of development.

Again Maslow and need theory is helpful. It is through the satisfaction of one's social belonging and love needs that a still higher level of need satisfaction becomes dominant, the need for a sense of self-esteem. Thoughtfully, Maslow observes, "Satisfaction of the self-esteem need leads to feelings of self-confidence, worth, strength, capability, and adequacy, of being useful and necessary in the world. But thwarting of these needs produces feelings of inferiority, of weakness, and of helplessness. These feelings in turn give rise to either basic discouragement or else compensatory or neurotic trends."[34] Recall from our earlier review of need theory that Maslow held that needs are of genetic origin.[35] While Maslow did not posit a life stage link with his hierarchy of needs, he did recognize a tie between satisfaction of higher need levels and age. Simply put, he concluded that a maturity associated with age and experience was necessary in order to progress to the highest levels in his hierarchy.[36] In describing the need for a sense of self-esteem, he broadens the concern to include a sense of independence and freedom.

Here we wish to digress a moment and expand on the notion of generativity by further noting Maslow's ideas. We do so because of the world-wide changes that are occurring as people of the world, particularly those enslaved, are seeking greater freedom and independence.

Maslow was not sure whether the need for a sense of independence and freedom was a part of the need for personal esteem, that is, whether it was a universal need at this level in the hierarchy. He contemplates the matter as follows:

> Whether or not this particular desire is universal we do not know. The crucial question, especially important today, is, Will men who are enslaved and domi- nated inevitably feel dissatisfied and rebellious? We may assume on the basis of commonly known clinical data that a man who has known true freedom (not paid for by giving up safety and security but rather built on the basis of adequate safety and security) will not willingly or easily allow his freedom to be taken away from him. But we do not know for sure that this is true for the person born into slavery.[37]

Maslow wrote these words some forty years ago. While we still do not know the answer to his question, his words today, as they did then, have a prophetic quality to them.

While in its fullest sense, generativity deals with a sense of mutuality to all and a sense of responsibility for another, it, too, has a negative aspect: stagnation. Erikson puts it:

> Generativity thus is an essential stage on the psychosexual as well as on the psy- chosocial schedule. Where such enrichment fails altogether, regression to an obses- sive need for pseudo-intimacy takes place, often with a pervading sense of stagnation and personal impoverishment. Individuals, then, often begin to indulge themselves as if they were their own—or one another's—one and only child; and where conditions favor it, early invalidism, physical or psychological, becomes the vehicle of self-concern.[38]

Developmental Activities

The notion of domains of life is useful in thinking about this stage of life and the activi- ties associated with dealing with the crisis of **generativity versus stagnation**. For most people, the domains would include the family and the rearing of children, and work and community service, among others.

To deal positively with the crisis of this stage, the individual must feel good about her- or himself, and her or his life situation. Some interesting research has been per- formed in this area. It is also the general area in which your authors have done much of their research. For example, some interesting work has been done on satisfaction and problems with marriage, parent-child relationships, and work. A finding of interest is that happiness in marriage is consistently related to overall happiness and life satisfac- tion.[39] Our own research supports this position, especially the relationship between mar- ital satisfaction and job satisfaction. A particularly interesting finding in our study of job satisfaction among child welfare workers was the strong relationship between marital satisfaction and job satisfaction. In fact, marital satisfaction was the single strongest pre- dictor of job satisfaction.[40] Simply put, those workers who were feeling good about their marriage were feeling good about the job and vice versa. Our research design did not permit us to determine the specific relationships involved, but we assume they are interactive. On the negative side, our research suggests there is a relationship between marital satisfaction and the susceptibility for job burnout.[41] Thus, while there are several domains of activities in which the crisis of generativity versus stagnation is played out, these domains appeared to be closely linked.

Barbara and Sam are now fifty-eight years old. Ann is divorced, is rearing two children alone and lives in Dallas. Like her mother, she too is a social worker. Paul has not married; he is an architect, loves his work, and lives in San Francisco. Barbara and Sam moved to Chicago over ten years ago primarily because of unusual job opportunities they both found. Also, Chicago was one of their favorite towns; it was where they went to school, fell in love, and married. Sam is district sales manager of a steel company; Barbara did realize her ambition and is now Executive Director of The North Care Mental Health Center. Both of Sam's parents have died as has Barbara's father. Her mother is still vigorous, but did move close to the Joneses, "Just to be close to family."

Barbara and Sam have just finished meeting with their attorney after having made some changes in their will. Trust funds have been set up for both their grandchildren to help with their educations. They have also set up a small trust for their church, and Barbara has set up one for the school of social work. Driving back home Barbara remarks, "We have had a good life; I just hope that Ann and Paul have as good a life. I so worry about Ann and the kids. She would be so much better if she would let us help more" (the interface). Sam laughs and reminds Barbara of the difficulties she had with his mother. He goes on to reassure her that Ann and the grandchildren seem quite happy. He adds, "You know that Ann is a lot like you. She is going to do it her way."

Later that evening and still "taking stock" of their lives, Sam asks, "Next to the kids and our life, what is the thing that you have done that has given you the most pleasure?" Barbara smiles, saying, "That's not hard. I really have enjoyed my job and the people at the center. We are like a big family and, believe me, are really making life better for our clients. I am especially proud of our new day-care program for the children of staff and our clients. I remember how important the Children's Center was for me after we had Ann. Did I tell you that they have asked me to chair a state task force to see if we can get state funding for this service? One of my ambitions is to see it made possible for every mental health center to develop a day-care program for children for both staff and clients. I don't think there is anything I have done that has been more appreciated by staff than starting this program. Can you imagine the research opportunities that it could open up?"

Barbara and Sam continue to grow, and as they do, their attention is starting to shift and to broaden. While concerned about their own children and grandchildren, they are increasingly thinking about other children and other people generally; they are wondering how their own lives can be used to make the world just a little better. Also, by establishing trusts for their grandchildren, their church, and Barbara's school, they are insuring some continuity of their contributions after they are gone.

Late Adulthood

Late adulthood completes the life cycle according to Erikson. It starts at roughly the time the person enters retirement (of whatever sort) and ends with death. At the time Erikson wrote, there was a very modest amount of scientific literature dealing with old age. To some extent, this meagerness of literature may reflect a society that placed relatively little value on its elderly. Old people, in a manner of speaking, had made their contribution and had been "put out to pasture." There would be a physical decline and the inevitable death; "What more is there to say?"

Erikson did not share such a conception of later adulthood. For him, it was an important time of life. It was a time for reflection and a time for putting it all together as well as a time for a continuing contribution.[42] Other psychosocial theorists, noting the increasing length of life and related changes, have added one or more additional stages to the life span.[43]

Psychosocial Crisis: Ego Integrity versus Despair

Erikson connects the first life stage (trust) with the last (integrity) by offering a dictionary definition of trust—"the assured reliance on another's integrity."[44] The cycle is thus completed. The healthy child should not fear life if her or his elders have achieved a sufficient sense of personal integrity so as not to fear death.[45]

In recent years, there has been a significant growth in the scientific literature on the sociology and the psychology of aging. Similarly, there is a growing interest in schools of social work and in other professional schools on death and dying. Many schools, in fact, teach courses on the subject of dying; we do in our own. Our interest here is only to call your attention to the growing importance of this final life stage in terms of knowledge building, research, and as a field of practice. As reported earlier (Table 1.1), just over three percent of our NASW respondents practice in the field of aging. We believe this field will undergo rapid professionalization in the years ahead and become a major growth area for professional social work. Why? Among other reasons, our society is rapidly aging and "seniors" are becoming a powerful political force. More importantly, it is a critical life stage; people are living longer, are in better health longer, and they are becoming economically more secure. There are enormous opportunities for improving the quality of life for this segment of our population so they, in turn, can contribute further to society. In short, the issue is how to help people in this stage of their life achieve a sense of ego integrity.

Integrity is not easily achieved. It requires a favorable ratio of successes in dealing with each of life's stages. Poetically, Erikson puts it in the following way: "Only in him who in some way has taken care of things and people and has adapted himself to the triumphs and disappointments adherent to being, the originator of others or the generator of products and ideas—only in him may gradually ripen the fruit of these seven stages."[46] As the person grows older, she or he develops a sense of her or his own mortality. For most people, this meaning starts evolving during middle adulthood and adds pressure or urgency to successfully deal with the crisis of generativity versus stagnation. At this, the eighth stage, there is the realization that time is running out. There is not time to start over, no "trying to get it right the next time." It is this realization, that there is no more time to get things right, that accounts for the despair and the fear of death in many.

Conversely, for those who have been fortunate enough to have "ripened the fruit" of the previous seven stages, an opportunity is offered for a final quest—true wisdom and self-actualization.

Developmental Activities

With retirement, with the death of one's parents, and some colleagues and friends, there is a reduction in the systems through which one plays out this final psychosocial crisis. There is another handicap: the role definition held by society of being "old." For it is through the societal roles that a person is given, that the crisis is confronted. As indicated, in ours, and many other western and industrialized societies, the role of being an "old person" has essentially been a negative one. This is now changing and part of the credit for this goes to people like Erikson and others who see the potential for a contribution to be made.

For many people, retirement offers a whole new set of opportunities to pursue. Where there had been children, they are now grown, as are the grandchildren. This is the time of great-grandchildren and somewhat less of responsibility than there was in being a grandparent. Increasing numbers of retired people can travel and volunteer their time. In short, this stage provides a time of choice, a time of greater control over one's life. This is also the time that one contemplates and evaluates the past and prepares for death. It is in this latter case that society is recognizing the importance of choice over how one dies. Death is the final experience. It needs to be handled in a dignified, caring, and sensitive way. The rapid growth of hospice programs in recent years is an expression of the growing importance of death as a life event, as a completion of the life cycle over which the terminally ill person exercises control.

We now visit the Joneses for a final time. Barbara is now eighty-four and, while still living independently, has been informed that she has terminal cancer. Sam died three years earlier from a heart attack. Ann did remarry and had a third child whom she nicknamed Wendy, after her own lifelong friend. Ann returned to Midtown and, following in her mother's footsteps, became and is currently director of the Midtown Mental Health Center.

After retiring, Barbara became an active volunteer. In addition to her church, she served on the advisory body to the school of social work, serving eight years as chair. She also was very active in the mental health movement, both at the state and national levels. For two years, she served as secretary for the American Alliance for the Mentally Ill. Throughout her professional life, Barbara had two special areas of interest, children's programs and programs for the seriously mentally ill.

Upon learning of her terminal cancer, Barbara started making final preparations for her own death. She sold the house in which she and Sam had spent so many happy years, and moved back to Midtown to be close to Ann. While Paul never married, he was always attentive to both his parents. He remains in San Francisco with a thriving practice as an architect. Since learning of his mother's illness, he visits her monthly.

Barbara accepted Sam's death. He had two previous heart attacks and so the final one came as no surprise. While death is always hard to accept, especially when it comes to one so dear, Sam's own acceptance of his coming death helped. At times they would reminisce of their times together, both good and bad. He would still tell her, "You are still one hell of a woman and I love you!" Sam continued to surprise Barbara with red roses. She still has pressed in her Bible the final rose Sam gave her. Barbara is tired, at peace, and she misses Sam.

Barbara and Sam, as the Joneses, met and satisfactorily resolved each of their life crises on the positive side. As they contemplated their eventual deaths, Sam used to kid Barbara, "At least in a small way, Barbara, the world is a little better place for our having been here."

SUMMARY

In this chapter, we have provided an outline of psychosocial theory from a social systems perspective. Building primarily on the work of Erikson, eight life stages have been reviewed. Each stage is treated in outcome terms. The psychosocial crisis of each stage results in a change and, it is hoped, a further positive development of one's sense of selfhood. The crisis is primarily played out in a series of developmental activities associated with the societal role that is assigned to each of these life stages. It is the role that provides the structure through which the developmental activities take place. The role is always associated with other roles within the various social systems' activities during the stage. For most people, the family is the dominant system. Each individual brings her or his own genetic and experiential background into the stage. This is played out against and with cultural expectations and within a series of different social systems, each with its own suprasystem. The result, in every instance, is a unique human personality.

GLOSSARY

Autonomy   The ability to think and act independently.

Autonomy vs. shame and doubt   The psychosocial crises associated with the post infancy life stage. Resolution leads to either a sense of self-control and freedom or an overwhelming sense of self-doubt.

Basic trust vs. basic mistrust   The psychosocial crisis associated with the life stage of infancy. The infant, through the relationship with the primary care giver, develops a fundamental sense of confidence in others, or a sense of unpredictability, fear, and basic mistrust which affects one's perception of self.

Developmental activities   The means employed by a system to deal with the psychosocial crisis at each life stage.

Ego integrity vs. despair   The psychosocial crisis associated with late adulthood, the completion of the life cycle. Ego integrity conveys a final sense of wholeness or completeness of self. Death holds no fear. Despair, the counterpart, represents the final recognition that death is near but the sense of personal wholeness has not and will not be achieved. Death is feared and there is the final despair.

Generativity vs. stagnation   The psychosocial crises associated with the middle adulthood life stage. Generativity, the positive resolution, deals with a sense of mutuality to all, of continuing to grow through giving. Stagnation, the negative pole, is a lack of growth, a sense of personal impoverishment.

Identity vs. role confusion   During the life stage of adolescence, the psychosocial crisis involves the establishment of a personal sense of self on the positive end. An inability to establish any unified sense of self or to integrate various roles is the result of a negative resolution.

Industry vs. inferiority   The psychosocial crisis of the school age life stage is resolved through a sense of pride and accomplishment in one's capabilities (positive) or through a negative self-evaluation and sense of incompetence.

Initiative vs. guilt   The pre school stage psychosocial crisis in which initiative is an active investigation of the environment and guilt can be viewed as an adverse consequence of initiative.

Intimacy vs. isolation   The psychosocial crisis of early adulthood. A positive resolution results in the ability to give of oneself to a relationship in a full sense of mutuality without fearing the loss of oneself in the process. A negative resolution is the diminishment of the potential of selfhood as one remains psychologically distant from others.

Life stage   A developmental level which corresponds to a period of life. In psychosocial theory, each life stage is associated with a psychosocial crisis which must be resolved.

Polarity   The resolution of the psychosocial crisis of each stage will result in an individual possessing personality (self) features falling somewhere between the positive and negative poles.

Psychosocial crisis   The designation of the natural state of tension associated with the different sets of expectations and coping capacities associated with each life stage.

Selfhood   A process which continues throughout life and is impacted by the resolution of the psychosocial crisis of each life stage.

NOTES

1. This is an ongoing research effort involving the authors and Dr. Srinika Jayaratne. For information dealing with methodology and implications for social work see, for example, Srinika Jayaratne, et al., "A Comparison of Job Satisfaction, Burnout and Turnover Among Workers in Child Welfare, Community Mental Health, Family Service and Health Settings," *Social Work* 29, no. 5 (September–October 1984): 448–453; and "Private and Agency Practitioners: Some Data and Observations," *Social Service Review* 62 (June 1988): 324–336. The authors are repeating the survey every four years. The most recent survey was conducted in 1989 and the next one is scheduled for 1993.

2. *The Social Work Dictionary* (Silver Spring, Md.: National Association of Social Workers, 1988), 130.

3. See particularly, Erik Erikson, *Childhood and Society*, 2nd ed. (New York: W.W. Norton & Co., 1963). This is Erikson's most important work and contains the most comprehensive presentation of his theory.

4. Ibid., 15–18.

5. Ibid., 247–274. Erikson labels the chapter dealing with the life stages as the "Eight Stages of Man." For consistency purposes, it is useful to treat the eight psychosocial crises identified by Erikson as constituting his designation of the eight stages that comprise psychosocial theory. In other words, the psychosocial crisis of the stage is also the name given to the stage itself., 274.

6. Ibid. The position we are adopting here is consistent, in our opinion, with the one advanced by Erikson. He identified a series of ego qualities associated with a favorable outcome for each of the life stages. For example, a person favorably resolving the psychosocial crisis of initiative versus guilt would exhibit the ego quality of purposiveness.

7. See Chapter 9 for a review of the stages employed by Freud in psychoanalytic theory.

8. Ibid., 247. For a further development of this point also see Erik Erikson, "Identity and the Life Cycle," *Psychological Issues* 1, no. 1 (1954): 64.

9. For a review of this research and the model used, see particularly Srinika Jayaratne and Wayne Chess, "Job Stress, Job Deficit, Emotional Support and Competence: Their Relationship to Burnout," *The Journal of Applied Social Sciences* 10, no. 2 (Spring/Summer, 1986): 135–155; and Srinika Jayaratne, David Himle, and Wayne A. Chess, "Dealing with Work Stress and Strain: Is the Perception of Support More Important Than Its Use?" *The Journal of Applied Behavioral Science* 24, no. 22 (1988): 191–202.

10. Erikson, *Childhood and Society*, 11–19.

11. Robert J. Havighurst, *Developmental Tasks and Education*, 3rd ed. (New York: David McKay, 1972), 2.

12. Don E. Hamachek, "Evaluating Self-Concept and Ego Development Within Erikson's Psychosocial Framework: A Formulation," *Journal of Counseling and Development* 66 (April 1988): 354–360.

13. Ibid., 366.

14. There is an extensive and growing literature in this area. For example, see S.K. Clarren and D.W. Smith, "The Fetal Alcohol Syndrome," *New England Journal of Medicine* 298 (1978): 1063–1067.

15. Erikson, *Childhood and Society*, 72–80.

16. Erik Erikson, "Reflections on Dr. Borg's Life Cycle," *Daedalus* 105: 23.

17. Erikson, *Childhood and Society*, 252–253.

18. For a useful introduction to the charting of the maturational process, see A. Gesell, *The Embryology of Behavior* (New York: Harper and Row, 1945).

19. Erikson, *Childhood and Society*, 255.

20. Ibid., 259.

21. Ibid., 261.

22. See particularly Charles Horton Cooley, *The Two Major Works of Charles H. Cooley— Social Organization and Human Nature and the Social Order* (Glencoe, Ill.: The Free Press, 1956).

23. Ibid., 184.

24. Erikson, *Childhood and Society*, 262.

25. Barbara M. Newman and Philip R. Newman, *Development Through Life: A Psychosocial Approach*, 4th ed. (Chicago: The Dorsey Press, 1987), 319–413.

26. Ibid., 352–359.

27. Erikson, *Childhood and Society*, 265.

28. Ibid.

29. Abraham Maslow, *Motivation and Personality*, 2nd ed. (New York: Harper and Row, 1970), 35–95.

30. Ibid.

31. Erikson, *Childhood and Society*, 265.

32. Ibid., 266–268.

33. Ibid.

34. Maslow, *Motivation and Personality*, 45.

35. Ibid., 77–95.

36. Ibid., 150.

37. Ibid., 45.

38. Erikson, *Childhood and Society*, 267.

39. See, for example, Gerald Burin, Joseph Veroff, and Sheila Feld, *Americans View Their Mental Health* (New York: Basic Books, 1960); and J. Veroff, E. Douvan, and R. Hulka, *The Inner American: A Self-Portrait From 1957 to 1976* (New York: Basic Books, 1981).

40. Wayne A. Chess and Julia M. Norlin, *Child Abuse and Neglect in Oklahoma: A Study of*

the *Department of Human Services Programs Aimed at Identifying, Controlling and Preventing Child Abuse and Neglect* (Norman, Okla.: The University of Oklahoma, 1981), III, 70–79.

    41. Ibid.

    42. Erikson, *Childhood and Society*, 268–269.

    43. For an interesting discussion and for someone who has written extensively in the area see Bernice Neugarten, ed., *Age or Need: Public Policies For Older People* (Beverly Hills, Calif.: Sage, 1982).

    44. Erikson, *Childhood and Society*, 269.

    45. Ibid.

    46. Ibid., 268.

PART IV

THE FORMAL ORGANIZATION

The Social Systems Model

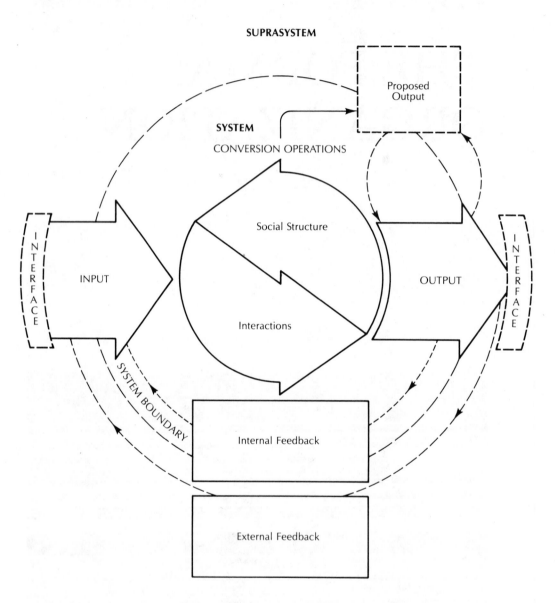

Part IV addresses the importance of formal organizations to the lives of all people and to the practice of social work and the other helping professions. Most people's entry into life is through a formal organization (a hospital), as is their exit (through a funeral home) and every day in between. Every day we are enmeshed in formal organizations and our lives are affected by them, many times for the better, sometimes for the worse.

Yet for all their importance, comparatively little is known about formal organizations and the effects they have on the people who comprise them or the societies they serve. Organization—servant or master? Only recently have there been attempts at the systematic study of organizations and the professional practice of administration.

Sometimes overlooked is the fact that social workers and other helping professionals are typically employed by a formal organization, and their practice is vitally affected by the policies of their agencies. Also of great consequence is the fact that social work administration is a major practice method.

In Part IV we track the main lines of theory development and identify the implications of this content to the shaping of the social systems model. With the distinctive features of the model noted, the model is then applied to a formal organization.

Chapter 11 introduces you to what we mean by a formal organization. Definitions are provided, as well as a review of some of the key concepts discussed earlier, namely Gemeinschaft and Gesellschaft. Also introduced in this chapter is the general notion of authority, an approach to conceptualizing social power.

With this introduction, the dominant lines of theory development applicable to the formal organization are identified. The chapter concludes with a summary of how organizational and administrative theory development has helped us shape the social systems model so that it can be applied to the formal organization.

In Chapter 12, the social systems model is applied to the formal organization. As in the previous applications, the eight concepts comprising the model are discussed. Here our attention is on the features that distinguish this form of social organization from others. Simply put, the characteristic features of this type of social organization relate to its formal and legal status.

Chapter 13 concludes Part IV and is devoted to a discussion of system dynamics. These dynamics take on their special features from the formal and legal character of the organization itself.

Chapter 11

The Formal Organization: An Introduction

OUTLINE

Background

The purpose of this chapter is to introduce the formal social organization. In developing the background for this chapter, it is helpful to remember the distinction between so-called primary and secondary forms of social organization. The term *primary group* had its origins with Cooley[1] and pertains to relationships among group members that are personal in nature, carried on for their own sake, and usually face-to-face. Examples include the family and small friendship groups. Secondary groups, in contrast, tend to be formally constituted, delimited in their functions, and with the capacity of much of the work being performed without face-to-face contact among group members. The type of social organization described as a formal organization in this chapter serves as a prototype of a secondary group, and would include General Motors or a family service agency.

Before proceeding further, it is important to note that we are treating the formal organization as a distinctive social entity apart from the individuals who may comprise it at any given time. The premise that a formal organization can be treated as a social entity is fundamental to the application of the social systems model to be developed later. The separation between the organization and the particular individuals who comprise it is also one of the most fundamental distinctions between a primary group and a formal organization. For example, if the members of a friendship group should renounce their association with each other, from a social systems perspective the group would cease to exist. In contrast, if all of the staff of a local family service agency should simultaneously quit, the agency as a formal organization would not cease to exist as a legally constituted social entity. If such an event did occur, the board of directors could simply hire a new executive and have that person hire a new staff. While services would be temporarily disrupted, the act of all the staff leaving would not, in itself, affect the existence of the organization. More about this feature later.

Gemeinschaft and Gesellschaft

Gemeinschaft and Gesellschaft are two other concepts useful in distinguishing the formal organization from other forms of human association. Recall that it was Ferdinand Tönnies who developed these concepts to contrast two basic types of social relationships.[2] While not categorized as an organizational theorist, Tönnies's work provides a useful starting place to develop our definition of a formal social organization, and for tracking development of organizational and administrative theory. His contrast of the Gesellschaft character of relationships within formal organizations with the Gemeinschaft nature of relationships among members of natural/primary groups is particularly useful. In the words of Tönnies,

> It [the formal organization] is never anything natural, neither can it be understood as a mere psychical phenomenon. It is completely and essentially a social phenomenon and must be considered as composed of several individuals. Capacity for unified volition and action, a capacity which is demonstrated most clearly as competency to pass resolutions, characterizes it. Just as the thinking individual is capable of making decisions, so is a group of several individuals when they continuously agree or agree to the extent that there prevails and is recognized as a definite will as the will of all or sufficient consensus to be the will of the social organization or corporate body [sic]. Thus, the volition of such a group can be represented by the will of a natural person behind whom the will of the whole social organization or corporate body stands.[3]

Tönnies's position with respect to formal organizations is similar to the one we have adopted. The formal organization can be treated as a social entity and is essentially independent of those individuals that may comprise it at any one time. In this same sense, and like an individual, the social organization can and does enter into relationships with other social organizations and with individuals, for example, employment contracts with employees and contracts with clients. These relationships will possess both Gemeinschaft and Gesellschaft features.

In the quote by Tönnies, he says that a formal organization ". . . is never anything natural." In this sense the social organization is contrived, created as a means to achieve some specified end. It follows that the relationships these organizations enter into are Gesellschaftlike. These features are highlighted by the rationalist position in organizational theory, which will be addressed shortly. The point is that Gemeinschaft and Gesellschaft should be viewed as constituting dimensions of social relationships generally. These two concepts can be treated as representing the extreme points on a continuum; and, just as both features are found in personally based relationships, so also are they found in relationships entered into by formal organizations. So while the Gesellschaftlike relationship may appear to dominate in formal organizations, it is the Gemeinschaft dimension to these relationships that helps overcome the unnatural (contrived) qualities of such organizations. It is these personally based (natural) relationships that help bind people together so that they are able to work collaboratively in order to achieve the goals of the formal organization. Later we will characterize these personally based feelings as constituting an important part of the core of the maintenance features of a formal organization.

Definition

We noted a distinction between primary and secondary groups. Unfortunately, no consensus exists on a more detailed typology of organizations generally, or of formal organizations in particular.[4] This lack of a commonly agreed-upon classification system characterizes the general state of development of organizational theory. Therefore, we begin by sharing our definition of a formal organization: a form of social organization deliberately and formally created to achieve relatively specific and delimited goals. Further, establishment of a formal organization entails the following activities. First, a specific and deliberate action is taken to create the organization as a recognized social and legal entity. Usually the organization is created under state law as a public entity or through the filing of legal papers that register the organization under relevant laws as a nonpublic or private organization or corporation. Second, a written statement sets forth the general purposes and sphere of activity of the organization. In a publicly created organization the statement of purpose will appear (either implicitly or explicitly) in the law, while in a nonpublic agency it will usually be found in its constitution and bylaws and/or in its articles of incorporation. Third, a governance structure is created. In this instance, the notion of formalization deals with the relationships among the organization's members in terms of how authority is exercised and how work is conducted. The governance structure will be specified in the law that creates the public organization; in the case of a nonpublic agency, it will be delineated in its legal charter.

In short, formal organizations represent one of the major ways in which people formally band together in order to perform functions or to solve problems that may not be accomplished or solved through individual efforts (or at least not as efficiently or effectively). Within the definition given, these organizations take many forms and sizes, ranging from the United Nations to county government, from General Motors to a local used-car dealership, and from the federal Department of Health and Human Services to a local child guidance center. It is important to recognize the number of formal organizations that exist, their varied purposes, and the effects they have on all our lives. In a complex industrialized society such as ours, people are immersed in webs of such organizations that vitally affect all aspects of life.

Understanding the importance that formal organizations have in people's daily lives, the question still arises as to why social workers and other human service professionals should study them in any direct way. The answer occurs at two levels. First, most social workers conduct their work within a formally constituted organization, for example, a mental health center, hospital, or welfare department. As employees, they are members of a formal organization. This organization shapes how their professional practice is conducted and whom they will serve, for example, by applying program eligibility standards. Not only does the organization affect the client-worker relationship, it has direct effects on the worker. In this sense, the worker is immersed in a work environment that has multiple features, some positive, for example, a feeling of self-fulfillment, and some negative, such as developing symptoms of burnout.[5] Thus the worker needs to understand how organizations behave in order to participate organizationally in ways that advance both direct practice with clients and personal and professional development of staff.

Second, the organization is a human creation—a potentially powerful tool that can be differentially used for the relief of social problems. In this instance, the social worker is still in a helping role but working as an administrator and/or manager rather than as a therapist. The social worker needs to understand organizations and how they are managed in order to practice competently as an administrator. Human service agencies, for instance, a community mental health center, are the chief means available to deal with large-scale social problems, such as mental illness, or to assist people in realizing their potential by promoting mental health. The practice of social work administration offers unusual opportunities for professional practice.

In Chapter 1 (Table 1.2), data were presented indicating that administration is a major practice method among professional social workers who are members of NASW.[6] Given the rapid growth occurring in the area of practice, there is an added urgency that additional attention be given to knowledge building in support of social work administration. For some this rapid expansion of social work into organization and interorganizational forms of practice is of concern. Here the thought is that the profession is moving away from its so-called traditional concern with the individual and with direct forms of practice. We do not share this position nor do we consider it an accurate perception of the profession's historical roots. Social work has from its beginnings sought human betterment through both direct and indirect forms of practice, that is, directly with clients and indirectly on behalf of clients through administrative and community forms of practice. For us, the interest in administration and community practice is a healthy development, one that is restoring a better balance to the profession's practice base.

Organizational Theory and Practice

The scientific study of formal organizations is a rather recent development. Commenting on this development, Scott observed, "It is safe to conclude that until the late 1940s, organizations did not exist as a distinct field of sociological inquiry."[7] Weber's works were translated into English during this period and probably were the single most important influence in the development of organizational theory as a distinct field of study.[8] This is not to say that there were not influential writings in this field prior to the 1940s, but these writings will be treated here as precursors to the development of modern organizational theory. (Here we are drawing a distinction between the development of organizational and administrative theory.)

Given the rather recent interest in the study of formal organizations, it is not surprising that there is no widely accepted agreement on a theory of organization. Similarly, there is no agreement on a theory in the applied area of administration. There is, however, intense activity in both the basic and applied areas. In this section we will briefly review the main lines of theory development, but emphasis will be given to the developmental trends that have contributed to a social systems perspective. Our contention is that many of the earlier contributions to organizational theory can be viewed as part of a dialectic process in which the social systems perspective can be treated as the synthesis.

The German sociologist Max Weber is generally recognized as the father of modern organizational sociology.[9] His writings also have formed important foundations to administrative theory (management of organizations). Weber's inquiries focused on the processes of formalization and legitimization. Given our attention to formal organization in this chapter, the work of Weber in the area of the formalization and legitimization of organizations is particularly important and will be reviewed at some length in the following paragraphs.

Authority

Weber is perhaps best known for his model of bureaucracy. Before describing this model, it would be helpful to review his conception of the three forms of authority, since his notion of legal authority and the legitimacy attendant to this form of authority serve as a cornerstone to his model of a bureaucracy. **Authority** as defined by Weber is "the probability that a specific command will be obeyed."[10] The notion of authority is developed in the context of **legitimacy**, which means an acceptance on the part of those being commanded that the person commanding possesses that right.

It might be useful to stop for a moment and recognize that the term command as used by Weber has a troublesome and negative connotation when employed to describe a feature in social relationships. From our perspective, Weber identifies and develops a very useful classification of ways in which human volition is exercised. His classification of types of authority also formed an important source for the study of social power—the ability of one person to influence the actions of another. For the immediate purposes of this chapter, we are interested in examining the exercise of authority (social power) in formal organizations.

Weber identified three pure types of authority: legal, traditional, and charismatic. These should be treated as distinct analytical models for examining authority as it pertains to organizational behavior. It should also be noted that each type of authority tends to be associated with different types of social structures.

Legal authority, according to Weber, is most clearly evident in the behaviors of bureaucracies. (In this context, we are treating the notion of bureaucracy as a type of formal organization. Weber's concept of a bureaucracy will be developed later in this chapter.) One characteristic of a bureaucracy is that the exercise of power is within the framework of established laws, rules, and other such objective sources of governance.

Earlier it was noted that formal organizations have a legal existence that establishes (sanctions) both their purpose and arrangements for governance. It is assumed that those who voluntarily accept membership in formal organizations are contractually bound by its formal arrangements for governance. The exercise of authority flows from these governance arrangements and the basis of legitimacy is established by contract (written or understood).

In order to understand the concept of legal authority and its relationship to legitimacy, it is important to grasp some of the more subtle features of Weber's reasoning. For example, while his writings focused on the importance of the assignment of authority to the office (position) as opposed to the individual, the assumption is that each office is occupied by a qualified person. There is the further assumption that the person occupying a given office was appointed through known and objective procedures and was selected because of being the most qualified person available for the position.

Legitimacy, as noted earlier, pertains to the acceptance of orders, usually in the form of commands or requests, by those occupying a subordinate office to the one issuing the order. The exercise of legal authority rests on the right of the person occupying the office to give a particular order. The acceptance of the order by those affected legitimizes the authority—the person accepts the order because he or she believes the person issuing it has the right to do so and that he or she has the corresponding responsibility to accept and comply. There is a subtlety involved that is important in terms of the administrative implications involved. While Weber focused on the legal source for this exercise of authority, there is another dimension to the acceptance of authority—the assumed qualifications or expertise of the person exercising the authority of their office. In essence, Weber combined the notions of the authority of position and the authority derived from expertise into his conception of legal authority.

An example of these two dimensions of authority is a decision by a casework supervisor to transfer a case from one worker to another (assuming the administrative authority and a professional judgment based on good cause). In the first instance, the worker might not necessarily agree with the decision, but would recognize the right of the supervisor to make it. By accepting the transfer decision based on the rights inherent in the position, the worker legitimizes the exercise of authority. In the second instance, if the worker believes the supervisor is incompetent or not qualified for the position (for example, the supervisor does not possess a professional degree or was appointed through an assumed act of favoritism by the agency director), the exercise of authority might not be legitimized by the worker involved. In such an instance the worker might contest the decision, not because the legal right to make the decision is not vested in the supervisor's office, but rather because the supervisor did not secure the position through established procedures or is not qualified to make the kind of decisions vested in that office. Similarly, the worker might accept the transfer only because to do otherwise would run the risk of the act being defined as insubordination and possibly result in loss of the job. In such a situation, the supervisor's authority would not be legitimized. In any event, the conditions noted in the example are those that seriously affect the exercise of legal authority in a formal organization.

The second form of authority identified by Weber is derived from a belief of sacredness in the social order, with compliance to expectations of behavior being rooted in piety. He labels it **traditional authority**. Patriarchal authority represents its purest expression. Historically, the rule of estates by feudal lords and monarchs clearly represents this form of authority, a divinely given right. In its purest form, power is lodged in one person, with all others being dependent on that person in all matters. The constraints on the exercise of authority are rooted only in the sacredness of tradition. It should be noted that a person can occupy an organizational position in which legal authority is vested and still exert power based on traditional authority as well. The authority of the Pope is an example; a portion of his power can be understood in terms of the position held, but the vastness of the power is most clearly understood in terms of traditional authority.

In a problem mode, the parent who physically abuses a child may feel justified in this behavior in terms of traditional authority. Here children are viewed as essentially without legal rights, and what takes place between the parent and child is a private family matter—"This is the way I was raised and this is the way I am going to raise my kid." Another example in a problem mode would include authority relationships in family-owned businesses. Here some expressions in the exercise of authority can be best explained by traditional authority vested in property rights, not in legally based prerogatives—"It's my money so do it my way or get out." In such situations, personal loyalty, based on tradition (or fear), not law, may be the controlling variable in the exercise of and acceptance of authority.

Charismatic authority is the third and final pure form of authority identified by Weber. Here authority is vested in a particular person because of the personal qualities possessed by that person, not because of the office or tradition. The war hero or human-rights leader, the prophet, or the demagogue is each an example of a charismatic leader— Pericles, Joan of Arc, Napoleon, Gandhi, Martin Luther King, and others. The charismatic leader can be very powerful, as history has shown. The tie between leader and followers is a personal one; the office held by such a leader is incidental; the tie is to the person, "I would follow him (or her) to the ends of the earth."

Weber made a significant contribution to the study of social organization with his identification of the sources of authority. His work has also served as a foundation for investigations into the more general area of social power and particularly the notion of leadership.[11] Formal organizations as we have defined them will always have some specified means for governance, or in Weber's terms, an authority structure. What he provides are three distinct models for examining this structure and its legitimizing features. Legal authority, according to Weber, is the most stable. Here the governing body is either elected or appointed, and the rule-making procedures are formalized; similarly, there are established procedures for the change or modification of rules. The notion of legitimacy is rooted in acceptance by those affected by the rules and the procedures through which the rules were made and exercised.

In legal authority, the rules are assigned to an office for enactment, not to a person. In contrast, traditional authority and charismatic authority are vested in an individual and in this sense can be less stable than legal authority. In the case of legal authority, both the individual exercising the authority and the person being affected are bounded by the same rule. Not so in the same sense with either traditional or charismatic authority; in each of the two instances, the person exercising the authority has much greater leeway for action and less personal accountability. Similarly, the loss of confidence in the legitimacy of the person is far more serious in traditional and charismatic authority than it is in legal authority. In the latter instance, the person can be removed from the office with relatively little effect on the office (as in the resignation of Richard Nixon from the presidency); not so with traditional and charismatic leaders (for example, television evangelists Jim and Tammy Bakker).

Several matters should be kept in mind when viewing Weber's contribution to the study of authority. Perhaps most important is that it is a presentation of pure types of authority. In any application, one form is likely to dominate, but this does not suggest that features of the other two might not be in evidence. For example, the willingness of a caseworker in a large public agency to follow suggestions of her supervisor in the handling of a case may appear to be a clear expression of legal authority. However, in a given instance, this may represent only a part of the authority relationship between the two. The supervisor may be viewed as a great person in her own right as well as a skilled supervisor, and thus her authority (her ability to influence) over the worker is extended through the personally based charismatic qualities attributed to her by the worker. Similarly, the age and other characteristics of the association between the two might have qualities suggestive of a mother-daughter relationship. In such an instance, there might be a feature of traditional authority that would help explain the caseworker's reactions to suggestions made by her supervisor.

The Weberian Bureaucracy—The Rationalist Perspective

With Weber's conception of authority as background, the following provides an overview of key features of the Weberian model of bureaucracy.[12] These features have served as foundations for the study of modern organizations and the subsequent development of organizational theory. Given the historical setting of his study, Germany in the year 1900, and its principal subject, the Prussian bureaucracy, it is not surprising that the model underscores the rational features of behavior to the point of suggesting "machine-like" qualities.

Because of the so-called rational foundations of Weber's model of a bureaucracy, its key features here are identified and explicated as constituting the core of the rationalist perspective in organizational theory.[13] Weber's conception of a bureaucracy also identifies characteristics that, in our judgment, are found in some form in every formal organization. For this reason, we use this opportunity to identify and provide examples of how these characteristics are seen in human service types of organizations.

A Hierarchial Authority Structure

In his model of bureaucracy, Weber further develops and operationalizes his notion of legal authority. Legal authority becomes the chief means through which control is exercised over the organization's component parts and through which its goals are pursued. According to Weber, legal authority is vested in a single position, for example, the agency's executive director. From that position, authority is delegated downward, giving the organization its typical hierarchial and pyramidlike form. Utilizing Weber's concepts, structurally the bureaucracy can be viewed as organized around two axes—one vertical, the other horizontal. The vertical axis is the hierarchial authority structure; the horizontal axis represents a division of labor. Offices along the vertical axis are organized by levels of graded, legally based authority, with people located in higher offices supervising the work of those located in lower offices. This gradient of authority is typically referred to as the **chain of command**. Within this chain of command, the number of positions (persons) being supervised by a given supervisor is generally referred to as the span of control.

In the hierarchial authority structure, there is a supervisor for every office (position). The top office in the pyramid, the agency director, typically reports to an elected or appointed board of directors or in some cases to an individual who is either elected or appointed, for example, a state director of public welfare may be responsible to the governor, who is elected by the people of the state. The central point here is the identification of a vertical chain of legally based authority that reaches from the top of the structure to its bottom and thereby affects every person employed in the agency.

In administrative theory, it is the hierarchially organized authority structure that provides the official sanction for the administrative process known as *control*. In systems language this is part of the feedback loop that provides information about progress being made in meeting organizational purposes. The control process consists of those actions taken to assure that organizational behaviors conform to organizational expectations and purposes. From a role theory perspective, the authority structure becomes a means of seeing that role enactment conforms (within limits) to the normative expectations established by agency policy, for instance, that all case records are kept up to date.

Division of Labor

The notion of **division of labor** as used by Weber has its clearest origins in the economic theory of Adam Smith and pertains to breaking down a given task or function into its component parts and then assigning persons to perform one or more of these subtasks as opposed to the total task. In Smith's celebrated analysis of pin making, he calculated that ten persons each performing a specialized part in the manufacturing of pins could produce 48,000 pins per day.[14] For example, one person would draw the wire, another would straighten the wire, another would cut it to the prescribed length, another would shape the head, another would solder the head to the shaft, and so on. If, on the other hand, each person had to perform all of these tasks, that person, according to Smith's analysis, would be lucky to produce twenty pins per day. A more familiar example of the notion of division of labor would be in building a house. Plans need to be made (architect), excavation must be performed (heavy machine operators), foundations laid (masons), utilities incorporated (plumbers and electricians), framing put up (carpenters), exterior walls and siding put in place (siding specialists and bricklayers), a roof put on (roofers), interior work completed (wallpaper hangers, painters, carpet layers, etc.), and so forth. While some individuals possess the knowledge, skill, and time to build a house themselves, most people would have the work done for them by a general contractor and a team of specialists as indicated.

Weber understood the vast potential for assembling specialists in the sense suggested by Adam Smith and coordinating their work organizationally. It is this functional division of work that becomes the horizontal axis of the organization. Recall that every formal organization has been consciously created to perform some task(s) or function(s).

It is the breakdown of this overall organizational task into all of its component subtasks and the assignment of these subtasks to specific workers that constitutes the notion of division of labor. This process is sometimes referred to today as *work simplification*. The vertical axis or authority structure provides the means to coordinate the multiple subtasks so that the total function is performed. In effect then, each position in an organization is assigned some subtasks to perform (division of labor) and is allocated a specified amount of authority (hierarchial authority structure) that relates to the performance of those subtasks. In administrative theory literature, this is referred to as the *organizing process*.

According to Weber's position, assignment of the work to be performed (division of labor) and assignment of authority to see that the work is performed is always made to a position, not to an individual. In a bureaucracy, this process results in a specification of the knowledge, skills, and authority required to carry out each of the various organizational roles. This specification is then used to select those individuals with the qualifications needed to perform the duties required by the role. Weber's central notion is the separation of the position from the person. In other words, the organization can be viewed as a system of functionally interdependent roles.

Utilizing the earlier example of a caseworker, the division of labor concept would be illustrated by an agency organizing its staff so that some caseworkers would specialize in intake, others in providing ongoing treatment services, and still others in providing aftercare services. The division of labor would be an alternative to having all caseworkers being generic, that is, each worker providing all services as needed in each case.

Standardization of Role Performance

Not only is there an allocation of function and authority to each office, but role performance is standardized. This notion is perhaps most clearly seen in **job descriptions**. The rationalist position builds in part on an assumption that it is possible to determine a point where both efficiency and effectiveness are optimized—the one best way for performing a task. The notion of standardization of role performance becomes the specification of method, or the precise way to perform a given task. Operationally, every person assigned to the same role would carry out that role essentially the same way—presumably producing a standardized outcome. A typical example is the person performing a job on an assembly line. Every person performing the specified job would do it essentially the same way. These highly prescribed procedures become one method of quality control—every product produced in a given classification is identical with every other product in that same classification. Why? Because precisely the same procedures are used. Such procedures can be helpful from the vantage point of the consumer, whether it is in buying a new car (you don't want a lemon) or a MacDonald's hamburger (a Big Mac wherever it is purchased). As we will see later, the notions of standardization and the specific tasks associated with role performance and the division of labor can (and frequently do) create very boring types of work, and these create problems for both the worker and the employer (e.g., high job turnover rates).

For a role to be standardized, the function of that role (its outcome) must be clearly delineated. For that reason, many roles do not lend themselves to precise specification, for example, university professor, community organizer, family therapist. There are, however, many examples of the concept of standardization of role performances in the human services field. The role of the child protective services worker tends to be highly prescribed because it pertains to conducting an investigation for determining whether a child has been physically or sexually abused. The reasons for the levels of specification of role behaviors are quite clear—the overall function of the role is to protect the child from (subsequent) abuse and to determine whether or not a specific allegation of abuse took place. Also, since court action may be involved, there are prescribed procedures that the worker must follow in gathering and presenting evidence.

Inherent in the concept of standardization of role performance is the ability to match human capabilities with organizational requirements. In the rationally based logic employed by Weber, people looking for work are matched differentially to the work requirements for each available position. Carried to its logical extreme, if all the knowledge, skill, and personal features of job applicants were known and all the role requirements of jobs within an agency were known, it would be possible to design a perfect fit between the individual and the organizational role. Putting aside for the moment the desirability of such an approach, the intent here is to identify the underlying assumptions and key features of that logic employed in the rationalist perspective. The assumption is made in this view that it is possible and desirable to get the best qualified person for the job.

At an organizational level, particularly in large agencies, personnel departments are formed, in part, to help carry out the function of standardizing role performance. Included in this function is preparation of job (role) descriptions, recruitment and hiring, establishing work performance standards, and monitoring the regular evaluation of employees in accordance with established performance standards. Similarly, state licensure of professions (including social work) is related to this concept. Typically such laws specify the practice being licensed, the general methods employed, and the qualifications necessary to practice the profession.

Depersonalization of Position

The notion expressed earlier that a formal organization can be characterized as a system of roles has its intellectual roots in the work of Weber. From his position, people are hired into jobs based on the related job requirements, not on personal characteristics. Weber also saw positions in bureaucracies as requiring the full-time attention of the incumbent in the work role. The combination of the depersonalization of office and viewing the position as needing the full-time attention and devotion of the office holder has become part of a force that has resulted in the professionalization of many work roles.

In Weber's model of a **bureaucracy**, all roles in the organization are depersonalized so that relationships pertaining to the authority structure as well as those related to the functional distribution of work are guided by work (Gesellschaft), not personal (Gemeinschaft) determinants. From a conceptual perspective, Weber used the notions of depersonalization and dehumanization in a different manner than is currently used in the human service professions. In Weber's words,

> When fully developed, bureaucracy also stands, in a specific sense, under the principle of *sine ira ac studio*. Its specific nature, which is welcomed by capitalism, de-

velops the more perfectly the more the bureaucracy is "dehumanized," the more completely it succeeds in eliminating from official business love, hatred, and all purely personal, irrational and emotional elements which escape calculation. This is the specific nature of bureaucracy and it is appraised as its special virtue.[15]

An example of **depersonalization of position** would be case assignments by a casework supervisor to her or his workers. The assignment, based on this conceptualization, would be premised on objective criteria related to caseload standards and practice skills rather than personal features of the relationship; that is, the supervisor would not make preferential assignments because of her or his personal feelings about a specific caseworker.

The interrelationships between Weber's concepts should be clear by now. In his view, for an administrator to select the best qualified person for a given job, the specifications for that position should be standardized and the role depersonalized. The administrator must be free of all prejudices and other such personal biases so as to choose the person entirely based on objective and specified standards (obviously, the good old boy network would not thrive under such conditions).

As we will see later, some very serious questions arise when these concepts are put into action. For example, does the depersonalization of an office contribute to feelings of depersonalization of the office holder? If so, under what sets of conditions and with what adverse effects to the officeholder and to the organization? More specifically, does the depersonalization of the position of caseworker in an agency tend to foster feelings of depersonalization on the part of the worker—losing a caring attitude toward clients and treating clients like impersonal objects, that is, being burned out?[16]

Decision Making Guided by Rules Based in Law and/or Administrative Policy

The notion here is that decision making and related forms of organizational actions are based on legal (or quasi-legal) forms of authority. Weber's concept embodies the principle of fixed and official jurisdictional areas of responsibilities. Authority is vested in the position, not in a person per se. The notion also includes the principle of the delimitation of authority and the right to appeal a decision to a higher authority. In this sense, the areas within the bureaucracy in which authority is exercised are not open-ended but are limited to a given and known jurisdictional area. For example, a supervisor has the right to exercise authority over how agency cases are handled, but has no authority over actions by her or his caseworkers after working hours and on matters not pertaining directly to agency interests, for instance, how these caseworkers handle their own family matters or conduct their own private practice.

One of the most powerful insights to be drawn from Weber's work is recognition of the relative independence of the person and position. Whereas the primary group is a form of social organization comprised of patterned behavior among specified individuals, the bureaucracy is a contrived pattern of behavior composed of vertically and horizontally linked offices—not persons; a system of roles—not individuals. In Weber's formulation, humans are the temporary occupants of roles, with the determinants of who should occupy a given role based on organizational, not personal, concerns. Following from this position, the lifespans and development patterns of such formal organizations are not to be understood in human terms but from quite a different perspective – an organizational perspective. The Catholic Church, nearly 2,000 years old, is a familiar example of the independence of the organization from those who may comprise it at any given point in time.

Before proceeding further, it would be useful to stop a moment and examine Weber's model of a bureaucracy in terms of Tönnies's concepts of Gemeinschaft and Gesellschaft. Viewing social life from a historical perspective, Tönnies suggested that as social life becomes more complex, there is a shift in social relationships from possessing Gemeinschaftlike to Gesellshaftlike features. It can be argued that Weber, observing the same shift, fashioned a model of organization embodying the Gesellschaft features described by Tönnies. Weber's model of a bureaucracy is essentially a pure model of such relationships – one that systematically excludes the personally based Gemeinschaft relationships. The rationally conceived bureaucracy could thus be viewed as a potentially powerful social tool ideally suited for dealing with the ever-growing complexity of the modern world. It should also be noted that Weber foresaw both the power and the danger in this new creation; like a Frankenstein, a human creation that has potential for harming its creator.[17]

In concluding this section, we remind you that Weber's writings have been used to develop the rationalist perspective in organizational theory. Weber was a scholar, and as such was primarily interested in the development of knowledge for its own sake. Writing at about the same time (but before Weber's works were translated) were other writers who, unlike Weber, were primarily interested in the application of knowledge to the problems faced by managers of industrial and business enterprises. These writings helped establish the beginnings of management theory, or what might be termed applied organizational theory. The views of some of these writers were very similar to those held by Weber, and so will be noted in this section. Best known among this group was Frederick W. Taylor.[18] Taylor, whose background was in engineering, is known as the "Father of Scientific Management." His contributions to organizational and management theory were developed during the late nineteenth and early twentieth centuries. Taylor spent time with workers in the factory as they performed their duties; just as an engineer might design a new machine, Taylor sought to design a worker-machine combination that would result in the most rational and scientific way of performing the job. His application of science to the study of management is perhaps most clearly reflected in time and motion studies. Using a stop watch, the physical movements of the worker in performing a task were charted and timed in order to design the best possible way for accomplishing that task.

From a conceptual position, it is important to note that Taylor operated on the assumption that workers were motivated primarily by economic incentives, that is, earning wages that would be used to meet basic, survival-level needs. He reasoned that if production levels could be increased and costs reduced through worker-related actions, it would be possible for management to share these extra profits with workers; the task became one of precisely (rationally) designing the work environment so that workers would adopt new work procedures and work their hardest in order to make more money (e.g., adopting a "piece rate" basis for computing wages). In Taylor's words,

Perhaps the most prominent single element in modern scientific management is the task idea. The work of every workman is fully planned out by the management at least one day in advance, and each man receives in most cases complete written instructions, describing in detail the task which he is to accomplish, as well as the means to be used in doing the work. And the work planned in advance in this way constitutes a task which is to be solved, as explained above, not by the workman alone, but in almost all cases by the joint effort of the workman and the management. This task specifies not only what is to be done but how it is to be done and the exact time allowed for doing it. And whenever the workman succeeds in doing his task right, and within the time limit specified, he receives an addition of from 30 percent to 100 percent to his ordinary wages.[19]

Given the assumptions and a rational model for viewing organizational and human behavior, Taylor's thinking became popular with administrators, owners, and with many organizational theorists. Taylor's work is helpful in that it extends a line of reasoning about worker motivation that is associated with the rationalist perspective. In short, both workers and management can profit by optimizing working conditions, procedures, and incentives. This position is also predicated on the theoretical assumption that there is no inherent conflict between organizational goals and the goals of workers. There were many other writers in addition to Taylor who made contributions to the rationalist perspective. These particular efforts will not be reviewed here, but include such well-known names as Henri Fayol, Henry Gantt, and Herbert Simon.[20]

The Human Relations Perspective

Criticisms of Weber's model of bureaucracy and of the rationalist perspective focused on its view of human actions being driven essentially by rational considerations. It was argued that humans simply do not behave within formal organizations in the manner suggested. To borrow again from Tönnies, the rationalists gave little consideration to the personal or Gemeinschaft features of social relationships and their effects on life within the organization. In introducing this criticism, it is important to recall that from Weber's perspective, the systematic exclusion of personal determinants in decision making was what gave the bureaucracy its superiority over other organizational forms. In his words:

> The decisive reason for the advancement of bureaucratic organization has always been its purely technical superiority over any other form of organization. The fully developed bureaucratic mechanism compares with other organizations exactly as does the machine with the non-mechanical modes of production.[21]

It is not surprising, given Weber's position and that of other writers holding the rationalist perspective, to have it sometimes referred to as the "Machine School of Organizational Theory."[22] Nor is it surprising that these criticisms resulted in further investigations into the subject area. These inquiries led to development of what became known as the "Human Relations School." Elton Mayo is generally credited with the development of this school of thought.[23] Central to the establishment of the human relationist perspective were findings from studies conducted at the Western Electric Company's Hawthorne Plant in Chicago between 1927 and 1932. This research has come to be known as the Hawthorne studies. Initially the studies were aimed at testing hypotheses generated from the rationalist perspective. In a now famous study, the researchers were seeking an optimum level of illumination for workers assembling telephone relay equipment. The results were unexpected and confusing. In Mayo's words:

> The conditions of scientific experiment had apparently been fulfilled—experimental room, control room; changes introduced one at a time; all other conditions held steady. And the results were perplexing. . . . Lighting improved in the experimental room, production went up; but it rose also in the control room. The opposite of this: lighting diminished from 10 to 3 foot-candles in the experimental room and the production again went up; simultaneously in the control room, with illumination constant, production also rose.[24]

Left without a scientific explanation for their perplexing findings, the researchers turned to their subjects for help. These employees were so pleased with the interest shown in their work by the researchers and by the company they reciprocated by trying to do their best, thus creating what has come to be popularly referred to as the "Hawthorne Effect." Also discovered through the Hawthorne studies was the presence within the formal organization of an informal organization. For our purposes here, this informal organization can be thought of as comprised of loosely coupled social groups—natural as compared to contrived groups. Tönnies can again be helpful in understanding the origins and the nature of such groups.[25] The relationships among members of the informal organization were personally based, essentially conducted face-to-face, and dealt with the personal needs of members, particularly those needs associated with their work setting and actions by management. The relationships were primarily Gemeinschaft in nature and represented a kind of balancing of the formal or Gesellschaft relationships that typified the contrived structure of relationships within the formal organization.

Findings from the Hawthorne studies and related work posed serious questions about many of the assumptions associated with the rationalist perspective. Arising out of the questions were assumptions that became foundations to the human relationist perspective. These assumptions have been summarized as follows: (1) worker effort is a function of social, not physical capacity; (2) noneconomic rewards vitally affect worker motivation; (3) high levels of specialization are not necessarily the most efficient means for organizing work; and (4) workers tend to relate to management as group members, not as individuals.[26] The Hawthorne study has taken on historical importance because its findings challenged some of the key assumptions of the rationalists. The study also was important in that it helped demonstrate the contribution that empirical research could make in building a theory of organizational behavior.

As with the rationalist position, the human relationist perspective was represented by a group of writers who shared similar, but by no means identical views regarding the behavior of formal organizations. As previously noted, a central concern expressed by this collection of writers was the emphasis placed on the rational features of the organization; they felt that the rational model was both incomplete and misleading in its portrayal of organizational and human behavior. As suggested by their name, the human relationists focused on the individual as a member of a work group. Postulated as a central thesis by these writers was that the social norms that developed within the work (natural) group were key determinants of individual behavior in the work environment. From this position, the work group took on critical importance in understanding the behavior of the total organization. This attention to the work group led in turn to explorations into worker motivation and the influence of leadership on a group's behavior.[27]

The rationalist and human relationist perspectives have both contributed significantly to the development of management theory and to the general development of organizational theory. At this point it would be useful to examine their similarities and their differences. In the most fundamental sense, both schools of thought accepted an underlying rationality in seeking the kind of structural arrangements that would most efficiently and effectively produce the formal organization's intended outcomes. The rationalist position rested in part on an assumption that workers were primarily motivated by economic gain (as were their employers), so that the best structural arrangement would be the one that maximized economic returns for both management and labor.

The human relations argument was not against the thesis of organizational rationality in its most fundamental sense, but on some of the assumptions pertaining to the role of humans in this calculus. Their argument was that the rationalist view of the worker and human motivation was incomplete and misleading. Their position was that workers were not motivated primarily by economic gain and that workers did not relate to the work situation only as individuals, but rather as members of a work group as well. In this sense, the organization was seen as possessing both a formal administrative (rational) structure *and* an informal (natural) social structure. It was therefore deemed necessary to consider both structures and their respective needs to understand organizational behaviors and their outcomes. From the perspective of the human relationist, satisfaction of the worker's social as well as economic needs were necessary in order to create an optimum organizational environment. Simply put, satisfied (happy) workers would be productive workers.[28] Conceptually, the assumption was made that worker and organizational needs were reconcilable and that an optimum balance could be struck. Finding and maintaining this balance was essentially a management function and expressed through the leadership behavior of the manager.

Before leaving the discussion of the similarities and the differences between these two perspectives, it would be useful to tie them to their historical antecedents. Earlier, mention was made of Tönnies and his identification of two contrasting types of social relationships. Gemeinschaft characterizes those behaviors found in primary or natural groups. These relationships evolve informally, are based on sentiment, are spontaneous, and are engaged in for their own sake. The origins (motivation) for the development of these relationships are to be found from a conceptual position in the nature of the person himself or herself. The human relations writers are in the tradition of such other social theorists as Rousseau, Proudhon, Burke, and Durkheim.[29] Gesellschaft relationships, according to Tönnies, are characterized by rationality and calculation and are means for achieving a specified end. The rationalists are clearly in this tradition. Here the intellectual roots go back to such social theorists as Hobbes, Lenin, and Saint-Simon.[30]

For us, the contributions of the rationalists and the human relationists constitute a dialectic process, with social systems theory representing a synthesis. Some writers include a third major school of organizational theory in their reviews of theory development—the structuralists.[31] Typically, the structuralist view is treated as a view arising out of deficiencies in the human relations position and represents an attempt at synthesis of the rationalist and human relationist perspectives. This synthesis is seen as occurring along three main lines: (1) recognition of the importance of both the formal and informal features of social structure; (2) the importance of the organization's environment as a variable that affects its behavior; and (3) the role of conflict as a significant process employed in dealing with inter/intragroup differences. We have found the contributors to the structuralist position helpful, but treat the position as a precursor to the social systems perspective.[32]

A Social Systems Perspective

In Part I we identified a social systems perspective. Here we extend this perspective as it applies to the formal social organization. To do this, the social systems perspective is treated as an overlay and applied first to the rationalists and then to the human relationists, to obtain a set of comparisons as to how each differs from the social systems perspective.

When the systems overlay is applied to the rationalist position, two major differences appear. First is what we might refer to as the relative *tightness of fit* among the social units. From the rationalist position, there is a tight fit, with every position being related to every other position in a specific and logical way. The logic of the fit is drawn from the legal charter of the formal organization. Positions are related to one another both vertically and horizontally in terms of the most efficient and effective means of achieving the organization's goals. The rationalists' portrayal of the formal organization suggests that it might have been designed by an engineer—it is precise, it is neat, and it is logical. Like a machine, the organization's design and specifications draw their logic from the job to be accomplished. In contrast, the fit, or relationships linking member units, has much more slack when viewed from the systems perspective. In short, the fit between member units is not precise, neat, or logical. From the systems view, the fit is loose, frequently sloppy, and at times illogical; in other words, humanlike rather than machinelike.

Second, the rationalist perspective focuses on the formal organization. The social systems perspective takes a much wider view and focuses on the formal organization in an environmental context, that is, the system in relationship to its suprasystem. Given this difference in focus, stability and fixed relationships among member units are the desired normal state of the rationalists. In contrast, change is the normal state from the systems perspective. To summarize, when the rationalist perspective is viewed from the systems overlay, the organization appears to be that of a relatively closed system. Individual behavior in terms of enactment of organizational roles is clearly related to organizational needs and purposes. From a closed systems perspective there is little "leakage" into the system from outside sources. Such leakage, if it should occur, would be treated as a negative deviation, and efforts would be made to control and thereby insulate the organization from it. The social systems perspective of all forms of social organizations is that they be treated as open systems. The perspective is always of the organization in an environmental context. In this sense, it represents an extension of the notion of "human behavior and the social environment." In other words, human behavior is to be understood relative to individual and environmental determinants; each acts on the other in a cyclical and reciprocal fashion. The systems perspective holds that the formal organization is a social entity not unlike the individual and is to be understood in terms of the interplay of organizational and environmental factors.

Earlier, the human relationist perspective was described and contrasted to that of the rationalist. Here the social systems perspective will be treated as an overlay and applied to the human relationist perspective. Writers associated with this position gave special attention to the individuals who worked in formal organizations, their needs, and their propensity to join together in social groups. The group not only was viewed as a medium through which individuals satisfied their social needs, but dealt with organizational stresses and strains as well. In contrast to the focus on Gesellschaft relationships by the rationalist, the human relationist focused on the Gemeinschaft—those relationships dominating in social groups.

Viewed through the systems overlay, the human relationists tended to treat the formal organization more as a social group or a natural, rather than a contrived system. It was suggested that the formal features identified by the rationalists to distinguish this type of organization from others were overstated. In turn, the human relationists held that those features typifying social groups were understated in terms of their presence and influences in so-called formal organizations. Commenting on the perspective of viewing formal organizations as natural systems, Scott comments, "The whole thrust of the natural system view is that (formal) organizations are more than instruments for attaining narrowly defined goals; they are fundamentally, social groups attempting to adapt to and survive in their particular circumstances."[33] Scott's observations help identify another major difference between the human relations perspective of the formal organization and the rationalist view. The human relationists noted the tendency of formal organizations to change or modify their goals. This tendency was treated by the rationalist as a deviation or distortion of the basic nature of such organizations. In contrast, this tendency toward goal displacement, substitution, or modification was seen by the human relationists as strengthening their contention that the formal organization could be more appropriately treated as a special form of a social group rather than as a distinctive form of social organization. This argument reduces to a means-end or Gesellschaft-Gemeinschaft conception about the distinction between these two organizational forms. In commenting on this argument, Gouldner notes:

> The organization, according to this model [the natural systems perspective], thrives to survive and to maintain its equilibrium, and this striving may persist even after its explicitly held goals have been successfully attained. This strain toward survival may even on occasion lead to the neglect or distortion of the organization's goals.[34]

From this position, survival is the most fundamental of all organizational goals and overrides all other considerations; given this position, all organizations, including the formal ones, are self-serving and thus should be treated as means as opposed to ends. In other words, while formal organizations are constituted as means for achieving specified ends, in effect they are self-serving, and their continued existence is the end state.

Viewed through the systems overlay, the means-end argument is spurious and arises from a closed system perspective held by both the rationalists and the human relationists. Both positions focus on the organization, with only scant attention given to the environmental determinants of organizational behavior. While the human relationists argued for greater attention to the needs of the workers and to the importance of social group formation within the work place, they treated organizational goals and purposes as essentially fixed; goal substitution, modification, or change are treated as distortions or deviations from the organization's main character.

The social systems view of the organization in its environmental context would not necessarily consider goal modification or change as a deviation but simply as part of the constantly changing relationship that the organization has with its supporting environment; the systems view is that change is the normal state. Further, the observation that formal organizations engage in self-serving and self-maintaining behaviors should not be treated as a deviation from their alleged main character and thus evidence that they could be best treated as natural systems. Rather, the social systems perspective holds that formal organizations must expend a portion of their resources to meet the personal needs of their workers and to maintain and strengthen the organization itself; according to this view all organizations that behave like social systems confront the survival imperative by addressing both task and maintenance goals.

Given the above comparisons as background, we view the social systems perspective as more than just a larger and more comprehensive framework through which to seek understanding of the behavior of formal organizations. The systems perspective is a synthesis of these two perspectives with the synthesis representing a disjuncture in the mode of thought used to understand organizational behavior.

In the paragraphs to follow, we will summarize some of the concepts that have helped shape the social systems model being applied to formal organizations. Earlier references have been made to the distinction between primary and secondary groups or between natural and formally constituted social systems. Here the concept of emergence is helpful. The concept of emergence holds that each higher level of social organization develops from a predecessor level and retains features of that level and is thus dependent upon it. Further, the newer and higher level of organization develops properties that are not found in its antecedents. These new and distinctive features emerge in the higher organization and thus require that it be considered as something different from its parts. The thinking behind this concept is antithetical to a reductionist logic that would hold that the higher level entity can be explained through disassembly and analysis of its component parts. More will be said about the reductionist logic later.

The oft-quoted "the whole is more than the sum of its parts" is premised on the assumptions underlying emergence. In seeking to explain what is meant by this phrase when applied to social groups, Buckley argues:

> Thus, if social groups are not "real entities" then neither are individual organisms, organs, cells, molecules or atoms, since they are all "nothing but" the constituents of which they are made. But this "nothing but" hides the central key to modern

thinking—the fact of *organization* of components into systemic relationships. When we say that "the whole is more than the sum of its parts," the meaning becomes unambiguous and loses its mystery: the "more than" points to the fact of *organization*, which imparts to the aggregate characteristics that are not only *different* from, but often *not found* in the components alone; and the "sum of the parts" must be taken to mean, not their numerical addition, but their unorganized aggregation.[35]

To recapitulate, all forms of social organization are created by the interactions of individuals. The ordered relationships that evolve and the meanings participants attach to these ongoing relations constitute what is herein called *social organization*. At the social group level, the notion of emergence would hold that the characteristics of a specified group are derived from the particular individuals who comprise it, for example, the family comprised of Mary and John Smith. While the Smiths as a family unit are inseparable from the interacting individuals Mary and John, the behaviors of the family unit are not fully explainable based solely on their individual physical, social, and psychological characteristics. The explanation lies in the combining and the resulting organization of their respective characteristics.

A new whole or oneness is formed, providing a capacity to achieve ends not accomplishable or otherwise explainable in terms of the two individuals. In this sense, the relationships formed are assumed to possess synergetic capacities, for example, a love (or hate) that transcends the initial individual's capacities for such feelings. It should also be noted that while Mary and John Smith comprise a special social group called the Smith family, the Smith family is not codeterminate with the respective personalities of Mary and John Smith; each has a separate and distinct existence as individual personalities as well as comprising a social entity called the Smith family. It is Mary and John in their respective family roles as husband and wife that constitute the social entity the Smith family, not Mary and John as total personalities.

Similarly, the formal organization is comprised of individuals. These individuals, in turn, are enacting functionally related roles that comprise the social structure of that organization. Earlier, distinctions were drawn between primary and secondary groups (formal organizations). Three of these differences are important in the present instance: (1) formal organizations are contrived; (2) they possess a legal authority structure; and (3) they pursue relatively specific and delimited goals. While both primary and secondary groups are comprised of individuals, the primary group is comprised of specific people, and each has a (direct) relationship with every other group member; this is not the case with formal organizations. Specific roles within formal organizations (family therapist) are drawn from its contrived nature (a mental health center), not from the personal needs of those who may work there. Therefore, the roles are independent of any particular person and thus are interchangeable. The depersonalized character of roles helps give the formal organization its uniqueness.

Consistent with the notion of emergence, we hold that formal organizations are comprised in part of social groups which, in turn, are made up of individuals. This is not to argue that all individuals relate to the total organization as group members; the position is that the formal organization is comprised of one or more social groups and its distinctive features have emerged from the social group level. From this position we argue that the principal finding from the Hawthorne studies was the discovery of groups imbedded in formal organizations. The difficulty that followed in the development of the human relations perspective was the lack of recognition of the distinctive qualities possessed by the formal organization; in other words, it was not to be understood as a "super" social group comprised of smaller, loosely coupled groups.

The previous paragraphs have summarized the concept of emergence. The concept and its related features pose important empirical questions; for example, does each higher level of social organization develop out of a lower level and develop unique features not found in its antecedent components? Is the whole greater than the sum of the parts? The attempt here is not to answer these questions. Rather the purpose is to formulate a model of social organization based on previous theory construction that is sufficiently explicit to have practice relevance. As a secondary consideration, we hope that the level of explication will permit testing of the validity of these concepts within the context of practice.

One of the most comprehensive applications of a social systems perspective to formal organizations has been made by Daniel Katz and Robert L. Kahn.[36] They characterize their approach as open systems theory, a theory of social behavior that emphasizes the systemic qualities and the influence of the environment on social behavior. From their position, formal organizations represent a special class of open systems with their own distinguishing features. The notion of "open" helps to differentiate the approach from what has been described earlier as closed systems. From our position, open systems theory represents a response to the previously mentioned deficiencies in closed systems as represented in the rationalist and human relations positions. Katz and Kahn explain: "Our basic model of a social system is a structure that imports energy from the external world, transforms it, and exports a product to the environment that is the source for a reenergizing of the cycle."[37]

The open systems formulation by Katz and Kahn has been helpful in shaping the application of the social systems model being developed in this section. For example, many students have difficulty in distinguishing the organization from the people who comprise it at a given time. The difficulty is complicated because the formal organization as a social entity cannot be discerned through the human senses. What is observable are buildings, furnishings, people in interaction, and so on. Katz and Kahn address this problem by distinguishing between levels of description and explanation and the corresponding levels of conceptualization and levels of phenomena. In the current application, the formal organization is conceptualized as a social system. At the level of phenomenon are the behaviors of individuals, the flow of information, the use of space, and so on. Phenomena, unlike concepts, have existence and can be known through the senses. The concept level tells us what data to gather at the phenomenon level and why.

For example, a social systems perspective applied to a formal organization versus a social systems perspective applied at the interpersonal level might both utilize data obtained from a specific caseworker. Depending on the exact purposes of the investigation, quite different data might be collected and used in quite different ways. In the case of an organizational study of decision-making processes, the caseworker might be asked— "How are treatment cases assigned to workers? Do you make the decision, does your supervisor make the decision, is it made jointly, or is it handled in some other manner?" Similar data gathered from other caseworkers might then be aggregated to determine whether or not there is a common (agencywide) pattern evident in this aspect of decision making. At an interpersonal level, and assuming the caseworker is in treatment because of problems with authority figures, the worker might be asked, "How do you feel about your supervisor as a person?" Here the interest is at a feeling level, and the use made of the data would pertain to the treatment goals of the client and the therapist. In this latter instance, how other workers feel about their supervisor would, in most cases, be considered irrelevant. In both instances data are gathered at the phenomenological level, but the conceptual level determines the exact information to obtain and the meaning that may be derived.

Katz and Kahn also are helpful in their formulation of the growth stages of formal organizations. Three stages are identified: Stage 1—primitive collective responses to common problems; Stage 2—insurance of stability of structure; and Stage 3—elaborated supportive structures.[38] Through these three stages they suggest it is possible to track the growth and development of formal organizations, with particular reference to the evolution of specialized structures, for example, those associated with the performance of maintenance and task functions.

According to Katz and Kahn, two conditions set the stage for the initial development of social organizations: (1) a commonly defined environmental problem; and (2) the needs and abilities of the population. The position being advanced by Katz and Kahn is very similar to the position we have taken with respect to how all social organizations come into existence (e.g., see Figure 3.3 in Chapter 3). In short, there is a problem or opportunity that is commonly defined, the resolution of which is determined by those affected to be best addressed through some form of collective versus individual action. The functions to be performed generate the particular tasks to be accomplished; and the needs, interests, and capabilities of those available affect the assignment of duties. During Stage 1 it is the continuing environmental pressure to solve the problems that maintains the conditions necessary for the pursuit of cooperative actions; these same conditions facilitate the evolution of the social structure most advantageous to the accomplishment of the desired goal. An example of an environmental problem might be persistent vandalism and assaults on residents living in the same apartment complex. Calls to the apartment owner and police have proved ineffective, so those living in the complex decide to band together and find ways of defending themselves and of protecting their property.

In this first stage, the relationships are tenuous, and their continuance is understandable in terms of a commonly defined danger, both to property and to person. Here it is important to draw a distinction between the evolution of a primary (natural) versus a secondary group (formal organization). In this example, the evolution of the organization is driven by external circumstances (the commonly defined threat), and the cooperative activities among members are functionally related to dealing with this threat. The evolving organization has been consciously created as a means to accomplish an agreed-upon end state—the control of vandalism and assaults. In contrast, recall that in the formation of a social group it is the personal needs of participants that act as the catalyst. The satisfaction of social needs by the group members represents the end state. In other words, the group exists principally to satisfy the needs of its members. Caution should be exercised here; all forms of social organization have both internal and external orientation features. What is being illustrated are some differences in emphasis that affect their development patterns.

To return to the example, in this first stage the members perceive their cooperative relationships to be effective vis-à-vis the external threat; then the conditions are established for the second stage—insurance of stability of structure. As indicated by the name given to the second stage, the effort here is to control the variability of behaviors so that a required level of organizational stability is achieved. For example, if some rotation of "watch" by members of the concerned group is agreed on as a step toward mutual protection and some people fail to take their turn, the system of protection is threatened. Katz and Kahn suggest that the bases for the development of the primitive cooperative structures (the conversion operations of the social systems model) are the shared values and normative expectations of task performance for those dealing with the common problem. These features are not enough to assure the stability of the evolving social structure. Interfering at the individual level are a host of competing problems and time demands ("I can't 'watch' tonight, this is my night to bowl."), and perceptions of how serious the current problem is and how successful the coping efforts have been. Arising out of these crude and tentative initial efforts at cooperation will be, according to Katz and Kahn, the beginnings of a formalized authority structure; its aim is the formulation and enforcement of rules to reduce the variability and instability of the behavior resulting from the emerging social structures. Examples would include the election of a chair, agreement on regular meeting times, publishing a roster of members, a dues structure, and so on. If the cooperative efforts continue to prove successful, and some level of stability of the emerging social structure is achieved, a decision might be made to further formalize the structure by creating a constitution and bylaws and having the organization registered as a not-for-profit organization under state law. The development of a legal authority structure as the dominant form of authority further distinguishes this organization as a secondary as opposed to a primary or social group.

The point of special interest here is that if the fledgling organization survives, it is this primitive authority structure that becomes the basis of the organization's management subsystem. In social systems terms, the focus of the emerging legal form of an authority is on task goals; in the example used, it is mutual protection. The exercise of the authority structure diminishes in varying degrees the choices of actions available for those participating. Participants no longer are pitching in and helping out as they see fit. Rather, a series of organizational roles has evolved, and the individual is now being fitted into this system of roles. Further, augmenting the normative expectations of role performance is a set of rules backed up by a legal authority structure—"If you don't pay your dues, your apartment will be dropped from those being watched."

If the primitive social organization is to survive, attention must be given to efforts at maintaining the social structure. A new function emerges within the authority structure, that devoted to the maintenance of the structure itself. This growth feature is what will be referred to as part of the process of differentiation—the elaboration of specialized subsystems dealing with the special problems being confronted by the social organization as it seeks to survive and then grow.

At this point in its development, the authority structure has two distinguishable functions—one devoted to the task and the other to the maintenance function. The maintenance function in our example would be someone functioning as secretary. This person (also a part of the authority subsystem) would be responsible for taking minutes and otherwise recording decisions (rules) made by the group. Other maintenance functions would include such things as holding workshops for the orientation (socialization) of new members, recognition through awards of the special contributions made by members, and so on.

The assumption is that the maintenance function within the formally constituted authority structure is never fully and continuously successful in meeting both the organization's needs and those of its members. This deficit gives rise to what is termed the organization's *informal social structure*. In the social systems model, the informal structure comprises an important part of any formal organization's maintenance function. This informal structure is comprised of a social group, or a natural system. A large formal organization may be comprised of any number of loosely coupled social groups. The communication linkage among such groups has frequently been termed the *grapevine* when contrasted to the organization's formal communication network.

Unlike the formal features of the organization's authority structure, which relate to members in their organizational roles, the informal structure links people to each other as total personalities. The informal organization also tends to focus on tension points between organizational and human needs and thus can be very helpful in performing the maintenance function of the total organization. An example would be in the social support that members provide each other in dealing with work-related sources of stress, preventing or reducing burnout.

The focus of Stage 2 deals with stabilizing the social structure, and this is accomplished largely through development of a legal authority subsystem. In other words, rules and rule enforcement procedures are added to shared values and task requirements as the means through which the social structure becomes stabilized. In a more stable (predictable) environment there is the tendency for additional elaboration of task-related structures to occur; this, in turn, spurs further development of the related supportive (maintenance) structures. For purposes of illustration, let us assume that the organization originally formed for the protection of the apartment dwellers has proved quite successful. The organization became incorporated and now has a paid staff of several people. The organization and its paid staff are supported by a monthly fee paid by members who receive protection services. The elaboration of the task function is evident in the existence of specially trained and paid personnel as opposed to the previous use of volunteers. Further, the paid staff not only provides security services for members but also checks daily on the well-being of the older residents.

According to the Katz and Kahn formulation, Stage 3 focuses on the elaboration of the organization's supportive structure. Conceptually, the elaboration is related to the open systems nature of social organizations. It is the input-output relationship that the organization has with its suprasystem that forms the basis for the elaboration of its various subsystems. On the input side is the tendency for subsystems to develop related to the procurement of needed resources. In very small organizations, this typically takes the form of expanded features of selected roles; for example, the executive of the agency assumes responsibility for fund-raising activities. On the output side, the tendency is toward the development of subsystems concerned with the marketing/disposal of system outputs. Again, in small systems this is most likely to be evidenced by organizational members taking on additional duties related to the suprasystem's acceptance of the system's output. An example would be an agency that provides work training services to have one of its staff members take on additional duties as a job developer. In this example, the primary function of the agency would be to teach work-related skills. When clients become work ready, the problem is finding them suitable jobs, and this would be the added function of a job developer.

To expand on the earlier example of the organization formed to provide security services, on the input side would be the evolution of specialized functions associated with the screening and selection of new staff, attempts to obtain federal or state grants pertaining to the specialized security services being offered elderly residents, contact with suppliers offering new technology in the area of security, and so on. Relative to output would be such efforts as marketing the security services to nearby apartment dwellers and local business establishments and consulting with the police, courts, and other community agencies on the specialized functions of the security services.

SUMMARY

This chapter is devoted to a presentation of some of the writings and theoretical support that serves as background to modeling the formal organization as a social system. The intention is to establish the position that the formal organization can be viewed as a special form of social organization. The distinctive feature of these types of organizations is their designation as formal. The term *formal* refers, among other things, to the recognition by society of the social organization as a legal entity. This legal recognition, depending on its exact form, carries with it certain rights and responsibilities as well as sanctioning the organization's right to exist. Although an aspect of its legal character, the specificity of goals is another major distinguishing feature of formal organizations.

Early in the chapter, Tönnies's concepts of Gemeinschaft and Gesellschaft are used as background in distinguishing between types of relationships associated with primary and secondary groups. Weber's models of authority structures and the bureaucracy are then introduced because of their historical importance in the development of organizational theory.

Two perspectives contributing to the development of organizational theory are identified, the rationalists and the human relationists. Both are compared with a social systems perspective. Utilizing a dialectic process, we have treated the social systems perspective as the synthesis resulting from the two positions. In preparation for the discussion of the social systems model applied to formal organizations, attention is given to selected works of Katz and Kahn and others who have helped shape the model's development.

We have in this chapter distinguished between the development of organizational theory and administrative theory. The latter can be usefully viewed as an applied version of the former. In both instances our primary concern is in identifying content that we have found useful in developing our model of a social system and its application to formal organizations. Implicit in our approach has been an effort to shape the model in a manner that will enhance its usefulness to the practitioner.[39]

GLOSSARY

Authority   An expression of social power; the ability of a person to influence the actions and thoughts of others.

Bureaucracy   A conceptualization of formal organizations from a rationalist position, for example, formal organizations characterized by a hierarchically organized legal authority structure and explicit rules that serve as the basis for its rational actions.

Chain of command   The legally based and hierarchically arranged authority structure in bureaucratic types of formal organizations.

Charismatic authority   A form of social power derived from personal characteristics perceived to be possessed by the person exercising the power.

Depersonalization of position   The removal of personal considerations in the assignment of duties, work performance, and the evaluation of work performance – the rationalist perspective.

Division of labor   The breakdown of work or a function into its component parts and the assignment of this work to different people or "work units."

Job description   The specification of duties, performance standards, and qualifications needed to perform the work (also referred to as work role specification).

Legal authority   A form of social power identified by Weber that derives from the legal foundations of formal organizations.

Legitimacy   Acceptance of the exercise of authority by reason of the belief that those exercising authority have the right to do so, that is, the acceptance of authority by those affected by it legitimizes the authority.

Traditional authority   An exercise of social power in which the source of power is vested in the sacredness of the social order.

NOTES

1. Charles Horton Cooley, *Social Organization, A Study of the Larger Mind* (New York: Charles Scribner's Sons, 1910), 26–27.

2. Ferdinand Tönnies, *Community and Society (Gemeinschaft and Gesellschaft)* trans. and ed. Charles P. Loomis (1887; reprint, New York: Harper Torch Books, 1963).

3. Ibid., 258.

4. Marvin Olsen, *The Process of Social Organization* (New York: Holt, Rinehart and Winston, 1968), 57–69.

5. See Srinika Jayaratne and Wayne Chess, "Job Stress, Job Deficit, Emotional Support, and Competence: Their Relationship to Burnout," *The Journal of Applied Social Sciences* 10 (Spring, Summer, 1986): 135–155.

6. Wayne A. Chess, Julia M. Norlin, Srinika D. Jayaratne, "Social Work Administration 1981–1985: Alive, Happy and Prospering," *Administration in Social Work* 11, no. 2, (Summer 1987): 67–77.

7. W. Richard Scott, *Organizations: Rational, Natural, and Open Systems* (Englewood Cliffs, N.J.: Prentice Hall, 1981), 8.

8. Ibid.

9. Ibid.

10. Max Weber, "The Three Types of Legitimate Rule," trans. Hans Gerth, in *A Sociological Reader on Complex Organizations*, ed. Amitai Etzioni and Edward W. Lehman, 3rd ed. (New York: Holt, Rinehart and Winston, 1980), 4.

11. For an overview of leadership theory and research from a social work perspective, see Barbara J. Friesen, "Administration: Interpersonal Aspects," in *Encyclopedia of Social Work*, vol. 1, 18th ed. (Silver Spring, Md.: National Association of Social Workers, 1987), 17–27.

12. Max Weber, "Bureaucracy," in *Critical Studies in Organization and Bureaucracy*, ed. Frank Fischer and Carmen Sirianne (Philadelphia, Pa.: Temple University Press, 1984), 24–39.

13. Writers have classified organizational theories, particularly those pertaining to formal organizations, in a number of ways. The approach being taken here builds in part from the classification approach suggested by Scott, in *Organizations*. For an example of alternative approaches, see Amitai Etzioni, *Modern Organizations* (Englewood Cliffs, N.J.: Prentice Hall 1964), 4; and Thomas P. Holland and Marcia K. Petchers, "Organizations: Context for Social Service Delivery," in *Encyclopedia of Social Work*, vol. 2, 18th ed. (Silver Spring, Md.: National Association of Social Workers, 1987), 204–217.

14. The example is found in Adam Smith, *An Inquiry into the Nature and Causes of the Wealth of Nations* (London: Strahan and Cadell, 1776). For a brief discussion, see Amitai Etzioni, *Modern Organizations*, 22.

15. Weber, "Bureaucracy," 32.

16. For a discussion of burnout within the general context suggested here, see Barry A. Farber, ed., *Stress and Burnout in the Human Service Professions* (New York: Pergamon Press, 1983). For a review of a model in which the authors discuss the relationship of depersonalization to burnout, see pp. 126–141.

17. Weber, "Bureaucracy," 35–39.

18. Frederick W. Taylor, *The Principles of Scientific Management* (New York: Harper, 1911).

19. Frederick W. Taylor, "Scientific Management," in *Critical Studies in Organization and Bureaucracy*, Frank Fischer and Carmen Sirianni, eds. (Philadelphia, Pa.: Temple University Press, 1984), 72.

20. Henri Fayol, *General and Industrial Management*, trans. Constance Stours (1919; reprint, London: Pitman, 1949); Henry L. Gantt, *Industrial Leadership* (New Haven, Conn.: Yale University Press, 1916); Herbert A. Simon, *Administrative Behavior*, 2nd ed. (New York, Macmillan, 1957).

21. Weber, "Bureaucracy," 31.

22. Ibid.

23. Etzioni, *Modern Organizations*, 32. For additional information on the development of this line of reasoning, see F. J. Roethlisberger and W. J. Dickson, *Management and the Worker* (Cambridge, Mass.: Harvard University Press, 1939).

24. Elton Mayo, *The Social Problems of an Industrial Civilization* (Boston, Mass.: Graduate School of Business Administration, Harvard University, 1945), 69.

25. Tönnies, *Community and Society*.

26. Etzioni, *Modern Organizations*, 32.

27. Friesen, "Administration."

28. Etzioni, *Modern Organizations*, 39.

29. Scott, *Organizations*, 101.

30. Ibid.

31. See particularly Etzioni, *Modern Organizations*, 32–49.

32. For a discussion on the contributions made by the structuralists to systems theory, see particularly Scott, *Organizations*, 123–124.

33. Ibid., 80–81.

34. Alvin W. Gouldner, "Organizational Analysis," in *Sociology Today*, ed. Robert K. Merton, Leonard Broom, and Leonard S. Cottrell, Jr. (New York: Basic Books, 1959), 405.

35. Walter Buckley, *Sociology and Modern Systems Theory* (Englewood Cliffs, N.J.: Prentice Hall, 1967), 42.

36. Daniel Katz and Robert L. Kahn, *The Social Psychology of Organizations,* 2nd ed. (New York: John Wiley & Sons, 1978).

37. Ibid., 55.

38. Ibid., 70–75.

39. For a review of organizational theory in terms of its application to social administration, see Burton Gummer, "Organization Theory for Social Administration," in *Strategies of Community Organization,* 4th ed., ed. Fred M. Cox et al. (Itasca, Ill: F. E. Peacock Publishers, 1987), 427–449.

Chapter 12

The Formal Organization as a Social System

OUTLINE

Introduction

In earlier chapters the social systems model was applied first to a professional counseling relationship and then to a family. In both of these applications the individual, or more precisely, the role the individual was enacting as a counselor, client, or family member, was the focal social unit. It was the totality of these roles and their relationships with one another that comprised the whole—the social system. The scale in this application is larger. The focal unit, in most instances, is a work group that is comprised of individuals enacting specific organizational roles. The work groups are administrative units essentially derived from the organization's formalized structure and carry such designations as departments, divisions, bureaus, sections, project teams, quality circles, and so on. Attention is given to the social groups that form in the work context and that also are part of the social system. The point is that the scale of the typical formal organization does not lend itself to an approach in which the individual role is the focal unit of attention. This is not to deny the importance of the individual in formal organizations, but rather the importance of the individual can be best understood as enacting a role within an administratively defined work group. It is the interaction of such groups that represents the calculus of formal organizations as presented in this model.

There are many types of formal organizations. For example, it is possible for a social worker to form a corporation for purposes of conducting a private practice. In such an instance, the formal organization might be comprised of the practitioner and a part-time secretary. The approach presented in this chapter would not be suitable for modeling such an organization. To deal with this kind of definitional problem the authors offer a simple classification of formal organizations: Type A and Type B. Type A, the subject of this chapter, is characterized by: (1) formal/legal existence; (2) a hierarchically organized legal authority structure; (3) functionally differentiated roles; and (4) a multigroup structure. Type B is comprised of all other forms of legally constituted social organizations.

Formal organizations categorized as Type A can become quite large. For example, many such organizations have members numbering in the hundreds, thousands, and in some instances in the millions, for example, an army. Given the scale and scope of formal organizations, we have decided to use the administrative subunit as the primary building block for the structural presentation of the model. It is important to recall that these subunits can, in most instances, be treated as subsystems of the system being examined. In addition, all such subsystems are comprised of individuals playing organizational roles. It is only because of the relatively stable patterns that these roles take in formal organizations that it becomes possible to cluster them unit by unit and/or group by group for purposes of model construction and usage.

An example would be a large county welfare department employing a thousand people and made up of twenty different administrative units. One such unit, intake, might have thirty caseworkers each performing the intake function for establishing financial eligibility of clients for the Aid to Families with Dependent Children program. Given the federal and state regulatory features of this law, it can be assumed that all thirty caseworkers are going to enact their work roles in essentially the same way. In this intake unit there would be approximately six supervisors, each responsible for five workers and each carrying out their role in a similar manner. These six supervisors would, in turn, be supervised by a program director. Given this administrative structure, if the model focused on the individual role (position) as its unit of analysis, there would be a thousand such units, with thirty-seven professional roles in the intake unit alone. Such size would render the model extremely complex and perhaps useless as a practice tool. For most applications, the intake unit itself could be treated as the unit of attention and a structural building block for purposes of modeling the total agency as a social system. This is possible because of the assumed comparability in the role behaviors of the thirty caseworkers and the six casework supervisors. As indicated earlier, the focus of the model is on the common patterns characterizing role behaviors, not the individual features of the human personality. By focusing on the administrative units, the model would be examining relationships among twenty social units rather than a thousand. In such an organizational application, the role of the intake program supervisor is treated as representative of the functions of the thirty caseworkers and six supervisors comprising that social unit. Some detail is lost in such applications, but what is gained is an ability to grasp and better understand the larger and more complex patterns of behavior of the total organization.

If, in our example, it became important to better understand what was happening within the intake unit, that unit would be designated as the system, with the remaining organizational subunits becoming part of its suprasystem. At this level of inquiry, the individual role would become the unit of study and thus the structural building block for the inquiry. In large formal organizations, the model assumes a "nesting" of systems within systems (subsystems). Given this structural feature, the model permits inquiry at various levels of specificity, something like the use of a microscope employing various levels of magnification. However, it is important to keep in mind that it is not possible to understand the total agency by examining each of the subunits of that agency one by one; the whole is more than the sum of its parts.

The discussion of concepts comprising the model that follows will focus on the special features of the formal organization as contrasted to other types of organized social behavior. The single most important characteristic that distinguishes this type of organization from others is the degree of formality in relationships among its member units, the Gesellschaft as distinguished from the Gemeinschaft nature of these relationships. For purposes of context, you should recall that the formal organization is contrived, a social tool that has been formally created in order to respond to some social problem or social opportunity existing in the suprasystem. The underlying assumption is that this problem or opportunity can be most successfully addressed through a formal type of collective action as opposed to individual actions or individual actions coordinated informally. The contrived nature of this form of social organization and its assumed relationship to a social problem or a social opportunity also provide an explanation of the functional interdependence that the system is assumed to have with its suprasystem.

The paragraphs that follow are organized under the various concepts that comprise the model—namely boundary, suprasystem, interface, input, output, proposed output, conversion operations (structure and process), and feedback.

Boundary

As indicated earlier, the concept of boundary is treated as a specialized aspect of the system's structure; its principal functions are the control of input and output exchanges with the suprasystem and protecting the system from disruptive and destabilizing influences. The notion of boundary is also closely associated with the identification of the social organization, and, as such, is the logical starting place for any application of the model. In other words, the identification and specification of the organization to be modeled as a social system typically starts with a determination of its boundaries. Once this has been completed, everything inside the boundary is considered part of the system and those external social units affecting output-input exchanges, its suprasystem. This seems obvious enough, but in most instances, the specification of boundary is more complicated than it would appear. Recall that social organizations as defined here have no discernible physical structure and so cannot be identified directly via the human senses. The boundary of a social system is identified primarily through the role behaviors of those system members who perform a boundary-maintenance function. In other words, the boundary of a social system is not to be found in physical structures (a building) but in the selected patterned social behaviors of those who comprise the system. In short, interactions among insiders are different than those between insiders and outsiders or among outsiders; the task becomes one of identifying those behaviors that are aimed at distinguishing insiders from outsiders. This task is made easier when one understands that the boundary-maintenance function is aimed at helping to preserve the essential character of the system, and this is largely accomplished through the control of input and output exchanges between the system and its suprasystem.

Prior to illustrating the concept of boundary and the boundary-maintenance function, it is important to identify the distinguishing features of boundary when applied to formal organizations. These characteristics are associated with its legal status. To start, the name of the organization is legally registered in some fashion. As a part of this same chartering process, selective information pertaining to purpose and governance is specified. Key features of boundary build from these attributes. For example, the clearest determination of boundary is whether any given individual occupies a formal role in that organization. This is most clearly expressed if a person is employed or otherwise officially recognized as holding some form of membership in the named organization, for example, a client. The boundary-maintenance function is evidenced whenever there is effort made to determine who is or is not a member of the specified organization. Normally each member is given a membership card, badge, or some other means of organizational identification. Recall that in large organizations people will not necessarily know each other, so some formal means of identification are used in performance of the boundary-maintenance function. Examples include badges that have the organization's name and the employee's picture and Social Security number, and the special identification cards that are used like keys to access closed doors or parking lot gates. Depending on the possible consequences of outsiders entering the organization undetected, some organizations go to great lengths to screen all persons seeking physical entry, for example, the presence of armed guards and sophisticated screening devices at airports. Such boundary-maintenance activities are not necessary in most small human service agencies but are becoming commonplace in larger public agencies such as a public welfare department or hospital. The reasons for tight security range from such matters as the confidential nature of client records to the physical protection of staff and clients.

As an attribute of size, formal organizations frequently develop subsystems charged with the boundary-maintenance function. An example is an agency's security force. People employed in such a unit might perform a variety of boundary-maintenance functions, including checking people in and out of the agency, patrolling the grounds and parking areas, serving as night watchmen, and so on. Another common example of boundary maintenance in human service agencies is found in the role performed by an intake unit. The principal function of these units is to screen requests to determine the client's eligibility for agency services. In social systems terms, this is the control of inputs—a vital part of the boundary-maintenance function.

It should be helpful at this point to provide a more detailed example of the concept of boundary and the performance of the boundary-maintenance function. Historically, a state mental hospital has served two general functions: (1) to provide protective care and treatment for the seriously mentally ill, and (2) to protect the community from people determined to be troublesome and perhaps dangerous. The latter function is not usually stated, but the literature clearly supports this definition of function.[1] State hospitals have also tended to become quite large. Prior to the introduction of psychotropic drugs and other modern treatment methods, many of these hospitals had patients numbering in the thousands. Given such size, it was not possible for everyone in the hospital to know everyone else. However, given its function, the need to clearly distinguish between staff and patients and, more generally, between insiders and outsiders becomes readily apparent.

Typically, the state hospital occupies a large tract of land, is comprised of a number of buildings, and frequently is located in a rural or semirural setting. In the past, these hospitals frequently had their grounds fenced with gatekeepers strategically located to control movement in and out of the hospital by staff, patients, relatives, vendors, and others. Through its boundary-maintenance functions, the hospital was able to help confine patients to its grounds and generally keep them under observation. Similarly, these arrangements kept hospital patients from wandering into the community and possibly frightening or troubling townspeople (control of input and output exchanges with the suprasystem).

Although the state hospital's fence and gatekeeper are now relics of the past, they are useful in illustrating the concept of boundary and performance of the boundary-maintenance function. For example, does the presence of the fence at the hospital mean that the fence should be treated as a feature of the boundary? Not necessarily. The answer is only to be found in the behaviors of staff and patients at the hospital. If staff, especially the gatekeeper, utilize the fence and its gates to screen insiders from outsiders, then the fence becomes a part of the hospital's boundary. In other words, fences, property lines, buildings, or any other such physical structures may or may not be an aspect of boundary; it depends entirely on how they are used. Boundary, in this model, is a social and not a physical concept, and boundary maintenance is a social behavior.

To continue the example of the traditional state hospital, admission procedures were likely to be legally defined, for example, court commitment, competency (sanity) hearings, and so on. The extent and specificity of those structures affecting admission (controls of inputs) as well as those pertaining to discharge (control of outputs) attest to the importance of the boundary-maintenance function to such institutions, and illustrate how carefully and precisely boundaries can be drawn and the boundary-maintenance function prescribed.

In no way are we suggesting that all formal organizations have boundaries with the kind of high profile suggested by this example. What we are indicating is that the social systems model includes the concept of boundary, and that every social organization that behaves like a social system has a discernible boundary and will expend energies in the maintenance of that boundary. Understanding the amount of energy expended in boundary maintenance and the relative openness or restrictiveness of the boundary will in part be found in the purposes served by the formal organization.

To illustrate the latter point, let us change the example from a traditional state hospital to a modern community mental health center. For purposes of this example, the assumption is made that the center will stress caring for the client (rather than patient) in the least restrictive environment and will make an effort to maintain the client's social functioning in as many areas as his or her condition permits (for example, as parent and/ or employee). If the client should require inpatient services, that area might more resemble a family living area than a hospital room. To the casual observer, it would be very difficult to tell the difference between clients (patients) and staff. For example, both clients and staff would be dressed in street clothes. The only distinguishing feature might be the color-coded name tags (for example, clients may wear green name tags, and nurses wear white tags). Both staff and clients would move freely around the building and on and off the grounds. It would also be possible for this community mental health center to be occupying space in buildings that had previously housed the state hospital cited in the earlier example. In this instance, while the fence and gate might still be present, they would not be associated with boundary or the boundary-maintenance function; their only function would be decorative. In this example, boundary would most likely be defined in terms of employee and client status in the organization. The boundary-maintenance function would show in such things as the conditions included in the form of admission to the center, the helping contract (which would specify something of the role of client and therapist and other staff in the helping effort), name tags, and billing procedures.

In the above examples, employee and patient/client status are both used as a way of designating boundary, and the role definitions of staff and patients show how features of the boundary-maintenance function are performed. Such specifications are typical when identifying boundary in formal organizations. While these represent reasonably clear designations of boundary, there are many less clear determinations that may need to be made in deciding where to draw the boundary in any given application of the model. For example, are clients always to be considered as part of the social system, and if not, under what circumstances? Or what about agency volunteers, consultants, and contractors—should they be considered insiders or outsiders? There is no one answer, except that the decision needs to be made in each application; the guide is the use of the model.

Suprasystem

Once the system has been designated and its boundary identified, those individuals, groups, and agencies relevant to its output-input exchanges become the suprasystem. Being modeled is an open system, one that is continually influencing and being influenced by its external environment. The identification and explication of these external relationships form the basis of the concept of suprasystem. The input-output exchanges between the system and its suprasystem constitute the focal point of this examination.

The formal features of the social organization being modeled are utilized as the beginning point for describing the suprasystem. The initial assumption is that a problem or opportunity exists within the environment, and the organization being examined represents a specific and formalized social response to that need or opportunity. Every formal organization exists to serve some purpose, and this purpose has its ultimate origins in a need or opportunity in its external environment, that is, outside the subject organization. This assumption results in the formulation of a mutually interdependent relationship between the organization and its relevant environment. The organization's output represents the response to this need or opportunity. This output is then exchanged either directly (money) or indirectly (political support), for resources (inputs) required by the organization to continue to serve its purposes. The additional assumption is made that the needs or opportunities existing in the subject organization's environment are constantly changing, thereby requiring the organization to monitor the changes and to adjust its outputs so they remain responsive to these ever-changing needs and opportunities. The model presented here incorporates this functional formulation of input-output exchanges as the basis of conceptualizing the relationship of the system to the suprasystem. By extension, these input-output exchanges among all individuals and their social organizations become a functionally based explanation of the existing social order.

The above conceptualization of system-suprasystem relationships would be misleading if suggested that a tight fit exists between a system and its suprasystem. The model presumes a level of functional interdependence, but considerable slack exists in these relationships. Further, the model does not assume any fixed set of relationships between the system and its suprasystem, only that such functional relationships exist, they are dynamic, and they represent the fundamental determinants of organizational behavior.

Two examples are offered to illustrate system-suprasystem relationships. The first builds on the example of the state mental hospital that was used to describe boundary. The second is Chrysler, an automobile manufacturer. The latter example was selected to illustrate some differences as well as similarities between public and profit-making organizations in terms of their ties to the suprasystem.

In the example of the state hospital, boundary was evidenced in the way selected social roles were enacted between staff and patients and between staff and outsiders. The hospital's fence and gates were used to illustrate how physical barriers can be employed in the boundary-maintenance function. In effect, the example was intended to convey a relatively closed system. The system was able to maintain its comparatively closed position vis-à-vis the suprasystem through a well-developed and tightly drawn boundary and the vigorous maintenance of that boundary. For the concept of suprasystem to be useful, it is necessary to identify those individuals and particularly those other organizations in the suprasystem that are involved in its input-output exchanges. The model is thus constructed on the assumption that the system's suprasystem is represented by those that affect its input-output exchanges. On the input side (signal) for the state hospital would be those people presumed to be mentally ill. Communities have specialized agencies and sets of procedures used to formally screen potential patients. In the instance of a severe mental illness, the local probate court is likely to be involved in the determination of the patient's mental status and need for care. Given this function, and for most applications involving the hospital, the court is a vital component of its suprasystem. For example, any significant change in court procedures that affects the number of persons being committed to the state hospital is of critical concern to the hospital's staff.

Up to this point, the example has focused on signal input, the patient. The state hospital must also secure maintenance inputs—money, staff, information, and knowledge of new treatment procedures—all of the resources necessary to maintain operation of the hospital. Conceptually, all of these inputs are derived from the suprasystem. In this example, the assumption is that the state hospital is one of a series of hospitals operated by the state department of mental health. This department's needs are included with all other state department needs in an executive budget submitted by the governor to the state legislature. The legislature, in turn, makes yearly appropriations based on various political and economic considerations as well as department needs as set forth in the governor's budget. Once the state department of mental health receives its yearly allocation, it will, in turn, allocate money to its various operating units including the state hospital used in the example. The point here is the *indirect* connection between the hospital's task output, that is, condition of patients following discharge, and the generation of resources for input. In other words, state hospital patients don't pay the cost of their care; it is borne largely by the taxpayers of the state. The Chrysler example to follow will illustrate the direct connection between the system's output and its exchange for resources required on the input side.

Continuing on the input side, the availability of professionally prepared personnel will be a vital issue for the state hospital. Given this need, the hospital will tend to have close ties to nearby universities having professional programs in such areas as medicine and psychiatry, nursing, social work, and psychology. For many organizations, these other agencies that compete with them for inputs (signal and maintenance) will also represent vital features of their suprasystems. In this example, the state hospital is deemed to have few competitors; the mentally ill with personal resources will seek admission to private mental hospitals. However, the state hospital could expect to compete with other programs within the mental health department for department-controlled resources. Many human service agencies do not, as a feature of their suprasystem, have competitors for their clients. Their monopoly over a specified area of service can be useful in understanding the hospital's behavior as an organization.

On the output side, the families of patients represent a key feature of the hospital's suprasystem. In our example, it can be assumed that hospital staff will work with the families of patients to prepare them for the return of their family member (conceptually, discharged patients are the hospital's task output with the patient becoming input into the family system). Because of this output-input relationship, families of former patients become critical features of the hospital's suprasystem. In terms of model usage, those social units that serve as consumers of system outputs will always be considered as vital parts of that system's suprasystem. Any disruption or alteration of this relationship is likely to severely affect the subject organization. If the families receiving members back home have positive feelings toward the hospital and if former patients feel likewise, they will tend to be supportive of the hospital. These positive feelings will likely be communicated formally and informally to state legislators, officials in the state department of mental health, and others who have a role in affecting inputs to the hospital, for instance, legislative appropriations. Similarly, if former patients and their families are critical of the hospital and believe it not to be adequately fulfilling its function, this will be fed back and likewise will tend to have an effect on hospital inputs.

Former patients represent a high risk group for subsequent admission (readmission). Given this relationship, the hospital needs to be vitally concerned with the support systems their former patients have that will affect their community adjustment. Thus, agencies that receive referrals of patients discharged from the state hospital represent vital features of its suprasystem. As just indicated, how well these other community agencies serve the former state hospital patient will be a factor in the subsequent adjustment of the patient to community life. In recent years, there has been growing pressure on state hospitals to return patients to the community as soon as possible. Many patients do not have families to return to, nor do they possess the capacity to take care of themselves. In this situation, a surrogate of the family must be found to provide the support needed to sustain the patient outside the hospital. This surrogate can take many organizational forms, but for all, the client will be its signal input, and thus the interdependent relationship based on output-input exchanges with the state hospital is established. Currently, state hospitals are discharging some of their patients without viable families to so-called bed and board homes. In other instances, hospitals are discharging patients without families and without means for care in bed and board homes directly into the streets. These former mental patients then become a part of the community's homeless, the disaffiliated street people who live in abandoned structures and under bridges, and who receive assistance from community food centers and temporary shelters like the Salvation Army. Such mentally incapacitated and vulnerable people were historically sent to hospitals and were retained there indefinitely if no community or nonhospital alternative were available. Given current practices of many state hospitals, there is likely to be some tension developing between the hospital and the communities they serve. Each will argue the other is not fulfilling its role (loss of steady state). From the position of this model, there is a breakdown in the output-input exchange between the system and suprasystem. As this problem grows, some changes can be expected in these relationships as the systems seek a return to steady state.

To conclude this example, other organizations that would comprise the state hospital's relevant suprasystem would include those that have some regulatory authority and those representing special interest constituencies. In the former instance, it would include agencies such as the Joint Commission on Accreditation of Hospitals. This agency would prescribe standards to which the hospital would have to comply in order to receive reimbursement from Medicaid and other third-party funding sources. The assumption is that every organization through its input-output exchanges will develop sets of special interest constituencies. Such constituencies are especially important to public agencies such as the state hospital since they can advocate for its continued existence and development. Included here would be such constituencies as its state mental health association, local chapter of the National Association of Social Workers, state nursing home association, and key vendors. Some or all of these constituencies can be expected to have paid lobbyists who will seek to influence legislative appropriations to the state mental health department and more specifically the state hospital.

Chrysler Corporation is the second example used in formulating the notion of suprasystem. The intent of this example is to identify and further explicate the common features of the suprasystem as used in this model and also to indicate some of the differences that result from how output-input exchanges are accomplished. In the case of Chrysler, its principal task outputs are motor vehicles. These vehicles must then be purchased by individuals or other organizations at a price sufficient to permit Chrysler to produce more cars. Conceptually, Chrysler's output of cars constitutes an input for the various social units that comprise key components of its suprasystem. Simply put, a need exists in the suprasystem for people to be transported from one place to another. Chrysler has responded to this opportunity with a product that satisfies this need. An interdependency is thus created between Chrysler and those who buy its products. Just as in the state hospital, Chrysler's suprasystem is defined in terms of those individuals and organizations affecting its output-input exchanges. The difference in the Chrysler example is that the output-input exchange is more direct and occurs under what is usually referred to as market place conditions—a customer chooses to buy or not to buy the car. If the car is purchased, it is at an agreed-upon price, and the proceeds are used by Chrysler as an input to satisfy its maintenance requirements as well as to purchase all of the task input requirements needed to produce its next production cycle of cars. In the case of the state hospital, the exchange of outputs for inputs is indirect and is mediated by intervening organizations such as the state mental health department and the state legislature. These actions by mediating organizations do not alter the fundamental dynamics but create what we refer to as slack in the exchange process. Among other things, this slack affects the immediacy and clarity of feedback, for example, expressions of customer satisfaction.

To continue on the input side, Chrysler is affected by the behavior of all of its suppliers, so they become vital features of its suprasystem. The banks, investment houses, and other organizations providing credit and information are important aspects of the suprasystem. Like every other organization, Chrysler must find and employ talented workers and managers. As a consequence, Chrysler has a vital interest in those organizations that educate and train these people, such as schools of business and engineering.

Like the state hospital, there are regulatory agencies and constituent groups who have a vital interest in Chrysler. In the first instance, various federal and state agencies will set standards of worker health and safety as well as standards for its cars. Various special interest groups such as unions and associations of dealerships will seek to influence Chrysler. All such organizations are conceptually a part of Chrysler's suprasystem.

The Chrysler Corporation is a useful example because it came close to bankruptcy in 1979. Significant changes occurred in its suprasystem that Chrysler apparently misread, for example, the lingering effects of the oil embargo, changes in customer preferences, governmental regulations, and so on. This is a simplification, but it illustrates the constantly changing and at times volatile nature of the suprasystem and its vital effects on every organization. In this instance, Chrysler came close to not surviving as an organization, in other words, loss of steady state.

In practice terms, the systematic attention a system gives to its suprasystem is usually referred to as **environmental scanning** or *mapping*. This effort is directed at defining the key external relationships that the system has to its suprasystem and attempting to understand and control these relationships as they pertain to output-input exchanges.

In concluding our discussion of the concept of suprasystem, we want to introduce a still larger organizing scheme. Most of us are used to thinking in terms of individuals and families; less familiar is a way of thinking that involves agencies, communities, and societies. For many, thinking in world terms seems a long way from helping individuals and families with their personal problems. We do not think so, and for two reasons. First, professional social work does involve more than working at the individual and family level. We also work at the agency, community, and societal level. Some social workers are even working at the international level.[2] Our conception of practice must be sufficiently broad to include systems that comprise from as few as two people to a concept suitable for viewing intervention at an international scale. Second, we, as well as the model, assume existence of a larger and dominating ordering process that operates at a world level. It is described in this chapter as being applicable to all levels, sizes, and types of social systems.

Earlier we mentioned that in this model the notion of environment is treated as comprising the larger contextual or setting factors. This is true whether the model is being applied to a family or to an international organization dealing with the worldwide effort to understand and control the spread of AIDS. The concepts we will introduce you to are derived from **ecology,** a branch of science dealing with a study of the interplay between organisms and their environment. It is from ecology that an ecosystem's conception of this interplay developed.

It was a botanist, A. G. Tansley, who introduced the term **ecosystem.** As with von Bertalanffy, Tansley and others associated with the development of ecological theory were dissatisfied with the ability of linear cause-and-effect theories to explain the growth and change in living organisms.[3] From its origins in botany, ecological theory has been applied to the study of all living organisms and in recent years has become important in the study of humans. Currently, ecological theory represents a major school of thought within sociology.

From the beginning, the focus of ecological theory has been on the interdependence that seems to characterize everything sharing the same habitat. Sociologists became interested in ecological theory because it offered a way of examining the effects of environment on social organization and thus an approach to the general study of social change. There has also been a growing interest in ecological theory or more particularly, an **ecological perspective,** in social work.[4]

Our approach in relating the ecological perspective to the social systems model builds particularly from the ideas advanced by such writers as Duncan and Micklin.[5] Their approaches helped us in formulating what we have described as the setting factors or influences that affect all forms and sizes of social organizations.

Simply put, the ecosystem is comprised of four classes of variables: (1) Population; (2) Organization (social); (3) Environment; and (4) Technology. The formulation is frequently referred to as the **POET model,** with the acronym being drawn from the first letter of each of the four variables. The ecosystems formulation can be applied at a world level, from examination of sociocultural evolution and the apparent worldwide interdependence of societies to microscale applications involving such social units as a neighborhood.

Figure 12.1 represents our formulation of an ecosystem as it might be applied at the highest level, our world. Each of the four variables is viewed as acting upon themselves as well as acting on and being acted upon by the other three. In a relative sense, the formulation is of a closed system. To the right of the diagram is what we call "calculated effects." By using the model, it is possible to make rough approximations of changes in the ecosystem from time A to time B. For example, a complex problem like world hunger can be simply described as too many people and not enough food. Increasing populations (P) damage or pollute the environment (E) — the same environment that is expected to produce the food supply. Technological advances (T) or governments (O) may reduce the stress on the environment through antipollution processes or legal regulations. A measure of the extent of world hunger might be considered as a measure of the quality of life on earth. A world hunger measure taken today might be then compared to another measure a year from now and used as a rough guide to changes occurring in the quality of human life. By this we mean if the second measure of world hunger showed an increase, we would treat this as an indicator of a decline in the quality of human life on earth; or if the second measure showed a reduction in hunger, this would be taken as an increase in the quality of life. With appropriate modifications for external influences, the model could be similarly applied to a nation or to a community, for example, the quality of human life in the United States or Chicago.

FIGURE 12.1 The Ecosystem: POET Model

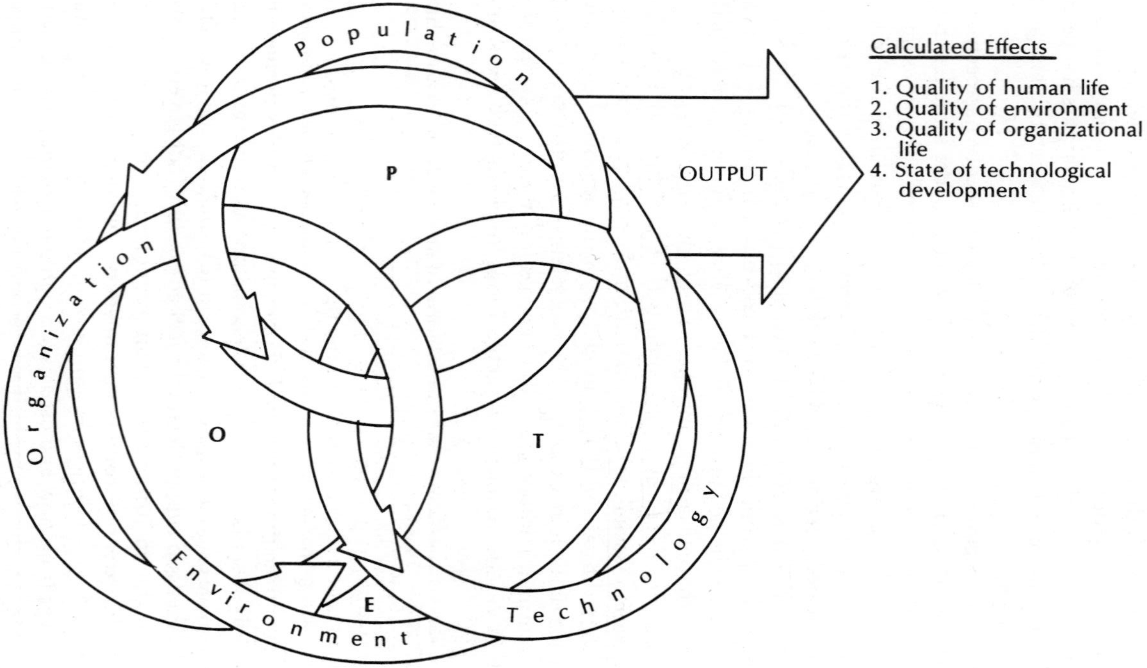

OUTPUT

Calculated Effects
1. Quality of human life
2. Quality of environment
3. Quality of organizational life
4. State of technological development

Population

Organization

Environment

Technology

P

O

T

E

For us, an ecosystems perspective offers a useful way of thinking about interdependence on a world scale. The POET model is a simple but helpful aid for thinking about matters that are incredibly complex. It is also useful in seeking a sense of the larger order to which all systems, social and physical, relate. At a more practical level, the POET model offers a way of thinking about the growing interdependence among not only the nations, but the people of the world. Seldom does a day go by that we are not reminded through the media of how events occurring halfway around the world affect us as individuals, for instance, the oil-pricing policies of Oil Producing & Export Countries (OPEC), a terrorist act, the spread of AIDS, or the dismantling of the Berlin Wall. The ecosystems formulation is simply a crude way of examining this growing interdependence. It also provides a way of thinking about how larger forces in our environments such as industrialization and urbanization continually affect our behaviors as individuals or as members of social organizations.

Consistent with the use of the systems metaphor, the ecosystems formulation stresses functional interdependence among all parts of the environment, the nonliving as well as the living. To help get across the level of interdependence suggested in an ecological perspective, data in Figure 12.2 suggest some possible relationship between two of the variables, P (Population) and T (Technology). As shown in this figure, in 5000 B.C. the world's population was estimated at less than 20 million people. By the time of Christ's birth, the population had grown to 200 million and by A.D. 1300, it had doubled to roughly 400 million. As indicated in Figure 12.2, the upward slope of the population curve between 5000 B.C. and A.D. 1300 (6,300 years) was a very gradual one. Historically, this was a time in Western Europe in which people were organized in tribes and later in extended families living under protection of feudal lords. The level of social organization was tied to the land, especially in the latter part of this period. By A.D. 1300 the world's population was being drawn somewhat closer with the advent of trade among the people of the world. Advances in technology (T) permitted construction of the great sailing ships that facilitated world trade and contributed to the growth of England into a world empire (O). Using the ecosystems model, one could diagram this simply as $T \rightarrow O$.

Since A.D. 1300 there has been a rapid upward swing in the population curve. By 1850, the world's population was estimated at 1.2 billion. In just over 500 years the world's population had tripled. More importantly, the world's population was increasing at an ever more rapid rate. Historically, we had moved from the mercantile to the industrial era. Perhaps most importantly, the Industrial Revolution occurred. Technological advances, for instance in health care, were being made along many fronts, which resulted in more people being born and living longer.

In 1987 the world's population was estimated at 5 billion and by the year 2000 it is expected to top 6 billion. To say that technology caused the rapid growth in the world's population of $T \rightarrow P$ would be a massive simplication and one based in linear reasoning. The model is cyclical and not intended to demonstrate cause-and-effect relationships. Rather, it is simply a way of examining or thinking about possible associations among these four variables. Nevertheless, and from a common sense perspective, there does seem to be some relationship between a rapidly growing technology and rapidly growing world population.

Our special interest is in modeling the effects of the environment on social organizations. Before leaving the ecosystems model, let us look at a set of relationships that

FIGURE 12.2 World Population Trends: 5000 B.C. to A.D. 2000

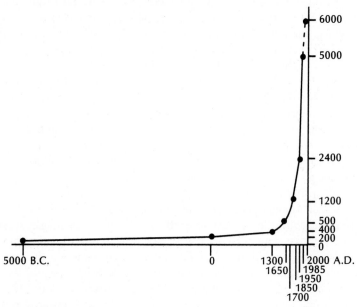

Population in millions*

All population figures are rounded and should be considered as approximations. For population estimates, see Ralph Thomlinson, *Population Dynamics: Causes and Consequences of World Demographic Change* (2nd ed.). New York: Random House, 1976, pp. 13–29.

includes the social organization OPEC. We have traced population growth through the year 2000 and have noted some possible relationships between technology and population. One can argue that an ever-growing population (P) is going to need ever larger amounts of energy required for the technology (T) used by that population, for example, fuel to drive automobiles and heat homes. A primary source of energy is a fossil fuel, oil. Oil is a natural resource, a component of our environment (E). At this point we have an interplay between P, T, and E. Or, an increasing number of people (P) are making use of an ever-growing technology (T), which depends on a natural resource, oil (E); also, someday oil will be exhausted. As it turns out, most of the world's oil reserves are located in several Middle Eastern countries, like Saudi Arabia. Recognizing the effects of the interplay of P, T, and E, these countries joined together with some other oil-rich countries to form OPEC. Here we have an example of P, T, and E acting on each other and the creation of a new organization (O) whose function appears to be one designed to exploit these effects in a manner that would benefit its membership. In short, a cartel was formed to seek control of the production, distribution, and sale of oil. Although a macroscale application, in this instance we have all been affected by OPEC—the size of the cars we drive, the costs of fuel, our general sensitivity to environmental concerns. We are not arguing that the above scenario explains the creation of OPEC; what we do propose is that the POET model offers a way of thinking about such matters in systems terms. At the largest scale, the model helps to formulate the underlying order to what we are designating as the *environment*.

Our use of the POET model is similarly useful to illustrate the forces of social change at the highest level of organization and of the growing interdependence of all components of the ecosystem. It helps to show how each year the world grows ever smaller and how events or change halfway around the world may affect us as individuals and as family members. In our social systems model, the POET formulation provides an approach for thinking about our contention of an ever-changing suprasystem and an ever-changing environment of which a specified suprasystem is but a part. The ecosystem model also provides a context for examining some of the larger contextual features of change as we concentrate on the more immediate and direct exchanges that occur between a subject system and its suprasystem.

To conclude our discussion of system-suprasystem relationships, let us again return to the example of the state hospital. Just as OPEC represents the creation of a new form of organization having its origins in the interplay of POET, so is the state hospital a dying or at least changing organizational form. In systems terms, it is losing steady state. In many parts of the country, the state hospital is a vestige of our past, having been replaced by the community mental health center. The state hospital was essentially a closed system and, as changes occurred in POET, the hospital failed to adjust and is now becoming progressively less functional.

The example of Chrysler and the other American automobile companies have been and will continue to be affected by POET. Competition is now worldwide and, because of technological and organizational factors, American auto makers are in fierce competition and are losing market share. The point we want to establish is that the POET model offers a way of examining change and social ordering on a world scale. These changes do impact throughout the system, including the family and the individuals that comprise the family as, for example, when a family member loses employment due to a plant closing.

Interface

You will recall that, conceptually, interface designates a boundary segment that one system shares with another. It is through this shared boundary and the mutually performed boundary-maintenance efforts that two systems work toward achievement of some mutually held goal. In contrast to the social group, formal organizations exhibit Gesellschaft features in the social behaviors associated with the performance of this function.

The concept of interface differentiates the various relationships that a given system maintains with other systems comprising its suprasystem. As indicated earlier, we assume that social organizations tend to deal specifically, not generally, with those individuals, groups, and agencies that comprise its social environment. Interface, then, is the explication of these specific relationships as they are manifested in the mutual performance of the boundary-maintenance function.

We have used the state mental hospital and a community mental health center as examples of formal organization. The local court has been used to illustrate the concepts of boundary and suprasystem. A specific court and a specific mental hospital can also be used to illustrate what we mean by interface. Each state has provisions for court admissions or "commitments" of seriously mentally ill patients to hospitals. The rights of the individual patient are specified in the law, as are the responsibilities of the court and hospital. In other words, the relationships of the principals are formal, not informal — Gesellschaft, not Gemeinschaft, in character. There may be informal features to these relationships, but the formal features dominate. It follows that if there is a breach or if the patient's rights are alleged to have been violated, the matter will be adjudicated based on whether the formal procedures have been followed, not on whether the informal ones were followed; the latter may, in fact, be the source of the problem or the breach of the person's rights.

Within the framework of state law, each court and the mental hospital(s) it serves are likely to jointly work out specific policies and procedures that affect how court admissions to the hospital will be handled. Interface, then, is represented by these largely formalized arrangements through which the patient passes across the boundary of the court and the boundary of the hospital and becomes a hospital patient. In summary, the court and the hospital are each vital parts of the other's suprasystem. They have a common purpose to see that the client's rights are protected and that both the court and the hospital conduct their community roles in a manner that is in the best interest of all concerned. In a given year, several hundred clients may pass from the court into the hospital. The formalized arrangements between the court and the hospital are designed to assure that each client is handled in essentially the same way. This is accomplished through mutually agreed-upon procedures, or interface.

Every formal organization has multiple interfaces. This is no more than another way of saying that every organization evolves specific arrangements for dealing with other organizations that comprise its environment. Given the open-system formulation of this model, these arrangements need to be understood in order to understand the behavior of the organization itself.

Input

The term *input* refers to all resources required from the suprasystem for the system to accomplish its purposes. Given the construction of the model, input for the subject system always represents output from other systems comprising its suprasystem; as indicated previously, this input-output exchange helps define the mutually interdependent state existing between a system and its suprasystem. Conceptually, every system has some specialized means for screening inputs so that their relevance to system purposes is established. This screening has previously been described as associated with the boundary-maintenance function.

Inputs are classified as either signal or maintenance. Signal inputs are always clients in human service agencies, though not necessarily so in other organizations. *Signal* is a generic term and simply means that the presence of such inputs activates (serves as a signal to) the subject system. As used in this model, *signal inputs, task inputs,* and *through-*

puts are synonymous terms. Each is used to identify and distinguish those forms of input that are processed by the system as opposed to those that are employed in processing, that is, maintenance inputs. An example of a signal input would be a customer entering a restaurant. This person activates the system, that is, he or she is cordially greeted by the restaurant's hostess, escorted to a seat, presented with a menu, and so on. In other words, the person is identified as a customer, passes through the boundary and is dealt with by the restaurant's staff through prescribed behaviors designed to satisfy the customer's need for food, drink, social contact, and so on. The intention is that the customer will pass through the system (throughput), have all his or her relevant needs satisfied, and then leave the restaurant as a satisfied customer (task output).

Inputs are always defined as such by the function performed by the subject system—a restaurant serves food and drink; those needing food and drink represent potential signal inputs. They become signal inputs only after they pass through the system's boundary and activate its conversion operations.

Maintenance inputs are also always acquired from the suprasystem; they represent the resources needed to process signal inputs and generally to maintain the system. In the restaurant example, maintenance inputs would represent everything required to produce satisfied customers—space, time, staff, foods, drinks, recipes, and so on. Maintenance inputs also include everything needed to sustain and develop the system itself, that is, new knowledge, skills, new products, and particularly money. While signal inputs in human service agencies are always people (clients), maintenance inputs will appear in three forms: (1) human resources, the helpers in professional and staff roles; (2) physical resources, including money and credit; and (3) nonphysical resources—culture, time, and specialized forms of information. Also in a conceptual sense, signal inputs always leave the system in some processed form, for example, a satisfied customer. At a conceptual level, maintenance inputs do not leave the system, at least as task outputs; they are utilized or consumed in some fashion during the system's conversion phase. In other words, maintenance inputs are combined with signal inputs in a predetermined way to accomplish the task output. More will be said about the disposition of maintenance inputs in subsequent sections of the chapter.

The state hospital is again used as an example in conceptualizing input. As a formal organization, it came into existence as a means of dealing with the problem of mental illness and in response to those requiring help in dealing with their mental state. As a formal organization, it is a contrived social tool having its justification and existence tied to a problem or state of need evident in people in the suprasystem. In fact, the particular organizational form the hospital takes, along with its approach to treatment, is affected by the definition of the problem or need existing in the suprasystem, that is, it is culturally defined. As this definition of the problem and the need changes, so will the organizational form taken by the hospital, for example, the conversion of many so-called state hospitals to comprehensive community mental health centers. As these definitions change, so does the composition of signal inputs.

Signal inputs for the hospital are people classified as being mentally ill, or at least possessing personal difficulties that suggest a mental problem of an order requiring further specification. In the latter instance, the court may authorize the patient be held in the hospital for a specified period for observation and determination of subsequent actions. In any event, the patient represents signal input to the hospital and assumes the role of patient and all that may mean vis-à-vis those other roles that comprise the hospital as a social system.

Maintenance inputs to the state hospital include all resources to help the client and to maintain and develop the hospital as an organization. Its human resources include all of the mental health professionals, support, and administrative staffs along with others who directly help the hospital achieve its purposes. In any given input cycle, for example, the fiscal year, only a few new staff members are likely to be hired. Physical and fiscal resources are necessary to both attract new as well as retain existing staffs. For most purposes, money is the medium for obtaining maintenance inputs. Just as in the case of staff (money is used to hire new as well as to retain existing staff), so is money required to sustain a vast variety of other continuing requirements of the hospital. The point is that the concept of maintenance inputs pertains to all resources needed to sustain the system in a given cycle of activity. In other words, the term is not confined to new resources.

In addition to personnel and physical forms of maintenance inputs, the hospital needs and receives other nonphysical forms of input. The hospital develops, over a period of time, its own culture. This culture is derived from the society of which it is a part. Conceptually, this hospital developed its own culture by selectively taking as inputs aspects of its societal culture. Features of culture in the hospital secured as inputs are those shared meanings that guide social behavior generally in society. For example, all of the general roles played by those comprising the hospital's social system have their origins in similar societal roles. Thus, the role of mental patient is derived from society; the more specific feature of this role, vis-à-vis other roles in this particular hospital, is developed internally and is part of this state hospital's subculture.

Other nonphysical forms of input include time and information. For example, the court frequently specifies how much time a patient must remain in the hospital under a particular form of admission, perhaps ninety days or six months. The time is given to the hospital in order to achieve a specified output. Here time is treated as an input and later will be used in some specified way as a structural feature of the system's conversion operations.

Information comes in many forms and is used in various ways as inputs. In this model, information generated from the system's last organizational cycle pertaining to outputs is called *feedback* and is treated as a key form of maintenance input. The concept of feedback as applied to formal organizations will be further developed later. It is sufficient to say, at this point, that the hospital has both formal and informal means for ascertaining how successful it has been in achieving its goals (proposed output). This information, which is gathered internally and externally, is fed back into the system and treated as a maintenance input. Feedback, as indicated earlier, is the primary means employed in this model for maintaining steady state.

Other forms of information will be obtained by the hospital and treated as input. In this example, it is assumed that the hospital has a small planning staff. This group of people is constantly scanning and mapping the hospital's suprasystem. In so doing, they are obtaining and processing information that might help the hospital better serve its patients as well as simply helping the hospital to maintain itself as a viable organization.

Output

We will develop the concept of output prior to discussion of the system's conversion operations. This arrangement of content derives from the fact that the model is organized around output. In short, an understanding of a system's conversion operations is pursued by examining what the organization actually does (output) and then comparing this with what the organization purports to do (proposed output). This approach has particular utility when applied to formal organizations, since some specification of function is contained in the definition of such organizations—"a type of social organization deliberately and formally created to achieve relatively specific and delimited goals."

The notion of output is based on the previously noted assumption undergirding the systems perspective, namely, that all forms of social organization are functionally related to the environment in which they exist. Incorporating this assumption, a system's continued existence is to be understood in terms of how well it performs its function vis-à-vis consuming units in its environment, and how well those constituting the subject social system have their needs satisfied. These two need categories give rise to two forms of outputs, task and maintenance. Task outputs are processed signal (task) inputs and represent the system's reason for existence. Maintenance outputs are processed maintenance inputs; their processed form is a consequence of their involvement in the production of task outputs. The notion of maintenance outputs has been developed in this model in order to recognize the effects of system activities on maintenance inputs, that is, on the system itself. Simply put, just as clients are affected by system activities, so are their helpers. The concept of maintenance output refers to the status of maintenance inputs at the end of a specified organizational cycle, for example, the end of a budget period.

The final form of outcome addressed in this section is referred to as waste. It is a designation of negative or inappropriate outcomes, wasted inputs. Conceptually, the intent is to capture and account for all system outputs. Utilizing the notion of efficiency, the ratio of maintenance inputs to task outputs becomes a definition of **efficiency**. Assuming an organizational standard, a negative deviation from this standard would, in this model, be treated as a measure of waste (an efficiency level not conforming to agency standards). A definition of **effectiveness** becomes the ratio that task outputs have to proposed task outputs. Since professional standards of effectiveness are in an early stage of development, most agencies evolve their own standards, for example, last year's performance. An example in the area of child protective services is the proportion of perpetrators who commit a subsequent act of abuse to the total number of perpetrators seen during a specified period. Given this situation, an agency's task objective for the next year might be to reduce the recurrence of abuse by known perpetrators by 10 percent over the previous year's experience. If the actual reduction turned out to be 5 percent, then the difference between the actual output of 5 percent and the proposed output of 10 percent would be considered waste. In other words, the agency did not perform as effectively as it had intended. The notion of waste should be thought of as the means for identifying and systematically collecting helpful information to be used to improve agency services in the future.

Technically, waste becomes a measure or statement of negative feedback returned to the system as a maintenance input. The purpose of this form of input is to provide information necessary to take corrective actions during the system's next cycle of activity. The notions of efficiency and effectiveness can be combined into a performance measure that attempts to optimize both. An assumption is made that a relationship exists between efficiency and effectiveness, and that some trade-offs are necessary in order that both standards be optimized. Assuming no change in maintenance inputs, the higher the caseload of a child-welfare worker, the lower the dollar cost is for servicing each case (efficiency). But beyond a point the quality of work is assumed to diminish as a consequence of the increased size of caseload (reduced effectiveness). From an output perspective, what is sought is a level at which both efficiency and effectiveness standards are optimized. This approach to the measurement of performance is sometimes referred to as **cost-benefit** or **cost-effectiveness analysis**. From a conceptual perspective it is useful to assume that it is possible to optimize output from both efficiency and effectiveness standards; waste then becomes the negative deviation from this optimum point. In the human service field, much has yet to be learned about how to help people most effectively and with the most efficient use of scarce resources. Given this situation, the notion of waste, while helpful, must be used with great caution.

In the previous paragraphs, an overview was provided of the three forms of organizational output: task, maintenance, and waste. Attention is now given to a more detailed discussion of task and maintenance outputs.

Conceptually, task outputs in human service agencies providing direct services always refer to the condition of clients following a specified cycle of organizational activity. In most instances, this refers to the condition of the client at the time of discharge from the agency. Typically, the client's status at discharge (output) is described in terms of the conditions that resulted in the person coming to the agency in the first place. This statement is provided by the professional helper and is usually set forth in terms of the mutually agreed-upon goals of the intervention effort (proposed output). For example, a discharge summary might read: "Mr. Smith came to the agency addicted to drugs. He has been drug-free for six months; this fulfills the terms of our treatment contract, so the case is closed." The worker might then check a box on the agency's discharge summary sheet dealing with successful closures: "Goal achieved; no further services indicated." Examples of unsuccessful closures might be "Client terminated services; condition unchanged," or "Client failed to return; condition unknown." Just as the condition at discharge for an individual client represents a system's output for a clinical application of the model, so would the conditions of all clients of an agency discharged during an organizational cycle, for example, those discharged during the previous month or fiscal year. Here an example might be: "During the past year intervention goals were achieved in 68 percent of the cases, in 22 percent of the cases goals were not achieved, and in 10 percent of the cases clients did not follow through with their proposed treatment plan."

Typically, the concept of task output is applied to clients who have been discharged from the agency following a period of treatment. This need not be the case. The concept of output is applied to ascertain results, both good and bad, following completion of a processing cycle by the organization. For example, some clients stay in an agency for many years and in some instances for the remainder of their lives, such as in a state hospital or a nursing home. Given such situations, it becomes important from time to time to obtain measures of client progress, or lack thereof, presented in output terms. Usually such statements are formulated as goals or proposed output to be achieved during some specified reporting period, such as a yearly budget period or completion of a particular program. An example at the clinical level would be a client who is mentally retarded but possesses potential for relatively independent living through employment in a sheltered workshop. A statement of proposed output might be "John H. will complete our job readiness program for Level B work activities and will earn, as a workshop employee, $45 per week by June 30." Here, output would be John's actual weekly earnings as of June 30 even though John will be continuing as a workshop client. Again, at the organizational level, output would be the achievements (or lack thereof) of all such clients as of June 30. In such an instance, the output might be summarized as follows: "Seventy percent of all clients who entered the job readiness program successfully completed Level B preparation, and by June 30 were earning an average week's wage of $45." This output would then be compared with what had been stated as proposed output to determine the relative success of the agency during the specified organizational cycle. Thus, if the proposed output had been 70 percent, actual output would have been right on target; if the goal had been 80 percent, the target would not have been achieved. In the latter instance, the difference between the 80 and 70 percent would be an indication of waste and treated as negative feedback.

Recall that maintenance outputs are the effects on the social system associated with the production of task outputs. For example, levels of job satisfaction and burnout would, in this model, both represent maintenance outputs—one a positive, the other a negative outcome (waste). The notion of maintenance outputs is simply the means employed in this model to recognize the interactive effects of the work situation on the system itself. Organizational accounting practices recognize these effects by assigning worth to the agency's physical assets and then regularly adjusting these values based on some schedule. An example would be a depreciation schedule that specifies yearly the value of the agency's building and its other physical assets, such as cars and other equipment. The value of an agency's physical assets at the end of a budget year or some other designated organizational cycle would represent a part of that agency's maintenance outcome. These physical assets are usually converted into their dollar worth, so that year-by-year comparisons can be made. These comparisons become feedback and are treated as inputs for the next organizational cycle. The social systems model utilizes this same reasoning but extends its application to the organization's social assets as well, its employees and others who comprise the social system. We are aware that most formal organizations do not usually submit statements of the worth of their human/social assets. The point is that the model recognizes that such values exist and that they are constantly changing. While accounting practices have not as yet been fully developed to systematically assign values and otherwise record these changes, the model user needs to be sensitive to the changing social worth of the system being addressed.

The writings from those associated with the human relations perspective provide part of the theoretical foundations for highlighting the human dimensions in formulating maintenance outcomes.[6] Quite simply, workers have needs as do clients; and the organization will inevitably affect these needs either positively or negatively and vice versa. In operationalizing the concept of maintenance outcomes, the assumption is made that every system produces maintenance outcomes. Actual maintenance outcomes are then stated in terms of what had been proposed.

We present some examples to develop the notion. In introducing the examples, it should be noted that maintenance outcomes do not usually leave the system. Conceptually this is not a problem because, as used here, the term *outcome* pertains to the status of a maintenance input after a specified cycle of organizational activity. In other words, the concept of maintenance output is merely a convenient designation given to the tracking of selected maintenance inputs (for example, staff) through the system. The notion of maintenance outcomes is used to compare the status of maintenance inputs to a subsequent status. For example, in what ways are staff different after a year (or two or three) of experience? In most instances, the assumption would be that they are more capable in dealing with their clients and thus more valuable to the agency. The concept of a maintenance output is no more than a recognition and specification of this change in status.

At an organizational level, one of the most frequently used statements of a maintenance outcome is an agency's staff turnover rate. This rate is compiled by comparing the number of employees who voluntarily leave the agency during the year with the average number of people employed by the agency in the same period. Simply put, if an agency had 100 employees at the start of the year and 50 people quit during the year and were replaced, it would have a 50 percent turnover rate. The assumption is generally made that the turnover rate is a rough measure of how satisfying a job is or how workers feel about their agency.[7] Thus, a high turnover rate is generally considered bad, and a low one, good. This greatly simplifies the matter, because a low turnover rate may be a measure of general economic conditions in a community and the lack of alternative employment as opposed to the measure of job satisfaction. This distinction is not important at this point. The assumption being made is that the turnover rate can be a very useful global measure of organizational health and can be treated as a maintenance outcome.

To develop the example, let us assume that the subject organization set a maintenance goal of reducing its turnover rate for the coming year from 50 to 35 percent. At the end of the year, the rate was determined to be 40 percent; that figure represents a maintenance output. The assumption is made that a connection exists between that figure and the myriad of organizational experiences that workers had in that agency last year. The assumption is also made that certain organizational actions took place during the course of the year that were aimed at reducing the turnover rate. In this instance, those actions did not fully meet the goal (perhaps wages were considered a factor contributing to job turnover and so an increase in wages was granted). For whatever reason the goal was not reached, so the difference between the goal (35 percent) and actual performance (40 percent) would be considered waste (5 percent). This negative outcome is treated as negative feedback and as such flows back into the system as a maintenance input for further assessment and corrective action. In this example, we are not arguing that the goal of reducing the turnover rate from 50 to 35 percent was realistic; it may not have been. The point is that the goal represented a professional judgment by management as to what could be accomplished. It was not accomplished, and this information is fed back into the system to determine what, if anything, should be done in the next cycle.

Organizationally speaking, the assumption is that workers should become increasingly more valuable as they gain experience and skill at what they do. Conceptually, and consistent with the principle of negative entropy, an organization's human resources should appreciate in value over time rather than depreciate as is usually the case with many physical resources. The model incorporates this assumption by providing for the specification of maintenance outcomes. By calling attention to what is considered a natural consequence of experience, the intent is to focus on the development of those experiences that are most likely to be challenging to the worker as well as helpful to the organization.

Another example of a maintenance outcome would be the number of workers in the agency who, by the end of the year, complete the requisite hours of professional supervision and pass a licensing examination. The goal might read: "Our goal is to have 75 percent of the agency's noncertified social work staff pass the state social work licensure examination by the end of this year." The actual percentage of staff passing the examination would represent actual output. This is an example of a maintenance output because it contains the assumption that the agency's general capacity for serving clients is enhanced through the professional certification of additional members of its staff. The percentage is considered an outcome measure because it certifies an achievement level to be accomplished at the end of an organizational cycle.

The final example of a maintenance outcome involves physical resources. The maintenance goal might have been for the agency to acquire during the next year additional space so that workers could have private offices as opposed to being located in a bull pen area. The actual maintenance outcome would be the office arrangements of these workers at year's end. It is a maintenance outcome in the sense that it was deemed to strengthen the system's capacity to professionally serve clients. In this instance, the direct beneficiary is the system; the assumption made is that the change helps meet the worker's need for professional recognition as well as provides the level of privacy required in professional work with clients.

The notion of maintenance outcomes has been stressed in the preceding paragraphs. Our intention here is to highlight an important aspect of organizational behavior—the effects that the organization has on itself; most particularly, we want to call your attention to the effects that the organization has on the people who comprise it. In Chapter 2, "A Social Systems Perspective," we set forth an assumption that read: "When fully developed, all forms of social organization display self-maintaining and development characteristics." Our use of the concept of maintenance outputs is one of the ways we seek to operationalize this idea. In a related sense, our use of maintenance outcomes is also intended to help operationalize the concept of negative entropy, that is, the propensity of systems toward growth and development. We will develop these ideas further in the next section, Proposed Output.

Proposed Output

The concept of proposed output was utilized in the previous section. Given the general discussion of this concept in both Parts I and II, we trust that the reader understands the notion and appreciates the difficulty of discussing output in this model without mentioning what had been proposed as output.

The presentation of the concept focuses on its particular application in the modeling of formal organizations. The importance of proposed output is highlighted in the definition of a formal organization: "A form of social organization deliberately and formally created to achieve relatively specific and delimited goals." In essence, this type of organization is a consciously created means to achieve a formally stated end. Delimited goals are the intended end states and are synonymous with our use of proposed output.

Our approach to the formulation of proposed output builds from and extends the reasoning set forth in Chapter 3. There the notion of a hierarchy of outcomes was introduced as the means to formulate proposed output. In short, the approach represents a way of operationalizing the key features of the definition of a formal organization: "formally created to achieve relatively specific and delimited goals." Before proceeding with these ideas, we reiterate that while such organizations may have formally stated goals, it does not follow that organizations do not also have unwritten and informal goals; nor does it follow that the formally stated goals are the more important of the two. Further, we are aware that some formal organizations go through the motions of formulating goals and objectives and then promptly ignore them. The point is that in this model, proposed output merely establishes an anchoring point to help understand how an organization behaves. Simply put, we start our application of the model by determining what an organization formally identifies as its goals. We then seek to establish what, in fact, it did accomplish during a specific organizational period, for example, the past month or year. Once determined, the results are then compared to what had been proposed. With these two reference points, we seek to understand how the actual results were achieved. In doing so we maintain as a point of orientation what the organization had said it was going to do and how it was going to do it. The differences between proposed and actual outputs are typically revealing and provide insights to the actual behavior of the organization.

The notion of a hierarchy of outcomes also has useful practice implications. With this in mind, we will again present the approach, but with an application to a formal organization, our hypothetical Midtown Mental Health Center.

The essential ideas of the hierarchy are set forth in Figure 12.3, The figure embodies the concept that every formal organization has its origins in some existing need or opportunity within the suprasystem and that the continued existence of the system depends on some degree of satisfaction of these needs. In this presentation, the problem is one of adverse conditions within the community of Midtown that are negatively affecting the quality of life and the mental health of its citizens. As indicated in the section of the diagram designated "Problem," it has been determined that, among others, a disproportionate number of the community's poor and minority group members are mentally ill. Here an assumption is made that an assessment of community needs has been done and that this is one of the conclusions reached. The desired outcome of this helping process is an improvement in the overall mental health of all community members, but with special attention to the problems of the poor and minority group members. Again, an assumption is made that an assessment has been made, and that the barriers and deficits have been identified and goals have been formed representing the desired outcomes. In this presentation, the social system is our hypothetical Midtown Mental Health Center. In short, the agency is being modeled as a social system, and its mission is to improve the quality of life for the citizens of Midtown. The system is contrived in the sense that it draws its sanction from community needs, and the agency is a "social tool" created and supported by the community in order to help its citizens live a fuller quality of life. The agency's signal inputs are the citizens of its **catchment area** (the area served by the agency), who are in need of mental health services. Its intended task outputs are an improved quality of life for those clients who have made use of the center's services.

Section II of Figure 12.3 diagrams the concept of a hierarchy of outcomes as was done in Chapter 3. Section III provides examples of task outputs for each level of the hierarchy. Its mission is "To improve the quality of life of the residents of the Midtown catchment area through the provision of comprehensive and quality mental health services." Conceptually, the second or goal level of the hierarchy is formed by framing the mission statement as a question: "How can this center improve the quality of life of Midtown's citizens through the provision of comprehensive and quality mental health services?" The answer to this question represents an operationalization of the mission statement and suggests areas of priority consistent with the community's needs and resources, and the agency's capabilities.

In this example three goals have been identified. Goal 1 has been further developed to illustrate the notion of a hierarchy of outcomes. Using the same technique as in the mission statement, the goal is converted into a question: "How can this center reduce the incidence and prevalence of mental health problems among the residents of its catchment area?" The third or objective level indicates that the agency has adopted, under Goal 1, three objectives for the coming year. While not shown, the same process would be used for each of the other goals. As suggested by the definition of an objective, these objectives are specific, attainable, appropriate, measurable, and are to be accomplished by a certain date. Completing the hierarchy is specification of the activities to be performed in order to accomplish these objectives. For purposes of an example, we have taken the first objective and operationalized it by converting it into a question: "How can this center reduce the incidence of mental illness requiring inpatient care from 18 cases per 1,000 population to 15 per 1,000 population by December 31, 19__?" The answer provided in this example represents the planned activities to be engaged in by the center's staff, or in other words, the specific programs and services to be offered that should result in reduction in the numbers of new cases being admitted into the center's inpatient service. Obviously, the question is very complex and technical, the kind of question that only a professionally qualified and experienced staff could answer. The answer also represents a priority statement as to what services the agency will provide during the coming year.

Note that a qualitative break occurs in the hierarchy between statements of objectives and activities. The system's purpose, goals, and objectives all pertain to future end states or outcomes; activities, on the other hand, pertain to the proposed means selected by the agency for achieving those ends. For many, the distinction between outcomes and the means for achieving the outcomes is difficult to grasp. In our illustration, promoting programs of early detection of mental health problems assumes that by detecting these problems early, it may be possible to help some of these people without placing them in the hospital itself, for example, by keeping them on an outpatient basis. The early detection program is thus a means; the end state is a reduced number of people requiring

FIGURE 12.3 Proposed Output as a Hierarchy of Outcomes: The Formal Organization

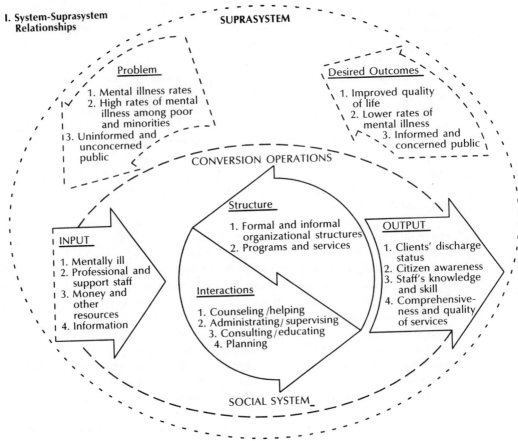

I. System-Suprasystem Relationships

SUPRASYSTEM

Problem
1. Mental illness rates
2. High rates of mental illness among poor and minorities
3. Uninformed and unconcerned public

Desired Outcomes
1. Improved quality of life
2. Lower rates of mental illness
3. Informed and concerned public

CONVERSION OPERATIONS

Structure
1. Formal and informal organizational structures
2. Programs and services

INPUT
1. Mentally ill
2. Professional and support staff
3. Money and other resources
4. Information

Interactions
1. Counseling /helping
2. Administrating/ supervising
3. Consulting /educating
4. Planning

OUTPUT
1. Clients' discharge status
2. Citizen awareness
3. Staff's knowledge and skill
4. Comprehensiveness and quality of services

SOCIAL SYSTEM

II. Proposed Output as a Hierarchy of Outcomes

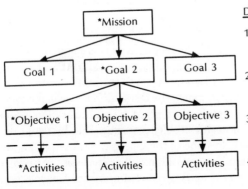

Definitions:

1. Mission: A broad philosophical and inspirational statement of intended output which guides all practice activities.

2. Goals: Long-range qualitative statements of intent pertaining to a component or aspect of the mission statement.

3. Objectives: Statements of intended accomplishments that are specific, attainable, appropriate, and measurable.

4. Activities: A program or plan of (professional) services directed toward accomplishment of each objective.

III. TASK OUTPUTS

MISSION: To improve the quality of life of the residents of the Midtown catchment area through the provision of comprehensive and quality mental health services.

GOAL 1. To reduce the incidence and prevalence of mental health problems among catchment area residents.

GOAL 2. To increase the level of personal self-sufficiency of the chronically mentally ill in order that they may increase their ability to function in the least restrictive environment.

GOAL 3. To increase citizen knowledge, sensitivity and commitment to an improvement in the mental health of all citizens.

OBJECTIVE 1 (Goal 1). To reduce the incidence of mental illness among catchment area residents requiring inpatient care from 18 cases per thousand population to 15 per thousand by December 31, 19 __ (date specific).

OBJECTIVE 2 (Goal 1). To reduce the readmission rate for inpatient services among the poor from 56 per 100 readmissions to 45 per 100 readmissions by December 31, 19 __ (date specific).

OBJECTIVE 3 (Goal 1). To reduce the readmission rate for inpatient services among minority group members from 37 per 100 readmissions to 30 per 100 readmissions by December 31, 19 __ (date specific).

ACTIVITIES:

(OBJECTIVE 1). Effective January 1, 19 __ to initiate programs of early detection of mental health problems through educational programs directed toward physicians, clergy, social workers, and teachers.

(OBJECTIVE 1). Effective January 1, 19 __ to increase staffing in that the center can provide on-site twenty-four-hour-a-day emergency services.

(OBJECTIVE 1). Effective January 1, 19 __ to expand the center's outpatient department by adding an aftercare unit that will provide case management services to special needs clients.

IV. MAINTENANCE OUTPUTS

MISSION: To improve the quality of life to the residents of the Midtown catchment area through the provision of comprehensive and quality mental health services.

GOAL 1. To develop and maintain a professional staff dedicated to provision of quality mental health services.

GOAL 2. To develop a comprehensive range of quality mental health services.

GOAL 3. Through programs of research, to increase the quality, efficiency, and effectiveness of the center's mental health services.

OBJECTIVE 1 (Goal 1). To increase from 70 to 80 percent the proportion of the center's current professional staff holding terminal degrees in their respective disciplines by December 31, 19 __ (date specific).

OBJECTIVE 2 (Goal 1). To employ twenty-five additional professional staff members who possess terminal degrees in their respective disciplines by December 31, 19 __ (date specific).

OBJECTIVE 3 (Goal 1). To reduce the job turnover rate among the center's professional staff from 26 percent to 20 percent by December 31, 19 __ (date specific).

ACTIVITY 1 (Objective 1). Effective January 1, 19 __ to·adopt a tuition reimbursement program for all Center staff willing to obtain a terminal degree in their discipline.

ACTIVITY 2 (Objective 1). Effective January 1, 19 __ to grant twenty days of professional leave per year to all Center staff able to complete requirements for a terminal degree in their respective discipline on a part-time basis.

ACTIVITY 3 (Objective 1). Effective January 1, 19 __ to grant one year of professional leave with one-half pay for the Center's staff working to complete terminal degree requirements in their respective discipline.

inpatient care. The assumption is that people who can be helped in a less intensive form of care enjoy a higher quality of life than those who must undergo more intense forms of treatment for their problems.

The examples provided in Section III were of task outcomes. Maintenance outputs are illustrated in Section IV. Here our focus in the mission statement changes from its "ends" dimension—the improvement of the quality of life of the residents of the Midtown catchment area—to the "means" to be employed, that is, the provision of comprehensive and quality mental health services. Now our effort is to operationalize what we mean by "comprehensive" and "quality" as they are used in this mission statement. Our approach is reviewed under Task Outputs. The question becomes: "What kind of comprehensive programs are needed and what levels of quality are required to improve the quality of life of the residents of our catchment area?"

Three goal statements have been formed in answer to our quality question. The first goal focuses on the center's professional staff, and it has been used as the example for development of three objective statements. Finally, Objective 1 has been used to identify the various means selected to accomplish this objective.

We have in this section discussed the concept of proposed output and how it is operationalized through use of a technique we call a hierarchy of outcomes. Proposed output provides the functional orientation to the system, that is, it serves to specify, in advance, system-suprasystem relationships. Also to be noted is the wholeness that is embodied in the formulation. The totality of intentions and the means to accomplish those intentions form an interdependent whole, itself a system. In effect, what is created is an "idealized whole" or system that then serves as a comparison with the "actual whole" or system. By actual whole we mean the actual results achieved and the actual behaviors engaged in that produced those results. We will further discuss this matter in the final two sections of this chapter.

Conversion Operations

The three preceding sections have dealt with the concepts of inputs, outputs, and proposed outputs. The discussion to follow addresses, in systems terms, the means by which inputs are converted to outputs. The focus of this content will be on those processes that dominate this transformation in formal organizations. Recognizing that a social systems model is a conceptual scheme, a useful place to start a discussion of conversion operations is with a question: What is the controlling (dominating) variable for explaining an organization's arrangements for transforming its inputs to outputs? The answer has been alluded to previously—the organization's actual output.

Structure follows function; therefore, the first step in seeking to understand conversion operations is to determine its outputs, that is, what the organization actually produces. Given the formal nature of the subject organization, the second step as mentioned earlier is to establish what the organization formally intended to do. Third, with actual and proposed outputs as reference points, retrace from output to input the conversion process itself. Conceptually this is a functional view of the conversion operations; it represents a systematic explication of the means employed to achieve the organization's results during a specified cycle.

The model is of an open system, one that is always influencing and being influenced by forces in the suprasystem. In other words, the conversion process is continually being affected by inputs from the suprasystem, and similarly, the conversion process always involves actions to influence selected aspects of the suprasystem. To put the matter in another context, the conversion operation should not be thought of as being like a room with two doors, one through which inputs enter with the door closing, followed by a period of conversion activities taking place without outside influences, with the processed inputs achieving output status by leaving through the second door. A better analogy would be a baseball game, complete with fans, cheerleaders, umpires, and so on. The structural features of the conversion operations would include the game rules, roles of the various players, the batting roster, overall game plan, and the layout of the baseball field. Game play (interactions) would be influenced by the preceding structural features and the personalities of the individuals enacting their respective roles. In addition, game play would be affected by the fans, cheerleaders, the weather, and a host of other suprasystem influences. In addition, the players and their managers could be expected to attempt to influence the suprasystem and its effects on the game, for example, protesting an umpire's call or inciting the fans to cheer.

A clinical example might also help to convey the implications of an open systems view of the conversion process. In short, the actual outcome would be the condition of the client at the conclusion of the therapeutic process in relation to the person's condition at the time of entry. Reference would be made to the goals of the therapeutic process and an excursion would then be made back through the treatment process in an attempt to explain its outcome. In so doing, the conversion operations would be explained. Given the open systems formulation, the excursion back through the therapeutic process would not be exclusively concerned with what took place between the therapist and client, for example, diagnoses, theory of intervention, treatment plan, number of interviews, experience of therapist, characteristics of client, and so on. Rather, attention also would be given to the hosts of suprasystem influences—work experiences and relationships with friends and family, among others. In addition, attention to suprasystem influences would not be confined only to those affecting the client, but the therapist as well—in other words, on environmental effects on the helping system itself.

This clinical example can be extended to the clinical unit of the mental health center. Again, the same basic approach would be used, but applied to all patients treated during a specific organizational cycle, for instance, during the last calendar year. As a starting place, attention would be given to proposed output and to actual output (in this example, rates of readmission). With this information as a reference point the variety of internal and external influences would be examined as the means of explaining actual output.

There is one other cautionary note that pertains to addressing a systems model for conceptualizing its conversion operations. Just as causality should not be sought in closed systems terms, causality should not be pursued through linear-based reasoning, that is, similar end states being derived from similar processing steps and similar initial conditions. As you will recall, Bertalanffy's concept of equifinality is helpful in dealing with this.[8] In essence this concept holds that final states may be reached in different ways and from different initial conditions. The concept is helpful in recognizing the distinctive features of social organizations when modeled as social systems, particularly their open system characteristics. The concept of equifinality is also useful in understanding the criticism of the rationalist perspective and its linear-based scientific thinking that suggested pursuit of a perfect means-end set of organizational relationships; the one best way of designing and managing a formal organization.

With these cautionary notes in mind, the model presented is organized around outcome: both what the organization anticipated it would accomplish and what actually was accomplished. As in previous applications, the conversion operation is comprised of structure and interactions. These two features are like two sides of a coin. Each side has distinctive characteristics but the two comprise a whole. The dynamic relationship between structure and interactions also needs to be understood—each acts on the other in a circular fashion. The notion of structure represents, in part, a set of normative role expectations of how all of those people comprising the social system will interact, one with another; interactions are the *actual* behaviors that take place. Here personality, situational, specific organizational, and related suprasystem factors are added to the mix and become variables that help account for the interactions that take place. *Interactions* refers to the actual behavior of the people playing organizational roles. Based on the dynamic and open qualities of social systems, the assumption is made that normative expectations and actual behaviors are never quite the same. Normative expectations are historically based and are constantly affected by current and anticipated events. Attention to this process is also helpful in understanding the dynamic nature of social systems. Through role enactment, the role is constantly being altered, which in turn affects future role expectations, and so on.

Structure

We made the point earlier that social structures have no physical existence—that structure is only discerned by examining social interactions. It is the relatively stable and ongoing nature of this social behavior that constitutes evidence of structure. The role is the fundamental building block in conceptualizing structure in a social system. Simply put, social systems are systems of roles. The distinctiveness of structure in formal organizations stems from the formal and legal foundations of these roles. Because of these formalized features, the concept of structure is somewhat more easily understood when applied to formal as opposed to other forms of social organization.

Given the importance of the concept of role in the formulation of structure, a brief review would probably be helpful. A role as used in this model will always have three distinguishing features: (1) it will always represent a location in the social system; (2) it will be comprised of a more or less integrated set of behavioral expectations (norms) and; (3) the behavioral expectations will represent a specialized aspect of an ongoing functional process.[9] A role is always to be understood as representing one position in a social system comprised of two or more positions. The behavioral expectations are always held toward the occupant of the counter role(s) as well as to oneself, and they are always mutual. In short, the functional process can only be accomplished by each role encumbent carrying out his or her respective role in a prescribed way. A *relationship* is a key notion in the field of human services. As used here, a relationship is a mutually held and stable set of behavioral expectations associated with a specified functional process.

An example of the role features described above would be the relationship between a caseworker and her or his supervisor. These two roles can be found on an organizational chart of the agency—the location feature. Each role is comprised of a more or less integrated set of behavioral expectations—the worker understands that she or he is to submit for review selected aspects of work. The supervisor is to conscientiously review the submitted material and share her or his judgment with the worker as to whether it meets agency standards. Both roles can be understood as comprising two aspects of the same functional process—supervision, the administrative process of determining whether the work performed meets agency standards.

At a more fundamental level, the question arises as to the derivation of the mutual sets of behavioral expectations that comprise functionally interdependent roles. A general answer would be that the roles are derived from the function to be performed; they are shaped by cultural values and evolve informally and historically largely through trial and error methods. Roles take on their more distinctive features in specific forms of social organizations and in specific sets of circumstances. In the paragraphs ahead attention will be given to the distinctive attributes of formal organizations and how these attributes impact on the development and modification of organizational roles.

The social systems model views organizational roles as having three major determinants: (1) contextual, (2) formal, and (3) informal. It is the second of these, the formal, that largely accounts for the distinctive features of formal organizations.

Contextual

The contextual features of social structure include, among others, culture, time, space, and physical structures. It is these contextual qualities that continually affect and shape all forms of social structure and, in so doing, social interactions. By culture, we mean the totality of meanings shared by people in the same society. Given the open systems nature of the model, the assumption is made that the organization's culture is constantly changing, based in part on the changing nature of societal culture. An example here would be the changing gender roles in our society and their impact on work roles. Traditionally in human service agencies the caseworker role has been seen as possessing features of empathy, caring, and acceptance—characteristics of the traditional nurturing role held by women. In contrast, the administrative role in such agencies has been viewed as one requiring skills and behavior associated with the male role—decisiveness, objectivity, and aggressiveness. Now, as the cultural definitions of gender roles have changed, so have the work role definitions.

Time, space and location will always represent important influences on how roles are shaped and carried out. They are contextual in the sense that all social behavior has time and space dimensions. Neither time nor space should be viewed as essentially passive or neutral in terms of how they affect social behavior. Using the caseworker-supervisor example again, assume that because of agency cutbacks and increased demands for service, the supervisor has had to assign twice the number of clients to the worker as has normally been the standard. Given an unchanged eight-hour work day and no relief from other duties, the worker simply has less time to devote to each of his or her cases. In short, something has to give. The worker's role, with clients and the supervisor, will likely be changed and, as a consequence, changes will occur in the other roles. To extend the example, let us assume that to save money the agency's staff moved to smaller quarters. Here, rather than each worker and supervisor having a private office, all are located in an open space with only book cases and filing cabinets separating workers, and workers and supervisors, from each other. Given this reduction in privacy and the general loss of space, an assumption can be made that the roles of all comprising the social system will be affected. The example also indicates how physical features of the work environment affect roles and their performance.

Formal

Perhaps the clearest example of a formal determinant of role behavior is the legal basis of formal organizations. Of the type being modeled here, all are either registered under law as formal organizations (for example, private not-for-profit corporations), or are created under law as public agencies (for example, a state-operated mental health center). Thus, all the roles comprising such a social system have their sanctions in society's legal system. More importantly, the duties and responsibilities associated with these roles and their performance have a formal existence with ultimate ties to the organization's legal origins. For example, a caseworker and the organization employing the worker can be sued by a client for malpractice if the worker's role is conducted in a harmful, inappropriate, or incompetent way.

Attesting to their formal status, roles in large agencies are typically set forth as job descriptions or job specifications. In systems language these are role specifications. To use an earlier example, both the caseworker and the supervisor would have job descriptions for their respective roles. These descriptions would, in general terms, set forth the expected role performances of each, vis-à-vis the other. In short, the job descriptions are a feature of structure designed to serve as a guide on how the individuals fulfilling those roles should behave toward each other. As will be pointed out later, the actual behaviors of those enacting roles is what is herein referred to as the interactive feature of the conversion operation.

Other formal features of structure include relevant laws, administrative rulings, policies, procedures, plans, and contracts, to mention but a few. These features have a physical existence in the sense that they appear in written form; they are considered a part of the social structure because they are designed to shape interactions among those holding organizational roles. To return to an earlier example, state laws specify how a mentally ill person is to be admitted to a hospital. The law prescribes how a series of roles will be performed relative to the alleged mentally ill person, including that of the police who may transport the person to the hospital, the judge who may legally commit the person to the hospital, and the psychiatrist who may make a medical determination of mental status.

In the preceding paragraphs, the concept of role has been highlighted with the point made that the model conceptualizes a social organization as a system of roles. While roles represent a key component of social structure in this model, as noted previously, they are not the only feature. With this as background, the remaining portions of this section will be devoted to those structural features that help provide the overall form to the system, the coordination and sequencing of roles. It is in this area that we are indebted to the contributions the rationalists have made to organizational theory.[10]

Of central importance was the recognition by the rationalists of the legal charters of formal organizations and thus the legal roots to the authority structure. It is the legal authority structure that provides the foundations for the control and coordination functions needed to pursue organizational goals. Also to be highlighted in the following paragraphs is the division of labor within the conversion operation, in other words, how work is partialized and sequenced as a strategy for the efficient and effective completion of the overall work task.

Figure 12.4 has been prepared for use in examining features of the overall form of an organization when modeled as a social system. Represented are the formal relation-

FIGURE 12.4 Formal Administrative Structure: The Midtown Mental Health Center

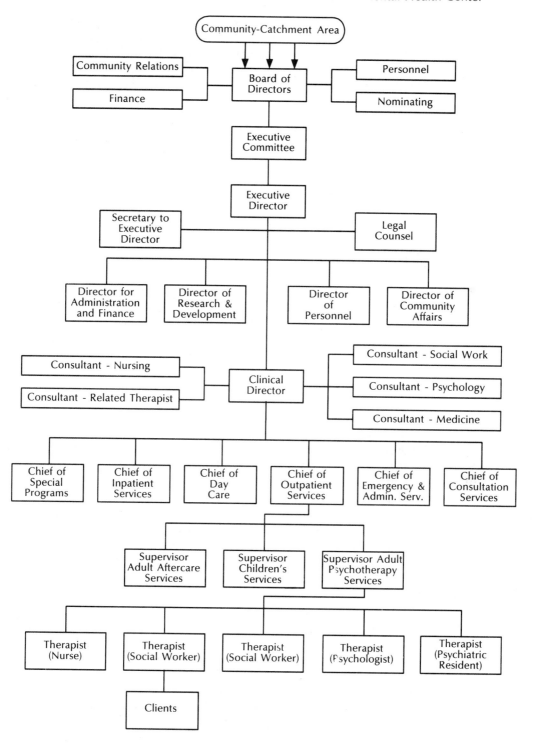

ships among roles in our hypothetical organization, the Midtown Mental Health Center. Through this diagram the following concepts are illustrated and discussed: (1) policy versus executive functions, (2) delegation of authority, (3) chain of command, (4) line versus staff positions, (5) span of control, and (6) the functional allocation of work.

Policy versus Executive Functions   Conceptually, every system is a subsystem of a larger system to which it is connected through input-output exchanges. In this example, the Midtown Mental Health Center is a formal organization whose function is to meet the mental health needs of the people residing in its catchment (service) area. The center's **Board of Directors** is constituted by representatives from this catchment area and from other key segments of its suprasystem. Using this perspective, it is useful to view the board as constituting a microcosm of the center's relevant suprasystem. Through use of the board generally and through the individuals comprising the board particularly, the center possesses a capability of maintaining contact with relevant constituencies in the suprasystem, for example, the local medical society, politicians, the mental health society, industry, and welfare rights groups.

The board can be viewed as providing an oversight function, helping the organization to pursue the purposes for which it was originally sanctioned. The board has a **policy** function, that of formulating agency goals and the general plans to be followed for achieving those goals, for example, responding to the changing mental health needs of catchment area residents. The diagram shows how this board divides up its policy work through actions of several subcommittees, including community relations, personnel, and finance, for example. The diagram also indicates that the board operates through an Executive Committee that deals regularly with the board's chief administrative officer, the Executive Director.

At the operational level, the Executive Director usually recommends and otherwise assists the board in the development of the agency's statement of goals (hierarchy of outcomes); but it is the acceptance of these goals and related policies by the board that constitutes sanction to operate under these policies. In summary and based on its constitution and bylaws, the board formulates overall policy (structure), and selects the center's Executive Director, who it then empowers to execute its policies. It is then left to the Executive Director to develop the narrower range policies and **procedures** to flesh out the broader policies adopted by the board, to develop and/or sanction the agency's objectives and activities for the coming year. The Executive Director is then held responsible by the board to secure the staff and in general to see that the center accomplishes its intentions.

Delegation of Authority   The term **delegation of authority** is closely associated with the concept of the rational/legal authority structure. The legal basis for this authority in the above example is found in the agency's constitution and bylaws. In its constitution, authority is first vested in the Board of Directors which is given the right to empower the Executive Director to carry out the board's policies. To do so, the Executive Director hires key staff (usually those reporting directly to him or her) and *delegates* authority to these respective positions. This delegation/empowerment process moves downward until it reaches the lowest level positions. The authority structure thus connects all positions ultimately to that of the Executive Director. Both conceptually and practically, the person holding the position of Executive Director is responsible to the Board of Directors for everything that happens in the center—both good and bad.

Chain of Command   The process of delegating authority results in what is typically referred to as the chain of command. It is the vertically organized authority gradient created to control and give direction to the agency. The notion of chain embraces the structural linking of positions one with another from top to bottom. In Figure 12.4, the chain of command is represented by the vertical line connecting the Executive Director to the five positions reporting directly to him or her, the Director for Administration, Director of Research, Clinical Director, and so on. This line extends vertically connecting every position eventually to the Executive Director and the legal authority of every position is ultimately derived from that delegated down by the Executive Director.

Line versus Staff Positions   **Line positions** are those related one to another vertically, the chain of command. These positions are those directly related to production of task outputs. In the example, line positions are those with vertical lines connecting with the Executive Director, for example, the Clinical Director. In Figure 12.4, staff positions are connected horizontally to line positions; denoted by this horizontal line is a supportive relationship between line and staff members. Typically persons in **staff positions** do not make administrative decisions or perform work directly related to task outcomes; frequently, staff positions are filled by specialists whose job is to advise people in line positions of the technical factors associated with a given decision or action. This function is depicted by the relationship the Legal Counsel has to the Executive Director. In such an organization, the role of counsel would be to advise the Executive Director of the legal implications for a given course of action (decision).

Span of Control   **Span of control** refers to the extent of the horizontal administrative control, that is, how many positions a given administrator supervises. The concept pertains to the exercise of the legal authority by a specified administrator. The concept is illustrated by the number of people being supervised by the Executive Director—five line and two staff positions. The Clinical Director in turn supervises six line and five staff positions.

Functional Allocation of Work   As used here, the notions of **functional allocation of work**, division of labor, and departmentation are all essentially synonymous. Reference is to a differentiation process in which the total work of the organization is divided up into natural or logical units and then assigned to groupings of people to be performed. The grouping of these work activities and their assignment is given an organizational designation, for example, a department. This process proceeds downward, and at each administrative level the work is divided and assigned horizontally. Ultimately, all of the organization's work is assigned. These assignments become key attributes of all organizational roles. It is in this sense that the organization can be viewed as a functionally dependent system of roles. Each role represents a specialized aspect of a particular functional process, and each role becomes dependent in varying degrees on the performance of other roles comprising that process. It is this process that gives the system its chief feature, functional interdependence.

Figure 12.4 illustrates the vertical and horizontal axes of a formal organizational chart. In this example, the Executive Director has divided the work of the Midtown Mental Health Center into five functional areas and has placed a director in charge of each of these areas: administration and finance, research and development, clinical (treatment), personnel, and community affairs. From a conceptual position, each of these units is at the same level in the organization's authority structure, and therefore each director is presumed to possess roughly comparable amounts of authority. These five functionally derived units constitute the second level of administrative authority (the Executive Director occupies the top or first level).

The position of Clinical Director illustrates the third level in this agency's formal organizational structure. Here program/service has been employed in the differentiation process rather than the administrative function as the rationale for dividing up the work. In short, all of the center's clinical work is assumed to fall into one of these six categories—that is how the board has operationalized the concept of *comprehensive* (see mission statement in Figure 12.3). Again, a supervisor is placed in charge of each of the clinical programs with that person reporting to the Clinical Director. All of the positions vertically related to the Clinical Director are designated as line positions and constitute a part of the chain of command described earlier. (For purposes of further elaboration, the position of Clinical Director has been placed lower on the axis so that the staff positions could be illustrated.) In contrast, positions horizontally connected to the Clinical Director are staff positions. Persons occupying these roles advise the Clinical Director on matters pertaining to their particular area of professional expertise (for example, the social work consultant would advise the Clinical Director on policy pertaining to the role of social work in the center's clinical program). It should be noted that these consultants have no line responsibility over the people in their professional discipline. Typically such consultants, while administratively reporting to the Clinical Director, serve as consultants to people in their own discipline. They might also be responsible for holding workshops and other forms of inservice training for members of their discipline (the maintenance function).

The position of Chief of the Outpatient (Services) Department (OPD) is used to illustrate the fourth level of organization in this agency. This unit is also organized by program/service with a supervisor responsible for each service. The fifth and final level is organized by treatment modality (in this instance psychotherapy). Notation has been made of each therapist's professional discipline. Given the scheme for organizing the work—providing psychotherapy—the individual's professional discipline, while noted, is considered to be incidental. Here an assumption has been made that the person occupying the role of therapist is professionally qualified to perform that role. Finally, at this level the work is divided by number, for example, the number of clients comprising each therapist's caseload.

Two points are instructive at this juncture. First, it is only at the fifth level in the organization's formal structure that direct client contact (treatment) occurs. The four higher levels constitute the administrative arrangements needed to provide a comprehensive and quality range of services to clients. Second, this chart is the formal presentation of structure; there are innumerable ways for organizing the center's work—this is merely one of them. Finally, it does not follow that the center actually functions in the manner suggested; it may in some instances, it may not in others. Recall that one of the criticisms leveled at the rationalist position was the neglect of the informal structural features in understanding organizational behavior.

Figure 12.4 is also intended to illustrate how systems are imbedded in systems (as subsystems). For example, the Clinical Director is responsible for the center's Clinical Department (all clinical services). It would be possible to model this department as a system, with the remaining administrative parts of the organization treated as key features of its suprasystem. Similarly, the Chief of OPD heads another administrative unit that could be examined as a social system, and so on. With each step down in the administrative hierarchy, the analysis can become more detailed. The open systems approach maintains the relationship of the system being examined to its environmental context (suprasystem). For example, modeling the Outpatient Department as a system would have limited value without reference to how its activities (input-output exchanges) relate to the rest of the center and to other relevant features of its suprasystem. Again recall the assumption that the whole is more than the sum of its parts; the center is not to be understood only by understanding each of its component parts.

Informal

The role is the central feature comprising structure in this conceptualization of a system's conversion operations. Up to this point, the focus has been the roles comprising the system's formal organization. These roles have been prescribed and related to one another on a functional basis—what the system is supposed to accomplish. Here the content has been largely drawn from the rationalist perspective. There is another system of roles comprising the system's informal organizational structure. Here role specification is drawn from the human needs of those persons actually occupying roles in the formal structure. Assistance in developing this feature of structure is drawn from the work of the human relationists. Roles in the informal organization are loosely linked, there is no formal vertical and horizontal structure, and they are not related to one another via a legal authority structure. Here the relationship among people is Gemeinschaft in character. People relate to one another more as total personalities as opposed to their formal role designations, such as therapist. While similar to what is generally referred to as a *social group*, there is the added dimension of the association being work-related, that is, shaped by organizational variables in addition to personal ones. In other words, while the informal organization arises out of the personal needs of its members, one of the functions of this association is to mediate members' needs with the demands of the organization. In some instances this function becomes formalized, for example, as a union. Other functions served by the informal organization include social support (help in dealing with organizational and personal stressors) and communication (the grapevine).

In modeling a formal organization as a social system, attention is thus given to its informal as well as its formal system of roles, the former being implicit, the latter explicit. The two features of structure are treated as interactive, each operating on the other and thus collectively affecting outcome. There is no counterpart of the formal organizational chart for this informal system. It is discernible only by observation and by examination of its effects. The important point to be recognized here is the assumption that, due to its contrived nature (unnatural), the formal organization is unstable, and it is largely through development of the informal organization (the natural system) that stability is maintained. Also, the further assumption is made that these two interacting structural features pursue different ends and are driven by different power sources, for example, rational/legal authority versus other forms of authority (charismatic) along with personal needs.

Interactions

In the previous section, that part of conversion operations termed *structure* was discussed. In short, structure pertains to all of the features and forces within the social organization that serve to guide or otherwise shape the behavior of those involved in the conversion process. There are a host of structural features ranging from the layout of work spaces and the goals and objectives of the organization to its legal authority system. All of these features influence and give substance to roles, the chief structural component of a social system. But, as indicated earlier, roles have no physical existence; they cannot be seen, touched, or heard. Rather, they represent normative sets of expectations as to how a given person will behave in a specific situation. These expectations are shared in the sense that all those comprising a role set will hold roughly comparable expectations toward one another in performing functionally related tasks. Interactions represent the counterparts of structure. It is only through the observation of people and the assignment of meaning to their interactions that the structure of the social system is discernible.

The structure is evidenced by the ongoing and reciprocating patterns of interactions of individuals carrying out their organizational roles, each toward the other. In formal organizations, by reason of their degree of differentiation and complexity, these same reciprocating interactions take place between the formal and informally constituted groups of which the organization is composed. For example, just as there will be a discernible pattern of reciprocating behavior between a specific therapist and a specific client in a mental health center's outpatient department as they enact their respective roles, so will there be an overall pattern in the interactions of all of the therapists and their respective clients in the outpatient department itself. In no way does this suggest that the behaviors of all of the therapists and their respective clients will be identical. What is being suggested is that there will be many similarities and that these similarities constitute a discernible pattern and that this pattern is associated with the systemic features of the outpatient department itself, vis-à-vis other departments within the center. In other words, if the mental health center behaves as a social system, its member parts, as subsystems, will also behave as systems with all that that implies.

At the department level, attention shifts from interactions at the individual scale to interactions of those who represent groups of people. For example, the interactions on a policy matter between the chief of the outpatient department and the chief of inpatient services can be viewed as each representing the interests of all those people comprising their respective departments. Given the legal authority structure of a formal organization, the department head is administratively responsible for all that occurs within the department, which could, for example, include the work of forty employees. In this role, the department head has particular responsibility for the input-output exchanges that occur between the department and other administrative units comprising the center as well as other components of its suprasystem. In an application of the model to formal organizations, administrative units or social groups become the primary units of attention, not the individual in a specific role. In so doing, the administrative head of that unit and that person's interactions with his or her counterparts can be treated as representative of all those members comprising the subject unit. Technically, the legal authority structure of the organization provides for this type of representativeness. Similarly, the recognized leader of an informally constituted group can speak and act on behalf of those he or she represents.

Certainly some of the richness and detail is lost by focusing on the interactions of larger social units via the behaviors of those who represent the members of these groups; what is sought, however, is an understanding of those organizational behaviors that help explain system outputs. To do this, one starts by seeking to explain or understand the interactions among the member social units. As with the total system, there will be input-output exchanges, and the totality of these exchanges are functionally related to the outputs of the total system.

We will continue our use of the Midtown Mental Health Center as our example for explicating the concept of interactions and its tie to structure. One objective of the center for the coming year is to reduce the readmission rate for inpatient services among the poor from fifty-six per one hundred readmissions to forty-five per one hundred readmissions. This objective was proposed to the Board of Directors by the center's Executive Director, Dr. Sarah Shields (an interaction occurring between Dr. Shields in her role as Executive Director and members of the Board of Directors in their respective roles). Prior to bringing the recommendation to the board, Dr. Shields had held extensive discussions (interactions) on this matter with her various department heads and they in turn with their respective staffs. In part, the objective pertaining to readmission had its origin among community agencies who felt that many of the center's poor clients were being discharged prematurely and as a consequence were unable to make satisfactory adjustments even with the considerable support provided by community agencies. In this instance, the interactions occurred between Dr. Shields representing the Midtown Mental Health Center and executives representing the interests of their respective agencies, for example, the department of welfare. Also, several members of the center's board had brought up in a board meeting what they felt might be a problem—an apparent high number of poor clients being returned to the center within a year of discharge. Conceptually, this would suggest some output-input exchange breakdown between the center and its suprasystem (the community of Midtown). Officially, the board asked Dr. Shields to look into the matter and report her findings back to them at their next meeting, again an interaction between the board and Dr. Shields acting in their respective roles.

Let's assume that gradually over the last several years the staff of the center's OPD began concentrating their services on those patients interested in and needing long-term psychotherapy. The OPD Chief, Dr. Fred Edwards, was aware of this trend and was informally supporting it because of his own conviction (a feature of structure) of the value of long-term psychotherapy versus other intervention methods. Dr. Edwards was also psychoanalytically oriented in his treatment of clients (theory also being a structural feature), and this approach was well suited to long-term treatment. Because of his theoretical orientation, he felt that long-term treatment was necessary to bring about lasting changes with clients.

To make time (structure) available for clients in long-term psychotherapy, the OPD staff gradually reduced the time they were spending with the center's chronic clients, those not having good verbal skills, like many of the poor and more generally those needing a variety of supportive services including the supervision of their medications. As a consequence of this change in OPD, the center's inpatient unit found that many of their referrals to OPD, particularly those who were poor, were not being picked up. According to OPD staff, these clients were not following up on referrals or were not showing an interest in OPD services, for example, they lacked "motivation." Because of the pressure to discharge clients, the inpatient staff began to discharge many of their most vulnerable directly into the community rather than sending them to OPD (an interaction). In this instance, a change in one part of the system (OPD) produced changes in other parts (inpatient), again an interaction. As a consequence of the growing practice of the staff of the inpatient unit to discharge those clients unable to profit from long-term psychotherapy directly into the community (once the patient's symptoms were stabilized on medication), there was increasing concern by various community agencies about the number of homeless people sleeping under bridges and in doorways, and eating out of garbage containers. Many of these people were thought to be former mental patients.

This example is an examination of actual output – the discharge of many patients directly into the community without follow-up and without the necessary forms of community supports needed to sustain the former patient in the community. Many of these former clients would be classified as poor. Consequently, a higher than usual number of these patients were returning to the center's inpatient unit for readmission. The phrase "higher than usual" indicates presence of an objective or some standard to which actual output was being compared (this comparison is also an interaction). The comparison suggested that something was wrong (negative feedback), and an examination of the center's conversion operations started. This examination by Dr. Shields led to a determination that a shift had occurred in the role played by the OPD in relation to other departments, particularly the inpatient department. This role shift had occurred in the actual behaviors of the therapists comprising the OPD staff. There had been no formal structural change as evidenced in a change of job descriptions or in the role expectations of these therapists by the center's Clinical Director, Dr. June Mason. This example shows how deviations can occur between structural expectations and role enactment. It was the effect of these changes in role behaviors that were evidenced in the center's actual output that brought the matter to the attention of its board.

Once the source of these changes had been identified by Dr. Shields and her staff, discussions (interactions) were held as to what should be done. It was agreed that during the coming year priority would be given to reducing the center's readmission rate of the poor (a priority decision resulting in establishment of a specific objective related to the center's goal of reducing the incidence and prevalence of mental health problems among catchment area residents). Once the objective had been agreed upon and confirmed by the board (an interaction), a plan (a structural feature) had to be agreed upon and actions taken to implement this plan. Conceptually, the plan represents the set of interrelated activities that are always associated with achievement of an objective – the means employed to achieve the proposed outcome. In this instance several related plans (sets of activities) were adopted. One was to expand the center's OPD to provide for a unit concerned with the provision of long-term psychotherapy and another to provide aftercare services to the center's clients with special needs, the poor. A new professional title and role, Case Manager, was created for those working in the aftercare unit. The assumption was made that, through the creation of a new helping role (new element of structure), the kind of advocacy, supportive, and empathic behaviors called for in the performance of this role would be responded to by clients with special needs. Also the type of relationships formed would help these clients adjust to community life, and thus they would be less likely to return to the center's inpatient service.

The adoption of the new role, Case Manager, led the center to also adopt a new maintenance outcome objective for the coming year, namely, "to have eight staff members be certified as mental health case managers." To achieve this maintenance objective, the staff involved were to attend four two-day workshops offered by the National Association of Case Managers. In this instance, the maintenance outcome objective and the proposed workshops represent structural features of the center's conversion operations — one an end, the other the means selected to achieve that end.

Feedback

The social systems model is an output-driven representation of social organization, and it is through feedback that information is obtained about the effects of output. In short, feedback provides the data needed by the system to maintain its orientation and its movement toward the achievement of its goals. Because of their legal nature, formal organizations can be particularly helpful in developing the notion of feedback.

Conceptually, feedback refers to evaluative information pertaining to the extent that actual outputs conform to proposed outputs. This information is gathered formally and informally from inside the system and from the suprasystem. The term *feedback* is instructive in itself. It conveys that something is fed back. What is fed back is not part of what was produced, but intelligence about how that which was produced was received by the consuming or receiving units in its suprasystem. In human service applications, task outputs are former clients, thus former clients or their representatives are an important source of feedback.

Because of the legal status of formal organizations, their proposed and actual outputs are more easily identified than in other forms of social organization. As indicated earlier, this is not to suggest that a formal organization's statement (if it should have such a statement) of goals and objectives represents an accurate statement of intentions. It may or may not. What is being said is that the formal character of such organizations provides at least a starting place for determining intentions. Further, the formal status of such organizations provides the formal communication lines that can facilitate consensus on intentions and the transmission of information on actual outputs.

Implicit in the foregoing discussion is that feedback requires two reference points: the first, what was actually produced, and the second, what was intended to be produced. No comparison is possible in the absence of these reference points. Use of the systems model is premised on the determination of such reference points; and, importantly, feedback only pertains to information generated through this comparison process. Information not related to proposed or actual output is treated, from the feedback perspective, as noise, and effort is made to filter it out so that the feedback process is not impeded. The technique for formulating proposed and actual output in this model is through use of the concept of a hierarchy of outcomes; this concept has been discussed in detail in earlier sections.

In formulating the concept of feedback, it is important to be reminded that it is not necessary to have consensus on what is intended as an organizational outcome and what is actually produced. What is necessary is that a position is taken by the person using the model on these two reference points. It is assumed that the position would be arrived at by examining the organization and a best judgment rendered. To put this matter in another perspective, various organizational constituencies are likely to hold somewhat different views on both the organization's intentions and what it actually accomplished. This is particularly true in human service agencies and other such agencies that provide services as opposed to more tangible products (for example, improved mental health versus an automobile). Given the presence of such diverse views, the model user/ practitioner renders a professional judgment with regard to these two reference points. This judgment is made bearing in mind the critical systemic features of the agency, particularly those involved in its input-output exchanges.

For example, what do the consumers perceive to be the agency's proposed and actual outputs? What about the agency's major funders? What about the position of its governing board, its chief administrator, staff, and others? To the extent that there are significant differences regarding the agency's intentions and accomplishments among these constituencies, the model user has to be cautious about any judgment made. The existence of such differences among key constituencies does suggest the possible presence of other tension points throughout the agency and endangerment of steady state.

Formal organizations of the type being modeled here are multigroup in character. While our central interest in this section is the feedback mechanism that guides the total system, it must be remembered that the model assumes that these administrative units and/or informal groups comprising the total system also behave as systems. In other words, these subsystems also possess feedback loops that are output oriented. In such instances, the output of a subsystem will usually represent an input into another of the system's subsystems. An example would be clients seen by an agency's intake unit; once eligibility has been determined, these clients would represent output of the intake unit and input to the agency's service unit. Another example would be the work of an agency's business office in the processing of a payroll. Money (an input) budgeted (a structural feature of conversion) for meeting payroll would be processed by staff in the business office (an interaction feature of conversion) and then distributed to employees (a task output of the business office). In this example, feedback is information fed back to the agency's business office relative to the distribution of payroll (for example, were checks received on time?). The multigroup nature of formal organizations represents one of its distinguishing characteristics and this feature has particular relevance in conceptualizing feedback. At the agency level, feedback on task outputs is relevant to all of the agency's subsystems.

If feedback is positive, the tendency is for all subsystems to take this information as confirmation of the way they are currently performing their specific functions. In this sense, the feedback returns as a critical feature of input, suggesting that the next processing cycle should be performed in essentially the same manner as the one that produced the positive feedback (assuming comparable goals and objectives). Given this use, it is important that feedback be returned to the system in a form that facilitates its confirming nature. Generally, the design of formal feedback subsystems and the distribution of feedback as input is a general management function. For example, if the Midtown Mental Health Center has a computerized management information system (MIS), which includes measures of client outcomes, then these data have implications for central management but most particularly for the therapists who have delivered the client services. Similarly, if the feedback is negative, it must be distributed in a manner that makes it useful as input for all the system's subsystems. Negative feedback is more complicated in the sense that it indicates that system intentions were not fulfilled (presence of waste). Normally such feedback does not indicate why, or even if the intentions were realistic in the first instance. These questions are just as important in viewing positive feedback, but as a practical matter they take on more importance when the feedback is negative.

Recall that from the perspective of this model, organizational behavior is reciprocally cyclical and mutually determinant as opposed to being linear in form. One feature characterizing this behavior is that as a consequence of an event of interaction, the cycle of that interaction reaches closure in a manner that creates a new starting position for the next cycle. Two points are relevant in terms of feedback: first, evaluative data pertaining to that cycle of interactions is returned as inputs to the individuals or social units involved in those interactions; second, the feedback comprises only a part of the inputs upon which the next cycle of organizational activities will be based. Conceptually, it is the feedback portion of inputs that is critical for determining whether any structural changes are indicated in the next processing cycle.

Implicit in this formulation is that feedback, like all other forms of input, represents the raw materials that are processed by the system's conversion operation. It does not follow that all feedback is processed in a manner that improves the system's next cycle of behavior; the feedback may have been distorted, incorrect, or improperly processed. Nor does it follow that feedback ever enters the system as input, or if it does, that it is properly routed. To the extent that a system is closed, its conversion operations are correspondingly more self-contained and thus primarily dependent on internal as opposed to external sources of feedback. Given this general feature of closedness, an assumption is made that such systems will tend to experience entropy forces as opposed to the forces of negative entropy.

The Midtown Mental Health Center will again be used to illustrate the various forms that feedback can take. Assumed is the existence of a hierarchy of outcomes comprised of both task and maintenance forms of outputs. One task objective is "to reduce the readmission rate for inpatient services among the poor from 56 per 100 readmissions to 45 per 100 readmissions." This objective was derived from one of the center's goals, which read, "to reduce the incidence and prevalence of mental health problems among catchment area residents." Several assumptions need to be made in support of this objective. First, that the center has an automated data system that would permit the collection, processing, and reporting of the information required by this objective. Second, that the comparisons are made on identical characteristics (variables), for example, a definition of "poor." Third, the objective represents a priority judgment of what should and can be done by the center to better serve the citizens of Midtown.

Now, relative to the concept of feedback, the objective indicates that the first condition is satisfied, that is, existence of a statement of proposed output. The second condition is also assumed, the existence of an information system that will indicate the actual output—the number of clients discharged from the center during the past year who have been returned to inpatient status. Given the prior specifications of outcomes (the objective), existence of last year's data on comparable clients and the specifications of readmissions occurring during the current year, the system is now capable of making the comparisons that constitute the feedback. The example is one of formal and internal feedback. It is formal in the sense that it is planned, systematic, and relatively precise; it is internal in the sense that it is under the control of the center. A formal type of external feedback would be that performed by the Joint Commission on Accreditation of Hospitals (JCAH). Here it would be formal in the sense that the feedback would be on compliance to previously known and specified standards (proposed and actual outputs). It would be external because the feedback was provided to the center by an agency in its suprasystem.

Internal and informal feedback would be remarks made by staff to each other, say over lunch, relative to the previously cited objective. "This place is just a big revolving door; clients are on the street one day and back here the next," or "We really do a job here; clients come back to tell us how well they are doing—not that they can't make it and need to be readmitted." The feedback is internal because it is generated by staff, and it is informal because it is spontaneous, imprecise, and irregular. Finally, an example of external informal feedback would be comparable statements made by persons not associated formally with the center.

The focus of remarks on feedback has been on its main dimension, outcome. However, we have built into our model the assumption that outcome forms of feedback are always accompanied by process types. By **process feedback**, we mean feedback on the activities performed during the conversion of inputs to outputs. Here the question becomes: "Have the agreed-upon activities and methods been performed in accordance with specified standards?" The question assumes existence of a standard (proposed output); the answer to the question represents actual output. Again, a note of caution is offered. We hold that in its informal state, this type of feedback is always present in social organizations having systemlike features and thus its inclusion in the model. Conceptually, the reason it is always there is the assumption that there is an evaluative dimension to all role enactment; in other words, the judgment made by the actor as to how successfully the counter role was performed in a given interactional situation. The preceding question would represent existence of a formal type of process feedback. An agency may or may not have in place a formalized means for producing feedback on the processes performed, for example, the number and type of medications provided clients during the past year.

Now to return to the previously stated objective of a reduction in the center's readmission rate. Here we make the assumption that the center relies heavily on the use of medication provided by physicians and supervised by case managers employed in the aftercare service. The aftercare service not only provides medication, but supportive services, including center-related self-help groups comprised of former clients. Given this background, a process form of feedback would include such information as the number of clients seen in the aftercare clinic each month, the number of medications dispensed, the number of clients attending self-help groups, and so on. These numbers represent process feedback or measures of the means provided; they are not to be confused with actual task outcomes or end conditions. The latter will always pertain to the condition of a client, not to how many services were provided aimed at producing that condition.

Our example has been developed to illustrate the means-ends relationships that exist between process and outcome forms of feedback. We suggest that process forms of feedback are essentially meaningless except as they provide information on outcomes or end states. In other words, the fact that the center may have provided aftercare medication services last year to 1,235 individual clients and that 853 meetings of self-help groups took place is simply an activity count, a statement of effort made. The issue is the end resulting from this selection of means; or, what was the mental health condition of these clients resulting from the services rendered? Similarly, data on the ends achieved, the percentage of people not being readmitted to the center within one year, are relatively useless without information on the kind and number of services selected to achieve that outcome, in other words, the means employed to help former clients function at a level that did not require their readmission.

In concluding this section, we note developments in administrative theory and practice having implications to the concept of feedback as utilized in this model. For example, the concept of cost-effectiveness or cost-benefits is frequently used as an approach to the measurement of organizational outcomes.[11] As applied in this model to feedback, these concepts refer to a ratio of maintenance inputs to task outputs. The development of such a ratio is no easy task. It would require an assignment of a dollar value to all inputs having a direct bearing on the achievement of a specified unit of output. In the example used earlier, "What is the average cost to the center to provide a treatment program that would result in an additional one percent of its clients not being readmitted to an inpatient service within one year of their discharge?" Few human service agencies currently have the capacity to answer such a question, but the model provides the conceptual scheme for addressing it.

At a somewhat less complicated level are feedback systems that provide cost data on activities performed. Generally referred to as "unit costs," feedback is designed to provide information on the dollar cost to produce a defined unit of care at a specified level of productivity. Examples would include the cost per fifty-minute family therapy session or a medication check. It is important to note that these examples are not of outcomes; rather they pertain to formal and internal systems designed to provide feedback on the costs of the means being employed. These measures are typically taken during the conversion process. In short, these measures represent the ratio of maintenance inputs to units of services provided.

SUMMARY

In this chapter, the social systems model has been applied to a formal organization. The distinguishing characteristic of this type of organization is its formal and legal status. Clearly, Gesellschaft types of relationships dominate in this form of organization, but not to the exclusion of Gemeinschaft. We have stressed that formal organizations are contrived, that is, they are human creations, designed as a means to accomplish some acknowledged end state. Once formed, though, they take on a life of their own. It does not follow that they always pursue the wishes of their creators, any more than a child will grow up and meet all of his or her parents' expectations. Formal organizations, like people, have a propensity to "do their own thing."

The eight interrelated concepts comprising the model have been used to show how any formal organization can be viewed as a social system. Building on our focus of seeking understanding of human behavior by examining it in an environmental context, we characterize the current chapter as addressing the behavior of formal organizations in their social environments. The model builds on this approach by assuming a cyclical, a mutually deterministic, and a functional relationship between every social organization and its environment. Given this emphasis, the model is driven by a functional conception of system-suprasystem relationships and utilizes the concepts of proposed and actual outputs as forming the basic organizing scheme.

We have used several examples to illustrate the model's basic concepts, but particular attention has been to our hypothetical formal organization, the Midtown Mental Health Center. Figure 12.5 is a visual presentation of the center modeled as a social system.

GLOSSARY

Board of directors   The governing body of a formal organization, typically of a private as opposed to a public agency.

Catchment area   A term associated with community mental health centers, the geographical designation of the location of the population to be served by that agency, a critical component of its suprasystem.

Cost-benefit/cost-effectiveness analysis   A cost control measure in which both efficiency and effectiveness measures are employed, that is, the cost to achieve a specified outcome.

Delegation of authority   The assignment of authority by an administrator to a subordinate.

Ecology   A branch of science that addresses the reciprocal relationships between organisms and their environments.

Ecological perspective   A very general approach for examining systematically the reciprocal relationships between organisms and their environment.

Ecosystem   A systems formulation of the reciprocal relationships between organisms and their environments.

Effectiveness   The ratio of a system's task outputs to its proposed task outputs.

Efficiency   The ratio of a system's maintenance inputs to its task outputs.

Environmental scanning   The process of mapping and assessing by a system of its suprasystem.

Functional allocation of work   The administrative process of logically dividing and assigning the work among those who comprise a formal organization.

Line position   Positions within the social system directly associated with producing its task outputs.

FIGURE 12.5 Midtown Mental Health Center Modeled as a Social System

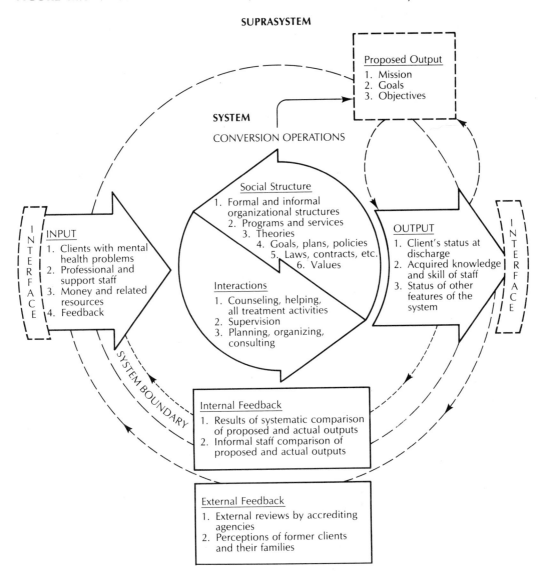

SUPRASYSTEM

Proposed Output
1. Mission
2. Goals
3. Objectives

SYSTEM

CONVERSION OPERATIONS

Social Structure
1. Formal and informal organizational structures
2. Programs and services
3. Theories
4. Goals, plans, policies
5. Laws, contracts, etc.
6. Values

Interactions
1. Counseling, helping, all treatment activities
2. Supervision
3. Planning, organizing, consulting

INPUT
1. Clients with mental health problems
2. Professional and support staff
3. Money and related resources
4. Feedback

INTERFACE

OUTPUT
1. Client's status at discharge
2. Acquired knowledge and skill of staff
3. Status of other features of the system

INTERFACE

SYSTEM BOUNDARY

Internal Feedback
1. Results of systematic comparison of proposed and actual outputs
2. Informal staff comparison of proposed and actual outputs

External Feedback
1. External reviews by accrediting agencies
2. Perceptions of former clients and their families

POET model An ecosystems formulation of the ordering process resulting from the interaction of four classes of variables: (1) population, (2) (social) organization, (3) environment, and (4) technology.

Policy A general plan of action to achieve a system's goal(s), a guide to decision making in pursuit of a system's goals.

Procedures A set of detailed rules or activities to be followed within a policy, for example, forms to be completed to apply for vacation leave.

Process feedback Information generated on activities performed pertinent to accomplishing task and maintenance outputs, that is, measures taken of the "means" utilized to achieve a system's "ends."

Span of control   The number of positions supervised by a given administrator.

Staff positions   Positions within the social system where advice is given to those in line positions on matters pertaining to achieving both task and maintenance outcomes.

NOTES

1. Joint Commission on Mental Illness and Health, *Action for Mental Health: Final Report of the Joint Commission on Mental Illness and Health 1961* (New York: Basic Books). See particularly pp. 24–35 and 60–71.

2. For a review of the development of practice on an international scale, see Katherine A. Kendall, "International Social Welfare Organizations and Services," in *Encyclopedia of Social Work*, vol. 1, 18th ed. (Silver Spring, Md.: National Association of Social Workers, 1987), 969–996.

3. For an interesting presentation of the relationship between general systems and ecological theory, see Geoffrey L. Grief, "The Ecosystems Perspective 'Meets the Press,'" *Social Work* 3 (May–June 1986): 225–226.

4. A helpful introduction to this perspective is contained in Carel B. Germain and Alex Gitterman, "Ecological Perspective," *Encyclopedia of Social Work*, vol. 1, 18th ed. (Silver Spring, Md.: National Association of Social Workers, 1987), 488–489.

5. Otis Dudley Duncan, "From Social Systems to Ecosystem," in *Urban America Conflict and Change*, ed. J. John Palen and Karl H. Flaming (New York: Holt, Rinehart and Winston, 1972), 4–12; and Michael Micklin, *Population, Environment and Social Organization: Current Issues in Human Ecology* (Hinsdale, Ill.: The Dryden Press, 1973), 3–19.

6. See Stephen P. Robbins, *Organization Theory: The Structure and Design of Organizations* (Englewood Cliffs, N.J.: Prentice Hall, 1983), 19–41.

7. See, for example, Srinika Jayaratne and Wayne A. Chess, "Job Satisfaction, Burnout, and Turnover: A National Study," *Social Work* 29 (September-October 1984): 448–453. For a more detailed presentation of the concept of turnover and its meaning, see Herbert G. Heneman III, et al., *Personnel/Human Resource Management* (Homewood, Ill.: Richard D. Irwin, 1980), 161–166.

8. Ludwig von Bertalanffy, *General Systems Theory* (New York: George Braziller, 1968), 40.

9. Alvin L. Bertrand, *Social Organization: A General Systems and Role Theory Perspective* (Philadelphia: F. A. David Company, 1972), 35–43.

10. See discussion in Chapter 11. For additional detail see W. Richard Scott, *Organizations: Rational, Natural, and Open Systems* (Englewood Cliffs, N.J.: Prentice Hall, 1981).

11. For a discussion of measures of organizational outcomes see Ronald D. Sylvia, Kenneth J. Meier, and Elizabeth M. Gunn, *Program Planning and Evaluation for the Public Manager* (Monterey, Calif.: Brooks/Cole Publishing Co., 1985).

Chapter 13

The Formal Organization: Systems Dynamics

OUTLINE

Introduction: Steady State

In this final chapter of Part IV, our interest is in the distinguishing characteristics of formal organizations in terms of how they maintain steady state. In our previous discussion of steady state we identified its origins in the works of Talcott Parsons.[1] He identified four universal problems confronted by every social organization: goal attainment, adaptation, integration, and pattern maintenance. Simply put, the actions by the organization to deal with these four problems becomes an explanation of the structural differentiation apparent in all organizations. In effect, then, this differentiation causes to be formed four subsystems that continually are called upon to deal with these never-ending problems. Parsons' use of this four-problem paradigm is far more complex than suggested above, and is a feature of his formulation of a theory of action. We have drawn from this important work of Parsons to develop our explanation of system dynamics. Recall that Parsons identified goal attainment and adaptation as functions having an external orientation, that is, to the suprasystem, and that integration and pattern maintenance were functions having an internal orientation. Also, the four problems have means and ends relationships to each other and to the system itself. Goal attainment and integration are the ends, serving a consummatory function; while adaptation and pattern maintenance are means, or serve an instrumental function. For more information on this paradigm you may want to reexamine the presentation of Figure 4.1.

Conceptually, steady state is linked to the notion of feedback because feedback represents the process of comparing intended with actual outputs and the return of this information to the system as input. Steady state is also linked to the process of entropy in that the loss of steady state is accompanied by an increase in the entropic process and the eventual loss of systems status, its ordering. Correspondingly, negative entropy characterizes steady state, an increase in order.

Emery is helpful in developing the concept of steady state when applied to formal organizations by identifying two characteristics he believes to be possessed by systems in steady state: (1) constancy of direction in goal achievement, and (2) an acceptable rate of progress in goal achievement.[2] The notion of constancy of direction recognizes the open nature of social systems. Every social organization exists within a constantly changing environment. Assuming its open system features, these environmental changes will have effects on the subject organization. Given this conception of reality, every organization must therefore make changes if it is to maintain a level of "constancy of direction" in its environmental relationships.

There is a subtlety involved that needs to be understood. While it is necessary for organizations to be in a continuing state of change in order to maintain constancy of direction in functional ties to their environments, the core patterns of organization must be maintained, and must remain stable. Suggested is that certain relationships within the organization with close ties to influences within the environment may be more subject to changes than those relationships deeply imbedded in the organization itself, for example, staff working in an intake unit versus those in a treatment unit. Steady state in an organization is also characterized, in our opinion, by favorable output-input exchanges. This means that the organization is achieving its goals at a level that results in an exchange of its outputs for the resources required to produce the next cycle of outputs plus contingencies. The notion of contingencies is intended to convey that the output-input exchanges are not an identical exchange of values; rather, over time there is a surplus created on the input side. This margin of safety enables the organization to deal with unexpected happenings that place demands on its resources, for example, a lawsuit against the agency or a budget reduction resulting from a shortfall in state tax revenues.

The previously cited conceptualization of steady state has been incorporated into our systems model. The assumption is that every system seeks to maintain steady state, and the loss of steady state is associated with entropic forces that result in the "death" of the system, or nonsystem status. In formal organizations the loss of steady state occurs when the organization ceases to exist as a separate and distinct social and legal entity. This can occur in either formal or informal ways. On an informal level, the people comprising the organization can simply renounce their association and walk away. More typically, the termination of such organizations occurs formally—by an official vote of the governing board, bankruptcy, merger, sale, and so on. Given the formal existence of the subject organizations, the loss of steady state and systems status is usually accompanied by some specific legal action that recognizes the removal of the legal sanction of an organization to exist. In a sense, these actions are not unlike those associated with the death of a human, which include the signing of a death certificate and specific legal arrangements for the distribution of the deceased's belongings. Since formal organizations typically possess assets and debts, special legal actions are usually required to dispose of their obligations once the organization ceases to exist. In short, social systems that exist are characterized by steady state; loss of steady state represents loss of system status. Given this position, the development of the concept of steady state becomes a means of seeking to describe and to understand those behaviors of organizations aimed at helping them to survive and to grow.

In the paragraphs that follow, the four functional problems will be developed. Two assumptions are made that undergird the discussion of this four-problem paradigm: (1) the four problems are never solved in any absolute sense, and (2) the problems are dealt with simultaneously—there is no inherent linear or serial relationship existing among the four problems, that is, they are systemically linked. Also, while the four problems are never finally solved, the status of problem resolution creates the conditions under which the system operates "for better or worse."

Goal Attainment

THE PROBLEM: How to Achieve a Level of Output that Through Exchange Produces the Inputs Needed to Sustain and Enhance the System

The problem posed in goal attainment provides a useful starting position. It also identifies the controlling variable in the model—task output. Formal organizations are social tools deliberately created as means to respond to some opportunity or problem perceived to exist. Given this purpose, goal attainment represents both an external and a consummatory function. It is external in the sense that the opportunity or need that caused the system to be created in the first place exists in the suprasystem. It is consummatory in that goal attainment represents the satisfaction of that opportunity or need.

Conceptually, all the structural features of the system pertaining to performance of the goal attainment function are collectively and systematically engaged in dealing with this problem. In approaching the study of steady state from a practitioner's position, it is probably not helpful to view Parsons's paradigm as constituting the logic for understanding the main structural configuration of an organization. Rather, the paradigm should be of greater help in understanding a structural dimension of the system in relation to each of the identified problems. To cite an earlier example, the Aftercare Unit of the Midtown Mental Health Center is considered to be primarily involved in the performance of the goal attainment function. Its job is to help the seriously mentally ill residents of Midtown to remain in the community with their families and, to the extent possible, function in their usual community roles, as wage earners, for example. As outlined here, this administrative unit has an important external and consummatory function.

Similarly, those features of roles played by the center's staff dedicated to this function are also external and consummatory in the orientation. In this formulation, it is important for you to distinguish between the notion of "orientation" and the totality of the role (status position) and its location in the administrative hierarchy. The fact that the role is primarily played out in an office located in the center and that the formal organizational structure identifies units and positions located within the system is incidental to the point being made here (goal attainment is external and consummatory).

Perhaps a review of the notion of role and its derivation would be helpful in clarifying this point. Conceptually, roles represent the structural creation of a social system in which the specialized tasks to be completed are functionally assigned to two or more persons (for example, to restore a mentally ill person to an improved level of mental health requires the role of client and the role of therapist). Role enactment is thus dedicated to an improvement in the client's mental health status.

Now to return to the example. With respect to orientation, it is external; that is, the source of the roles and their respective tasks exist in a need located in the center's suprasystem. The orientation is also consummatory in that the performance of the function is dedicated to the satisfaction of that need located in the suprasystem. To put the matter another way, the therapist-client relationship does not find its primary justification in the maintenance of the social system itself or in meeting the needs of the therapist, but in meeting the needs of clients.

As suggested in the example, roles possess several dimensions with respect to this four-problem paradigm. It does not follow that each role or each social unit is equally involved in dealing with each of the four problems. In the above example, the therapist role in relation to the client role is primarily oriented to the goal attainment function, but certainly not exclusively so.

In conceptualizing the notion of goal attainment, it is important to note that goal attainment assumes that the system's output matches the needs and/or expectations of those units existing in the suprasystem. In other words, the consummatory dimension of the concept implies that not only has an output resulted from the system's activities, but that the output has been accepted by consummatory units located in the suprasystem. Finally, the value of the system's output is of an order that an exchange for inputs must occur (directly or indirectly) which is sufficient for continuance of the system. In the example used, goal attainment would be evident in the maintenance of clients in the community as opposed to being returned to the center as inpatients. It would further be assumed that the families of these clients and other community agencies dealing with them accept and support them in their family- and community-relevant roles; only in this sense is the consummatory function acknowledged. To put this another way, if the center simply released their clients to function as best they could in the community, sleeping under bridges and eating out of trash cans, this condition would not fulfill the consummatory function as used here. In fact, such actions would lead toward a loss of steady state in that a community would not consider these behaviors a part of successful intervention.

Adaptation

THE PROBLEM: How to Modify the Suprasystem in Ways that Optimize Goal Attainment

The problem is external in the sense that it pertains to conditions existing in the suprasystem that represent barriers to, or at least not optimal conditions for goal attainment. The problem is instrumental in the sense that the focus is on those means that will result in goal attainment.

In understanding the adaptation function, it is important to keep the open systems features of the model in mind. The system comes into existence to serve some need in the suprasystem. The suprasystem is constantly changing, and thus the previously noted need state is constantly changing, thereby affecting the subject system. The problem to be solved is one of seeking to control those suprasystem influences that may have adverse effects on the subject system, and more importantly to attempt to modify the suprasystem in ways that optimize the system's goal attainment efforts. The notion of adaptation is helpful because of its stress on the dynamic interplay between the system and its suprasystem. As used in this model, the adaptation function is proactive not reactive in its basic orientation. Conceptually speaking, the system's posture is that if change is needed (for goal attainment), it is best that the suprasystem change as opposed to the system itself. As a practical matter, changes typically tend to be made externally as well as internally. The central point is that the model assumes that to maintain steady state, every system must address changes occurring in its suprasystem that bear on its reasons for existence. Further, the system will seek to modify the suprasystem before it seeks to modify itself, that is, in terms of dealing with those suprasystem influences that may hinder goal attainment. We are not saying that all formal organizations behave in the prescribed manner, only that the model is so designed. The implication is that, to the extent that an organization does not take such a proactive stance, it deviates from behaving as a social system as set forth in this model. More importantly, if the model is correct in its portrayal of reality, then to the extent that a system is not successful in performing its adaptation function, it increases the chances of a loss of steady state.

Continuing the use of the example of the Midtown Mental Health Center, case managers in the Aftercare Unit will expend some of their time seeking to manipulate the environment of their clients in ways that will enhance the achievement of interventions or treatment goals. An example at the level of the Aftercare Unit itself would be negotiations between the Case Manager with the local welfare department that would result in their workers taking food stamp applications at the client's home as opposed to requiring the client to go to the welfare office; also having the welfare department's volunteers take selected center clients shopping each week for food and other such requirements. Again, these activities pertain to the goal of maintaining clients in the community and, in so doing, reducing the number of such clients returning to inpatient status (the goal attainment function).

A final example of the problem of adaptation would be actions on the part of the center's Executive Director to get the director of the local welfare department to contract with the center to provide mental health consultation services for the social service staff of the welfare department. The purpose of this consultation would be to enhance the capacity of the staff of the welfare department to recognize mental health problems among welfare clients, a high risk group. In so doing, more thoughtful and appropriate referrals could be made between the welfare department and the center. The intended result of this association between the two agencies would be more effective and efficient use of the center's resources and would be evidenced by greater proportions of Midtown's citizens with mental disorders being maintained in the community as opposed to being admitted for more intensive care in the center's Inpatient Unit.

In each of the above examples, the efforts have been aimed at the modification of the center's suprasystem and, in that sense, are external in their orientation. Also, in each example, the actions have been instrumental in relationship to the center's goal attainment function. Finally, it is important that a value judgment not be attached to the adaptation function, that is, that it is manipulative, driven by self-interest and therefore bad. Our position is that the function is inherent in the behavior of social organizations seeking to maintain steady state and thus its inclusion in the model. Also, the function can be performed in a manner that is injurious or hurtful to others, but this is true for all of the functions pertaining to the maintenance of steady state.

Integration

THE PROBLEM: How to Achieve that Alignment of Systems Components that Satisfies its Maintenance Requirements

The problem statement serves both to focus attention on a problem that all systems must solve as well as to highlight the interrelationships among these four problems. The problem could be reformulated as follows: how to achieve that alignment of system components that satisfies maintenance requirements in a manner that does not adversely affect goal achievement. This formulation suggests some tension between the satisfaction of a system's task and maintenance needs, that is, trade off of one for the other. Another possible formulation of the question would be: how to optimize satisfaction of the system's task and maintenance needs. This formulation assumes existence of such an optimal point and the lack of inherent conflict between satisfaction of task and maintenance needs.

The integrative problem represents another way of conceptualizing the task and maintenance issues addressed earlier: the rationalist and the human relationist perspective on organizational behavior. The integrative problem addresses both the internal and the consummatory functions. It is internal in the sense that the needs are those of the system itself, its components including but not limited to the personally based needs of those individuals enacting organizational roles. The problem is consummatory in that it pertains to an end state—need satisfaction.

Now, to continue the example used to illustrate the goal attainment problem. The Aftercare Unit is a part of the center's Outpatient Department and as such has relationships to other units comprising that department, for example, Outpatient Counseling Services. Assumed is that as a subadministrative structure, the Aftercare Unit enjoys a certain status within the administrative and social hierarchy of the center. Assumed also is an affinity that this unit has with other units, derived by forces pertaining to the satisfaction of the social needs of the various social units involved. Similarly, this same affinity is assumed to exist with respect to the social needs of the various individuals enacting organizational roles within the unit. The clearest theoretical support for this assumed affinity is found in the hierarchy of human needs advanced by Maslow and reviewed earlier.[3] Maslow suggested that these needs were genetically based and were thus universal. One of the identified basic needs was to belong, to be loved, to be needed. Maslow advanced a psychological perspective, the presence of a motivational force existing within the individual; but satisfaction of the need to belong is a social experience. Assumed is that, in part, the formation of primary groups is explained by the social needs of those comprising the groups. Further, Gemeinschaft relationships characterizing primary group members are supportive of the social needs identified by Maslow; in other words, they are based on sentiments that are pursued for their own sake.

Earlier the social group was contrasted with the formal organization. Two points are instructive here. First, relationships in primary groups are Gemeinschaft in character, that is, the relationships constitute an end in themselves. They are consummatory for those involved. Second, formal organizations are comprised of groups and, as suggested by the human relationists, these groups have primary- as well as secondary-group characteristics. Inferred from these structural features and the systems perspective is that the Gemeinschaft feature of primary groups (the affinity of individuals toward one another within the group) will have its counterpart in relationships among groups comprising the formal organization. The inference is based on the emergence phenomenon assumed to characterize the various forms and levels of social organization.[4]

Returning to the problem identified as integration, an assumption is made that every formal organization must satisfy the maintenance needs of its component parts, that these needs are social, and they are reflected in an affinity that the system's components have toward one another. At the core, this affinity is viewed as being driven by Gemeinschaft types of relationships, but with an overlay of Gesellschaft dimensions. Here it is important to recall that all groups or administrative units comprising a formal organization can be viewed as subsystems and thus connected by input-output forms of relationships. Thus, by definition, these groups will have Gesellschaft (means-ends) relationships as well as Gemeinschaft.

Now, to return to the example, the Case Managers comprising the center's Aftercare Unit have personal needs that in part are satisfied through their work roles, for example, social belonging and self-esteem. This example is intended to convey that the Case Manager roles do not have an exclusive goal attainment orientation. These roles also comprise a system, and there will be an integrative function performed. In other words, features of the worker-client relationship will meet the personal needs of the worker and client. As indicated in the introduction of this section, depending on one's theoretical orientation, goal attainment pursuits can be viewed as adversely affecting integration efforts and vice versa. The point is that both represent system problems that must be constantly addressed.

Prior to leaving discussion of the problem of integration, another more specific example might be helpful. The Midtown Mental Health Center has a Personnel Department, and this department has the primary responsibility for hiring staff, developing job descriptions, making salary and promotion recommendations, administering the center's leave and professional/staff development policies, and so on. The Personnel Department also administers a day-care program for children of staff members working at the center. Conceptually, this department can be viewed as possessing a primary orientation toward dealing with the system's problems around integration. Again the problem is internal, consisting of needs arising from the social system itself, and it is consummatory because the effort is directed toward the satisfaction of those needs.

Pattern Maintenance

THE PROBLEM: How to Maintain in a Constantly Changing and at Times Volatile Environment the System's Most Important Structural Features, Those that Provide Its Unique Identity/Status

We take the position that every social organization is a separate and distinct social entity and that the preservation of those structural patterns that provide for the essential identity of the organization must be maintained if steady state is to be accomplished. The problem as outlined above deals with the basic structural features of the system; in this sense, it is internal in its orientation. The effort is directed toward the maintenance of core relationships among system components, thus its instrumental character.

The concept of pattern maintenance arises from assumptions made about social organizations and humans who comprise them. It is useful to think of the multiple relationships comprising a social system as possessing various levels of importance. A simple example in a formal organization would be the exchange of work for pay. While there are a variety of relationships that workers have with their employers, one of the most fundamental is the exchange of work for pay. Should that relationship be altered by the employer reducing the pay of his or her workers, there is a likelihood that serious difficulties would follow. The workers might leave their positions, and if all workers left, there would probably be the loss of steady state. Given the importance of this structural feature in formal organizations, the assumption can be made that even during a fiscal crisis every effort will be made to meet payroll—even if payment of some other bills are delayed.

A university offers another more complex example in the relationship that it has with its professors. Historically, it has been thought that the pursuit of knowledge and truth can be best accomplished in an environment characterized by academic freedom. Accordingly, professors have considerable latitude in how they teach their courses and the areas in which they conduct their research. The professor is largely guided by professional ethics and the rules of science, for example, as opposed to administrative rules. The notion of pattern maintenance would hold that academic freedom is so fundamental in the relationship that professors have with their university that it must be maintained at all costs. In other words, goal attainment of the university rests fundamentally on an atmosphere of academic freedom, the means upon which the end of goal attainment rests. In this instance, the assumption would be made that the loss of academic freedom in a university would result in the loss of steady state. In other words, it would no longer be a university.

The final example is based on our hypothetical Midtown Mental Health Center. Fundamental to maintenance of a helping relationship is trust between the therapist and client; clients need to know that information shared with the therapists is confidential. The notion of pattern maintenance would hold that, irrespective of what the external pressures might be, the center would make every reasonable effort to maintain the confidentiality of its records. If clients could no longer trust that what they said in therapy interviews was held as confidential, then the center would no longer be viewed as a mental health center, and it would lose steady state.

The previous examples of pattern maintenance discussed externally based threats to the organization and those organizational responses that sought to protect and maintain essential relationships, perhaps at the expense of those deemed less essential. The final threat to pattern maintenance can be viewed as arising from the system components themselves. Assumed is that every system component is characterized as possessing two opposing forces: one that draws social units closer together, resulting in increased levels of interdependence, and the other that presses for greater amounts of independence, autonomy. Again Maslow is helpful in his assertion of a hierarchy of human needs. This hierarchy can be viewed as constituting a hierarchy of related states of independence, with survival level needs representing the greatest level of dependence on others and self-actualization representing the highest level of independence of others—dependence on self.[5]

Utilizing the logic summarized in the section on integration, we have built into our model an assumption that all systems' subsystems will have propensities toward increased levels of independence. Given this tendency, there is an ever present threat that basic systems patterns could be altered, resulting in the loss of steady state. An example of this tendency toward increased levels of autonomy would be the interest of the staff of Midtown's Outpatient Department in maintaining client fees in a departmental account rather than their going into the center's general account. The reasons offered by department staff stressed the importance of having control over the use of this money so it could be used to meet department needs. The argument was advanced that department control over the use of these funds would provide the incentive for staff to make greater efforts to collect fees from clients.

SUMMARY

This chapter has focused on the dynamics of organizational behavior, the patterns that should be discernible in any formal social organization. The approach builds from Parsons's four-problem paradigm: goal attainment, adaptation, integration, and pattern maintenance. These four concepts identify four problems that every social organization must constantly address in order to maintain steady state, that is, the ordering that distinguishes that organization. These problems are never solved in any final sense, and they are always present. Sought is a steady state, in which the continuing efforts toward resolution represent an ongoing optimization of the four solutions.

Given the assumed universality of these four problems, one should be able to find the arrangements for addressing these four problems in every organization. Given the formality of our so-called formal organizations, the identification of these subsystems should be easier than in, for example, the social group. We believe this is so. Figure 12.4 was used to illustrate the formal organizational structure of our hypothetical Midtown Mental Health Center. Assuming a rational and logical relationship between means and ends, the formal structure should represent an agreed-upon means to achieve the center's mission—"to improve the quality of life of the residents of the Midtown catchment area through the provision of comprehensive quality mental health services." According to Figure 12.4, the Executive Director of the center has five directors reporting to her. Clearly the Clinical Director is the one who has the responsibility to deal with the goal attainment problem—how to improve the quality of life of the people of Midtown through the provision of mental health services. The problem of adaptation seems to fall generally under the purview of the Director of Community Affairs. Normally it is in such a department that an agency's public relations, community education, and community fund-raising functions are lodged. Also rather easily identified is where the responsibility for dealing with the problem of integration rests—the Director of Personnel. We would accept the argument that in most agencies the Director for Administration and Planning or his or her counterpart is also vitally involved in efforts aimed at dealing with the integration problem. Less clear is the administrative assignment of primary responsibility for dealing with the problem of pattern maintenance. Given the vital importance of this function, it may well be that this function is essentially retained at the highest level of management in formal organizations. We do, however, believe that certain aspects of this function can be identified particularly within large organizations. Many formal organizations have what is typically called a "quality control" unit. To the extent that this unit seeks to maintain and enhance the agency's most vital sets of relationships vis-à-vis its function, it is addressing the problem of pattern maintenance. An example of a quality control effort in a professional social work agency would be one in which monitoring would be done to assure that the agency's helping efforts are performed in accordance with specified professional standards.

NOTES

1. See the earlier review of Parsons's concepts and our use of them in Chapter 4. For another review of the use of these concepts in a social work practice context, see discussion in Fred Cox, "Introduction," in *Strategies of Community Organization*, Fred Cox, et al. eds., 4th ed. (Itasca, Ill.: F. E. Peacock Publishers, 1987), 187–212.
2. F. E. Emery, ed., *Systems Thinking* (Baltimore, Md.: Penguin Books, 1969), 10.
3. See discussion of Maslow's theory of a hierarchy of needs in Chapter 2.
4. The concept of emergence has been referred to earlier; see particularly Chapter 2. For a particularly useful discussion, see references in Walter Buckley, *Sociology and Modern Systems Theory* (Englewood Cliffs, N.J.: Prentice Hall, 1967), 111–112 and 142–144.
5. This relationship was diagramed in Figure 2.3, Maslow's Need Hierarchy.

PART V
THE COMMUNITY

The Social Systems Model

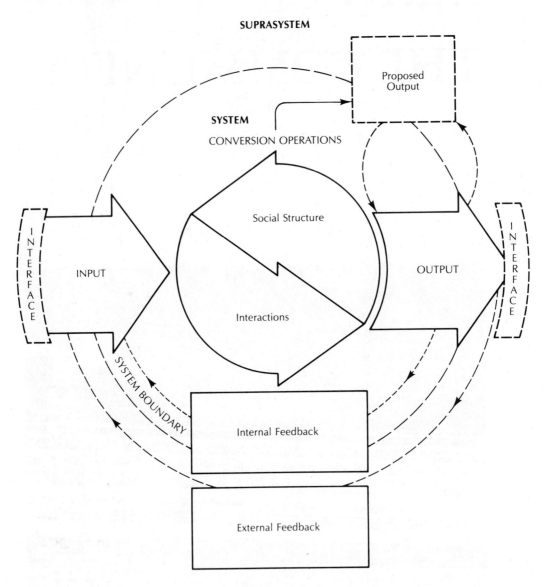

In the final part of this book the social systems model is applied to the community. As in each of the previous parts, we have identified characteristics that distinguish a particular form of social organization from others. The two features that characterize the community are: (1) place, and (2) scope of functions performed.

Given your familiarity by now with the basic concepts comprising the model, we are varying the format by including a practice application of the model to a hypothetical community.

As in each of our earlier parts, the initial chapter is devoted to an introduction of the organizational form being addressed. This is our focus in Chapter 14. Following a brief review of definitions of community, we summarize what we consider to be the main lines of theory development. We make the observation that community theory is less well developed than that applicable to the individual, group, or formal organization. The state of community theory development thereby poses problems to the professional practitioner concerned with community-scale change efforts.

Chapter 15 is devoted to the application of the model to the community. In contrast to the format utilized in earlier chapters, we combine a discussion of the concepts comprising the model with system dynamics.

In Chapter 16 we conclude our discussion of the model with a community application. Our definition of a community focuses on place. It is the common needs, the common problems, and the common opportunities of people who share common living spaces that give rise to the form of social organization that we call the community. Our application of the model focuses on a community's effort to confront a common problem—the maltreatment of children. Specifically, the model is applied to a community subsystem, the child protective services system.

We take the position in Part V that most professional practice at the so-called community level is not with the total community, but rather with some segment of it. With this assumption in mind, our approach could be more appropriately defined as an application of the model to a subsystem of the community, addressing the problem of the maltreatment of children.

Chapter 14

The Community: An Introduction

OUTLINE

Overview

In each of the earlier sections we have mentioned problems in knowledge building posed by lack of consensus on key terms. Knowledge building without clear definitions is like attempting to pick up mercury, a slippery and difficult task. As indicated earlier, our approach is a pragmatic one. We review the definitions of others, offer our own, and attempt in our subsequent discussion to be faithful to that definition.

Like *group* or *formal organization*, everyone is familiar with the term *community*. In fact, if defined in terms of an urban space, almost everybody in this country lives in a community. However, as one starts to probe the meaning of the term, the extent of the problem of definition becomes apparent. For some the concept is associated with a nostalgia of the past, an intimacy of associations in which all people know, care about, and help one another. Frequently this nostalgia is tied to a concern for what is perceived to be happening in urban life today—a loss of community and a growing sense of **anomie**. For others, community and city are synonymous. While this perspective is straightforward, problems arise in any attempt to systematically analyze the community using it. The most evident problem is that a municipal boundary does not always coincide with boundaries of the principal organizations operating within the city, for example, the school system, the mental health catchment areas, the welfare and health districts, the United Appeal service area, and so on.

Some writers do not restrict the concept of community to a place, but include all of

373

those who might share a common interest, have a common heritage, pursue the same profession, and so on. These functional communities (as distinguished from geographical communities) would include such diverse examples as the business, Christian, Irish, gay, and social work communities. The problems with usage of the term have become so severe that one leading scholar has questioned the continued use of the term in social science research.[1]

Our position is that, while the multiple uses made of the term community are troublesome, its level of familiarity and the common elements of its meaning are great assets and far outweigh its liabilities. In part, the multiple uses of the term can be viewed as attempts to capture the essence of a social phenomenon pertaining to interdependence—the need people have for one another. What is needed is a renewed effort aimed at developing a schemata of the community—one that recognizes and builds from the notion of interdependence and is based on the common needs of those sharing the same habitat. Such a schemata would serve the practitioner as well as the researcher. In fact, our position has been derived in part from the rich tradition of community work performed by practitioners representing a number of different professions. Implicit in their work is the notion that the community is a social entity and one that significantly affects people's lives. The work of community practitioners, while focused on this elusive concept, "community," is ultimately aimed at improving the quality of life of the individual. These professionals operate under a variety of different names—community developers, community planners, community organizers, and community health specialists, to mention but a few.

Many community practitioners and those who write about community forms of practice observed and discussed the systemic qualities of the community long before systems theory was fashionable. For example, in social work, over thirty years ago, Murray Ross observed, "The community is a complex whole, all parts of which are related, interact, and influence one another. To select one part of this whole and identify it as the primary cause of integration or disintegration is not possible."[2] Ross was writing about the practice of community organization, one of the recognized methods of practice in social work. Unlike casework, where a specific client is the object of the change effort, the community, or more likely some aspect of the community, is the object of change (for example, a neighborhood). Again, unlike casework, the form of practice is indirect (planning, organizing, and coordinating the work of various groups) as opposed to direct (for example, counseling, which involves one-to-one contact with a client). While in both instances the client is the ultimate intended beneficiary, community organization change efforts are aimed at organizational or interorganizational features of the community that are perceived to adversely affect clients.

The distinction between direct and indirect forms of professional intervention is crucial in building a practice-relevant definition of community. The differences in practice approaches relate to where the problem is assumed to be located and/or where intervention should be focused. In community organization (and other professional forms of community practice), the problem is seen as existing primarily in the social structure of the community, not in the social or psychological makeup of an individual or a group of people. An example might be a community in which those who are thought to be mentally ill are temporarily placed in jail to await a court hearing to determine whether they should be committed to a mental health center. A community assessment of this situation concludes that this action reinforces belief systems among those jailed that complicate subsequent helping efforts (i.e., jailed mentally ill people believe that they have done something wrong and are being punished or that people are after them). In such a community, the target of social work intervention would be the community values and legal system and the related police and court practices that result in treating the troubled person like a criminal. While the form of intervention is essentially organizational or interorganizational, the beneficiaries are a class of people residing in the same locality and possessing similar problems—mental illness. This vignette assumes there is an entity called "community," and intervention is focused on organizing or reorganizing how the community goes about dealing with the problem of mental illness. As indicated earlier, the problem in its essence is that there are existing forms of community practice but a lack of consensus on theory that supports and enhances that practice.

Social work is not the only profession that trains people for community practice; so does medicine, nursing, law, the ministry, and so on. Historically, perhaps public health is the profession best known for community practice. Early in the development of this country there was a recognition that community life posed significant health hazards because of the level of interdependence and physical closeness of people. In tracing the history of public health, George Rosen noted:

> The major problems of health that men have faced have been concerned with community life, for instance, the control of transmissible disease, the control and improvement of the physical environment (sanitation), the provision of water and food of good quality and in sufficient supply, the provision of medical care, and the relief of disability and destitution.[3]

Public health practice for a number of professional groups was a response to these community problems. Unlike the personal health care of the individual, the focus of public health is on the community—on a population at risk with respect to one or more health hazards. In public health, efforts are aimed not only at ameliorating existing or potential health problems, but also at promoting health and the general quality of community life as well.

Many significant public policy enactments have been premised on a conception of community. These laws not only assume the existence of community but support the notion that the community is the object of social intervention efforts by professionals.

The passage by the federal government of the Mental Retardation Facilities and Community Mental Health Centers Construction Act of 1963 represents one of the most important of these policy enactments.[4] This law not only recognizes the community by title, but sets forth a national strategy rooted in attacking the problem of mental illness (and mental retardation) and the promotion of mental health within the context of the community. Significant in our approach to a definition of community is an implicit assumption in this legislation that treats the community as a microcosm of society—but more of this later.

Definitions

In the paragraphs ahead we will review some of the approaches utilized to define and study the community. Our attempt is to share the ideas of other writers who have helped to shape our approach to modeling the community as a social system. Before proceeding, let us set forth our definition: "A community is a territorially based social organization through which most people satisfy their common needs and desires, deal with their common problems, and through which they relate to their society." The definition reflects the outcome orientation of the social systems model. It answers the question: What does a community do? There are also several distinctive features to the definition:

1. It is a form of social organization that is tied to a physical or geographical place. In this definition, the concept is not extended to groups of people sharing an interest or cause.
2. It focuses on the people who reside in and/or are identified with a common place. The community should have as its highest purpose the improvement of the quality of life for those who live there.
3. The interdependence that is inherent in the notion of social organization is linked to the presence of common needs, common problems, and opportunities for growth and development. In short, the community is viewed as a form of social organization that has come into existence in part because it provides comprehensive arrangements through which and by which people can meet their common needs and deal with their common problems. It follows, then, that cooperation and competition are the main social processes. It should also be noted that at a narrower range recognition is given that other forms of social organization can provide for the satisfaction of selected needs and the means for seeking resolution of selected problems, for example, a mental health center. Also, while cooperation and competition are the principal social processes, there are others, including conflict.
4. The assumption is made that the community is the dominant (but not the only) intermediate organization through which the individual relates to his or her society and through which society relates to the individual. In a conceptual sense, we view the community as a societal subsystem.

Our definition of community borrows heavily from Maslow in terms of operationalizing the concepts of needs and desires.[5] Barriers to need satisfaction and desires form the bases of common problems. The notion of relating to society refers to the medium through which individuals encounter and deal with society—how they learn about their societal role(s) and discharge their societal responsibilities (such as voting, paying taxes, and otherwise carrying out the role of citizen).

With this general introduction and presentation of a definition, we will proceed with a review of some of the community theory literature that led us to this definition and to our particular approach to modeling the community as a social system.

Community Theory: Lines of Development

The search for a definition of community offers a well-worn but intriguing path for writers. The dictionary, as is so frequently the case, offers a useful and convenient beginning point—"a unified body of individuals: the people with common interests living in a particular area: an interacting population of various kinds of individuals in a common location."[6] Webster's definition does not restrict the concept of community to place: it also includes the notion of functional communities, "a group linked by a common policy: a body of persons of common and especially professional interests scattered throughout a larger society." It would appear that these definitions would accommodate such diverse community forms as people of the Roman Catholic faith, people residing in San Francisco, people visiting Disneyland, recipients for Aid for Dependent Children, and all of the nation's dentists. These diverse definitions also help to illustrate the problem that must be solved if a social systems approach or any approach is to be employed to work with the community—the lack of consensus on what is meant by the concept "community."

How have other theorists and writers approached the definition and study of the community? Weber in his insightful and parsimonious approach focused on the economic interdependence among people and viewed the community as a social structure that evolved to provide for the regular exchange of goods. In its essence he saw the community as a marketplace.[7] From this perspective, the community can be viewed as a particular form of social organization, shaped in large part by common human needs and the increased interdependence of people caused by society's moving from agrarian to mercantile, and later to industrial forms of economies. Weber is helpful in drawing attention to the interdependence of people in terms of their needs and in understanding the contrived nature of the community as a form of social organization.

Robert Ezra Parks is also helpful in terms of extending an examination of the interdependence among people sharing the same locale.[8] He moves beyond a focus on the economic forms of this interdependence in his ecological conceptualization of the community. Perhaps more than any other theorist, he helps to examine the tie of humans to a physically defined place. In building his conceptualization, Parks views the essential features of the community as: "(1) a population, territorially organized, (2) more or less completely rooted in the soil it occupies, (3) its individual units living in a relationship of mutual interdependence that is symbiotic rather than societal."[9] Parks moves attention on the interdependence of humans beyond their economic and social dimensions to the broader interplay of these dimensions with the physical and "man-made" aspects of the environment. His concentration on the relationships between human behavior and other features of the habitat are especially useful in community intervention efforts aimed at improving environmental conditions and the balance of people and nature.

Israel Rubin, on the other hand, disregards the territorial element of the community and its purpose of providing for the daily needs of its members and views the community as a form of social organization that serves a mediating function between the individual and society.[10] In developing his position, he draws on Durkheim:

A society composed of an infinite number of unorganized individuals that a hypertrophied State is forced to oppress and contain, constitutes a veritable sociological monstrosity. For collective activity is always too complex to be able to be expressed through the single and unique organ of the State. Moreover, the State is too remote from the individuals; its relations with them too external and intermittent to penetrate deeply into individual consciences and socialize them within. Where the State is the only environment in which we can live communal lives, they inevitably lose contact, become detached, and thus society disintegrates. A nation can be maintained only if, between the State and the individual, there is intercalated a whole series of secondary groups near enough to the individuals to attract them strongly in this sphere of action and drag them in this way into the general torrent of social life.[11]

Rubin argues that individuals relate to their societies through nonterritorial as well as territorial structures. He views the action of some theorists to tie the concept of community to place as limiting and one that detracts from the central function of a community—that is, providing the medium for the individual to relate to his or her society. While we do not share Rubin's concern about the territorial ties of the concept, we do find his arguments regarding the need for intermediate structures between the individual and society helpful in conceptualizing community output and for viewing the community as a primary societal subsystem.

By definition, social organizations are comprised of interdependent and interacting parts. Harold Kaufman's thoughts are helpful in examining community processes.[12] His writings complement those of Rubin's by demonstrating ways that the individual operating in a community context relates to societal forces. Kaufman suggests that the community be viewed as an "interactional field." The elements in his formulation include individuals, associations (formally and informally constituted groups), and stages and phases of their actions. In short, the field consists of a network of actions conducted by people working through various organizations and aimed at problem solving for the local community. We found that Lewin's field theory provides a helpful background to Kaufman's formulation of the community.[13]

Kaufman introduces several ideas that are useful in the construction of a definition of community: (1) community actions are conceptualized as problem solving; and (2) problem solving is aimed at securing a local adjustment to the broader changes that occur at the societal level. The community operates like a microcosm of the larger society, and individuals working mainly through community-based associations seek forms of adjustment to a constantly changing society; and (3) the principal social units through which community action takes place are locally based formal and informal associations. In other words, the individual participates in community activity largely through organizational roles.

In contrast to the rational features of community processes identified by Kaufman, Morton Long, in a classic essay, likens the community to an "ecology of games."[14] Using game playing as an analogy, he examines the interactions among people and their organizations in the community. Rather than a single game being played, Long suggests there are many, but all loosely related in a symbiotic manner. There is the political game, the school game, the business game, the social work game, the police game, and so on. Each game has its own set of rules, strategies, and tactics imbedded in culture and in symbiotic relationships. As a consequence, the behavior of each game player is predictable (assuming you know which game is being played). In fact, knowledge of how other people play their games is crucial in how successfully a given player (or a group of players) can play his or her own game. For example, the person playing the business game must be aware of how the banking, legal, and political games are played; because to play the business game well, the person will sometimes need the assistance of these other game players, or at least not their opposition. Similarly, for those other players to do well in their respective games, they will need the assistance of those playing the business game.

We found several features of Long's game-playing analogy especially useful in conceptualizing the community. First, nobody is in charge of the overall game—there is no central authority, and, in fact, there is no single overall game or overall winner. Second, the coordination that occurs between the games is more unconscious than conscious (reflecting the symbiotic relationship among units); and the results, while largely unplanned, are generally functional for the many games and game players. Third, the relationship of the games to one another differs from a natural ecology because of the existence of a territorially based general public. To some extent, the game players play their game with one eye on the scoreboard and the other on the general public (the fans). While the general public does not normally exert any direct formal control over how the game is conducted, the public does evaluate performance and thus has an influence. This influence is most clearly seen in play of the social game. It is through the social game that social standing is obtained. Fourth, while territorially based, most games, except the newspaper game, have a specific rather than general territorial interest and concern. This is important because the newspaper can alert and gain the attention of the general public. As a consequence, it is the one game that can set a communitywide agenda and to some extent influence how others play their respective games. Finally, perhaps most importantly, Long's game-playing analogy introduces the ecological concept of **symbiosis** to the construction of community theory. In so doing, he introduces an approach for the study of the interdependence that characterizes the various organizations and groups that share a common habitat.

One of the most comprehensive theories of community has been set forth by Roland Warren.[15] He defines the community "to be that combination of social units and systems that perform the major social functions having locality relevance."[16] The definition contains several key features: (1) it builds from the notion of place (the community is territorially based); and (2) definable social functions are performed in support of the daily living requirements of the people and organizations sharing the same habitat. To the extent that these social functions have locality relevance, they pertain to and are part of the community. Warren identifies five major functions that have locality relevance.[17]

1. Production-distribution-consumption
2. Socialization
3. Social control
4. Social participation
5. Mutual support

According to Warren, it is the network of individuals, organizations, and other social units performing or making use of these functions in a particular locality (place) that constitutes community. While the performance of these five functions should be thought of as constituting a whole, each can be identified as a functional area or subsystem. Further, Warren notes that the performance of these functions can be carried out by formally and informally constituted groups, and that one social unit (like the family) might be involved in the performance of several of these functions (socialization, social control, and mutual support).

Warren carefully makes the point that the community does not necessarily exercise specific responsibility for, or exercise specific control over the provision of these functions. In many if not most instances, control rests outside the community. An example would be a General Motors automobile assembly plant located in a specific community, for example, Oklahoma City. The decisions regarding numbers of people to be employed or monthly production quotas for the local plant would not be made in Oklahoma City, but rather at the corporate headquarters of General Motors in Detroit. Nevertheless, the provision of local employment opportunities and the purchase of locally available goods and services by that plant would represent key features of the performance of the production-distribution-consumption function for that community.

Warren's formulation of the community is as a social system, and thus it makes a special contribution to the conceptualization being developed here. He incorporates both a horizontal and vertical dimension in his formulation. It is through the vertical connections that community-based organizations are attached to their parent organization, as in the General Motors example. Similarly and conceptually, it is through these external ties that the community is linked to society and in effect functions as a societal subsystem. Warren and Long are both helpful in thinking about how subsystems might be conceptualized in a social systems model applied to the community.

In reviewing the literature on community theory, one is struck by comparisons between the community and two other forms of social organization, the social group, particularly the family, and the formal organization. Historically and until recently, the family performed to one degree or another all of the locality relevant functions noted by Warren. Particularly in agrarian economies, the family in its extended form was an economic unit and was much more self-sufficient than the nuclear family of today. In the past, the family has had a much larger socialization and social control responsibility over its members than is the case today. Finally, the social participation and mutual support functions were also more clearly exercised in earlier family forms in contrast to the role of today's family. As modern societies have evolved and become more specialized, the community has emerged as a principal structure for performing essentially similar functions as earlier provided by the family. While the functions are being performed by specific (groups of) organizations, these organizations share three things: (1) the same locality; (2) the people who reside in the locality who are dependent upon them; and (3) their dependence on each other.

Contrasting the concepts of community and formal organizations can also be instructive. The most obvious difference is that communities are territorially bounded while formal organizations are not. While all formal organizations occupy physical space, the connection between that space and the organization is tenuous. The building can be sold or the lease terminated, and the organization can be moved to another location. Not so with a community—its physical location is central to its identity (notwithstanding the few instances in which communities have been moved because of natural disasters, dam construction, and so on).

The notion of "formal" gets at another major difference between communities and formal organizations. The latter organizations are formally constituted under law; they are specific legal entities; communities, like a social group, are a conceptual designation. Depending on their legal status, they can be bought and sold, can enter into contracts with one another, and can engage in a variety of other activities specified in their legal charters; not so with communities. In a formal organization, someone is in charge and that person is responsible for setting the agenda; no one is in charge of a community. The relationships between member units are established by contract and are assumed to be related to one another in terms of an agenda—the organization's goals. In short, they are essentially Gesellschaft in nature; in contrast, Gemeinschaft relationships dominate in communities.

Communities and formal organizations also differ in terms of goals. In relative terms, the goals of a formal organization are explicit, specific, narrow in scope, and sanctioned by a legal charter. In contrast, the community's goals are implicit, broad, vague, and without formal sanction.

Finally, next to societies, the community is the most inclusive of all forms of social organization. In this respect it differs from the exclusive character of formal organizations.

We have based our approach to modeling the community as a social system on the following distinctive features of the community. Communities:

1. are territorially based
2. are characterized by relationships among member units that are not usually formally or contractually based; rather the relationships are symbiotic and pertain to the needs of those sharing the same habitat
3. are a subsystem of society and, while more inclusive, the society is organized in a structural manner similar to the community
4. are essentially flat structurally; that is, the social units comprising the community are horizontally related to one another with a relatively undeveloped vertical pattern. (In this sense, structurally the community more resembles a social group than a formal organization. In this same sense, recognition needs to be given to the strong ties that individual social units of the community may have to other organizations external to the subject community, for example, a local plant's ties to its home office.)
5. do not have a formally constituted goal structure, but one can be derived from the common needs and problems faced by people sharing the same habitat
6. tend to be similarly structured, the structure being derived from the society of which it is a part and the common needs of people who share the same habitat
7. integrate the social units in two general ways: (1) through sharing a similar culture, and (2) through symbiotic (interdependent) relationships
8. like all other forms of social organization, derive their energy from the individuals who comprise the community and their efforts at need satisfaction. Although the community lacks vertical organization, every community has decision-making structures that informally are vertically organized and are popularly referred to as "power structures."

Community Practice Theory: Lines of Development

In the section just concluded, we reviewed the writings of several community theorists. The effort was to identify some of the lines of theory development that helped shape the definition of community and the approach to conceptualizing the community as a social system. In this section there is a similar intent, but this time the aim is to identify the main lines in the development of community practice theory. One might think that practice theory would build from a general theory of community. Given a comprehensive and unified theory of community, this might be the case. As noted earlier, this is not the case; so what we have are two relatively independent lines of development.

Recall that in the systems model, theory is treated as a feature of structure; like all features of structure, it is a guide for behavior. In other words, a particular theory of community will affect what data are gathered by the user of the systems model and how that data will be organized and perhaps interpreted. Similarly, the model user will be affected by his or her theory of community practice. Our position is that the systems model provides a useful framework for integrating community theory and practice theory. It should therefore be helpful at this point to briefly survey community practice theory. A logical starting place is the Community Organization Curriculum Development Project sponsored by the Council of Social Work Education. In writings resulting from that project, Perlman and Gurin[18] identify four views of community practice: (1) Strengthening Community Participation and Integration, (2) Enhancing Coping Capacities, (3) Improving Social Conditions and Services, and (4) Advancing the Interests of Disadvantaged Groups.

Strengthening Community Participation and Integration

Ross is cited as a principal spokesperson for this conception of practice.[19] Writing in the mid-1950s, Ross was one of the earlier authors to adopt a social systems perspective in formulating community practice. The approach is captured by his oft-quoted definition of community organization: "a process by which a community identifies its needs or objectives, orders (or ranks) these needs or objectives, develops the confidence and will to work at these needs or objectives, finds the resources (internal and/or external) to deal with these needs or objectives, takes action in respect to them, and in so doing extends and develops cooperative and collaborative attitudes and practices in the community."[20]

The conceptualization of community organization by Ross applies to both geographical and functional communities. As suggested by the definition, the approach embodies a problem-solving methodology and relies primarily on cooperative processes. The community problem conditions are seen as general ones having their origins in the twin forces of industrialization and urbanization. The effects of these forces in the quickening pace of social change is an erosion of the social ties among people—a loss of a sense of community. In keeping with our earlier references to Tönnies, the concepts in Gemeinschaft and Gesellschaft relationships are again helpful.[21] In these terms, movement was from Gemeinschaft to Gesellschaft relationships among community members.

Ross defines community organization as a social work process. He also considers the several social work methods as having a great deal in common. In this connection, he notes:

> Thus, while the context in which the caseworker, group worker, or the worker in community organization operates is quite different, fundamentally the objectives they seek and the means they use to achieve these ends have a good deal in common. If we were to adapt to casework our statement defining community organization, it would read: "The caseworker seeks to help the individual identify his problems, develop the confidence and will to deal with these problems, find the resources (internal and external) to deal with these problems, take action in respect to these problems, and in so doing increase his understanding of himself and his capacity for integration." We should then be defining approximately what the caseworker or psychotherapist attempts with an individual client.[22]

From a social systems perspective, the Strengthening Community Participation and Integration approach emphasizes open system features; it suggests that to deal with substantive changes occurring in the suprasystem, the community needs greater structural elaboration and integration. The approach is distinguishable based on its general developmental character. Strategically, the focus is on maintenance forms of proposed outputs, for example, enhancement of the system itself. The model emphasizes the creation of structure and relies on consensus-seeking strategies involving the total community for building this structure. In such a conception of community change, the practitioner is primarily an enabler and secondarily a teacher. Geographically based examples of this approach to practice may be found in Third World communities adjusting to the demands of industrialization and rapid urbanization; small communities in the sunbelt of the United States experiencing rapid growth and the effects of particular forms of technology, with firms moving into the community producing computers and other "high tech" products; and transitional neighborhoods in established communities.

Enhancing Coping Capacities

Lippitt is considered to be a principal representative of this approach to practice.[23] He and his colleagues formulated a general theory of planned change that would help people improve their level of functioning. Lippitt examines change efforts at four levels: the individual personality, the face-to-face group, the organization, and the community. Much of the current popularity of the terms **client system** (those being helped) and **change agent** (the professional helper) can be attributed to Lippitt.

This theoretical approach to practice as proposed by Ross emphasizes an open system perspective. The client system at each level is viewed as being affected by a world in rapid change. Lippitt and his colleagues make the assumption, however, that in relative terms, each level can be regarded as a closed system for purposes of intervention.[24] In other words, problems are seen as arising in part because of the rapid changes taking place in the suprasystem and because the four levels of systems being studied tend to have a conservative bias that causes them to resist change, to become closed systems. In short, old coping patterns are not effective in handling the new problems that constantly arise. As a consequence, problems mount and outside assistance is needed.

This formulation of the community is defined in political and ecological terms and is comprised of a variety of interacting parts. Beyond its systemic features, Lippitt has little to say that would contribute to community theory; his attention is focused on development of practice theory.

This approach to practice makes important distinctions between the helping efforts aimed at improving the relationship between the client system and its environment and those focused on changes in the system's internal processes. As evidenced by the name given this approach (Enhancing Coping Capacities), the ultimate aim of practice is an improved capacity of the system to cope with its environment, that is, to move from a closed to an open system state.

In examining helping efforts focused on internal relationships, Lippitt identifies three problem areas:[25]

1. Faulty internal distribution of power (decision making)
2. Ineffective mobilization of energies (motivation)
3. Faulty communications (incomplete/inaccurate feedback)

Intervention efforts are based on the correction or amelioration of these problems.

Three categories of problems are also identified that pertain to the client system's orientation to external relationships:[26]

1. Correspondence between internal and external reality
2. Correspondence between goals and values for action of the client system and its environment
3. Inadequate skills and strategies for action of the client system

Planned change efforts that are conducted through a relationship with the client system are directed toward dealing with one or more of these problems.

Lippitt suggests that every type of client system possesses characteristic patterns of growth and development. Communities are viewed as possessing at least three distinct phases: (1) growth and expansion; (2) stability; and (3) periods of decline. The particular phase in which a client system is operating is important, according to Lippitt, because it has an effect on the kind of change that can be undertaken. In the approach suggested by Lippitt, five general phases of the change process are identified:[27]

1. Development of a need for change ("unfreezing")
2. Establishment of a change relationship
3. Working toward change ("moving")
4. Generalization and stabilization of change ("freezing")
5. Achieving a terminal relationship

Lippitt and Ross both did their writings in the 1950s, and their approaches have many common features. Both give evidence of an underlying therapeutic model of change, domination of cooperative processes in the change effort, and adjustments by the client system to the changes and other influences in its external environment as opposed to efforts aimed at changing features in the environment. It is essentially a reactive as opposed to a proactive formulation of community behaviors. From the perspective taken in the systems model developed in these writings, little attention is given to the notion of adaptation, that is, the manipulation of the suprasystem in terms of the goals of the subject social system.

Improving Social Conditions and Services

The approaches to community practice suggested by Ross and Lippitt stress maintenance goals—building the capacity of the community to be in greater harmony with its environment and thus better able to meet the needs of its residents. The authors who are representative of the final two approaches to practice wrote some ten years later (mid-1960s), at a time when the nation had grown increasingly more concerned about its massive social problems.

Morris and Binstock are considered representative writers of the approach called Improving Social Conditions and Services.[28] Their concern is with the behavior of formal organizations, their policies and procedures, and the means of bringing about changes in such organizations. Their approach to practice is from the position of a planner, although according to the authors, "it is difficult to distinguish planners from their employing organizations. In some measure, their interests, motivation, and means are those of their employers."[29]

Morris and Binstock give more attention to the notion of power and of conflicting interests and needs within the community than did either Ross or Lippitt. Organizations and communities are viewed as possessing power structures with special interests and concerns. These "dominant factions" both within organizations and between organizations are key determinants in any effort at social change. The planner, a technician, seeks an understanding of the interest and behaviors of these dominant factions in formulating and pursuing social change goals. The following pathways for influencing dominant factions are identified by the authors:

   a. Obligation
   b. Friendship
   c. Rational persuasion
   d. Selling
   e. Coercion
   f. Inducement

Similarly, a series of resources are identified and available to the planner for use through one or more of the pathways just identified:

   a. Money and credit
   b. Personal energy
   c. Professional expertise
   d. Popularity
   e. Social standing, political standing
   f. Control of information
   g. Legitimacy and legality

In this approach to practice, the planner possesses expert knowledge and skills in organizational and interorganizational change. Organizations are the tools for dealing with social problems, and thus become the focal point for changes that help them become more relevant in terms of the needs of those they were designed to serve.

From a social systems perspective, the community is viewed as structurally mature and functional. In this sense, the main structural features of the community are considered functional in terms of community resources and goals (inputs and proposed outputs). Also, communities are viewed as culturally diverse with various contending interests. In contrast to the positions noted by Ross and Lippitt, this approach envisions a more complicated and volatile environment for planned change efforts.

Advancing the Interests of Disadvantaged Groups

Grosser is a representative writer espousing this approach to community change.[30] This conception of practice is predicated on the need for basic structural changes in the community. Those advocating this position hold that wealth, power, knowledge, and other such resources are unequally distributed in society and thus in communities. As a consequence of this inequity, there are people in the community who are unable to satisfy their needs and deal with their common problems. In short, they are oppressed by those who control the community. The aim of this approach is a realignment and a more equal distribution of resources. Unlike Lippitt, who stresses the "enhancement of coping capacities" in a **nonzero-sum** context, Grosser's approach operates from a different premise and requires the use of different strategies. His approach is essentially **zero sum**—there are winners and losers. Helping efforts seek to engage the poor in the decision-making process of the community, both to overcome apathy and estrangement and to realign the power resources of the community by creating channels through which the consumers of social welfare services can define their problems and goals and negotiate on their behalf. Conflict strategies (strikes, boycotts, public demonstrations) become dominant processes as opposed to cooperation. The professional roles employed emphasize the activist, advocate, and broker as opposed to the enabler or expert.

From a social systems perspective, the community is viewed as structurally mature but relatively closed to the interests and needs of specific groups within the community. In short, selected structural features of the community are considered dysfunctional to the needs of the poor and not subject to change through use of education and related cooperative strategies. This assessment suggests use of contest strategies that force change in the targeted structures.

In concluding their review of these four approaches, Perlman and Gurin note: "Our examination of practice has persuaded us that there is no single methodology that fits all the dimensions of this field and that there is little consistency in the extent to which the various dimensions of practice are correlated with one another."[31] These authors then formulate an approach to practice that contains three principal features:

1. Purpose
2. Method
3. Context

Building from an earlier conception of practice by Lane, they view the purpose of community intervention as a redistribution of resources, functions, and decision-making power. Any or all these factors may represent a target of intervention. In other words, the inability of community residents to satisfy needs or deal with their problems can be traced to one or more of these factors.

The method of intervention is problem solving, which is conceived as:

a. Defining the problem
b. Establishing structural and communication links for consideration of the problem
c. Studying alternative solutions and adoption of a policy
d. Developing and implementing a program plan
e. Monitoring and feedback[32]

The application of this problem-solving approach is seen as possessing a circular (spiral-like) as opposed to a lock-step pattern. Steps blend into one another with adjustments constantly being made because of an ever-changing environment (suprasystem).

Perlman and Gurin also argue that most of the variations in practice can be accounted for by the organizational context in which it is conducted, for example, the organization that employs the practitioner. These authors identify the various contexts and then illustrate how these different settings affect the purposes and methodology of practice. The three contexts of practice identified are:

1. Voluntary associations (State Mental Health Association)
2. Service agencies (Department of Welfare)
3. Planning organizations (Health and Welfare Planning Council)[33]

Community practice is typically conducted by persons who are employees. Thus, the work of Perlman and Gurin is particularly helpful because they identify the agency as a principal variable affecting how practice is conducted. Similarly, the Community Organization Curriculum Development Project was helpful in providing an opportunity for the profession to take stock of its efforts in formulating a theory of community practice.

One of the best known classifications of approaches to community practice is found in an anthology authored by Cox, and others.[34] In the lead article, Rothman with Tropman identifies three models of community organization: Model A—Locality Development; Model B—Social Planning; and Model C—Social Action. His analysis of these three models is based on a set of eleven practice variables. The matrix produced provides a useful way of describing and comparing the three models.[35]

The three models can be summarized as follows:

Model A—Locality Development

Rothman's Model A embodies many of the practice concepts advanced by Ross and Lippitt. Other writers cited by Rothman who suggest a similar approach to social change include the Biddles,[36] Goodenough,[37] and Cary.[38]

Model A is premised on a developmental model of social change and relies on broad-based citizen participation in all aspects of the change process. The change agent is an enabler and convenor, a person who believes in and practices self-help techniques.

The people sharing the same locality are helped to identify common problems and to set an agenda to advance the common good. The change agent/helper also serves as a teacher, offering help in a "community application of the problem-solving process." Strategically the helping process is focused on developing a community problem-solving capability. The assumption is that as community members see what they are able to accomplish through these cooperative group efforts, they will apply this capability to other community problems, and the general development process will be continued.

From a social systems perspective, this model focuses on developing through group processes community structures that assist those people sharing the same locale to more effectively meet their common needs and deal with their common problems. The name given to the model is instructive—locality development. Conceptually, the problems arising can be viewed as an absence of or a partially developed community infrastructure needed by people to meet their needs and to solve their problems.

Model B — Social Planning

Rothman's Model B parallels the previously cited writings by Morris and Binstock. Other authors employing essentially similar formulations of the change process include Wilson[39] and Perloff.[40]

Model B embodies a technical approach utilizing a problem-solving methodology and focuses on substantial community social problems—housing, delinquency, illness, and child abuse, for example. The change agents are the technocrats, who apply their knowledge and skill within the framework of large complex social welfare organizations. The assumption is that these social problems are understandable and that knowledge and technology exist to ameliorate them. The focus is on the delivery of goods and services to those in need. Where problems are found to exist, these problems are explicated and actions taken to "fix" them.

Task goals dominate the change effort in Model B. Relatively little attention is directed toward capacity building through broadly based community participation. The assumption is made that the capacity for change is within the sanction and capabilities of the organizations vested with the change effort, for example, the statutory authority of a welfare agency. Similarly, this model does not build from any assumption of a need for major structural changes in society or in the community. In short, Model B does not include a radical change philosophy or methodology.

From a social systems perspective, the model assumes that the necessary community infrastructure is in place and operative. Feedback is crucial in the operation of this model. The model also assumes a consensus on community goals. Also, as in Model A, an open system stance is taken. The importance of planning is premised in the need for the community to be able to adapt to a constantly changing and at times disruptive suprasystem. Crucial in this formulation is that the community structures (organizational and normative) are flexible and functionally adaptable to the aims of the planned change efforts.

Model C — Social Action

The earlier cited writings by Grosser provide the parallel to Rothman's social action model of change. Other writers contributing to this model of change include Alinsky,[41] Haggstrom,[42] and Weisner.[43]

Model C involves not only a substantial departure in methodology, but in ideology as well, when compared to the other two models of change. Contest and conflict tactics dominate this change strategy. Use of this model is predicated on an assumption that a subpopulation of disadvantaged and oppressed people exists within the community and that existing structures are either unresponsive, impotent, or systematically victimizing this population. The change agent's roles are derived from this formulation and include advocate, broker, negotiator, and/or agitator. The strategy relies on raising consciousness so that the client system defines itself as the victim of oppressive community-based actions. The victims must also come to believe that through collective action they can overcome these victimizing practices and create a more just community. Both the locality development and social action models rely on an empowerment strategy involving those who possess the problem—the client system, or those we would designate as "signal inputs." In Model A, a nonzero-sum formulation of power is made; as a consequence of collective action (organization) the total power of the community is enhanced and all citizens benefit through gaining more control over their own lives. In contrast, Model C is a zero-sum game. The problem is grounded in an unequal distribution of power so that some people can and do oppress others to their own advantage. The empowerment of those who are victims (using organizational techniques) results in a loss of power by other factions and thus the increased ability of the powerless to control their own lives.

Utilizing a social systems perspective, the problems of the clients are not of their own making. Rather, they result from interactions with the social environment—structural features of the community itself. Racism and sexism resulting in job discrimination and related practices are examples. The model is premised on the assumption that the community structures—organizational and normative—are well developed (in contrast to Model A), but are not subject to change utilizing one of the other models. In short, the change must be forced, and thus the rationale for use of contest strategies. The model suggests that in relative terms the community has taken on closed system features, feedback has not resulted in the maintenance of steady state, and the forces of entropy are in evidence.

Rothman's formulation of three models of community organization is especially helpful as a classification effort and represents a useful step in building a theory of practice. As Rothman notes, it is important analytically to view each approach as an attempt to construct "pure" forms.[44] The intent is to build a model in which the distinctive features are highlighted as a means of assisting analysis. In actual practice, and based on a series of considerations, the likelihood is that the approach taken might include features of each of the models.

Rothman's three models of practice are easily related to a social systems formulation of the community in the sense that each model can be viewed as resting on assumptions about the structure of the community. Each model aims at a change effort focusing on these structural features; all aim at helping people residing in the community to more effectively meet their needs and deal with their common problems.

The final conceptualization of community practice to be summarized has been set forth by Chin and Benne.[45] Here the focus is not on the community, but on all systems levels—from the individual to society. The authors identify three types of strategies of planned change, each based on somewhat different assumptions and each focusing on different tactics in the change effort. The three categories are: (1) empirical–rational; (2) normative–reeducative; and (3) power–coercive.

Empirical–Rational

No single writer is credited with the origins of this approach to planned change. Rather, the orientation is imbedded with the orientation of the Enlightenment and of Classical Liberalism in Western Europe and in this country. Ignorance and superstition were the barriers to human progress with science and education being the tools to overcome these barriers.

The fundamental assumption underlying this approach is that people are rational and are moved by self-interest. Planned change builds on the additional assumption that people will follow their rational self-interest once it is revealed to them. At a societal level in this country, the strategy of a free public education for all children rests in large part on this strategy of change. The public school is the vehicle for transmission of knowledge, skills, and values to the young as they prepare for societal roles. Societal progress toward human betterment is rooted in scientific knowledge building and the transmission of this knowledge through varied educational techniques.

Barriers to social progress include the pace of scientific development along with the special problems associated with the transmission and application of knowledge. Having the right person in the right job is critical in this formulation. The writings of Weber on bureaucratic forms of social organization are instructive from this perspective.[46] Here Weber cites the importance of proper preparation for organizational positions with appointment and promotion to such positions being based on merit as opposed to personal considerations. The applications for community-scale interventions include efforts aimed at securing qualified people as office holders and removal of the unfit from their offices.

The writings cited by Morris and Binstock flow from the traditions of the empirical–rational strategy. This is also the core of the social planning model formulated by Rothman. Also in this tradition have been the Utopian communities. Here the attempt is to extrapolate from the advances of science to a Utopian community life.[47]

Normative–Reeducative

The normative–reeducative approach to planned change builds from the foundations of the empirical–rational position. Rationality and self-interest are not denied but rather operate in a larger cultural context. All people do not share the same values and beliefs. The argument is that change efforts must understand and deal with the normative structures that support existing behavior patterns if change is to occur. The common features of this strategy of change include:

a. The involvement of the client system in the change effort;
b. The problem confronting the client system cannot be assumed to be solvable only through provision of new relevant information;
c. Mutuality by the change and client systems in defining the problem, determining goals and working toward the achievement of those goals;
d. Nonconscious features of the problem must be brought into consciousness and resolved; and

e. Knowledge and technology of the behavioral sciences must be differentially and appropriately used by the change agent and the client system in the resolution of the confronting problem and in preparation for handling similar problems in the future.[48]

In short, this approach can be viewed as a therapeutic conception of change adapted to a community scale of intervention.

Power–Coercive

The authors note that social power (the ability of person A to get person B to do something he or she would otherwise not have done) is a feature of all social behavior. The form and the central place that power has distinguishes the power–coercive from other approaches to planned change. Knowledge/information is the power resource in the empirical–rational approach to change. Here, the growth of knowledge and its transmission is the vehicle of empowerment of people and the chief means for societal betterment. The notion of power is also inherent in the normative–reeducative strategy of change, but the focus shifts. Added attention is given to the noncognitive sources of behavior and power. There is great potential and thus energy and power within the individual. Via the contribution of the behavioral sciences, these power sources are understood, explored, and refocused.

It is the use of the coercive forms of power that chiefly distinguishes the power-coercive from the other approaches to planned change. In short, change is imposed. The imposition is typically in the form of economic and political sanctions. The players in this contest are usually organizations. The use of the court system to achieve the desegregation of schools and the organized demonstrations that led to the nation's withdrawal from Vietnam represent historically significant examples of this strategy. A rent strike against a slum landlord would be a community-scale example of the use of this strategy.

Those who use this strategy recognize the vast power inherent in a society's economic and political institutions. It is the massing and focusing of this power to force change that is the center of this strategy. Also recognized are the normative structures of society that undergird societal institutions and determine what is good and bad in social life. For example, in a nation founded on the belief that all people are created equal and are guaranteed certain rights under the Constitution, it is both legally and morally wrong to deny these rights because of racial or gender differences. Under such a formulation, not only may economic and politically coercive force be used, but moral coercion may be used as well. Mahatma Gandhi and Martin Luther King, Jr. are recent historical figures who sought to use moral coercion to force change.

The work by Chin and Benne fits nicely into a social systems perspective. Their attention to planned change assumes an underlying order or patterning in human associations. There are two critical characteristics of this association: the interdependence of member units and the dynamic quality of the association. A systems perspective is merely a way of conceptualizing this order. The notion of planned change carries with it a human effort aimed at controlling the direction, pace, and character of change.

SUMMARY

In this chapter we have identified the lines of development in community and practice theory. We have not attempted to be exhaustive but rather to note those that have contributed to our thinking and our forming an application of the social systems model to the community. You will have observed by now that the lines of theory development, at least from our account, are less well formed than those applying to the formal organization, the social group, and particularly to the individual. In fact, it has been our observation that as one moves from the individual to the social group to the formal organization and finally to the community, the lines of theory development are less well developed and have less practice utility.

Given our attention to the basic model and its application, the meagerness of theory development at the community level itself is not as troublesome as it might have been otherwise. In other words, our assumption is that the community as we have defined it is a separate and distinct social entity, and thus any given community can be modeled as a social system.

We believe that there is one particular strand identifiable in the various theories reviewed in this chapter, and that is the use of the notion of system. While the uses of the term varied by author, its importance in the community literature has made our task easier.

GLOSSARY

Anomie   A loss of connectedness, a feeling of being isolated and lacking purpose.
Change agent system   Typically a professional helper and the associated organizational support.
Client system   Typically the system possessing the problem and the anticipated beneficiary of a professional helping effort.
Nonzero-sum   A situation of contest in which no one loses but everyone gains something. Participants in the contest experience a net gain.
Symbiosis   A state of existence of different organisms with forms of relationship that are mutually advantageous.
Zero-sum   A situation in which the gain of one side involves a corresponding loss to those on the other side—there are winners and losers.

NOTES

1. G. A. Hillery, Jr., "Villages, Cities, and Total Institutions," *American Sociological Review* (1963): 779–791.
2. Murray G. Ross, *Community Organization: Theory, Principles, and Practice*, 2nd ed. (New York: Harper and Row, 1967), 105.
3. George Rosen, *A History of Public Health* (New York: MD Publications, 1958), 25.

4. For a discussion of the act, see Thomas M. Meenaghan and Robert O. Washington, *Social Policy and Social Welfare: Structure and Applications* (New York: The Free Press), 182–205.

5. Abraham H. Maslow, *Motivation and Personality*, 2nd ed. (New York: Harper and Row, 1970).

6. *Webster's New Collegiate Dictionary* (Springfield, Mass.: 1976), 228.

7. Max Weber, "The Nature of the City," in *Perspectives on the American Community*, ed. Roland Warren, 2nd ed. (New York: Rand McNally, 1973), 9–11.

8. Robert Ezra Parks, "Human Ecology," in *Perspectives on the American Community*, ed. Roland Warren, 2nd ed. (New York: Rand McNally, 1973), 32–44.

9. Ibid., 34.

10. Israel Rubin, "Function and Structure of Community: Conceptual and Theoretical Analysis," *International Review of Community Development* 21–22 (1969): 111–119.

11. E. Durkheim, "Preface to the Second Edition: Some Notes on Occupational Groups," trans. George Simpson, in *Division of Labor in Society* (Glencoe, Ill., 1964), 28.

12. Harold F. Kaufman, "Toward an Interactional Conception of Community," *Social Forces* 38 (1): 9–17.

13. For a review of field theory see Chapter 2. For a more detailed discussion see Kurt Lewin, *Field Theory in Social Science*, ed. Darwin Cartwright (New York: Harper & Brothers, 1951).

14. Morton E. Long, "The Local Community as an Ecology of Games," *American Journal of Sociology* 64 (November 1958): 251–261.

15. Roland Warren, *The Community in America*, 3rd ed. (Chicago, Ill.: Rand McNally and Co., 1978).

16. Ibid., 9.

17. Ibid.

18. Robert Perlman and Arnold Gurin, *Community Organization and Social Planning* (New York: John Wiley and Sons and The Council for Social Work Education, 1972).

19. Ross, *Community Organization*.

20. Ibid., 40.

21. Ferdinand Tönnies, *Community and Society (Gemeinschaft and Gesellschaft)*, trans. and ed. Charles P. Loomis (1887; reprint, New York: Harper Torch Books, 1963).

22. Ross, *Community Organization*, 61–62.

23. Ronald Lippitt, et al., *The Dynamics of Planned Change* (New York: Harcourt, Brace and World, 1958).

24. Ibid., 6.

25. Ibid., 21–48.

26. Ibid., 51–68.

27. Ibid., 130.

28. Robert Morris and Robert Binstock, *Feasible Planning for Social Change* (New York: Columbia University Press, 1966).

29. Ibid., 17.

30. Charles F. Grosser, "Community Development Programs Serving the Urban Poor," *Social Work* 10 (3): 15–21.

31. Perlman and Gurin, *Community Organization*, 55.

32. Ibid., 58.

33. Ibid., 76.

34. Fred M. Cox et al., eds., *Strategies of Community Organizations*, 4th ed. (Itasca, Ill.: F. E. Peacock, 1987).

35. Ibid., 10.

36. William W. and Loureide J. Biddle, *The Community Development Process: The Rediscovery of Local Initiative* (New York: Holt, Rinehart and Winston, 1965).

37. Ward H. Goodenough, *Cooperation in Change: An Anthropological Approach to Community Development* (New York: Russell Sage Foundation, 1963).

38. Lee J. Cary, ed., *Community Development as a Process* (Columbia, Mo.: University of Missouri Press, 1970).

39. James Q. Wilson, "An Overview of Theories of Planned Change," in *Centrally Planned Change: Prospects and Concepts*, ed. Robert Morris (New York: National Association of Social Workers, 1964), 12–40.

40. Harvey S. Perloff, ed., *Planning and the Urban Community* (Pittsburgh: Carnegie Institute of Technology, 1961).

41. Saul D. Alinsky, *Reveille for Radicals* (Chicago: University of Chicago Press, 1946).

42. Warren Haggstrom, "The Power of the Poor," in *The Mental Health of the Poor*, ed. Frank Riessman, Jerome Cohen and Arthur Pearl (New York: The Free Press, 1964), 205–223.

43. S. Weisner, "Fighting Back: A Critical Analysis of Coalition Building in the Human Services," *Social Service Review* 57(2): 291–306.

44. Cox et al., *Strategies of Community Organizations*, 8.

45. Robert Chin and Kenneth D. Benne, "General Strategies for Effecting Changes in Human Systems," in Benne, et al., *The Planning of Change*, 4th ed. (New York: Holt, Rinehart, and Winston, 1985).

46. Max Weber, *The Theory of Social and Economic Organization*, trans. A. M. Hendersen and T. Parsons, ed. T. Parsons (New York: The Free Press, 1947).

47. Note B. F. Skinner, *Walden Two* (New York: Cowell-Collier and Macmillan, 1948).

48. Ibid.; and Robert Chin and Kenneth D. Benne, 31–38.

Chapter 15

The Community as a Social System

OUTLINE

Introduction
Boundary
Suprasystem
Interface
Input
Output

Conversion Operations
Feedback
Steady State
Summary
Glossary
Notes

Introduction

In our previous application of the social systems model, member components were either individuals, as in the social group or formally constituted administrative units and informally constituted groups, or formal organizations. The member components are not as simply or clearly identifiable in the model's application to the community. The member components of the community include: (1) all individuals enacting community roles; (2) all of those social groups and other such social units that enact or perform community-related functions; and (3) all formal organizations either in their entirety or that component that performs community-related functions. Our identification of the member components of the community has been influenced by the earlier mentioned writings of Harold F. Kaufman and his interactional conception of the community.[1] For the notion of community function as referred to above we are indebted to Roland Warren.[2]

These conceptual distinctions are of perhaps more importance to the researcher and those concerned with theory development than to the professional practitioner. In this chapter our focus is on presentation of the social systems model and its application to the community. Our attention more than before will be directed toward the distinctive features of the community and the special implications these features have in the way the model is used. We will also be departing somewhat from the format used in the previous parts. In this chapter we consider both the concepts comprising the model and its dynamics. We also make less use of examples, but will devote the final chapter of Part

395

V to an application of the model to a community. In so doing, we hope to further explicate the model by showing its practice utility.

Before proceeding, let us take a moment to review our definition of community—a territorially based social organization through which most people satisfy their common needs and desires, deal with their common problems, and relate to their society. The key attributes of this definition that identify the community as a distinctive form of social organization include: (1) it is territorially based; (2) the nature of the interdependence of those who share the same habitat is found in their own needs and the problems and opportunities they share. It is in this sense that the relationships that link people and their various forms of social organizations are symbiotic in character; and (3) the commonality of human needs, problems, and opportunities gives rise to similar goals and structural arrangements for attaining those goals. It is the commonness of these patterns that we believe makes the systems model a particularly useful approach for conceptualizing the community.

Boundary

The systems model requires the designation of boundary to distinguish it from its suprasystem. Similarly, the model specifies that every system engages in the boundary-maintenance function. It is particularly useful in an application of the model to conceive of primary and secondary means for determining boundary, and thus the means for distinguishing insiders from outsiders. Our position is that each classification of social organization tends to have a dominant or "first cut" means for establishing a boundary. For example, in formal social organizations, each member is carried on some form of membership roster. In other words, there will be some legal or quasi-legal means for determining whether any given individual (in a defined role) should be considered inside or outside the organization. The first cut or starting position for identifying who is on the inside and who is not is simply who holds formal membership in the organization. Similarly, for human service agencies, if a client has an open case, he or she is typically included in the system. We want to stress again that it is the model user who makes the determination of what constitutes the system, and this decision will depend largely on the purposes being served by use of the model. The central point here is that the model user needs a practical starting point to determine who is to be included inside the system and who is not.

Utilizing the same notion of a "first cut" with the community, it would be whether or not an individual, organization, or other social unit physically resides within the boundaries of the community. There may be other important considerations, for example, some people live in one community but work in and otherwise identify with another community. What we are saying is that in a practice application, too much can be made of such issues. Until we get better theoretical foundations we have to be guided by the practical and professional judgments necessary to get the job done. For instance, many programs require that a "community needs assessment" be performed to establish existence of a community problem and to justify requests for monies to deal with the problem. The request may be for improved health services, services to the elderly, education services, or any number of other such programs. The problem confronting the practitioner is determination of the actual boundaries: What is to be placed in the system and what goes into the suprasystem? Needs assessment typically involves counts of people and estimates of conditions existing among specified groups of people.[3] Frequently the question becomes which existing boundary lines should be used—county lines, municipal lines, census tracts, United Fund collection areas, mental health catchment areas, and so on. In any event, one cannot start counting people measuring their needs, or inventorying resources until the boundary designation problem is solved.

In spite of the critical need for specifying boundaries that capture a natural community, the practitioner must usually make some compromise. On the one hand is the conceptual issue of what constitutes the natural community for a given application. On the other hand, such matters as programmatic considerations and data availability may become the primary determinants for specifying system boundaries. If the practitioner is influenced too much by practical considerations and convenience, the designated boundaries may not represent a community in any useful sense. In other words, the individuals, groups, and organizations in the designated area would not be meaningfully related to one another in terms of need satisfaction and problem resolution—the area would not contain a community as we have defined it, and the application of the model would not be appropriate.

Suprasystem

The suprasystem is comprised of those aspects of the environment affecting output-input exchanges with a designated system. In the systems model, the concept of suprasystem is broadened to include all relevant aspects of the environment that affect the behaviors of the community being examined. The notion of relevance is included and represents a judgment on the part of the model user in terms of those aspects of the environment that have the most influence or are most helpful in understanding the community under study.

In a community application of the model, the specification of the suprasystem is complex because of the level of inclusiveness of the system. The notion of viewing the community as a microcosm of society helps to suggest the number and complexity of its ties. Earlier it was stated that the society was the most self-sufficient and inclusive of the various forms of social organization, with the community being the next most inclusive. In conceptualizing the notion of suprasystem, it is useful to consider the community as a societal subsystem with multiple ties to society, the next larger social system. Further, the community and society can be viewed as possessing many structural similarities. The vertical ties between the community and its society can then be assumed to follow similar structural lines. For example, the economic system of the community tends to have its primary ties to the society's economic system. Some of the horizontal structures that serve to coordinate and integrate the activities of the community's economic system have their counterpart at the societal level (for instance, the local chamber of commerce and the National Chamber of Commerce or the local United Fund and community welfare council and United Funds and Councils of America).

Viewing the system-suprasystem relationships in terms of the ties between their respective structural components can be useful to the practitioner. For example, the national counterpart of a local agency, as with United Funds and Councils of America, can be an important source of consultation and technical assistance around a variety of community human service problems. At another level, certain community problems cannot be effectively dealt with locally, for example, unemployment and drug abuse. What is frequently required for effective intervention is a societal or sometimes an international effort. Typically what occurs is a national effort that builds down to the community, as in drug abuse prevention, or builds up from community interest groups in order to provide a nationwide attack on a problem. The point is that these vertically organized connections tend to follow similar structural lines at the local and national level. This is important for the community practitioner to understand and to use strategically.

Interface

The concept of interface is particularly useful when the model is applied to a community. Given the number and scope of functions performed by the community, interface as a shared segment of boundary offers a useful way of particularizing system-suprasystem relationships.

Roland Warren is again helpful in identifying some of the distinctive features of interface, as evident in an application of the model to the community. He contends that the community is characterized by multiple and strong vertical ties to what he terms **extracommunity systems**.[4] Illustrative of such ties would be a local plant that was a unit of a much larger industrial enterprise with home offices in another community or perhaps even in another part of the world. An example of the latter would be a local plant assembling Toyota cars but with a home office in Japan. As a consequence of the strength of the vertical tie, the behavior of the local affiliate is dominated by external influences as opposed to those arising out of the community itself. While our use of *interface* is somewhat different than that of Warren's "extracommunity," his attention to the dominating influences of the suprasystem on the community is instructive.

In our use of the concept, *interface* refers to a shared boundary between two systems. In this instance, it would be between a community and another social unit comprising its suprasystem. Further, both systems perform boundary-maintaining functions that affect input-output exchanges that cross their mutual boundary and both work to exclude influences that would be disruptive to their cooperative arrangements. An example would be the receipt of a federal grant by a community agency to provide drug abuse counseling and educational services. The agency receiving the grant has negotiated arrangements with the local school system to provide drug education programs for its students. In addition, the agency receiving the grant has close working relationships with all community-based agencies addressing the community's drug problem. The agency actually receiving the money is providing with others a community service, one that is directed toward the amelioration of a community problem. In this example, the contract with the federal funding agency constitutes an interface. Although the contract is between two agencies, the local agency has in place various horizontal relationships that, in fact, create a community subsystem dealing with a community social problem — drug abuse. This contract in fact affects a community subsystem. The notion of interface is evidenced in the sense that the contract affects input-output exchanges between the two systems, for example, money, progress reports, and so on. We can also expect both the community and the federal agency to protect their shared boundary from disruptive forces so that their shared function can be pursued.

The above example describes one interface; a community, depending on its size, may have hundreds or thousands of such formal arrangements. We are not suggesting that all such arrangements are in harmony, or all are pursuing similar and agreed-upon purposes. Our experience is quite the opposite. There will be linkages between community agencies and external groups that may be overlapping or even working at cross purposes. In part, the practice of community organization is to identify these linkages and to help develop a more systematic set of relationships both among agencies within the same community and among these community agencies and those other agencies and groups that they relate to outside their community.

Before leaving the concept of interface, it is important to remember that interface refers to all of the mutual boundary-maintaining behavior that occurs among a subject community and external social units that affect it functionally. Many of these relationships are informal and Gemeinschaft in character; others, like the previously noted contract, are formal and Gesellschaft in nature. Our formulation is of an open system, and interface is the concept used to identify the specifics of the exchanges that occur and to characterize them as cyclical and mutually deterministic in nature. Finally, and as shown by our example, the community boundary-maintaining function may be largely evident in the behavior of a single or lead agency. Assumed in such an instance is that the lead agency is acting on behalf of the community.

Input

Conceptually speaking, the community has many similarities to the social group. In fact, some theorists have approached the study of the community as a group.[5] It is in this sense that, as in the social group, in a community application of the model the individual is considered both a signal and maintenance input. For purposes of this notion, the reader may want to review the material on input described in Chapter 7. Conceptually, the model views communities as having effects on the people who comprise them. These effects can be either positive or negative. The processes causing these effects take place in what we designate as conversion operations; so, the concept of signal inputs is applied to the condition of people before they are affected by community processes.

Maintenance inputs include relevant aspects of culture, money, material resources, information—particularly that pertaining to feedback—and so on. Every social organization incorporates aspects of culture, for example, values derived from the society of which it is a part. In the present application, the community is viewed as having a major responsibility for transmitting culture. This responsibility is seen most clearly in the operation of its educational system. By law, all of the community's children of a given age must attend school. It is through schooling that specific knowledge, skills, values, and other features of culture are transmitted to the community's youth. For the most part, these aspects of culture are not generated in the community; they are *imported* from the larger society but "worked through" in the community, and vice versa. It is important to view this process as dynamic, with changes constantly occurring in the larger society and fed into and acted upon by the community. An example of a cultural form of input would be those features of culture that pertain to the changing role of women, for example, the right to choose a professional career as a single person instead of marriage and motherhood. While this might be treated as a general cultural value, it becomes operationalized in a somewhat different fashion in each individual community. In other words, this aspect of the larger culture is likely to be incorporated somewhat differently in San Francisco, California, than in a Bible belt community such as McAlester, Oklahoma.

A more specific form of maintenance input would be a federal grant to help construct a community hospital, fund a mental health program, or conduct research on AIDS. Another typical example would be state tax monies that are allocated to communities in support of their system of public education.

In an application of the model, it is important to understand that a system is able to maintain negative entropy by reason of its capacity for importing resources from the suprasystem—thus the notion behind input. While communities are relatively self-sufficient when compared to most other forms of social organization (for example, they raise taxes to support some of their functions), they are modeled as open systems relying on substantial inputs from the suprasystem.

Output

The social systems model is organized around output. From the perspective of output, the user of the model seeks answers to three questions: (1) what was the proposed output?; (2) what was the actual output?; and (3) what is the explanation of the differences between the two? Output as conceptualized in this model is the reply to the second question. The difficulty presented in a community application of the model is determining the answer to the first question. As indicated earlier in this chapter, by their very nature, communities do not have explicitly stated and agreed-upon goals. In the absence of knowledge about what was proposed as output, questions two and three become moot. The approach we develop in this chapter is that while communities usually do not have explicitly stated goals, they are implicit in the definition of community. That is, a community goal structure must pertain to the satisfaction of common human needs, the resolution of commonly held (community) problems, and the carrying out of selected societal roles. In short, if there are common needs and common problems, then communities will tend to share common goals, that is, the satisfaction of these common needs and the resolution of these common problems. We also depart from the format utilized earlier by discussing the concepts of proposed output and output under the same heading. In so doing we hope to better convey the relationship between the two.

We did not find the literature on community particularly helpful in operationalizing the notion of community outputs. Warren has commented on the general problem of specifying community outputs as follows:

> How is it possible for citizens working to improve their own communities, or for professional community development workers, to operate effectively? How can

they set realistic goals, and measure progress toward them unless they have, even in general terms, a clear conception of what the community would be like that they are striving for?[6]

Perhaps the most relevant work on the problem of community goals or output has been done at the national level, particularly that body of work associated with the social indicator movement.[7] Here the effort was aimed at the construction and measurement of societal goals. During the 1960s not only was there considerable scientific interest in societal goals but political interest as well. President Lyndon B. Johnson pledged his administration to the goal of building the Great Society. Again the question becomes: What are the goals of a Great Society and what are the indicators that can be used to track progress in achieving those goals? We have taken the position that the community operates as a subsystem of society and may be considered a microcosm of society. Therefore, much of the work in the construction of social goals and indicators at the societal level has application at the community level as well. The above societal question can be rephrased: What are the goals of a Great Community and what are the indicators that can be used to track progress in achieving those goals?

The 1960s and 1970s were also a period when those in the field of human services gave considerable attention to the purposes of services, their definition, their classification, their interrelationships, and their effectiveness. One such effort was the development of a taxonomy of social goals and human service programs called United Way of America Services Identification System (UWASIS).[8] UWASIS was formulated in systems terms and sought to link collective human helping efforts to societal goals:

> UWASIS is a system for identifying, classifying and defining individual organized human endeavors in relation to major goals of society. It can be said that all organized human endeavors—characterized here as human service programs—can be traced to one ultimate purpose or goal overriding all others, and that is, to enable individuals to live a well-adjusted and satisfying existence and to enable them to realize their full potential.[9]

In keeping with the above-noted purpose, eight societal goals were established to which the various programs pertain:

1. Optimal income security and economic opportunity;
2. Optimal health;
3. Optimal provision of basic material needs;
4. Optimal opportunity for the acquisition of knowledge and skills;
5. Optimal environmental quality;
6. Optimal individual and collective safety;
7. Optimal social functioning; and
8. Optimal assurance of the support and effectiveness of services through organized action.

While these goals were formulated and treated as societal goals, the UWASIS authors created a framework that was designed for use by American communities. As stated earlier, the intent was to develop a taxonomy of social goals to which human service programs could be related and evaluated. In effect then, these goals were treated as both societal and community goals.

The logic used in this chapter for operationalizing proposed output builds on the work associated with the social indicator movement and UWASIS, among others. The logic is also implicit in our definition of community—a territorially based social organization through which most people satisfy their common needs and desires; deal with their common problems; and relate to their society. Based on this definition, output should pertain to the satisfaction of the needs and desires, level of progress made in dealing with common problems, and ways that community members relate to their society.

With this background in mind, the following has been selected as the community goal structure for use in the model. As in other applications, a hierarchy of outcomes format is used.

Purpose To improve the quality of life of community members through development and provision of facilities and services that contribute to the satisfaction of their residents' needs and desires, and that help them cope with their common problems in ways that advance themselves, the community, and society.

Goals

1. *Work/employment.* To encourage development of an economic system that will provide equal opportunities for all citizens to obtain healthy, safe, and satisfying remunerative work.
2. *Health.* To create and sustain those physical, social, and environmental arrangements that maximize the health and physical fitness potentials of all residents.
3. *Nutrition.* To assure that sufficient quantities, types of food, and required nutrients are available and usable so that suitable nutritional standards are maintained for all residents.
4. *Safety and security.* To create the social conditions and the associated systems that satisfy safety and security needs of community residents through assurances of protection of human and property rights.
5. *Social welfare.* To provide a comprehensive and quality system of social welfare services that contributes to the strengthening of human resources of all people and that assures that the basic needs of all residents are satisfied.
6. *Education.* To provide a comprehensive range of educational programs and facilities that assures that all people have access to educational opportunities consistent with their needs and potentials.
7. *Housing.* Consistent with individual preferences and means, to encourage provision of housing for all people that is esthetically pleasing and meets standards of privacy, health, and safety.
8. *Social participation.* To encourage provision of the spaces, programs, and facilities that will permit all people to have access to opportunities for need satisfaction related to their psychological, social, and cultural development.
9. *Transportation.* To provide access and ease of movement for all to community facili-

ties, spaces, organizations, and services in ways that are environmentally healthful, convenient, safe, economical, and personally satisfying.

10. *Citizenship*. To encourage participation of all people in activities that promote a sense of community and societal citizenship.

Consistent with the definition of community, the goal structure is comprehensive, thereby taking into consideration those functions required for satisfaction of common human needs and for efforts toward resolution of commonly held problems. While not shown, under each goal there would be a series of objectives and activities (see Figure 10.1). We make the assumption that, while communities share common goals, important differences would occur among communities in terms of how objectives would be formulated to achieve common goals and how goals and objectives would be prioritized. In using the model and consistent with community needs, the practitioner would develop the third level of the outcome hierarchy (statement of objectives). Similarly, a practice application would also include a designation of the plans (activities) needed to achieve each objective.

As indicated earlier, goal statements in this model are considered a feature of structure. In this sense, goals are targets that guide system behaviors aimed at goal attainment. Output is the current state of affairs and for presentation purposes would be organized under each goal statement, for example, a mayor's "state of the community" message. For example, conceptually, under the work/employment goal there would be a subgoal structure comprising a series of objectives that would operationalize such concepts as "equal opportunity," and "healthy, safe, and satisfying." An objective aimed at operationalizing "equal" might read as follows: "By June 30, 19__ there will be a 25 percent increase in the number of employers who certify that all of their employees are paid in accordance with the principle of 'equal pay for equal work.' " In this instance, output would include the actual percentage increase over last year of community employers who have made this commitment. The sum total of all the data available under each of the goal categories at a specified time would represent actual output.

The notions of maintenance and task outputs are also necessary components in conceptualizing the community as a social system. Maintenance outputs, as you will recall, pertain to those outcomes that strengthen and enhance the capacity of the system itself. In this application, need satisfaction and resolution of problems would be considered maintenance outcomes for the people residing in the community. Task outcomes would be thought of in terms of the levels of preparation people achieve in their various societal roles, for example, mother, teacher, citizen, and so on. People are socialized into societal roles within a community but these roles are (or should be) relatively independent of any particular community. Such preparation can be deemed functional in a highly mobile society. For example, people trained as physicians, bricklayers, ministers, social workers, or laborers should be able to assume those same roles in any community.

Examples of maintenance and task objectives would probably be useful at this point. The work-related example previously cited—equal pay for equal work—would be considered a maintenance objective. These data would pertain to efforts aimed at strengthening a community subsystem (in this example, the economic base). On the other hand, measures of how many high school graduates went on and completed college and subsequently received graduate degrees would, in most applications, be considered a task output. The measure would be of people who have been prepared, via community processes, for assumption of various societal roles. Another example of a task objective might include the number of people in the community who vote in state and national elections. Here the assumption might be that these data would be a measure of how well the community has prepared its residents for their responsibilities as citizens.

A final form of output utilized in the model is waste. Conceptually, the attempt is to account for all resources expended in converting inputs to outputs. Waste is the measure of inefficient or inappropriate use of resources. This measure becomes incorporated as feedback and is channeled back into the system as a maintenance input—information that should result in improved (less wasteful) outputs in a subsequent cycle of the system. To cite an earlier community example, waste would be the money lost by women, minorities, and others not receiving equal pay for equal work. Waste, in this example, would be the cost of undeveloped and underutilized community resources, that is, people. Other examples would include the psychological damage done to a young person unnecessarily sent off to a prison or a reformatory due to the absence of a community-based treatment program. In each of these instances, to be treated as waste, an assumption must be made that the damage to the person could have been prevented or reduced by some form of community action. At a practical level, there will always be waste. The model highlights the evidence of waste because it becomes the basis of or justification of professional forms of intervention aimed at improving the quality of life of all community residents.

In concluding our discussion of output and proposed outputs, it is important to remember that these concepts apply to a designated cycle of system operations, for example, a calendar or fiscal year. The use being made of the model will, in most instances, determine the cycle of conversion operations to be used.

Conversion Operations

Every social system has a means of transforming inputs to outputs. The assumption made in developing the model is that the most useful approach for the assessment of an organization is to make a comparison between what actually happened versus what was intended to happen. In each instance the comparisons start with proposed output being compared against actual output. To understand the differences between what was proposed and what actually occurred leads back into the system's conversion operations.

In this section the content will be subdivided into two parts—structure and interactions.

Structure

When the model was applied to a formal organization, the principal structural features were administrative units, for example, departments and divisions. In a community application of the model, the principal structural units are organizations or parts of organizations. As an aid in understanding some of the distinctive characteristics of community structures, we will briefly review how these features build on and extend the structural components of less complex systems. The least complex social system is comprised of two functionally interdependent roles. Two people determine they need each other in order to achieve a given purpose, such as, a client and social worker. Conceptually, this can be viewed as a task in which the total work to be performed can be systematically allocated to the performance of two different roles. With each person carrying out his or her role in coordination with the counter role, the goal is pursued. In such an application, the role is the chief structural feature. It is comprised of a series of interrelated norms that are, in turn, derived from the task to be performed.

In modeling more complex forms of social organizations, the same basic logic is used. Tasks are to be performed that require the coordinated work of a number of people. Depending on the number of tasks and their level of complexity, the work can involve hundreds, thousands, or tens of thousands of people (for example, General Motors building several million cars each year). The individual who enacts an organizational role is the smallest building block. Individuals performing similar work roles are grouped, forming ever larger social units. These units, in turn, are related horizontally and vertically in ways that pertain to the efficient and effective ways of achieving the organization's goals and objectives. Conceptually speaking, the social units comprising the organization can be viewed as linked through individuals who have "linchpin" features to their roles. A social work supervisor is an example in a formal organization. One aspect of this supervisor role pertains to facing inward and downward in the unit, that is, supervising and coordinating the professional work of the caseworkers. Another feature of the linchpin role has the supervisor facing outward and upward to his or her supervisor (an **intramural** role or role feature). In larger and more complex organizations, the supervisor also relates laterally to other supervisors performing similar duties, and in most instances they all relate to a common supervisor (frequently called a program supervisor or administrator).

The linchpin analogy can be particularly helpful in conceptualizing how organizations relate to one another at the community level. The chief administrative officer of an organization also faces in three directions. The person faces inward and downward in terms of supervising the work of those employed in the organization. This administrator faces outward and laterally to other administrators operating similar agencies but who must (or at least should) work with one another in terms of their own agency's goals or some larger interest, such as community or societal goals. In an organizational application of the model, the role attributes of the administrator that pertain to matters outside the agency would be considered as relating to the suprasystem. In a community application of the model, these features represent key structural features of the community. In other words, there are linchpin roles that coordinate with and link various organizations in terms of the pursuit of community goals.

Thus, the basic structural units of communities are organizations or parts of organizations. Organizations become formally (by contract or law) and informally (by tradition or symbiotically) related as they work toward achievement of community goals/outputs. Administrators also face outward and upward in terms of their **extramural role**(s). For example, an administrator may be responsible to an agency board of directors. Here the administrator faces upward to a group of people who are representing a broad community interest and who have the job of relating the agency to overall community needs. The president of this board and the administrator will both have complementary extramural features of their roles that pertain to relating the agency to external funding sources, to other community agencies performing similar or related functions, and ultimately to some broad conception of community interest.

While the individual can theoretically be located in the model, for practical purposes major attention is given to organizations or the functional groupings of organizations. Just as there are groupings of social units within a formal organization (departments, divisions, bureaus, and so on), so are there groupings of organizations within a community. In our model these groupings are treated as subsystems of the community. The work of Warren is helpful in conceptualizing this structural feature of the community.[10] Before examining Warren's work, brief attention is given to other features of community structure.

Conceptually, all aspects of social structure ultimately become integrated into a role that is then activated by a person. The following structural features have an existence of their own but only assume meaning when they affect the behavior of people enacting a role relevant to the community. These other aspects of structure include culture, laws, contracts, policies, and so on. For example, every community can be viewed as importing, in a selective way, its culture from that of the larger society. The cultural features of a given community in its entirety can be treated as a subculture of the larger society. All this suggests is a level of individuality of the community. In other words, the culture of any given community differs from that of the larger society as well as from other communities in identified ways. For example, the societal value (an aspect of culture) that holds that "all able-bodied people who can work should work" may be held at different levels of intensity by different communities. The differing levels of intensity may then become helpful in understanding why communities differ in terms of how they deal with unemployment, underemployment, and related problems pertaining to work. The central notion here is one that assumes that all communities differ in terms of selected cultural features, particularly in the dominance of certain values. It is important to understand these differences because they become fundamental determinants of the other and more specific structural features of a community—laws, policies, and so on.

All laws should be thought of as structure in the sense that they formally establish rules of conduct between people and other social units (organizations). Here the concern is with those laws, regulations, and other forms of administrative rules that affect the behaviors of individuals and organizations within the community. A typical example is the requirement that drivers adhere to posted speed limits in the community. To do otherwise is to run the risk of a fine or, if found to be an habitual offender, losing the right to drive an automobile. The point is that one cannot explain through an understanding of their psychological makeup (an internal source of explanation for the specific behavior), why most people adhere to speed laws in school zones. Rather, the explanation is essentially externally based—it is in the law and in the supportive normative structures; it is the expected way for the individual to behave in a given set of circumstances. Another example on an interorganizational level would be all of those laws that pertain to how a mentally ill person should be treated in a given community. Such laws would include those state statutes that define mental illness, specify the role of mental health agencies in the provision of services, establish the procedures used by the courts in the admission and discharge of patients from mental health facilities, and so on. The issue is not the source of law, but rather its application, the "guides" that affect the way organizations and agencies relate at the community level. In this example, one would expect to find an interplay of federal and state statutes as well as local ordinances in terms of the effect that law has on how a community goes about dealing with the problems of its mentally ill. Similarly, laws pertaining to mental illness deemed not to have community relevance would not be considered as structure. In this model, all policies based in law or administratively rooted are considered features of structure. However, only those policies relevant to an understanding of community outputs would be treated as structures in a given application. It is also helpful to treat policies and plans as essentially synonymous terms. That is, those plans that affect the behavior of individuals, groups, and organizations within the community become structural features in the model.

The definition of the community includes the concept of place. The assumption is then made that the unique physical aspects of the community, man-made and natural, affect social interactions among community members. An example of a policy/plan that embodies this assumption is a community's (city's) general plan or master plan. Typically, this plan represents a compilation of ordinances that guide land use within the city. The plan exerts a major influence on the interactions among construction firms, real estate agencies, banks, and all residents who may want to buy a house, rent an apartment, build an addition to their house, or start a new business.

Up to this point, mention has been made of the various features of structure with little attention as to how the member units are related functionally. Conceptually, the matter is complex. As indicated earlier, there is no one "in charge" of the community, no organizational chart that specifies functional relationships among units or that shows who is responsible to whom. In short, and on surface examination, there are a variety of relatively autonomous groups and organizations sharing the same locale. However, on closer examination, one finds symbiotic relationships among units that suggest functional groupings of organizations not unlike that alluded to by Long when he compared the community to an "ecology of games"[11] and by Warren in his identification of the five "locality relevant functions"[12] performed by communities. With this in mind, our model is premised on the existence of natural groupings of agencies and organizations that share the same habitat and that are symbiotically related in terms of how they serve or otherwise affect the quality of life of those who reside in the community.

The specific approach for modeling community subsystems builds on the work of Roland Warren. As noted earlier, Warren linked his definition of community to the performance of five locality relevant functions: (1) **production, distribution, and consumption**; (2) **socialization**; (3) **social control**; (4) **social participation**; and (5) **mutual support**.[13] While conceptually viewed by Warren as functions, here they will be treated as horizontally organized community subsystems through which specific outcomes are achieved, that is, related to the previously mentioned goal structure. Complicating the conceptual scheme is the fact that any given social organization in the community may be involved in the performance of two or more locality relevant functions. The school, while clearly performing a socialization function, can also be seen as performing social control and social participation functions. On the other hand, there is a similar conceptual problem in fitting an individual into the various social structures within which he or she operates (for example, teacher, mother, wife, president of The League of Women Voters). Role theory helps in examining the interplay between individual and organizational behavior. In a similar way, role theory can be helpful in viewing social organizations or parts of organizations as playing various community roles, for example, the school performing both a socialization and a social control role. Such an approach also helps to account for the level of coordination and integration that is evident in communities.

In the section to follow, the various subsystems of the community are summarized. We examine these subsystems in terms of their structural role in contributing to the community goal structure identified earlier.

Production, Distribution, and Consumption

This subsystem includes all of the formally and informally constituted organizations involved in the production, distribution, and consumption of goods and services within the community. It includes such diverse forms as a barber shop, a post office, a trucking concern, a steel mill, and an individual consumer. Depending on the purpose of an application, it might or might not include an unlicensed day care program operated in a family home. For some applications of the model, such social units might be seen as constituting a part of the community's mutual support subsystem. The basic test for inclusion in what might be more simply described as the economic subsystem is whether the output was primarily associated with the function being performed by this subsystem.

The linking of production, distribution, and consumption conveys the natural interdependence of these components in forming a community subsystem. In short, not only must goods be produced, they must be distributed and made accessible to customers; finally, these goods must be purchased and consumed (need satisfaction). The exchange of monies for such goods energizes this subsystem, making the production of more goods possible. The production, distribution, and consumption function is also the subsystem in which most of the community's jobs are located. In this sense, the subsystem is critical with respect to the achievement of the work/employment goal (1) (see earlier discussion of goals in the section on output). Because of the exchange of labor for money, the production, distribution, and consumption subsystem is also important to all of those other goals that make use of the marketplace for need satisfaction, for example, goals 2 (health), 3 (nutrition), and 7 (housing).

Finally, not all of the the goods and services produced by a given factory are to be retained in the community (Detroit does not use all of the cars its factories produce). Attention, however, in modeling the community as a social system is on understanding the effects of community behaviors on the people residing in the community. Therefore, a given company's products as they move beyond the community are not of particular concern in this model.

Socialization

This subsystem includes all formal and informal organizations devoted primarily to accomplishing educational outcomes aimed at helping community residents prepare for their many community and societal roles. **Socialization** includes the transmission of all knowledge, values, and behaviors presumed to prepare and sustain people in relevant community and societal roles. In this application, the terms *education* and *socialization* can be considered synonymous. The term *socialization* is preferred because it generally conveys a more inclusive process with education tending, in popular usage, to refer to formalized learning activities. For example, the family and the church are considered to be the primary organizations in this society charged with performing the socialization function, but the public school comes to mind when the education function is discussed.

In a rapidly changing and developing society, the socialization function is critical in helping to assure that needed levels of value consensus exist, that people are prepared with sufficient knowledge and skills to fulfill the increasingly more technical roles that are emerging. Examples of formal organizations comprising this community subsystem include the church, public and private elementary and secondary schools, colleges, and vocational technical schools, to mention only a few. A day-care center for children might be included as a unit of a community's socialization subsystem, or, depending on the purpose of the application, it might be treated as a unit of the mutual support subsystem. The determination would be based upon the function performed by the center. If the primary purpose of the center was educational, it would be as part of the community's socialization subsystem. However, if the purpose was to provide for the health, safety, and social development of the child, it might be better treated as a part of the mutual support subsystem.

The socialization subsystem would have primary responsibility for the achievement of goal 6 (education) and would play a supportive role in the achievement of most of the other goals, particularly 1 (preparation for work/employment role), 8 (social participation), and 10 (citizenship).

Social Control

It is useful to think of **social control** as a backup to the socialization system, "the enforcer." It could be argued that if every member of society was perfectly socialized, and therefore acted in ways that were fully in accord with the prevailing cultural standards, there would be no need for a social control subsystem. In other words, socialization pertains to the development of internalized controls that result in behavioral compliance with established norms, while social control pertains to external forms of control aimed at securing compliance to these norms. To use an earlier example, if the driver of a car were not socialized in a way that resulted in obeying speed limit laws (it's the right thing to do), he or she might conform only because of a fear of arrest and loss of a driver's license (being punished for not complying).

The police power, the inherent power of government to exercise reasonable control over persons within its jurisdiction, is probably the best example of a formal method of social control at the community level. The family, social groups, and other informal types of organizations play major roles in performing social control as well as the socialization function. In contrast to the formal exercise of police power, these latter groups exercise the social control function informally, as in the discipline of a child by a parent. In any application of the model, both formal and informal types of social organizations must be considered in conceptualizing the social control subsystem.

Finally, the social control subsystem would have primary responsibility for goal 4 (safety and security) and a supportive responsibility for most of the other goals.

Social Participation

Consistent with Maslow's position, we hold that the distinctive features of humans are socially acquired and must constantly be supported throughout life.[14] For the majority of people, the community provides the daily access to those organizations and groups that perform a social participation function. The church is an example of a formal organization involved in the performance of this function. Other examples would include such diverse forms as a city's recreation department, the family, and the local Welcome Wagon Club. To some extent, every organization in the community is involved in the performance of this function.

As with all other functions, this subsystem has both formally constituted organizations as well as informal groups concerned with provision of the social participation function. The need for social contact is so fundamental to human life that it is easy to overlook its pervasive character and the fundamental role the community plays in providing people-to-people access. Because of its pervasiveness, it is difficult to separate this function from other functions provided by the same organization. For example, should the community's senior citizens' center be viewed as primarily involved in performing a social participation or a mutual support function? While the social participation subsystem has primary responsibility for achieving goal 8 (social participation), it plays a major supportive function with all the goals (for instance, consider its relationship to the maintenance function in all forms of social organization).

Mutual Support

Warren's formulation of community recognized that there are times when community members or their families are unable to perform their usual responsibilities in the expected and needed way. Therefore, the community provides organized arrangements to help those persons during their times of need. The aim of this effort is to assist the persons to overcome their problems so that they might resume their usual roles and community responsibilities. The community hospital, local welfare department, and local churches would represent formal organizations primarily engaged in performing the **mutual support** function. The family, as with most other functions, would be the dominant informal organization performing this function. As a matter of clarification, the notion of mutual support is similar to but not identical with the concept of social welfare. As used here, mutual support is the more inclusive of the two terms; it includes informal as well as formal helping efforts.

Informal features of this subsystem include such activities as residents getting together to help take care of a sick neighbor during a period of convalescence. Unlike its formal counterpart, "neighborliness" is spontaneous, relatively unorganized, lacks formal sponsorship, and is offered rather than requested.

The notion of "networking" can also be viewed as an informal component of a community's mutual support subsystem. Here the tendency is for people sharing the same kind of problem, concern, or interest to locate one another and enter into relationships (a network) that are mutually helpful. The assistance offered is usually in the form of social support, information sharing, and related forms of help. The concept of community is useful in viewing the notion of networking and its utility in helping to deal with some of the common problems shared by people residing in the same locality. An example would be a local Alcoholics Anonymous group. Output of the community when viewed as a social system pertains to need satisfaction and problem resolution. Here the notion of networking is premised on the existence of common needs or problems for which new and strengthened ties become a key feature bearing on problem resolution among those who share the need or problem.

The mutual support subsystem has primary responsibility for goal 5 (social welfare) and a supporting role for other goals such as 4 (safety and security) and 9 (transportation).

Like all subsystems, these community subsystems are interdependent when viewed from the perspective of output, that is, the relative states of well-being of the community's residents. The Smith family can be helpful in illustrating the kinds of connections and interdependence that exist among community units. When the Smith family moved into the community some five years ago, they would, in systems language, be considered a signal input. Their sense of well-being and adjustment in any and all of their community relevant roles at any given time would be considered output. They would also be considered output if they should leave the community. But here the focus is on structure and the use of Warren's five locality relevant functions. Mr. Smith is an accountant with a national firm located in the community of Midtown. Mrs. Smith is a social worker employed in the local office of the state welfare department. They have four children—two attend the local community college and two attend high school. The family is active in the Methodist Church as well as in a variety of civic and professional groups. Mrs. Smith's mother lives with them. She is just recovering from cancer surgery that was performed at the local hospital. Mrs. Smith's mother has also been quite active in a local support group comprised of other community members who have cancer. In this vignette, each of the locality relevant subsystems are represented as well as their interdependent relationship.

The position held by Mr. Smith and the accounting services rendered by his firm would be part of the community's production, distribution, and consumption subsystem. Also, the majority of the goods and services the Smiths purchase locally would be derived from this system—their home, utilities, food, clothing, and automobile. Mrs. Smith's position would be in the community's mutual support subsystem as would the hospital and mutual support group used by Mrs. Smith's mother. The accounting services purchased by the local hospital from Mr. Smith's firm and the contribution by his firm to the hospital's building fund indicates the interrelationship ties between the two subsystems. The church, high school, and junior college attended by the Smith children are located in the socialization subsystem, as would all of those interactions between the children and their parents that were aimed at "bringing them up right"—everything from toilet training to how to cook. Mrs. Smith's daughter is planning to become a professional social worker, which indicates the interdependent relationships between the socialization and mutual support subsystems. The Smiths' role in their church and their regular attendance at the community theater and a bridge club illustrate the importance of the community's **social participation** subsystem to them. Both of the Smiths participate in the bowling teams that are sponsored by their respective employers, again illustrating the interdependent relationships between these respective community subsystems. The Smith family was required to obtain a building permit and a zoning variance from the city when they built two rooms onto their house to accommodate Mrs. Smith's mother. This experience, along with Mr. Smith's recent appearance in traffic court, represented their contact with the community's social control subsystem.

In terms of the use of this model, the assumption is made that the community of Midtown can be viewed as a distinct social entity. As such, there is an interdependent relationship among all members of this community (individuals, families, and organizations). The effects are differential, that is, while there may be common goals, the experiences pertaining to these goals are experienced differentially by each person. Some of these effects are negative (harmful) while others are positive (growth enhancing). The model also contains the assumption that the behaviors of the community and its impact on people and organizations are sufficiently understandable to permit professional intervention. The aim of intervention is always directed at improving the quality of life of those who are members of the community and/or are affected by the community; but the effects of intervention are manifested only in the *actual behaviors* that result from these structural changes. It is the actual behaviors of member units that will be the subject of the following section on interactions.

Interactions

The previous section on structure was intended to summarize those features that serve as guideposts or establish parameters to social behaviors. These guides, as indicated earlier, represent the expected or normative way that an individual, organization, or groupings of organizations, as in the case of a community, would be expected to behave in a given interactional situation. An analogy would be the banks and bed of a river that provide direction and contain the actual flow of water. But as the river waters flow, the banks and bed are always being altered and thereby affecting the subsequent waters that flow. Similarly, as interactions occur among people, the structures that serve as guides for those interactions are also being affected and thereby affecting subsequent interactions.

The role has been the focal point for describing structure. The enactment of a role by a given individual or by extension to an organization or a grouping of organizations is what is termed *interaction* in this model. Role enactment always involves communication with another person or persons either as an individual or in an organizational role. In its simplest form, it is a meaning sent by a person enacting a role and a meaning received and acted upon by another person in a reciprocating role. This does not mean that the meaning sent was the meaning received—only that there was an exchange of meanings. The cycle is completed when the person sending the communication receives some response in the form of a derived meaning from the receiver(s) of the message or those who represent them. In other words, the exchange of meanings does not always involve direct exchanges between the sender and receiver; it can be and is frequently indirect. Nor does it mean that the message sent was in verbal or written form. It could be in any form—a physical movement or in doing nothing. The point is that an exchange of meaning has taken place.

For example, a city council may pass an ordinance calling for a tax increase to pay for the construction of bike paths and nature trails. Whether the electorate passes or fails the bond issue, the city council members acting collectively will derive a meaning from their actions. This meaning will affect subsequent dealings by the council with their electorate. Another example of an indirect form of communication would be a commercial involving the opening of a new specialty restaurant. If patrons show up at the designated time and order the advertised specialty, the person representing the organization sponsoring the commercial would derive a meaning from the response and would be so guided in future dealings with this public. In this instance, the time of day aired, the amount of time the commercial was on, and the script of the commercial would all be aspects of structure. The person actually reading and interpreting the script on television and the actions of the public would represent interactions.

The social systems model is simply a way of seeking to understand the effects that various forms of social organization have on people and on each other. As stated earlier, the model is a device to answer three questions: (1) what was supposed to happen? (proposed output); (2) what actually happened? (actual output); and (3) what accounts for the difference between the two? Much of the answer to question three is to be found in examining the interactions that take place and comparing them with those structural features of the conversion operations that were to serve as guides.

To illustrate the interactional component, consider a community that is having far more traffic fatalities than might be expected (a comparison of proposed and actual output). There are local and state laws about such things as driving speeds, use of seat belts, driving while intoxicated, and so on. The police manual specifies how the police officer is to behave whenever confronted with a situation in which one or more of the laws are broken. However, when the *actual* behaviors of local drivers and police officers are observed, people may be found to be ignoring the law and the police ignoring the violators. The result is a proportionately greater number of traffic accidents and deaths resulting from the accidents. The problem is not to be found in the goals, structure, policies, and procedures of the police department or in the law, but rather in the actual driving habits of community residents and the behaviors of the police. Only by observing and understanding the actual behaviors is light shed on the discrepancies between proposed and actual outputs.

The sheer size and complexity of most communities requires that observation be restricted to only the most critical and relevant forms of interactions. The guides to what is critical and relevant are usually contained in the purpose under which an examination of the community is being undertaken, for example, a needs assessment pertaining to the problem of child abuse and neglect. Within the framework of the purposes of the assessment, the community's goals and objectives would be examined along with what actually happened, for example, in the previous year. The relevant community goals would be those pertaining to safety and security (goal 4) and social welfare (goal 5). The community subsystem principally responsible for achieving those goals would be social control (goal 4) and mutual support (goal 5). As a further guide in determining which interactions might be most relevant, the subgoal or objectives under each goal statement would be examined (assuming they existed for a particular community). Again for purposes of illustration, let us assume the following objective existed under the safety and security goal: "The rates of confirmed child abuse and neglect shall be less than the state average for the year 198X." The state average for 198X was 7.5 cases per 1,000 children while the rate for Midtown was 10.8 cases (actual output). Rather than being less than the state average, the rate was much higher. Something appears to be seriously wrong; the question becomes "What?" In such an instance, the practitioner would determine the key structural features of the community as they pertain to the social control and the mutual support subsystems. Once these structural features were identified (typically subsystems of the court, police department, office of the district attorney, hospital emergency rooms, public child welfare agencies, public and private family counseling agencies, and so on), an examination of the interactions that occur both within and between these agencies would take place. The focus of this examination/observation would be to try to understand what produced the higher than expected rate of child maltreatment.

Such an examination might have revealed that as a consequence of a series of meetings among civic, professional, and agency leaders (interactions), the community planned to undertake a comprehensive program aimed at the prevention of child maltreatment (a new structural feature). One assumption behind their approach was that persons who used harsh physical punishment against their children represented a high risk group for subsequent acts of abuse in which the child might be severely injured. A sizable number of these people were reported annually to the public child welfare agency. Because of the relatively low level of severity of these acts and because of various other work pressures, large numbers of these cases were never officially reported into the system by the caseworkers or, if entered, were reported as representing an "unconfirmed" case of child maltreatment (less paper work was involved). The investigations of the alleged act of maltreatment and the subsequent entry or lack of entry of the results of the official investigations into an official record would all be considered interactions. The fact that the decision not to enter the case into the official file or to label a relatively less severe case of maltreatment as being unconfirmed might all be at variance with state law and agency policy (elements of structure that are assumed to be specific guides to role behaviors). While the interactions (role behaviors) were not in keeping with agency policy, they may well have been in accord with community and agency norms.

As a consequence of the implementation of this new program of prevention, caseworkers were now more likely to enter these less severe cases into the official registry and to label them as confirmed as opposed to unconfirmed cases. By so doing, these cases would be referred for services on the assumption that they represented a high risk group for subsequent and more severe acts of abuse. While the goal was to reduce the amount of child maltreatment in the community through a program of prevention, the actual output showed an unintended result—an increase in the recorded rates of child maltreatment. In this example, the increase was a reporting artifact (interaction). But, the artifact would only be discovered through an examination of the structural features of this community and the actual behaviors that were taking place in their efforts at controlling the problem of child maltreatment.

Feedback

Feedback represents the information generated by the system and its suprasystem by comparing proposed and actual output. This information is then returned to the system as a maintenance input. Two problems must be confronted by the model user in applying the concept of feedback to a community. Both of these problems stem from the nature of the concept of community itself; first, the scope and complexity of the community goal structure; and second, typically community goals are not formally adopted. Given this situation, a special responsibility is placed on the model user to confront and resolve the issues associated with these problems early in any practice application. The major step in the resolution process is deciding precisely the boundaries of the designated community and determining the goal structure to be used in the application.

Relative to the first problem, few if any communities will have in place the kind of formalized comprehensive goal structure described in the model. The value of the goal structure is essentially conceptual; it provides the practitioner a way of thinking about the community as a whole while working in a more narrowly defined area (for instance, the problem of child maltreatment). What the model user is likely to find is that "bits and pieces" of a community goal structure are in place and can be built upon. This assumption is premised on the definition of a community. The community is, in all applications, an ongoing form of social organization. It has a past and a future. The model is simply a tool for thinking about community and trying to understand its behaviors. The first problem is not likely to be as overwhelmingly complex as it first appears.

The comprehensive community goal structure is deemed implicit in the very nature of the notion of community. At a practical level, the model user is only going to use the comprehensive goal structure as a way of thinking about the community as a whole, while concentrating his or her helping activities in a much narrower area of current community interest, such as AIDS, teenage pregnancies, the homeless, racism, and so on. Given an agreement on the designated problem and a related goal structure, the practitioner may find it strategically useful to help the community formalize or otherwise upgrade its feedback arrangements. In so doing, the community becomes better able to gauge its progress toward goal attainment and be more systemlike in its behavior.

The second problem dealing with the formalized adoption of goals is also less complex than it might otherwise seem and for reasons similar to those noted above. Communities as we are using the term are comprised of member units that are symbiotically not formally related to each other. Given this characteristic, the sharing of goals becomes strategically related to the dynamics underlying the symbiotic ties that member units have with each other. In this sense, the absence of formally adopted community goals becomes an incidental rather than a central problem. Again, and assuming some agreement on the problem and the related goal structure, the practitioner might help the community by suggesting ways of improving feedback arrangements among those community units most closely and symbiotically related to the problem. In many instances this will not require the creation of new feedback systems but merely the sharing of information among agencies that have the same community goals, like the prevention and control of the maltreatment of children.

The forms of and the extent that feedback is used vary greatly community by community. What can be suggested at this point is that as communities increase in size, and become more complex and formalized, they will tend to increase their reliance on formal and more inclusive feedback systems.

Steady State

In this chapter we are including discussion of steady state as a part of the larger discussion of the model and its application to the community. In the same sense as discussed previously, the community in the pursuit of its purposes will be confronted with four ever-present problems. These problems are never solved in any final sense, but the resolution efforts provide the avenue for understanding the dynamics of community behaviors and the more general process of community growth and development, that is, negative entropy. This investigation also offers an avenue for exploration of the reverse process of community disorganization—loss of steady state or entropy. We will, as before, discuss steady state under the four problem headings.

Goal Attainment

THE PROBLEM: How to Achieve the Community's Task Output of Improving the Quality of Life of Its Citizens Through the Provision of Facilities and Services that Will Help Satisfy Common Needs and Cope with Common Problems

The premise on which this problem has been formed is that most people reside in what we are designating as a community. And it is through the facilities and services contained within the community that most people go about seeking satisfaction of their needs and dealing with their problems. At one level the community can be likened to a very large self-help or self-development group. Undergirding this contention is the degree of interdependence characterizing people and social organizations who share the same habitat.

In developing the goal structure of the community, we referred to the United Way of America Services Identification System, UWASIS, and to the social indicator movement. Implicit in both of these approaches is a condition that can be usefully defined as "quality of human life" and the fact that this condition is measurable. We have found this position useful in conceptualizing the community and its function. Now, in developing the notion of steady state, we start with the question of how well the community is doing in helping its citizens to improve the quality of their lives. If satisfactory progress is not being made, we further assume that this will lead to a progressive loss of steady state. If not corrected, the result will be continued out-migration and carried to its extreme, creation of a ghost town.

Goal attainment as used in the model is an external and consummatory function.[15] At a conceptual level, goal attainment is a system effect, an end state, for example, how citizens judge the contribution their community has made to the quality of their lives. Two points are helpful in applying the model. First, when applied to the community, citizens are considered both signal and maintenance inputs. Recall that this is also true in applications of the model to a social group. From this position, the community residents answer the question: "What have been the effects that the community has had on the quality of my life?" Second, and in all applications of the model, the output is the designation of the effect following a cycle of organizational operations. Assuming existence of a community goal structure, a measure of goal attainment would be the answers that community residents would give to the following question: "All things considered, over the past year how would you rate the contributions made by this community to the quality of your life?"

While approaches to the measurement of the quality of community life are in their infancy, the notion has important practice implications. The most important and perhaps most exciting is the belief that by working with the community, it is possible to affect positively the quality of the lives of the people who live there.[16]

Integration

THE PROBLEM: How to Optimize Satisfaction of the Community's Maintenance Outputs

The problem is an internal and consummatory one. This problem is a particularly important one for communities because of the looseness and perhaps weakness of its horizontal structures. We referred to this problem earlier in this chapter; it has also been highlighted by Roland Warren.[17] Approaching this problem from a practice perspective can be helpful. We have argued earlier that the formulation of the locality development model of community organization can be viewed as focusing on this problem.[18] This model of practice focuses on community capacity building, integration, and, more generally, on the accomplishment of process goals.[19] The accomplishment of process goals is very close to integration.

Examples of community efforts at dealing with the problem of integration would be the festive events that communities typically celebrate—Founder's Day, the Fourth of July, the Community Art Fair, naming of the "Community Volunteer of the Year," and so on. These events bring residents together to celebrate their community, to recognize those that have served the community, and to feel good about themselves. Other examples dealing with the problem of integration include support of the local high school's football team or the community's professional baseball team. All such efforts can be viewed as helping to build and to strengthen relationships among the components of the community. In so doing, citizens, and particularly those in organizational roles, feel good about themselves, the organizations they represent, and their community.

Adaptation

THE PROBLEM: How to Optimize Community Goal Attainment by Modifying the Suprasystem or if Necessary by Modifying Community Structures and Goals

Adaptation is defined as an external and instrumental problem. The focus is on the community's external environment, and the effect is directed toward the creation of conditions that help achieve community task outputs (goal attainment). A familiar example would be the promotional efforts made by community groups to convince outsiders that their town would be the best place to locate new industry and for people to live. These efforts are viewed as designed to help the community achieve goal attainment, more and better paying jobs and an increase in the quality of life, for instance.

The notion of adaptation is particularly helpful in conveying the dynamic and open system nature of organizational life. Suggested is a continuing interplay between every social organization and the social context in which it functions. Several features of this interplay are important:

1. It is proactive—the system is not viewed as a passive recipient of changes imposed by the suprasystem. The basic stance built into the model is proactive;

2. The focus of activity on the part of the system is to create receptivity in the supra-system for its outputs; and,

3. The nature of interplay (interdependence) has a strong symbiotic character (mutual need–mutual benefits).

The model incorporates the assumption that, if it is to maintain steady state, every organization must seek to control/adapt its environment to facilitate its input/output exchanges. This is the problem to be resolved. If the problem is not solved at a satisfactory level, the social organization does not survive. The concept is not intended to convey that only the suprasystem is adapted or that only the system is adapted to the needs of the suprasystem; rather, only that the problem resolution process starts with efforts at controlling features of the suprasystem central to a "successful" input/output exchange. The notion of adaptation should be thought of both as designation of a universal problem to be solved in the quest of steady state and as the dynamic processes associated with the resolution of this problem. Recall that system-suprasystem relationships are deemed as mutually determinant.

Pattern Maintenance

THE PROBLEM: How to Maintain in a Constantly Changing and at Times Volatile Environment the Community's Most Important Structural Patterns, Those That Provide Its Unique Identity

Pattern maintenance is an internal and instrumental problem. It is internal in the sense that the problem pertains to the maintenance of the crucial features of the relationships that bind member components to each other. It is instrumental in the sense that these relationships form the means by which system needs are satisfied (the integration problem) and through which goal attainment is pursued.

The concept of pattern maintenance is helpful because it distinguishes two interrelated features that are considered inherent in all forms of social organization (these features are assumed to be ultimately derived from the innate needs of the people who comprise social organizations). As applied to the community we hold that:

1. Every community has core distinctive qualities that distinguish it from all other communities.

The concept of pattern maintenance as employed in this model assumes that if these core features are lost, steady state is lost and the system ceases to exist (at least in its earlier form). A hierarchy of relationship features is assumed. Faced with adversity and the need for adjustment to preserve steady state, accommodations start with the least sensitive sets of relationships and progress up the hierarchy toward the core. If the core is violated, the system ceases to exist. In conceptualizing the core, it is helpful to view it as comprising those relationships most fundamental to achieving the organization's highest (most important) purpose.

2. Every social organization has within itself general patterns that guide growth and development.

Contained in this notion is the tendency of every system to push toward growth and development along specified lines. Associated with this notion is that the growth patterns will include those associated with the defense of its distinctive features. Taking this assumption of thrust toward growth and increased autonomy as a given, it follows that each of the system's subsystems will also display tendencies toward increased states of autonomy—the counter movement of the force described earlier under integration. Carried to its logical conclusion, each subsystem would achieve system status itself— becoming detached from the parent system. An example is the behavior found among neighborhood associations as they are formed within communities. The model would assume that there will be a force (pattern maintenance) that will result in the association seeking higher states of autonomy, such as control over the schools in their area, the police, fire personnel, and so on. Carried to its ultimate conclusion, a new community would be formed, by deannexation. If every neighborhood association were able to accomplish this level of autonomy, the original community would cease to exist. Therefore, the community must exercise some control over this thrust of its subsystems or its basic character would be violated and a threat to its own survival would develop.

A community example of the concept of pattern maintenance might be the responses made by community members to the shutdown of a major industry. The shutdown would affect all community subsystems through the loss of jobs, tax revenues, and so on. The model would hold that a hierarchy of adjustments would be made until steady state was again achieved. If the core features of the community were violated (governance, water distribution, police protection, education of the young), steady state would be lost, and the community would cease to exist. A ghost town would be created.

The concept of pattern maintenance incorporates the notion of hierarchy, which guides both development (negative entropy) and decline to nonsystem status (entropy). The concept as we apply it in this model does not include a single lock-step form of growth and decline, but rather one that is specific to each class of social organization, yet follows the general pattern outlined.

SUMMARY

This chapter has provided an application of the social systems model to the community. In Figure 15.1 we identify the concepts comprising the systems model as it might be applied to our hypothetical community Midtown. This is the fourth and last application to be made. Each application has built from a social systems perspective. Having its philosophical and conceptual roots in general systems theory, the perspective represents a way of looking at the ordering characteristics of social phenomena. Given the applied orientation of this book, we have presented a social systems model as a way of conceptualizing the interplay between human-behavior and the social environment. While the model represents a way of thinking about human and organizational behavior, it is offered as a way of examining any particular social organization, whether it is a professional helping relationship between a worker and client or a community.

Each application, while incorporating the general ordering characteristics of social organizations, focuses on the features distinctive to the class of organization being modeled. The special qualities of the community pertain to its ties to place and the scope of the function performed. The community also shared with the social group the feature that individuals represent both its signal and maintenance inputs. Communities are formed by the interactions of the people who comprise them, their citizens. Similarly,

FIGURE 15.1   The Community of Midtown Modeled as a Social System

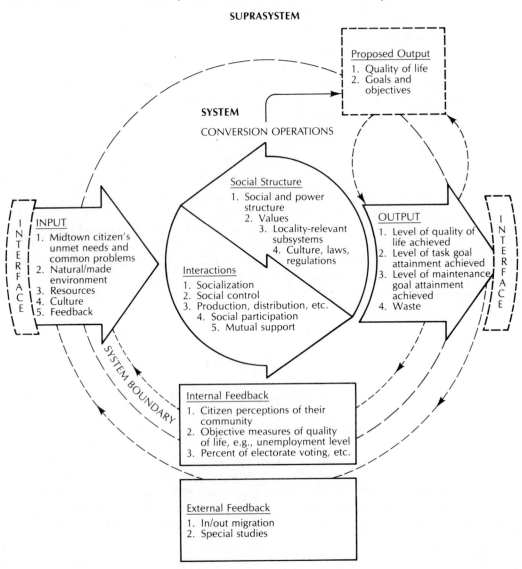

this interaction affects these same people for better or worse. It is another way of saying that the individual is both the cause (input) and the effect (output) of all forms of social organizations.

GLOSSARY

Extracommunity systems Systems external to which a social system is vertically linked (e.g., a local subsidiary's relationship to the parent organization).

Extramural role Role enactment that occurs primarily with others external to the system (e.g., a traveling salesperson).

Intramural role Role enactment that occurs primarily within the social system (e.g., a casework supervisor).

Horizontal patterns The concept as used by Roland Warren is essentially synonymous with what we designate as a community's internal structuring. These horizontal linkages or relationships relate functionally community-based groups and organizations to each other.

Mutual support One of the locality-relevant functions identified by Roland Warren and roughly comparable to the notion of social welfare.

Production, distribution, and consumption A locality-relevant function identified by Roland Warren and roughly comparable to a community's economic system.

Social control The means utilized by a system to secure compliance to its rules (normative expectations). Conceptually compliance is sought through socialization measures. When these measures are unsuccessful, they are, so to speak, backed up by social control measures.

Socialization The process by which individuals acquire and internalize the values, knowledge, skills, and related matters necessary to function successfully as members of a society.

Social participation A locality-relevant function identified by Roland Warren. Reference is made to the community-based arrangements through which people are provided opportunities for social interaction.

NOTES

1. Harold F. Kaufman, "Toward an Interactional Conception of Community," *Social Forces* 38 (1): 9–17.

2. Roland Warren, *The Community in America*, 3rd ed. (Chicago, Ill.: Rand McNally and Co., 1978).

3. For a useful summary see Larry M. Siegel, C. Clifford Attkisson, and Linda G. Carson, "Need Identification and Program Planning in the Community Context, in *Strategies of Community Organization*, 4th ed., Fred Cox et al. (eds.) (Itasca, Ill.: F. E. Peacock, 1987), 71–97.

4. Warren, *The Community in America*, 240–246.

5. See particularly E. T. Hiller, "The Community as a Social Group," *American Sociological Review* 6 (1941): 189–202.

6. Roland Warren, "The Good Community – What Would It Be? *Journal of the Community Development Society* I (1): 15.

7. For a review of the social indicator movement, see Robert J. Rossi and Kevin J. Gilmartin, *Handbook of Social Indicators* (New York: Garland STPM Press, 1980).

8. United Way of America. UWASIS II. (Alexandria, Virginia: United Way of America, Planning and Allocations Division), November 1976.

9. Ibid., 7.

10. Warren, *The Community in America.*

11. Morton E., Long, "The Local Community as an Ecology of Games," *American Journal of Sociology* 64 (November 1958): 251–261.

12. Warren, *The Community in America.*

13. Ibid., 9.

14. Abraham H. Maslow, *Motivation and Personality,* 2nd ed. (New York: Harper and Row, 1970), 299.

15. For an earlier discussion of the conceptual origins of this four-problem paradigm, see "Steady State" in Chapter 4.

16. For examples of studies of the quality of community life, see Robert W. Marans, Don A. Dillman, and Janet Keller, *Perceptions of Life Quality in Rural America* (Ann Arbor, Mich.: Institute for Social Research, 1980).

17. Warren, *The Community in America.*

18. Fred M. Cox et al., eds., *Strategies of Community Organizations,* 4th ed. (Itasca, Ill.: F. E. Peacock, 1987).

19. Ibid., 10.

Chapter 16

The Community Problem of Child Abuse and Neglect: A Practice Application

OUTLINE

Background

The inclusion of a chapter dealing with a practice application of the model to a community problem is a departure from the format used elsewhere in this book. The reason for doing so is that for many the community is the most difficult of the various forms of social organization to model. We believe there are two principal reasons for this difficulty. First, like the social system model itself, a community is a conceptual designation – it stands for something. For example, New York City is a municipality, a special type of formal organization; in this sense the designation is of something real, with legal and political existence. New York as a community is not the same thing. Depending on the use being made of the term, it may include New York as a municipality but usually much more (for instance, all the people who identify themselves as New Yorkers). Because of the many meanings and uses of the term, community may or may not correspond exactly with something that is "real."[1] As we will point out in our example, modeling the community as a social system requires the model user to apply the term community to something that has existence. Practically speaking, we would not find it useful to try to model system-suprasystem relationships without first identifying the subject system and agreeing on what constitutes its boundaries. Second, the community, as we have defined

423

it, has the most comprehensive set of functions and is the most functionally differenti-ated of all the forms of social organization to which the model has been applied. Com-pounding these problems, the relationships among member units of the community are typically not formally constituted. This means that the relationships are essentially infor-mal. What further complicates the matter is that those engaging in informal relation-ships may not know each other. Given the size of many modern communities, we must assume that the functional interdependence among the many components comprising the community is not dependent upon either formal or informal (personal) relationships. We characterize these relationships as symbiotic in nature. Unfortunately we do not as yet have a set of concepts or coherent theory that helps to explain in human relationship terms what is meant by symbiotic. For example, in applying the model to the social group and to the formal organization we employed the concepts of Gemeinschaft and Gesellschaft to describe the key features of these relationships. We were able to further develop these characteristics through use of various psychological and sociological theo-ries. There is no counterpart set of well-developed concepts or theory that the model user can employ to the community, at least no theory *specific* to human social behavior.[2]

The problems just summarized might suggest that the community practitioner has few if any guides upon which a professional approach to practice can be grounded. We do not subscribe to this position. Our approach is premised on the assumption that when the concept of community is applied to a form of social organization it can be modeled as a social system. In other words, the so-called community possesses the same general characteristics of order as all other forms of social organization. The model itself can be useful to the practitioner. The limitation is in theory development that helps explain the distinguishing characteristics of the community in ways that extend the model's practice utility. Even here we believe that it is easy to understate development of relevant community and community practice theory.

Prior to undertaking an application of the model, it is important to recall distinc-tive features of the community that affect professional intervention efforts. Perhaps the most important feature is that the community is not formally organized, and so there is no established authority or decision-making structure. As a consequence, no person is formally empowered to set an agenda, to "fix" things that may need fixing. Instead, the community is comprised of an indeterminant number of autonomous but interdepen-dent social units of varying size and complexity (from families to corporations). The organization that develops among member units within a community is to be under-stood as a consequence of the seemingly symbiotic relationships that arise out of the common needs and problems confronted by people sharing the same habitat. Their in-terdependence is central to the definition being employed—a community is a territorially based social organization through which most people satisfy their common needs and desires, deal with their common problems, and through which they relate to their society.

At this point it might be helpful to illustrate the notion of a community problem by contrasting it with an individual's problem, or problems confronted by a formal orga-nization. Two features will be used in drawing the comparisons: (1) the focus of the problem, and (2) the resources/capacity for problem resolution. At the individual level, the problem and its effects are primarily focused on the individual and the individual's capacity for resolving or at least reducing the adverse effects of the problem (with or without outside resources). There are a myriad of such problems ranging from those that are essentially intrapersonal to those arising out of a lack of knowledge or skill (examples include both divorce and being passed over for a job promotion). Similarly, organizational problems are those that pertain to the formal organization itself and not primarily to the individuals who comprise it. As with the individual, it is within the capacity of the organization (its resources and sanctions) to resolve or at least deal with the problem. Again there would be a myriad of examples ranging from such commonplace ones as bankruptcy, to a law suit alleging discriminatory hiring practices, to high job turnover rates among employees. By contrast, community problems are those that have adverse effects on the community and those who comprise it. Similarly, the assumption must be made that the community, through the coordinated work of its member units, has the capacity to deal with the problem. But unlike the individual or the formally established organization, the community has no authority structure with sanctions to address the problem. Because of the lack of a formalized structure, the community is confronted with special problems in all facets of the usual problem-solving process. The first and perhaps most serious difficulty is establishing that a problem state exists. For purposes of subsequent discussion, the following is offered as a definition of a community problem: A condition adversely affecting a significant number of community members and about which members feel that corrective action is possible and desirable through some form of collective effort.

In the sections that follow, maltreatment of children is conceptualized as a community problem, and the social systems model is employed to illustrate features of the model that are relevant to practice.

Child Abuse and Neglect

Nationally, over one million children are reported to be maltreated every year. Of that number about 200,000 are physically abused, 60,000 to 100,000 are sexually abused, and the remainder are neglected. As a measure of the seriousness of the problem, some 2,000 children die each year as the result of being abused or neglected.[3] Maltreatment is thus one of the leading causes of death of young children. The enactment of P.L. 93-247, The Child Abuse Prevention and Treatment Act, was signed into law in 1974. This action defined child maltreatment as a social problem requiring a national effort aimed at its control.[4]

Frequently, a community social problem is given a problem status through legislative action taken nationally, as is the case with the problem of child maltreatment. Federal law has encouraged and supported public awareness campaigns to sensitize citizens to the problem of child maltreatment, thereby helping communities define child maltreatment as a community problem and to take collective actions. In addition, governmental support has spurred research and related efforts aimed at extending and strengthening service delivery systems. It is also important to note that the identification arrangements and service delivery systems that deal with the maltreatment of children are located in what we are calling the community, for example, the court and child welfare agencies.

The question might now be asked—why is child maltreatment being considered a community problem as opposed to an individual (family) or an organizational problem? At the individual level, the child is the victim but possesses little or no capacity for resolving or otherwise dealing effectively with the problem. The local public child welfare agency may have the statutory responsibility for investigating allegations of abuse and neglect, but for the most part any effort at intervention must be with the consent of the court. In other words, the problem encompasses more than the responsibilities assigned to any one agency. Further, most child welfare agencies do not possess significant specialized treatment capacities. These capacities tend to be located in the community's various mental health, health, and family service agencies. In short, the local child welfare agency and the other agencies serving maltreated children can be conceptualized as comprising an interdependent network of agencies that have a collective responsibility for helping to protect the community's most valuable resource, its children. From this perspective, each agency is both a separate and distinct social organization as well as a component of a community subsystem that works in a coordinated way with other community agencies to prevent and control the problem of child abuse and neglect. From the perspective just described, the notion of community becomes a helpful way of designating a collectively sensed problem and a collective and mutually agreed-upon response.

Modeling a Child Protective Services System as a Community Subsystem

The social systems model will be applied to our hypothetical community called Midtown. This mythical community is located in a midwestern state and has a population of 601,953. Midtown was recently shocked with a series of front-page stories dealing with the maltreatment of children. The most shocking was the beating deaths of twin infant girls by their mother. Consequently, there was a call from various community leaders to ascertain the extent of child maltreatment in the community and to determine what could be done to prevent or control the problem. Midtown's Health and Welfare Planning Council and the local office of the State Department of Child Welfare (DCW) cosponsored a public forum dealing with the maltreatment of children. Coming out of that meeting was a proposal for the creation of a representative group of community leaders who would study the problems and report their findings back to the community. It was suggested that the study group seek answers to the following questions:

1. What agencies are involved in the community's effort to prevent and control child maltreatment and what are their respective functions? (What is the community subsystem responsible for dealing with this problem?)
2. What was the incidence of child maltreatment in the community last year? (signal inputs)
3. What were the results of last year's efforts to prevent and control the maltreatment of children? (actual outputs)
4. How much money is the community receiving annually to deal with the problem of child maltreatment? (maintenance inputs)

5. What can be done to prevent and control the problem of child maltreatment in this community? (proposed outputs)

An Ad Hoc Committee for the Prevention of Child Abuse and Neglect was convened by Midtown's Health and Welfare Planning Council. The committee was representative of the major agencies having an interest in the problem of child maltreatment as well as others representing civic, business, professional, religious, and political interests. The committee elected as its chair Judge Faire, Midtown's Juvenile Court Judge. Also on the committee was the wife of the community's leading industrialist, Meg A. Bucks; along with the associate editor of *The Daily Express*, Midtown's only daily paper; the president of the Midtown Ministerial Alliance; and others. The committee was staffed by a planner from the Health and Welfare Planning Council. The planner, Mr. Eddie State, was a recent social work graduate and was familiar with utilizing a social systems model for conceptualizing the community, assessing the problem, and mounting an intervention approach. Given the nature of the problem to be addressed, the level of concern, and the structural development of the community, Mr. Eddie State suggested to the committee an intervention strategy incorporating locality development and social planning features (see earlier discussion of these models in Chapter 12).

After a three-month study the committee issued its findings. The centerpiece of the report was a delineation of the organizations and agencies having primary responsibilities for dealing with the problem of child maltreatment and the key features of their relationships. Figure 16.1 identifies the agencies and sets forth some of their relationships. The report reviewed and discussed the problem of child maltreatment by conceptualizing this network of agencies as a subsystem of the community.

The Social System

Centre County, in which Midtown is located, was determined, for planning purposes, to be the community. The community included all of the people who had their primary residence in the county plus all of the groups and organizations located within the county. This decision was made because Midtown's population comprised 85 percent of the total and 89 percent of the portion under age 18 of the county's population. Also, the county was utilized in the planning activities of the Midtown Health and Welfare Planning Council and the state's DCW was organized on a county basis as were many of the other agencies dealing with the problem. As a consequence, most of the data on the maltreatment of children were reported by county.

The identified community subsystem that dealt with the problem of the maltreatment of children was determined to include selected parts, such as administrative units (subsystems), of the following organizations and agencies: Midtown General Hospital, Centre County Juvenile Court, Midtown Police Department, Centre County's Office of the District Attorney, Midtown's Public Schools, Centre County DCW, Midtown Mental Health Center, Midtown Family Service, Catholic Charities, Midtown Ministerial Alliance, Poteau Indian Tribal Council, and the Parents Assistance Center. The staff members from the preceding agencies working in the area of child protection along with all the protective services clients were included in the designated subsystem.

FIGURE 16.1   Midtown's Child Protective Services Subsystem

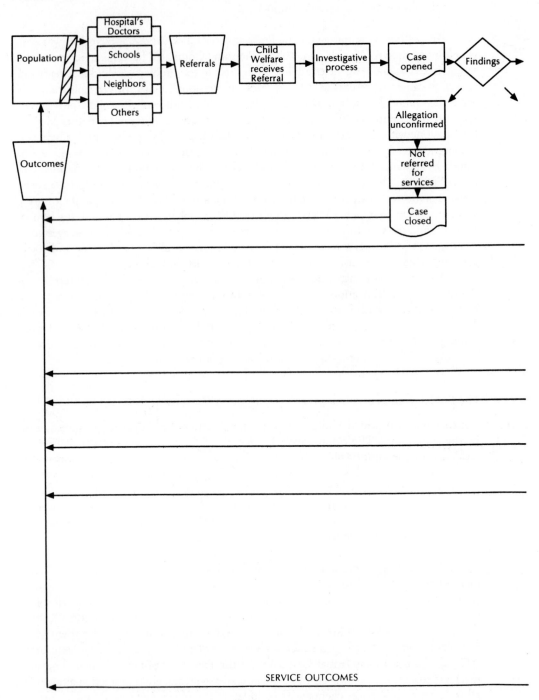

SERVICE OUTCOMES

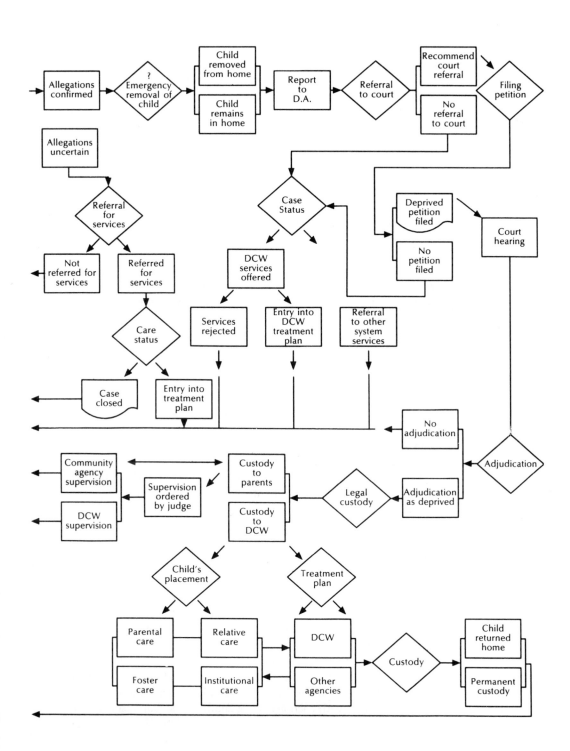

Input

The committee's report showed that of the 601,953 residents of the community, 175,402 or 29 percent were under the age of 18. State law defined a child as being a person under the age of 18. Therefore, the 175,402 children of Midtown were determined to be the "population at risk," those who could experience an act of maltreatment. Of that number, last year reports alleging maltreatment were received on 3,684 of those children, a rate of 21.0 reports per 1,000 children at risk. Based on state law, Centre County's DCW opened a case on each of these children. Following investigation of each of these cases, a confirmed finding of maltreatment was made in 52 percent of them (1,916 or a rate of 10.9 per 1,000). In the remaining cases, maltreatment was "not confirmed" and no further official action was taken.

In this instance, signal inputs were the 3,684 children and their families (a total of 11,736 individuals). Maintenance inputs included all of the staffs of all of the agencies comprising the community subsystem [estimated at the equivalent of 653 full-time equivalent positions (FTE)]. Other maintenance inputs included the estimated $15,412,678 the community through its various agencies had budgeted in the support of this subsystem (staff salaries, transportation, space—all direct costs attributed to dealing with this problem). Also included as maintenance inputs were the knowledge gained about the problem and other information and data secured as feedback, for example, data on the number of confirmed cases of maltreatment that occurred in the community last year.

Under the input heading of its report, the committee noted that it had plotted on a map the location of each reported case of child maltreatment. This map indicated a high concentration of reports in the poorer area of the community, particularly in neighborhoods located just north of the central business district (CBD). The committee observed that Midtown's General Hospital is located in this same area, and this probably accounted for the large proportion of child abuse referrals that came from that hospital's emergency room. In summarizing the input section of their report, the committee indicated that the children in this area of the city should be considered a high risk group and that subsequent work should target this area in an effort to better understand the social, psychological, and environmental determinants of child maltreatment.

Conversion Operations – Structure

The committee's report identified eleven major agencies that were determined to comprise the principal units of the community's subsystem dealing with the maltreatment of children. The committee likened this network of agencies to an organizational chart, saying that it represented a structural portrayal of those agencies dealing daily with the problem of child maltreatment in Midtown. Many other agencies and groups had some involvement with this problem, but according to the report, these eleven agencies were the principal players. The report also identified the equivalent of 653 full-time positions (roles) that were devoted to dealing with this problem. The report noted that, while each of the eleven agencies was autonomous, they operated with a surprising level of cooperation (symbiotic relationships) with each agency assuming leadership responsibility over certain aspects of the process. For example, the emergency room of Midtown General Hospital was a primary source of referrals of children who had been seriously abused or neglected. The pediatric unit of that hospital was the place where most of the seriously injured children were taken for care and assessment. Also, and by state law (structure), the Centre County DCW received, investigated, and rendered findings on all of the alleged acts of child maltreatment that occurred within the county. Because of their key role, the committee designated the Centre County office of the state DCW as the lead agency in Midtown's child protective services system.

In summarizing the structural features of the community subsystem, the report tracked the typical flow of clients through the network of agencies. They noted that all of the 1,916 cases in which the investigation resulted in a finding of "confirmed" were referred by DCW to the District Attorney's office (DA). Of that number, the DA filed petitions on 1,686 or 88 percent of the cases (the DA concluded that there was insufficient evidence for filing in the remaining 12 percent). Juvenile Court scheduled hearings on all of these cases, with 1,214 (72 percent) resulting in the child being adjudicated as deprived. In 973 (80 percent) of these cases, legal custody was granted to the State DCW and carried out by their Centre County staff. In the remaining cases (241), custody remained with the parents or was granted to a relative. Supervisory responsibility over these custody arrangements was evenly split between the state DCW and other community agencies, for example, Catholic Charities and the Poteau Indian Tribal Council.

Conversion Operations – Interactions

The committee commented (interaction) that there were a number of concerns that arose during the course of their study. For example, while state law (structure) required that all instances of suspected child maltreatment be reported to the local DCW office, the physicians of Midtown were determined to be referring (interaction) very few suspected cases. According to research performed nationally, physicians generate approximately 5 percent of all referrals of suspected cases of child maltreatment; in Midtown, physicians accounted for fewer than 2 percent of the referrals. Similarly, educators in the Midtown School System referred (interaction) far fewer cases of child maltreatment (4 percent) than did their colleagues nationally (14 percent). The committee observed that the professional roles (structure) of physician and educator usually call for the professional to be an advocate and protector of the child and so they were unsure why these professionals were not more active in the referral process. Central to the committee's concern was the theory (structure) that early detection of the problem of child abuse is critical in terms of preventing or at least reducing the severity of subsequent acts of maltreatment.

The matter that most concerned the committee was high caseloads and high job turnover rates among the child welfare workers located in the Centre County DCW. According to standards (structure) suggested by the National Child Welfare Association, each worker in such an agency should have an average of twenty active cases per month. In the county office, the caseloads averaged thirty-two per worker. The committee observed that based on their inspection of records (interaction), it took Centre County's child welfare workers an average of four days from the receipt of a referral to establish contact with the child and his or her family (interaction). State DCW policy (structure) called for such contact to be made within forty-eight hours. Further, the committee observed that case records (structure) were frequently incomplete. For example, in over half of the cases examined, there was no evidence of the establishment of treatment goals or a coherent treatment plan. Another consequence of excessive caseloads was a greater tendency of Midtown's child welfare workers to recommend (interaction) foster homes and other out-of-home placements for children than was the practice nationally. The committee noted that whenever possible, supervised in-home placements are preferred to out-of-home placements. The committee observed that in-home placements require much more intensive supervision and counseling by the worker than do out-of-home placements. In short, the committee concluded that because of workload demands (a structural feature), many children were inappropriately being placed (interaction) in foster homes, group homes, and other such out-of-home arrangements. The committee also observed that the job turnover rate last year for Midtown's child welfare workers was 42 percent, far above state and national averages for such workers.

Actual Output

The committee's report highlighted some of the results of the community's child protective subsystem. For the year ending December 31, 19__:

1. The incidence of child maltreatment increased from 9.3 last year to 10.9 per 1,000 children at risk. (In many instances this would represent an input statement, but because of the committee's concern with prevention, this was also considered an output statement—a result of lack thereof of preventing the maltreatment of the community's children.)
2. The percentage of persons committing a second act of maltreatment within a period of one year increased 12 percent over last year's figures.
3. Eighty-five percent of all children adjudicated as deprived were put in out-of-home placements, an increase of 11 percent over last year's figures.
4. Sixty-seven percent of all children placed in out-of-home placements were returned to their own homes within a period of one year. The previous year's percentage was 76.
5. Etc.

The above data were categorized as task outputs. With respect to maintenance outputs, the committee reported that for the year ending December 31, 19__:

1. The various agencies comprising the community's child protective services system spent a total of $16,337,439, or an increase of 8 percent, over last year's expenditures. This figure represented 106 percent of the amount budgeted. Both the Centre County Juvenile Court and the Centre County DCW received supplemental funds from the State because of expenditure of all of their original allocations.
2. Twenty-seven percent of all professionally designated staff positions were filled by persons professionally certified to hold those positions, an increase of 3 percent over last year's figures. The range of professional staffing was from a low of 15 percent in Juvenile Court to 100 percent at the Midtown Family Service Agency. The professional staffing was also determined to vary by discipline. For example,

85 percent of those persons holding the position of psychologist were licensed as psychologists under the State's licensure law. The counterpart of this figure for social work positions (all agencies) was 20 percent.
3. Staff turnover rates for all positions identified in the community's child protective services system was 34 percent, a 6 percent increase over last year's figure and a five-year high.
4. Etc.

Proposed Output

Central among the conclusions reached by the committee was that child maltreatment was truly a community problem. No single agency was found to have sole responsibility for dealing with the problem, so the committee concluded that progress was only going to be achieved by the coordinated work of a number of community agencies supported by a caring and concerned citizenry. Specifically, the committee called for establishment of a standing committee within the Health and Welfare Planning Council concerned with the well-being of the community's children. The following statement of a hierarchy of outcomes was suggested:

Purpose To improve the quality of life of the children of Midtown to the end that each child is able to develop to his or her full potential as an individual and as a citizen.

Several goals were suggested in areas such as family life, health, safety, and education (task). Other goals were suggested to improve and update the services and facilities serving children and their families (maintenance). Under each goal statement, the report listed a set of specific, measurable objectives, and for each objective a set of activities (a plan) was suggested for achieving that objective. For example:

Task Goal To assure that all children live in a safe, healthful, caring and growth-enhancing environment.

Task Objective To reduce the incidence of child maltreatment from 10.9 children per 1,000 at risk to 8.8 children by July 1, 19_.

Task Activities

1. To develop a profile of high-risk features associated with child maltreatment.
2. To promote use of the child abuse hot line for parents desiring help in dealing with their children.
3. Etc.

Maintenance Goal To improve the delivery of child protective services in Midtown through the professionalization of agency staffs.

Maintenance Objective To increase from 20 to 35 percent the number of licensed social workers holding social work positions in the child protective agency system in Midtown by July 1, 19_.

Maintenance Activities

1. To meet with state and local agency officials to encourage agency officials to develop employment standards that give preference to professionally qualified applicants.
2. To provide testimony at the legislature and testimony at the United Fund hearings attesting to the importance of establishing professional standards for key child welfare positions.
3. Etc.

Suprasystem

The committee observed that, while there were eleven primary agencies comprising the community's effort at protecting children, many of the key decisions affecting how those agencies operated were made by decision-makers located outside the community. For example, the lead agency, Centre County's DCW, is the county office of the state DCW. While the local director has some control over her operations, major program and management and financial decisions are made in "State Office." It is thus very difficult for the local director to coordinate the work of her agency with other community agencies. To one degree or another, all of the agencies comprising the community's child protective services system were found to have strong ties to agencies and organizations located outside the community. In some instances, like DCW and the mental health center, they were county units of a state agency. In these cases, staff in state office and the state legislature vitally affected local operations. In the instance of Catholic Charities, the local agency is simply one of a number of subagencies under the control of the bishop, who is located in another community. Even Midtown's Community Hospital (a public hospital supported by the taxpayers of Midtown) is operated under contract by a hospital management group located in Chicago.

Interface

Because of strong links that each of its agencies has with out-of-community organizations, the committee concluded that its planning and programming would have to have both vertical and horizontal dimensions. Similarly, the committee concluded that interested citizens would have to take a much more active role in local and state political activities if they were going to be able to influence decisions affecting operations of local agencies, for instance, helping to elect candidates for public office who were interested in the problem of child maltreatment, and testifying before legislative committees making budget decisions affecting local agencies (adaptation).

The committee was particularly sensitive to the importance of the state DCW in achieving community goals. In discussing the matter, the committee noted that the community and DCW shared many of the same goals and that by working more closely, both the community's and the department's goals could be advanced. In the course of these discussions, staff pointed out that DCW and the United States Department of Health and Human Services had financial grants to help communities deal with the prevention and control of child abuse and neglect. After studying the matter, the committee, working through the Midtown Health and Welfare Council, submitted and had funded a research and demonstration project aimed at the early identification of, and services to children at high risk of being maltreated. Given the success of their initial effort, the committee asked its planning staff to identify other possible sources of funding that would permit interfacing with other outside groups.

Feedback

In the course of developing their approach in dealing with the problem of child maltreatment, the committee determined that they would need to include a feedback system in order to monitor their goal attainment efforts. One of the committee members was an executive in a locally based computer firm. As a contribution, her firm provided technical assistance and equipment to the committee, which resulted in a computer-based linkage of all the agencies comprising the community's child protective services subsystem. Using the local contribution as a match, the committee, through the Midtown Health and Welfare Planning Council, was successful in obtaining a federal grant for a three-year pilot program. The purpose of this program was to develop and test a performance-based feedback system that would serve as a model for other communities making similar efforts in behalf of their children.

Steady State

Early in committee deliberations Judge Faire, the group's chair, had observed that the community problem that they were addressing was difficult, complex, and of long standing. He noted in addition that to be successful both committee members and the community would have to make a long-term commitment to their resolution efforts. Consistent with this position, the committee later recommended that the Midtown Health and Welfare Planning Council establish a permanent advisory body to provide the continuity suggested. In implementing the committee's recommendations, the council's president, Dr. Betty Kule, reminded Judge Faire of his earlier remarks about the importance of a long-term commitment and asked him to serve as the chairperson for the newly created advisory body on child maltreatment. The judge accepted, but only after extracting a promise from Dr. Kule that the former committee's staff assistant, Mr. Eddie State, would provide the professional staff services to the newly created advisory body.

Judge Faire explained to Dr. Kule that during the course of the committee's work he had come to rely on and admire Mr. State's planning and organizing abilities. He recalled particularly how helpful he had found Eddie State's use of "GIPA–the Four Horsemen that plague every organization and every community." GIPA, the Judge added, was the acronym that Eddie had coined for the "Four Horsemen." According to the judge, Eddie explained that the idea of the "Four Horsemen" had come to him when he was taking a course in graduate school on social systems. One of the points developed by the professor in that course was that every social organization is plagued by four problems labeled (1) goal attainment; (2) integration; (3) pattern maintenance; and (4) adaptation. According to the professor, any one of the four problems could lead to the so-called death of the organization. "As Eddie explained it to me," the judge went on, "the professor's use of the word plague had reminded him of the legendary 'Four Horse-men,' the four plagues that the Bible speaks of that confront mankind." Continuing, Judge Faire added, "I have also found the idea of GIPA and the Four Horsemen useful and will look forward to continuing my work with Eddie and with you, Dr. Kule."

Half amused and half intrigued, Dr. Kule said, "Wait a minute, judge, you are not leaving until you tell me what these four problems are all about." Using the recently completed work of the Ad Hoc Committee for the Prevention of Child Abuse and Ne-glect, Judge Faire summarized the four problems as follows:

Goal Attainment

The problem we faced was the maltreatment of our community's children, in most instances parents hurting their own children. The family is the community's basic institution, and this problem, if left unattended, poses a basic threat to the family and thus to our community. For most of us it is a sign of social disorganization. Goal attainment then was all of our activities directly related to the prevention and control of the maltreatment of our children. Examples would include among others the temporary placement of children in foster homes, the counseling of their parents, and the public education efforts aimed at the education of our citi-zens about this problem. Simply put, if we are not successful in attaining this goal, we are in serious trouble as a community and as a society.

Integration

This problem is really our problem as a community, the ability to join together to work cooperatively toward a better, healthier, and safer community for our chil-dren. Each of our agencies and groups tend to get caught up "doing their own thing." We all have our own petty jealousies and jurisdictional concerns. I think to some extent we as a community have not done as much as we can to strengthen family life and thus to promote a better and caring community. Eddie was very helpful to our committee by helping us see that the maltreatment of children was a problem that we all had a stake in solving; in fact none of us working alone could solve it; we had to learn to work together as a community. We had to build a community capable of helping agencies feel good about working together. In many ways communities are like families, as members feel good about the family they become more caring about each other. Similarly, when people feel good about their community, they start caring even more for each other, especially for the children of the community.

Pattern Maintenance

The family is the basic institution in this community, as it is in every community. If we forget this we are in deep trouble. As a community, through our churches, our schools, all our institutions, we must work to strengthen the family. By strengthen-ing our families, we not only strengthen each other but we strengthen our sense of community. The reverse is also true, if the family is weakened the whole fabric of our community, of our society, is weakened. That is why I am so concerned about the problem of the maltreatment of children; for me this feels like a sign of family disorganization and if not controlled, it is like a plague and a threat to all of us, and future generations as well. If there is any one pattern to be maintained in our community, it is that of a caring family. If we lose that, we lose our whole sense of community.

Adaptation

Eddie used to remind me that as a community we could not solve this problem by ourselves. Nor could we just sit by and wait for somebody, like the federal government, to help us. Eddie's point was a good one; first, and based on our understanding of the problem, we had to decide what we wanted to do about it—our goals. Second, we would mobilize our own efforts to attain those goals; but we would not stop there, we would seek help from all sources both in and outside our community. In effect, then, we would try to "adapt" other organizations and groups so that they shared our goals. In reality we tried to adapt to each other's goals, and in so doing jointly sought to help children and their families find a better life, one in which there is no place for violence.

Judge Faire stopped after summarizing his understanding of what "GIPA" meant. He laughed and said, "You know I must sound more like a preacher than a judge." Dr. Kule laughingly agreed and added how pleased she was that he had shared Eddie State's notion of GIPA and the Four Horsemen with her. She concluded by saying that she prefers to look at the positive side of "GIPA": "By working together to solve these four problems we are given a special opportunity to do something far more than just survive as a community; by working together we can build a more just and caring community— one that increases the quality of life for everyone.

SUMMARY

The preceding hypothetical example of a community application of the systems model was intended to illustrate the practice utility of the model. While not representing a theory of community or of community organization, the model offers a way of conceptualizing both the community and an approach to intervention. The model is also viewed by the authors as essentially free of content. The model user adds content in the form of additional concepts or theories and, in so doing, increases the utility of the model for specific applications.

For the practitioner, the model offers two different opportunities. First, for the eclectic it offers a framework upon which appropriate concepts, theories, techniques, and so on, can be related to one another for purposes of developing an individualized theory of practice. Second, for those having a special interest in general systems theory, the model provides an avenue for developing a social systems theory of practice. These two approaches are not mutually exclusive, but rather represent a difference in emphasis. In the latter instance, the focus is on evolving a theory of social organization within the general theoretical framework of general systems theory. The use of other concepts and narrower range theories would be secondary in such an approach, and such concepts would have to be compatible with the precepts of general systems theory and a social systems perspective. From our position, the important matter is having practice grounded in theory. The particular approach to theory building is less important than starting somewhere. Community and practice theory are in relatively early stages of development. Given this state, the practitioner must proceed with caution but proceed he or she must. Similarly, the practitioner must view him- or herself as a contributor to theory construction, a partner with the researcher and the theorist. The process will only serve to enrich both practice and theory.

NOTES

1. For a recent review of community theory and its relationship to practice see Jack Rothman, "Community Theory and Research," *Encyclopedia of Social Work*, vol. 1, 18th ed. (Silver Spring, Md.: National Association of Social Workers, 1987), 309–317.

2. We find the ecological perspective helpful, but chiefly in examining relationships in the most general sense. We have not found it particularly helpful in operationalizing the distinctive human features of "human behavior" and the "social environment." For a review of this perspective, see Carel B. Germain and Alex Gitterman, "Ecological Perspective," *Encyclopedia of Social Work*, vol. 1, 18th ed. (Silver Spring, Md.: National Association of Social Workers, 1987), 488–499.

3. Center for Social Work Research, "Child Abuse and Neglect in Oklahoma," School of Social Work, The University of Oklahoma (p.II-1); U.S. National Center on Child Abuse and Neglect, Department of Health and Human Services, *Recognition and Reporting of Child Maltreatment: Findings from the National Study of the Incidence and Severity of Child Abuse and Neglect* (December 30, 1980); and Jeanne M. Giovannoni, "Child Abuse and Neglect: An Overview," in *A Handbook of Child Welfare*, ed. Joan Laud and Ann Hartman (New York: The Free Press, 1985), 193–212.

4. See Henry L. Gunn, "Administration in Child Welfare," in *A Handbook of Child Welfare*, ed. Joan Laud and Ann Hartman (New York: The Free Press, 1985), 309–310.

Index